Lessons From A Tour Bus Presents
# THE ACTION SANDWICH

## Alan Frew
### with Sharon Brennan

To MARCY
with ♡

## Binea Press

MARCY@MARCYS.TV

*For my beloved wife Marcy whose love and friendship has been the perfect support for an imperfect man.*

Published in 2008 by
Binea Press, Inc.
512-1673 Richmond Street
London, Ontario, Canada N6G 2N3

Tel: 519.660.6424
Fax: 519.660.4449

E-mail: bineapress@bellnet.ca
www.bineapress.com

Distributed by:
Binea Press Inc.
519.660.6424

Library and Archives Canada Cataloguing in Publication
Frew, Alan
The Action Sandwich
A Six Step Recipe For Success By Doing What You're Already Doing
Alan Frew, Sharon Brennan
Foreword by Tim Long
ISBN 978-0-9783012-4-8
1. Success.  I. Brennan, Sharon, 1961-  II. Title
BF637.S8F69 2008    158.1    C2008-903191-1

12  11  10  09  08    2  3  4  5  6
Second Edition

Design by Response Generators
London, Ontario, Canada
Tel: 519.432.4932
www.rgdirect.com

Printed in Canada by Friesens Corporation
Altona, Manitoba

*"There is no worse place out of hell than that neighbourhood."*
A writer's description of
Coatbridge, Scotland, (My hometown).

## A SPECIAL THANKS:

With Tony Robbins I hit the goalpost, with Napoleon Hill I was leading at halftime, but with Jack Canfield's, *The Success Principles* I won the Cup! It's a basic, fundamentally sound, honest, practical book filled with truth and commonsense. Thanks Jack, you're the Paul McCartney of all of them.

*"I want to sing my song, for you, for everyone."*
Alan Frew, lyrics from Glass Tiger's *My Song*.

# ACKNOWLEDGEMENTS

This book is the result of the RECEPTIVITY, DESIRE, BELIEF, INTENTION and ACTION of my business partner, co-author and loyal friend, Sharon Brennan. Thank you for your dedication, PASSION and perseverance in getting me to do this. It would never have happened without you. You never faltered, not a single time in staying true to our purpose. This is only the beginning.

A special thank you to all of the musicians that I have worked with professionally in the making of my favourite band, *Glass Tiger*, especially Wayne, Al, Sam and Michael. Without all of you I have no Rock 'n Roll tales to tell.

And so to my wife and munchkin thank you for making each day richer and richer still.

A special thank you to my dear son Gavin, who has walked by my side through many of these stories and so much more. Much love to Ryan whose journey is only now beginning and to my brother Gordon and sister Christine, our family is truly an "original." I always knew our wackiness meant something. To my dear parents Gracie and Hughie who are at last, together again.

Finally to Scotland for "your wee bit hill and glen" gave me my gift of the blether.

Sharon would like to thank her brilliantly gifted husband Peter and beautifully spirited daughter Jessica for their patience and support, and her parents and friends who have been so lovingly interested in every step of this process. Thank you Alan for giving me the chance to craft these precious stories with you, for unlimited access to the renewable resource of your enthusiasm and for the daily opportunity to be who I am called to be. We are creators. That's what we do.

Together, Alan and Sharon would like to thank the amazing Tim Long, our publisher, Richard Bain, of Binea Press for his guidance and wisdom, Peter Watson, Amanda Jean Francis and the team at Response Generators, Cynthia O'Neill, Deane Cameron, Wayne Gretzky, Rod Knight, Jacques Villeneuve, Keith Pelley and our dear friend and fellow-thug "Manchester Dave" Nolan who gave us the mighty UK stamp of approval.

# TABLE OF CONTENTS

MY SONG – *Opus 6*

# FOREWORD

Here's how you know you've made it in life – the guy whose music you failed to get laid to in high school asks you to write the foreword to his book.

I first encountered Alan Frew whilst sprawled on my parents' couch in Exeter, Ontario, in the mid-'80s, watching MuchMusic. The video was, of course, *Don't Forget Me (When I'm Gone)*, and I instantly recognized Alan as handsome, charismatic, and wildly talented. The kind of person who really gets on my nerves.

Cut to some eighteen years later, and I meet Alan at a late-night party at the Canadian Comedy Awards. It soon becomes clear that in addition to the aforementioned talent and charisma, Alan is also friendly and thoughtful. Plus he dresses well, smells great, and really seems to care what I have to say. By now, this guy is totally starting to piss me off.

Three more years pass, and Alan calls and asks if I would read his upcoming book and write the foreword. I agree instantly, because a) he's Alan friggin' Frew and b) I am a whore. But soon I'm gripped by an overwhelming fear: What if the book he's written is really, really good? As a professional writer and a fantastically small-minded person, how will I deal with that?

Not well, it turns out. As I drain the remnants of my third gin and tonic, it gives me no pleasure to report that the book you hold in your hand is – *sigh* – wonderful, full of hilarious anecdotes and priceless wisdom.

It turns out Alan Frew is one of those people who just sort of has things figured out: he knows what it takes to rise from hardscrabble Coatbridge (like him) or not-so-hardscrabble Exeter, Ontario (like me), achieve everything you've ever dreamed, and have fun doing it. What's more, he's generous enough to share that knowledge with the rest of us.

So read the damn book – it's great. Now, if you'll excuse me, I'm going to go fix another drink (my fourth) (okay, tenth) and start teaching myself how to write songs and play the guitar. Hear that, Frew? If you're gonna move onto my turf, I'm gonna move onto yours. You're a wonderful man… and you've written a gem of a book… but you're going *down*.

Tim Long
Executive Producer, *The Simpsons*
Former Head Writer, *David Letterman*
Los Angeles
April 2007

# PROLOGUE

When it was announced that Deane Cameron was to become the President of EMI (Capitol) Music Canada, I was happy for him. He surely deserved it more than most. Deane literally knows the business inside out, for back in the '70s he started out as a warehouse employee packing vinyl albums into sleeves and driving the fork lift truck to load vast quantities of product onto skids that were on their way to the nation's record stores and eventually into the homes of music lovers all across the country. So here was a true rags to riches tale of a young man working his way up to becoming the man in charge, the President. My happiness for his success was also a little self-serving, for I knew that as the President of the label he would have the opportunity to meet all of the stars who were signed to his company including of course, *him*. GOD... ok, not The God, but my favourite, my idol. And there was no doubt in my mind that as President, Deane would actually meet him in person, shake his hand and actually, speak to GOD.

Being a so-called Pop Star in my own right carried with it a few perks, one of which was that I had managed to score second row floor seats to see him in concert in Toronto the following month. To say I was excited about attending his concert would be a bit of an understatement but actually meeting him, well now, THAT would be out of this world, no wait, THAT is another galaxy entirely and Deane, I knew would get to do just that...the lucky sod!

So the next time I was in his office I asked if and when the time came to meet GOD, would he be kind enough to get me an autograph signed to yours truly. I couldn't help it, I would not normally do something as contrary as this, but after all it was GOD, and I was helpless to resist the temptation. Deane said he would be glad to and I left it at that. The day of the concert came and I was surprised to receive word from EMI that there was going to be a press conference and an invitation had been put aside for me to attend and listen-in as GOD answered questions from the media. I thought I'd died and gone to, well, heaven, I guess, and so with a childlike skip in my step I headed down to the stadium.

The room was jammed, the atmosphere palpable as he entered the pressroom. Was there a living soul among this throng that was NOT a fan? Impossible! I had caused a tiny stir myself when I had entered earlier because *Glass Tiger* at the time was at the peak of its success and many, if not all, recognized me and enjoyed the novelty of having a so-called celebrity in the room with them waiting for GOD to enter. When he did, I was soon forgotten, but quite frankly I didn't care. He answered any and all questions, carefully, playfully and with the ease of a well-seasoned veteran. In what seemed like the blink of an eye I heard a woman say, "Last question please!" and then in a flash, it was over and he was gone.

Suddenly, I became fodder again for the attention of many of the reporters who wanted my take on all of it. I couldn't answer them, I did not wish to answer them, for I wanted to sit and bask for a moment in the fact that I had been in the same room as GOD and that answering their questions was just not something I wished to do. Then someone came to my rescue. A short, well-dressed woman, "Miss Last Question Please", with a clipboard in hand. She cried out in a very strong English accent, "Capitol Records, party of six and an Alan Frew!" I remember thinking, "What's an Alan Frew?" But wait! That was me! What the hell did she want with me?

"I...I'm an Alan Frew," I said, swallowing the large lump that had just leapt into my gaping mouth.
"Come on then," she said authoritatively.
"Where?" I asked.
"Where else, but to meet HIM of course?" she answered turning on her heel and leading the way.
My mind was a blur. How could I possibly meet HIM? What would I say to HIM?
I began to rehearse in my mind, "Errr, thanks a lot for being, well, you know...you. I am such a fan of, you know, HIM, well you are HIM, and I'm

- 4 -

sure you know that, but thanks a lot anyway." I was in trouble, but my legs seemed to be moving and I was indeed making my way down a long corridor following "Miss Last Question Please" at a rapid pace.

It seems that Deane had gone well above and beyond the call of just getting me an autograph and had made arrangements for me to go back to a secluded little room with the others from his company and have a private audience with, "Oh my God... GOD!"

No money, no accolades, no amount of record sales, could have replaced that moment in time for me, for I had dreamed of this since I could remember the sound of his voice blasting on the tiny transistor radio that sat beside the kitchen sink in our old prefabricated post-war home back in Scotland.

My dad was hilarious on these cold mornings, getting dressed in the kitchen, by the oven. I remember the time when singer-songwriter Jose Feliciano's version of "Light My Fire," originally written by Robby Krieger and Jim Morrison of *The Doors*, crackled out of our little radio.

"In the name of the wee man, who the hell is that?"
"Jose"
"Whoosee?"
"No Jose! Jose Feliciano, Dad, isn't he fab?"

In his version, at the end Jose would repeat over and over almost ad nauseam the line "Light My Fire, Light My Fire, Light My Fire..."
Causing my dad to inevitably say, "For Christ's sake will somebody light that laddie's fire and while yer at it...light ours!"

We'd be huddled at the oven or the little kerosene heater because coal was expensive and would never be burned for something like getting dressed in the morning.

"Fab? Turn that bloody rabble off!"
"But Dad, he's brilliant," I would plead.

"Brilliant my arse!" he'd reply.

How ironic this was, for by 1986 he would live vicariously and passionately through his son's pop-fame, and would become well versed, and learned regarding the world of pop music.

As I walked down that hallway towards the legend, my mind searched for an appropriate opening line but nothing would come to me. I knew that my wits had never let me down in the past and I was sure they wouldn't here, so I decided to just let providence guide me. "I'll bet it's easier meeting the Queen or the Pope!" I thought to myself.

Suddenly the door opened and he was the first one in front of me, his back turned, facing one of Capitol Record's representatives, who upon seeing me spoke up.

"Ah, here he is, this is one of our nation's top recording artists. Please let me introduce you both. Alan Frew meet…"

FOOD FOR THOUGHT

*"It's About The Performance, Not The Applause"*
ALAN FREW

# THE MAN WHO WOULD BE BING

My life is a true success story. This book is a true success story. Last night's dinner is a true success story, as was that hug my baby girl just gave me. Come to think of it, just getting up this morning was a true success story, for let's face it, there are many who did not. The completion of any desired outcome, attaining that which you set out to attain, no matter how small or seemingly insignificant at the time is, again, a true success story.

Does it sound like I am oversimplifying? Perhaps. But then again, perhaps not, for life cannot possibly be all about the toys, the accolades, the houses, cars and the money, can it? I pray not. Surely it is not about who has the most. If that were so then would it not follow that Bill Gates is a success and everyone below his net worth is a failure? A preposterous notion I know, but what then would you call success, a million dollars? Fifty million? Three billion?

Let me ask you this. Is the dude who is pulling in a high seven-figure salary from Wall Street, who owns a Donald Trump condo and is driving to work in his special edition Lamborghini while making a call to his personal pilot to ready-up the Gulf Stream jet that will scoot him to his second home in the Turks and Caicos Islands a success, just because of the money and goodies he has?

Conversely, is the guy who is presently deep in a forest somewhere in Northern British Columbia living in a turn of the century shack that leaks like a bugger with no running water and no electricity and who still has to "snag" dinner if he intends to eat that night, not caring about money or the toys of life -- is he a failure because of his lack of material and financial abundance?

The answer of course is too diverse and has too many variables for us as outsiders to decide. But let's suppose for argument's sake that the Wall Street dude is addicted to cocaine, stressed out to the point of having blackouts and is separated from his wife and children due to his anger and violent outbursts. Jeremiah Johnson on the other hand is there in the Canadian wilderness eating organic food and vegetables living meditatively with his wife of thirty years eagerly awaiting the arrival of his children and grandchildren who make him happier than any job ever could. So now, if asked to decide, who would you say is the success and who's the failure?

I believe that living a truly successful life centres around one major factor: control. How much say do you have over your life and its outcome? How much control do you have over where you work, how you work, why you work at what you do, where you live, how you live, where you go, how much free time you have, how active or inactive you DESIRE to be, how much money you have and any number of the endless events that make up your life? Do you control these things, or do they control you?

Oh don't kid yourself. I love the bells, whistles and the trimmings of success. However, they are simply the by-products of achievement. Successful people know this. They know it's about the journey and not the destination. They know it's all about the performance and not the applause.

Oh yes indeed. I have always loved toys, why as a matter of fact...

Wavy lines, wavy lines...waaaavvvyy llliiiiiinnnes....

Once upon a time, my mother took me shopping into the city centre of Glasgow, some nine miles and a bumpy double-decker bus ride away from my hometown. I was all of five years old, two feet tall and toothless. My baby teeth had fallen out when I was fifteen to eighteen months old, and by age five, my new ones had yet to grow in. The song "All I Want For Christmas Is My Two Front Teeth" is something that to this day I equate to finger nails being scratched across the full length of a chalk board, though perhaps the Walt Disney tune, "It's A Small World After All" is even more unbearable, for I would rather take a stick in the eye than have to listen to that bugger ever again. Perhaps one day I will tell you why.

The bus ride into the centre of Glasgow was uneventful, other than the performance put on by the token drunkard at the back of the upper deck of the bus. A bus ride to and from Glasgow without a drunk on board is like a scruffy dog without a flea. Scolding and singing, singing and scolding, that is their forte.

"SEE YOOOZE PEOPLE," he says, squinting as though he can't decipher if there are two or twenty-two on board.

"Yooooze people think yooooze are better than me...don't yooooze?"

This is always followed up with a little expletive.

"Well .........PISS OFF THEN!"

Now comes the song, usually a little Bing Crosby, Al Martino, Englebert Humperdink or if you're really lucky, some Jolson.

The Scots, especially those that are from the city of Glasgow (known as Glaswegians), are a breed unlike any other. Poets who can fight like lions, drunkards who can sing like larks, dropouts who can solve problems like Pythagoras, and wasters who can debate like Churchill, they are human encyclopedias. Walking libraries of information ranging from the mundane to the extraordinary. To this day I am fascinated by the fact that you can walk into any one of hundreds of pubs and see that same, wee scruffy drunk bastard, who is nothing short of a master in the art of debating. And yes, he's in EVERY single one of them. I kid you not. It's like cloning at its finest, and no matter how drunk, incapacitated or mentally challenged he may appear, he is a walking literary enigma, stacked to the hilt with facts and answers to questions ranging from "What was Plato's real name?" to "Which character has been on Coronation Street longer than any other?" Then, just for good measure, he'll give you a wee lecture on how Einstein got it wrong in his theory of relativity just before telling you what Geronimo had for breakfast prior to the battle of Little Big Horn.

Of all the races of people on this earth that I have had the fortune to come across, the Glaswegians stand out as a people who seem to know exactly who they are, and what they are doing here, even when they are talking a load of shite.

"SEE YOOOZE PEOPLE...yoooze people think am drrrrunk, don't yoooze? Well I'll show yoooze who's drunk!"

He then proceeds to tell you name for name, every member of the Scottish Football Team that beat England at Wembley in 1928!!!

As a matter of fact, the whole trip into and (for my mother), out of the big city that day was insignificant and uneventful right up until the moment when she arrived back at the house with bags in hand, only to be greeted by my father with an urgent question.

"Where's Alan?"
"Christ almighty!" I'm sure she said, "I forgot him! He's still in the store!"

And indeed I was, even after the manager had closed it up for the night, and headed home for a well-deserved fish supper with his wife and kids. For me there were two significant reasons why I didn't give a flying duck that I had been locked in a large department store all alone, at the tender age of five-and-a-bit.

The first was the fact that a light had been left on in the back storage room. The second was that the back storage room was where the toys were kept. My mother had to contact the police (by going to the police station in person since we had no phone), who in turn found the manager, who grumpily re-opened the store, amidst quite a bit of huffing, puffing and panic. Totally oblivious to this was a boy at peace, a boy in bliss, a boy who at times had a voice loud enough to take the ears off a donkey. Yet here he was quietly playing with a toy farm set that featured a plastic farmer, a barn and fence, and cows, sheep, horses, ducks. And yes, a donkey. No panic. No fuss. No fear.

At no other time was it more apparent that I was destined to find the fortitude to take care of myself in this world than at that moment.
"He doesn't seem very worried, does he?" observed the police officer.
"No, he gets very focused on things he likes... as if nothing else exists," replied my mother, somehow distant.
"I could have finished my dinner by now!" grumbled the store manager.
"Come on then sonny, let's go home," said the giant policeman to the toothless two-foot loner. So, with a little undetected smirk on my face, I was soon once more on the bus with my mother, this time headed home.

What a success story! Oh yes dear reader, a success story, for as I said earlier, success is the completion of any desired outcome, and you see, I neglected to tell the policeman, the store manager and especially my mother that my pockets were stuffed with plastic cows, sheep, and other livestock, and that indeed, "Old Macdonald had a farm, Ee i ee i oh!"

Being here to tell you this tale and to write about *THE ACTION SANDWICH* (a six-step recipe to success, by doing what you're already doing) is not only a success story, it is most likely the greatest story of my life, for I come from a place and from a time where success seemed like a stain, reviled, criticized, even feared. I come from a place where your friends were named anger, wits, fists and survival. Trying to attach a dollar figure to the success held between the pages of this book would be incalculable. This is a tale of how *THE ACTION SANDWICH* helped the boy to become a man, the fighter to become a healer, the storyteller to become a public speaker, and the singer to become a rock star.

The recipe for *THE ACTION SANDWICH* is simple and deliberate. Since embarking on this new pathway as an author and public speaker, I have talked to literally thousands of everyday people about life and the challenge of living it. We have also talked about books; the self-help, take-charge, be-godly, attract-wealth, release-the-lion-within motivational books, of which I have *inhaled* more than my fair share.

One thing that seems universal to our discussion is how absolutely overwhelming some of them make the adventure of living your best life seem. Just when you finally decide to reach out for help because you are feeling stressed, depressed, frustrated and at your wits' end, the instruction manual comes along and has you keeping journals, writing in diaries, sending out chain letters and so forth. And although I truly am not knocking this philosophy, I just know that for many people (including myself by the way) this just doesn't feel practical. I can NEVER stay on track when I attempt to keep journals or use mind-mapping techniques. I get frustrated and feel like I'm failing before I begin. So give me good old-fashioned, simple, practical directions, suggestions, affirmations and so forth, that I can read, digest and place into my mind and heart without having to stand on one foot while drinking a glass of water, hiding sticky-notes on bathroom mirrors or carrying painted rocks in my pockets, and I promise you I will get further. These techniques that do not work for me however, do work for many people, but for those of you who cannot make them work for you, I'm here to tell you that all is not lost. Abundance is for you as well.

I was at a seminar recently and I swear I couldn't tell where the motivation began and the infomercial ended. People high-fived and hugged their neighbours, "whooped and hollered," and got caught up in the frenzy of the moment. And, again, if this works for you then knock yourself out. But, personally, I do not want to be yelled at. I don't want to repeat little phrases like a parroting karaoke singer. I don't want to high-five and hug strangers while I am at a seminar. But that doesn't mean I don't want abundance or that my heart isn't open to teachings. It just means I like to think for myself.

For example, "The Bible" of so-called motivational books for me is *The Success Principles* by Jack Canfield. It is a simple, direct, honest, basic technique and Mr. Canfield by no coincidence also happens in my opinion to have the same simple, direct, honest, basic style to his speaking, which is why I am attracted to his teachings and why I look up to him as my mentor. It's a "take what you need and discard the rest" approach. It works for me and I know it can work for those of you who respond to this type of teaching.

I've made the principles of my book simple because IT *IS* SIMPLE and it is part of a lifestyle that anyone can adopt for everyday living. This book is not just for the enlightened business-savvy sector using information like this for reminders or top-ups for the success-plan that they have already implemented. This book is for everyday people, who work in all kinds of jobs. It's for bartenders and cab drivers, grocery clerks and waiters, nurses and bank tellers. This book is for people like my family, who still live within the clutches of the well-known acronym, "J.O.B." (Just Over Broke). This book is for those who struggle with the challenge of living, families who question philosophies, people who mess up, then move on. This is a book for you and for me, and just for good measure, I hope to make you laugh or perhaps shed a wee tear along the way. I have written this book to share some of the things I have learned in my journey thus far, and I have also peppered the pages with childhood and Rock 'n Roll stories that I hope will touch your heart or funny-bone. I hope you will read this book with an open mind and take from it whatever it gives you.

# WHO ARE YOU? WHO, WHO, WHO, WHO?

Who are you?
What do you want?
No, what do you really, really, want?
Do you know? If so, do you know how to get it?
Do you need to change the direction that your life is heading?
If so, how will you change it?

It's all a bit frightening isn't it, the "who, what, where, why, and how" of your life? Have you ever had the courage to ask yourself questions like these, and then followed through with trying to find the answers? Some ask them and then leave it at that. Countless others never ask them at all. Successful people ask them all the time and they do not stop until they find the answers.

It's tough isn't it, dealing with this thing called life? The fun, the laughter, the sorrow and the pain, the anger, violence, love and hate, the "in sickness and in health 'til death do us part" of it all? We call it life's ups and downs, as though life were a roller coaster -- challenging, overwhelming and, yes, even terrifying.

Let me tell you how I have come to feel about it these days...I love it. That's right...I love it. The fear, frustration, pain, sorrow, as well as the love and the joy -- the PASSION of living. I love it, difficult as it can be. I'll take it all. This journey, this jigsaw puzzle we call life. I, for one, would not have it any other way.

First of all, what's the alternative to loving it? Choose anything else and you might as well dig a hole in the ground and get in. Why? Because you are here, and this is now, and that is a fact. You see, it does not matter if the divorce is pending or the cancer is spreading or the ship is sinking. All that matters is what you are going to do about it and how you react to it. So, what ARE you going to do about it? How much longer are you willing to stay this way? Is your life important enough to you, to do something about it? If your answers to these three questions are, "I'm going to do nothing", "I'll wait forever" and "no, my life is not that important", then pal here's the shovel, go dig. Hopefully as you read on you'll discover that my credentials are in order and you'll realize that I have the proper lineage to back up an understanding of what defeatism and bitterness can breed.

-Poverty? Check.
-Family history of alcoholism? Check.
-Violence? Check.
-Abuse, segregation, bigotry? Check.

This book is not rocket science. In fact, none of the so-called motivational books are. They are all based on fundamentals like common sense, right and wrong, good and bad, clever and stupid. Besides that, as you're about to find out, the amazing thing is that when it comes to the questions of life you already know most of the answers.

I really hope this book motivates you to live a better life, but be careful of the "motivational" label, for all too often we think that a book or a speaker is going to be a quick fix, our miracle pill. However, they are not. As I sit here, dear reader, alone in my writing room, I often glance at my bookcase where I see the names of past and future legends; Chopra, Hill, Dyer, Myss and Canfield, to name but a few. Such wonderful, visionary and inspirational teachers universally connected to a common source, the apex of light, and of spirit, INTENTION, goodness and wisdom. These books, however, do not live in the space between the slight of hand and the disappearing playing card; they are neither potions nor the stuff of magic. They are not written from visions or the remains of tealeaves in the bottom of a china cup. On the contrary, they represent the journey, the toil, the dedication, the hard work, the stuff of real life that lives between the question and the answer.

So the principle of this book is based on the concept that we are already using the recipe to make ourselves things that we do or do not wish to be. Your life to date is a culmination of using this recipe. If you are stressed, fat, unemployed, incarcerated, addicted, lazy, or _____ (fill in the blank), you are all of these things as a result of choice. So why not choose to use the recipe to make yourself empowered, fit, rich, charitable, energetic and passionate? Just as it takes as many if not more muscles in your face to frown as it does to smile, so it is with THE ACTION SANDWICH, for it takes just as much if not more effort to live a life of redundancy and stagnation as it does one of abundance and vitality.

Is this a "how-to" book? Perhaps, but I prefer to think of it as a "Do It Yourself" book because I don't know "how-to" get you to do anything, nor would I force you to try. Besides, I'm too busy trying to figure out "how-to" myself. To be successful and live the best life you possibly can, you're going to

---

be asking and answering and "how-to-ing" until they put you in that hole that the other guy is digging. It never ends, but that's the beauty of it. That's the space between the question and the answer, that's the journey. So come on, grab your hat and let's get started. Don't be afraid, fear is not an enemy. Fear is a signpost and in many cases an ally. Or, dare I say, a friend? Is that possible? Can fear be your friend? I know this much, the only people who never fall are the ones who never stand up. Come on, get up and let's go.

# DR ROBERT

Very early in my career, fear was my one true nemesis. Without a doubt the biggest challenge I faced each and every night was going out on stage in front of an audience. I was so terrified that I carried a little medical bag with me everywhere I went that I affectionately called Doctor Robert's Bag. It was filled with prescriptions and potions that I felt would help me combat fear and nervousness. Pills, sprays, tonics: you name it and I had it.

Back in the very beginning, a lifetime ago and then some, a few local musicians heard me singing at a party and offered me the chance to audition for the role of lead singer of their band. I was more than receptive to this notion but I was also young, naive and incredibly inexperienced when it came to being a musician. Though I was soon the band's singer, it didn't take long before I grew a little uncomfortable with the idea, and on more than one occasion when they would come to pick me up for rehearsal, I would have my mother go to the door and give the excuse of my impending death from some exotic twenty-four hour flu, or tell them of a problem I was having with constipation or the mange. So you see, right off the bat, my RECEPTIVITY, my DESIRE and my BELIEF were not balanced with living the truth about who I was or wanted to be. When it came to getting up in front of an audience I was a wreck, and within moments my gag reflex would kick in and I would go through this awful wrenching motion consistent with the feeling of needing to vomit. It truly was terrifying, so much so that in a world of readily accessible medications, I turned to my family doctor, who willingly handed out pills. I also remained aware of the fact that if they didn't quite do the trick, street drugs like pot, hash, uppers and downers were easier to get than money for a cup of coffee, and I would willingly try those if need be, for there was ALWAYS someone in the drug world that loved to hang out with musicians. To gain your favour, they would graciously offer to get you high if you so desired. So Mr. Bag of Nerves here set off into the world of Rock 'n Roll fully stocked.

Anyone who has known me through the years would understand that this was a strange dilemma, for I have always been a confident take-the-lead type of a guy. And even stranger was the fact that I truly love to entertain people and know with all of my heart that I am good at it. I had worked in an adult world since the age of fifteen in a variety of jobs. I'd been a shoe salesperson, a factory worker and a milkman. I'd recently started a job as a hospital orderly, which I enjoyed immensely. But entertaining, musically in particular, was my driving force. So being a guy that couldn't get up in front of an audience without showing them what I ate for supper that night was driving me crazy.

## COMING TO TAKE YOU AWAY

We set off in 1977 on what truly was the quintessential Magical Mystery Tour -- so young, so green and oh so naïve. There I was, running back and forth to the wings of the stage (if there was a stage) or behind a guitar amplifier to periodically do an impersonation of a returning Emperor Penguin attempting to regurgitate the day's meal for the benefit of its offspring. Every few minutes I would dive behind the cover of the amp, then return with weepy eyes and some drool on my chin. They must have thought I was a lunatic. On one crazy occasion I was so fearful before the show that I allowed myself to smoke some hashish with one of the locals, which then led to what will go down in history as one of the shortest performances ever for a professional rock band. It went something like this...

Band takes the stage; crowd cheers; drummer starts a solid beat; crowd cheers louder; guitar riff to "All Right Now" kicks in; crowd goes wild; bass guitar joins in as if to say, "Let's get ready to rrruuumble!" The crowd is in a frenzy. Lead singer (yours truly) steps up to the microphone looking cocky, sexy and ready for some Rock 'n Roll ACTION; and the crowd goes wild again. But, wait a minute!

What the crowd does not know, dear reader, is that inside this young Rock-god's head he is fighting the paranoia between two questions. One, "What do they want from me?" and, two, "On whose head am I going to plunk this dollar-forty-all-you-can-eat-with-dessert-included-lunch." Let the show begin!

THE SINGER SINGS

"There she stood (gag) in the street (ga-gag), smiling from (gag, gag) her (gag) head...(gaaaaaag)...to her (gggaaaaagagag)."

THE SINGER SPEAKS

"Ladies and gentleman we're gonna take a short break and we'll be right back!" Length of show: thirty-four seconds.

THE SINGER RUNS

A mad dash for freedom ensues as the singer makes a break for it faster than Keith Richards can run up a bar tab. He is closely followed at near Olympic pace by a guitar player who is attempting to show why a guitar is nicknamed an axe, followed by a drummer whose wild attempts to "drop him" by firing drumsticks in his direction is beginning to look vaguely like a vintage episode of "Audubon's Wildlife Theatre," (you know, the one where the natives of Australia boomerang that unsuspecting Kanga to death), and finally a bass player who has also smoked the peace pipe with some locals, who is so stoned thinks the band is still on stage performing the show, while running.

"Get back here, you idiot, we're doing a show!"
"No!" (Gag)

Hyperventilating and sweating profusely, the singer makes it to his room, which is on the upper level of this not so high class BAR and OTEL (the letter H had fallen off back in '68) and locks himself in, only to be found in the fetal position some twenty to thirty minutes later when a furious bar owner grabs a screwdriver and removes the door from its hinges.

"Get back down there", they scream.
"I can't," plead I.
"Yes you can."
"No I can't, I can't remember the words and besides, I'm going to be sick all over the people in the front row."
"They're used to that!" cries the owner.
"Don't care, I can't do it!" (gag). "I can't do it!"
The night was explosive to say the least. No wait, I stand corrected. The night was a bomb.

Surprisingly the manager did not fire us. It took a long time for me to sufficiently recover and go gagging on again. However, this little story doesn't take the cake in my repertoire of facing fear. No my friends, sometimes it truly does have to get a lot worse before it can get better. Fear and I had another formidable showdown, but I will save that anecdote for a little later.

After telling you this, am I mad to say that today I believe fear can indeed be an ally or, better yet, a friend? It most certainly can. You see, you and fear have just got to come to a little arrangement. Read on dear reader, read on.

## A DAY IN THE LIFE

In this book you are going to discover a simple strategy for success that I use each and every day and have been using all of my life, even when I was completely unaware that I was doing so. You see we're all using it, every day, constantly. You cannot escape it. It's like breathing. It's not something you have to be conscious of, but at times, like sticking your head under the water at the lake, or when climbing Everest, it suddenly becomes an incredibly conscious necessity. I mentioned earlier that we know the answers to the questions we ask ourselves like, why am I fat? why am I irritable? why don't I have a job? But knowing the question and the answer isn't the difficult part; it is the space between the two that is the challenge. It's the ACTION you take between the question and answer that counts. It's not that we don't know the answers. It's just that at times we simply won't face up to them. The truth, as they often say, can hurt. Why? Because it can be embarrassing, revealing, or perhaps hurtful. And in order to tackle it head-on, two key things that all of us dread are required -- fear and change. Or, more accurately, fear OF change. Fear of change always tilts our balance at first. For many of us, even when change clearly shows us that it will improve our lives, we opt to remain in a bad situation.

*THE ACTION SANDWICH* not only addresses the place where fear of change dwells, it's the place where it can be embraced and overcome. Understanding that change and fear may come as a package for this journey is the beginning step on the pathway to overcoming it. It's the hammer that lives between the hand and the nail. It's the paint between brush and canvas. It's the step between your foot and a walk in the park. Simple, humble, unassuming yet, when focused, practiced and built upon, leads to the Eiffel Tower, the Mona Lisa or the Boston Marathon. It's reorganizing the day-to-day practical things you're already doing in your life that allows you to accomplish amazing results. The true magic of this formula is that you are using it now. You cannot escape it and it will remain with you for the rest of your days. Hence the description, *a six-step recipe to unlimited success by doing exactly what you're already doing.*

You are using this blueprint in every success and yes, even in every failure that happens in your life. I have given it a name but I certainly cannot lay claim to its essence, for it has been with humankind for millennia. To use it effectively you must face up to and challenge head-on all of the unsettling questions that I asked you at the beginning of this book. Yet let me ask you this: how many wildly successful people do you know? Not many? Why is that? Because it is not easy. In fact it is extremely difficult, confusing and exhausting to face life-altering questions honestly, passionately and with determination and focus. And yet when you master this tool, you hold the key to an exhilarating, revolutionary and unlimited pathway to a successful life. I call it *THE ACTION SANDWICH*.

# THIS BOY

I was recently booked to speak at an event that had a beautifully designed brochure resting at each of the invitees place-setting containing a welcome from the foundation's president, an itinerary of the evening's events and various silent and live auction items. Within the brochure was an Alan Frew Bio for folks to browse through to get a handle on who I am and on what the hell I was doing there. Let's face it, although I am a seasoned communicator, I am relatively new to the public speaking circuit and if I'm on the bill, I usually have a band behind me. As you read these words I thank you, for I am also extremely new at being an author.

Through the years I have had thousands of interviews with thousands of members of the media. I have had tens of thousands of words written about me in various magazines and newspapers and it is more than just a crap-shoot when it comes to whether or not they will get it right, and I DO mean even the simple stuff.

"Lead singer Alan Frey, sixty-two, said today that his '80s pop sensation Glass Eye is finally thinking of calling it quits, after it was discovered that Frey, a native Mexican, wishes to return to his homeland and settle down with his long term love interest, Frank."

Meanwhile, what you actually told them was that upon hitting fifty you wanted to settle for a quieter lifestyle and you were thinking about cutting back on the touring a bit, to enjoy some home life while taking some precious time to do some traveling with your family. I often think back to a time, more than just a few years ago, when I was sharing the spotlight with the phenomenal vocalist Steve Perry, when both of us were being interviewed at a radio station in San Francisco. Steve was asked what his opinion of concert reviewers was and he said, "Why do I need to wake up and read about what some newspaper thought of my concert the night before, when twenty-thousand ticket buyers gave me an instantaneous review?" My sentiments exactly, Steve. "Good on ya!"

I sat at dinner that night and opened up the brochure that was on my plate. This little Bio was written not by a paid professional but by a woman who was a volunteer for the foundation. And yet in all of my years I truly feel that who I am, where I come from, how I got here and where I am going has never quite been captured more simply and more honestly (except of course in this book) than in this woman's words. So I am going to pretend for a moment that I am awaiting the opportunity to come and speak to you and I will let her introduce me. Mrs. Volunteer, if you please:

"As with many success stories, Alan Frew took a rare and unlikely route to becoming an empowering, professional public speaker and author. Born in Coatbridge, Scotland, a town described by one author as, 'no worse place out of hell than that neighbourhood,' Alan's story of rising from a life of religious and social segregation, fueled with a sad abundance of anger and violence, to his becoming an award-winning, multi-platinum selling artist, is edgy, yet heartwarming and thought provoking. Alan had every reason to grow up angry, yet was an eternally optimistic boy, with only himself to truly rely on. He successfully learned to negotiate his way through an adult world of hardship, where a real man was a violent man, a woman belonged in the kitchen or, when needed, the bedroom, and as for children it was simple, they should be seen but never heard. He claims 'telling the tale of his life is easy but that surviving to be able to tell it was the hard part.'

Moving to Canada in 1972, he went on to become a registered nurse turned rock musician whose music reached millions. A natural leader and motivator, his first public speaking engagement happened purely by chance when he was hired to sing at a conference for a major pharmaceutical corporation, and was casually discussing his personal success formula with the management at a cocktail party. When the President of the company overheard his message he hired him on the spot to speak formally to his VPs the next morning. With nothing prepared, he used his wit, charm, business and street smarts, matched skillfully to his old country roots and entertaining past to captivate, motivate and enlighten a tour bus of high stakes business executives without missing a beat. It was an unrehearsed magical session, which without knowing it actually gave birth to *LESSONS FROM A TOUR BUS*.

He has entertained and been entertained by royalty. He has sung for and put his arms around the young people serving in the Armed Forces in places like Bosnia and the Middle East, and on more than a few occasions he has cared for and entertained the elderly, infirmed and the dying. Truly he has already lived ten life times and will surely live at least ten more before it's over. Milk boy, shoe salesman, factory worker, orderly, registered nurse, rock star, entrepreneur, actor, author, please meet the ever-inspiring Alan Frew."

There you have it, no Harvard degree, no doctorate in psychology, no Nobel Peace Prize (yet), but a lot of miles on the tour bus of life. I have to my credit adapted a combination of street-wise vision, common sense and tireless energy, and managed to turn it into my tour de force, my tale of a kid from a small town who does well, and I have been blessed to have experienced tremendous success along the way.

This book reflects who I am and what I know from living the life I have led. I know that truth lies within each bite *of THE ACTION SANDWICH* and I know that *THE ACTION SANDWICH* lives within the space between your questions and your answers. But this book is not a book of group hugs or high fives, nor will it win any awards from the Moral Majority any time soon. That's not where I came from. I came from the raw reality and hardcore nature of life on the streets, and I managed to parlay it into a successful and abundant life filled with everything my heart desires. I make no apologies for its rawness, for that would constitute apologizing for its honesty, which I cannot do. This story is living proof that abundance and success are truly for all, even, I might add, for a cheeky wee bastard from Coatbridge.

If you are truly committed to parting the waters of confusion, by understanding how to use the elements of *THE ACTION SANDWICH*, where RECEPTIVITY deciphers the signals the universe is sending to you and if you DESIRE the type of BELIEF system that you once had in yourself and if your true, unwavering INTENTION is to live the absolute best life that you can live, and you are committed to taking ACTION to make it all happen, then this book is indeed for you.

You may notice that although I have devoted a chapter to each of the six ingredients of *THE ACTION SANDWICH*, there remains at times an overlap, where perhaps I am speaking about INTENTION when suddenly you get a flavour of PASSION. Likewise I may be talking about DESIRE and before you know it, you get a little taste of ACTION. Why is this, one may wonder? Well, it's simple really. How can you possibly eat a sandwich and not taste all of the ingredients at one time? You can't pop it into your mouth and separate the chicken from the lettuce or the lettuce from the mustard. And besides, why would you want to? *THE ACTION SANDWICH* is no different. Each individual ingredient stands fresh and savory alone, yet when chewed, or lived if you will, the combining flavour comes alive in your mouth, invigorating and nourishing, giving you life and energy. Think of it as a bite of life, with your personally chosen combination of flavours giving you not only your originality but your individuality as well.

Success by doing exactly what you've always done? It sounds crazy doesn't it? I mean, if you are the first one to stand up and say that you are not successful, then how can I claim with certainty that you can indeed be successful by doing exactly what you are and always have been doing? Well, let's explore.

# YOUR SONG

You've already read this book. In fact you have LIVED this book, getting to where you are today. You are living it ...AND you would continue to live it even if you didn't read another page. Think of your life as a song, think of the message in this book as the notes of that song. Think of me as no more than a fellow songwriter; a music coach if you prefer, here to communicate with you in a way that gets results, to inspire and empower your song to its fullest potential and together work to make a hit.

As any musician will attest, it is astounding and seemingly infinite, how no two songs are ever the same. Even when you think it's impossible that more songs can be written with only the eight notes of the scale, another comes along, and another and another, all unique. So it is with your *ACTION SANDWICH*, an exclusive version of your own priorities, passions and personality, written and executed with the precision of a master composer, through the discipline of positive thoughts, energy and INTENTION, all the while reflecting the humility, worthiness and wishes of your true self.

*THE ACTION SANDWICH* is being prepared and consumed by every single solitary soul on this planet today, no matter where they come from, what their social or economic status is, what religion they may follow, what sex they are or what their sexual orientation may be. It is with you ...ALWAYS. You are using it, so why not use it properly? Why not use it to be the very best that you can be? Why not use it for success instead of failure? Enjoy wins as opposed to losses, highs instead of lows and strengths instead of weaknesses. Why not use the same simple steps to bring about a fantastic result as you would for a mediocre one? You are expending the energy required to create the life you have, so why not redirect it and create the life you want?

The good guys use it and the bad, the skinny and the fat, the rich and the not-so-rich, yes even the downright poor, the motivated are pumped on it and the complacent, well, they just drag it along with them. In fact the only people not using it are the dead!

This book is here to help you not only discover and understand this recipe, but also to guide you in its use to a life of total abundance and unlimited success, whatever that means to you. It is of the utmost importance to understand that success can mean many different things to different people. This book can point you in the direction of fame, wealth, houses and cars if that is what success is to you. However, if success to you means getting a promotion at the grocery store, or coaching your son's baseball team to the playoffs, or figuring out how you can raise money for your local church, then that is also true success.

There are six mouthwatering, savory ingredients in *THE ACTION SANDWICH*, and the good news is that you already have all of these ingredients in your fridge. The problem is that so many out there never take the time, never have the inclination, never have the direction nor the energy to make a healthy sandwich. In this fast-paced, media-driven worldwide web of supply and demand, they are more attracted to Bob's Triple-Bacon, Double Cheese Burger and Heart-Attack combo (usually washed down with a diet-something-or-other). It just does not register, for is there anyone over the age of twenty-five that doesn't know how they feel ten minutes after eating junk food?

Success is NOT built upon the foundations of instant gratification. It is built upon RECEPTIVITY, DESIRE, BELIEF, INTENTION and the ACTION of living somewhere between where we are and where we want to be. We live in the world of MORE -- more people, more gadgets, more options, more possibilities, more opportunities than ever before. Why then is there more poverty, more anger, more hunger, more violence and LESS TOLERANCE, than at any other time in our history? Are we so catered to, that just opening our mouths and being fed garbage is acceptable? Has entitlement blinded us, so that we have lost sight of who we truly are and what our purpose really is? Here's an old-fashioned thought: are we lazy? Are we so obesely slow and unpurposefully driven, that we will follow the most extreme ideas and doctrines? Is it just me or do there seem to be more self-proclaimed leaders out there, for just about ANYTHING you can make up? Why does most of society seem so willing to let others decide it ALL for them? Here comes one of the simplest dictums for living the best life you can, filled with abundance and all you DESIRE. Are you ready? Decide for yourself. As Shakespeare said, "There's the rub." For by deciding for yourself, you are brought back to the issue of control and of how much say you have in your own life.

As children, we are taught that RECEPTIVITY equals education. BELIEF means "do what everyone else is doing and you'll be fine." DESIRE is reserved for money, the house and the car, and incidentally it is often associated with greed. INTENTION, being elusive and totally misunderstood, is not acknowledged at all, and ACTION means "get a job!" PASSION? Well you can forget about that, for it is only for the lucky, certainly not you. Often it is portrayed as an intensity to shy away from. After all, what do you have to be so passionate about anyway?

We limit ourselves then, because we have been taught since childhood to choose boundaries that make others feel comfortable with our pathway. But if you knew that you could tap into a life of unlimited abundance, why would you choose boundaries? There's only one thing stopping you and that's you. Just you. Your life can change right now. I know this as positively as I know that I love breathing, singing, writing or those plaid hipsters I've been hanging on to since 1976. Hey, go easy, they'll be back.

The doubters among you will already be trying to think of exceptions to this rule, even though you yourself are likely not an exception. Of course there are those who through absolutely no fault of their own find themselves at the mercy of their environment, specifically those in this world subjected to poverty, hunger or perhaps an oppressive society or government. However, no matter what your social, economic, mental or environmental situation is, you're using the formula. Even my little two year-old daughter knows how to use it, and as a matter of fact she is an expert at using it, for she puts no boundaries or limitations on anything that she desires.

You might be amazed to discover how those who seem to be in desperately hopeless situations can utilize the recipe for *THE ACTION SANDWICH*. Those who at one point in their lives felt like all hope was lost and that they were doomed to a life of despondency and failure, yet managed to reach inside and find their power, their source if you will and went on to rise from the ashes of pain and suffering, despair and hopelessness and proceeded to achieve successes beyond even their wildest imagination. People like Oprah Winfrey, Nelson Mandela and Terry Fox come to mind. It is from this source we all share that heroes come. If it can power a young man with only one leg and a body ravaged with cancer across the vastness of a country like Canada, then just think of what it can do for you and me.

---

# TRUE COLORS

In its infancy *Glass Tiger* (then known as *Tokyo*) had a dual existence. The formation of the group happened when musicians from two separate bands became one, and it happened that the drummer of the newly formed *Tokyo* had also been the lead singer for his group, very similar to what Phil Collins, drummer for *Genesis*, started doing after Peter Gabriel quit that band. He drummed and sang, but eventually smartened up and became one and not so much the other. (Note to young musicians: Never form a band where the drummer is the lead singer, it looks goofy, and the band's timing suffers. It's a little like driving the car from the trunk. Got that? Good.)

So when the two bands merged, our drummer was rather reluctant to relinquish his duties as lead singer even though the band had a singer, namely me. The idea of change for him was too difficult to deal with and to accept, so our band would perform songs with me as the lead singer, then I would exit the stage for one or two numbers and he would take over. We continued this way for the longest time.

Our styles were different. I would be up there singing British pop and rock songs from *The Police*, *U2* and *Duran Duran*, then he would perform metal songs by *The Scorpions*, *Def Leppard* or *Ozzy Osbourne*.

If it sounds like a dog's dinner, it was. Not only was it disjointed and confusing, but it was extremely disconcerting to the audience as well as to any record company thinking about signing a new group. After months of this I was compelled to address the issue and tell them that I felt that our true color was one that had a lead singer who was also the front man. And I laid it on the line that I should be that guy. I told them that if they didn't agree, I would leave the group. They have all confided since then that it was the right move. Even the drummer went on to admit so, but it did not diminish the fact that he found the change painful and difficult.

A few years later it became apparent to him that the front man gets most of the attention. This made it even more unbearable for him, an even bigger change, and by all accounts he made an even bigger mistake when he quit the band and tried to go it alone.

News flash: None of this is easy. If an easy life with little effort is what you're looking for, this is not the journey for you. Making the choice to use *THE ACTION SANDWICH* correctly means that never again can you play small in this world. It means that you have finally acknowledged your place as being important. If you don't mind trading a few bumps in the road for a life full of PASSION and rich in abundance, then this recipe is for you. Are you ready? Let's get started on making that sandwich shall we?

---

# HUNGRY LIKE THE WOLF

Everyone knows what hunger feels like. Your tummy rumbles, you have that empty feeling inside of it that sets off a trigger between your stomach and brain. You hear yourself say, "I'm hungry!" What you are really doing is showing RECEPTIVITY to the internal feeling of hunger. You think to yourself, "I want to eat something." Simply put, you DESIRE food. Certainly you know that you're entitled to eat, everyone is, so you have the BELIEF that you can and will take care of this hunger by eating. You get the bread, chicken and the lettuce and tell the world that it is your INTENTION to eat.

With knife in hand, you begin to make your sandwich. You've done it a thousand times, right? Now that you've taken ACTION, success is just around the corner and your hunger will soon be gone. It is the ACTION of putting it all together that is the key ingredient and the backbone to being successful, for indeed if you do not get up off of your backside and actually do the making of the sandwich you will continue to suffer hunger. You must DO to get DONE!

So there you are making the sandwich that will take away your hunger and make you a happy camper. However, even when you are really hungry it is highly unlikely that you will just take the chicken and slap it on two slices of bread and eat it. Dry bread and chicken would take away your hunger and sustain you, but it is the mustard, the mayo, the relish or even the good old ketchup that adds the taste that seems to make it all worthwhile. It is the vast array of condiments that bring the life and energy and taste to our sandwich.

THE ACTION SANDWICH is no different, and I invite you to experience a special condiment that I have added for you, which, like mayo, mustard or relish, not only enhances the flavour but also allows your success to taste even sweeter. The condiment I am referring to is PASSION, and here comes the best part. The beauty of this condiment is that while one person's ham might simply be just another person's ham, the condiments make the experience unique for each and every one of us. My mayo can be your mustard, which in turn is her relish, and so forth. And the good news is that the condiments are limitless. You can smother your ACTION SANDWICH in all of the joy and charisma that PASSION has to offer while maintaining your uniqueness and individuality. As a footnote you will discover that PASSION goes hand in hand with DESIRE and BELIEF. It is difficult not to be passionate about something you really DESIRE and believe in.

So pull up a chair, grab a stool, a bench or some lawn and join me as I present to you the recipe for THE ACTION SANDWICH: A six-step recipe to unlimited success by doing exactly what you're already doing. I hope you're hungry!

With the fullest of INTENTION of making this team, I took to the field one day for my one big shot at it, and in short order managed to turn several defenders inside out and score a couple of goals, which led to the coach telling me that I could join the squad.

I went home ecstatic. "Dad! Dad!" I cried as I blasted through the front door, "I made the school team, THE school team, and I need a pair of football boots!"

Of course I would have been just as well off saying, "Dad! Dad! I'm opening my own safari park and I need money for a hippo!" For the end result would have been the same. "Are you kiddin'? Where the hell do you think I'm going to get money for football boots?" He then proceeded to tell me that a guy he knew at work had a son who didn't play the game anymore and that he had a pair of football boots that were going to waste and he was sure he could get them for me. Now at this point I wish I had been opening up a safari park for God knows I am sure he could never have gotten me a hand-me-down hippo no matter how hard he tried. The football boots that came into our home the very next day looked like something Moses brought down with him from Mount Sinai.

"God says he's not quite finished with the Ten Commandments yet," cries the weary leader of the Hebrews. "In the meantime he wants you to have...THESE!"
"You said you'd bring us the very words of God," cry the people.
"I know I did," says Moses. "But while we're waiting, let's have a game of football!"

Like many kids, I knew hand-me-downs all too well, so well in fact that they were a way of life for me. My sister laughs to this day over a certain pair of corduroy trousers that went from a lad several years my senior to his younger brother, then to me! When I wore them the hem was so big that my mother would gradually let it down in increments as I started to spurt. Those trousers went from a ten-inch to a two-inch hem with me in them the entire time.

I drew the line only once when I was forced to wear a pair of swimming trunks that had belonged to my older cousin Jim. They were made of wool!! Can you believe that? Wading out into the frozen North Sea in woolen swimming trunks? My God, even the Spanish Inquisition never thought up torture that cruel. I actually took them off while still in the water and pretended that the ocean had scooped them away. It was easier and more bearable to walk naked back to my towel than it was to wear a sheep over my balls in the freezing cold water. Having to wear a shirt, pants or a jacket however from a neighbour didn't bother me so much unless some other mother insisted on calling me for dinner thinking I was hers.

"No Mrs. Murphy, it's me, Alan. I'm only dressed like your Harry!"

The football boots were however a completely different matter. They were brutal.

The modern boot came into being in the sixties, when footwear looked sleek, and the cleats were replaceable screw-ins made of nylon, but this was not the case with these babies. Imagine if you will a steel-toed, ankle high work boot from 1945 worn by Ko-Ko The Clown in his circus routine, complete with nailed in cork cleats, and you might come close to getting the picture. By the way, my father had neglected to tell me that the son of his friend was nineteen and these boots were six sizes too large for my nine-year old feet.

"We'll stuff them with paper," said my rocket scientist father.
"Oh, no!" said I.

When I went to the first game my sweater drowned me, my socks went all the way up to my knees then folded and returned all the way back down to my ankles, then folded again and went all the way back up to my knees! Hold on though, for it gets better. My shorts, my soccer shorts, had to be held up with a belt! Already mortified, I brought out the boots. My goodness, times like these can seem so painful to the best of us but to a child it can be excruciatingly so. It is at such crossroads of life that character, willpower and soul can be constructed or perhaps destroyed. I knew that if I could just get past all of this peripheral junk and not internalize the mocking that was coming my way from some extremely amused older boys, that my skills could do the talking for me. I remained optimistic in the face of adversity and indeed went out and played what we call "a blinder", known more often as a great game. I remained on that team for the rest of my days at that school, eventually becoming the leader and captain.

After one match, I was traveling home as usual on a double-decker bus, when I decided to deliberately lose my boots by leaving them on the upper level. I must have looked like that little guy in the movie *The Omen* who was really Satan, as a wicked smirk formed on my pursed lips and I silently said goodbye to that cobbler's nightmare forever. When I arrived home my father asked me where my boots were.

"Oh no! I've left them on the bus Dad, sorry. Oh well they'll be long gone now," I emoted, hoping to make a believer of him.
He was already pulling his jacket on.
"Come on then," he said.
"Where we goin' Dad," I inquired.
"To the bus depot!"

Now, understand folks that this is Coatbridge, Scotland I am speaking of, known widely for its thugs, delinquents and thieves. Most have a demeanor that is one hinge away from the door falling off. Some of these people would not only steal the eye out of your head, but would have the nerve to come back to you and ask for a refund because when they got it home it was the wrong colour. Go back to the opening page of this book for a second. Do you see it? "There is no worse place out of hell than that neighbourhood." Never a truer sentence was ever written. It seemed therefore pointless to go trailing up to the bus depot for the boots would surely be on the feet of a well meaning thief by now. But go we did. On the way there my dad felt the need again to tell me how I should be more careful with my belongings.

"Football boots don't grow on trees you know!"
These ones did, an ancient, smelly, ugly football boot tree.
We approached the lost and found desk at the depot.

"Excuse me," my father said to the lady behind the counter. "My son was playing football earlier and..."

"Are you looking for these?" she asked, as she pulled out the boots.

My eyes were like saucers looking through a magnifying glass. Agog doesn't come close. Awestruck, maybe. Astounded, definitely. You see, when I left the precious cargo for all to see and hopefully take, I did so with the bus still having to complete another thirty stops! These free-to-a-good-home relics had traveled the entire length of the town and back again and not a soul had touched them! No sir, there they were in her hands right before my wide eyes and gaping mouth.

"Ah, lovely," said my father. "A wee bit o' luck eh son?"

---

# NOWHERE MAN

Here's an interesting notion. At first when I was creating *THE ACTION SANDWICH*, I was inclined to use the word knowledge as opposed to the word RECEPTIVITY, my logic being that in order to set off on a formula for success the first thing one would require would be a great knowledge of the subject at hand. This seems more than reasonable, does it not? I do not, however, feel this way today and I will tell you why. Putting a demand on yourself that you must have knowledge about whatever it is you DESIRE can, if not approached cautiously, set you off on a pathway that I refer to as the pathway of "always getting ready to." Always getting ready to be, to try, to trust, to deliver, to see, to give and goodness knows how many other excuses. "I promise you," she says, "I'll start very soon just when I get a bit more money, a bit thinner, a bit better, a bit smarter, a bit more together." "Trust me", he says. "As soon as I get a bit stronger, wiser, faster, richer, leaner, funnier, you name it...and I'll be right there." I call this "Victim Speak" and victims are always easy to spot.

# I'M JUST LOOKING FOR CLUES

Do you relate to these excuses? Do they sound familiar? Do you use them yourself? They are the voices of the "always getting ready to" talking. They are victims and they have two major qualities. First, they always live their lives as if life happens to them as opposed to them creating it for themselves. Second, they always have their fingers simultaneously on the blame and excuse buttons, ready to push them rather than owning up and taking responsibility for everything that has and will happen to them.

If you think of yourself as a victim, then you are one. How can you believe you will achieve great things if you don't believe you are full of greatness? It just won't happen. Don't look to your past for excuses to use for your future. What was may effect what is, but has nothing to do with what will be if you change your attitudes and actions now and move on.

RECEPTIVITY requires that you allow yourself to see the world through a variety of perspectives. When I stand on stage and look out at twenty thousand people, I have a different perspective than the audience does when looking at me. Sometimes before a show or while another act is on I will quietly wander out to the back of the venue and take in the view from the audience's perspective so I can be receptive to their vantage point. The venue remains the same regardless of where you observe it from, however the perspective of the viewer impacts the experience. Everything we do in life has different perspectives and the more open we are to various points of view, the more knowledge we will gain from the journey. RECEPTIVITY however doesn't necessarily require high levels of knowledge. In fact I would say that at times it doesn't require it at all. RECEPTIVITY is about watching for clues and living in the moment so you do not miss an opportunity that comes your way. It's about being fully awake, not wishing or hoping but rather being in tune with what is true and real in your life, from every perspective.

# MATTED SPAM?

Let me share a couple of short stories with you. Look at the following image. What do you see – squiggles and dots on a page? Gobbledygook? Matted Spam? Well you're not alone because I cannot decipher it either. Yes, of course it's music, but what music? When you find out the answer could somebody please let this musician know? Thank you.

Of course I am being facetious, for I do indeed know that this is the music for a song that took the world by storm in 1986 when *Glass Tiger* made "Don't Forget Me (When I'm Gone)," a number one smash hit. But if you jumbled this musical score up with dozens of others and brought them all to me I would not be able to find it again because I cannot read music! This is where RECEPTIVITY lives, because as some of you may already know... I, along with Sam Reid and Jim Vallance, wrote this song, in fact I have written hundreds of songs. And yet to this day I still cannot read music.

So what would have happened if when I was approached to join my first band I had turned my back on the moment, been unreceptive to the opportunity I was being given, and asked them to wait for me until I received my degree in music? Would they have waited for me? I think not. Musicians are an excellent example of people who are receptive to the idea of *being and doing* while having limited or in some cases *no* knowledge prior to becoming. They just do it. They learn as they go. They know what an instrument is and that if you strum it, beat it, blow it or plunk it you'll get noise out of it, so they do have a certain amount of knowledge to begin with. The rest they refine as they go. John Lennon and Paul McCartney fell into this category while they created the greatest pop legacy in music's history... *The Beatles.* Even when they were writing "She Loves You," "I Want To Hold Your Hand," "Help," and so on, they too could not read music. So I ask you, knowledge or RECEPTIVITY?

# TAKE ME TO THE PILOT

I was recently on a flight over the Rockies and I am not the best flier, but when I am in a small matchbox with wings attached and it has Bob's Airlines written in crayon on the side of it, I am even more of a wreck. Obviously, dear reader, since I'm here writing to you, we landed safely and I took it upon myself to speak with the captain after the flight. Our conversation went something like this. "Excuse me Captain, I have a question for you." "Yes Sir! Fire away."

"Well, since there are only six of us on a flight like this, in the case of a terrible emergency, why don't you give each of us a parachute?"

He looked at me as if I was pulling his leg.

"Are you serious, sir?"

"As a heart attack, Captain."

"Well sir, apart from the added cost let me ask you this, have you ever used a parachute? Have you ever jumped from a plane before?"

"Errrr... NO Captain I have never jumped from a plane and I have never used a parachute."

"Well, you see sir, you have no experience, no perspective, no *knowledge* of how to use a parachute."

"That may be true Captain," I said respectfully. "However I also have no experience, nor perspective nor indeed no knowledge of having my arse fly into a mountain at six-hundred mph either! Give me a parachute and I will take my chances and learn on the way down!!"

Isn't it the truth? Would you not take a chance with a parachute the moment you are told that the plane is going to crash? It is my BELIEF that knowledge, extremely important as it is, should be considered more of a journey, a life-long journey, than an immediate experience. I sincerely believe that if someone handed me a parachute screaming "Quick…put it on and pull this and if that doesn't work pull that!" I would jump and succeed in my very first sky diving lesson.

I am not making light of the power of knowledge. I happen to love it and the opportunities it can bring. I take every opportunity I can to learn new things. But in life you need to take the plunge sometimes and learn on the way down, or up, or even sideways if need be.

# I'D LIKE TO TEACH THE WORLD TO SING

Being receptive is immediate. It lives in the here and now, and the beauty is that it contains knowledge but allows you to gather more as you go. It is important to note that being receptive does not mean letting everything under the sun that comes your way affect you. RECEPTIVITY with *selectivity* is what is most important. To enjoy a successful life you must raise the drawbridge and deny entry to the limitless negative influences that the information age wishes to feed you.

To be successful with your life, it is imperative that you control your own programming in order for you to control your own destiny. It is equally imperative that you spend at least the same amount of time culturing and nurturing your personal growth as you do on things like television and the Internet. We are bombarded by negativity everywhere we turn. Pick up a newspaper and see how difficult it is to find a story that is positive. I was appalled recently to read an article that a Toronto paper publishes each month titled, "One Month of Reasons Why The World Is Getting Worse." It lists an entire month's worth of disasters and disturbing things, like serial killing, famine, violence or just good old celebrity gossip garbage. Just what kind of message does this send out? Would an article called, "One Month of Reasons Why The World Is Getting Better" not sell enough newspapers?

Even if you choose to believe that the world is getting worse, does it not seem logical that if that is all we are prepared to focus our attention on, then we will simply create and receive more of it in return? People change the world and often one person taking a stand is all it takes to form a group of people who can make an incredible difference. People like Rosa Parks, who simply say "enough." People like Mahatma Gandhi or Nelson Mandela. These people are no different than you or me; they are not perfect and may not be highly educated, yet they believe as Gandhi said, "they must be the change they wish to see in others." Does it not follow that if you change something about yourself, no matter how small or seemingly insignificant, that you therefore change the world? Our planet as a whole is what it believes itself to be and if it believes it is a place of anger, war and bloodshed then it will follow that pathway. Conversely, if it believes it is a place of peace, kindness and abundance then that shall be our destiny.

# MONEY, IT'S A HIT

In 1974, when Muhammad Yunus decided to loan $27.00 from his own pocket to poor women in Bangladesh who needed to buy bamboo to make and sell furniture, the spark of an idea was born. By 1976 he had formed the Grameen Bank (*Grameen* meaning rural area or village) and launched the beginning of micro banking, administering tiny loans, 97% of which were going to women. This was unheard of in a country where most women did not even borrow money from financial institutions, but Yunus believed not only that they were credible borrowers, but that in giving them this money he could stop the growth of poverty in Bangladesh.

The figures now speak for themselves. Borrowers own ninety-four percent of this bank, and the government of Bangladesh owns the other 6%. The bank has 6.61 million borrowers, 2,226 branches that cover 71,371 villages and employs 18,795 people. Yunus was correct in his assumption that these high-risk loans were actually not so high-risk at all, as the bank boasts a loan recovery rate of 98.85%, much higher than most North American financial institutions. Since inception, total loans distributed amount to $5.72 billion, of which $5.07 billion has been repaid. In 2006 the Nobel Peace Prize was divided into two equal parts, won by none other than Muhammad Yunus and the Grameen Bank for their efforts to create economic and social "development from below." Yunus knew that breaking the cycle of poverty by giving people needed funds to grow their businesses was the only way to improve his community while advancing the cause for democracy and human rights.

What a wonderfully fulfilling and inspiring story. Did you see that one on the front page of your daily newspaper?

The theory of the Butterfly Effect is that the flapping wings of a butterfly might cause tiny changes in the atmosphere that can eventually lead to a tornado on the other side of the world. The theory also states that the same flapping of the butterfly's wings might also prevent one from occurring. The

Butterfly Effect is a perfect analogy for the story of the Grameen Bank, for today similar banks are sprouting up in all corners of the world. Changing the world is about commitment to the positive creation process each and every day, in everything you think, say and do. We get frustrated because we cannot see how the world could possibly improve. We begin to point fingers at charities or celebrities, saying they are not doing enough or that they are self-serving. This is not the path to improving the planet. We do not know what is in someone else's heart. Albert Einstein said, "All meaningful and lasting change starts first in your imagination and then works its way out. Imagination is more important than knowledge." Change yourself, your words and actions and the world will change. Forty-two families with $27.00 each became almost $6,000,000,000...go figure!

# LET IT BLEED

I grew up surrounded by hate in a religiously segregated world where Protestant and Catholic sectarianism and sometimes violence were the order of the day. I ran with some heavyweights who were always looking for a new notch to put on their rifles. Violence was like dinner to these guys and on many an occasion I even got caught up in the war with rival factions myself. In some cases it was simply survival. Fight or be beaten, literally. Soccer hooliganism and violence was at an all-time high in the late sixties. I witnessed horrors that today I can scarcely imagine. There is a saying that ignorance is bliss, and on rare occasions that may well be true. But ignorance is mostly a travesty. I recognized this, thank goodness, early on in my hooligan phase and even within that darkness as a twelve- to sixteen-year-old, RECEPTIVITY shone a tiny pinhead of light, showing me the way to go, eventually engulfing and eradicating the darkness that was my world.

I have chosen not to fill the pages of my book with descriptive commentaries of how I've witnessed people being seriously harmed, especially since in this day and age our television screens and computers are filled with it. It would be remiss of me however not to at least touch on the topic, because as you'll witness I could have been receptive to a very different pathway at that juncture of my life and only the heavens themselves know what would have become of me. But I didn't. At that tender and impressionable age I chose to use the power of *THE ACTION SANDWICH* for success, not failure, and for light, not darkness. I was already receptive to the idea that violence was a one-way ticket to more violence with the outcome being pain and most likely prison. I wanted a better life and I believed that I was different than those who by choice lived farther from the light. I chose to separate from those who enjoyed the violence even if they were still immature, perhaps even still children. I intended to get out of that pattern of violence no matter what others thought of me for doing so. Finally I took ACTION. I joined a group called "The Boys Brigade" (very similar to the Boy Scouts), where the focus was on self, community and helping others. I got a job in the clothing division of a large department store that kept me busy, off the streets and put money into my pockets. I used all of my communication skills and did more than a few song and dance routines to talk my way out of violent encounters rather than participate in them. On more than one occasion I convinced bigger and tougher guys that I was indeed the leader and they were the followers. If they must fight, the leader didn't have to. The generals always sat atop the hill and watched the battle, right?

This wasn't a perfect solution, and this new direction didn't happen overnight. I brought a lot of that street toughness, Scottish heritage and anger with me as a young adult when my family moved to Canada. It was not uncommon for me to lash out and violently beat a perpetrator for mocking me for being a foreigner or for being different, for it was the Coatbridge way. It was how we handled situations like that. Many of my co-workers in the early seventies were not shocked to see me limping at work since my foot was still sore from an altercation the previous weekend, or that I was sporting heavily bruised or cut knuckles from "that party" I was at the night before. I always knew though, deep in my being, that this was not the answer. Violence truly only begets more violence. You send it out, and you get more of it in return.

On one dark outing I entered a bar to meet my girlfriend when two seated men noticed I was wearing a toque with a Toronto Maple Leaf logo on it. I had just arrived after watching the Leafs win game seven of a playoff series on television with some buddies. (Remember those days?) My friends walked ahead of me but I stopped to listen to what the two had to say to me.

"Hey you! Where did you get that goof ball hat?"
"Sorry, come again?" I asked.
"Oh, RRRRight then laddie and the goofy accent too!"

They each had a beer bottle in front of them and as I focused deep eye contact with them, I gently brought one of their bottles closer to me.

"Look lads, I am in a good mood," I said. "My team won and I am here to have fun with friends, ok?"

Suddenly one of them put his hand up and flicked me under my chin pompously to dismiss me.

"AYE RRRRRight you are then why don't you just piss off, Scotty-boy back to the fields or wherever the hell you came from."

It was over in a matter of seconds. I need not give you gory details but in brief, number one got the beer bottle and number two got a "Glasgow Kiss" – a brutal head-butt to the face. Both were down and out but number one was doing some serious bleeding. As usual I tried to defuse things by pretending that I had no idea what had just happened. I saw my pal and my girlfriend look over with that, "Oh God, not again" look, as I made my way over to the bar and calmly ordered a drink. A girl screamed in the background and a waitress came over to me with finger pointed.

"You animal!" she yelled at me. "You animal, I saw that! I saw what you did!"
"What are you talking about?" I said with my innocent tone.
Just then the barman leaned over to me, "Alan, you better go...now!"

I took a deep breath and headed out at the very moment I saw number one being carried towards the washroom, blood pouring from his face. When I got home, I called the bar and asked for my girlfriend who came on the phone and started giving me regular reports on what was transpiring. She told me that "number two" was back on his feet, bleeding but standing. "Number one" was still in the washroom. She had taken a close look at him and it wasn't pretty. There was no police involvement as of yet, but she thought she overheard an ambulance being called. I felt sick deep within the pit of my stomach, as I had done many times before when these things happened and I admit that they had happened all too often. The feeling of wondering if you had harmed someone to the point that they might have lost an eye, or far worse, was awful, and the waiting for the doorbell to ring and the police to arrive to arrest you for assault causing bodily harm was equally debilitating and nauseating. I detested it. What became of the incident? Nothing. No charges were ever laid and I never saw those lads again.

I can only surmise that like many I had grown up with, they were accustomed to playing rough and that this incident had just been a losing battle on their part and they moved on. Difficult as it may seem, for you dear reader to understand, it was "how things were done" where I came from. Sadly it must have been that way for them as well.

Retaliation is such a natural human instinct. In sport, interestingly enough, especially soccer, it is usually the retaliator rather than the perpetrator who catches the referee's eye and inevitably gets reprimanded. The 2006 World Cup Final quickly comes to mind, and Zinedine Zidane's now infamous head-butt on Italy's Materazzi, which led to his ejection. It is now his cross to bear forever as he retired following that game from the sport to which he has given so much. If given the chance would he take it back? Only he knows for certain, but for my money I'm sure he would be receptive to a much different outcome.

I believe that we are obligated by everything that nature truly stands for to try and make this a better world to live in. Try harder than ever before, to catch yourself when you bask in the negativity of things like anger, revenge and obsession that the world feeds you – and turn it off!

"Are you joking?" you ask me. "I get up in the morning and watch the news, get in my car and listen to talk radio all the way to work, read the paper at my 10:00 a.m. break, put CNN on at lunch to get any breaking news I've missed and just for good measure, you can find me at six and eleven, staying up-to-date on what's going on in the world."

Well, what would happen if you didn't? What if you didn't know about an earthquake or train derailment? What if you didn't know about the disgruntled office worker who has just killed ten of his colleagues before turning the gun on himself? What if you didn't listen to Washington's spin-doctors for a little while? Has your knowledge of this in the past ever helped you? Have you ever personally saved anyone of these victims because you happened to be watching at the time? Have you EVER felt better watching one of these horrendous reports, fed to us ad nauseam, than you did before turning it on?

I want you to try a little experiment. I know it's not easy but I guarantee you, you will feel just a bit more liberated, refreshed and replenished if you can accomplish it. I'm asking you to try not watching the news or reading the newspaper for one week. Just seven days without letting the media and the news influence your life. It's an experiment to see how it affects your outlook. In place of the media I want you to notice every good thing that crosses your path no matter how small, because that's the news no one tells you about. I'm telling you it will change your perspective and your life. As Dr. Wayne Dyer said, "When you change the way you look at things, the things you look at change."

If you find that you must get your fix of the *News according to...* then so be it. However if after the fact you find yourself focusing on the negative of what's wrong with the world or your life, ask yourself a positive question about all that is right with it and all that your life has to offer you and those around you. Perhaps even hundreds of times a day you will need to bring your attention back to the positive things that enrich your journey to combat the negativity that came with your news fix.

If you adapt to this practice of switching negativity to positive thinking, eventually it will become second nature, eradicating your defeatist attitude and filling your life with the kinds of things that you really want by matching your new experiences to the thoughts you are projecting.

# I'M ASKING YOU SUGAR, WOULD I LIE TO YOU?

This is not a book of exercises. However, here is a simple little choice you can make when you awake in the morning and just before closing your eyes at night. Focus on something positive, no matter how small or insignificant it may seem. Be receptive to what made it a great day. It could be that you woke up early and worked out, went for a walk or perhaps helped your little one solve a problem with his or her homework. Perhaps it is how you felt coming home tired from a hard day at the office to your wife's pot roast or maybe even the success you had in making one for her. *THE ACTION SANDWICH* will work to improve your golf swing, your marriage or our planet. Your RECEPTIVITY to troubling issues and their possible solutions, your DESIRE to make things better, your BELIEF that we can have a greater world, your INTENTION to do all you can to accomplish that, your ACTION to give of your time, encouragement or indeed your money, whatever you have to give, and being passionate about helping others, will effect change.

Focus on the life you want. Be the change you want to see in others. When your positive thoughts include being grateful for the life you have or tapping into a PASSION you have for helping others, you will reach your goals even faster.

Did Lance Armstrong have the legs for winning the Tour De France seven times before riding a racing bike? Why did Warren Buffet tell his middle-class wife way back in the early sixties that they were indeed going to be wealthy beyond imagination in such a matter-of-fact manner, as if they were indeed already rich?

The late great actor Jimmy Stewart was a stage hand on the movie set when he was asked by a director to be an extra in a scene, which led to more extra work and then to some solid acting roles. Upon meeting Spencer Tracy on the set one day, he said he was going to leave the movie lot for a while and use some of the money he had made to take acting lessons and become a full-time actor because he loved it so much. Spencer Tracy said, "Are you nuts? You already are an actor. You're working aren't you? Act as you go." He was receptive to the advice and became the legendary actor we all know and love.

If you cannot swim I don't advise that you dive in at the deep end, but get in the water! Start at the shallow end. Splash, feel what it is like to put your head under, get comfortable with water, find someone who can teach you to swim, be receptive. Watch for the signposts and knowledge will follow. Pay attention. Try this simple exercise. Listen more. Speak less. Listening is a tool for success. Many times the words of others contain the clues you are looking for. Allow the perspectives of those you respect to give you a wider view on each decision in your life. Ultimately, trust your heart, your instincts, your intuition and your gut, and NEVER let fear be the beacon that lights your stage.

Remember I promised you the tale of when fear and I had our final showdown? Well, if you liked the story of the shortest show in the history of Rock 'n Roll just wait until you read this!

## CAUTION: MAY CAUSE NERVOUSNESS

Kingston, Ontario, Canada circa 1977, at Queen's University. They had a very happening pub there that offered bands a six-night stint Monday through Saturday, which was very common in those days. The bar scene back in the seventies and eighties was extremely vibrant and most offered live entertainment.

As a fan myself, I used to see great bands like *Rush*, *Triumph* and *April Wine* all play the local scene before hitting the big-time, and I loved it. We were far from the big-time and usually when you got a six-night gig you used the first three nights or so to win people over and hopefully after word of mouth had spread you would get a happening Thursday, Friday and Saturday night. That is exactly how this particular gig began. Monday night we entertained four people, three of whom were staff (the other was the University outcast), but we rocked. If there is one thing I have learned through the years, it is that you give your best show to everyone. Four, forty, four thousand or forty thousand, I have played them all. One thing remains a constant: concentrate on the performance, not the applause. Go on stage, give everything you have to give and leave nothing behind. So on this Monday evening the outcast and the staff got the best show in town, so much so that the next night, Tuesday, saw at least the outcast, the staff and ten others in the pub for our show. We were winning them over. Wednesday saw at least fifty for what turned out to be a great evening, setting Thursday up for more of the same. Word was flying around the campus and we were told to "get ready for Friday, it's gonna be a zoo!"

Ah…"a zoo": music to a musician's ears right. But what about Gag-man? Remember him? Doctor Robert's bag was still with me but I knew I daren't try to street medicate to get through the evening, not after the debacle in Quebec weeks earlier. This event called for something the doctor ordered.

I truly was a bag of nerves, pacing up and down, stopping to stare at myself in the mirror and say, "You can do this, you can do this, you can do this." But wait! There was an echo. "No you can't, no you can't, no you can't," said that other voice, sounding so familiarly like mine. What was a boy to do? I was an absolute wreck. Fear had become so painful for me, so controlling, that I just could not seem to cope. It was a battle that I was now losing before even taking to the battlefield. I couldn't stand it.

"Okay let's see," I said to myself as I slowly opened my little black bag. Inside I had an array of goodies to help me combat my fear. I decided to take a few things. There were some little blue pills that promised to settle my nerves and I think a red one that was specifically for the nerves in my stomach. Are they not all just nerves? I popped them and for good measure I decided to clear my sinuses by inhaling some menthol vapour nasal spray, of course failing to notice that written along the side of the container were the following words: "Caution: may cause nervousness."

That's just what I needed. It seems this stuff can cause nervousness all on its own, and here I am prescription medicated to the hilt and without knowing it have a healthy dose of nervousness racing me to the stage. Here we go again, it's show time!

The drug combination was beginning to have a serious affect on my system. I felt a warm tingling sensation in my ears, nostrils, and eyeballs. My tongue was forked and my hair suddenly wanted to stand up all on its own. My heart raced and, just to add insult to injury every minute or so, our one and only roadie would come up to me to say, "This is gonna be grrrreat!"

The pub was jammed, with as many lined up outside the building as had been inside the previous four nights. The other lads in the band were pumped.

Faster and faster my chest pounded and I thought to myself that if I slipped out now, before the gig started, I could run the three hundred and fifty kilometers home to Toronto and be tucked warm and cozy in my bed before anyone even knew I was missing, but I bailed on that idea when I took a moment to look down and realize that my feet were missing. I had to be hallucinating. I mean my feet were still there, right? I decided against running, just in case. Suddenly the moment of truth arrived.

The band takes the stage; crowd cheers; drummer starts a solid beat; crowd cheers louder; guitar riff to "Alright Now" kicks in; crowd goes... Oh never mind, by now you get the picture.

What followed was so far into fear that really no words can do it justice. However this is a book and words are necessary, so here goes. I swear I couldn't be more scared sunbathing on the Iran-Iraq border. I had just entered hell and found that it is full of Queen's students with 1970's hairdos.

I was sweating profusely, yet had been on stage all of thirty-one seconds. The band was rocking but I had yet to sing a note. I leaned into the bass player.

"Wayne", I yelled over the blasting music.
"Yeah man?" he yelled back.
"Wayne, they're all staring at me."
"Who?" He enquired without missing a note.
"THEY ARE!" I said in disbelief.
"They're supposed to man," said Wayne. "They're the audience!"
He urged me to relax and to get up to the microphone as the band could only keep this intro going for so long before it melted. I slowly, painfully approached my spot. Girls were smiling and winking, guys were cheering and howling. The world was ready, willing and very able to rock!
I clenched my fists and low and behold out came my first words.
"We're gonna take a short break and we'll be right back!!!!"
And the Lord said, "When in doubt...Runnnnn!!"

I was off again like a U.S. border guard as they continued to play the intro. When I reached the dressing room I began to board it up by grabbing anything that was not bolted down. Benches, tables, waste bins, anything would do. Suddenly I heard the voice of our roadie on the other side of the door begging me to come back to the stage. I could hear in the distance that the band had begun to play "Rocky Mountain Way" by Joe Walsh, which was the one and only song that the guitar player could do without me, so it was a race to see if they could get me back up there before the well ran dry.

"Hey man, come on! Please come back to the stage, they're going to riot and we'll get our asses fired." By this time I was boarding up all the air vents just in case they tried to come in that way. I had completely lost it. On stage the lads heard the following message coming through their vocal monitors.

"Alan is not coming back."

Meanwhile, back in the dressing room...I passed out. Fear, it seemed, had its final victory.

When I came around it felt like *War Of The Worlds* and I was the alien. My body drenched in sweat was under a bench in the far corner of the room. The lads were getting the last of the gear together and were obviously shuttling things to our little van outside. The silence was deafening.

"What happened?" I asked the bass player.
"Oh, we played "Rocky Mountain Way" for about forty minutes until they booed us off the stage."

He continued taking his stuff out to the van. Upon his return he looked down at me again.

"Oh yeah, by the way we also got fired. We're in the van. You comin'?"

The journey home was a nightmare for me, as I was still tripping. Our van consisted of a driver in the driver's seat, someone in the passenger seat and someone in the middle seated on a milk crate. The rest of us were huddled together under jackets and blankets in the back as the Canadian winter howled up at us through the large hole in the van's floor. On this occasion, I huddled alone.

Thinking my music career was surely over, I laid low for days. Not only was I convinced that the guys would certainly not want me anymore, I was equally convinced that something was severely wrong with me and that perhaps I just was not cut out for this business of being in the public eye. Yet, amazingly enough, I still knew that I was good at it and that somehow it was what I was meant to be doing. A week or so later I got a call that we had an offer to do a gig way up north in a tiny town called Temagami.

"Is there any point in taking it?" I was asked.

I felt it was better for everyone to give them relief and say the right thing and turn it down. I should say no.

"YES! Yes, let's do it!" I said almost immediately.

Where the hell had that come from? Why did I say that? I was supposed to say no. They wanted no, and I wanted no!

---

# OH NO NOT I, I WILL SURVIVE

As I write this book I have performed live for over twenty-five years and for literally millions of people. As part of *Glass Tiger*, I have looked out over audiences at festivals numbering in the tens, twenties and thirties of thousands. We have performed on national holidays for one hundred thousand and more. I have toured and performed with Rod Stewart, Tina Turner, *Journey*, *The Moody Blues* and dozens more who consistently have hundreds of thousands of people come out to see them. I was the first ever voice to sing live at Toronto's huge domed stadium, the Skydome, now known as the Roger's Centre, when *Glass Tiger* was part of the opening ceremony. If you take into consideration home viewing audiences who have seen *Glass Tiger* from the comfort of their living rooms on the wide array of shows we have done, then I have indeed sung live for hundreds of millions through the years. How then did I do it? How did I win the battle against fear? How did I get the courage to tell the director of the Skydome opening ceremonies that we would do it only if I could sing live (knowing that this would make me the first to do so) or the courage to do the same with the director of an enormous Latino show filmed out of Miami that had a viewing audience of some seven hundred million world wide?

How did Gag-man beat fear? Well, the answer is simple. He didn't, for you don't beat fear. Ask any soldier on the front lines and I am sure he or she will tell you that he is scared each and every time he goes into battle. Ask any firefighter, police officer or search and rescue team, and I am positive they will tell you that they have fear when faced with life-and-death situations. Fear is not a sin. Fear is human. You do not beat it, you accept it, acknowledge it, and understand that it is present. It is what tells you that you are alive and in the moment and that what you are doing is not mundane, or stagnant and certainly not common. It's part of the "if it were easy, everyone would be doing it" category. Successful people know that fear is not the beacon that lights their way, but rather a caution sign that says, "Stop!" but stop doesn't necessarily mean retreat, go back, or give in. Stop means evaluate, question and *think*. Fear is a powerful tool that we have all used even if we don't recognize it as such. Remember your first day of kindergarten. Better still, if you are a parent, think of your child's first day, for that is fresher in your mind. Was he or she afraid? Of course. Most recently, my little one entered a kindergarten class clinging to her mother's leg, but by day's end she was telling us to "go back, not finished yet, Mummy."

Was fear a sign that we should not start school? Of course it wasn't. What about elementary school or, God forbid, that first day of high school? I remember it all too well, being an alien, a foreigner, someone from another land, that thinks, looks and speaks differently from everyone else. What a living nightmare that was! Fear was present in all of these scenarios, yet you overcame it; you worked through it and grew from it.

So that's what happened to me some twenty-five years ago or so back in that little dive in Temagami. I gave myself permission to feel the fear that accompanied going onstage and performing before the public. I looked in the mirror again only this time I said, "If you are going to be sick, then be sick." Moving to the back of the stage for a few seconds to be sick could not possibly be worse than running for the hills and destroying the gig. And what do you think happened? Correct, nothing happened. After coming to terms with the fact that doing something extraordinary carries with it a sense of fear and that this fear is normal, human and acceptable, I never gagged again. I never was sick again. I never popped another pill to get me on stage ever again. Today do I have fear before going on stage? You're darn right I do. Does it prevent me from performing? Never.

What will separate you from the crowd is seeing fear and pain for the guidance it brings you instead of using it as an excuse to be negative, or to quit. Any negative thought, or any chosen suffering will hold you back from the growth you are seeking and the goals you have set for yourself. Peace Pilgrim in her amazingly simple way described following the right path as, "If you should be doing something, start it. If you shouldn't be, stop it." How is it that the simplest things to understand are often the most difficult to implement? The fact is that once you start using *THE ACTION SANDWICH,* when you see things you should be doing, you will get to the point where you must do them. Your new headspace will not allow you to do things you are not meant to do, just those things that enrich your path.

Stop waiting to live! The show is *always* on and it is performed in front of a live audience every moment of every day.

# TALKING HEADS

What must it have been like for Jackie Gleason, Art Carney, Milton Berle and all the other pioneers of early television, when everything was live in front of thousands and eventually millions of viewers. I will bet that if you asked them, they would tell you that they NEVER felt more alive than at that moment when the red light went on and the cameras started rolling. I implore you to ask yourself what change you can make no matter how small or insignificant it may seem. Do it right now, at this very second. Try following the little "think it, do it" rule. This is where you implement something immediately upon thinking of it and not give procrastination a chance. The speed that you move from "thinking" to "doing" is equivalent to the speed in which you will fulfill that which you DESIRE and in turn determines the speed at which your dreams are fulfilled. RECEPTIVITY to the need, not only to "think" but also to "do" is like discovering the gas pedal in a running car. "Thinking it" expedites the process of not having to find the keys, open the door and start the car but it still remains up to you to push down on the pedal determining how fast you go and how much road you will cover each day of your life.

Not too long ago I wrote a line in one of my songs: "Years are only days holding the seconds of each passing hour, history is now for all I know." Simply put, the clock is ticking and as we get older it ticks at what seems like an alarmingly faster rate. What is important to you and worth doing in the time you have left? Are you important enough to yourself to make the change?

Stop the blaming. Kill the excuses. Be receptive. As the eloquent Maya Angelou puts it, "This experience, this life, is our one time to be ourselves." The one time not the dry run or the practice or the dress rehearsal. You do not have to know everything that is going on under the hood in order to be able to drive the car. Let's go! The journey begins now. See, you are hungry aren't you?

# TEN STEPS TO RECEPTIVITY

1. MIND YOUR OWN BUSINESS - RECEPTIVITY should be for things over which you have true control or influence. Understanding, and being sensitive to global issues is important, however, worry and negativity over things that you have absolutely no control, is useless, draining and unproductive. Dude, the dinosaurs are dead. Let it go.

2. I HEARD IT THROUGH THE GRAPEVINE - Your ears remain two of the greatest tools you will ever carry in your toolbox. There is a vast difference between hearing and listening. Many times, more clues lie within what you are being told than what you are saying. Listen.

3. SIGNS, SIGNS EVERYWHERE A SIGN - The universe responds to what you send out in the form of thoughts, ideas, dreams and wishes. Don't ally with luck, coincidence or things that you can't measure. Your RECEPTIVITY should match with who you know yourself to be and who you are becoming. Look for signs that not only uncover what is on the surface of your mind but also dig deeper into what is hidden or dormant. Sometimes our greatest talents live there and only need to be awakened. Wake up.

4. THE GREAT PRETENDER - Acting as if you are already where you need to be or that you already have all that you DESIRE, raises the bar on how your subconscious mind perceives your place in this world and improves your ability to send out higher quality messages to the universe, thus raising the level of your RECEPTIVITY. Don't have it? Act as if you do.

5. DARE TO TRUST - Innocent until proven guilty. Give the world around you the benefit of the doubt by entering into negotiations and new relationships from a point of trust in yourself and in others. You cannot be receptive from inside a bubble. Inevitably at some point you may be hurt, let down or disappointed, but that is called life. By its incredibly positive nature, trust will always bring you more riches than rags, more light than darkness and more success than failure. Trust yourself.

6. SMELL THE ROSES - RECEPTIVITY is your gut's sense of smell. When the situation feels skunky trust your gut instinct and walk away. Toxic people and situations will drain you dry. Lose them.

7. C'EST WHAT? - "Well Mr. Smith, I'm afraid you're dying"
"Can I get a second opinion, Doctor?"
"Ok, you're ugly too!"
Being receptive means not succumbing to or taking for granted that the first answer is the ONLY answer. Question yourself, others, and the universe as much and as often as it takes to find the only true answer, regardless of how the truth makes you feel. Speak up.

8. FEELINGS, WOO-O-O FEELINGS - As someone who was raised in a world where, "Big Boys Don't Cry", I can attest to the fact that it is essential to be receptive to your own feelings as well

as the feelings of those around you. On this road to a life of abundance and success there is no room for blocking out your sensitivities and ignoring those of others. If you do, you will damage your natural relationship with the universe and limit the level of experience that this world can offer you. Feel it.

9. TAKE THE TASTE TEST - Savour every moment and everything in between that is wonderful in your life no matter how small or insignificant it may seem. If you cannot enjoy, love, cherish and appreciate your life then WHAT'S THE POINT? No one's last words are, "I wish I'd spent more time with my nose to the grindstone!" Be receptive to meager treasures, for it's on their shoulders that true fortunes rest. Taste it.

10. GIVE A LITTLE BIT - So you want to get? Then give. It is an indisputable fact that the only way to receive anything of worth in your life, is by giving. Want more love in your life? Give love. Short on cash? Give something to charity. Want more happiness? Easy, make someone happy. Whatever it is that you want on your journey is exactly what you need to send out to the universe through thoughts, ideas, dreams, goals and passions. Give.

# MY SONG
*Opus 1*

### 1976 - 1979

Here's a question for you. What would you have to be given in order for you to be receptive to living above a bar that fills each and every night with a crowd of biking enthusiasts whose taste for illicit activities such as prostitution, illegal pornography, extortion, drug trafficking, and good

old fashioned retribution in the form of murder and mayhem while
filling their human engines with the fuels of their creed, such as, alcohol,
marijuana, cocaine and heroin as they anxiously await your arrival in
order that you might entertain them? What would you want in return, if
asked, to live in a place where the bed is a battlefield for bugs and fleas
that decide to call a truce during your stay, in order that they might
share the spoils of your torso? What about a place where the exotic
dancers keep you awake at night as they begin the toils of their second
trade as exotic hostesses for many of the clientele from downstairs. What
would it take to get you to live in a situation in which eating something
like uncooked macaroni from a box held under some hot running water
because there is no oven, is still considered a luxury? In this place, on
any given night you might find a rat or even the occasional mole in bed
with you trying to stay warm. Would you consider yourself lucky if your
room sat above the filthy kitchen, where the heat from the deep fryer
leaked through the floor boards, giving much needed warmth? Of
course smelling like a giant french-fry is a cheap price to pay in order
that you don't freeze your butt off, so what would it take to get you to
do it, a million dollars, ten million, fifty million plus a lifetime
membership to the "Looney Of The Week Club?" Let me ask you this.
Could you love something enough to be willing to live there for fifty
dollars a week? What about twenty? What about NOTHING?

In some eastern traditions the word for PASSION has two symbols, the
symbol for love and the symbol for suffering. To say that I find that
poignant would be an understatement. LOVE AND SUFFERING, is that
truly what lies between the question, "Are you passionate about what you
want from this life" and its answer? Is it necessary to suffer in the name of
PASSION? Perhaps not, but would you, if you had to? What road lies
between indifference or apathy and the magic of PASSION? I want to
take you on a journey with me. It is a journey of two symbols, LOVE and
SUFFERING. It is a journey of PASSION, which in turn means it is a
journey of true purpose for when all is said and done, true purpose is the
real meaning of this thing we call life. This will be the story within my
story. I call it my Opus and it is readable as one continuous story or as I

prefer, it can be "staggered" which I hope will cause you to anxiously await what comes next. Here we go, follow me.

## I'VE GOT THE MUSIC IN ME

Hearing The BEATLES for the very first time and being given my first guitar as a boy had a profound effect on my psyche, although it took years for it to manifest itself into the form of true purpose. From the stories I tell in this book, I'm sure you will soon get the impression that even as a child, music played a leading role in my existence. The performing for friends and classmates, my father putting on living room shows for family, friends and stragglers alike, the transistor radio being our early morning inspiration as we gathered around a single paraffin heater to dress in the unbearable cold and damp conditions of good old number 16 Kirkshaws Avenue. And of course there were the television shows like *Top Of The Pops* or *Sunday Night At The London Palladium* that were such mainstays in our lives, allowing us to forget the times and places we were living in, and to live vicariously through the PASSION of such a wonderful array of entertainers who had the ability to elevate our spirits and our souls. They made us smile, sing, dance and laugh in the face of adversity and the challenge of living hand to mouth day in and day out. Entertainment made living in hard times, in this hardman's world, just a little bit easier. Looking back it still amazes me how we were riddled with debt and constantly facing the challenges of poverty yet STILL we managed to have an old telly functioning, around which we gathered to be transported away from our worries and woes.

Music however, between the ages of twelve and seventeen was nothing more than a pleasant distraction but I certainly would not rank it higher than my love for football (soccer). I enjoyed it, was good at it but that's where it ended. So what happened?

What suddenly made me receptive to living my life through art and music? What was the epiphany that sent me on the pathway that I remain on to this very day some thirty years later?

## 1973

Within a year of landing in Canada, I met a chap named Martin
Ridgely who was a fine entertainer in the tradition of the classic folk
singer/songwriters of the late '60s and early '70s. Martin and I took to
each other very quickly and soon struck up a friendship. We would get
together several times a week and share our love of music by Elton John,
*The Beatles*, David Bowie and new up-and-comers *Queen* and
*Supertramp*. He taught me several new chords and pretty soon we were
taking our guitars to parties and playing for anyone who cared to sit
around and listen to us. It was however, still very Karaoke-like in as
much as we were merely performing our own interpretations of songs
written by others. Then, it happened one night while sitting around
plunking on my guitar. I hit a chord (it was an E chord, not that it
matters) and I sang a little melody. There's nothing unusual about that,
but this melody wasn't just any old melody, in fact this melody wasn't
anyone else's melody. This one was mine. I continued with these
original lah, lah, lahs, until words started flowing from my mouth that I
was not familiar with. They weren't McCartney's or Taupin's, Jagger's
or Taylor's, they were Frew's.
"Holy shit! I'm writing a song! My first original song! What do you
make of that, world?"
"Hey Mum, Dad, guess what? I've written a song!"
"That's great, hey nip out to the liquor store for me and get a 'wee'
forty-ouncer would ye? And hurry back!"

I played it for Martin.

"That's cool," he said enthusiastically. "Let's write more."

And so, we did. That was the moment, a little magnificent magical,
unadulterated original moment, when my lah, lah, lahs, became my very
first song called, *You're The One*. That's it, without question, the
moment where my DESIRE in music and entertaining was ignited and
it all went from being a pleasant distraction for me to becoming my true

purpose, my PASSION and it has remained so ever since. For any of you out there that care, I finally recorded *You're The One* in 1994 for a solo CD I did called, *HOLD ON*.

Martin and I continued writing our little ditties and continued entertaining and even got our first paying gig at a wedding for a friend of ours, although if memory serves I am not sure if money or beer was the remuneration.

# CHAPTER TWO

## 2

*"DESIRE is the starting point of all achievement,
not a hope, not a wish, but a keen pulsating DESIRE
which transcends everything."*

NAPOLEON HILL

# CHAPTER TWO: DESIRE

The next step to achieving success in anything you put your life force behind is DESIRE. Now this part always sounds and looks simple on the surface. I say, "What do you want?" and you say, "I want a million dollars...cash, and a yacht and a summer home in Tuscany. Oh yes, and a Rolls Royce and a large dog called Fetchmyslippers." Well, let me tell you something. It is perfectly reasonable for you to DESIRE all of these things. However, if I ask you what your next move is on your journey to obtaining all of these things and your answer contains the words *casino*, *lottery*, or *race track*, or if it has anything to do with a nylon stocking over your head the next time you visit the bank, then I will say that we need to talk. Step into my office.

The late great George Bernard Shaw once said, "Hope is DESIRE with an expectation of accomplishment." Now although I am not a big advocate of hoping as a means of achieving, I love this quotation, for it contains the beautiful and profound notion of having to have an "expectation of accomplishment." In other words, your desires must have some connection to that which we call *common sense* in order that you can give them the type of structure needed for success. "Sense and Sensibility" are just as important today as they were in the time of Jane Austin. It is still more than reasonable for me to learn to skate at my present age, but to DESIRE, believe and intend on securing an NHL contract would be pushing it. It does not border on ridiculous; it IS ridiculous, and therefore has zero expectation of accomplishment. For a teenager it is possible, but for me to exert my power and life force behind a notion of skating anywhere other than the frozen pond near my home is a total waste of time and energy. So the fast cars, the luxury yachts, the home in Italy, or whatever your desires may be are very possible, however don't forget that an expectation of accomplishment must come with it. DESIRE anything you want but it is better to DESIRE those things that remain within the realms of common sense. You must be able to believe that you can have the things that you tell the universe you want.

Desires can and should be established incrementally. What you want today may be different than what you'll want once you're a millionaire, because how can you know what you will want as a millionaire when you've never been one? Work towards your attainable desires in the moment and you cannot go wrong. Desires with expectations of accomplishment based on common sense will lead to achieved goals as you negotiate and conquer each rung of the ladder on the way to a successful life. Today you want to prepare the most important proposal you have ever written so that tomorrow you will close your largest business deal, which in turn will secure that raise, which someday will help pay off the mortgage. Remember the thousand-mile journey? One step at a time, my friend. A journey to success is no different. DESIRE, BELIEF PASSION all are just steps on the stairs of life and it's perfectly okay if it is three steps up and one back, because that's also part of the journey. Life isn't one staircase negotiated at breakneck speed from bottom to top all in one go.

The crime being committed day in and day out by literally millions of adults all over this planet is that so many have no DESIRE at all because they have no idea what they want out of their lives and they have no INTENTION of finding out why this is. Give me an eighty-five-year-old dude who has his *ACTION SANDWICH* knob turned to "ten" desiring to be a male model in Milan and I say, "Good on ya mate!" While most of us might chuckle at the idea, I would also admire his courage, his tenacity and perhaps even his suit. However, show me an eighty-five-year-old who lived an entire life of "always getting ready to" and who never ever knew what he wanted from this world, and I will show you a human tragedy. I'm striving to be at it like Andy Rooney, who at eighty-seven still has a voice, or Charlotte Hamlin the seventy-five-year-old long distance cyclist who is telling the world that fitness is essential for everyone.

Once ignited, DESIRE is an ageless and renewable resource. It grows within you and when satisfied becomes restless again with the need to achieve more. Successful people are in tune with this concept and use it to build empires. Bill Gates doesn't stop at twenty, thirty, or forty billion dollars. He continues the journey that he loves and is so very passionate about.

Promise yourself right now that you will not fall prey to society's definition of success. You must define it for yourself in order to be happy. For Bill Gates that means billions, but for others it's a two-bedroom cozy cottage.

Don't try to fix your dissatisfaction in one part of your life by distracting yourself in another. If your DESIRE is to have a great marriage, a bigger house and faster car will not fix it, if things are not all right at home. If your DESIRE is to have a healthy relationship with your children and you're failing, all the money in the world will not make it better. Align your desires and actions, and do not assume that the answer to everything is monetary. Your ultimate goal must be to live YOUR life to YOUR standards, whatever they may be, and your gut is your best gauge.

## EVERY STORY TELLS A PICTURE

Being in a vocal booth at a recording studio was nothing new to me. In fact you could say it was old hat. I never lose sight of the fact that I am blessed to be able to make music that so many people listen to and enjoy. Having sold so many CDs, and hearing my songs on the radio still thrills me, so being in THAT vocal booth on THAT particular day felt like I was doing what I was meant to be doing. On that day though, I was sharing the space with another singer, for my vocal part on the track was already in the can, as they say in the industry – completed, secured, and I didn't have to re-sing any of it. So what was I doing in THAT vocal booth you might ask? Well, THAT singer was going to put his part down for me and turn my song into a duet, and he had asked me to come in and sing as he warmed up to the track and learned his part. When he was ready to go I would leave the booth and come out to the front and just listen, but for now I was there to guide him through my lyrics. There was one particular moment, however, that I will never forget as long as I live.

The vocal booth was dark except for one small light shining down on the lyrics of my song sitting on a music stand. I could have been anywhere, in any number of studios, in any city in the world. But I wasn't. I was in THAT city, in THAT studio, with THAT singer, and for a moment the silence was broken as he decided to do a little warming up of his precious vocal chords by performing some bluesy and R&B type scats; that is to say, some off-the-cuff non-lyrical lah, lah, lah's and oohs and ahhs, which he did so effortlessly, ahead of singing the song for the first time. I closed my eyes. A soft chill went down my spine and the small hairs on the nape of my neck tingled as I listened to THAT voice in my headphones.

My heart raced. Suddenly, as the singer continued his warm-up, in the darkness of my mind a bright light began to shine way off in the distance and an image became bright and crystal-clear. I remembered the scene so vividly at that moment, as it had been back in 1969 when it all took place for the very first time.

Ah, there's my dear old dad sleeping on the chair after having a well-deserved supper. He had pork chops tonight. I on the other hand had soup with lots of bread in it to fill my hungry twelve-year-old tummy. But after all, he is my dad and he deserves the pork chops and besides, I know I will get to chow down on whatever he leaves.

There's my mum at the sink. Boy, she looks young. Funny I've never thought of my mum as ever having been young before but that's silly isn't it? She just got home from work not long ago, as both of them have to work to make ends meet. In fact my dad holds down a second job at a betting office on Saturdays, where men come to gamble on horse racing and greyhounds. That job causes such arguments here because my mum swears that "That tart who works with your dad on Saturdays is after him." He says it's a load of "bollocks" but it sure does cause grief around here. Sometimes they fight so ferociously that I am terrified and it usually ends with my mother asking me to "decide" whom I want to be with. "Him or me," she'll say. It's a loaded question because even if I say him, she'll grab me by the hand and say, "No you're coming with me," and then we'll walk the length of the town to my grandmother's.

Still the singer continues his warm-up.

There I am, over there, on the floor in front of the television. Boy, I look so tiny! It must be Thursday, because I am glued to something other than football so it has to be, yes I see it, it's *Top Of The Pops*, a weekly show featuring the music world's biggest stars and new up-and-comers. I love this show and I couldn't be any more receptive to its PASSION and power than I already am. Look at my young face and my eyes. They are literally dancing to the music. It would be fun to do THAT someday. There is no doubt in my mind that I DESIRE attention, for I love to entertain people so much that when the teacher at school asks who will come up and entertain the class I am always the first to put my hand up. Then, taking charge, I bring Willie, Davy and Ian up to be *The Beatles*, to the delight of the entire class. Of course, we have only air guitars but that's okay as the class doesn't even notice or care. By the way, I am always Paul.

Man, this guy beside me can really sing.

I have been waiting for this great new artist who has been number one for the last few months. I love him. Some day I want to be just like him, having hit songs, making music, entertaining people, and one day I will even sing with him. Now that would be success. I don't care what it takes; I just want to do it. What an entertainer this guy is on our old black and white telly as he struts his stuff up and down the stage in his tight leopard pants and sings with THAT voice, that one-of-a-kind, bluesy, raspy, R&B voice that could only belong to...

"Alan, hey Alan! I'm ready man, let's start the track and go for it."

Suddenly, back in the moment, I jumped and shook my head a little like you do when returning from a deep sleep.

"Where am I?" I wondered. Ahh, yes, I am here, here where I belong, doing what I was born to do, and I am working with him, THAT singer. "Okay, Rod, let's do it," I said confidently, masking the fact that I cannot believe for one second that I am doing a duet with none other than my friend Rod Stewart.
"I was just watching you on the telly," I said.
"Where, when, what the hell are you talking about?" says Rod confused.
"Never mind" I say sheepishly. "Who'd believe it?"

The *ACTION SANDWICH* would.

# AM I HEARING VOICES?

What separates DESIRE from the realm of wishes and hopes is the concrete foundation it builds as it burns within your heart and mind and the core of your body, as opposed to existing only within your passing thoughts. It is fuel for the fire that is yet to come. It is a very delicate piece of the puzzle and it is easily driven in a downward spiral by self-sabotage or a negative voice within. Have you ever driven through a beautiful neighbourhood or walked by a car showroom and as soon as you hear that little voice in your head say, "Wow I'd like to have that," there's another one that says "Yeah right, that'll be the day?" Well, that's the daydreamer talking to the self-saboteur. As easily as one hopes for it, it is sabotaged by a sense of unworthiness, disbelief or failure. This can be one of two things. It can be your own insecurities at play trying to sabotage your goals or just a lack of true DESIRE. You must decide which it is. It would be like me in a Ferrari showroom. I don't really care about Ferraris. I can appreciate the beauty of the car and the momentary ego-boost it provides, but for me when that little voice says, "Right, that'll be the day," it is correct. Because I should be focused on another model of vehicle. I do, however, have a tremendous DESIRE to be a working actor; therefore *THE ACTION SANDWICH* formula has kicked in full steam ahead and when it comes to acting there are no negative self-sabotaging voices of any kind in my head...period!!

I cannot stress enough the importance of that voice within your head. It is fair and reasonable if it is saying *NO* to you for the right reasons i.e. "No, Alan, you don't want a Ferrari." However, a voice such as, "No, Alan, you don't deserve a Ferrari" is simply not acceptable and would never stand a chance inside of my head. You must not let it exist inside of yours. Chat with it, wrestle with it if you must, look at where it comes from but at all cost you must take the time to acknowledge, dominate, defeat and rid your mind of it.

We all experience this but it is the focused, motivated and well-intentioned who take the time to understand and rid themselves of their self sabotaging thoughts and then go on to succeed. I'm telling you that if you don't let yourself DESIRE all of the great things you could have in your life you won't get them. Success is dependent upon DESIRE. DESIRE is dependent upon an expectation of accomplishment. Things must make sense. Whether it is to make a lot of money from a particular idea that you have, or to make beautiful music, if you are receptive to it and DESIRE it then you are on the road to success.

Let's see, you are now receptive to a particular outcome that you wish to achieve and you have the fire of DESIRE burning in your belly. You now know what you really DESIRE. Is this enough? No, DESIRE alone is incapable of moving you to a state of INTENTION. What must come next is BELIEF: true, unwavering, undeniable BELIEF. You must truly believe that you are capable, worthy, entitled, and deserving of success and of the life you DESIRE. So let's meet BELIEF. Where's my sandwich?

# TEN STEPS TO DISCOVERING YOUR DESIRE

1. I'M STARTING WITH THE MAN IN THE MIRROR - Knowing what it is that you truly DESIRE is essential. Desires should not be fleeting thoughts but rather penetrating experiences built on solid foundations, infused with deep emotion. Reinforce this message and image of the happiness you seek as you go about your day. Be aware.

2. FLY ME TO THE... TOWER? - It's perfectly fine to DESIRE the moon but I ask you this, "Will it fit in your living room?" Having a sensible expectation of accomplishment is essential on the journey to success. DESIRE must be attainable. If need be, increment your desires as you would your steps on a journey. Grab the Eiffel Tower, then the moon.

3. DECISIONS, DECISIONS, DECISIONS - What does success look like to you? That's really the secret to a prosperous life. Never come from a place of wishing and hoping but rather from believing and knowing exactly what it is that you need in your life to feel successful. Deciding is the first step to achieving. Decide.

4. MY POGO STICK, PET ROCK, BELLBOTTOMS, LAVA LAMP AND OH YES, MY LAWRENCE WELK COLLECTION - If you could only have five things, what would they be? Decide today and plan to go and get those five things. Have you signed up for the class, called the travel agent, bought the cookbook or joined the club? Go get five things you want and when you succeed, pick five more and go get them. Go.

5. IT'S MY LIFE - Every thought starts with you, and you alone. Don't wait for someone else or some profound circumstance to bring you what you want. Remember self-responsibility doesn't necessarily mean going it alone. Soliciting help or partnership may be the difference between success and failure. Be open.

6. BIT BY BIT - Accomplishing small goals allows you to feel successful immediately. Skyscrapers are created one brick at a time. If necessary walk success before running it. Create.

7. MY PLACE OR YOURS? - What constitutes success? You do. To some being in the pit is a lifelong dream while others can only be satisfied behind the wheel of the roaring Formula One engine. But in order to win the world championship all of us must be the best at what we do. Excel.

8. I KNOW I KNOW I KNOW - Don't let THEM, IT or THAT get to you. Do what you know you should be doing regardless of what the chatter around you is saying. Stay aimed at your target, focus, persevere and smile because you are doing what you love and that my friend is success. Love it.

9. DON'T SURROUND YOURSELF WITH YOURSELF - Never stop helping others in the achievement of their dreams. When assisting others you are focused on manifesting a positive outcome not only for them, but also for you and indeed, the universe. "Butterfly Effect" my friend, "Butterfly Effect."

10. FRIENDS IN LOW PLACES - Critics, back-biters, fault-finders, skeptics and toxics have no place in the life of someone who is committed to success, abundance and living the best life they can. These detractors are dedicated to helping you stand still or lose ground. Dump 'em.

# MY SONG
*Opus 2*

## COME TOGETHER

By 1976 I was approached by some musicians who asked me to join a band, not as a guitar player I might add, but as their singer. They arranged a band rehearsal, yet neglected to tell their regular singer that it was happening, making this all very clandestine indeed. I sang one song with them, "Get Back" by none other than *The Beatles* and they became putty in my hands. The deal was done. The original singer, who I swear to you, had the last name of Singer, was doomed. They took a vote. To this day, *Glass Tiger's* bass player claims he didn't vote as it was already unanimous by the time it came around to him, for you see dear reader, Mr. Singer, the now ex-singer, was at the time his closest friend. Et tu, Brute?

Such is the way of bands as they weave the web that the world becomes entangled in. By the time I recorded my first CD some twenty years after getting into the business, I had only been in two bands, yet within the makings of what finally became *Glass Tiger*, I have probably worked with fifteen or twenty guys.

As I mentioned earlier, I didn't take to being in a band immediately and on many occasion I would dodge rehearsal preferring to sit by the fire and watch *Hockey Night In Canada* or a good movie instead. Finally though it was the emergence of our first original song as a band that sent me back on the pathway to becoming successful. It didn't hurt I might add, that I had just seen what the world was calling a video of a concert filmed live in the famous Budokan, in Japan. The band was called *Cheap Trick* and the concert is now legendary. They were adored and worshipped by thousands of screaming girls and when you watch the footage of them performing you just know they are working at their true purpose. I looked at the screen and said without any hesitation, "Oh yeah! I want that job!" My epiphany was about to become a pilgrimage.

You see, once true PASSION takes over, you are helpless in an attempt to fight it. No question. You will suffer until you fulfill your DESIRE. You obsess with the need to do something, love someone, try something, and be something. Your stomach knots, your heart aches, you lose sleep, you're in a fever, driven uncontrollably to follow the path that love puts you on.

PASSION made Shakespeare the Bard of Avon, put Armstrong on the moon and caused Martin Luther King to change a generation. It drove a deaf Beethoven to write symphonies and a Gandhi to his demise at the hands of his assassin. Yes LOVE AND SUFFERING absolutely are the two symbols of PASSION.

I sit here today, fifty years of age, somewhat matured, very reflective yet deeply content and I feel equally as empowered by my true purpose today as I did as a scrawny twenty-year-old, back what seems like a million years ago, yet only yesterday. When I ask myself the question, "Am I doing what I love?" the voice that asks the question is indeed a fifty year old one, but yet the echo that returns a resounding "YES!" is that of the Believer, the Desirer and the Intender, and it is ageless. It has no number attached to its being. It is constant. It is immortal.

They say be careful what you wish for, for you might just get it. I know what they mean. Wanting that job and working at that job, were two entirely different things.

We decided right from the get-go, that we wanted to look and sound like a 'real' band, a big-time band, which meant having to rent a bona fide sound system, a great lighting rig and a small crew to run them. The cost usually ate up whatever we were being paid that week, sometimes even exceeding the amount of our payment, forcing us to dip into our own pockets to make up the difference. On infrequent occasions, we might manage to bring it in under the wire, leaving ourselves a small wage. No wait, a "wee" wage, no that's not it, a tiny, miniscule, minute wage of ten to twenty dollars, which of course was to feed, intoxicate or numb you, depending on your preference, for the entire week. Remember now we were not at home and this scenario would be taking place far away, perhaps in the frozen tundra's of northern Ontario or Quebec. I always threw caution to the wind when I was handed that ten or twenty dollar bill, and I would immediately order a steak dinner and a few beers and use it all up in one sitting, then the game was how I was going to eat for the rest of the week.

Now this isn't the story of a choirboy, nor is it a tale of the boy most likely to be high school president. This is a tale of a guy in 1977, singing in a band, doing his thing, working the room, holding up his end of the bargain and living under a huge billboard sign that reads, "Sex, Drugs and Rock 'n Roll, Right This Way" with a big arrow pointing right at him. All this boy wants to do is stay alive. Stay alive and live to tell the tale someday.

## MONA LISAS AND MADHATTERS

"God bless groupies!"
"What did you just say?"
"You heard me, I said God bless groupies. Oh yes and strippers too!"

Think what you want folks but if it was not for so-called groupies and the girls of the dance-pole, I am certain beyond any doubt that I and many like me in the music industry, would have been nothing more than a group of performing skeletons. The dancers simply made tons and tons of money. Yes I know some of them had an extra job on the side, a job that many do not approve of, the oldest known profession on the face of this earth but what the heck, who are we to judge? So they were loaded, and they had mercy, which they lovingly bestowed upon the starving musicians along the hallway. A pizza, a sandwich or a cup of tea was always most welcomed by the lads in the band. These young women were generous, sweet and kind. They knew we were broke, it wasn't hard to figure that out and so they helped us. Due to their numerous costumes that they wore on stage, they were all quite proficient seamstresses and they would gladly help sew a hem, stitch a button or put in a patch, as your clothes slowly fell apart around you. Ironically, I can't recall any instances where sex took place between any member of the band and these girls, even though sex was their trade. We all truly bonded as entertainers, road warriors, just trying to make a living, just trying to get a foot on the bottom rung of the ladder of success. They were our peers and I always think back on them fondly.

Now groupies, they are an entirely different breed. I am certainly a man of the world, not prudish in any way and I definitely don't believe in censorship except on behalf of our children and I most certainly cannot deny that my promiscuity in those times, reveled in the sheer number of women that came out to see us play. The groupie thing goes far beyond the mere concept of two people finding each other attractive enough to have instantaneous, intimate relations together, for the groupie syndrome goes deeper, much deeper than sex. These girls begin to behave as surrogate girlfriends or even mothers uncaring of the fact that there may be a significant other or even a spouse at the home of the musician. I have and never will understand the mentality of anyone who feels compelled to somehow lay claim to a guy in a band by sleeping with him and in doing so then believes somehow that they two, are now one, a couple, at least until he leaves town on Sunday!

I am not about to dedicate page upon page to the distorted mindset of the groupie, however it is relevant to my story to note that they wanted something and of course I wanted something, so the playing field and the rules of the game would be set pretty darned quickly. Within minutes you were new best friends, like you had known each other since childhood as opposed to only the last seven minutes. Her desires usually had something to do with you, your jeans and her bedroom, while on the other hand, your DESIRE usually had something to do with her kitchen, her pantry, her washer and dryer and God bless her, yes her bubble bath! Oh yes, there was sex, lots of sex, but even sex isn't as great a motivator as hunger. Borderline starvation will bring out the 'tramp' in you pretty fast and so it was that I would carefully place myself in a group of females knowing all too well that one, two or perhaps all of them would be fishing for one of the boys in the band and as they chatted eagerly divulging who they were, where they came from and where they lived, I would listen for keywords.

"Cooking." (There's one.)
"Roast beef." (Lovely.)
"Mashed Potatoes and gravy!" (Music to my ears.)
"Bubble bath!" (THAT'S IT! I'm going home with her.)

And so without fail, I would end up staying at "Sally's house" and we'd live like the couple next door, playing the role of 'your neighbours,' doing everything except inviting the in-laws over for tea. My clothes were clean and my belly was full and I was ready to face whatever 'crack house' we had decided to go to next. Sad really, yet at the time, it was as normal as my life is today.

During this period of my life I decided out of the blue that if my career as rock star was going to evade me that I should "become" something else and so I decided that the something else I should become was a doctor.

By this time I could have said male stripper because God knows, I had all the moves down pat, from watching the dancers, but I didn't, I said doctor instead. And so I applied to medical schools and colleges around the province of Ontario and very soon thereafter letters of rejection came flooding in. I swear some were like, "Dear Mr. Frew, We are sorry to BWA! BWAH! BWAHAHAHAHAHAH!!"

It was at that moment I wished I had taken things just a little more seriously back in my high school days, for it was now apparent that although smart, my school marks did not speak of intelligence and to boot I had basically no credits in the fields of science and biology. Every one of them told me to forget it but I think you know by now that I am not very good at that and so I had to draw up fresh battle plans.

## WHO'S CHEATING WHO?

"Ladies and gentlemen, I give you employee of the month, Alan Frew!"

My dad looked at me rather skeptically out of the corner of his eye, for he knew I detested this place and had only taken this job out of necessity and that I had always attempted to do as little as possible here, so how then, was it remotely feasible that his son, yours truly, had been selected as employee of the month for turning in the highest quota of freshly cut tubing? Simple really, however before I tell you the answer, let me tell you where I am.

It's a large tubing factory where my job is to take twenty-foot long rods of steel tubing and cut them into pieces six inches long. It was the worst job I had taken since working in a plastics factory a few years earlier where I had twelve-hour shifts watching plastic form into rolls similar to what a toilet roll looks like only these were huge. I got so delusional there one time I deliberately cut my hand only to be taken to the hospital, stitched up, and relieved of duty for two whole weeks.

This steel tube cutting job wasn't much better and indeed I even went as far as to do a smaller hand cutting job on myself to get out of it for a few days. Insane as this sounds, this job was a family affair, for my father, mother, brother and brother-in-law all worked in this hell hole at the same time, the only difference being that they worked the day shift while I on the other hand worked nights. My God I hated it and so I started a campaign of phoning the local hospital to ask if there was an opening for an orderly or porter position, my logic being that if I could just get into a hospital I may be able to plan my next move as to how to become a doctor! I was relentless, calling sometimes two or three times per day. It got to the point that as soon as they answered the phone in the office and I said a word, they knew who it was.

"Hello!"
"No Alan. As I told you two hours ago, there are still no openings," she would say, referring to me on a first name basis.

I began purchasing medical and science magazines that I would read during my spare moments and while on my breaks. Of course as always, I found lots of humour in this factory and had lots of laughs within its walls. Still I never lost sight of where I wanted to go next and so every day I would call, while every night I would cut, well I would kind of cut. On night shift, which I disliked immensely, I would sneak off to the toilet for forty winks or read my magazine. Upon my return I would look at the quota of the two shifts prior to mine and then I would add a whole lot of their work into mine, basically fabricating my count.

Now I am not advocating cheating and of course it was inevitable that if this process were to continue over a period of time, that my misconduct would be discovered and my backside would be shown the door, but these were desperate times for me and I did not care, for I was getting a job in the hospital and I was going to be a doctor and that was that!

Looking back on it, I would have handled it differently, by actually cutting above and beyond my quota of tubes and in doing so, becoming the employee of the day, the month and even the year if need be. By doing this I would have left an indelible mark of positivity behind that would have allowed me to know that I had honestly done my best in a place that I detested and under painful circumstances I would still have shown integrity. They in turn would have lost a good worker, who they would have spoken highly of, sending out the right message to the universe on his behalf, instead of the negative one they would surely send upon discovering a cheater who had wronged them by fixing the numbers.

"Sorry Alan, still nada!" the lady in the hospital employment office would say regularly.
"Okay let's see then, how many did I cut tonight?" Said the tube cutter.
"Six hundred and sixty seven. Okay time to log that into the records."
He writes 9, 9, 7....
Hey! What's a six but an upside down nine, right?

My father looked at me out of the corner of his eye, for he knew me all too well.

"Alan, with an astounding tally," said the foreman, "Has cut more tubes this past month than anyone else in the entire workforce. Why it's as if he's cutting for all three shifts!"

(The employees all smile as the tube-cutter clears the back of his throat).

The days past and the nights were long. I had cut back on gigs due to the fact that I was working steady nights but I did continue to rehearse and rehearse and rehearse with the lads as much as possible. Then one night not long after being caught sleeping in the toilet, (again), for which I received yet another warning, I was told to go to the office.

"Shit, they're on to me!" I said under my breath on the long walk to the head office. I entered cautiously and addressed the staff.

"Someone sent for me?"
"Hey Mr. Employee of the month," said one of the girls from behind her desk. "You have a phone call."

I was a little worried for it was still only 6:30 a.m. and so I was afraid that something was wrong at home.

"Hello?"
"Alan?"
"Yes."
"This is York County Hospital...Do you want a job?"

## THE FIRST CUT IS THE DEEPEST

"What are you doing son?"
"Easy, I am aligning my actions with my dreams."
"What are you thinking?"
"Simple, I am thinking about what it will be like when I am one."

"And what exactly is it that you are going to be?"
"Why, a doctor of course."

As a youngster I had a curious fascination with the human body. No not that. That came later. I am talking about biology, the ins and outs of how we are "put together." Interestingly enough, I remember as a child a lady came to our door and told my mother that for the fair sum of sixpence and a cup of tea, she would "read" the tea leaves in the bottom of my mother's empty cup, telling her, her future and what lay in store not only for herself but for her family. Tasseography as it is called, has been around for centuries, originating in Asia, Ancient Greece and the Middle East and it was not uncommon for a woman to earn her living, going door to door, offering her psychic services to others who were in dire need of good fortune and my mum of course, was one of them.

Now I admit that I have always been a bit of a skeptic around those purporting to have such powers and since the Seer basically looks at the pattern of tea leaves in the cup before allowing her imagination to play around with the shapes suggested by them, I haven't changed my position and to this day I remain skeptical. However, something was said that day to my mother that I will never forget and it's one of those things, those eerie things, the kind that can leave even the most skeptical among us, wondering if perhaps, it just may be real after all. She looked in the cup and said as she nodded in my direction,

"That one's going to be a doctor."
"Alan? Are you sure?" said my mother.
"Oh, yes dearie, I sees it all here, a doctor he'll be."
"Oh, I don't think so," said my mum confidently.

What the hell did she see in the bottom of the cup exactly, Dennis The Menace with a rubber glove on one hand? Who's to know, of course at that time she would have made as much sense saying that I was going to be the Prime Minister, but a doctor? I hated doctors and I was terrified of her too, so I scampered off as fast as I could leaving her and my mother pouring 'seconds' and getting ready to find out if my dad really was having a fling with that blonde tart in the off track betting shop he worked on Saturdays.

"Me, a doctor?" I thought to myself. "That'll be the day."

# CHAPTER THREE

## 3

*"You can have anything you want
if you will give up the BELIEF that you can't have it."*
ROBERT ANTHONY

# CHAPTER THREE: BELIEF

Sadly, this quote from Robert Anthony fits all too well with the day-to-day lives of so many of the multitudes of people that I meet in my travels. "Victim-speak" oozing from their pores, telling me why they are stuck, why they are broke, why they live with abuse, why they will never get ahead, why they will never own a business, why, why, why, why and almost always at some point they bring up the topic of BELIEF and worthiness even if they are not aware of it. Interestingly enough, when I was formulating *THE ACTION SANDWICH* I once again was tempted to insert knowledge here as opposed to BELIEF, and yet once again I resisted, held firm and did not. There are those who say that BELIEF is knowledge with an option, meaning you will believe as long as things seem to be going forward as planned, but as soon as life throws out a knuckle-ball you drop the bat, walk off the playing field and quit. I whole-heartedly disagree with this assumption and say that BELIEF is knowledge with certainty.

You cannot fake ideology. You cannot half-believe. You either do or you don't believe. There's no out-clause. You can force yourself to suppress, you can cover up true INTENTION, you can delude yourself all you want, but you cannot hide from that which is true. Now don't think for a second that it becomes automatic that if indeed you believe in something with total certainty that you will necessarily succeed, for BELIEF is not enough in and of itself. Remember, there are many parts to *THE ACTION SANDWICH* and it's all about the performance in all of these areas not just the applause at the end of the day. But BELIEF isn't interchangeable. BELIEF is concrete; again, you either do or you do not believe. You must know with conviction that you are on your right path every single day, and believe that your choice is taking you to your perfect outcome.

In fact, I'm going to tell you that the truly successful people in this world don't give personal gain much of a thought. They are passionately absorbed in the journey that they are on each day of their life. Each morning these rare souls can't wait to get out of bed and get working on what they left waiting from the day before. They love their work and their lives and the financial gain and the accolades are simply a bonus and byproduct of their efforts. Frank Sinatra sang because that was his gift to honour, not because he wanted to make a million dollars. Anthony Hopkins is an actor who happens to be a millionaire as an outcome of his PASSION. Stephen King writes, because an author is who he is. And you, too, have a gift, a reason for being that will fulfill your heart's DESIRE each day as well as pay life-dividends along the way.

> *"Life is like a box of chocolates,*
> *you never know what you're gonna get."*
> FORREST GUMP

The ACTUAL outcome in life is never completely one hundred percent within your control, no matter how much you may believe. I do not care who you are, what you do or how rich you may be, you cannot with certainty predict the outcome of everything and get it totally right.

Everything changes, so learn to love it and once you get good at implementing the formula of *THE ACTION SANDWICH*, you need to also be one step ahead of yourself, knowing what you want next, because there is no end. Bill Gates is indeed super-rich, yet is he finished being rich or is he going to be even richer? And if so, just how much richer is he going to be? Even he cannot know with certainty. However, what he can say is that he believes he is on the right pathway to becoming even richer than he is at the present time. When he was a teenager dabbling in that which was to become Microsoft, do you really think for a second that he knew with certainty that it was going to lead to his amassing some fifty BILLION dollars? There are an infinite number of outcomes to the same opening in any game of chess. So focus on the matter at hand. RECEPTIVITY is just one part of the journey; DESIRE another, as is BELIEF and knowledge and PASSION. Honesty, integrity and yes, anger, violence, pain and suffering all have their place and must be handled appropriately. Remember *THE ACTION SANDWICH* is working regardless of who you are and what your intentions may be.

Do you get my point? Life is not just black and white or hot and cold. Answer me this, how good is good? How rich is rich, how talented is talented? And by the way, how do you know when you've arrived? You would drive yourself crazy trying to figure it all out, would you not? Outcomes lead to more outcomes and change – that is the one thing you can count on. Successful people don't get their lives set up and then follow a particular pattern from then on. The successful ones look to attain "control." That is to say, they decide to have as much "say" as possible in how their lives are going to play out, but sometimes the universe has plans for them that even they cannot predict.

## MAMA WEER All CRAZEE NOW

Here's a question for you. What do Mother Teresa and Osama Bin Laden have in common? No, I am not crazy. Just answer the question. What if I told you that I believe that they have a lot in common – would you agree with me? Probably not, yet I truly believe that they have a common denominator not only with one another but with countless other highly motivated and exceptionally successful people. In fact, with you. Well, what exactly? Let's see, RECEPTIVITY to purpose, unwavering DESIRE to succeed, BELIEF with certainty that the pathways chosen are the true ones, and INTENTION that enough force, focus and willpower fueled by great ACTION leads to the highest levels of achievement in their respective fields. And as for PASSION, need I say more? So the only major difference between the two of them on a strictly superficial level: outcome. One endeavored to spread human kindness, love and peace at the highest level of energy, while the other is the antithesis wreaking havoc, causing mayhem and inflicting death on those he calls infidels. As a matter of fact, his strategy is so powerful that he can convince many, many others that his RECEPTIVITY, DESIRE, BELIEF and INTENTION is also theirs and so they apply their actions to doing his bidding for him and of course history has shown us all too well how deadly and dangerous that can be.

Yet I say to you, they both have shown the highest level of commitment to what is or was important to them. Does my comparison of these two energies shock you? Good. It's meant to. Now I wonder if those searching for Bin Laden are as receptive, desirous, believing, intended and passionately "actioned" as he is, about catching him?

Everything depends on how the formula applies to you and only you. What do you believe your purpose is? What journey do you believe is the right one for you? The only way you will accomplish great things in your life will be to believe, to KNOW without doubt that what you DESIRE will happen for you.

Take the time to make yourself answer the difficult questions of life such as those I posed to you at the beginning of this book. Give yourself the gift of a turning point in your life. Find your purpose and be clear with yourself about who you are right now, and who you want to be as you grow. You are either rich or you are not. You are in shape or not in shape. You are either focused or you are not. Face up to what is, so that you can make good decisions about what can and will be. Then let "what is" go. *THE ACTION SANDWICH*, as I mentioned, is already working for you regardless of whether you are aware of it or not. It works for the good guys and it works for the bad guys and it also works for the indifferent. The only difference is the outcome. The pathway you choose to take towards the outcome is what is important. Did I know with certainty that when I chose to be a musician I would write one, three, seven or ten hit songs? Would I earn $100 or $100,000 or even $10,000,000? Of course I did not know. Did Wayne Gretzky know for certain that he was going to be known as the greatest to ever play the game of hockey? I say no. However, what I am certain of was that both he and I and all other successful people are on the right pathway to our successes and that everything else like the money, the fame and the accolades are all just by-products of that BELIEF in our choices and in ourselves.

> *"Sometimes I've believed as many as six*
> *impossible things before breakfast."*
> LEWIS CARROLL

Please remember that money is a natural outcome but it is not a life force and deserves only the attention that is required to use it for its intended purpose. Don't focus on it, fret over it or pine for it. (Try not to steal it either!) It is inanimate. Your real currency is your thoughts, because they attract more in kind and inspire you to make the moves in your life that bring inanimate objects like money, cars and houses to you. If your thoughts are constantly on the next achievable step, and they are moving you towards your ultimate goal, then each expectation of accomplishment will ultimately take you there.

Here is something I find truly fascinating. Have you ever heard anyone talking negatively about something they truly believe in, even if the outcome is something negative? Sound confusing? It isn't really. Let's say the topic is a negative one like "I believe I am too fat and I believe that I will never be thin." It is usually said with such positive conviction that the person saying it succeeds in their BELIEF, thus staying fat. You see they are using the rules of the game and are mapping out their destiny. *THE ACTION SANDWICH* is working just as hard for them in keeping them exactly where they have decided they belong as it does for overweight people who truly believe that their purpose is to lose weight and will take the necessary steps to accomplish that. You must eliminate the power of any thought, ACTION or person in your life that does not inspire you to believe in yourself and your goals. "Whether you believe you can or you can't, you're right!" said Henry Ford. Truer words were never spoken.

I want to go back briefly to what I call "victim-speak" and share with you a true story and a classic case of someone whose BELIEF system is so far out of whack that she abandoned her journey and her purpose long ago.

I recently chatted with a room full of prospective business owners in a small town in Ontario, Canada. During my break I chatted with a woman who was sitting in a chair that was no more than fifty feet from the room where the conference was taking place. Within two minutes of saying hello to me she was telling me how dull her life was pouring coffee and waiting tables in a diner. She lived alone with three dogs and said she wasn't pretty enough to meet someone. She believed that everyone else had it good while she did not. Then she said something very interesting – to me it was like a siren going off. She said that nothing ever happened around these parts, and the only thing worth doing was saving her money because there wasn't much out there to spend it on. I told her there were a whole bunch of people just like her in the other room finding out about the possibility of taking their capital and applying it to owning their own businesses. I mentioned that perhaps she could look into that idea for herself.

I was getting excited for her. Here she was just a short walk from an opportunity, or at least on the edge of what she could turn into a life-changing thought process. But then she did what so many often do. She discounted the idea that she could have a better life. Even though I thought she could improve her life, she didn't want to hear me or believe me. "Are you kidding?" she said. "Me, own my own business? Get real, I'm not smart enough to do that!" As she put on her coat and prepared to leave I got bold enough to ask her a question that was burning in my brain. "If you don't mind me asking, just how much have you managed to save over the years as a waitress?" With her back to me, and already well on her way to the sliding doors she answered back, "About seventy-five thousand dollars," and toddled off.

Seventy-five thousand dollars?! Empires have been built on less. My father, in all of his eighty-six years, never saw that much money in one lump, and he probably earned the better part of a million dollars in weekly wages, maybe even more if we took the time to try and add them all up. No, this woman was smart enough, frugal enough, disciplined enough and dedicated enough to save seventy-five thousand dollars, yet could not conceive remotely of the notion of taking control of the helm of her own life. What a tragedy. She couldn't walk the twenty steps to hear about an opportunity or even spend the thirty minutes to explore it or the positive ideas that may have come from it. This woman did not recognize the most fundamental truth. Everything she needed to be successful, she already had within her. If her choice is to believe in herself, then the sky truly is the limit. If not, then it merely is limited.

It takes as much energy to believe you CAN'T as it does to believe you CAN. As you learn to be positive, it will become even clearer to you just how exhausting it is to be around negative people. Their flaccid personalities will have you wanting to shout, "Make it stop!" You can feel the life force draining out of you as they speak with jaundiced enthusiasm about the gloominess and "doominess" of life.

---

## YOU'LL FIND THAT LIFE IS STILL WORTHWHILE, IF YOU JUST SMILE

*"Te audire no possum,*
*musa sapienum fixa est in aura."*

To this day I am fascinated by people who can find the ability to laugh at themselves or are able to find humour in some kind of drastic situation or disaster. Brits and those from the Republic of Ireland seem to be particularly adept at this. Give them long enough and they'll find the funny side of virtually anything. I like to think of it as part of the therapy that we call healing. It bonds us with those sharing our pain and also with those that we may have lost. Most recently, my father's passing on Aug 11, 2006, exemplified this notion when after his funeral people were coming up to me and saying, "Alan, please don't take this the wrong way, but I had a great time! This is the best funeral I have ever been to!" My father would have loved that, and of course is probably a bit pissed off that he wasn't there. Humour in the face of tragedy has been a part not only of legendary careers but also part of the everyday lives of countless folk just like, well, these three for starters.

Murphy and Fagan are standing outside Patrick O'Reilly's little hobbit-sized home in the middle of nowhere, Ireland. O'Reilly is on his deathbed and the lads are here for a visit to cheer him up.

"Now whatever you do Fagan," says Murphy, "don't mention the words death or dying now, ye hear, 'cuz Paddy doesn't know that he's dying see, and we don't want to give him any terrible thoughts or ideas."
"Aye of course I won't," says Fagan. "You won't hear them from me lips."
And so they head on into the tiny cottage, ducking as they go because their height causes them great difficulty to move with any ease. As they sit by the bedside, O'Reilly is a mere skeleton of a man, weak, feeble but quiet and content to hear from his two old pals.
"Sure yer lookin' good, man," says Murphy
"Aye, grand," says Fagan. "Why, I'll bet you'll make the bingo this Friday night coming, don't you think so Murph?"
"Why sure 'n' all, I declare he will."

This goes on for quite some time and indeed O'Reilly seems to be almost picking up his spirits from all of the positive feedback he's been receiving. But soon it is time to leave and the boys prepare to say farewell.

"Well, Patrick, we must be off, but we will see you at bingo Friday, never fear. And remember to wear your tie boy'o for we're off to the pub and the dancing afterwards with all of our winnings."
"Right, we're off then, Patrick."

The two men stand quickly and Fagan completely forgets about the need to duck and so when his head buries itself into the ceiling above with a mighty thud, he blurts out...........".Jaayzus boy, how in the name of God are we ever going to get a coffin oot o' here?"

Laughing in the face of adversity is precisely how I handled having to look constantly into the face of anger as a child growing up. I laughed at it. I sang to it. I played and I believed.

But what was there to possibly believe in, in a place filled with such bitterness? I guarantee you that if you go to Iraq right this minute that somewhere, some way and somehow good and decent people are finding a way to still laugh and to smile and cheer each other up all in the face of such unbelievable horror. May their God love them, for they certainly deserve it.

So I refused as a boy to believe that everything had to be dark and frightening and angry and violent. I NEVER conformed, ever. It is not within my nature to stay connected to indifference and anger and pain. Of course, as a youngster I listened to those around me and said that I believed what THEY believed, and so as the songs were sung and the battles were fought we children too had our heels dug in and lines drawn in the sand.

"Proddy dogs eat the frogs," they would say with all the venom they could muster.
"Catholic cats eat the rats!" was always the reply.

And so when elders teach children that dying for a cause such as for "God and for Ulster!" or for "God and for Ireland" is worthwhile, they believe it. Funny how poor God always seems to get roped into all of this mayhem isn't it? But throughout all of this bigotry I still had pals who were Catholic and the extent of my mayhem was usually no worse than a wrestling match or a bloody nose. Best of all, I would befriend my enemies, make them my BEST pals and then teach them songs, Protestant songs. THEN I would tell them to go in and sing for their mums and dads as I watched through the window. It never failed.

"Alan Frew, I will kick your arse. Get back here!"

And so the chase would ensue, with me running like the hammers of hell with somebody's mammy chasing me with some object that would "brain" me if ever they caught me... they NEVER caught me. That doesn't mean however I was never caught. Word would spread to my house and inevitably my mother or father would be waiting for me.

My mother did most of the spanking. I liked that. Why in the world would I say that I liked my mother doing the spanking? Well, it meant that my dad wasn't doing it, for when my father spanked it was always memorable. When he was after me I would stand out front near our little gate by the street, while he stood in our front doorway. Usually I had done something *trivial* like hitting a lamppost with a hammer. The kind of lamppost that hums when you put your ear to it and contains all those meaningless electrical wires and stuff that short circuits the entire neighbourhood when hit by a hammer, leaving every bugger in the dark part of town even darker. *That* lamppost. The kind that can get your parents prosecuted for damages to government property.

"Get in here," he would command.
"Nope."
"Alan, get in here now!"
"You'll hit me!" I would reply.
"I won't hit you." He would say unconvincingly.
"Aye, you will!!"

This seesaw of words would continue until he would vanish back inside. From my vantage point, I could see the open door of our little washroom beckoning me to safety. I would run like a bugger, similar to one of those poor bloody wildebeests, trying to make it across the flooded plains of the Serengeti, all the while trying desperately to not become an afternoon snack for some famished predator. Nine times out of ten I would be way too fast and much too slippery for "the hand" that would emerge just as I was passing by the living room door. But he had to nab me only once and this little "wildebeest" would find it very difficult to sit on his "Serengeti" for quite some time.

My mother on the other hand "cuffed" my ear almost daily. Doctor Goldie our family physician, examining me:
"Mrs. Frew, do you ever hit your son?"

My mother: "Just with my hands, doctor."

She never ever hurt me. Come to think of it, she couldn't stop talking long enough to give you a good one because she always liked to tell you why you were getting hit as you were getting hit.

"See (hit) you (slap, slap) ya wee (hit, slap) shite, (hit) that was (hit, hit, hit) my favourite hat (slap, hit, slap) you gave away (hit) to those Gypsies (hit, hit, hit, hit, hit)."
Time out.
Puff cigarette.
Continue: "It's ruined (hit, slap) because they cut holes in it (slap) to fit it over the ears (hit, slap, hit) of their donkey!!"

My granny on the other hand was a combination of my mother and my father. Standing all of four foot six inches, she was a human dynamo. She had the talk-as-you-slap-ACTION down to an art, but always ended with her secret weapon, a crescendo of arse-numbing whacks, bumps and thumps, ranging from kicking you with her woolly-slippered toe, to hacking at you with whatever was within her diminutive reach. A book, a boot, a rolling pin, a chair or a dog, it didn't matter because if she could pick it up, you were getting hit with it. Fending her off took an entirely different strategy, and I came up with some sheer artistry.

The best one ever, came after watching one of my favourite movies, like *Bataan* or *The Sands of Iwo Jima*. I went out into the back yard to dig a hole, not just any old hole mind you, this one was like the Japanese soldiers dug during jungle warfare, (minus, of course, the spikes in the bottom that would normally be used to capture and kill elephants, tigers or American soldiers). They would cover them with twigs, leaves and dirt and await the enemy or victim. Yes this was a special kind of hole; this was a J.J.G.T, A Japanese Jungle Granny Trap.

When I was an infant, my father cared about his garden. When I was a toddler, he cared somewhat less. Later, when I was a boy, he just didn't care at all, and thus provided me with my very own private jungle just outside my kitchen window, which was probably an aesthetic nightmare for our neighbours. But for a boy it was nothing short of marvelous!

So take one smart remark bestowed upon one axe-murdering granny, then run like hell. She usually gave chase, but not for long. On one particular occasion however she was relentless for not only did she chase me down our garden path and out the gate, she followed me all the way across the street and into Mrs. McDougall's front garden.

"Hello Mrs. McDougall," said I to the wee head sticking out her kitchen window.
"You'll never make it!" she calls to me with mirth. Then to my granny she calls out, "Do you want me to set Kim on him Chrissie?"
Kim was her big black slobbering mongrel killer-dog that bullied and terrified our entire neighbourhood. The animal however was afraid of only one person, and *SHE* was chasing me!
"No, it's okay Iza," says my granny. "I'll get 'im."

I ran back through the front gate but she was still on my tail. I headed for my jungle and the large bush beside the shed, yes *that* shed, the one I will set on fire a bit later in my life. Is she gone? Nope. Okay, drastic measures. A little "deke" to the left, a quick head fake to the right. That's it, let her almost grab you. Closer, closer...RECEPTIVITY to the fact she'll kill you if she gets you, DESIRE not to get caught, BELIEF in your skills at hiding holes, INTENTION meet ACTION...and...
"There she goes ladies and gentlemen, right down the old Japanese Jungle Granny Trap!" *THE ACTION SANDWICH* strikes again!

Like an old vinyl record with its needle stuck, I repeat. Do what you do because you're meant to do it. Do it because you can and because you love it. By following the path in front of you and focusing on where you're going rather than where you have been, you are sowing seeds for the future, for there is ALWAYS a future.

# WITH OR WITHOUT YOU

God bless you Mrs. Biggart, you old bastard! For if it wasn't for you and that bloody umbrella I would never have been in Rock 'n Roll.

It's 1965 and I am told, not asked, that it is time for me to join the youth division of The Orange Order, a Protestant fraternal organization founded in Loughgall, County Armagh, Ireland in 1795, the same year Coronation Street first aired. The "Juveniles," as they are called, took part in many of the marches, the major one taking place each year on the twelfth of July to commemorate the outcome of the famous Battle of Boyne, which occurred in 1690 when protestant King William III defeated Catholic King James II. Coincidentally, 1690 is the same year that Scotland last qualified for the World Cup. Look it up if you don't believe me.

Interesting how most of the crap that the world is still entrenched in today almost always seems to stem from the antiquated wounds and principles from those of centuries and indeed millennia ago.

Anyway, there I am all dressed up in my best duds and I am told that I am going to be one of four kids having the honour of carrying one of four cords attached to a huge decorative banner identifying the branch of the fraternity which in turn is to be carried by two strong men from the Lodge. If you were to ask me what the images on the banner were symbolic of, I would not be able to tell you because it all comes from the hidden world of secret societies and secret hand shakes. God knows I still get a kick out of chatting with the funny handshake club members like the Freemasons and Lodge guys. I have family and friends to this day who are members and in fact two of my best pals in the whole world, *Brother Bryce* and *Brother Kenny*, are members.

Me: "So what does that symbol mean?"
Them: "Join and find out."
Me: "C'mon, I won't tell on you, it's a riddle right? What's the big secret?"
Them: "Well for starters, it's *not* a secret, because the truth is that the answers

to the symbol, in fact to *all* of our symbols are right in the Bible!"

They make it sound so simple. Just match the symbol to the significant clue in the Bible – easy, peasy. Now let's see, the banner's symbol is a painting of a young virginal woman, with one eye in the middle of her forehead and she is dressed in a long, flowing robe, one breast exposed, and she is standing on one of the heads of a six-headed ram. In her left hand she's carrying a sword, while in her right she is holding a book with the word "Freedom" on its cover, only it's upside down – the word that is, not the book. Behind her is a dragon standing on one foot and in the talons of the other foot is a serpent that has an upside-down pyramid on its head and blood pouring from its mouth. Two eagles are flying above them, one has fire coming from its ears while the other has just dropped twin baby boys from the sky and, miraculously, they appear to be landing safely on the branch of an apple tree that has one apple hanging on it. All the other apples have fallen to the ground and are being devoured by a one-eyed white tiger, which appears to be smiling right at you.

So you open up the Bible and immediately say, "right, there it is, that's smashing, okie-dokie, I've got it then, thanks. I'll just get going now." I mean get a grip lads, I can't even find Waldo. Give me a break.

Right then, so we have the banner, the men, the cords and the kids and with the responsibility of carrying the cord comes "Your best behaviour!"

"Right you are, Mrs. Biggart. My best behaviour."
"The single most frowned-upon crime that a boy can commit," she says in a flurry of spit, "is dancing and swinging that cord to the sound of the band. Do you understand me, ALAN FREW?"
Why is she singling me out? It's not like I'll do anything wrong. Hold on! We're off. And a left, left, left right, left.

The parade consisted of a large flute band followed by a lot of people in bow ties and bowler hats followed by big heavy banners carried by large sweaty men. They were surrounded by children being chaperoned by Helga the S.S. Queen, formally known as Mrs. Biggart, followed by hundreds more bow ties, bowler hats, kids with cords, and chaperones who are all being followed by thousands of the general public. Of course, there was the occasional detractor popping his or her head out the window to shout abuse at you or empty out the potty filled with the morning's constitutional. All very civilized, wouldn't you say?

"What's that sound? It's drums and flutes. That's magical and I like it, yes, I do. I like that very much. It makes me want to, waggle my bum a wee bit. Look at me, for I've got a skip in my step. This is great. Let's see what I can do with this corrrr..."

"BANG!"
"What the hell was *that*? Good God, I'm blind and deaf and if I'm not mistaken I think I've also pissed myself!"
Helga's umbrella had entered my ear with a crushing thud, sending it on its way to somewhere other than Coatbridge. And as if that's not bad enough, here comes the craziest part. No one cared. Not one single solitary soul gave a monkey's damn about me, my ear, or the fact that I was nine years of age lying on the ground with a bleeding ear drum and the perpetrator of the crime was this old drill sergeant five times my age and twenty times my size!

"What did he do then?" says the bowler hat.
"He swung the cord Alec! THAT is what he did. So I just had to put him down!" says Helga.
"Right you are then," says the hat. "Keep moving!"
"You heard the Grand Master then, young Frew. Keep moving!"

And move I did, off like the clappers as fast as my wee legs would carry me, much to the consternation of Helga and the bowler hat. But do you know what? I remember it now as if it was yesterday. The second the umbrella attempted to introduce itself to the grey matter of my brain via my ear canal, and I felt like someone just stuck my head into a pan of frying chips, two thoughts came to mind instantaneously. One was, "Ooooooooohhhhhhhya baaaaastaaaaard!" And the other?
"Piss on this. I am joining the band!"

And so I did. I decided right there and then that if I could not beat them, they could follow me. And so it was that I took up the flute immediately and never went back to the lodge, ever. And so was born my musical career, thanks to a cord, a maniac and an umbrella.

If you don't love it, then don't do it. If you don't believe it, then it cannot happen. Never did it occur to me that I was destined to stay in that place, with those people. I always knew that one day I was going to leave it behind. And do you know why? The answer is simple. I believed.

*"You Can't Always Get What You Want"*
MICK JAGGER

*"Yes You Can"*
ALAN FREW

One of the fundamental yet most often misunderstood and unaccepted laws of the universe is this: "What I think about, I get." Well, I have news for you – IT'S TRUE. What you DO indeed think about you WILL indeed get. Now this doesn't mean that if you think about a cool million in cold hard cash, you'll wake up to find it lying beside the bed in the morning. What it means is that if your focus and your energy are applied positively toward the BELIEF and worthiness of wanting something (yes, even a cool million) as opposed to being applied to all of the reasons why you cannot or should not have it, it stands to reason that you at least have a fighting chance of figuring out the ACTION required to get a million dollars. Some people, when asked why they play the lotteries against such seemingly insurmountable odds reply, "If you don't buy a ticket, you cannot win." Well, you know what folks? In that, they are 100% correct. So I ask you this, if you don't believe that you can ever have a million dollars or if you don't believe you are worthy enough for a million dollars (or, for that matter, a dollar) then how can you ever possibly get it? Surely if I focus all of my energy on never having something then I will succeed and never have it. It is the focusing on and the sending out of energy from within me that says, "I want, I deserve, I am worthy of and I believe that I can and will have," that sets me up for answers that will direct me to the

ACTION I need to take in order to set off on the required pathway to my DESIRE of anything at all, never mind a million bucks. Think of it like sending a telegram, making a phone call, or like hitting the send button on your email. Of course this may require a leap of faith on your part, but ask any successful person about leaps of faith and I am positive you'll get a mountain of answers regarding when they took theirs.

Have you ever noticed how you feel when things just seem to be going your way all the time? Funny isn't it? You start wondering and questioning why this is so. "What did I do to deserve this?" you ask. But I ask you: can it possibly be just coincidence and luck and just plain old good fortune every single time something great happens to you? Conversely, is it simply coincidence and bad luck when things go wrong all of the time? No it is not. You ARE creating it, all of it, the good, the bad, the ugly and the indifferent.

Look, it's easy. If the mailman came to your front door with a smile on his face, and gave you a pleasant, "Good morning," and you said "Bug off! Leave me alone!", he probably would and you would get what you want. If you did the same to every single colleague at work, you would get the same result. If you went on a local radio station and told all the listeners the same thing, you would again get the same response. National television? Ditto.

Energy. It's ALL energy. The energy of communication, which includes what you are thinking, what energy you are "giving off" or "sending out" to the universe, received by the energy of others, the human listener, in fact the universal listener, which is simply the gateway to telling the world to give you what you're asking for.

We all, at one time or another, have had the feeling that someone was giving off a bad vibe without even really knowing them or perhaps without them having even spoken to us. Have you ever returned from an event or perhaps a meeting to be asked, "So how was it?" and found yourself replying, "Hmm there was a weird vibe in the room. It felt hostile yet nothing bad actually happened?" What is that? Coincidence? Bad luck? Of course not; it's energy. You can't deny it, can you? So why believe it of others and not of yourself?

Focus your thoughts and your energy with the same care you would give your bank account and if you don't have a bank account worth talking about, then focus on fixing that. Just concentrate on what you want. If you are thinking about some "thing" that you DESIRE, then you are going to get *something* back in return. However, if you're thinking about nothing, or the lack of something, then guess what you're going to get? Hmmm, where the hell's that lottery ticket? I know I put it here somewhere.

Once you declare your BELIEF in something, you WILL be challenged. You can count on it. People will challenge you, and so will life. There is a phenomenon that happens as soon as you say, "I believe" – something or someone will come along to challenge the depth of your commitment. This challenge is there to help you. Defending your beliefs and having to stay the course through thick and thin reinforces your resolve, which benefits all areas of your journey. A little leap of faith perhaps?

Believe that you can have it, do it, deserve it, and are entitled to it and it shall be. Surround yourself with people who have strength and their strength will be yours to draw on. Avoid the toxic nature of others, as their weakness will become a part of you and will drain your strength. People like Nelson Mandela, Deepak Chopra, Richard Branson, Angelina Jolie and Mother Theresa are role models of tremendous strength. What do highly successful people possess that attracts more success? I believe they channel the same force that was powerful enough to take a pinpoint single bang and turn it into a sprawling universe some twenty billion light years across. To some, it is God and I respect that with all of my conviction. I believe it is the same force that brings a man and woman together and creates a beautiful newborn child, or that transforms the caterpillar into a butterfly. Sound heavy? It is. Welcome to the world of INTENTION.

# TEN STEPS TO BELIEF

1. YOU GOTTA HAVE FAITH - Go on, dare to believe in something wonderful. What's stopping you? You may get disappointed? You may believe in something that doesn't happen? So what, change your tactics and try again and again if need be. BELIEF in nothing is nothing. So believe.

2. PLAY BALL! - Hit the ball three times out of ten and you're a Hall Of Famer. I have had about 10 hit songs in my life yet I have written a thousand! Missing the mark and rejection are a part of success. How many strikeouts did Babe Ruth have, or game winning shots did Michael Jordan miss? How many light bulbs never lit up for Edison and yet they rank as three of the world's greatest believers. Never quit.

3. I AM, YOU AM, HECK! WE ALL AM - Don't wander aimlessly without questioning who you are and what it is you truly believe about this world and your place in it. Take an inventory of what you have to offer, your gifts, your skills and your talents. Believe in and nurture each thing on that list no matter how small it may seem. Honour your BELIEF.

4. IMAGINE - Visualize the outcome you DESIRE in your mind before it arrives. Create the picture and set an anchor to it. Make it strong, passionate, healthy, and the most beautiful thing you have ever seen. Taste, smell, hear and feel it all for this is what it will be like when you get there. Put yourself in the picture. Click.

5. HEY JUDE, DON'T MAKE IT BAD - Take a sad song and make it better. Does your inside voice tell you that you are too old, too fat, too broke or too late? If so then you must fight it,

argue with it and tell it to get lost. This is non-negotiable. Lose this voice, or lose.

6. I'M JAKE THE PEG - If you have a deep conviction about something then nourish it with the highest regard. Step outside the circle and find your own truth. If society says you are trying to fit a square peg into a round hole then so be it. It's your peg.

7. 10, JACK, QUEEN, KING...? - Don't be wishy-washy. Take a leap of faith, even if that leap is small. Get used to experiencing what that leap feels like because one day the stakes are going to be much higher and in order to turn over the ace you'll need faith in spades. Ready, jump!

8. KEEP YOUR EYES ON THE ROAD - Money and the things it can bring are by-products of being on the right pathway. Do you want lots of money and things? I do. Focus on the highway not the destination and let the means by which you arrive be the universe's job. Life really *is* a highway.

9. THIRTY-DAYS HATH SEPTEMBER - Life and death, fear and calm, happiness and sadness, are all just extreme ends of the same energy. All required, all necessary, all normal. Stay on your path and focus on living your life each day. In 30 days you will have had the best month of your life. In twelve of those months...you know the rest. Being alive and living each day are two different things. Know the difference.

10. BUT TOMORROW MAY RAIN SO... - Change is frightening but completely reliable. You may not realize it at the time through the anger, tears or sense of loss, but change can be a gift. Look deeper and turn it into an opportunity. Embrace it.

# MY SONG
*Opus 3*

### THERE'S A WHAT IN MY BUCKET?

On my first day at the hospital, I was notified that we were short three orderlies, due to two quitting and one being fired. They were so understaffed that I was asked to start immediately in on-floor training, as opposed to the two or three weeks of orientation and classroom studies normally afforded a new employee. In my case, Jake, the head orderly trained me as I just stood by his side watching. Now this may not seem like a big deal to you but can you non-medical folk out there imagine that you are told to leave your office, or department store, or perfumery or whatever line of work you are in and go immediately to the city hospital, whereupon you are then told to go into a patient's room and shave and prep his groin for a hernia operation? Oh, and just for good measure, you are to also give him an enema! Still think it's no big deal? One minute you're a grocery clerk or a bank teller (or a tube cutter) and instantaneously without any classroom instruction you are actually doing these kinds of things! It seemed madly surreal, yet it was my baptism. So there I was, fresh from factory work, dressed in whites, doing things so unbelievably foreign to me that I was dazed and confused by the whole thing. Here's a doozey. Near the end of my first shift, Jake's pager went off so he called to receive instructions from the switchboard.

"Right, okay, will do," says Jake and he hangs up the phone.

"What is it?" says the ex-tube-cutter.

"They want an orderly to go to the operating room and pick up a specimen to be taken down to the morgue for disposal."

Now dear reader, although this activity was to become second nature to me, on this day, this my very first day, I was petrified that he might say, something crazy like he wanted me to do it.

"I want you to do it."

"What?" I replied shakily.

"I want you to go pick up the specimen, take it downstairs to the morgue and place it inside the freezer. It's your job," said Jake very matter-of-fact.

"ME?"

"Yes...you... now get going!"

That wasn't a question, so off I went to the operating room sweating profusely as I cursed myself for being so diligent with my calls to this place. This antiseptic filled, clinical, medicinal place, where they give ex-tube-cutters "things" in buckets to take down to a place where they keep dead people!

"Oh no! What in the name of the wee man have you gotten yourself into?" asked the voice inside my head.

"The hospital," I replied.

Suddenly the voice inside that cranium of mine burst into guffaws of laughter.

The bucket I held in my hand was of average size. It was white. It was opaque. It made a sound, a squishy, slop-slop sound that intensified as I walked. It sounded positively icky.

"What in hell's bells is in this bucket? What is this thing?"

SLOP-SLOP-SLOP.

I entered the elevator on the fourth floor. There was one person on board.

"Hello," she said.

SLOP-SLOP-SLOP

"Hello," I replied, quietly.

"And just what do you have there?"
"I don't know, they didn't tell me."

The door to the elevator opened on the third floor and as she exited she said,

"Hmmm, curiosity would kill me. If I were you I would just have to look inside. Bye now!"

The doors closed and the elevator resumed its journey to take me to the basement.

"No, I can't, I said to myself. I can't just open it... can I? That would be wrong, wouldn't it?"

SLOP, SLOP, SLOP, I couldn't stand it. It was killing me. I just had to peek.

Slowly, ever so slowly I pried the lid up. I closed my eyes until they were little slits, as if squinting would help me.

SLOP-SLOP-SLOP.

"Okay", I told myself. "On the count of three, open your eyes and look. Are you ready? I'm ready. Here we go. ONE...TWO...THREE...Oh dear God, it's a... "

## FATHER AND SON

"Zeppelin!!"

"C'mon man, do some Zeppelin will ya?"

The battle cry of the masses roared, the bar-crowd the audience.

What of course they were really saying was, "I don't give a shit about you and your original songs, play me something I know!"

The bar owners didn't help matters either, for they loathed original material even more than the patrons did. The idea of a band trying out original material only meant fewer patrons, which of course equals less beer and liquor sales. The bottom line was if you want to work here, play music by bands that already have hits on the radio. By now I was a fully-fledged orderly in a hospital working days instead of the graveyard shift, so I was also back taking gigs and playing for the 70s generation, the one that made John Travolta, and *Pet Rocks* famous. Now you younger readers probably think I am speaking of a band by that name, however I am in fact referring to the 1970s fad conceived by a California advertising executive who sold ordinary gray pebbles bought at a builder's supply store as pets.

Each "creature" came accompanied by a training manual, with instructions on how to properly raise and care for one's newfound pet. The people who purchased them usually gave them names, talked openly to them, petted them, and then said that they were teaching them to perform simple tricks. Mercifully, the fad lasted only about six months, but it held in long enough to make the creator a millionaire.

We had left the swinging '60s and entered the super '70s and unless you played *Zeppelin*, *Hendrix*, *Fleetwood Mac* or *Foreigner* bar owners simply did not care. I had also married my childhood sweetheart at the ripe old age of 19 without anyone of maturity stepping forward to try and bring me to my senses by telling me that I was still a kid, growing, developing and hopefully maturing. We tried to be man and wife at 19 and 17 respectively, I holding down a full time job as an orderly while singing and performing in bars. It was a very stressful time for a young couple of such tender years. We struggled. We struggled hard and just when it seemed like it couldn't get any tougher...it did.

"Push, c'mon, you can do it...P-U-S-H! That's it, that's it, there we go!"

"Congratulations! You have a son!"

It was 1979 and I had been slogging it out now as the Rock Star orderly for going on four years becoming depleted, worn out and broke. The music scene wasn't paying me but costing me, as the bills and the debt were mounting. To emphasize just how bad it was, on the very evening that my son came into the world, the bass player was waiting for me in the maternity ward because we had to drive to a town in Quebec obligated by contract to perform in some flea bag pub, leaving my wife and not yet two hour old son at home.

Meanwhile back at the hospital something interesting was brewing. Upon my return I was asked if I would like to go on down to the morgue and witness an autopsy, something that not only fascinated me but also gave me a leg up (pardon the pun) on the biology needed for my quest to become a doctor. I readily agreed. I had seen numerous autopsies by this time and had witnessed death first hand throughout my four years on staff, so off I went to the place where I had taken that little bucket on my very first day. You know, the one containing that...oh never mind. So when I got there I was asked to gown-up and within minutes I was receiving requests from the pathologist.

"Hold this please."
"Grab that, would you?"
"Can you hand that to me? Thanks."

Shortly thereafter the doctor asked me if I felt I was cut out (again with the puns) to do the job of assisting him and his colleague due to the retirement of their regular assistant. I told him of my goal to one day attend medical school and he assured me that he would always leave the most interesting autopsies to last so that he could take the time to teach me as much as possible.

"You have a deal," I said shaking his hand.

So now the plastic molding, tube cutting, orderly, Rock Star... was "Cadaver Man!"

This was a turning point for me in more ways than one, because it was at this point I threw in the towel, waved the white flag in the face of Rock 'n Roll and said, "I surrender!" Or so I thought.

I called it quits. Enough already, although things were dodgy at home and my wife and I were really just like acquaintances. I adored my son and wanted him to have his daddy around full time. I told my wife that I was quitting music for good, told her that I was going to apply to nursing college as a mature student and that along with my orderly experience and autopsy experience I felt I was a shoo-in to get accepted. She, on the other hand told me she was moving out.

It was of no real surprise to me that the break up had come, for we were living separate existences, with separate friends and interests. I was however a little bruised in the macho department, due to her being the one to say, "I'm outta here!" My ego got the better of me and talked me into saying something ridiculous like, "Well I'm telling you, if you go out that door, then there's no coming back!" (I cringe, even now just writing this).

And so off she went to her new life and off I went to nursing college, never the twain to meet, but alas, she had my son with her and that was a dagger in my heart. True love has no boundaries, walls cannot contain it nor keep it from penetrating, and the love I had for that baby boy was all of that and more. I made up my mind right there and then, that not only was I going to be a doctor but that I would not lose him in the process. I knew in my heart I would undoubtedly be the better parent for my son. I decided in my mind that he was coming to live with me. I was of course told by many that I had no chance of fighting a system, which in 1979 could not comprehend giving custody of a child to a father when the mother was available to give care, but nevertheless in my mind, he was going to live with me. My RECEPTIVITY, DESIRE, BELIEF, INTENTION and of course my ACTIONS were of a man who had his son living with him as a single parent and so that is what I told the universe. It was non-negotiable.

So let's see, I'm broke due to the fact that my student loans are garnisheed to cover debts that my band has incurred. I'm a full time student again at age 23 in a school with 300 females (that's another book entirely). I'm holding down a full-time job as an orderly and a part-time job as a pathologist's assistant. I see my son only by popping into his mother's home every day on my way home from school and on my way to work to then begin an eight-hour shift until midnight. I've moved back in with my parents. What the hell else could possibly happen?

"Alan?"
"Yeah."
"It's Wayne."
"Yeah."
"Sittin' down?"
"No."
"Could you?"
"Yeah."
"Are you?"
"No."
"Will you?"
"Yeah."

"Ready?"
"No."
"Wanna join a band..."

Was he insane? He had to be. I had just given that all up. It had drained me dry, physically, emotionally, mentally and financially. I had popped pills, smoked pot, drank like a fish, not to mention lived with people I didn't even know and taken bubble baths all in the name of Rock 'n Roll.

"Just come and meet them," said Wayne. "That's all I'm asking. Just a meeting."

How could I not say no?

I was supposed to say no. You must say no.

Go on, say no.

"Yeah, Okay, I'll meet them."

PASSION. Pain and suffering. How prophetic. Needless to say I met with them and I sang for them.

The singer, "Okay, I'll join your band, but on one condition."
The band, "What's that?"
The singer, "That it's just a hobby for I am never going back on the road!"
The band, "Okay, great!"

So now the nursing student, autopsy assisting, single dad is also a rock 'n' roll singer in a band....again.

## I'M SO TIRED

I graduated from nursing college in 1982 and was given a full-time job on day shift as Alan Frew R.N. I was and still am very proud of those letters.

In the meantime I had faithfully visited with my son on every possible occasion, so much so that my soon to be ex-wife was now very comfortable with me having him stay at my place every available chance. My work was certainly cut out for me now. I was working dayshifts that included rotations of seven straight shifts in a row at times. My band was working full time at night, Monday through Saturday. I was also being called in on Saturday and Sunday mornings to assist in autopsies. It was a frantic pace. Death on two legs actually and something had to give. A typical week had me going into work for 6:30 a.m. and working in an already overworked, under staffed environment and finishing at a frantic pace somewhere around 4:30 p.m.

I would then pop in my car and drive over to see my son for one hour before hopping back in the car and driving up to wherever we happened to be gigging that particular evening. Sometimes the gig might be as far away as a two-hour drive. Typically we would go on around 9 p.m. and finish around 1:30 a.m., at which time I would get in my car, drive back home, get in around 4 a.m. only to sleep "upright" on a comfy chair until my alarm went off at 6:00 a.m., at which time I would splash water on my face throw on some clean clothes and head back to the hospital to begin it all over again. Tell me, can you see the train wreck coming?

I had met my wife as a fifteen year old when I myself was only seventeen. We dated, we married and we split. We had a beautiful boy who by now was spending more and more time at the home of my parents and myself. After our separation, she was finding more and more joy in going out on weekends and partying, content in the knowledge that our son was at my home as opposed to being in the hands of a babysitter. The periods that he would be with us, would stretch longer and longer until one day I suggested that he stay with me and that she could come by anytime she chose to see him or pick him up. She agreed, and the living arrangements changed which made me extremely happy on the inside even though by now I was killing myself with work.

It seemed like I was always awake, either while nursing, singing or dissecting some poor soul who had met his demise the night before. It was relentless. On one occasion I was with a patient and the last thing I remember was leaving the room to grab a face cloth.

"Can I help you Alan?" said the voice.
Suddenly I stirred from what seemed like a deep sleep.
"Are you ok? Can I help you with something?" she said again.
I found myself behind a curtain of a patient's bed area. There was a nurse from a completely different floor attending to an elderly woman. I did not recognize this patient as anyone from my floor.
"What did I do?" I asked the nurse. "What are you doing on my floor?"
"You did nothing," said the nurse. "You simply walked in here and stood there, staring and I am not on your floor, you are on mine!"

Good God, I had actually walked from my patient's room on the fifth floor, taken the elevator or the stairs and made my way to the fourth floor, entered this room all while asleep. Shaking I immediately went to my supervisor and told her I felt ill and must go home. It was a terrifying experience and I can only thank the heavens that I did nothing that led to discomfort, injury or indeed something worse for any of my patients.

On the other side of the coin the band was making great headway and I on a personal basis now had credentials that a medical school would take a look at without laughing. I had my son living with me as I had intended but what else, oh yes! Now I remember, I was coming apart.

## LOOK INTO MY FATHER'S EYES

Gary Lyman Pring was a man who entered my life as a then unknown manager of decent, hardworking bands and yet by the time he left my life he was my father, or at the very least, that part of a father that I never had.

The band was officially called *Tokyo*, from a little southern Ontario town called, Newmarket, and I was never going on the road, not ever, as it was just my hobby, my side-line, for I my friends, was going to become a doctor.

This was the beginning of a new decade, the '80s, and styles were changing rapidly from the rocking '70s. Techno was happening and at a rapid pace. There was a bit of a Japanese thing going on in clothing with headbands and oriental symbols and I believe this is where our inspiration for the name *Tokyo* came from, although we loved to tell people that it was because we had heard that there was a band from Tokyo called.... "Newmarket."

We were good. We were very good. And after we worked out who the final lineup should be and who the lead singer was, and what our style would look and sound like, we started to come into our own.

Gary had asked on a handshake if he could become our manager and he told us that he would deliver us a record deal within six months or the handshake was null and void. We agreed and he went tirelessly to work on the Record Labels in Toronto. Soon *Tokyo* was packing them into the bars on the local scene and was being wooed by several major recording companies with Island Records leading the way, founded and headed by the legendary Chris Blackwell who went on to start the careers of Bob Marley, *U2*, Steve Winwood, Melissa Etheridge and *The Cranberries*.

Capitol Records who had played the wooing game, even going as far as to dedicate our own label representative to us while funding our demo's had all but resigned to the fact that Island Records had us in the bag, but they never refused an opportunity to come out and see us perform in the hopes that they might still persuade us differently. I admit I always enjoyed Capitol's company and loved sitting down at their table, partaking in their hospitality, which knew no bounds. It was decided that Blackwell himself was going to fly in from Jamaica to hear the band, just prior to putting pen to paper, a formality really, and one which the head of the Canadian label looked forward to, for he felt that after meeting the "Legend" himself, we would have no reservations signing the contract.

And so the stage was set. A small club in Bradford, Ontario would serve as our stage, for we were certainly local heroes there and the place was jammed to the rafters every time we played. Capitol Records came along that night, just in case.

Crummy little flea-ridden rooms were our dressing area, all very normal though and still a sign of our times. We hit the stage around 9pm and did a blistering set that left us invigorated, drenched in sweat, deeply satisfied and most certainly "Masters of our Domain." As the lads basked in a bit of adoration from the crowd I was quickly whisked away to meet the man himself. It was short, sweet and to the point.

He extended his hand and we shook. This was the exact moment however, that I knew that he had no INTENTION of ever putting his ACTION into signing our band to any contract.

He finished up with a few pleasantries and went on to meet the rest of the guys, before heading back in his limo to the airport and straight back to the Caribbean. I was sitting with the Capitol team having a beer, before his arse had settled into his limo seat, but how could I possibly have come to the conclusion that his words and handshake were saying two different things? Well the truth is, I don't know. Was it what I call a clammy handshake, one that seems, weak, damp and somehow deceitful? Perhaps. Or was it the sound of his voice? Did it waver or seem to stumble as he searched for what he was going to say to me? Who knows? But whatever it was he was sending out thoughts and desires and INTENTION that this meeting between us was to be the first and last and my RECEPTIVITY was picking up on all of it. My gut therefore knew full well that this was the last time that I would ever see him again at least on any professional level.

I was correct, for soon after that fateful meeting he claimed that *Tokyo* was a bit too similar to the approach they were taking with a relatively new band he was grooming from Ireland called, *U2*. A huge step at the time for a man known for his love and development of the eclectic sounds of the islands.

At the time it was a devastating blow, but I do not look back with blame or ill will regarding his decision. *U2* became the biggest band in the world and all was good for Chris Blackwell, but one of his employees, the head of Island Records Canada, never fully recovered from losing us and will tell you so to this very day. My resolve to keep going was strengthened by this affair so back to the drawing board we went while Gary made what was to become a key move. It was never about the money for Gary. It was always about the journey. As a manager he could have had us exclusively but from the beginning he had brought his day-to-day partner Joe in, and in so doing split his commissions. He was now prepared to do it again.

Gary contacted a manager in America, an Englishman, called Derek Sutton, and told him if he knew what was good for him, he would make the trip to Canada to check out this new band that he was shopping around. Derek made the trip, saw the talent and almost immediately a deal was cut between himself and Gary making Derek our International manager. It didn't take long before Capitol made a move offering us a deal but it was a somewhat like a martini for indeed it had a little twist.

Gary and his partner Joe held a conference call telling me we were to go to the boardroom of Capitol Records that day, so off I went to meet the other lads to finally put to rest where *Tokyo* was going to belong.

Walking into that building still gives me a little buzz even to this day, but back when it was still Capitol Records it felt like the home of *The Beatles*. The foyer displayed *Beatles* awards and the whole atmosphere gave me goose bumps. I was quickly ushered into the boardroom to find Gary, Joe, Tim Trombley, our record rep, and…no band. Was I just early? The atmosphere in the room told me no. Something was afoot but I did not know what. We all made small talk with comments on the weather, the hockey game and world news when Deane, who was the head of A&R (Artist and Repertoire) at the time, entered the room.

"Well did you tell him?" asked Deane matter-of-factly.
"No we were waiting for you," someone spoke up.
"Tell me what?" I asked.
"Well here it is in a nutshell Alan. We are offering you a deal. Perhaps one of the guys, I'd say perhaps the guitar player, can hang with you, maybe, but I want to send you to England to join a great musician that we have over there and we're going to build a band around you."

My mind was racing, Deane's mouth was moving but I wasn't getting it all. I knew the musician he was referring to but I also knew Deane (being an ex-drummer) had a reputation for being hard on rhythm sections and splitting bands up because he felt insecure about many of them when it came time to sign contracts.

"So you see the rhythm section just can't cut it and they gotta go. So what do you say, is it a deal?" He again sounded so calm and to the point, and yet my head was spinning.

"I uh, I am not sure what to do."
Gary looked at me and shrugged his shoulders a little.
"Your call," he said, "but I'm backing you regardless."

Deane went on to offer me a signing bonus that at the time was more money than I could make in a couple of years as a nurse. He was however expecting an answer on the spot but I just couldn't do it.

"Can I have a little time to think about it?" I asked sheepishly.
"Sure", said Deane, "But soon, okay?"
I headed from the building in silence. Instead of going with Gary and Joe for a celebratory beer, I simply told them I would catch them later.

I tried talking it over with my parents but they were too detached to be able to give me sound advice. My mother was all for me taking it because I mentioned it was good money. She never understood the music industry and always thought that being an orderly was like being a doctor and constituted a real job. Her mind just could not comprehend what was going on. My dad on the other hand, simply said, "It's up to you and you'll know what to do." Of course at the time, I didn't think I did.

I knew this band had something. I knew we were good. I cared about these guys for they had become my friends. I didn't know what game the gods were playing but I decided not to call Deane back. Gary could if he wished to but I was staying with the band. The LOVE AND SUFFERING was beginning to feel much more like suffering and suffering.

Meanwhile back at the hospital, the staff was beginning to notice changes in my behaviour. It was obvious something was up, as I had dark patches under both eyes, which were sitting just above my upper lip, a dead give away of exhaustion. I also weighed around 130lbs, if I was carrying a golf bag full of clubs to work. It was hard to decide what I wanted most at this time for I truly did love being in medicine. My patients were my family and I enjoyed giving everything I could to help them heal. To many it would be difficult to understand but I loved that clinical smell of the hospital. I loved dealing with doctors and with crisis and with the drama of life and death. I loved being with my patients, one on one on a surgical floor or a medical floor, but I shocked my fellow staff members when I told them that my next move was to take the O.R. course and become part of the Operating Room Team, still seeing myself as a surgeon somewhere down the road.

"Who does that little Scottish prick think he is? Does he not realize what I am offering him? Isn't this what he always wanted?"

Gary told me Deane was furious and ended his rant by saying that all bets were off and that Gary could take us wherever the hell he wanted. Meanwhile Derek was calling in one very big favour to one of his peers in management, a favour that would finally change the course of my life forever.

There were however just a few more twists and turns still to go on this road to LOVE AND SUFFERING.

We continued to fill every bar we played and the owners could care less if we were original or not for their beer and liquor sales were going through the roof. The occasional record company guy would pop in now and then but the ACTION had cooled off quite a bit. My son, now living with my family and I full time, had seen his mother drift off into the sunset as I had always known would be the case. On any given night the bar where we were playing would be well stocked with hospital staff who still came out in great numbers to support me, which of course pleased the rest of the lads greatly because it meant a room filled with pretty nurses. On the surface, all seemed to be going well...then I hit the wall.

It all began when Gary called to tell us some exciting news. First of all we had a gig in a club that we loved to play in a town called Oakville just west of Toronto. The gig would run Monday to Saturday as it had in the past but we all wondered what was so exciting about that. "You can use it as a rehearsal for Maple Leaf Gardens," he said enthusiastically. "Derek has us two nights opening up for *Culture Club!*"

At the time, *Culture Club* with their more than flamboyant front man Boy George was one of the top bands in the world. They were selling out venues everywhere and Toronto was to be no different. A complete sellout for both nights and *Tokyo* would be there along with every major recording label in the country. My mind shot back to the first ever concert I attended at The Gardens, which was a double bill showcasing Johnny Winters and the madmen from England, *Slade*. I vividly remembered telling myself at that concert that one day I would hit that stage and knock 'em all dead. Seems that you do have to be careful what you tell that old universe you want because you just might get it!

Several years prior to all of this, back in my "Dr Robert's bag days" I had tried "speed", an amphetamine (stimulant) that is now used primarily in the treatment of narcolepsy and attention-deficit hyperactivity disorder. "Beans" or "Bennies" as we commonly called them, turned your brain's dial to ten. You were stimulated to the point of declaring yourself, the best or untouchable and you went out and gave the performance of your life. I went on stage one evening in a small town called Newcastle in Ontario and performed like Mick Jagger's wee brother "Flash." From the second I hit the stage I was like a jackhammer. I danced on tables and on chairs. I grooved like the grooviest. I was on fire and nothing could stop me. At the end of each song the crowd roared. Well I am sure the crowd would have roared if there had been one, for you see the only two people in the audience that evening, were the "Two Billy's," both my mates but you see folks, beans don't care what size an audience is.

"You on beans," said Billy number one.
"Yeah! Yes! Yeah! Uh huh! That's right I am, I am, I am, Oh yeah. By the way, how can you tell, how can you tell, can you tell?"
"Wild guess," said Billy number two.

This gig that Gary had for us had fallen on the exact same schedule as my seven day straight hospital shift, so my schedule consisted of me going from 6:00am to 4:00am non-stop. Working, driving, working, driving, it was horrendous. On the Friday evening I had several friends with me in my vehicle, including one who was visiting from Scotland so I needed to be "on." Rumour had it that several record labels were popping in, perhaps even Capitol, which I found hard to believe. The crowd was lined up for a block around the corner and the buzz in the room that night was electric. I popped a pill and then just for good measure...I popped another.

We were brilliant. Gary Pring was ecstatic about how good we were. He felt a record deal was just a matter of time. I wasn't so convinced of that when we set off in my car to return home, my nervous system on fire as I tried desperately to keep it all together, a far cry from the nervous systems of all who were crammed in beside me, for they dropped like flies almost immediately upon my starting up the engine of the car, each one falling into an alcohol induced sleep leaving me, my brain, my exhaustion and my "Beans" alone at the wheel with no one to assist in trying to keep me calm or awake.

I am sure that many of you out there have had the horrible experience of nodding off while at the wheel of a car. It leaves you palpating, shaking and discombobulated to say the least. Your eyes open and you immediately say to yourself, "Oh God, I'm driving!" You feel that you have just had some sort of "out of body" experience. Your eyes focus on the road ahead and even if not religious by nature you begin thanking heavens that at least you didn't hit a...
"WALL!"
"ALAN!"... A WALL!" someone screamed in my ear.

My eyes opened some twenty feet or so from the brick walled siding of a bridge we were going under and it was coming in fast! Normally, one would simply negotiate the curve in the road as the wall ran along side your vehicle. But we were not negotiating any curve. We were heading straight for disaster. Instantaneously I turned the wheel slamming the driver's side of the car into the immovable object. We scraped along for some twenty or thirty feet before I managed to steady things and get us back on the road again. I had flirted not only with my own death, but also inexcusably with the lives of others. I slammed on the brakes and stopped at the roadside to try and compose myself. A female friend beside me didn't say a word, she just held out her hand to take mine. I was shaking noticeably.

"Oh good, are we home?" said a voice from the back.

After dropping everyone off and returning home I went to my son's crib and just stared at him, imagining what in the world would happen to him if I had killed myself on this night. I drifted off to sleep in the fetal position on the floor beside his crib, thinking about how I had to make a decision about whether or not I should continue my medical career, not knowing that I would sleep in missing my work and that my boss would make that decision for me.

"Alan we love you here," she said reassuringly. "And firing you is not something I care to do. You are a fine nurse and will make a great doctor, but you are killing yourself and we are watching it happen right before our eyes. You have to choose I'm afraid. Doctor or entertainer, choose."

She told me to take a couple of days off to rest then upon my return she wanted me to give her my decision. Would I quit the music industry and continue on my quest of becoming a doctor, or would I do one final shift as an R.N., take an extended leave of absence, and pursue my LOVE AND SUFFERING?

I told her of the upcoming gig at Toronto's famous Maple Leaf Gardens and I asked her if I could make my decision after that performance. She agreed but in one of the greatest ironies of all time, the two super-shows fell on my schedule when I had to work midnights. This would mean being on stage at the Gardens in front of a huge crowd and then hauling my ass into the hospital at night. I couldn't help but laugh at the absurdity of it all.

Rumour had it that no unsigned band had ever taken that famous stage before *Tokyo* did. I cannot tell you if this is true but I can tell you that going on in front of 20,000 people at a venue worshipped by musicians (including myself) was as nerve-wracking as it comes. In that building I had seen *The Who, Queen, Bowie* and even comedian Steve Martin back in his, "Wild and crazy guy!" days. It was a shrine to say the least.

I remember standing in the shower of our dressing room not fearing going out to sing for them but rather being petrified of what I was going to say to them between songs. I had made one special request to the band for this gig. By today's standards it seems trivial but on that evening it was to prove a major player in our destiny.

"If we can only afford one thing for this gig," I said pleadingly. "Please make it a cordless microphone!"

Seems a silly request today doesn't it? I knew however that if I was not constrained by a mic cord, I could utilize the stage to its maximum. I could be Rod Stewart... I could be *Cheap Trick*... I could be... Alan Frew.

# 4

*"There is an immeasurable, indescribable force
which Shamans called "intent" and absolutely everything that exists
in the entire cosmos is connected to it."*
CARLOS CASTENADA

# CHAPTER FOUR: INTENTION

As the brilliant Dr. Wayne Dyer reminds us, "You can call it spirit or soul or consciousness or universal mind or source. It is the invincible force that intends everything into the universe. It's everywhere. This source is always creating. It is kind. It is loving. It is peaceful. It is non-judgmental, and it excludes no one."

Those of us who read books such as this one will know by now that the word INTENTION seems to be over-used and rather hip and chic at the moment. And here I am using it once again. To not use it in a strategy for living a successful life would be like not using the word love when connecting to your children, your mother, best friend or even man's best friend, which in my case is a funny little Lab-Poodle cross named Harry (who, by the way, just finished a movie with Freddie Prinze Junior, so even he's using *THE ACTION SANDWICH*).

INTENTION is the single most unassumingly humble, yet incredibly powerful source in the universe, regardless of whether you use it in a religious context or a spiritual one. My grandfather used it in the latter fashion. "Jimmy the Exorcist", they called him, because whenever he came over to your house, all your spirits disappeared. For me it has nothing to do with religion, yet for another it may be spoken of as God, Allah, Mohammed, Buddha or the likes.

By now you have probably deduced that I am not a religious man. Why not? Mainly because organized religion has never been a logical explanation for me. I do, though, understand why, when I discuss my thoughts and feelings on the topics of energy, higher power and INTENTION, those of you who do take comfort in and require an organized religion in your lives may feel that I am just using different words to describe a similar thing, namely God. So be it. I call it the Source, the Centre, INTENTION, and perhaps we are all talking about the same thing.

Dr. Stephen Hawking, probably the most famous living scientist in the world, has sold in excess of ten million copies of the tenth anniversary edition of his book, *A Brief History of Time*. For a book to sell so many copies is essentially unheard-of in the field of science literature. Those who have not read *A Brief History of Time* may be surprised to find that the book's central figure is God. Doctor Hawking tells us a perfectly sound explanation is possible for The Big Bang some trillionths of a second after it happened, yet none was possible prior to the actual moment. I wonder how many times this has been debated, at dinner tables, water coolers or over a cup of coffee. Even Albert Einstein relented and said that the necessity for a beginning must have required the presence of a superior power. One asks then, if everything that begins to exist must have a cause and if the universe began to exist, then does it not follow that the universe must have a cause?

Dr. Hawking, whom I respect immensely, is quoted as saying:

"It is difficult to discuss the beginning of the universe without mentioning the concept of God. My work on the origin of the universe is on the borderline between science and religion, but I try to stay on the scientific side of the border. It is quite possible that God acts in ways that cannot be described by scientific laws."

God, Allah, Buddha, the force that connects us…only you can decide which energy is for you. However, I guarantee that all explanations given for the existence of the universe will convey the message that any or all gods had great INTENT, so regardless of what doctrine you march to ladies and gentlemen, the meaning of life always comes full circle back to the power of INTENTION.

When you are raised within a divided community based solely on misinterpreted doctrines that are called religion, it makes for a very interesting childhood to say the least, for it almost inevitably leads to pain, suffering and heartache of some sort for some poor bugger. You only pray it's not you.

I know I am certainly not the first one to ask the question of how many people have suffered terrible fates in the name of religious intolerance. It's mind-boggling to those of us on the periphery, agape at the ridiculousness of it all. In the end, you just have to stay true to yourself and to your purpose and live the best life you can.

This reminds me of a little story about Sister Mary Margaret, who worked for the local Home Care Agency in her town and who was on her way to deliver a bedpan to one of the agency's bedridden patients. On the way there she ran out of gas, which brought to light the fact that she had forgotten to replace a small gas can that she kept in the trunk. But Sister Mary Margaret was an ever so resourceful type, so without hesitation she decided to take the bedpan with her to the nearby gas station. She returned promptly to her car and began pouring the gasoline from the bedpan into the gas tank. Just at that moment two Presbyterian ministers were walking by and saw her, which prompted one to say to the other, "I'm telling you, if it starts, I'm turning Catholic!"

# FATHER FIGURE

My first major introduction to religious differences took place when I discovered that my pal "Wee Peter Gallagher" had to regularly attend a thing called confession, while I on the other hand did not. This was something neither of us could seem to figure out. I mean for me it was a case of, "Why break it, steal it, eat it, or do whatever to it, if you then must tell someone that it was you that did it?" This wasn't an Einstein theory as far as I could tell, and confession made absolutely no sense to me and would probably have meant that, had I been born a Catholic, I would have had to spend every day at the chapel in order to keep pace with my mischief.

Wee Peter, although jealous, did not entirely believe me, so upon rounding up several other Catholic boys, which is never difficult in Coatbridge, we decided to put it to the test.

Every day, Father D'Arcy would ride his bicycle down my street either on his way to or from the chapel and so it was decided by the Catholics that the wee Proddy (that is, Protestant...namely, me) would jump out of the bushes, flash him my, "Dickie-Bird" (Hey, we were seven years old and that is what we called it), call him a bad name and then beat it to the safety of wherever the hell the nearest safety happened to be.

We toyed with vile and outrageous bad words to prove beyond a shadow of a doubt that the Catholic Church could not harm me. We thought long and hard. Bugger? No, not dangerous enough. Cross-eyed? Good, only he wasn't. Arsie? No, that won't do, 'cuz that's his name really, isn't it? Father D'Arcy.

Dickie-Bird, that's it! Perfect. After all, you're going to flash him with it, so why not call him it. We tittered and laughed at the very thought of it. Who would ever dare call a priest, their priest...a penis! After having done this, if I was not forced by my mother to go and "confess", then indeed I was not a Catholic and they would believe that confession played no role in my life.

We all agreed, so the game and this clever plan were afoot. As usual, my entrepreneurial skills kicked in and I decided that it should also cost them each a penny if I was going to do this, for it had to be worth something, right?

And so we hunkered down behind Mrs. McDougall's big hedge and waited. And we were not disappointed, for very soon along he came.

I neglected to tell you that I had my "bogey" with me. What, you may well ask, is a bogey? Well, it's what we in Scotland called a homemade go-cart. Basically a large plank of wood used lengthwise for the body of the vehicle, with two smaller pieces at each end creating the cross beams, each with an axle and two wheels. A wooden apple box served as the seat or the cockpit, and a piece of rope ran from the front axle into the hands of the driver, making it possible to steer. Since it had no engine and worked solely off of gravity, you just found a large hill, got in and held on for dear life. I still carry bogey marks to this very day from some legendary rides and crashes.

There I was behind the bushes, my "Dickie-bird" in one hand, my bogey's rope in the other, when Father D'Arcy came, cycling and whistling along on his merry way completely oblivious to the ambush that was awaiting him.

What did I think he would do? Nothing, I guess. Oh wait, hang on, as a matter of fact, I DID NOT THINK THAT PART OUT AT ALL! Out I leapt, almost giving the poor bugger a heart attack.

"Hello Father DICKIE-BIRD!" (Waggle, waggle, waggle). Could he see it? Was it big enough? The young priest stopped on a dime and I swear to this day he pulled a wheelie that made him look like he was riding a fine stallion as opposed to a woman's bike of the 1930s.

Envision if you will the following: It's today, and you look out onto your street from your kitchen or living room window, to see a young lad of seven years of age and he's running fast. In one hand he is holding on to a thick piece of rope that is attached to a soap-box cart bigger than he is, and he's clumsily dragging it behind him. Looking rather frantic, he repeatedly takes quick glances over his shoulder while trying to stay on his feet. In his other hand is his penis. Okay, have you got that image? Good.

Picture if you will again this young lad, rope, cart, glances, penis – and there is a young priest chasing him down the street! What goes through your mind?

Pedophile? Police? Fire Department? Marines?

But this is not today. This is 1961 and this is Coatbridge and this is as normal an occurrence for people to witness as seeing a dog with a blonde wig on, as it saunters down the street, stops, lifts its leg and pees on a drunk sleeping on the roadside. It's as routine as a baker, who as you are standing watching him, puts the holes in the top of his apple pies with his pipe, or perhaps the man at the bar whose stomach is a little queasy politely excusing himself, stepping out the front door onto the street, throwing up, taking a deep relaxing breath, and walking back into the bar to pick up where he left off.

So forget it kid, just because you're running down the street with your dick in your hand while being chased by a man of the cloth, don't think you're getting any help here.

Two ladies stand yakking at the garden fence.

"Hello Mrs. Anderson, hello Mrs. Gallagher!" I shout as the kid, the go-cart and the penis go whizzing by.
"Hello yourself, Alan Frew!"
"Did you see that Mary, he's got his willy out again?"
"Aye Betty, shocking!"
Now it's the priest's turn to cross their path.
"Good Morning Father," say the ladies.
"Good morning ladies," he pants, robes pulled up around his knees. "See you at mass later, Mrs. Gallagher?"
"Aye Father, that you will."
"Oh, he's lovely Mary, isn't he?"
"Aye, he's a real charmer, Betty."

The ladies resume their chat and the priest seems to be gaining on me. Drastic measures must be taken, for if this guy catches me he'll tie me up, put me in a sack, carry me back to the dungeon in his chapel and keep me there with all

the other kidnapped Protestant boys. How do I know this? My dad told me.
That's how!

I deliberately slowed my pace to allow the holy man to get to within about six
feet of me when suddenly I deked to the left, letting go of the rope and
leaving the bogey directly in his path. He didn't stand a chance. His
immediate reaction was to jump on it like a surfboard, as opposed to breaking
his neck by tripping over it. And for a brief shining moment he was doing
well. In his panic he then attempted to take the controls, but as the cart was in
full flight now and just about to head down the hill at the bottom of my
street, he ended up in a kind of luge position, you know the position those
maniacs in the Winter Olympics take when they lie on that skid and propel
themselves down the ice at the speed of light? Ok, well he was like that, only
BACKWARDS!

Now it's not every day, dear reader, that you see a priest facing backwards,
laying flat on his back on a speeding go-cart, flying down the street toward the
bus stop, and I must admit I was howling as I stood in front of our garden
gate outside the little house that I called home.

Suddenly I heard a voice, my father's,
"And what are you howling about then?"

I turned to face him just as poor Father Dickie-Bird vanished over the horizon
of the hill, denying me the chance to witness his landing.
"Nothing," I said rather sheepishly.
"For a boy that's laughing at nothing, you seem to be very happy."
"Ahh, it's nothin' Dad, really."
"All right then, get in here, yer dinner's ready."
"Ok, Dad."
I walked behind him in what seemed like those giant footsteps of his.
"And Alan?"
"Yes, Dad?"
"Put your dickie-bird away before anyone sees it, okay?"
"Right, Dad."

If you are part of an organized religion that brings you joy, I truly think that is a wonderful thing. I couldn't do it myself but make no mistake, I am a spiritual man and I know that there is a greater power, a greater INTENTION connecting me to everything and everyone in the universe, even to Father Dickie-Bird.

# NO DOUBT

INTENTION, when called upon through RECEPTIVITY, DESIRE and BELIEF, is a powerful force of natural energy that transports determination from the image in your mind to your desired outcome in the physical world. INTENTION carries everything you need from your "source" and brings it to the doorstep of ACTION, which produces your ultimate goal. INTENTION, however, will attach itself to whatever you are focused on. If you attach it to fear or a limiting BELIEF you carry from the past, it will take you to a destination that you do not want. This is why it is absolutely imperative that you know exactly what you want and do not allow doubt to erode your commitment to your goals.

I know of no one that doesn't believe in energy of some kind. Even the most die-hard of skeptics and pessimists will agree that energy surrounds us, passes through us and strengthens us. It's a scientifically proven fact. Why then would our thoughts be any less? They are not, and in many instances they are even more powerful than the energy required for physical accomplishments. If you send out thoughts like "I am no good at what I do; I have tried and keep failing", and you're in the coffee and donuts business, you are basically telling the world that your coffee and donuts suck and that we should not buy them. If I go to auditions in this the infancy of my acting career, with thoughts in my head that I cannot act, I am basically telling the director not to even consider hiring me. Does any of this seem remotely familiar to you?

Those of you who appear to fail at virtually everything you try should be interested in this because we stand at an important juncture in *THE ACTION*

*SANDWICH*. This is the moment where people destined for success send out positive thoughts and positive energy and emotion into the world. This is where achievers act and behave as if they have already achieved the outcome, and by doing so they add the intense power of INTENTION to their already positive thoughts and energy.

All right, so now you are receptive to what it is you want. You DESIRE it in your heart and you believe that you deserve it, that you are entitled to it...is that enough? I know that I am receptive to my tummy rumbling, and I really can DESIRE to have a sandwich and of course I believe that I deserve to eat. However, my plate remains empty. This is where the power of INTENTION must kick in and leave no doubt in my mind that the object of my DESIRE is attainable, for it is INTENTION that says, "There is no stopping me from having that which I DESIRE." At the moment when failure is no longer an option, INTENTION becomes the fuel for your dreams. Let me give you an example of this.

# FOOTBALL IS THE ONLY REASON, GOD GAVE US FEET

During the last World Cup I was the spokesperson for a sports network in a between-game segment called *Frew and Fans*. This happened purely because I intended it to. Rather cocky of me, one might think. But it had nothing to do with the network, at least not in the beginning.

I decided that I wanted to be part of what in my opinion is the most beautiful game. And so for over a year I would drop this idea into conversations at dinner parties, special events or with various business contacts, therefore intending it into being. I had my manager completely convinced it was happening long before we had our first meeting. I was receptive to the idea of being on a sports program. I truly desired this to happen. I believed that I would be an asset to any show covering soccer. I put all of the aforementioned criteria behind my INTENTION for this to come to fruition, and then I took

ACTION. I dropped the hint one day with a high-ranking contact who in turn fired my idea off the head of programming for the sports network. Shortly thereafter, I got the call. We set up a meeting, to which I brought all of the PASSION that I have not only for soccer, but also for communicating, promoting and performing. It was a cinch! I knew what the World Cup was, I love football; I wanted to be part of the World Cup and I believed that I was the guy for the job. When I included the power of INTENTION, it was like a door opening and lo and behold my goal stood before me. By the time the position was offered to me, three networks had joined forces to show the World Cup and all decided to use me.

I now bring this same recipe with me for my fledgling career as an actor. I bring it into the realm of public speaking, and it is how this very book came into being. You see *THE ACTION SANDWICH* was required in order for me to write a book about *THE ACTION SANDWICH*. Go figure!

As for the acting career, well, it brings every aspect of what this book is all about into play. In all of my life I have never felt emotions careening through my body as they do when having to perform an audition for a professional acting job. Man, it's nerve-wracking! Walking into a room with several people sitting behind a desk staring at you, a camera rolling, and you have to transform yourself into what the director desires.

"Okay, let's see, Alan. You're an Irish-Tibetan monk, totally addicted to Guinness, who secretly desires to be Donald Trump's personal massage therapist and......ACTION!"

Transformation is a word that I love. I'm not exactly sure why, but I do know that I love the way it feels in my mouth as I say it, and I notice that I feel a certain way after using it. It becomes like a little dose of positivism for me. Transformation means a change in form, appearance, or character, yet you know that it is grander than that, beyond the idea of mere change. When someone says, "he's changed," it just doesn't seem to reach the level of something like, "My God, what a transformation she has undergone!" Transformation Glasgow Style:

"Awwright, Willie?"

"Aye, Frankie. I'm doin' just fine, how's yourself?"

"Doin' great, Willie. Did ye' hear about Jimmy though?"

"Naw, I did not. What about 'im?"

"Well he's...goin' through one o' them transformations."

"Transformation? How so?"

"Well, it seems he's gone from being a prick, to being an absolute prick!"

# OH WHAT A LUCKY MAN, HE WAS

INTENTION is the purity of that moment when life itself came into being and joined the universal family. As a footnote remember this: from the perspective of the universe you were never intended to fail. The true INTENTION of so great a power is too positive for such a stance. Think of INTENTION and FAILURE for a moment. Now change that thought to INTENTION and NEGATIVITY. Or, for the purpose of this little experiment, change it to NEGATIVE INTENTION, which in my opinion now constitutes an oxymoron. All right, scholars out there don't get your knickers in a twist – hear me out. I say oxymoron because INTENTION is not about negativity. Saying someone intends to harm a child, kill another human being, rob a bank or rip off old people of their pensions, these are human frailties and weaknesses that bastardize the very nature of the word INTENTION, which in its purest form would be incapable of such dark acts.

INTENTION is the cancer's remission. It is the unexpected windfall you have just as you prepare to painfully borrow money from a friend. It is the great job offer that comes on the same day you take the stand and say goodbye to the job you know you should have never taken in the first place. It is the guardian angels that show up when you need them, and then slip away before you can even thank them. We call it luck, coincidence, six degrees of separation, chance, and a host of other names that make us feel comfortably disconnected from what is truly our spirit or, as I prefer to call it, our source at work. But make no mistake about it, INTENTION surrounds all living things and is most easily activated when you immerse yourself in and fill your mind full of positive thoughts about the outcome you DESIRE.

I was on a winter road trip last year with *Glass Tiger* and as part of promoting the show I had to visit several radio stations during the morning and afternoon, yet still sing in the evening. It was wearing me down. On one extremely cold evening in Edmonton, Alberta, I was asked, much to my consternation, to sing "live" on the drive-home show at 5:00 p.m. I reluctantly agreed. I was accompanied by a record company representative who was getting an earful from me on the way out telling him I was fed up of jumping through hoops. It was forty below outside; I was tired, freezing and hoarse.

You name it, I complained about it. As we exited through the main doors a van was blocking our pathway. I saw the driver slide back out of view and I wondered what this was all about. Suddenly two side doors on the van slid open and I saw this chap in a wheel chair. A few seconds later, an electronic-lift brought him to the ground and he approached me in his chair. He had only one arm and was a double amputee just below each knee.

"Mr. Frew," he said, "I have driven almost an hour to get here. Would you be kind enough to sign my CDs and photographs please?"
"Of course," I replied.
"I am one of your biggest fans, I love your music," he said with enthusiasm.
"Thank you," I almost whispered. Then I thought to ask him something, "Tell me, are you coming to the show tonight?" My idea was that if he was not I would offer him free tickets.
"Oh, I would love to," he said "But I gotta be gettin' back to town. I have to coach kid's hockey tonight, sorry though. Well, thanks kindly. Bye now."

He backed up his chair onto the lift, and within a few seconds he was gone. With no legs and one arm, there he was, heading back to town to coach kid's hockey, missing the concert of one of his favourite bands and doing it with PASSION and enthusiasm. He had driven over an hour just to come and say hello and get me to sign a few items. I stood silently for a moment watching intently as he pulled away in his van.

"He was meant to be here," I said trance-like.

"I beg your pardon?" said the record rep.

"That guy was meant to be here tonight. That was no coincidence. It was intended that he would meet me here at this precise moment."

"I don't understand," said the rep.

"That's okay, let's go." And so I headed back to the hotel deep in thought. Here I was complaining about being tired, having a scratchy throat and being worried that my voice might not make it through the two-hour show, while this fellow with no legs and one arm had driven over an hour just to spend a few minutes with me before heading back to coach hockey! It was just too powerful to be coincidence or luck. No, INTENTION put him in my pathway to remind me of how good my life is. This INTENTION was called up from a subconscious inner place on my behalf to bring me back down to earth and make me realize the blessings that I have and to remind me of just how grateful I should be. Incidentally when I got back to my hotel room there was a book I had not noticed stuffed into my bag. It was a book by Dr. Wayne Dyer called "The Power of INTENTION." I had left home in a rush and my wife had obviously seen it by the bedside and had stuck it into my case for me.

If you are at a roadblock that is causing you stress in your life, find a corner and a moment to yourself and think of something positive. It's there. Trust me. So look for it. Those of you who believe in and practice the art of meditation certainly have a leg up on those of us who don't. However, look for it, that special thing. It only seems like it's not there. I know it may be difficult right now, but if you have to, go back to when you were a child and life seemed so much more carefree, then feel what that was like. Let that feeling grow within you at this very moment. That child is still in you. That is still you. It is important to find this time. I do not meditate, but I always find time for myself to practice positive thinking. I do it while driving or when working out, or if I manage to get out and go for a relaxing massage.

# THE DAY THAT ALAN MEDITATED

Okay, what is my INTENTION here? Oh yeah that's it. I want to rid myself of this stress. Okay, now c'mon Alan, close your eyes, take a deep breath now. Go to silence. Ahhhh, that's it, deeper, deeper, deeeeeeeepppperrrr. Now chant softly. Ohmm, ohmm, oohmm, oohhhhmmmm, ohmmmmmmz! ohhmmmmzz! ohmmmzzz! ohmzzzz! zzzzzz! ZZzzzzzzz! ZZZZZzzzzzzzzzz!

# AND IN THE MIDDLE OF NEGOTIATIONS, YOU BREAK DOWN

I often tell my audiences that if ever they want to see expert negotiators and entrepreneurs at work, then look no further than little children, your own if you have them, but if you don't then little nieces, nephews or bratty neighbour kids will suffice. Watch how relentless kids are when they DESIRE. They begin by asking parent number one for whatever it is they DESIRE. If denied, they simply move on to parent number two. If that fails, they move perhaps to grandparent number one, then, if need be, number two. No luck? Back they go to parent number one, then number two, and again to the grandparents who, by this time, are more likely to break down or at least to take sides against parent number one. The child has already won because they know that the odds are they will get at least part of what they've asked for. They have made ground. If the adult still remains reluctant to give in, he or she will most likely carry the torch on behalf of the child to parent number two, who inevitably says,

"Oh, for Pete's sake, yes!"

Sound familiar? Parents reading this book know exactly what I am talking about.

Children are masters at getting what they want because they ask for it and if they do not get it they ask again, and again, and yet again. I haven't had a full, uninterrupted conversation with my wife for three years in my little daughter's waking hours. Oh sure, you can try the old, "Now sweetheart, Daddy and Mommy are speaking, so be a good girl and wait your turn!" Right, good luck! When they get something in their little heads that they want to ask for or tell you, then forget it. It is a relentless barrage of machine-gun talk until you give up and give in.

Asking for what you want works wonders. So why then do we stop doing it? Simple, because as we mature we become steadily more afraid of the fact that with asking can come rejection and with rejection can come pain and embarrassment. We become more and more fearful to ask. The outcome is never as bad as we think it is going to be, is it? You ask someone for something and they say, simply, no. Then what happens? A lightning bolt strikes you dead on the spot? You read it as a front-page headline in your local newspaper: "He asked and was told no, details page 18?" Of course not. Though you might feel a twinge of embarrassment or hear a nagging voice inside your head say, "See, I told you he'd say no."

So what if you break a heel and go flying, or exit a toilet dragging a roll of single ply. Is it not all just part of life? Of course it is. Why then is asking any different? Tell me, if you ask and you don't get, are you any worse off than you were before you asked? The answer of course is no. At the very least you are still the same. You don't have $20 so you ask Frank for it and he says no. You still don't have $20, but at the very least you might have discovered where not to go in the future to borrow money. Asking is as much a part of success as any other thing in this book, even if you have to take the occasional pie in the face.

People who have navigated the road to success certainly know the power of asking for the things they want and more than just a few of them have taken some pretty big pies in the "clock" on the way there. Yours truly is no exception. So do you want to know how to a get a recording-deal? Ask someone who works for a record company. Want to know how to start a business? Take a successful businessperson to lunch and ask them how they got started. Do you want to improve your golf swing but can't afford private lessons? Ask the best golfer on your street. Want to find out if you have what it takes to work in medicine? Go chat with the head nurse at your local hospital.

Do you want to know how to turn your $100 into $10,000? Ask Donald Trump! I'm serious. You will be amazed at how many people from all walks of life, regardless of social or financial status, will be more than willing to answer your questions. I know this because I have done it, especially in business and entrepreneurship. I have taken extremely successful business people to lunch for the specific purpose of picking their brains. And the best part is that they've known upfront that this is what I intended to do. I asked them ahead of time, and they agreed! Sure, some will decline your request but that's okay. Don't give it a second thought. Just erase them from your list and move on. It takes only one or two and you can have more answers to your questions than you had ever hoped for. One of the greatest topics that successful people love to discuss is how they became successful, so start there. This is useful information on your road to success. Inevitably, as you move forward on that pathway, you're going to have to negotiate at some time or another, and although listening is going to come in pretty handy when that time comes, having the ability to clearly define what it is you want and asking for it is equally powerful and necessary.

After you have successfully mastered the ability to ask for what it is you want from this universe, you will be challenged yet again. It is easy to fall into the trap of just asking indiscriminately for things and stuff and goodies. So be careful. Be selective. Think. We have all heard the term, "say no to the bad and yes to the good." Jack Canfield coined a phrase that raises the bar: "say no to the good and yes to the great!" All teachers of success subscribe to this adage although this kind of doctrine tends to make one fair game for the "easy for you to say" crowd. So be it. It's true and I know that it works.

Try this exercise of saying no to the good and yes to the great and you will be amazed to see how much "great" comes your way. It is the natural law of attraction. However this won't happen before a few tempting "goods" hit your world, for this is a universal truth. When you draw a line in the sand your life will definitely test the theory to see if it is true. Remember, what you ask for you get, and the more you ask for, the more of it you will get. So if you settle for "OKs and goods" then that is precisely what you will get. No matter what level you are at on the social economic ladder, this concept remains true.

# ALL GOOD CHILDREN GO TO HEAVEN

My school contained a wide array of characters from brainiacs with IQs off the charts to maniacs with the IQs of farts. As for me, I was always somewhere in the middle. Smart and intelligent enough to get to where I needed to go, yet tough enough that I could swim among the sharks and not get eaten alive.

I learned these skills so very, very, young. Wheelin' and dealin' becomes second nature when the street is your playground, whether by choice or necessity. Here's a lovely little example of what I mean.

At around five years of age, I liked the idea of having money in my pocket and I wasn't one of those kids who preferred shiny coins to bills, just because they glistened and were more fun to play with. No, I liked coins, but I loved bills. Still do as a matter of fact, but even as a child I knew you could do more with bills.

One day, approximately a hundred lifetimes ago, my parents took me to a museum dedicated to the life and work of a famous Scottish explorer called David Livingstone, most noted for being the first European to see Africa's wondrous Mosi-oa-Tunya waterfall, which he renamed (as if it needed it), Victoria Falls after his monarch, Queen Victoria. He also gets credit for locating the true source of the Nile (again as if the Africans knew only of the false one). Isn't it interesting that Africa is the oldest inhabited territory on earth, with many fossils and evidence of human occupation dating perhaps as early as seven million years ago and yet Africans are expected to thank their lucky stars that a European explorer came along to tell them all who they were and where they lived. I mean, they must have been at their wit's end trying to figure that out until a wee "Roman came roamin' over the hill."

First native: "Who are we?"
Second native: "How the hell should I know?"
First native: "Oh thank god, here comes a little white guy in a red dress and gold hat on his way to a parade no doubt. He'll know who we are."
Second native "Go on, ask him."
First native: "Hey! Who are we?"
Roman: "Well, I've decided that you are... Afri's."
First native: "And where are we?"
Roman: "Glad you asked. Since the Roman suffix 'ca' denotes 'country or land', I have decided that you live in... Afri-ca."
First native: "Well I am so glad that you cleared that up for us. I mean we've only been living, breathing, working, screwing, loving, laughing and talking for about a hundred bloody centuries, before your scrawny little white arse got here! But thanks for sorting that out for us."

Now, to a five-year old boy David Livingstone and his memorial was real John Wayne stuff. Looking back on it, it was a tiny space, but to this lad, it held all the treasures of the world and then some. Livingstone's bloody, worn-out uniform hung on the wall, for all to see. His sword and musket, remnants of a savage journey, were encased here. A hand-written letter, the penmanship exquisite, to his Queen, recorded his epic tale in fine detail. And of great curiosity to me, the very bone from his arm, which had been brutally ripped from his body during an attack from a ferocious lion, was also openly on display. It was marvelous. In fact, for a five-year-old, it was magical.

Yes indeed, my RECEPTIVITY to what I had seen in the museum had me consumed. I was equally receptive, however, to the existence of a willing clientele, including my parents, who had spent their good hard-earned money visiting this little gold mine from the Nile. My DESIRE therefore was to recreate it at home, and I had oodles of BELIEF in my ability to do so and in my own ability to sell it to a very captive audience. With unhesitating

INTENTION I took ACTION and here is what I did.

I took my grandad's old boiler suit, which was ripped at the elbows and knees, and smeared it with oil and splattered it with ketchup, then hung it up with a card saying "David Livingstone's Uniform." I wrote a letter to Queen Victoria, stained it with my granny's tea and signed it "Livingstone." I made a sword from two pieces of old wood. I broke the windshield wiper off of our first car (which I paid for later when my dad found out and not, I might add, with money) and I painted it blood red and declared on a card that, "This was the bone from David's arm." A few bells and whistles later and I had turned my grandad's garden shed into *THE DAVID LIVINGSTONE MEMORIAL* of all time. Now all I needed was my clientele.

Around the corner I went to the local pub, where spilling out onto the street was my wonderful old grandad and several of his cronies. The pubs opened at 11:00 a.m. and closed at 2:00 p.m., presumably to give the staff an afternoon break before opening again at 5:00. There was no one in this world like my grandfather (my dad came as close as you'll get); he was a truly unique piece of work. Gentle and caring, it seemed the drunker he got, the more lovable he became. I'll never forget the day several of my pals came running up to me, frantic, with that look on their faces that announced "I can't believe what I just saw."

"Yuh...yo... you ha...haaave to come ssseee this!" one of them said.
"What is it?" I asked. "A de...a dead man, we found a dead man!"
"Where?"
"At the bottom of the road, he's down there," one said as he pointed.
"And he's DEAD!" said the other, obviously excited.
"How do you know he's dead?" I inquired.
"Cuz he's hanging over a wall...he's GOT to be dead."
"Let's go!" I cried, and off we scurried to see the dead man.

Now to a boy some nine years of age or so, the prospect of finding a dead body ranks right up there with the flattened cat with maggots, the poop-in-a bag through the mail box or the stripped naked pal tossed into the girl's gym, so off we ran at top speed to the bottom of my street, and sure enough when we got there I saw the legs dangling over a small wall that he had obviously fallen over upon gasping for his last breath.

I looked all around me, wondering where the sniper was located that had so skillfully taken him out. Perhaps, though, he was a foreign spy who'd been poisoned at a spies' banquet and the drug had just kicked in, right here, at this wee wall on my street. Yes! That could be it. He was passing this wall and BANG! Down he goes, dead as a doorknob. I saw the legs and I stopped in my tracks, for I had never seen a real "live" dead person before, except the ones that John Wayne killed at the Alamo. Deep breath, here we go. Slowly, cautiously, I leaned over the wall to take my first peek. I couldn't see his face for his cap had fallen over most of it. I slowly reached down to remove it so that we might all get a good look at this corpse when suddenly... it decided to make a noise.

"Tccchhhhuh," it said, from that gargly spot in the back of its throat.
"Mammy, Daddy!" cried one of my pals.
"QUIET!" I commanded. "It's ok, I've heard they do that when they're dead."
"Tccchhhuh Too," it warbled again.
And yet again, "Tooch...Tooo."
Slowly, cautiously, defying my years, I reached down to uncover the dead man's face...when suddenly the corpse bellowed,
"TOOT TOOT TOOTSIE GOODBYE,
TOOT TOOT TOOTSIE, DON'T CRY."
"Jesus! It's Al Jolsen!"
"WATCH FOR THE MAIL,
I'LL NEVER FAIL,
IF YOU DON'T GET A LETTER, THEN YOU KNOW I'M IN JAIL," he sang at the top of his lungs.

Oh yes, my dear reader, I may never have seen a dead body up to this point in my life, but I had seen THIS one many, many times before. For this was my grandad. That sweet, loveable old man who adored me, who shared his roast potatoes with HP sauce with me even though he had very few of them on his plate. There wasn't much I couldn't get him to do. So on that day outside the pub, as the curator of the new Livingstone memorial, I knew I would have his full support in my venture.

"Come and see the wonders of darkest Africa!!!" I cried out. "Follow me gents, right this way!"

Now, if you think the real memorial was small, this one was a shoebox, but I kid you not, they filed in one at a time, some even turning around and going back for seconds.

Through my megaphone (a rolled up school notebook) I yelled,

"Come one, come all! Look if you dare!"

Soon other pubs had spilled out and my grandad was calling out to some others. "Frankie! Bob! Jimmy! My goodness, ye have tae see this, it's the bone oot of David Livingstone's arm!!"

I made a killing. It played for three days I think. Critics? They loved it ... even though they were tipsy. And my dad, well he went easy on me for the windshield wiper, but not that easy. Let's just say we cut a deal.

I still create David Livingstone's memorial today, only it's a song you can find on a CD, it's this book, or perhaps it's a concert in your hometown. It can be a speaking engagement or perhaps it's a piece of clothing I design or a painting done by my own hand. But it's all the same thing. The five-year-old entrepreneur, the twenty-five, thirty-five or one day sixty-five year old, they are all the same with the only difference being their circumstance and their ability to ask for what it is they want, while being able to negotiate with their surrounding world by being receptive, by having DESIRE, by believing, intending and taking ACTION, passionately towards the success that will not be denied them.

I love to tell the David Livingstone story. It comes from a time when life seemed so much simpler. Stress? What's that when you're a child? Was that not something your granny tied your grandad's hernia up with?

Think what it would be like to be happy beyond your wildest dreams. Close your eyes and be happy in your mind, body and soul, even if just for a minute. What is it that is stopping you from feeling this way for more than just this moment? The answer is, you, only you. Now I am not diminishing any or all the problems you may be facing, and indeed you may not feel responsible for all of them. However, I am saying that you are responsible for how you handle them and how you respond to them no matter how painful they may feel. If you detest your job, you are responsible for not leaving. If your husband beats you, you are responsible for remaining. If you have cancer, you are responsible for the fight against it. I know this can seem harsh and cruel but it is so necessary to understand and believe this, in order to be able to make different choices, towards different outcomes. Now hear this, if you take only one thing away from this book it is this: you cannot change what you do not acknowledge. If you want 100% of the "say" in your life, if you want 100% of the control in your life, then you must take 100% responsibility for your life. No ifs, ands or buts, period.

We are almost where we need to be. INTENTION is such a powerhouse of force, yet it should be obvious why I call this *THE ACTION SANDWICH*. For without the ACTION of getting up off of my backside and actually doing something like making the sandwich, I will remain hungry. You have to DO to get DONE! So I need to get up and go over to my fridge, gather the ingredients; then and only then will I be on my way to success and have in my possession a delicious sandwich. Remember now, THIS is the moment of truth. For if indeed it is a delicious healthy sandwich I DESIRE, then my ACTION will lead to my success. However, what happens if during my ACTION phase I get unfocused or lost or perhaps just plain lazy and instead I take a quick fix of, say, a large chocolate milk and a big helping of pie...what then? I may have removed that feeling of hunger, but at what price? I'm hungry! Let's talk some ACTION.

# TEN STEPS TO INTENTION

1. ORVIL OR WILBUR? - Somebody had to do it, right? Ever wonder how many people said to them, "Hey Orv! Willy boy! That thing'll never fly!" Once you are receptive to your DESIRE and BELIEF, your path is set. Let nothing negative in, ever. Don't doubt your creativity for this is INTENTION'S doorway. Invent your own Kitty Hawk.

2. IT'S MAGIC OF A KIND - There is nothing negative about kindness. One of the synonyms for the word kindness is good INTENTION. Spreading kindness synergistically creates power and positivism throughout the world. Again, *The Butterfly Effect*. By the way, don't forget yourself.

3. MONSIEUR PIERRE SEVERE - "This just in. Thomas Edison has finally given up! There will be no light bulb after all, news at eleven." Can you imagine? INTENTION requires perseverance, the steady persistence, and purpose in spite of difficulties, obstacles, or discouragement. This is non-negotiable. Get used to it.

4. YOU'VE GOT THE WHOLE WORLD IN YOUR HANDS - Try on occasion to think as part of one large mass of energy whose thoughts, choices and decisions ultimately affects the body of the universe as opposed to thinking about just yourself. Putting your thoughts on a grander scale not only elevates your decision-making but also raises the bar on INTENTION asking greater things in return. Elevate.

5. WE ARE EVO - Choose your pathway. Be prepared to evolve. Expand with the universe and you will open your RECEPTIVITY and awareness to an unlimited capacity, thereby

elevating INTENTION. Do this and you will accept that the universe is filled with abundance for all. You are sending out the message that says, "Nothing is beyond my scope. There are no limitations."

6. EMAIL FOR MR. UNIVERSE! - Give equal credence to the energy and power of your thoughts, as you would your arms or legs. Each thought is an email of your INTENTION notifying the universe of what your BELIEF and DESIRE is for any given choice or decision. This is where "I am who I know I am," lives. The universe will believe you and act accordingly. Be careful.

7. WHAT ARE YOU WORTH - If you are a $100 guy do not then accept $99.99 unless by doing so, you can see more than $100 value further down the pipeline. Jack Canfield says, "Say no to the good and yes to the great." You will be amazed what happens if you stay true to your self worth. Amaze yourself.

8. GET COMMITTED -
"I pledge allegiance to myself,
and to the life for which I stand.
One universe indivisible,
with RECEPTIVITY, DESIRE, BELIEF, INTENTION
and ACTION for all."

9. OF FLESH AND BLOOD I'M MADE - Change doesn't happen overnight. If you stray from the core of your INTENTION, go easy on yourself, but not too easy. Be firm in your resolve to evolve and start again. Use any mistakes or failures as guides to where not to go, on your journey ahead. Live and learn.

> 10. I CAN SEE FOR MILES - Visualize exactly how it's going to look, how it's going to feel, how it's going to be, when you get there. This process of creating internal mental images of how it shall be in the end conjoins you to INTENTION. It declares, "this is where I am, but this is where I shall be." Visualize.

# MY SONG
*Opus 4*

### GOD GAVE ROCK 'N ROLL TO YOU

"What are you doing son?"
"Easy, I am aligning my actions with my dreams."
"What are you thinking?"
"Simple, I am thinking about what it will feel like when I am one."
"And what exactly is it that you are going to be?"
"Why, a Rock Star of course."

### I'LL TUMBLE 4 YA

I wore a canary yellow suit that night, difficult for the audience to miss no matter where one might be sitting. Difficult to miss even for canaries. I know in my heart that my RECEPTIVITY, DESIRE, BELIEF and INTENTION were in complete harmony with everything that makes me who I truly am and as for my ACTION; well Monday's phone call answered that.

"Alan wake up. Alan, you have a phone call, wake up," said my mother.
"Who is it? Tell them I'm knackered. Tell them to call again."
"It's some man from Capitol Records."

I got up but it was painful for after both performances I was basking in a few minutes of glory with the lads before heading back to my hometown and working the night shift until 6:00 a.m. I remember chuckling at one of my patients saying, "Well, how did it go?"

"It was magic," I said, the sound of the crowd still in my head.

"Good for you Alan," he replied, as he reached beneath the sheets to remove a very full bedpan. Can you empty this?"

I groggily spoke into the phone.

"Hello?"

"You're a star," the voice said.

"Come again," I replied.

"You are a... star," it repeated.

I recognized it as being the voice of Tim Trombley, the A&R representative that had wooed the band from the very beginning. He was second in command to Deane Cameron and had been wounded by the split that had occurred upon my refusal to sign as a solo artist.

"Deane is on the line here with me Alan," said Tim.

"Hello Deane."

"Hello Alan," he replied a little conservatively. Then he delivered a phrase that was to become a defining moment.

"Well," he said gently. "I guess if I want the cherries, I'll have to take the whole pie!"

I stood silently, contemplating my world around me. I sighed deeply.

"Alan, gather up the troops and come on down and sign with Capitol Records."

Finally, a deal, a recording contract, a recoding contract with the label that signed *The Beatles*. Would this mean that I could still meet a Beatle? Can you imagine what it would be like to meet Paul McCartney?

It was a beautiful moment. A moment I will never forget. Yes this was something that should be shared with loved ones yet there I was, alone by the telephone, in my fruit of the loom Y-fronts all one hundred and twenty five pounds of me, with my hair looking like Elsa Lanchester's in the *Bride of Frankenstein*, with my son at school, my father at work and my mother... drunk.

"Thanks Deane, I'll see you soon."
I hung up the phone and crashed.
The following day I met with my hospital supervisor.
"You will always have a job here waiting for you," she said cheerfully.
I couldn't have asked for anything more than that, although I sensed one huge sigh of relief coming from her that kind of said, "Thank God, he's going." I had one last shift in me, one final, hospital gig and then the boy who was never going on the road, was about to do just that for a very long, long time.

## SOMEONE SAVED MY LIFE TONIGHT

"CLEAR!!!"
The sound of the defibrillator firing off its electrical surge into the chest of a dying human always made me quiver, no matter how many times I had taken part in resuscitations.

As an orderly I had been part of The Crash Team, which is a small crew responsible for attending situations within the hospital where patients have lost consciousness due to heart attack or stroke and assisted in many of these procedures, performing C.P.R. (think of *Baywatch* without the breasts). What was interesting was in all of my years in nursing, I had never been the one to actually discover the patient at the moment when the stroke or heart attack happened becoming the one to call the "code" that rallies the resuscitation team. This was to change on the very last minute of my very last shift as a member of the medical community.

As a favour I had been given only four patients in a four-bed ward, all of whom had surgery that day. My shift was called doing a "special," whereby I didn't have to work the entire floor but just attend to these four post surgery patients or "fresh bleeds" as we called them. I monitored wounds, measured fluids and blood pressures and up until the last minute of my shift everything had gone smoothly. Just as I was taking the last blood pressure of my nursing career, one of my patients turned deep red and his eyes rolled up into his head. He then gave an enormous grunting exhalation, his last breath before turning blue and spasm-ing violently. I leaned over him and hit the call button.

"Code 99! Code 99!" I screamed.

I dragged his limp body onto the hard surface of the floor and began administering C.P.R., working furiously until the team arrived and the doctor in charge took over. I continued to assist. After it was all over I sat at my desk and filled out the mounds of paper work required when such a thing happens. Unfortunately I had found out first hand a few years earlier what happens when you and your hospital are on the receiving end of a law suit, whether rightly or wrongly, from the family members of a patient who runs into difficulty during his or her stay in the hospital, and it's not pleasant. The administration needs you to do whatever you can to assist in keeping the hospital from being on the wrong end of the judge's decision. Once the hospital is free and clear, you're on your own! A nurse's notes therefore are the key to their ability to recalling the events of the incident in question and so I made copious notes on this one. The very last thing I ever did as an R.N. was to walk over to the Intensive Care Unit and see how the fellow was making out. He was alive, on life support but alive nonetheless.

Now, I was done. Finished. The milk boy who became a clothier who became the shoe salesman who became the tube-cutter, who jumps at the chance to be an orderly, who became a nurse, who did not become a doctor but instead became ... a Rock Star?

But hold on just a minute there Spanky for you're not quite a rock star yet, are you?

## I'M LEAVING ON A JET PLANE

The roar of the engine and a sudden burst of speed, so fast that one seems magnetized to the seat can give a guy, especially this guy, a feeling of helplessness, as some 200,000 pounds of steel grinds its way into the heavens and for a brief shining moment, your arse hangs in the balance like a little girl's doll, dangled over a balcony by her mischievous brother. I was on my way to my destiny.

Vancouver, British Colombia has since become one of my favourite places in the world, but back then on the day I made my first trip across this vast land, it was unexplored territory. Coming in over the magnificent Rocky Mountains was a sight to behold for this cheeky wee bastard from Coatbridge, and I smiled quietly to myself as I descended to the relative unknown. I was accompanied by Sam Reid and Al Connelly and it had been decided by Deane Cameron that we fledgling writers would work with a man who has since become somewhat of a legend in the business of song writing, Jim Vallance. Jim rose to fame as the behind the scenes songwriting partner of Bryan Adams as together they penned hit after hit, not only for Bryan but also for some of the biggest recording acts in the world. At the time Jim worked with us he was on the verge of stardom and had decided that he wanted to try his hand at not only co-writing with us but at producing as well. This session in Vancouver was to establish several things. Could we write great songs? Could we co-write with an established songwriter and was he the right man to take the wheel of our first major recording? It proved to be a week that changed my life, for in our first session together that lasted but a few days, we penned the two greatest selling singles of *Glass Tiger's* career: *Don't Forget Me When I'm Gone,* and *Someday.* Vallance was indeed "the man."

# 5

*"Suit the ACTION to the word,*
*the word to the ACTION."*
WILLIAM SHAKESPEARE

# CHAPTER FIVE: ACTION

If I were told I must give a one-word answer to the question, "What is the meaning of life," I believe the first word to leave my lips would be ACTION, for ACTION is the life force of all things. I repeat: You must DO to get DONE! If you're in the race and the starter sounds his gun, you have to run to have any hope of winning. Indeed, in the game of life, if you stop moving, you die. From the tiniest creatures to the mightiest galaxies in our heaven's energy, the pulse of life flows through all things. ACTION is a constant even when motion is not apparent.

*"Never confuse motion with ACTION."*
BENJAMIN FRANKLIN

# IT'S RIGHT IN FRONT OF YOU

Imagine this illustration for a moment. You're hungry, really, hungry. In the fridge you have all the makings of a great sandwich, yet you aren't making one. You're sitting on the couch thinking about how unfair it is that you're hungry. Your stomach is growling. You are actually starting to get a headache.

All physical, emotional and mental indicators point to the need for food, but still you sit there. You call your friends one after the other and say, "Man I'm so hungry."
"Why don't you make a sandwich?" they suggest.

But what do they know really? So you sit there and you start to think about that one time you made a sandwich and it didn't turn out very well.

"I might as well not even try," you say to yourself.
"That was such a terrible sandwich, I must not know how to make one."
"I don't really deserve a sandwich."
"My parents really never taught me how to make a proper sandwich and I failed home economics."

After a few minutes, you start to think some more about how hungry you are. "I could make a sandwich," you think, "but my husband bought the wrong kind of bread. So I guess I'll just have to be hungry." Eventually you die of starvation on that couch.

This may sound pretty far-fetched, but it's all too real for many people in real-life situations. Some people refuse to act because of the reasons I have mentioned, plus a thousand more. Imagine that there is something you really want, but you spend your energy on the reasons why you can't have it as opposed to actually acting upon the reasons you can and should have it. You have everything you need to start, but you don't. Often you have the support of your friends and colleagues, yet you discount their opinions while making excuses and blaming other people, allowing your ideas and dreams to die of starvation.

# OOPS SORRY, YOUR MISTAKE

When I was born, the term "politically correct" had not yet entered our vernacular. This, I know today for certain, because I can still remember those sweet, tender father-son moments, when my dad would take me up onto his knee, stroke my golden blond hair, pinch my soft dimpled cheeks, look engagingly into my glistening blue eyes and say, "See you, ya wee shite, you were a mistake!"

Ahh, isn't that special? Oh, now, please don't get me wrong; my father certainly did love me. It's just that in those times and that place, subtlety had also yet to debut in the lingo of Coatbridge. If you had subtlety in my town, someone would probably have gotten you cream for it, I'm sure.

How romantic to think that your dad came home late from the pub one dark and cold Friday evening, jumped into bed with your mother, who succumbed to his belches and farts – sorry, I mean kisses and charms – and, forgetting to wear his condom from the fifties, (which was easier to find than a Goodyear tire), they accidentally create you. How do you know all of this? Because he tells you, that's how. And he tells it to you like he's telling you a story about that other old belcher and farter, Santa Claus, who you know is really your grandfather, because he's wearing your grandfather's ring, watch, working boots AND horn rimmed bi-focal glasses! Isn't it also a dead giveaway when Santa says, "Ho, Ho, Ho, Ho, Gracie! Can you get Santa a wee whisky? I'm dyin' in this bloody suit!"

But what BELIEF I had and fun I shared with those men. The grandfather I speak of was the one on my mother's side of the family, making him my dad's father-in-law, but they were bonded closer than most fathers and sons – my dad loved him dearly, even more than he loved his own father. They were inseparable, and they were wonderfully entertaining.

"Dad, c'mon are you ready? The natives are getting restless out there."
"Hang on a minute son, ye canny rush greatness."
"Alan?"
"Yes, Grandad?"
"Get your grandad a wee whisky, would ya pal?"

And so it would go, time, after time, as my family prepared to once again make its own entertainment in the living room of the small, damp, pre-fabricated, bloody freezing, post-war house that I was born in.

This was 16 Kirkshaws Avenue, home of The Frews. Come one! Come all! My dad is about to enter from the kitchen, but he's no longer Hughie Frew. He's now the Vaudevillian Vagabond Burlington Bertie.

The original song "Burlington Bertie, with the Hyde Park Drawl" was performed in the old music halls of the early twentieth century, by the one and only Vesta Tilley, a male impersonator born in Worcester in 1864. Burlington Bertie was a young man about town, a dandy and a "toff" who stays out all night partying and doesn't get up till ten thirty in the morning. Vesta paid meticulous attention to detail when dressing and always took over an hour to get ready, padding and constructing her figure. Immensely popular with women, who saw her as a symbol of independence, she went on to make as much as £500 a week in the early 1900s! Meanwhile this old bugger, my father, was also taking about an hour to get ready and he wasn't even earning £500 a year – and this was the 1960s! I know I could write an entire book on the subject of my family, and perhaps I will one day. At any rate, he had a slew of characters inside him that he would bring out at random to entertain us. The other one I loved dearly was the "Red Shadow," a character that dated back to the early twenties, when Arabmania was abundant throughout the Western culture and the legendary icon Rudolph Valentino was the golden boy of the silver screen. My dad would dress up as an Arab, complete with the kitchen towel wrapped around his head, and enter singing "My desert is waiting…" from "The Desert Song." But here is the funniest part: my granny, my mother, my Aunt Sadie, Auntie Nan and any other woman who may have been jammed into our wee living room that night would all fight over who got to be his leading lady! True. It never failed to bewilder me. Now you see, if you didn't get to be Esmeralda, you got stuck being a mere dancing girl. Who the hell just wants to be a mere dancing girl when you can be romanced in Rudolph Valentino's arms? But what I am saying is it was really my dad in bed sheets and a towel!

"D-A-D, hurry up!"

"I'm comin', I'm comin'. You know you can't ru–".
"–Rush greatness. I know Dad, I know."

How I worshipped him; I can't explain it in terms that might make any sense for you, because he was not an attentive man per se and he didn't show his love or affection, as I would with my children. He didn't take any interest in how or what I was doing. I never kicked a ball with him. Never shared a bike ride. Never played a game with him and never did he help me with homework. Hugs and kisses were for sissies and I stayed out in the streets until the pitch-blackness of nightfall. I was always just one shout away from him coming to find me and that was never good news for my backside.

When I brought a report card home for his signature it could have read, Mathematics F, English F, Geography F, Everything F and under teacher's comments, "Dear Mr. and Mrs. Frew, Alan continues to exhibit behavioural problems. As a matter of fact, he killed little Billy Potter today with a ruler and a Bic pen and then proceeded to eat him in front of the entire class!" Still my dad would have gone straight to the bottom of the page where his signature belonged, and signed it.

"Right, well done! Keep it up!"
Yet I believed in him, for there was goodness in him. He always trusted people until they gave him cause not to. He always looked for the best in a person. He laughed at life and he always took the time somehow to acknowledge that I was marching to my own drummer, strongly and independently, and he liked that. He saw talent, an edge, a rawness in me that he always encouraged and never suppressed.

During the precious early years of my life, my mother spent an inordinate amount of time at her own mother's. It's just the way it was done. It was my father who became my pillar, my lifeline, and who made me most of my dinners, especially during the workweek. I was, shall we say, a bit of a menace, and so my parents would not allow me the key to the door. They did not want me in the house alone after school, as that would spell disaster. So I was always to play out in the street until one or both of them got home from work, and nine times out of ten that was my dad. I would see his working-cap peek over the crest of the hill and then his head and body would follow. He seemed so tall and straight, so upright and proud, and I would run as fast as I could to him. We had a little saying between the two of us that we would say each time like it was the first.

"Hi ya, scud," he would say.

"Hi ya, bud!" was always the reply.

It was a common event for my parents to catch wind of my mischief as they walked home after work. As they passed the houses on my street, any neighbour who happened to be home would announce from a window or garden something like, "I saw your Alan up on your roof earlier today and.......... it didn't look good."

"Aye, it's not for me to tell tales but I saw your Alan with a large piece of cable tied from your gate to your chimney and that boy is going to kill himself one day!"

"Hello, Gracie. There was a large flame that shot out your kitchen window about an hour ago. Alan ran like the clappers, missing some hair. He went that way."

Often I would "jimmie" the window and basically break in, only to go around to the front door and let a pal or two in the house.

On one occasion my dad came in, gave me the usual warning to "stop breaking in," then immediately proceeded to make my dinner. As usual, Mum was not home. So there was my dad and I sitting having our dinner around 5:00 p.m. when soft, muffled sounds began to become audible and I could see him rubbing his ear as if to say, "Is that a noise?" I'd heard it as well as "Lassie" could hear "WALKIES?" But I said nothing n-o-t-h-i-n-g.

"Mmmph!" says the noise.

Again, "MMMmmph!"

"What the hell is THAT?" says dad. "Do you hear something Alan?"

"No Dad."

"Mmmph! Hello? Mmmph! HELP?" squeaks the sound.

"You don't hear THAT?" he says again.

"Maybe."

"MAYBE?"

"MMMMPH! HEEEEELP!" the voice cries to the heavens.

"What in the name of Christ! WHO IS THAT?"

"John Kerr," I say poking at my dinner plate.

"JOHN KERR? And where the hell IS he?"

"He's locked in your wardrobe."

"LOCKED IN MY WARDROBE? WHAT THE HELL IS HE DOING LOCKED IN MY WARDROBE? Who locked him in?"

"Me."

"And how long has he been in there?"

"Oh, since about half past one. Hey, guess what, the teacher let us out early."

"Half past one? Alan, it's six o'clock. Go and let that poor laddie out of that wardrobe, right now!"

When I opened the wardrobe door, John was staring straight ahead, trance-like and shaking like a leaf. I knew he would be, as I had locked him in it many times before.

"Want a chip, John?"

# WE ARE FAMILY

Yes, there was never a dull moment around that wee house and I always believed my dad. I believed him when he told me that he was a World War II Flying Ace who had single-handedly shot down over one hundred German planes, or that he had fought with "Charlie Wingate and his Chindits" deep behind enemy lines within the jungles of Burma, when in actual fact the biggest war he'd ever fought was the one with the sleeve of his jacket when it was time to leave the pub. I found out years later that he had applied to join the army but was denied admission because tradesmen were needed at home to build the machines of war, not die using them. The fact that he never fought in the war always troubled him and he would become incensed if teased about being a coward and not going to battle.

I believed him when he told me he had fought for the Middleweight Boxing Championship of the World title, or when he said to me one time while sporting a black eye, "Don't worry Alan, I'll be all right. By the way, you should see the face on the other guy!" In actual fact he had been walking home from the pub drunk, took a stumble and hit his head on a big red mailbox. But then again, I always believed him.

"Alan, your big brother is coming home from Canada for a holiday. You have a little nephew now and so your brother, his wife and the little boy are coming home to meet all of us."

"Big brother? Nephew?" Waves of confusion swept over me, for I had never been able to get a handle on the concept of having a brother. You see, (and don't ask me why for the life of me), my brother, as a tiny baby, stayed over one night with my mum's parents, and basically that one night became the rest of his life before moving to Canada as an adult. As I said earlier, do not ask me how something like that can happen, but I do know the same thing happened to my father, who was also raised by his grandparents. I think it is based in some old country custom where the firstborn son went to live and help the elders of the family, rather than his own parents, who were younger, stronger and more able to take care of things themselves. And of course more than likely they would get pregnant again and have numerous children. So giving up the first-born wouldn't seem like such a big deal when you expect eight or nine kids.

Anyway, the fact that my brother was older than me by thirteen years meant that by the time I was four or five years old he was already a young man of seventeen or eighteen and since he did not live in my home, I could not for the life of me figure out who the hell he was. I called him Gordon Fleming, which was my grandparents' surname.

So the brother that I did not know came home, and he, my older sister and I were now all under the one roof for the very first time in our lives. At the same moment I got a new brother, I also got a new idol. It didn't take very long at all for me to want to be like him. He took me to see my beloved Glasgow Rangers play their bitter rivals, Glasgow Celtic, who were in the midst of dominating the scene from the late '60s to early '70s. And although they defeated us that night, I still loved it because I was with my big brother. Yes, he grew on me rather quickly.

Still, I was only a boy and my time with him was very limited. He, on the other hand, was a man and spent a lot of time in the company of our father and uncles, drinking, talking, telling tales of Canada, the New World, the Promised Land. It was during this time that he said something to my father that forever changed the course of all of our lives. He said it only in passing, and I am not sure if he was even serious. He said it to my dad, who in another off-the-cuff passing remark repeated it to my mother. I just happened to be on the floor playing with my GI Joes, who had all coincidentally decided that the Secret Agent Man my mother had bought me didn't fit in, and was to be taken out to the back yard some day very soon to be burned at the stake.

So what exactly was it that my brother said to my father just in passing? Five simple words: "You should come to Canada!"

## WORKIN' NINE TO FIVE

My father was already forty-nine years of age by this time. Certainly not old by any stretch, but no spring chicken either. He had now worked in the steel mill since the tender age of fifteen, and after thirty-four years a man starts thinking about the possibility of retirement with a nice big severance package, a gold watch, and a big pat on the back. He wouldn't get anything like that in Canada. He'd be out looking for whatever job he could, and at the age of fifty, that just wasn't very appealing at all. Oh yes, one other thing, we were broke.

When the topic of Canada came up he would declare,
"Me? Canada? Impossible. That's okay for younger men, know what I mean?"

This would be repeated ad nauseam any time he had a good amount of drink
in him.
"How in the name of God are we going to be able to afford Canada?" he'd
bellow. "It's just NOT going to happen."

Well, I have news for you Hughie Frew...It already has!

*"Whatever you can do, or dream you can, begin it.*
*Boldness has genius, power and magic in it."*
GOETHE

# NO REST

ACTION is impossible to escape and is one of the common denominators of all
living things. ACTION is the response that creates outcome. It determines the
drama of life. This is where the lion and the gazelle play out which one lives and
which one dies. This is where a Mother Theresa completely takes another
pathway from a Bin Laden or where the old saying comes from that the only
difference between a great con man and a great salesman is the outcome of their
actions. Their INTENTION has predetermined the type of outcome we will see.
ACTION puts INTENTION into play. Funny thing is, even if I ask you what
you are going to do today and you answer, "nothing, I am going to be a couch
potato today", well even that takes ACTION. You need to lock the front door,
get the chips and dip, find the clicker, shoo the cat, flick the channels...phew!
Sounds like a lot of work to me. Sleeping? Well, there is still a ton of ACTION
going on within your mind and body. Dreaming, digesting, growing, healing, cell
death, cell birth, and a million other duties being performed at levels we cannot
even fathom. So you see the light never turns off; in fact there is no "off" switch.
You are always "on" to some degree, so why not align this unavoidable ACTION
with your desires, beliefs, intentions and yes, even your dreams?

# OUR HOME AND NATIVE LAND

"What are you doing, son?"

"Easy, I am aligning my actions with my dreams."

"What are you thinking?"

"Simple, I am thinking about what it will be like when I get there."

"And where exactly are you going?"

"Why, Canada of course."

My brother returned to Canada in the summer of 1969 not knowing me all that much better than he had for the previous twelve years and ten months of my short young life. But for me it would never be the same. He had changed it forever without even knowing it, for I, this scrawny, scrapping, hand-me-down wheeling-dealing kid from Scotland was going to Canada.

"Right, tie his hands, you there, tie his feet and ask him if he wants a blindfold."

"Do you want a blindfold?"

"No, you bastards! I am braver than all of you guys put together! I don't need your stinking blindfold!"

Executions are always touchy things, aren't they? This one, I'm afraid, was going to be no different. GI Joe was the greatest, and was not only from different areas of the armed forces like the Army, the Marines and the Navy, he also came from different armies, like the German, Japanese and the French Foreign Legion. I had begun with only one GI Joe, that being GI Joe MARINE. However, when you bought accessories for the product you could save up stars that were attached to the box each accessory came in, and after saving the required amount necessary, you could send away for a free GI Joe. Coming from a family with no money, I had proven beyond a shadow of a doubt that what you think about you get, and between my David Livingstone Memorial scheme, my saving up pop bottles for refunds, and my playing the flute for tipsy protestants who only wanted to hear tunes in which mayhem, plague and murder were bestowed upon the Pope and his followers (where I made an absolute fortune because I could play them in my sleep), all of these and more allowed me to have six GI Joes! They looked cool. Their arms and legs were bendable, you could position them, you could dress and undress them in awesome uniforms, and the newest ones would bark voice commands when you pulled a cord in their backs. Yes, I loved GI Joe.

Secret Agent Man, on the other hand, was not bendable. He was stiff plastic and wore a painted-on suit. He had no uniforms, couldn't be positioned, and didn't speak! He just had to go.

They say it takes only a spark to get the fire roaring. Well, I have news for you. It may indeed take only a spark for the fire, but it takes a can of gasoline to get the attention of the local fire service. You see, a spark just doesn't cut it like a fire! So you get the can of gasoline that your father happens to have in the unlocked shed in the back garden, grab the matches, and you're all set. This burning at the stake will be underway very quickly, with just one wave of the can to get things going. I held it to my ear and shook.
"Good. It's almost full."
I unscrewed the cap, got it on its side and with a drum roll and a count I let it go.

WOOOOOOOSH!
"No more darkness, no more night,
Lordy, Lordy, I saw the light!"

Yes indeed, I saw the light all right! I saw it so closely it took an eyebrow with it. I didn't even have time to blink. My instantaneous reaction was to scream and get that can of gasoline up and away from me, saving the rest of my face for another day. The can, however, had further mischief in mind. It hit the side of the shed, my dad's shed, and I know you won't believe this but it set it on fire! It then introduced itself to the plant life.
"TREE'S ON FIRE!"
It ricocheted off of the shed-tree combo, landing next to the fence that was shared with our neighbours, setting it on fire as well. By now you probably know my modus operandi. I am amazed I never had tryouts with the British

Olympic track and field team, for setting fire to your dad's shed, fence and garden is a great training regimen for any young budding athlete. Once again, dear friends, I ran like the clappers around to the front of the house, in through the living room, settling at the kitchen table across from my father, who was engrossed in his newspaper. I looked over his shoulder, out through our kitchen window and observed what was now a full-fledged twelve-foot-high roaring fire.

"Dad?"
"Yes?"
"I'm going to Canada."

Just then a flame shot up in an attempt to kiss the hydro wires.

"That's nice son," he said never looking away from his paper.
"I'm serious Dad, in fact we're...(loud sirens were closing in on us)... we're ALL going to Canada."
"Aye that's good son. What's all that racket?" he said, inquisitively.

I could see several large firemen in our neighbour's yard preparing to blast the raging flames with water. Their siren was very loud indeed.

"What the hell's going on," said my father. "Hmm, there must be a fire somewhere, eh?"
Sherlock Holmes, your job is safe.
"Yes, Dad."

Gallons and gallons of water were dousing the shed, the trees, the fence and a big melted blob of soldiers...oh yes and a spy.

"Dad?"
"Uh huh?"
"Can we go to Canada – right now?"

# THREE JEERS FOR THE
# RED, WHITE AND BLUE

I have a little diary here at home that I actually found long before I ever thought of writing this book. It's a little pocket daytimer that someone once gave me. I'm not certain, but I get the feeling that it probably came from my mum and it is from the year 1969. Within its pages, written in my thirteen year old scribble, are things like "Going to Canada", "Sold table today", "Only six more weeks to go." When I read it I get such mixed emotions. I feel a sense of pain, sadness and even a little embarrassment for that boy, yet I am also proud, impressed and a little in awe of him. Let me explain.

You see, I didn't set foot on Canadian soil until August 18th, 1972. So why then was this boy writing things like "only six weeks to go" in 1969, and why was he selling off family belongings, much, I might add, to his father's consternation.

Well, it is very simple. I was so receptive, so desirous of, so believing in and so intended on going to Canada that all of my actions were those of a boy who was leaving his homeland, leaving all he had ever known behind and moving to a new world. When I think back on it, it is everything from warm and endearing to hilariously funny, yet painful too, for I had everyone around me convinced – and I mean EVERYONE – that my family and I were indeed leaving. And so everyone in my school, every pal in my street, their families, their friends and so on, all believed that I was indeed going to Canada.

I would pick a date, say, November 28th, 1969, and I would tell everyone that *that* was when we were leaving. I would offer them the chance to buy our couch, our bed, our teacups, even our dog, and come they would, one after another after another.

Man at door: "Aye, hello, I am here to see your couch."
My dad: "See my couch?"
Man at door: "Yes, your couch, the one you're selling."

My dad: "But I'm not."

Man at door: "Not what?"

My dad: "Selling."

Man at door: "Why not?"

My dad: "Because our arses will be sitting on the floor if I do! ALAN!!!"

And this would go on and on and still they came.

Stranger in our garden: "Hello."

My dad: "Hello, and what is it you think you're doing exactly?"

Stranger in our garden: "What does it look like I'm doin'? I'm digging up these here hedges."

My dad: "I can see that, but what do you plan on doing with them?"

Stranger in our garden: "Well, I'll plant what I need into my own garden and re-sell the others."

My dad: "Re-sell?"

Stranger in our garden: "Yes, sell what I don't use, to my neighbour."

My dad: "ALAN!!!!"

The dates would come and the dates would go and I would get tortured relentlessly. Finally, no one believed me. Not a single soul.

"You're not going anywhere! You're not going to Canada! You're a big liar, Frew!"

As I write about it for you, I still get that feeling of distress that was always so present for me during this time. The taunting, the jokes –and yet, never did I change my story. I would simply rub out the date and write in another one. I never changed my ACTION SANDWICH, not for one second. Every idea, every ACTION, every BELIEF and every DESIRE were those of a lad going to Canada.

The following winter my brother thought he was doing a good thing when for Christmas he sent home an anorak, today known as a parka, that not only stood out in a town like Coatbridge, but would have stood out in a town like

ANCHORAGE ALASKA because, my dear reader, it was an ALL FUR parka! Oh, but there's more, much, much more, for this big, hairy, monstrous covering also happened to be RED, WHITE and BLUE! I looked like a polar bear at a Republican convention.

Now, in today's world, Britain is post-revolutionary when it comes to Americanization. Hamburgers, cheeseburgers, fries, Budweiser, words like "yeah", "garbage" and "right on", all of these things have become not only acceptable, they are the norm. Walk down any of Glasgow's main streets and see a guy wearing a Miami Dolphins football shirt with a number sixty-five on it – he will not get a second glance. Television, movies, fast-food chains and especially the Internet have brought mainstream New York and Los Angeles right into the living rooms of London, Glasgow, Manchester or Belfast. It is ALL ONE WORLD.

But this was 1969, and this was Coatbridge, and their world wasn't ready for hamburgers and fries, not ready for sneakers and pop, not ready for a number on a team shirt to go any higher than number eleven, and God knows it certainly wasn't ready for a guy on his way to school in a RED, WHITE and BLUE FURRY COAT!

"Oh God, please, please, if you really are up there, could you do me this one small favour, please…yes…right now. Could you please just send a big ball of fire right here to my house and melt me to death...please?"

"Is it not bad enough that I am a Protestant totally outnumbered in a Catholic town nicknamed 'Little Ireland'? Is it not enough that a coat with a hood has never been invented as far as this part of the world is concerned? Is it not enough that everyone thinks I am a total bloody lunatic because I keep saying I am moving to Canada but never do? Is all of that not enough torture, dear God? How then have you found it within your mighty wisdom to SEND ME THIS F***ING RED, WHITE AND BLUE FUR COAT? ARRRRRRRRRRRGH!"

And so, with not a snowman or even a snowflake around for probably some five hundred miles in all directions, I set off on foot dressed as Frosty the Snowman's wee brother, *in drag*.

It was hard, it was very hard...and yet I believed. Three years had passed and still I filled my diary. Still I shouted it for all to hear, "I AM going to Canada."

But still we stayed. My dad exhausted himself trying to convince me not to do this to myself. And then it happened. He got laid off from work.

"BLOODY HELL! Are they kidding me?" he screamed. I don't think I had ever heard him this angry in my life.

"Eight hundred and fifty f***ing measly quid? Are they daft? And not even a goddamned handshake on the way out the door? Who the #^*@ do they think they are?"

He was seething, for after more than thirty years of service to this company, my dad was being shown the door with only eight hundred and fifty pounds (about two thousand dollars) to show for it. That was it. Done. He was gone and there wasn't a thing he could do about it.

Or was there?

"Well that's it! F***! THEM and F*** THIS PLACE. WE ARE GETTING OUT OF HERE, NOW!"

What had he just said? Was I dreaming? Did he just say that we are going to leave this toilet of a town? Is that what he just said? But to where?

"Where are we goin' Dad?"
"WE ARE GOING TO CANADA!!"

# IF YOU WANT TO SING OUT, SING OUT

If I told you that you must do one of the following, either rob a bank or visit children in hospital, the chances are you'd be visiting the children. If I told you that you must either clean the equipment in a fire hall or in a slaughterhouse, I think I know what most would choose. That's because when faced with such obvious scenarios we have little difficulty choosing where to apply our actions, especially when we have an outside force giving us very little choice. But when choice is available, I know that many of us struggle with the idea of the black and white scenario of this vs. that. No one can make these decisions for you. Only you can decide:

Will you work out and watch what you eat, or choose to be fat, unfit and risk a heart attack?

Will you quit smoking or risk an early demise from lung cancer?

Will you save at least ten percent of your income or keep blowing it on junk?

Will you run for city council and try to improve your community, or continue to be an armchair critic, pointing out the flaws of those currently holding office?

Identifying these types of obvious scenarios allows you to "get into the water" without necessarily being able to do the backstroke, but it's eventually doing the backstroke that gives you control over the situation that directly affects you. When I talk with people about this I often hear that it is a lack of confidence that keeps them from taking ACTION. Well, let me say this: do something, try something, attempt something, achieve *something*, and the confidence will follow. Make that a little mantra and trust yourself. How can you not gain more confidence if you are trying, attempting and achieving? They say that "practice makes perfect"; well, it also builds confidence.

# ALL IN ALL YOU'RE JUST A...

Why is it that those who are the best at any given skill or talent are not always the ones who succeed? Have you ever played soccer, football, basketball, tennis, darts, Trivial Pursuit or dominoes with someone so talented that it boggles your mind as to why they are not a legend, while some other "what-in the-name-of-God-is-he-doing-on-the-field" is out there making millions?

I have played soccer with guys who were so talented it was beyond my comprehension that they weren't playing professionally. Yet I would watch Rangers, Celtic, Manchester United or Liverpool and scratch my head as to why some "diddy" was playing and being paid pretty well to do so.

How many virtuosic guitar players are selling guitar picks in music stores? How many perfect tenors are delivering mail? How many teens are in detention centres instead of universities? The reason to me is clear. It comes down to choice, and choice is ACTION.

You are every choice you have ever made in your life up to this very moment, so if you are not happy with those choices then you must elevate them. You must make better choices.

So how do you do that? To choose the right things in life, it's very important to me to keep my thinking at the highest level possible. Elevated thinking inspires RECEPTIVITY, DESIRE, BELIEF, INTENTION and of course ACTION. It immediately improves my attitude and begs me to function at a loftier level. It commands me to be alert, aware, and receptive and to ask better, more enlightened questions of myself and of those around me. It places my desires on the top rung of the ladder. It says, "I believe in me!" Elevated thinking raises the bar and propels INTENTION motivating me to take immediate ACTION in pursuing my life's dreams.

That moment, or for some of you *this* moment, is the instant when we run out of excuses and must take responsibility for the shape of our lives. I have not arrived, and I struggle with many of the things you all struggle with and have the same questions and sometimes non-productive solutions that you do. But I have chosen to make each day better than the day before. I guarantee that if you work incrementally towards a better life, you will achieve it. There is no other possible outcome. So it is with those who I mentioned earlier, who have far greater talent yet are not always the ones who succeed. For what I neglected to mention was that I now know why the guys that I played soccer with, who were so highly skilled, didn't make the grade. They did not honour their gift. Instead they chose things like alcohol, anger, an undisciplined training and practice regimes, while those that I so misjudged as "diddies" actually honoured their gift and in doing so practiced all of the discipline required to succeed.

# THE LONG AND WINDING ROAD

Let me briefly revisit that moment on my way to the fridge when I must decide how I wish to execute my DESIRE to eat and stay on course with making a sandwich as opposed to grabbing the pie and chocolate milk.

ACTION is where one can really excel or, conversely, derail. In your head you can be as receptive as possible, DESIRE what you know to be true in your heart, believe you deserve, and INTEND until the cows come home, but without the discipline of ACTION, all that has come before is rendered useless.

Take the classic case of a recovering alcoholic who is receptive to the need to stop drinking and yet at the end of rehabilitation, takes the ACTION of heading to the bar and sabotages all of the hard work that *THE ACTION SANDWICH* put into his DESIRE to recover.

*THE ACTION SANDWICH* keeps fat people fat, poor people poor, rich people rich and so on. However, when applied with positive RECEPTIVITY, DESIRE, BELIEF and INTENTION, it will assist you to ACTION your way from fat to thin, poor to rich, depressed to happy – for it is an all-encompassing formula that I promise you, you cannot escape from. You are doing it regardless...ALWAYS. You are that which you know you are, nothing more, nothing less – the total summation of all of your choices. Use it wisely, my friends, for even ACTION falls prey to time and, as we know, time waits for no one. Use it continuously and thoughtfully, and never assume you've arrived. How many people have I seen in my industry who used the formula to become rock stars and then used it again to become drug addicts or alcoholics?

I like to think of my fulfilled goals and successes as tokens or rewards along my pathway of ACTION. I don't like to think in terms of "Oh, I must take ACTION", but rather that I am in a constant state of evolution, where being and becoming gives me a sense of always striving to move forward on this wondrous journey called life. You cannot strive backwards or even sideways. As soon as I find myself in a state of "being," my brain immediately asks "So what's next?" So here we are finally at the roller coaster of life. This is the holy grail: life in ACTION for the sake of goodness and fun and business and pleasure, loving, family, friends, rewards, good old money, and of course my favourite condiment, PASSION.

Ah, PASSION you're next.

## TEN WAYS TO TAKE ACTION

1. A THOUSAND MILLION QUESTIONS - A better question demands a better answer. Your brain knows all the answers. Stop avoiding the truth, accept responsibility and ask tough questions. Ask.

2. LIGHTS, CAMERA, ACTION! - Stop waiting to live. Talking about what you could do, should do, might do, or worse still, could have done, is useless and an unconstructive use of

ACTION. Decide on something, even *one thing* and move. Get going.

3. BEGIN THE BEGUINE - So you don't know how to start the dance of life, okay relax, it's not the end of the world, don't beat yourself up. Choose the steps that look the most appealing, even if awkward, and move. Clumsy feet in ACTION are better than no ACTION at all. Come dancing!

4. DID I TELL YOU THE ONE ABOUT - Your brain is way more important than your brawn so keep it involved constantly. Talk, dream, think, write or even sing about what you are doing, where you are going and how you are going to get there. Doing this only enhances and reinforces that it shall be so. The universe is listening. Speak up!

5. EIGHT DAYS A WEEK - Be prepared to step it up. Accomplishment asks for unwavering resolve and effort. Loving what you have chosen will help, but purpose, sweat and resolve will help you even more. C'mon!

6. POOR, POOR PITIFUL ME - Success evades those who feel unworthy simply because they focus on unworthiness. Keep putting one foot in front of the other no matter how muddy the trail is. Get off the pity train. I mean it.

7. TOMORROW, TOMORROW - Accept the fact that you are every choice and every decision you have ever made. You are the result of all of your yesterdays. Done? Good, move on! Now the good news, you will be the result tomorrow of what you decide today! Rejoice and decide.

8. HAND ME THAT MOP - If you don't love it, want it, use it, read it or care if you have it, then get rid of it. It's hard to take ACTION when you're lugging crap along for the ride physically or mentally. Lighten the load. Clean up your act.

9. ABRACADABRA! - Success isn't a rabbit pulled from a hat, nor is it a letter mailed to your door. Success is the culmination of efforts repeated over and over again. Ask the right question and get the right answer. Now commit.

10. A SIMPLE PLAN - Get up off your arse. You must DO to get DONE. Need I say more?

# MY SONG
*Opus 5*

### WE'RE OFF TO SEE THE WIZARD

New York, Paris, London, Madrid, sounds glamorous doesn't it? It is I guess. For the boy who ran away from Father Dickie-bird, and away from his granny and away from a furious band and away and away and away, was now running at these places, faster than he ever could run away. It was a whirlwind, a speeding train without the driver and a rocket doing what a rocket does best. We were hanging on for all we were worth.

The first tour was basically one where just myself and the senior representative from our U.S. label toured the entire continental USA in about six weeks, setting up the soon to be released recording for all of the major American radio stations. Occasionally one of the other lads would come out to join us, which was a great relief, but for the most part it was Jack, the record guy and myself. Never again would breakfast in New

York, lunch in Baltimore, dinner in Philly and cocktails in Chicago sound exciting, for that was achieved all in one day! We have a thing in our industry called "meet and greets" where you shake hands with hundreds of people that you are meeting for the very first time, either working the room or simply greeting fans or contest winners but this trip I christened, "meet and eat," for it seemed like that was all we did. You are repeating the same thing over and over again, trying to win the favour of each of the key players from the various radio stations in hopes that they will add your song to their play-lists. We worked it and it worked. The first release, *Thin Red Line* was a smash hit for the band. We toured and toured and toured, working with the likes of *Journey*, Tina Turner, Rod Stewart and yes, even *Cheap Trick* who had caused me to say years ago, "Now I want that job!"

There it is again. Tell the universe and it listens.

The pace was frantic. It was like going back to the "beans" days, only in a limousine, a jet or in a luxury bus. Having no boundaries, bosses, rules or limits, can be a deadly combination and has been for so many of my kind. Drugs and alcohol aplenty with no one to tell you no, can be a one-way ticket to doom. I had sessions that I look back on and gasp, as I realize how much was consumed without stopping. On one occasion I had tried cocaine, which got me so hyped up that I wrecked my room. The scene at the front desk was "Monty Python-esque" in its darkness and humour.

Desk Clerk: "Yes sir, how can I be of assistance?"
Singer: "Well, I've wrecked my room...your room."
Desk Clerk: "Very good sir, just let me get my note pad, and, okay go ahead then sir."
"Well let's see. I've smashed the telly."
"Very well."
"And the head board."
"Uh huh, got that."
"Smashed a window."
"Gooood."

"And I threw the mattress out onto the street from the 22nd floor."
"Right you are then sir, I'll send someone out to get that right away. Now if you'll just be so kind sir, to sign here for the damages, I'll have you on your way in a jiffy sir ... good. Well goodnight then sir, will there be anything else I can get you?"
"Yeah, ................a mattress."

## WRESTLING WITH THE IDEA OF BEING A ROCK STAR

I befriended one of the record reps in America called Terry who was based out of Atlanta, Georgia, a lovely man, who quickly became a great pal. We both had a great PASSION for music and an undying love of movies and movie trivia. He was charming and funny and very quick with his wit. We had verbal sparring that I loved. One evening he was entertaining several guests with yours truly when I accidentally knocked over a candle setting the table on fire.
"Terry I am so sorry," I said apologetically. "I spoiled the moment."
"No you didn't man," he replied. "You simply created another one!"
That was Terry.

On days off, which were few, I would pop out to Atlanta to see him and together we played hard. He was Mr. Promotion and was always working to have me be seen as much as possible. On one crazy occasion he got the two of us front row tickets to the wrestling match, which was just on the cusp of being the monstrous spectacle that it is today. Hulk Hogan, Roddy Piper and Randy "The Macho-Man" Savage were all coming into their own as stars of the ring and on this night I was getting caught on camera as the behemoths would toss each other out of the ring and begin battling right in front of Terry and I. In one particular match up, Ric Flair was fighting a wrestler called the "Iron Shiek," who would prance about the ring waving the Iranian flag, inciting the Americans who had long memories and remembered all too well, the Iranian hostage crisis in which members of the new Islamic regime held 63 diplomats and three other hostages from November 4th, 1979, through to January 20th, 1981.

ALAN FREW

The "Sheik" would yell at them, "ME HATE AMEERICA! ME HATE YOOOR COOONTREEE!" and the crowd would go insane throwing beer, pop, ice cream, you name it, and it hit us in the front row.

"Man isn't this great!" screamed Terry with a large ice cream cone lodged on his head.

"That's not quite what I would call it," I yelled back at the top of my lungs.

"What if the crowd gets out of hand and they riot? We could get mangled down here, don't ya think!"

"Man I hope so," barked Terry. "Think of the press!"

Sure enough Ric and the Sheik, brought their battle out of the ring and down to us, causing us to get drenched and caked and caught in the crossfire of a frenzy of abuse laid on the mad Iranian.

After the fight Terry said, "C'mon man, let's go!"

"Go where," I enquired.

"To the dressing room. I know the guys."

When we entered, Flair was the first to speak up.

"Hey Terry what's up man? Did you enjoy the fight?"

"Awesome!" replied Terry still buzzing from the spectacle.

Suddenly the mad Iranian "Sheik" came out of the shower area, looked straight at us and said, "Hey, Terry, long time no see man. What's up?"

"Hey Hoss," said Terry, "that was great man."

"Holy Moly," I thought to myself. What happened to, "Me hate yooooor coontreee?" Where did, "Me hate Ameerica go?"

This guy I swear had a Texas drawl going on.

"Hey thanks a lot guys for getting down beside us, it was great," said my friend.

"Any time T, catch you soon," said the American hater and then off he went.

Those crazy Iranian Sheiks fool you every time, don't they?

Terry asked me to be the best man at his wedding and six weeks later, he made me his pallbearer at his funeral.

It was in his home that I spent my short recovery period after my first knee operation and during that time he woke me up one morning, sparkling like a boy who has just been picked for the starting team. "Dude wake up," he yelled.

I was groggy, not only from sleep but from the after effects of the anesthetic and pain medication that I was on.

"C'mon man, let's go! We are going to Ringgold, Georgia!"

"What the hell's in Ringgold," I asked.

'My bride to be. I'm getting married!"

Ringgold is a city located in Catoosa County, Georgia, which as of the year 2000 census was still showing a population of just over 2000 residents. This story however takes place in 1987 and the little "cowboy town" of Ringgold looked mighty smaller than that. It was like something straight out of an episode of Bonanza. A "Smith & Wesson" carrying Sheriff who was a dead ringer for Gene Autry, the Singing Cowboy, married Terry and his fiancé. The ceremony took place with the Bride, Groom, Best Man (on crutches), Sheriff and a piano playing witness all in attendance in the Sheriff's office. Afterwards I took them both for traditional Wings and Ribs. I had never seen him happier than on that day at his Cowpoke Weddin'.

I left the comfort of Terry's home and set off on tour with *Glass Tiger*. The brace for my leg was now firmly a part of my life while he set off on married life with his new bride. Never, ever in my wildest of nightmares could I have imagined that this was the last time I would ever see him.

My life had already been scarred by tragedy a couple of years earlier while on tour with *Journey*. I was making my regular call home to make sure all was well with my son, when my dad's voice answered in a very strange way.

"Hey Dad, I don't have long, I gotta get going, everything okay?" I asked.

"Well, err, yes, it'll be fine. You err, you go on, and call back af..."

"What's wrong?" I demanded.
"Now it's probably just a scare. Go on and call home right after your performance, okay?"

After unsuccessfully prodding him for answers I reluctantly did as he asked. I did it by going to that place in an entertainer's soul where, "The show must go on" lives. It's a place I have been to, many, many, times.

When I got off of the stage, drenched in my own sweat I went to the production office and called home. My sister answered. She didn't have to tell me what I already knew.

She had fed the baby and put her down for a nap as she had done on any one of the other ninety-some-odd-days her little life had blessed this earth. Baby was still napping when her husband came home from work and after washing up immediately went in to her room for a little peek into her crib. What he found this time though was a blue and unresponsive infant.

Picking her up and screaming to his wife, they rushed this little angel to the nearest hospital only to have her pronounced dead from S.I.D.S. (Sudden Infant Death Syndrome) shortly after their arrival at the emergency department.

I was devastated. I was so devastated.
Now you question the meaning of it all, huh?

Our schedule was such that we had a three-day window coming up during which time we were supposed to hop off this grinding tour in the U.S., get on a plane, fly to Holland, do a live television performance, hop another plane, fly to London, do a breakfast television show, grab yet another plane, fly back to Florida and pick up the tour with *Journey* four days later.

Everyone in *Journey's* camp were incredibly sensitive to what had just happened and since we had two more shows before some time off, they told me they would try and find a substitute band.

I sat up in my room all night, calling home constantly hoping one of my calls might change the outcome of what had just happened. It did not.

In the morning someone from the production team came to my room to tell me that they had a flight for me late that evening, however the bad news (as if any news could be worse), was that they could not get a band to cover both shows, only one. I was being asked if I had the fortitude to get up on that stage just one more time before flying home to Canada for the baby's funeral.

## PEPPERONI, BACON AND DOUBLE MUSHROOM

I have never met *Bono*. I don't know *Sting*. I have never had a conversation with *Annie Lennox*. I do however know this. No matter who you are, there are times when as a performer you can be on stage, completely focused on the task at hand, singing your hit songs to the frenzied masses as the words are flowing out with precision and strength, while having a completely unrelated conversation with yourself inside of your head.
For example my mouth can be singing,

"You, you take my breath away, oh,oh,oh,oh,"
"Love, thinks it's here to stay, oh,oh,oh,oh,"

While my inner voice is saying,

"God, I can't wait to get back to the hotel and have a nice warm bath."
And as the crowds cheer, my mouth continues,

"Still so much for me to do,
And I can't stop loving you."

Just as my inner voice is saying,
"I think I'll order a nice, well fired.........pizza!"

Removing yourself mentally from a difficult, stressful, absorbing task is similar to the resting of your heart between beats. You don't have to tell your heart to keep beating, for it knows exactly what it is doing yet that little tiny rest between each beat is as necessary to sustain your life as the air that you breathe, or the water that you drink. In fact the rest period of the heart is considered in many ways, more important, if that's possible, than the beating part.

Great athletes talk of zoning-out or going on automatic, which doesn't mean they are any less focused on the task at hand but I guarantee you they are not saying. "Okay, move that foot, now that one. Good. Left hand up, now, jump." I will bet you Michael Jordan has ordered himself up a few pizzas from centre court while in the middle of some of the most important games of his life. This is how I managed to go onstage that night. This is how, although I knew my baby niece was dead, I managed to sing, gyrate, smile and rock! This is where "The show must go on" comes from.

Late that night I flew out of Miami back to Toronto, where just a few hours later, I was placing a little teddy bear at the side of the dead child. I was now pretty delirious from not having slept for close to forty-eight hours, a trend that was to continue right through this new day and into the evening spent around the kitchen table chatting at my sister's home. My family, like most dysfunctional families, still seem to do funerals and weddings extremely well. At least it brings us all together.

At the funeral I carried my niece's coffin to its resting place as a limo with its engine running, waited for me at the gravesite.

This death had of course brought me home unexpectedly and so I was seeing family, friends and my son, for the first time in weeks. I took him into the limo for a few minutes for a chat and some hugs before having to leave him again. I couldn't help thinking about what it would have been like if the call had come in that he had died, and not my niece. Would the show have still gone on? Would that have been possible? Does the "LOVE AND SUFFERING" infect you that badly?

There was a television show in Amsterdam followed by a television show in London and then it was back to Florida to pick up where we had left off touring America.

The bubble of touring is a well-oiled machine. The chain of command: Manager - Road Manager - Stage Manager - Sound Tech - Lighting Tech and Roadies become your family for out there, they are all you have. I found however, that the external demands put on me especially in the earlier part of our success kept me quite distant from the crew, meaning that usually I was off somewhere else, promoting, via radio and television, just about any time the band had a day or two off.

Once, when we were doing shows for Disney in Florida and California, and living in both locations for a month each time, Sam (keyboards) and I would hop up to Vancouver and work with Jim Vallance on new material for our second release. This pattern of always being somewhat separate from the crew continued for the duration of our band's success. It was on one of those occasions in Vancouver that I decided to pop home to Toronto to see my son. Tragedy had struck again as I learned about Terry.

He had been married about six weeks and was in the midst of a heavy work schedule. Record guys are a special-breed. Their job basically is two fold - schmooze radio guys into adding your band's song on their airplay list and schmooze the band guys when they are in your city. Always keep them happy. Needless to say, this lifestyle requires great stamina. On some occasions you could be out seven days and seven evenings a week working it. This is what he was doing the last week of his life. To add a little salt to his already exhausted wounds that week he was suffering from a bad toothache for which he was taking some prescription painkillers until he could have the tooth pulled. Combined with a substantial amount of alcohol he was unknowingly depressing his central nervous system as that is what alcohol and narcotics do, they slow you down.

On the fateful evening, in the wee hours of the morning his doorbell rang. It was a buddy of his who had just had a fight with his girlfriend and was looking for a place to vent his frustration and lay his head down. Terry welcomed him in and poured each of them a drink. The buddy then pulled out a large amount of cocaine. They snorted some lines of death before Terry's wife awakened and joined them. It was now around 4 a.m.

What happened next was positively creepy.

Terry had lit himself a cigarette as the three of them continued their conversation. In one of those moments where talking subsides and silence ensues Terry's wife noticed that his cigarette was actually burning into his finger without his reacting to it. The buddy started into another conversation but Terry's wife was now distracted by her husband's unresponsiveness to this cigarette burning into his hand.

"Terry, your cigarette, can't you feel that?" she asked.
He sat motionless. Speechless.
She arose and went over to him, putting her hand on his shoulder.
"Terry? TERRY!"
Sitting upright and without a single motion or hint of sound, he was dead.
What happened next must have been so terrifying for her, for the buddy panicked knowing that in a matter of minutes the place would be swarming with paramedics and police officers.
"Man, I gotta get out of here," he cried. "I can't be found with this shit on me, I gotta go!"
"Help me, don't leave, call an ambulance and help me," she pleaded but her plea fell on deaf ears for he was out the back windows, down the fire escape and gone before she had even called for help.

## A KODAK MOMENT

"Mr. Frew? There is a telephone call for you sir," said the waiter.
What a beautiful day it had been. I had my boy with me for some well-deserved father-son time and we went to a large park that had rowboats. Once on board our little boat we could finally be alone and not be followed by the throng of fans who had gathered to "look" at us. This was a strange time for me, this time of celebrity. Buying gas, going to the corner store, working out at the gym, going to the movies, walking in the park; all normal every day things to do, but I did them with a following.

"Hey man! You know who you are?" says the gas pump attendant, store clerk, bank teller and coffee shop guy.
"No Einstein, you want to say. Tell me, who am I?"
But you don't. You just keep smiling and walking, smiling and waving, smiling and paying, smiling and signing autographs. Everywhere I went the scene that would inevitably develop thwarted everything I tried to do in public. I learned during that time to never stop walking. Stop, and you're dead. Stop, and they've got you. It was very hard on my son because he just wanted to do all of the normal things that boys do with their dads. It didn't stop out on the streets but it made its way into my home on several occasions.

"Hold it up... (CLICK) okay, got it. My turn."
"Hey look at this, is this his?"
"Yes it is."
"COOL, hey! Get a shot of me with this, will ya?" (CLICK).
The strange voices were coming from the living room. I climbed out of bed in just my underwear and Elsa Lanchester hair (morning version) and tiptoed down the hallway to see what the hell was going on. What was obvious to me was that this was a family. A father, mother, son and two daughters and they were in our home. In our home and having tea and posing with my music awards, clothes, shoes and even my soccer ball!

My dad was sitting with them, refilling their cups of tea and topping up the juice for the kids.

"Pssssst! Dad, come here", I said quietly.

My father walked over to me while the family continued posing.

"Dad what the hell is going on? Who are these people?"
"They've come all the way from Newfoundland. The kids were asked what they wanted to do for their holiday and they said, find Alan Frew. So here they are."

I was amazed.
"But Dad, why did you bring them in here? Why did you let them in our home?"
"Well now, they were outside and it's cold and I thought a wee cup of tea and a digestive biscuit would warm them up."
"Dad, they have got to go! This is not right. They shouldn't be in here."
He didn't have the heart to do it. He was putting me on the spot. I threw some clothes on and entered the room.

The girls immediately got very excited.
"Folks you must leave," I said gently. "This is my home. This is where I live and I need a little privacy."

There was a bit of an awkward moment brewing. It was the moment where people cannot see beyond their own needs and desires. For these people it was about fulfilling the desires of their children regardless of how intrusive it may be. For me it was to not look like too much of a jerk and simply get them out of my home and on their way. I posed with the kids for a few shots and they left.

I cannot for the life of me ever imagine spending a vacation with my family trying to find Bryan Adams or David Beckham or even Paul McCartney, no matter how much I admire him and his music.

On other occasions girls gate-crashed my home by baking pies for my elderly mother whose mind was showing signs of deterioration. People camped out on my lawn. Girls conned my son into thinking they were his cousins in order that he would bring them home. Such is life when you step into the public arena. My experiences were mild compared to what *The Beatles* or Michael Jackson or other superstars go through but it left me so sufficiently scarred I cut down on activities that involved having strangers around me.

"Sir, you can take the call over here," said the waiter.
"Thank you," I replied as I followed him to a place behind the bar where the phone was located.
"Hello!" I said into the receiver.
"Alan," said my mother. "You know that friend of yours that you have down in America?"
"Yes."
"Well he's dead and you have to call New York right away. Okay? Bye."

My mother had never met Terry. My mother never knew the feelings I had for my friendship with him. My mother never knew sensitivity. Dead? Terry? Dead? My legs felt like they wanted to buckle beneath me. My stomach churned.

"Hey Alan smile!"

I lifted my head only to find some two-dozen people staring at me like I was the Gibbon at the local zoo. Some were snapping pictures of me. I wanted to scream at them,

"You bastards, don't you know my friend has just died? Don't you get it? Piss off!"

But of course I didn't, and twenty-four hours later I was standing by his casket looking at him, lifeless, gone forever. I wondered what this world was all about just as I had done so many times before while staring at cadavers in the autopsy room.

In my head I heard his voice saying, "Captain, remember the show must go on."
As I leaned over to plant a little kiss on his forehead my leg rubbed against the stigma of a flower that transferred pollen onto my pants, impossible to get out. I could hear Terry's voice from wherever he had now gone, apologizing to me for the stain that I never ever attempted to wash.

"Hey man," he said, "Sorry about that, I'm afraid I spoiled the moment."
"No you didn't Terry, you simply created another one."

What had killed my friend that night was described by the coroner as his heart basically exploding from the contradictory messages that the different drugs sent to it. On the one hand you had alcohol and pain killers telling it to slow down, take it easy and relax, while on the other the massive surge of the cocaine told it to speed up, get moving, put the pedal to the floor. By his estimation death had been swift, instantaneous and painless.

I was back at it within days, picking up the pieces and touring once again. I would miss my friend forever but the train was rolling and he would have been the first one to tell me to get my ass back on.

# CHAPTER SIX

## 6

*"They're not that different than any of you, are they?*
*There's hope in their eyes, just like in yours. They believe themselves destined for*
*wonderful things, just like many of you. Well, where are those smiles now boys?*
*What of that hope? Did most of them not wait until it was too late*
*before making their lives into even one iota of what they were capable of?*
*In chasing the almighty deity of success, did they not squander their*
*boyhood dreams? Most of those gentlemen are fertilizing daffodils!*
*However, if you get very close, boys, you can hear them whisper.*
*Go ahead, lean in; hear it?* Carpe Diem, *lads. Seize the day.*
*Make your lives extraordinary."*
FROM DEAD POET'S SOCIETY

# CHAPTER SIX: PASSION

## BUT I STILL HAVEN'T FOUND WHAT I'M LOOKING FOR

You did it – congratulations! You were receptive to something that you felt
would better your life, you desired it honestly and you totally believed that
you deserved to have it. You allowed INTENTION to flow fast and furiously
and you got up off of your backside and went out and got it! It's yours.
CONGRATULATIONS, now are you happy? I sure hope so. Let me ask you
this, though. Is it possible to do all of this and not be happy? Can such a thing
exist? Can you really appear to have, or worse still, *actually* have everything a
person could possibly want or need and STILL not be fulfilled? The answer of
course is "yes," and we see it happen all too often. We see the person who
seems to have everything, yet is miserable. Why is this so?

Well, there can be many reasons why someone who apparently has everything is still miserable. It can involve a whole variety of difficult, complex issues from the external world of personal relationships, family dynamics, professional choice and so on. But regardless of these things, if we follow our ACTION SANDWICH strategy, it's my BELIEF that somewhere along the way the miserable, the disillusioned and the disgruntled person is still missing a KEY ingredient. Your sandwich, my friend, needs to be garnished with that special condiment called...PASSION.

Anyone can eat to stay alive – dry bread will get you through – but would you choose to eat nothing but dry bread every day if you didn't have to? Your sandwich is so much more enjoyable, so much more desirable and believable with lettuce or honey mustard, or perhaps mayo, relish or one of a limitless number of other flavourful condiments that you can add. Why then should it be any different for *THE ACTION SANDWICH* - a slice of RECEPTIVITY, a slice of DESIRE...layered with BELIEF, smothered in INTENTION, heaped with lots and lots of ACTION, then topped off with a healthy portion of mouth-watering PASSION!! Mmmmmm, sounds delicious doesn't it?

You see, true PASSION is not a shopping splurge, nor is it fast food. It is not the latest fad, nor is it a quick fix. True PASSION can't be found on the street corner, nor can it be bought in a mall. It cannot be borrowed from a friend, nor loaned out for a price. PASSION is a slow-simmering delicacy that can take from minutes to lifetimes to reach its fullest potential before unleashing a taste so powerful that it can capture the taste buds of streets and towns, cities and countries and yes even worlds. It can build tunnels under oceans and rockets to the stars. It can find cures for deadly diseases and it can feed the starving. It can change the psyche of a generation and it can change the future. PASSION does not live in the external world; rather it comes from the INTERNAL one. Yet when unleashed into the external it can create feats of magical and legendary proportions. Socrates, Michaelangelo, Da Vinci, Shakespeare, Einstein, Chaplin, Churchill and Hawking to name so much less than just a few, all of whom were filled with an unbelievable love of what their true purpose was in the life that each was given, which in turn found its way out to the external world in the form of talent and PASSION, allowing them to live extraordinary lives, each reaching the pinnacle of success.

Now, PASSION doesn't give you a get-out-of-jail-free card, and I am not about to suggest that these people and the many others who reached the same levels of success were trouble-free. That would be a ridiculous notion. But for the moment we are talking about a compelling emotion that we should ALL feel at some point in our lives, for to live a life that has never experienced PASSION is, I fear, to have never truly lived.

Oh yes, and speaking of talent, extraordinary lives and PASSION, what about those four young lads from Liverpool who unleashed theirs on the world back in the early sixties, changing the face of music forever? What was their name again?...Ooooh, it's on the tip of my tongue...wavy lines...waaavy lineeeees.........

## MEANWHILE BACK AT THE PRESS CONFERENCE

Suddenly the door opened and the first one in front of me was God, his back turned to me, facing towards one of the Capitol Records' representatives, who upon seeing me spoke up.

"Ah, great here he is, this is one of our nation's top recording artists. Please let me introduce you both. Alan Frew, meet Paul McCartney. Paul, Alan."

He turned slowly in time with my heartbeat. *Bu-Bum*, his head and shoulders move. *Bu-Bum*, he's repositioning his feet. *Bu-Bum*, I can see his face. *Buuu-Buuum*, my God...it IS GOD! And he looks like...

"Hello mate," he said. "Paul McCartney. How're you doing?"

He extended his hand and took mine in a traditional handshake. Alan Frew. Great Communicator. Man of many words.

Orator extraordinaire, replied with...blank stare...silence... nodding...more blank staring...a little muted nodding and just for good measure another nod and a stare. Our hands though were still performing the handshake ritual as he repeated, "I'm Paul McCartney. What's up? Everything going well then, is it?"

The Great Communicator continued his mastery of the English language with the following oratory masterpiece, "Daaa, blaaaa, ummmmm, errrr." Darwin would have been so proud.
Still the handshake continued, for he was now locked in my vice-like grip.

"Listen. You hear that? No? I wonder why? Oh, I see, it's because I'm shaking hands with...PAUL McCARTNEY!!!!"

The Beatle politely managed to pry his hand loose and continued on his way, meeting others in and around the room.

"IDIOT! LOSER!" I screamed at myself inside my head. "This was THE moment of your professional life! Forget the albums, forget the accolades, forget the money, this is Paul McCartney and you blew it!"

Suddenly they were all posing for a photo-op when he looked at me and said, "Alan, come on, get in here beside me."
I pointed to myself.
"Yes you, come on over here and get in the picture," he said in that unmistakable Liverpudlian twang.
I went over, and a second later I was beside the legend himself. Not god after all, just a man.

The photographer snapped a few shots and the group disbanded. Paul was walking away towards his assistant and I hadn't even spoken a single word to him.

Is this what it has all boiled down to for me, was I about to let FEAR decide my fate and not speak to him? Surely I wouldn't, I couldn't let that happen. What did I have to lose? What's the worst that could happen? Successful people understand and accept fear as a factor, not a force. I had nothing to lose. So I went for it.

"Paul?" slipped out of my mouth.
"Yeah, mate," he asked.
I remember thinking at that precise moment how amazing it was that if you said his name, he not only recognized it but he answered!
"I have a poster of you here over on the table, would you be kind enough to sign it for me?"
"Love to," he replied, as though to say, "Oh, you CAN speak."

Shortly after that, and upon recognizing my accent as being from Glasgow or nearby, he got me talking about the city and about soccer and we had an unbelievable few moments together. He was gracious and attentive and I will always remember that. That is all I have to go on as far as my memory of our short time together, for there was no way that my brain could hang on to every word spoken between us, as my mind was racing way too fast. No, the only memory I was to be left with was the experience of speaking to him, and I remember thinking when I was being walked back to the room just prior to our meeting, that I so dearly hoped that he would be friendly and approachable. I was saying to myself, "Please, please, please, don't let him be a jerk." For, you see, I have a lot invested in *The Beatles*. Years in fact. A lifetime, actually. Watching them, listening to them, imitating them, loving them and all of that could have been destroyed in one aggressive, pompous, super-star moment.

What would have happened if he had basically given me a nod then dumped the moment? What would have happened if I had been told "don't look at him, don't speak to him and don't even think of asking for an autograph?" At the peak of my recording career, I have experienced that moment from the other side of the fence. When young fans were meeting me for the first time, it was a very big deal for them. How I behaved and reacted would ultimately be all that they would take with them after the meeting was over. The answer is as simple on stage as it is in life: manners, decency, kindness, listening are all human traits that cost us nothing to use.

Gracious, humble, polite and attentive – that is how I remember James Paul McCartney.

But what would it have really been about had Paul reacted in a way that I felt made him a jerk? How much of that luggage would actually have been mine and not his? Come to think of it, what about those people out there that think I'm a jerk? (Sniff) Hmmm…I smell the unmistakable aroma of burning Ego.

Ahhhh…Ego, that little image of who we have come to believe we are and how we distinguish ourselves from others, based on the input from the outside world, can sure seem to get in the way at times. Why is that, I wonder? And why is it that the more successful one becomes, the more negative the feedback seems to be?

Now it is not my INTENTION to go off on a wild tangent here about something as complex as Ego, but how, I ask you, can I tackle a book about abundance, purpose and great accomplishment and successful lives and NOT include Ego? Am I afraid? Scared I'll get in over my head? Damn right I am. Am I going to do it anyway? Yup!!

So here goes.

## LEGGO MY EGO

"Show off!"
"You big-headed bastard!"
"Thinks he's God's gift, that one does!"

I've heard them all in my time and I have to admit that I am guilty in the past of using them too. Come to think of it, is there one of us who hasn't used them? Let's see, show of hands right now, who hasn't used terms like those?

No, Jesus, put your hand down, you don't count.

Society seems to declare open season on so-called celebrities and super successful people, claiming that it comes with the territory. Yet where, I ask, is it coming from if not from the ego of society itself? Wasn't it society's ego that decided to give them celebrity status in the first place? Isn't it fair to say that society feels a need to create them? I mean, after all, they didn't do it themselves, did they? Of course not. They need a leg up, a BIG LEG UP, along the way. Sometimes I find it difficult to see where one ego begins and the other one ends in the celebrity tabloid world. What size of an ego does it take to grab a camera and stick it up the nostril of a movie star because there is a demand to see what his nose hairs look like or, better still, how he'll react to the unwanted photographer? Then there is the magazine publisher, whose ego is bigger than both the cameraman and the celebrity put together, willing to pay a small fortune for shots in order that he may satisfy the even more enormous ego of the collective society thriving on such events, displayed for all to see in the magazines we call the tabloids.

Once we point out the flawed ego of another person, we have merely activated our own by reacting to the messages we have received in an ego-based reality.

Jealousy is ego, but so is gratification.
Envy is ego but generosity can be as well.
Criticism is ego, but so is the need for approval and flattery.
Unworthiness is ego and so is self-importance.
It seems that in the world of the ego no one can win.

But what about poor old PASSION, then? Those who live the ego-less life would surely include PASSION into the ego mix, would they not? Hmm, it's so easy for it all to become very, very confusing when you begin to acknowledge and try to understand ego's role in your own life, and downright difficult when you try to understand it in others.

We certainly don't seem to be born with one, an ego that is. In fact the world at birth seems to be entirely opposite to the concept of self. It seems to be all about *the other*. When my baby daughter entered the world for her first out-of-the-womb breath, she certainly had no ego accompanying her that I could see. On the contrary, it was a moment that seemed more concerned with, "Who the hell are you?" But from that very second when I first met her, she began to receive and internalize feelings and messages that declared her something special, and so began the journey of self-awareness. And with this awareness of herself comes ego.

Two and a half years later it still fascinates me to watch her living life in a state of simply *being*. She has no inhibitions, no self-censorship, no self-consciousness; she simply does what she feels the impulse to do. For her life just *is*, although as each day passes her self-awareness increases and her ego becomes more apparent. Consequently, those of us around her, especially her mum and I, whether consciously or not, begin to define who we think she is, which in turn causes us to define what we will and will not tolerate. After all, the home, like society, requires rules. If she cannot have what she wants, the world according to her is disrupted and all hell can break loose. More and more it becomes a battle of egos as we the parents and she the child clash over the important things in life like another cookie, or teeth brushing or just one more glass of chocolate milk. This is as much a clash of egos as going toe to toe with your boss at work or with the coach of your basketball team or your wife or husband. This is part of the groundwork being laid for how the future will play out. At times it feels like she's saying, "Hey wait a minute here! You've both been telling me since the day I joined you two stressed-out, overworked, un-slept me-worshippers that I am beautiful, that I am clever and that I am an angel. So why then, pray tell, can I not smear this chocolate ice cream all over that plasma television, while one of you cleans up after me and the other runs to get me another one of these things?"

Ego has no problem in joining the party early, but in my generation when a child tried to make a stand for what he or she believed in, they played with the flames of a fire that was very likely to burn them. In the world of my childhood, adults crushed and squashed the spirit of children who tried to express themselves as individuals, especially if it made the adult feel uncomfortable or challenged in any way. Keeping the child in line with the same doctrine that had been hammered into them as children was extremely important.

"It was good enough for me, so it'll be good enough for you too!" was the battle cry of generations. This type of one-dimensional thinking leads to one-dimensional living, but thank God history is full of souls who did not conform, regardless of what the generations who came before them said. They faced the flames, got burned, and faced them again. They got crushed and squashed, but lived to fight another day. They stood up for what they believed in and for the people they believed themselves to be.

Here then lies one of the single most important philosophies on the journey to success.

You cannot possibly be who you or I or even society *says* you are. You can truly only be who you *know* yourself to be, and with that comes the "territory" to be negotiated along the way. This is where a guy like Donald Trump openly tells the world that he knows he is the best at what he does, then does things exactly the way he wants them done and the rest of us can go shit in our hats if we don't like it. But what does it all mean in the end? Well, it would seem to me it's a kind of paradox of nothing and everything depending on who's being asked – Donald or the rest of us. Ultimately though, the responsibility lies with the receiver of the information rather than the giver when it comes to how the response is going to play out.

For example, if I call you an idiot and you crumble and fall and your self-esteem drops off the radar, does that mean you really are an idiot? Of course it doesn't. It simply means that you had a certain response to my calling you one. When Donald Trump stands up and tells the world that he is the best at what he does, we all get so caught up in the drama and flair and audacity of it all that our knee-jerk response is to lash out and call him "big headed" and a "showoff." It's you and I, the "receivers," that seem to have the need to make the big deal out of it, no? I mean, if Donald quietly goes about his mission of making billions and feels the need to let us know that he's the best and our reaction is to take a big yawn and say, "Good for you Donny! Knock yourself out, son," would the drama of it all really rank up there with *One Life To Live*?

I have always prided myself on telling the world that there is not a single name or word that you can use to describe me or to try and hurt me with, that can ever penetrate my self-esteem, my mission, my purpose or my PASSION. And I MEAN THAT! When I fought during my other life, I fought because somewhere inside me I wanted to, not because somebody had thought up some words to rhyme together to insult or hurt me. I responded by fighting because I was a "scrapper," not because I was what someone else was saying I was. Make sense? My calling you a loser doesn't make you one, but punching me in the nose doesn't make you one either. The punch is coming from something and somewhere entirely unrelated to my using the word "loser."

Sometimes I feel sorry for PASSION. Poor old PASSION gets a bad rap way too often. A person's passion and willingness to "let it all hang out" gets misconstrued way too many times by receivers as something negative, causing an outburst and a backlash of unwarranted anger and abuse from those who feel the need to give us their take on it all, hence for example the tabloids.

But then again, only bad news sells right? Would you watch a newscast that began with, "Today in North America 67,352 flights took off from various airports all around the Continent, and they ALL landed safely!"

My God, I mean what would CNN do if at least one of them didn't fall out of the sky and land in a fireball on a school campus that had just been desecrated by a gun-wielding, disgruntled maniac who had just killed dozens of his school mates?

Powerful, complicated, complex stuff, this Ego and PASSION, huh?

Trying to get as close to an ego-less existence as possible is a worthy and noble challenge, and although I'm not there yet, I know the first step on the pathway to a successful and abundant life is that you must embrace the fact that you have an ego in the first place, accept it, and recognize that it is not something that has exclusivity. I've got news for you, Spanky. WE'VE ALL GOT ONE, and that's what makes the job of keeping them in check just that much harder.

So, if I know what is true in my heart, mind and soul regarding who I am and what my purpose is, what does your account of who you think I am mean? Well, I've got another newsflash for you, *nothing*. That's correct, I said nothing.

If I am taking the time and great effort to work towards a more ego-less life which will include my own recognition of the fact that I am not really who my ego thinks I am, why in the world would your ego-driven opinion of me matter? Think hard here, for I know that even writing something like this suggests that your opinion means nothing, stabs your ego in the arm, and makes you want to tell me even more adamantly that I am indeed a bigheaded bastard et cetera, possibly, God forbid, even AN EGOMANIAC!

Hey, blame that Freud dude, for he was the egomaniac.

Conversely, the good news is that what I think of you is equally meaningless. All that truly matters is that you know who you are and what it is that is significant and true to that knowledge. If I had left it up to others to decide who I was and what my future was to be, then my ship would have sailed into other waters, perhaps even dangerous waters, with a very good chance of finding the bottom of the ocean along the way. Now, I have never been adept at marching to someone else's drum and, of course, my ego floats in and out and back in again all along the way. Is this a bad thing? I guess that depends on who is being asked, doesn't it?

Okay, enough already. I said I wouldn't get too heavy, and here I am getting exactly that. I mean c'mon, who the hell do you think I am here? I'm just a simple, plain, ordinary, everyday, run-of-the-mill Rock Star. Gimme a break, will ya? God knows I gotta put up with all of you, talking and yakking and banging and ringing and clanging in my five-karat, diamond-studded ears, don't I? It's enough to make me want to jump into my Porsche 911 Turbo Special Edition and drive immediately to my private spa for a lavender-mocha exfoliation and butternut facial at the hands of a Peruvian goddess named Kalinda, whom I'm dating along with her sister, Dulcemer the super-model. I mean what's a guy supposed to do to get a little attention around here? But I digress. Where was I?

So what does it all mean? If I tell you I know for sure, that would be my ego talking because I know for sure that I don't. Just be aware that the road to success can be a very long one, and a rampant, unchecked ego has a tendency to make it even longer. There is a saying that "no one likes a show-off." Well, personally I like show-offs. To me, Tiger Woods is a show-off. Brad Pitt is a show-off. Michael Jordan is a show-off as is Gretzky, Clinton, Bono and, yes, even that Jesus guy – who else could make those five loaves and two fishes cut it after inviting five thousand strangers to dinner? Showing off or presenting great talent is what successful people do. The ego is merely the platter for that presentation. You're human; it will get away on you every now and again, but that's okay. Just try and remember that when it becomes more presentation and less talent you may become one of the so-called egomaniacs. They usually get found out in the end.

So the celebrity may be fair game, but if you feel the need to tell it to the world by gossip, blog or billboard then I've got news for you, you're a...

"Two fishes huh? What a guy!"

Perhaps living with just a little less of an ego is as far as I will get. I do know that just being aware of it has helped me ten-fold on my journey to a more successful and abundant life, and it can for you as well. It may take to my dying day, but perhaps before I leave this world I will know what it feels like to be ego-less. There I'll be, in the Twin Palms Nursing Home, having just finished a hearty helping of pureed potatoes, bacon and plums, a little drool escaping from my toothless head, having just peed myself; I'll take my last breath, and then head off to the big Rock Arena in the sky.

"Aw, he's gone," the nurse will say. "Poor, old, egoless, bastard. OH WELL, WHO WANTS HIS SLIPPERS?"

# I'VE GOT TO GET A MESSAGE TO YOU

Do you remember back at the beginning of this journey when I asked you which of the two guys was a success and which one a failure - the Wall Street dude vs. Mr. Wilderness guy? Well now, if it holds true that success cannot just be about the money and the toys, but rather about how much control or "say" you have in what you do, then what if you have put into play RECEPTIVITY, DESIRE, BELIEF, INTENTION and ACTION, and you get to make all of the decisions and have all of the say in how things are done, but you STILL hate what you're doing and have little or no PASSION for it? Are you still considered successful? I am going to make a bold statement here, and go out on a limb and say – NO. No, you are not truly successful. If life is not fun for you, if it's not enjoyable, then where is the success in that? A successful life is therefore in direct relationship to the joy it brings you, and a thousand or a million or even a billion dollars is not going to solve that for you. Money but misery, houses but no happiness, cars but no caring? PASSION bleeds of TRUTH, for it would seem all but impossible to be passionate about something that you dislike or don't want.

Do what you do because you are meant to do it. Do it because you can, and because you love it. By following the path in front of you and focusing on where you're going rather than where you've been, you are also sowing seeds for the future. This world is not a perfect place, so don't look for it to be. Just honour your personal growth and stay committed to each moment of each day. Try not to attach too much emotion to an imperfect world, or you will lose the energy that you will need to fuel your positive beliefs. Stay attuned to things that affect you and that you can affect. All too often people stress over that which they cannot ever hope to change. Let the outcome take care of itself. PASSION is a true ally of all of the elements contained within *THE ACTION SANDWICH*. It amalgamates, joins forces, and is the true reflection that tells the world that you are making the correct choices. I have tried and tried to get passionate about doing my taxes, but somehow it never seems to work. They get done eventually, but it is a horrible experience for me so I try to stay passionate about how I will feel when someone else does them for me.

Life should not be lived in misery; in fact, it should not even be lived in complacency. Your job and relationships are not meant to make you want to jump out of a window! You can be happy in all things if you remain receptive to that which makes you happy. Don't wait until the movie is two thirds over before buying your ticket. Don't wait until the end of the race to lace up your running shoes. Don't wait until the end to become an expert. Do it now, ALL OF IT, all of the things that make you happy. Go to night school. Learn that second language. Join a band. Take a cooking class. Learn to swim. SUCCESS isn't about the money or the toys..............is it?

Yogi Berra once said, "You've achieved success in your field when you don't know whether what you're doing is work or play."

If you think that this is a rather romanticized notion, let me tell you that I know there is truth to it. Living a life that includes forty hours a week of work you dislike or, worse still, hate, is hopefully harder for you to swallow than Yogi Berra's idea of success.

## TEN STEPS TO PASSION

1. ALL YOU NEED IS LOVE - Do you love what you do? If not then why are you doing it? You were not put here to live in misery. IF PASSION doesn't live where you work, then make sure it lives where you don't work. Remember no condiment...no flavour. Pass the mustard!

2. I'D LIKE TO THANK MY MOM FOR HAVING ME - Gratitude makes great kindling for a passionate fire. Reminding yourself how lucky and thankful you are for all that you have is tremendous fuel for attracting more of what it is you're grateful for. Always focus on what you have as opposed to what you do not have. Be thankful.

3. OH YES, YOU TOO - When you are handing out all that new found love and gratitude don't forget to pause at the mirror occasionally. Appreciating, loving and crediting yourself, reminds your true essence to shift the power back from the ego to the inner self. Love you too.

4. YOU MEAN LITTLE OL' ME? - Don't force your accomplishments on the world. Let it discover you on its own terms. It is but a short step from self-importance to self-pity. Practice a little humility. Egos shout. Deeds speak.

5. ALL OR NOTHING AT ALL - At some point in everyone's life PASSION asks you for "all or nothing." Why wait to be asked, get out on that stage, give everything you've got and leave nothing behind. Only then can you look in the mirror and say you truly gave it your best. As the song says, "All or Nothing At All."

6. AND THIS ONE IS LITTLE TOMMY - Display your PASSION with the same ease you would pictures of your children. Share PASSION with the fervor one would feel for a new car or the love of a newborn baby. Infect your whole world with it. PASSION, pass it on.

7. DREAMER - Go ahead and take yourself on a wonderful journey to the perfect life you see in your mind. Reinforce continuously the what, why, where, how and when of it all. By the way, you're dreaming anyway so don't hold back. Dream big.

8. PASSION NOT PEDIGREE - PASSION has no bank account, no fast car, no mansion on the hill. It wears nothing, costs nothing and dines nowhere. PASSION is your birthright,

like the blood in your veins and the air that you breathe. No one has exclusivity to it. Take a deep breath.

9. YOU ARE HERE - Don't know what to be passionate about? There has to be something! Is it walking, reading, cooking, checkers, juggling, pogo-sticking? Come on, you're not going to break PASSION so toss it around for a while. It's an environmentally responsible, completely renewable, nonexclusive resource. Do something! Begin from where you are!

10. REGRETS, I'VE HAD A FEW - Even unwavering PASSION can go a bit wobbly at times. Give yourself the freedom to question the direction you have chosen, the understanding that mistakes are made, the forgiveness for those mistakes and then make the changes required to get back on track. Let the record show, you took the blows and did it ...your way.

# MY SONG
## Opus 6

### I AM WITH YOU TONIGHT

By now my relationship with Gary was solidified. It had gone far beyond that of artist and manager and had become more like father and son. There was not a day that passed that we did not speak and if I happened to be off the road we would see each other almost daily. The PASSION we had for what was going on around us was strong. He was equally as driven as I, and although he still had a couple of other bands in his stable, it was *Glass Tiger* that remained his one true love.

He and his wife never had children of their own, so it was his two dogs and yours truly who filled that void for him. He would have done anything for me within reason. He was my biggest fan, my greatest sounding board and by now my closest friend. I kept nothing from him and that was a great feeling for a kid that had never experienced what it was like to have someone to turn to for advice or a shoulder to lean on. He had stood by my side during the death of my niece and of my pal in Atlanta. He took my calls in the wee hours no matter where I was calling from or how trivial the topic may have been. When you are lying in a cot in a Berlin hotel that resembles Stalag 13, with your family and all that you love back in your homeland, you can get pretty lonely. A voice that cares and understands what you are sacrificing in your endeavor can be the difference between calling it quits and understanding that what you are doing is indeed authentic and worthy.

His voice reminded me of home, and reassured me as to why I was doing what I was compelled and driven to do. He traveled with us on numerous occasions, which I thoroughly enjoyed and he always brought with him a voice of reason that could help settle me down especially since I felt the extra pressure of being the front-man of the band.

A bit of a "them vs. me" thing was developing even if not consciously vindictive in nature, but rather a bit of good old fashioned jealousy that can happen when someone seems to get most of the goodies that are going around the table. I seemed to need to fight a bit more for ideas and suggestions that I felt would benefit the band. One particular fiasco comes to mind that shows both sides of that coin. I remember it now as if it was....wavy lines...waaavvvy lliinnness.......

## BOTH SIDES NOW

It was July 16th 1988 and I had been invited to attend and sing at "The Great One's" wedding.

*Glass Tiger's* arrival on the music scene in 1986 coincided with the

*Edmonton Oilers* solidifying their claim to the term dynasty as they were about to secure their fourth Stanley Cup in the space of five years, led by none other than the greatest to ever lace up a pair of skates, Wayne Gretzky. I had met and become friends with winger Mark Messier a year earlier and through Mark I had spent a fair bit of time around the team, getting to know most of the lads. Many an evening was spent in a bar called Barry T's and little did I know that in that very place, somewhere on the dance floor was the girl who would eventually become my wife and the mother of my daughter.

Athletes, great athletes are enigmas. I have witnessed some of the top sports stars in the world partying long and hard into the wee hours on the eve of a big game, yet without skipping a beat they take the field or the ice and play the game the way it was meant to be played, tough, hard and selfless, perhaps picking up a hat-trick along the way just for good measure. I'm not condoning or condemning it, just reporting it. *The Oilers* could do this as well as most and of course *Glass Tiger* was well versed in this conditioning. So Edmonton became a little bit of a playground for yours truly.

One of the biggest thrills of my career was when I was asked to sing the national anthem at the Stanley Cup Final. I can still remember thinking about how my dad must have felt watching a sports event of that magnitude, hearing my voice over the top of those classic style images of athletes fidgeting with anticipation, the Canadian and U.S. flags flying and the crowd going wild well before the singer finishes his rendition.

Then came the invite to Edmonton's Royal Wedding.

The jabs came fast and furious even if not directly aimed at me. There is no doubt that I was the most recognized member of the band and certainly the most sought after when it came to the media.
Question, what's the drummer's name from the band *Aerosmith*? Ok you get my drift?

So with being the front-man of any popular band the bar is certainly raised and at this particular time when the perks were coming fast and furiously I was asked by the organization known as *Child Find* if I would be their National Spokesperson, to which I said yes.

MacLean's Magazine had voted me one of the top ten most recognizable faces that year and *Child Find* felt that this would add some reasonable clout to their message.

Meanwhile back at the Ponderosa a division was brewing among the ranks.

We were touring when I planned to attend Gretzky's wedding. I was going to fly in and out the same day leaving the guys to get ready for a show on the East Coast. It was also arranged that upon my return I would be picked up by representatives of *Child Find* and taken to visit some homeless kids before going to do a private autograph session signing posters from a shot taken with some of these kids.

I flew into Edmonton for an event that was the very embodiment of extravagance. This wedding ranked as close to the Charlie and Diana event as you could possibly get (without the ears of course).

Movie stars, music stars, sports stars, past and future legends were all in attendance. It was real Hollywood stuff. Many people think to this day that I sang at the church but I did not. It was in fact a fine singer by the name of Tim Feehan, however David Foster and I were to perform a *Glass Tiger* song together later that night. The reception line had other ideas though as Wayne and Janet were tied up taking photographs and participating so long in the receiving line that Foster and I were a little too "jolly" by the time we were to perform, so we passed on that idea for the betterment of all. It was no big deal and after a superb meal, a snuggle from my girl and well wishes from all, I was on a red eye feeling no pain and ready to do my *Child Find* duties.

Two little ladies greeted me at the airport. For the life of me I would never remember their names so for the purpose of my tale we'll call them Agnes and Betty.

Gary had stayed in touch with me the entire time and told me that although the boys were a bit miffed at my gallivanting they were going to do the local promotion and the sound-check at the arena, minus a singer of course (dig-dig).

I should have sensed danger when Betty and Agnes packed me into the back of a Ford Pinto on our way to visit a couple of the half-way houses for runaway, addicted and abused kids.

"So ladies, I am to do an autograph session later, correct?"
"Correct you are," said Agnes.
"And so tell me, what kind of promotion have you had, regarding this event," I asked inquisitively. "Radio ads? Television perhaps?"
"Oh," said Betty, "I must have told at least a dozen people or so and I know Agnes has told everyone she knows, and she knows everybody, believe me."

Instantaneously I knew I was in trouble. I have had autograph sessions with *Glass Tiger* that have been nothing short of riots and I have had autograph sessions with *Glass Tiger* that have been not so riotous at all shall we say. It all comes down to promotion. If you don't tell the public en masse, the public doesn't show up, en masse.

"You did do some radio promotion girls, didn't you?" I asked.
"Um… no," replied Betty in a matter of fact way.

"Don't think you'd need that here, son," Agnes piped in, "word of mouth works wonders here doesn't it Betty?"
"Oh definitely Agnes, why we know everything about everybody around here, don't we? Right, here we are then."

I entered the mall via the front doors thinking I was to be taken to a location perhaps in or near a music store but no, we walked right past all of them and we kept on walking...and walking...but to where? This was the decoy route right? What elaborate set up had they planned for my presentation I wondered?

The furniture department in Sears is a big place, especially when you have shrunk to the size of Stuart Little. Even the table, pen and especially the posters that I was to sign seemed enormous.

"Can I get you anything?" said Agnes.
"How about a gun or a large bacon, lettuce and cyanide sandwich to go please," were the words that filled my head while "a cup of tea please," were the words that left my lips.

Not only was I in the bloody furniture department, I was neatly tucked in behind the sofas and chesterfields surrounded lovingly by the standard lamps and armoires. Only one thing could have been worse than this and that would be to have it witnessed by *Glass Tiger* or heaven forbid, Wayne Gretzky!

I sat and stood then sat and stretched, then yawned, then sat some more. At one point a little man came along polishing the floors with one of those enormous flying saucer type cleaners that pulls the cleaner-person along as he buffs the floor from side to side. His curiosity was getting the better of him as he buffed closer and closer to me, straining his neck to catch a glimpse of the poster to see if he could figure out who the hell I was and what in god's name I was doing slap-dab in the middle of his flying saucer's buffer zone.

"Aye boy," he said in that unmistakable east coast twang.
"Hello, how are you," said the singer.
"And what do ye have there?" he inquired.
"Posters," was my reply.
"Hmmm and what might they be posters of?" asked the polisher.

"Me...and some great kids," I added with conviction.

Who, I wondered was he going to request that I personalize it to? His wife? Kids? You never know, perhaps he'd keep it for himself.

"Would you like one?" I asked.

Shamelessly, I added, "They're, free."

I was desperate.

He stopped his buffer, stared at the poster, took a deep breath and said, "Nope!"

He then fired up the flying saucer and buffed on his merry way to friggin' Mars I hoped.

"Would you like to keep the posters," asked Betty.

Back at the arena, the guys had not seen me since I left for Gretzky's wedding and of course there was a bit of the "wanderer has returned atmosphere" as I entered.

Some of the crew were mockingly bowing as someone yelled out, "It's the other great one!" Remember this dear reader, they thought I had just come from my own personal Rock Star autograph signing session for the masses. Little did they know I hadn't done one for the masses but for the Mrs.........Betty and Agnes.

Our drummer took the lack of attention harder than anyone. He was popular with female fans and never lacked for their attention but it was the recognition of the music industry and media that he desperately craved. We had several incidents that caused animosity within our ranks. On one occasion Sam and I had flown to New York to do the big stuff like Entertainment Tonight and CNN, leaving Michael, the drummer with the responsibility of doing local press in St. Louis where our next show was to take place.

When I arrived back at the St. Louis airport I was greeted by Gary and Derek who told me I had just enough time to get downtown to do radio and television newscasts prior to show time. It seems that Michael had refused to do it on the grounds that he should have gone with me to

New York. I was livid. I wanted to kill him. He was rooming with me.
He moved out.

We performed the show, with me still wanting to kill him. Later that
night Derek said that Michael wanted to speak to me and asked me if I
would let him back in the room long enough for him to do so. I agreed.

"I would walk over five hundred miles of hot burning coals to get my
face on the cover of a teen magazine," he said quietly, "while you get it
without even trying!"

At that moment I knew what it all really and truly meant to him. It
was about the fame, the adulation and the worship, not the craft...and
yet it was the most honest thing a band member had said to me in
quite some time.

Michael quit the band in Ireland, but the band had mentally released
him well before that. Still we toured. As a matter of fact a very short time
after he quit we had to go to Germany for a television show. We didn't
panic because the song was "Diamond Sun," which had at its core a
"drum loop", a synthesized sound created on the keyboard. We didn't
really require a drummer but the Germans weren't buying it. They
couldn't get it through the inner mechanisms of their minds that we
were now four instead of five.

"Fünf, ja?"
"No not fünf! Vier! We are now four."
"Fünf, ja?"

As luck would have it a Canadian band called *Chalk Circle* were there
and we asked their drummer if he would fire on a baseball cap and sit in
behind the drum kit to make the number "funf" and keep the Germans
happy. He said he would do it for fifty bucks!

He might as well have said $5,000 for just on the grounds of principle alone we told him to stuff it. My wife who was my girlfriend at the time said she would do it. She was deadly serious and so we sat with her showing her the rhythm while assuring her it would be easy. She pulled a baseball cap on as the television guys ran the playback for the first time. When the loop blasted out over the speakers the look of enlightenment was apparent as it dawned on the Germans that this song did not require a drummer, not even for aesthetics.

"Ahhhhh vier, ja?"
"Ja! Ja! Vier! Vier!"

And then, we were four.

I often regret trying to hammer it into them that we didn't need a drummer that day, for it would have been one of the better *Glass Tiger* trivia moments had my now beloved wife been our drummer that day.

The magical mystery tour continued and our third CD was released. The luster was wearing off however and confusion was setting in. I fought a losing battle to have the Rod Stewart duet released as our first single while the remainder of the band and the record company felt that we needed to release a classic rock song called "Animal Heart" which has a mountainous wall of guitars in it.

I had contributed to the song as I had for all *Glass Tiger* songs in the past but the style of this one never won me over. I felt it sent a confusing message and created an even more confusing image similar to the one that we had displayed years prior when we first met up and the drummer sang the rock songs and I the pop ones. Arguments ensued but my pleading fell on deaf ears.

"Animal Heart" was a hit in Canada but the USA wouldn't even release the CD. We began a nightmare tour of Europe opening the show for Swedish sensation *Roxette*, whose road crew treated us very poorly, which added to our misery. The tour as usual was a buy-on. This is when you actually pay them to be on their tour. As part of this arrangement we were to have a catered dinner only on gig days, not thinking for one second that they would refuse us a cup of tea or a piece of toast in the morning or perhaps a hot chocolate in the evening but refuse they did.

They held to the letter even when at night they were throwing mounds of food and drink out into the garbage. What made it most difficult was the fact that the bulk of the tour was in rural areas, which didn't offer us the chance at a late night pizza or sandwich. Who the hell am I kidding, a Swedish pizza?

We were on our own until the sun came up and someone could do a coffee run. Eventually I personally said, "screw this" and went marching in and made myself a bit of toast and poured a cup of tea, daring them to order me out. They never did and thus began a little trend of our guys quietly getting the odd bite of breakfast. I remember phoning Gary back in Canada.

"Get me home! Get us out of this!" I demanded.
"I'm coming to see you," he replied, "I'll be on the next plane."

He brought the band's pal Jimmy with him knowing full well that it would cheer the lads and I up. Jimmy looked after odds and ends for us, nothing overly important but I loved having him on the road with me. We had a lot in common, a love of sports, a love of history and a great love of movies and movie trivia. It was a brilliant move on Gary's part. We stuck it out together and got through it but the end was near.

## ALL BY MYSELF

"I'm quitting," I said matter-of-factly in our dressing room in Ottawa. "I'm going to go it alone. I have to."

Surprisingly, the one who seemed to take it the worst and was most insulted was Wayne our bass player. Sam immediately took the stand that it was the right thing to do. Gary, who was not aware of my intentions (I didn't want him to talk me out of it), walked beside me on the way to the stage.

"So what do you think?" I asked at the foot of the stage stairs.
"Well, it's painful but when all is said and done, I'm coming with you," was his immediate reply.

There was never any big announcement that *Glass Tiger* had split. We simply all slipped into a mode of doing our own thing. I was offered a solo deal with EMI and I took it. One of the first things I had to do was, you guessed it, go on the road.

I traveled to London England to do some writing then on to Los Angeles and then back again to England for some more. During a trip to England a good friend, someone who today would have been my brother-in-law, died from cancer. As I stood beside his casket among family and friends, Gary who was again by my side said something that was to be terribly foreshadowing.

"It's always the good guys isn't it?"

## GOOD ROCKIN' AT MIDNIGHT

My travels to Los Angeles secured my hiring of John Jones, a talented songwriter and producer to work with me on my first solo project. I literally moved to Los Angeles renting a home in the hills of Hollywood, leaving my son behind once again with family. "LOVE AND SUFFERING" was still driving me and I was unable to resist.

Los Angeles always held a mystical attraction for me. It also seemed to greet me in style for I was there for the O.J. Simpson verdict and likewise for the aftermath of the Rodney King riots. Mud slides? Done that. Brush fires? Been there. During the recording of my CD however, she held a surprise gift for me that still affects me to this day.

On January 17, 1994 at 4:30:55 AM Pacific Standard Time to be exact I was fast asleep in my bed knowing that I had much work to do the next day. Why am I so certain of this date and time? Well let's see, if you are old enough, do you remember where you were when J.F.K. was assassinated? What about when John Lennon was slain? For you younger readers, I bet you know exactly what you were doing and where you were when the Twin Towers came down on 9/11, correct? Well Jan 17th 1994 was a watershed moment for me.

Marcy, my girlfriend, now wife, had been down for a visit and I had taken her back to the airport the previous afternoon avoiding the freeway by traveling down La Cienega Blvd. That morning I had been finishing a vocal for John, when Marcy had entered the house claiming that she thought she felt a rumble beneath her feet while outside on the porch. We dismissed it and set off for the airport. I remember the traffic being so slow and for a few minutes we were at a standstill while under the Santa Monica freeway.

"My God, can you imagine if this thing came down during an earthquake," I said not thinking.
"Don't say that!" she replied.

I saw her off at the gate for her trip back to Canada and returned to work with John until midnight, at which time I called it a night and headed to bed. John left to go stay with his girlfriend that evening as opposed to staying in the little house he had down the hill from me.

My world was about to change.

To this day it still gets referred to as a moderate earthquake. Let me tell you, it might have been many things but moderate doesn't come close to what I experienced some twenty miles from its epicenter.

It had a magnitude they say of 6.7, and yet the ground acceleration was the highest ever recorded in an urban area in North America and to this day it remains the costliest earthquake in U.S. history. Cost doesn't enter your mind when your arse flies out of bed in the middle of a deep sleep, crashing you naked to the floor just prior to your home beginning a dance that causes it to rise and fall and sway and list, several feet in all directions. The thunderous noise is terrifying. It starts somewhere off in the distance and then comes for you. Thud! THud! THUD! THUD!

By the time it reaches you it sounds unlike anything you have ever heard. You are completely helpless, preparing to be swallowed at any moment. I thought my death was imminent. Something happened however at this moment that still amazes me to this very day for I had fallen with a bang onto the floor but I had landed on top of my telephone. I dialed Toronto, all hell was breaking loose around me and I thought I was going to die, so I dialed home. It rang, it connected, and I heard Marcy's sleepy voice.

"Hello."
"Oh! Marcy! Marcy! MARCY! MARRRCY!" was all I could muster.

To this day she tells the story of how for a brief moment she thought I had been stabbed or shot and left to die on the street. Then she heard the creature and its traveling noise.

"Alan don't talk, get out! You must get out!"

Naked I stumbled to my front hallway and out my door. I heard the loudest crash as one of the houses nearby succumbed to the grips of the quake and crashed down the hill. Suddenly it stopped. The silence seemed deafening. I began to yell for help as I was without glasses or contact lenses and blind as a tree stump.

My neighbour flashed a light.
"Alan can you see this?" she called out.
"Barely, but yes," I replied.
"Take your time and crawl towards it."

I reached her and she quickly wrapped a large blanket around my earthquake birthday suit.

"Sorry I didn't have time to dress for the evening," I quipped.

Shortly afterwards I checked her phone and unbelievably it had a dial tone.

"May I?" I asked.

I dialed Canada again and once again got Marcy who by now sounded more distraught than we were. I told her I thought it was over and not to worry. That is when it struck again with its mightiest blow and that was the last time I spoke to home for almost forty-eight hours.

My neighbour and I jumped into my car and we got out as fast as we could, tuning in the radio hoping for word from authorities that knew what the hell we should do. Suddenly it died again and the silence returned. We listened as they told us to stay calm and wait for further instructions. Stay calm? We were not to return to damaged homes, not to light any flames of any kind and to be prepared for the fact that this moderate earthquake might just be a precursor to a massive one.

We sat together for hours. Listening. Waiting. Thinking.

At one point helicopters flew overhead to inspect possible damage to the water reservoir and the dam that we lived beside. Wouldn't that be ironic, to survive Godzilla only to drown on Gilligan's Island?

After several hours I asked my neighbour a very important question.

"Do you drink?"

"Come again?" she said.

"Drink? Alcohol? Do you partake in the occasional nippy sweety?" I asked her.

"I used to enjoy wine," she replied. "But I haven't had a drink in years."

"Well listen up. I have to go get my glasses for I am blind without them. While I'm at it I am going to grab some pants, however, in my fridge, if

I still have a fridge, are six Heinekens and a bottle of white wine. I'm going to get them and we are going to have a little toast, one to survival and two, to kissing our arses goodbye if this thing returns."

"Deal," she said and off I went.

My house felt wounded. Strange creaking noises lurked everywhere. I found my way into my bedroom and found my glasses on the floor. I also recovered a pair of shorts before edging towards the kitchen. I could not see the extent of the damage but my foot hit cans and bottles scattered about. Getting down on my hands and knees I rummaged around, finding the wine and a couple of beers. I also found a large knife and a cup. Where's a corkscrew when you really need one?

Back in the car I opened the beer with the knife's edge and hacked the top off of the wine bottle. What a strange party this was. We drank, chatted and waited until finally it really seemed like it was over.

Around 7:00 a.m. we decided to re-enter our homes. We hugged and went our separate ways. Inside, it was strange how the pathway of death works in an earthquake. Pockets of my home were ruined yet other areas were untouched. My kitchen was devastated yet my living room practically unscathed. My washroom was a mess but my bedroom was fine. A vase full of tulips remained intact on my television, but all the petals had fallen off and the water had leapt out of the vase.

"What about the recording studio," I wondered.

I went downstairs with my eyes half closed for if I had lost over $100,000 of uninsured gear, I wanted to discover it slowly.

I counted to three and opened them. Unbelievably nothing had happened. Even our guitars were still leaning against the wall where we had left them and yet the little studio washroom was destroyed and the wall had caved in allowing you to step right through to the world outside. It was surreal.

Back home they had to contend with the waiting game of not knowing if I was alive or dead. I did not know if John Jones had survived until he walked through my door several hours later. We hugged and breathed a big sigh of relief before he said, "You do know that this is your fault, don't you?"

"What the hell are you talking about you goof!" I replied.

"I am serious," he said, "It's your fault!"

He hit me with a copy of the Los Angeles Times, which is no easy feat if you are familiar with the size of it. Get a grip L.A.; no paper should be the size of a small car and there on the front cover of the newspaper was the headline declaring the death toll and destruction from the previous night. There was also a map detailing the area, the epicenter and the fault lines responsible for the quake. I absorbed the map and read the following: "The quake started about nine miles underground and during the course of the main shock, ruptured upward and northward, spreading both eastward and westward. The northern end of the fault extends under the Santa Susana Mountains.

The Frew fault is one of several that could have been responsible."

"Are you kidding me?" I was dumbfounded. Spooked beyond belief. Even in Scotland my name is not that common. My first earthquake and it has my bloody name?

The death toll was 57, with 9000 people injured. The fact that the earthquake occurred at 4:30 a.m. greatly minimized the death toll. There was $44 billion in damages and $800 billion replacement value on taxable property.

22,000 people were now homeless and 9 bridges collapsed. Yes, the very section that Marcy and I had sat under in the traffic jam collapsed. No one was beneath it at the time.

I remained in Los Angeles to finish my recording, though for many Canadians a mass exodus ensued. Gavin, my son even came to visit and although we had fun, I was never quite the same. I never slept in my bed again, preferring the couch in the living room.

A few months later I had to return to L.A. for some cleanup work, a visit of only one week and I'll be damned but an after shock in the high 5s hit sending me into a state of panic.

The LOVE AND SUFFERING of my PASSION has taken me down many roads and the stories I have told you are but the tip of an iceberg, the size of which even I cannot begin to fathom. I tell these tales for two reasons. First, being a storyteller I hope to offer you a different perspective on what we would normally classify as a motivational book. Simply put, I want you to enjoy the stories. Second, I am attempting to show you that it is all about the journey, from birth to death, from RECEPTIVITY to PASSION, from a question to its answer, from the recognition of the need to change to the actual changing itself. It's trial and error, good and bad, mystical and mystifying, LOVE and SUFFERING, but it is worthy, you are worthy, the journey is worthy.

## SO BLIND

I have been tested, retested and tested again. Upon my return to Canada I prepared to launch my new solo project with a revitalized sense of artistry and stamina. Gary and I negotiated a brand new publishing deal for me and I recorded my first solo video. We were pumped and ready for the challenges ahead. We were a team.

My solo name did not have the clout of the *Glass Tiger* name but we were not deterred. Nothing would stop us now. Nothing... except the greatest test of all.

The songs contained on my first solo CD "Hold On" are without a doubt some of the finest I have ever written. The CD is beautifully recorded and the production is second to none. The musicianship is outstanding and includes the exceptional work of Mick Fleetwood, Steve Ferrone, Robin Le Mesurier and Jim Cregan to name but a few. We even had fun when Mickey Dolenz of *Monkees* fame joined in for some singing.

EMI stepped up to the plate and we spent world-class money. I flew to Jamaica to do one of several photo shoots and upon my return to Canada, Gary and I popped out to see Deane at the EMI headquarters in Toronto.

When we arrived at Deane's office he was conducting his business laying flat on his back on the office sofa suffering from a severe bout of sciatica, pain along the sciatic nerve usually due to a prolapsed disc in the lower spine. We talked about the upcoming launch and the never-ending cycle of touring when Gary uttered something new to me.

"I think I have sciatica as well," he said to both of us, "My leg's been giving me some awful pain recently too."

We concluded our business with Deane and headed out.

"You've never mentioned your leg before." I said sounding a bit like the dad.
"Oh, it's nothing, it'll pass."

In what seemed like the blink of an eye, we were in trouble. Both he and his wife didn't know it, but I knew it. I could see small incremental changes in his color, his eyes and his weight. I smelled cancer but could not bring myself to utter the word. I visited him almost daily although demands were coming in from EMI for me to start fulfilling promotional requests from the media regarding the new CD.

"What's the doctor saying?" I would inquire cautiously.
"Oh, not much. He has me booked for a scan in a few weeks."
"And he's not said anything, else?" I pushed.

"No, not really. You know the funniest thing happened to me outside the doctor's office the other day. My pants fell down. Imagine that, just right down they went."
I wish I could say I laughed...but I didn't. My heart sank.

## FUNERAL FOR A FRIEND

Progressively he got more and more uncomfortable. His face was gaunt and he had dropped a ton of weight. Still no one was saying the "C" word and I did not oblige in that way either.

My first video was launched and I flew to Calgary to shoot the second one. I was anxious and scattered, trying as hard as I could to stay focused on what we had to do for this new release. I knew in my heart that he was doomed but I couldn't bear the thought. I wanted to pull the plug on the CD but couldn't do that either.
My LOVE and SUFFERING was unbearable.

I would get calls from our office staff telling me that he was there but laying on the floor, in and out of sleep as he tried to instruct them on business. I would tell them to leave him be and that they should call me if they had any questions. Things went from bad to worse yet I was still working the new promotion for the CD. One day during the making of an EPK (Electronic Press Kit) in a studio in downtown Toronto, I was phoned and told that his breathing was very rapid and shallow and it was scaring the staff. I rushed there and was beside myself when I found him. I swear he was literally losing pounds per day. Every time I saw him, he was more and more skeletal.

"What's really going on Alan?" I was asked.
"He has cancer," I said for the first time, the words crushing me.
"He has cancer...and he's dying."

Gary Pring who in his hey day weighed in at about 230 pounds was now in my arms being carried upstairs to his living room. I placed him on the couch and found the number for his family physician. The secretary answered.

"Yes, my name is Alan, I am Mr. Pring's son, let me speak to the doctor please, it's an emergency."

"I am sorry sir," said the secretary, "The doctor is busy."

"That's ok I'll wait," I replied calmly.

"No you don't understand," she said, "He will be too busy to speak on the phone today. Give me your number and I will have him call you."

"No," I said, "I'm afraid it's you who does not understand. Get me the doctor, or I swear I will come down there, kick his door in and speak with him personally."

"Yes how can I help you?" he asked me.

"Doctor what exactly are you doing for Mr. Pring?" I asked, in what I'm sure was an accusing tone.

"Well I have a Cat Sca..."

"NO! I MEAN WHAT ARE YOU DOING FOR HIM?"

I asked him what he thought was wrong with Gary but got medical jargon back for a response. I asked if he'd seen him recently to which he replied no.

I didn't get very far. I did manage to establish that this doctor had booked him for tests but that was all. He never spoke of the obvious with Gary and his wife nor did he say the words to me. I do not know what his strategy was but on the surface, it sucked.

I told him that I had just carried Gary in my arms, all ninety pounds or so of him, wracked with pain up to the living room level of his home.

"What do you want me to do?" he asked me.

Incredulously I replied, "Be a goddamned doctor! I want him in a hospital. Send an ambulance for your patient now!"

When we arrived at the hospital they looked at me like I was an idiot for I had obviously brought a dying man into their world, which was already understaffed, overworked, with a lack of available beds. Gary should have indeed been at home, comfortably in his own bed, with the appropriate medications to keep him that way but we were desperate and he needed immediate help.

A doctor pulled me aside and said, "Why have you brought him here?"
"Because, he is dying and he is in great pain," I answered.
"Anyone can see he is dying," said the doctor almost mockingly. "My question is why have you brought him here?"
I stared him down.

"Because the last time I looked, the sign on your door said Hospital. He is a law abiding, tax paying citizen of this country and I want you to help him!"

He looked at me contemptuously as he said, "I don't think we can help him. Take him home and have his family doctor see him."
"Doc, Listen to me," I answered. "You don't know me and I am fine with that, but what I do for a living gives me great access to the media all across this nation of ours. Now if you turn us away and make me take this poor, ravaged soul back home, put him in his bed and attempt to get his family doctor who hasn't visited with him and who is completely oblivious to his dilemma, out to see him, I promise you that you and this hospital will be front page news before you can complete your backswing! Get me?
I have no choice. Help him."

Entering his room, Gary actually looked like a new man, which I enhanced by giving him a clean shave. Afterwards we chatted about music, Glass Tiger, and our new CD. He was weak and a little confused but all in all he still knew what was going on. Never once did he ever mention his illness or anything to do with dying. Later I said goodnight and told him that I would keep my appointment to finish the EPK that had been started the day before and then I would come see him. Even then he was still giving me support with a little "bossiness" Pring style, thrown in.

It was around 4:00 p.m. the next day and I was in the middle of an interview for the EPK when I was told that someone very upset was on the phone asking for me. I took the call to find Gary's wife on the other end.

"Alan, help us," she cried, "A doctor just left the room after telling us to get our papers in order! He says Gary is dying! He says he doesn't have long to go! My God, help us!"

"I'm on my way," I answered immediately.

Incredible as it sounds neither Gary nor his wife knew up until that moment just how bad this was. Call them naïve but this was the way it was and now it was a shock being told what I had known in my heart for months. Equally incredible was the fact that as soon as he was told, as soon as he heard from a doctor that his time in this world was nearing an end, he immediately deteriorated and by the time I got there some 45 minutes after receiving the call, he was already in the beginning stages of dying.

"Cheyne-Stoking" is when the breathing becomes a raspy panting as the body struggles to take oxygen in while the rest of the body begins the process of shutting down. I had endured over fifteen hours of this with my little granny and it is not pleasant, in fact it is down right horrible to witness. Gary had an oxygen mask on and was panting like a dog to keep going. I began a crusade to get the doctor to start a morphine drip on him that would make him comfortable while assisting his body to shut down. They fought me on this one and for the life of me I do not know why they persisted in attempting to give him medication orally. The long haul began. I had left him talkative, comfortable and clean-shaven just 12 hours before and now he was in the clutches of death. At one point after watching him struggle I lost all control of my emotions and in the arms of Jim from our office and Sam from the band my heart caved in and I sobbed, with gut-wrenching sobs, uncontrollably. Still he fought, still he hung on, still the hours passed.

By now it was impossible to know if he could hear us. His breathing was machine-gunning in the shortest of pants. He was sweating profusely and his pupils were pinpoints. Finally an order had come to begin a morphine drip. I was on his left side holding his hand as the nurse prepared to insert the catheter into a vein in the back of his right hand.

Suddenly he gave my hand a squeeze and we made eye contact.

"He's going to go now," I blurted out, "Grab Ilona, he's going now." The nurse stopped attempting to start an intravenous and stepped back to allow his wife to be on the opposite side from me.

I had witnessed the actual moment of death many times in my medical life and as sad and morbid as it can seem, witnessing life exiting this world is every bit as miraculous, equally as wondrous and just as humbling as witnessing its entry. I felt his power and energy pass from his hand into mine, traveling up and across my chest, into my body and my soul. His eyes rolled and he gave an enormous sigh.

"We love you Gary! We are all here with you and we love you!"
And then he was gone, but to where?

I will leave it up to you to decide. He has been given the answer to something that for me remains unanswerable. However I know his energy was honest and worthy, positive and good and it would serve him well on his new journey wherever that may take him. His death altered my life forever. I will miss him for the rest of my days and as painful as it was to lose him, I remain so grateful and I am a better man for having known him, this father and friend who showed up in my life when I needed him most.

I loved him.

# A note on GRATITUDE
## TO WHOM MUCH IS GIVEN

Almost 20 years ago I blew my knee out, badly, in what was supposed to be a fun, charity soccer match with a bunch of North American Rock 'n Rollers against a group of our counterparts from the UK. Not only was it a devastating blow to me in the short term but it also became life altering from that point on.

When the game began I was already tired from having to do a video shoot the night before, which lasted right up until one hour before taking the field. My body was exhausted and to this day I believe that I damaged my knee making the video and just did not realize it. But I had played this game all of my life and thought nothing of it. How wrong I was. I tore my anterior cruciate ligament, my medial cartilage and my medial collateral ligament...in layman's terms, "the big three." My leg spasmed uncontrollably and the pain was excruciating, but here comes the best part. The very next morning I was to fly to Atlanta, Georgia to begin a three-month tour of America working with British legends *The Moody Blues*.

As I lay on the hospital gurney the attending specialist whom I knew said, "Well Alan I am pretty sure you have torn your anterior cruciate but I won't know the full extent of the damage until I get in there and look around."
"You can't go in there," I said tentatively.
"What are you talking about?" he asked.
"Doc I gotta be on a plane tomorrow to the States. I am starting an American tour tomorrow."
"Are you nuts? Your leg is all but gone, I must go in and repair it."

I begged him for an alternative. Reluctantly, he acquiesced and gave me one.

"You have got to be kidding," was the general consensus.
"It'll be fine," I said, "Trust me."

I had arrived at the airport not only on crutches but I was also in a full length, groin-to-ankle fiberglass leg cast and still groggy from mounds of painkillers.

What followed was night upon night of relentless agony as I hobbled on stage in one hundred degree weather through Georgia, Florida and Texas, hundreds of miles night after night trying as best as I possibly could to keep my poker face on and give it my all. Some nights I would wear shorts so the crowd would know that I had a disability. On other occasions when I wore jeans, I would hit the microphone off of my leg, producing a loud thud throughout the stadium just to let them know that my funny walk was due to a leg cast and not because I had shit myself during the previous song. It was a nightmare. What I did not know was that the pain was getting increasingly more and more unbearable due to the fact that I was hemorrhaging tiny amounts of blood continuously into my knee cap, putting tremendous pressure on my knee now locked firmly inside a cast. Ironically word came back from Canada that the footage from the video we had shot weeks before at the time of the soccer match was mostly unusable and that the director wanted to re-shoot the band's scene entirely. A surgeon was hired to cut the cast off of my leg and assist me.

What a mess lay under that smelly old cast. It was revolting. The doctor told me he should look inside my knee. The leg was a weak, shriveled, and an emaciated mess, so I agreed.

They propped me up for the video re-shoot and I never moved. They simply panned a camera back and forth in front of me to capture the shots. I hated it and to this day I still hate the video and anything to do with the song.

I agreed to let the doctor at least take a look inside my knee. That evening we did a show in Memphis with me in a heavy leg brace followed by a flight back to Atlanta for my surgery. They opened my leg, cleaned things up a bit then recovered me from the throes of anesthetic to show me inside my leg on a video monitor while we discussed my options for repair. High as a kite, I was watching the old PAC-MAN video game as this little creature ate up all the bits of stuff inside my kneecap. The doc then proceeded to tell me what the plan for my leg was and how long the recovery process would be.

"Eighteen months," he said nonchalantly.

"Are you joking? Am I still under anesthetic and I'm only dreaming that I'm awake?"
"Doc I have got to be back on tour in four days!"

Once again I asked for an alternative and once again I got one.

Four days later I was on stage in Buffalo, New York in a leg brace that would have held Dumbo the Elephant up. I was again plodding across the stage like Lurch and this is how it continued for months on end. Even our triumphant return to Canada for two sold-out performances in Toronto were marred by the fact that my leg was useless and it was not being given the chance to repair properly nor was it receiving proper therapy. What they had done for me in Atlanta was minimal repair for that is all I would allow. The anterior cruciate ligament was hanging by a thread, which snapped completely a year later, and three more surgeries followed. Months and months were spent on crutches and my leg to this day has never been the same. A poorly functioning leg leads to poor posture and the favouring of one side over another. Night after night onstage and you get the picture. A bad back, sore ankles, sore shoulder and I'm thinking, "God, I've become my grandfather and I'm only thirty-five!"

Now here I am at fifty and I must admit to you that it has been such a drag all of these years living with pain and a pretty useless set of legs. Yes, the other one has since joined the party. So what do I do about it?

Well for starters, I give thanks for what I do have! I give thanks that I have legs! I am very grateful that I can still ride a bicycle and I am not in a wheelchair! I am happy to play golf even though I cannot kick a ball or run anymore. I used to laugh at golfers years ago when driving past the courses, but now I admire their skill and stamina, and am thankful for just having legs, albeit not the best! I am thankful that my voice is strong and that I am singing better than ever.

Be grateful for all that you have as opposed to bitter for what you do not have. No, it is not easy, and I am not professing that it will be. Sometimes it's tough to accept that you don't have what you most DESIRE but I promise you if you focus on what you don't have then you will keep on getting more of what you don't have. Conversely if you focus your thoughts on being thankful and grateful for what you do have, no matter how small or seemingly trivial, then you will start to invite more of such things into your life until more becomes a lot more. Successful people know this and apply it everyday to their endeavors.

Think of it this way. When you give someone a gift that makes them light up with joy and you witness just how happy you have made them, what is one of the first things you decide you want to do?

Give them another one right? You want to experience making them happy again.

So it is with ourselves. Being in a constant state of gratitude will not only empower us but it will bring us more of that which we are grateful for and we know gratitude is not just about the money or the toys either, is it? Of course not.

By all means if you have a lot of money and a big house and several beautiful cars then be very, very grateful, however what good are they without a strong beating heart, or healthy lungs or being cancer free? What good are they without loved ones and friends? While you're at it be thankful for your children, your wife, your guitar, your dinner and your dog, your eyes, hands, mind and yes... legs!

I am thankful that I am still able to take my sore legs and get myself up on stage to perform. Besides if I have to, I'll learn to walk and perform while standing on my hands.

"Oooh! Edith, look at that lead singer, he's singing out of his arse!"
"No love, 'e's not, the microphone's on the floor, see look, there's his head right down there where his willy should be."
"Oooh, he's not very good lookin' at all is he Edith?"
"Well 'e's upside down love, isn't he?"

Try to improve yourself constantly. Retire each night knowing you are a little better today than you were yesterday. It is invigorating. Take full mature responsibility for living your dream every moment. Find projects that make you proud and the rest will fall into place. If you do not love what you are doing, someone else will, and they'll love it with PASSION and be truly successful while you sit by and wonder why they can do so much more than you. Be grateful. Say, "Thank you", more.

Remember my last shift ever as an R.N.? The man whose life I helped save before leaving medicine behind forever? Let me share with you quickly one of the most memorable moments of gratitude that I have ever witnessed.

# COMING AROUND AGAIN

One day, at least two years or so after that last fateful shift I was rehearsing with *Glass Tiger* and I was taking a break and walking with Michael to a coffee shop when a lady and man were coming directly towards us walking in the other direction. The woman had the man by the arm assisting him on his obviously paralyzed side as he helped himself by using a tri-pod walking stick on the other. He had the classic look a person has after suffering a major stroke.

A curled, shriveled paralyzed arm and hand. Similarly with leg and foot, dragging as he struggled to propel himself forward, face and mouth drooping on one side. About six feet away from me he stopped dead in his tracks and started to shake and display a high level of emotion as our eyes met. He was incapable of speech but made loud groaning sounds, which were obviously upsetting his bewildered wife. She hadn't a clue what he was saying. But I knew. I knew what he was saying. For he and I were bonded.

Now dear reader you must realize something. Back on that eventful night in the hospital this man was almost a silhouette to me. I mean at no time was the room brightly lighted nor did we make close contact. He had after all only been post operative some eight hours prior to becoming my patient and was still extremely groggy and sore and so for his part, he spent most of my shift quietly sleeping in almost total darkness.

When he had his stroke at the end of the shift all hell broke loose and I paid little or no attention to his face. If I had been asked to pick him out of a line up the next day I would not have been able to do it and I can honestly say that he never saw my face with even the remotest clarity that night.

So how then could this be happening? I mean two years had gone by since I last had anything to do with this complete stranger and it had all gone from zero to one hundred in the madness of a blink of an eye.

I asked Michael to go on ahead without me and I approached the couple. Tears were streaming down his face. His poor wife was beside herself trying to figure out what was wrong for she and I had never met.

I got close.

"May I?" I asked his wife as I gestured for her to leave his weakened side to let me replace her. She moved aside letting me in.
"It's okay, I understand," I said gently. "I understand and I need you to know that I was just doing my job."
He sobbed and sobbed as I held him.
He was thanking me. He recognized me, he knew me and he was thanking me. Here he was, paralyzed and aphasic, emotionally wounded, a shell of his former self yet thankful to be alive.
"I was his nurse that night," I told his wife. "More importantly, I was the last living face he ever saw as he began to crossover to the other side."
Then I said, "He is thanking me."
"But how could he possibly have seen your face? He was having a stroke. He was *dying*," she asked astonished.

It was all rather implausible but yet here we were two years after the event and he did recognize me.
"He saw me," I replied. "Perhaps not with his eyes but he saw me."

Why be grateful for what you have? Well, incidentally I met them both again about a year later and once again he picked me out of a crowd and this time he was no longer aphasic and though slurred, he had the power of speech. Still somewhat paralyzed on one side he shuffled over to me without assistance from his wife and threw an arm over my shoulder only this time he took great pleasure in saying the words out loud... "THANK YOU."

Even when he had suffered terribly and was left as a bit of a shadow of who he used to be he was still nonetheless grateful and by showing that gratitude to the universe the universe was in return giving him more of what he was grateful for... life. He was mending.

Why did I tell you this story? I'm not sure really. I know how it makes me feel about the true power in all of us but yet it borders on the spiritual at such a level that it actually goes way beyond what the essence of this book is about and so I prefer to not attempt to share with you now my feelings about how this man could possibly have known me, for I am not qualified enough, I fear. I hope however, that it makes you think deeper about the connection between all of us, and with the universe both in life and in death.

A bit "spooky" huh? But it sure makes you think doesn't it? And you *are* thinking...aren't you?

# CONCLUSION

So there you have it, the *ACTION SANDWICH (a six step recipe to success, doing what you're already doing)*. Thank you for reading my book, which of course is now our book, for we are bonded if even just by the fact that together we know the content of these pages. We can bond further by implementing the strategy, by practicing the principles, by frequenting the same roads on our individual journeys, perhaps even crossing paths along the way as we have with this publication. It has been an arduous task writing this book, and an honour sharing it with you but now the true test begins. If when you started the first chapter you were unable to answer the questions I posed to you regarding your life, then I ask you them again.

Who are you?
What do you want?
What do you really, really, want?
Do you know? If so, do you now know what you must do to get it?
I have great BELIEF that you do.

At a certain point in life you just have to take stock of what this world has offered you. More importantly, however, there comes a time when you must take stock of what you offer this world in return. You must take responsibility for where you are today, no matter how painful it seems. You must look yourself in the mirror and take charge, which begins by taking responsibility. When you do, a remarkable thing will happen.

# WHAT ABOUT BOB?

Say hello to Bob. He's a regular guy, with a regular job, a growing family (four children and one on the way), a hefty mortgage and a maxed-out line of credit. His credit cards are so fed up with giving him five-minute majors for fighting that he's now been given a game misconduct and can't use them anymore.

RECEPTIVITY: Oh, he's got it all right, but unfortunately he is more receptive to what is happening in the lives of those on *Survivor* than in his own. He remains grossly overweight and is extremely unhappy with his job.

DESIRE: Sure he desires to lose weight, but right now it's just a word. His time is not his own and it just seems impossible for him to ever find the time to exercise. As for all those diet plans, well they just never work, now do they?

BELIEF: He believes he could have owned his own business as a chartered accountant if he hadn't listened to those around him telling him to get that crazy notion out of his head and go get a real job!

INTENTION: He wonders why he seems to be the unluckiest guy in the world. He tries focusing on bad things all the time to see if he can bring about a change, but the more bad things he focuses on, the more they seem to happen. He wonders why that is.

ACTION: Sure, successful people make their money work HARD for them, but Bob works HARD for his money, in fact he's the hardest working guy he knows. Is that not enough?

PASSION: Now what the hell does he have to be passionate about? He just can't win, can't get a break. His one true PASSION, owning his own business, was taken away from him when he listened to others, so why be passionate?

He is so stressed these days he cracks at the slightest provocation or challenge. His wife has taken to hating him, and his actions are so aggressive that she is fearful for her safety and for the safety of their children. She is planning to leave him shortly. Bob gets drunk way too often. He is sickly. He is rapidly losing all sense of self-respect and the respect of others. He seems only passionate about one thing, telling everyone who will listen what's wrong with the world. In Bob's eyes it continues to get worse.

People at work avoid dear old Bob at all cost, for to put it mildly, he's a downer. After his family runs for the hills, leaving him alone with his misery, Bob complains endlessly that he just can't go on. And of course now that he has to pay child support he will never be able to attend the necessary night school accounting courses required for him to be who he really wants to be. The sad thing of course is that it's not his fault. Don't believe me? Just ask him. It sounds like Bob's *ACTION SANDWICH* has some pretty skunky ingredients in it if you ask me. But Bob isn't asking me. The bigger question is "what is he asking of himself?" For I say again, he already has been using the formula of *THE ACTION SANDWICH* to put himself in the position he is in, and no matter how dark the scenario seems (and it can and will get even darker if he does nothing about it), he can use what he has already been using to get himself back in the game of life again.

Easy? No.
Doable? Absolutely!

# CH CH CH CH CHANGES

As we know from our first ingredient, if Bob does not show RECEPTIVITY for the need to change, then nothing will change. If he continues on this spiral towards the bottom of the well then, it's game over. If he continues behaving like a victim, the universe will support him and his cause by keeping him one. But say for the sake of argument that Bob has hit rock bottom and now realizes he needs to make a change. We have all heard it so many times before, but let's look at this old adage once more: you didn't get fat overnight, so you won't be thin overnight either. In other words, you didn't wreck your marriage, or give up on your dream in one day, you didn't lose the love of your children or the confidence of your friends and co-workers overnight, nor did you get to the level of debt that you have reached in the blink of an eye. So it will take longer than that to recover.

The good news is that Bob can decide right now to change his self-destructive behaviour, and then the improvement he seeks will follow. Now, if you are reading this and relating to Bob in any way, then also relate to the following: for this is a massive moment. This is the defining moment. This is the moment of truth and it must be non-negotiable. If Bob does not recognize the need to change, then I might as well stop writing about him right now, for he's finished. You must take 100% responsibility for your actions, and recognizing the need to change is the single greatest ACTION that Bob or anyone in his position could possibly take. Bob's decision to change is his and his alone.

Of course, help is just around the corner if he asks for it and seeks it out. But what must an alcoholic do prior to being helped by AA? Everyone with that problem must accept the fact that they are alcoholics, and they must decide that change is their only option. They must take responsibility.

So for the sake of not ending my book right here with old Bob on his way to hell, let's say that he looks himself in the mirror and says the magic words: "I must change." He tells himself and the universe that he wants to come back. Just like the patient who came back from the clutches of death, he must take his RECEPTIVITY and DESIRE, BELIEF, INTENTION and apply his greatest ACTION fueled by a PASSION that says, "I am going to change!" They cannot just be words. They must be the truth. The universe, like you, always knows the truth about you.

Now folks, I could make you an enormous shopping list of the various things that Bob can do, but quite frankly it could take a book on its own just to write them for you.

Things like calling the local AA, beginning the 12-step program. He could look into joining a men's group to assist not only with anger management but also with the need to be understood by other men who have been where he is at the moment socially, mentally, economically and morally. He could find a mental health practitioner, and if he cannot afford one then he could ask friends, his boss, his family including perhaps even his wife to help him with the cost, for I am sure they would all be ecstatic to know that he was willing to take such measures towards change and recovery. The opportunity exists to mend all things. Remember that.

He could decide to start eating twenty percent less at every meal. He may not be able to afford a gym, but walking costs nothing. He could start there. He could call the adult education centre in his community and ask about upgrading his skills or beginning night school or correspondence courses. Are you following me? It is endless and it is not easy, but it is doable, if you're willing to take responsibility. Stop blaming. Stop the excuses. Stop the old bus and get off. Like all of us, Bob is today what he put into play yesterday (consciously or otherwise) and so in order to have a better tomorrow, he needs to make changes now.

When he decides to make a change he will see that he needs a plan. He must begin by tackling his relationship with himself first. He must begin to respect and nurture the relationship he has with his own heart, mind, body and soul. From little changes come big effects. You'll be amazed at how they compound. You do not need to solve it all in one profound motion. The thousand-mile journey really does begin one step at a time.

It's really common sense though, is it not? Life is about small incremental changes every day. It's about undoing the damage you've done, one layer at a time, then improving your life systematically. If you make the conscious effort for little changes every single day, your confidence will begin to flourish and your relationship with yourself and the world around you will improve tremendously.

It's all about knowing when it's time to stop the "justs." That is to say, just thinking about it, just talking about it, just reading about it, perhaps even just complaining about it – start doing whatever "it" may be. It's allowing our sixth sense or our gut feeling to have a say, and not always squashing it because it makes you feel uncomfortable, stressed or frightened. It's a very simple concept, but it's not easy.

What *is* easy however, is to say that you'll start soon, or tomorrow, or perhaps next Monday, or after the holidays, or after you've lost twenty pounds or saved a little more money. Wrong! Its gotta be now! You must stop giving precious energy to excuses and procrastination and give as much as you can to making the changes necessary to turning things around and beginning to live the life YOU DESIRE.

When you take responsibility for your choices and their corresponding results you are given a fresh start, a new life so to speak, a point from which change can emerge, allowing you to let go of what was, accept what is, and embrace what will be. Sadly, for some this may not happen until it is almost too late, and that is a great human tragedy. That's sort of like convicted criminals who after exhausting all appeals for a stay of execution suddenly find God. What have they got to lose?

But where, I ask, was this faith, this BELIEF when they had the choice to live the best life possible? Why wait until you're another year older, or a month, or even a minute? Why wait until you are faced with a crisis situation before making a change?

It is never too late to rise above the pack and take responsibility for the position you may find yourself in. Not tonight or tomorrow or next January, and especially not when you're knocking on heaven's door, but now. Lives are changed, permanently altered, even lost in split seconds. Choices are no different. It truly is like turning one light switch off and another on, or like changing lanes on a highway. You simply need the willingness to do so and you will move forward like never before.

The tales held within the pages of this book are not those of a man who has arrived, but rather of one who continues the journey. It has taken me most of my life so far to reach the point where enlightenment and true self-awareness and understanding are things I DESIRE to pursue. Yet in doing so I have left myself exposed, vulnerable and open to attack, and you will too. This Achilles' heel seems somewhat less perilous when you realize that you are not alone on this journey. I know that this book was not written by a perfect man and I feel it is safe to say that it will never be read by a perfect reader, yet in that beautiful imperfection we are all bonded. Life is not easy, just look around you. When you read about its beginnings and middles and its yesterdays, you discover that it has always been hard, brutally so at times, and we are still not anywhere near bliss or nirvana. Hopefully that future lies ahead for generations to come. We are in the midst of a world changing at speeds beyond our comprehension. What is relevant today is becoming passé and obsolete by tomorrow. Ask any musician or even record company representative over the age of thirty to make sense of the music industry today and they will scratch their heads dumbfounded. Record companies are vanishing before our very eyes at an alarming rate. Websites like YOUTUBE and MYSPACE are driving nails into their coffins with no apologies. We are the generation witnessing the beginnings of changes that will have profound, everlasting effects on our planet and society's future. We all know that global warming is here, most likely to stay, and although I truly believe that each and every one of us must try our utmost to not contribute to its genesis, what is more important is how future generations will prepare to deal with it. Change scares us but I have great faith in our ability to handle these changes even if we must go through severe hardship in doing so.

I did not bring this book to you. You brought this book into your life and only you can decide if it feels true and meaningful to you. For you see, it's all about you. No one is defining what lies ahead for you. Only you are. Your life will be as satisfying as you design it to be. Your future is the future you have chosen to give yourself. When you are receptive to all of the abundance in this universe, and you identify what it is you DESIRE, when you believe you can have it and intend to bring it to yourself, when you act on it with PASSION, you truly can live a remarkable life. Use the simple *ACTION SANDWICH* to remind you to bring yourself happiness and joy. In this state of being alive, INTENTION thrives and you will manifest all that your heart desires.

# IMAGINE ALL THE PEOPLE LIVING FOR TODAY

So what are you going to do? Do you DESIRE the best possible life you can have? Are you important enough to obtain all that you want? To live the best life you can takes courage and stamina. You have to speak out, stand up, hold on, be strong, chase after, fall down and get back up again because that, my friend, is life. That is real. That is living.

In the movie *Braveheart*, William Wallace tells his love, "Every man dies, but not every man truly lives."
I offer this slight alteration to that beautiful line:
"Everyone exists but not everyone truly lives." For I fear that it is a far greater crime to just merely exist than it ever is to die. Don't just exist. Don't live a life that just happens to you. Make it happen. You have to DO, to get DONE!

Get up and do it! Make that sandwich. Smother it in PASSION. Live and enjoy the very best life you can.

Thank you, dear reader. Peace.

For Gary,

Alan


THE END

# EPILOGUE

Her name was Lettie, Lettie Douglas, "Sweaty" Lettie Douglas, and she was popular, very popular indeed, because without hesitation and for the measly sum of two cigarettes or one bright shiny sixpence, she would let boys look down her blouse for a whole thirty seconds, undisturbed, in a ritual that took place behind Mrs. McDougall's shed with great regularity. For you see, Lettie was a chain smoker. The Seven Wonders of the World may have belonged to the ancients but numbers eight and nine belonged to Lettie!

The problem I had every time this sacred communion would come around was simple. First of all, I was only seven and didn't smoke, and second, I never had a sixpence. And if I did, it would surely have gone into something that found its way into my stomach. But I sure wanted to see those wondrous hidden treasures that seemed to be worth so much to so few, for so many... pennies that is, six of them to be exact.

I would get in line behind the older boys in hopes that she would take pity on a boy whose hem on his trousers was taller than he was, and whose shirt originally belonged to her brother but alas, pity wasn't in Lettie's bag of tricks. I tried giving her a penny wrapped in silver paper once. It was a little trick I learned from my old granddad, who passed the occasional penny-wrapped shilling off at the local off-track betting shops as his wager. But he had my dad as an accomplice, for he worked in the shop and was the one who took the bet from him!

Lettie didn't fall for that and I only succeeded in getting a cuff 'round the ear from her and sent once more to the back of the line, though she kept my penny of course.

What does a boy have to do to witness such wonders, I thought to myself. What can I come up with?

Then the lights went off!

"Simmit" is an old colloquial term in Scotland used to describe a singlet or man's undershirt, while "drawers," on the other hand, as I am sure most of you know, is a word referring to boxers, briefs or underpants. I tell you this because these undergarments became the mainstay of my father's epithets in lieu of using really foul swear words at home; he would take the names of his, or perhaps even your, underwear in vain.

"Och! SIMMITS AND DRAWERS! Not again!" he'd yell out. But of course by then it was too late and we'd all be rooted to the spot in the pitch darkness of our home, waiting for him to spark a match and guide us all in, like moths to a street lamp. As mentioned earlier, I was born and grew up in an old post-war pre-fabricated home that had no central air conditioning system for summer or furnace for the winter. Now summer was no problem because Mother Nature looked after that by not giving us a summer. As a matter of fact, the four seasons in Coatbridge to this day remain rain, sleet, heavy rain and of course, "Cold Enough To freeze the 'Niagara Falls' off you!" So summer was taken care of, but winter, well that was like the planet Pluto with four paper-thin walls surrounding it.

Coal was not only scarce at times around our neighbourhood but also expensive, way too expensive to burn indiscriminately, and so on many a winter's night or morning, the little kerosene heater became your best friend, providing of course that you had kerosene. If not, a candle started to look pretty darned friendly. Barring that, the next best place was your bed with your clothes still on. The best however is yet to come, for you see the reason our lights would go off is quite simple. Our electricity, our only source of any and all the power that ran through the veins of our little home, was coin operated! That's correct, in order to have lights and power to any electrical outlets in our home, we had to put coins in a meter. Shilling coins, to be exact, before inflation pushed it up to two shillings! This process of your lights going out and a coin having to be put into the meter occurred approximately every four hours and it was common practice for families to keep jars of the much-needed tokens near the meter. We, however, opted for having a little stack of them on the mantle of our fireplace, and I use the term "stack" loosely, for that stack got raided continuously and on many an occasion provided the necessary loot for a fish supper when it was better to eat in the dark, than not to have eaten at all.

For me to raid the coin stack usually wasn't worth the risk, for they were almost certainly counted, and my arse just couldn't take that chance. But here comes the pièce de résistance, for you see the meter was attached to the wall out in our small hallway, next to our bathroom. But it also had a sort of cupboard built around it. Access to this meter meant that you had to open the door of the cupboard, which was around shoulder height for an average adult. I, on the other hand, needed a chair if I was asked to put a coin in. Now, if a coin happened to fall from one's grasp it did not fall onto the floor but rather down into the bottom half of this cupboard, into the darkness and into a space that was impossible for even the smallest of adults to squeeze into. Retrieving a missing coin was always a last resort and I will tell you, dear reader, exactly why.

If we had no money at all and our lights went out close to bedtime then off to bed we would go, for it was not worth wasting a coin that you couldn't get your complete four hours out of. However, if the lights went off when we needed light, this is usually how it would play out.

(Blink)...(Darkness)
"SIMMITS AND DRAWERS!"
(Spark)...(Moths fly to the light)

"Alan, run to Maggie next door and ask if we can borrow a shilling. If she says no, go across to the McDougall's and ask them. If they say no, come straight back here, okay?"
"Okay, right Dad!"
(Maggie's door)...(McDougall's door)...(our door)

"Dad! No luck."
"Right then", he'd say, "we're goin' in!" (James Bond, eat your heart out.)

We would then head to the cupboard where the meter was.

"Okay, Alan, you know what to do," he would say.
"Yes, Dad."
He would then hand me a match and have me sit on the floor so he could grab me by my ankles and lift me straight up in the air, turning me completely upside down.
"Now remember, don't waste your match. Wait until you're nearly at the bottom before you strike it, got that?"
"Right, Dad!"

And so it was that he would lower me down into the bottom of this hole for wayward coins, chasing away spiders and any mice who might get the wrong idea because I, my friends, had fire!

Have you ever lit a match while hanging upside-down in your father's hands? It's not easy. The flame rises up towards you and when you are in a cramped space like the hole for wayward coins, it's downright next to impossible not to burn your lip or your cheek or even your hair. But then the lights went off right in the middle of the football match, someone had to do it and that someone was wee, I mean, me!

Days passed since I last saw Lettie, but nothing happened to our lights. As a matter of fact, the meter inspector had been around to empty it and as always the family was given a little rebate of around five pounds. So for a few days after the big payday we were like millionaires, having chops or stew or something equivalent for dinner, instead of soup and bread. We were living the high life but I needed a disaster to strike soon or I might miss my chance forever, for Lettie might come into full bloom and get married, or worse yet, give up smoking.

"C'mon ACTION SANDWICH! This boy is receptive to, desirous of, believing in and fully intended on seeing those wonders of the world and God knows he is ready to take all the ACTION needed"...and then, it happened.

The stack had vanished. My mother as per usual was at her mother's. My dad and I were watching the big match on our wee black and white television. It was a fantastic game, 2-2 with fifteen minutes to go when–Blink!

"SIMMITS AND DRAWERS." And we had no coins.

# THE GOLDEN GLOBES

Waiting my turn at the end of the line, behind Mrs. McDougall's shed seemed to be taking unusually long.
"Were there more lads here than usual?" I wondered. "Nah, perhaps I am just extra-impatient today."
Eventually I stood before the buxom Lettie who was already looking at me distainfully, expecting my usual pleading to give me a flash without paying.

"So what do you want?" sneered Lettie.
"I want to look," I replied.
"Where's your sixpence?" she bellowed.
Much to her amazement, I held up not a sixpence but rather a bright, glistening brand-new 1963 shilling.
She paused for a moment, obviously quite taken by the fact that indeed I had a coin for her.
"Ok, come here then," she ordered.

She bent over as I raised myself up onto my tippy-toes for my first glimpse of any womanhood that didn't include my mother or my sister, the most exciting thirty seconds of my young life. If you can believe it, she actually counted your seconds down out loud. "Thirty! Twenty-nine! Twenty-eight! Twenty-seven..."

The British monetary system prior to the Decimal system coming into effect in 1971 was nothing short of a "wack job."
6 pennies = sixpence
12 pennies = one shilling
20 shillings = one pound
240 pennies = one pound. Absolutely no rhyme or reason to any of it.

But wait! Look again. A sixpence contains six pennies but a shilling has twelve or in other words, two sixpences.

"Oh, what bliss. Hallelujah! Sweet 'simmits and drawers', that means that whatever you can buy for one sixpence, you can buy two of for a shilling!"

"Three! Two! One! Okay that's it, you've had your money's worth," said Lettie, pushing me back as she readjusted herself to fit those rolling hills back from whence they came.

"Right then," she said, as tough as any boy, for those perks of voluptuousness certainly belied any hint of femininity, "your money, now!"

As she held out her open palm I placed the coin in the centre of her hand. We both stared at it for what seemed like eternity before she took a coin, half its size, and placed it aside my shilling. This was my change, my half-shilling, my sixpence. We continued staring for a moment when suddenly she broke the silence.

"What's your problem? Take your change, why don't you?"

For a brief moment thoughts of my sixpence had donuts, with soft powdery icing sugar dancing in my head, accompanied by a big box of Smarties, washed down by a gallon of cream soda. A boy could do much with sixpence in 1963. Suddenly her gulder awakened me from my candy-coated daydream. "Hey...what do you want then?"

With both my hands I reached out to her opened palm, and began to turn it into a fist, wrapping it around my sixpence and what was now her shilling. I felt a little smirk form in the corner of my toothless mouth.

"What are you doing," she asked. "What about your sixpence?"

"Keep it," I replied.

"Keep it, but why?" she quizzed me.

"Because whatever you can buy for one sixpence, you can buy two of for a shilling! I'm goin' in again!"

# FLUOROQUINOLONES IN THE TREATMENT OF INFECTIOUS DISEASES

# FLUOROQUINOLONES IN THE TREATMENT OF INFECTIOUS DISEASES

Editors

**W. Eugene Sanders, Jr., M.D.**
Professor and Chairman
Department of Medical Microbiology
Professor of Medicine
Creighton University School of Medicine

**Christine C. Sanders, Ph.D.**
Professor of Medical Microbiology
Creighton University School of Medicine

**PHYSICIANS & SCIENTISTS PUBLISHING CO., INC.**
Glenview, Illinois

Some of the information contained in this book may cite the use of a particular agent in a dosage, for an indication, or in a manner other than recommended. Therefore, the manufacturers' package inserts should be consulted for complete prescribing information.

Library of Congress Catalog Card Number: 90-60838
International Standard Book Number: 0-9244-2802-3

Physicians & Scientists Publishing Co.
P.O. Box 435, Glenview, Illinois 60025

Acknowledgement: Development of this book was made possible by an educational grant from Miles Pharmaceuticals, Inc., West Haven, CT 06516.

**Printed in the United States of America**

# CONTRIBUTORS

**Jørn Aagaard, M.D.**
Research Fellow in Urology
VA Medical Center
University of Wisconsin School of Medicine
Madison, Wisconsin 53792

**Jeffrey L. Blumer, M.D., Ph.D.**
Professor of Pediatrics
Division of Pediatric Pharmacology/Critical Care
University of Virginia Health Sciences Center
Charlottesville, Virginia 22908

**Larry H. Danziger, Pharm.D.**
Assistant Professor
Department of Pharmacy Practice
College of Pharmacy
University of Illinois at Chicago
Chicago, Illinois 60612

**Lawrence J. Eron, M.D.**
Department of Medicine
Division of Infectious Diseases
Fairfax Hospital
Falls Church, Virginia 22046

**Dale N. Gerding, M.D.**
Professor of Medicine
University of Minnesota School of Medicine
Chief, Infectious Disease Section
Veterans Administration Medical Center
Minneapolis, Minnesota 55417

**Larry J. Goodman, M.D.**
Associate Professor of Medicine
Section of Infectious Disease
Rush-Presbyterian-St. Luke's Medical Center
Chicago, Illinois 60612

**Faroque A. Khan, M.B.**
Chairman, Department of Medicine
Nassau County Medical Center
East Meadow, New York 11554

**Bruce E. Kreter, Pharm.D.**
Assistant Professor
Department of Pharmacy Practice
Temple University School of Pharmacy
Philadelphia, Pennsylvania

**Bennett Lorber, M.D.**
Durant Professor of Medicine
Chief, Section of Infectious Diseases
Temple University School of Medicine
Philadelphia, Pennsylvania 19140

**Jon T. Mader, M.D.**
Associate Professor of Medicine
Division of Infectious Diseases
The University of Texas Medical Branch at Galveston
Galveston, Texas 77550

**Paul O. Madsen, M.D.**
Chief, Urology Section
VA Medical Center
Professor of Urology
University of Wisconsin
Madison, Wisconsin 53792

**Knud T. Nielsen, M.D.**
Research Fellow in Urology
VA Medical Center
University of Wisconsin School of Medicine
Madison, Wisconsin 53792

**David E. Nix, Pharm.D.**
Assistant Director
The Clinical Pharmacokinetics Laboratory
Millard Fillmore Hospital
Buffalo, New York 14209

## Joseph A. Paladino, Pharm.D.

Director, The Clinical Pharmacokinetics Laboratory
Millard Fillmore Suburban Hospital
Williamsville, New York 14221

## Peter G. Pappas, M.D.

Assistant Professor
Department of Medicine/Division of Infectious Diseases
The University of Alabama at Birmingham
UAB Station
Birmingham, Alabama 35294

## Lance R. Peterson, M.D.

Professor of Laboratory Medicine and Pathology
University of Minnesota School of Medicine
Chief, Clinical Microbiology Section
Veterans Administration Medical Center
Minneapolis, Minnesota 55417

## Donna Przepiorka, M.D., Ph.D.

Associate Member
Pittsburgh Cancer Institute
Assistant Professor of Medicine
Department of Hematology/Oncology
University of Pittsburgh School of Medicine
Pittsburgh, Pennsylvania 15213

## Michael D. Reed, Pharm.D.

Associate Professor of Pediatrics
Division of Pediatric Pharmacology/Critical Care
University of Virginia Health Sciences Center
Charlottesville, Virginia 22908

## Keith A. Rodvold, Pharm.D.

Associate Professor
Department of Pharmacy Practice
College of Pharmacy
University of Illinois at Chicago
Chicago, Illinois 60612

## Kenneth V. I. Rolston, M.D.

Associate Professor of Medicine
Section of Infectious Diseases
The University of Texas System Cancer Center
M.D. Anderson Hospital and Tumor Institute
Houston, Texas 77030

## Christine C. Sanders, Ph.D.

Professor of Medical Microbiology
Department of Medical Microbiology
Creighton University School of Medicine
Omaha, Nebraska 68178

## W. Eugene Sanders, Jr., M.D.

Professor and Chairman
Department of Medical Microbiology
Professor of Medicine
Creighton University School of Medicine
Omaha, Nebraska 68178

## Jerome J. Schentag, Pharm.D.

Director, The Clinical Pharmacokinetics Laboratory
Millard Fillmore Hospital
Buffalo, New York 14209

## John Segreti, M.D.

Assistant Professor of Medicine
Section of Infectious Disease
Rush-Presbyterian-St. Luke's Medical Center
Chicago, Illinois 60612

## Thomas A. Stellato, M.D.

Associate Professor of Surgery
Case Western Reserve University
School of Medicine
Cleveland, Ohio 44106

## Gordon M. Trenholme, M.D.

Professor of Medicine and Pharmacology
Section of Infectious Disease
Rush-Presbyterian-St. Luke's Medical Center
Chicago, Illinois 60612

# PREFACE

The fluoroquinolones have been available for clinical use in the United States for only a few years. However, there are already thousands of original manuscripts, dozens of extensive review articles, and several multi-authored books in print. Given the relative newness of these agents and the extensive literature, one might reasonably inquire "What is the need for another book on the fluoroquinolones?" Answers may be found in the target audience for this publication and the extremely rapid pace of change in the field.

Our intent has been to provide an overview of the fluoroquinolones for individuals who are at the forefront of patient care: primary care physicians, specialists, pharmacists, clinical microbiologists, and other members of the health care team. In order to make this a quick reference source, liberal use has been made of subheadings, figures, and tables, along with a comprehensive index. Individual authors have attempted to distill clinically important material in the text while providing extensive references that will permit the reader to return to the original source for greater detail as desired. In designing the book, individual authors were selected because of their continuing "hands-on" experience in the laboratory and at the bedside or in the clinic. Many of the authors have contributed to the original literature on available fluoroquinolones and are presently involved in investigations of even newer congeners.

Each month dozens of new publications concerning fluoroquinolones appear in the world's literature. Reports confirm and extend our knowledge of available quinolones and describe the development and testing of new agents. The number of potential new uses for ciprofloxacin and norfloxacin continues to increase almost monthly. Possible future indications for these drugs are suggested throughout the book and are summarized in the concluding chapter. The legions of new quinolones marching our way are mentioned where appropriate. Agents with enhanced in vitro activity against gram-positive bacteria, chlamydia, or obligate anaerobes appear worthy of further study for several indications. The field is advancing extremely rapidly. We hope this publication will be a timely and useful vehicle to update broad segments of the medical community.

Following introductions to the microbiology and pharmacology of the new fluoroquinolones, chapters are devoted to uses in infections grouped first by organ systems and then by more specific clinical settings. The book concludes with discussions of adverse reactions, the profound pharmacoeconomic implications of these agents, and glimpses of the future in therapy. Individual authors have been remarkably consistent in their conclusions. The fluoroquinolones are believed to represent an important breakthrough in antimicrobial chemotherapy. The bactericidal activity resulting from their unique mechanism of action has translated into clinical efficacy against a broad array of organisms. The ability of many of these agents to penetrate into inflammatory cells and relatively inaccessible tissues has markedly facilitated the treatment of often recalcitrant infections. Efficacy against intracellular parasites such as the typhoid bacillus, or in prostatitis, is a direct result of the intrinsic activity and excellent pharmacokinetic properties of the fluoroquinolones. Compared with other classes of antimicrobial agents, the fluoroquinolones are as safe or safer. The oral fluoroquinolones have proven to be safe and effective alternatives in many infections that heretofore demanded parenteral therapy exclusively. The ability to substitute oral for parenteral therapy in certain clinical settings has resulted in dramatic reductions in expense. Clearly, the fluoroquinolones represent a major advance. However, as with all agents, the development of resistance is possible. In order to maximally prolong the useful "life" of these agents, they must be used judiciously. We hope this book will be one of the means to that end.

We gratefully acknowledge the assistance of two individuals: Brian G. Green, Editor-in-Chief of Physicians & Scientists Publishing Co., for his wisdom and infinite patience, and Carole Sears, for her secretarial skills and equal patience. Finally, we wish to dedicate this work to our mothers, Lois Brightman and Gertrude Sanders, whose love and inspiration are eternal.

**W. Eugene Sanders, Jr.**

**Christine C. Sanders**

# TABLE OF CONTENTS

# MICROBIOLOGY OF FLUOROQUINOLONES

# 1

*Christine C. Sanders*

## INTRODUCTION

Ciprofloxacin is a new 6-fluoro, 7-piperazino, 4-quinolone that is a highly potent, broad-spectrum, bactericidal agent. As a fluoroquinolone, it shares many features with other members of this group; however, it possesses many distinct properties as well. This chapter presents an overview of ciprofloxacin and chemically related compounds and will include discussions of mechanism(s) of action, structure-activity relationships, mechanisms of resistance, and antimicrobial spectrum and potency.

## MECHANISM OF ACTION

The mechanism of action of ciprofloxacin and related compounds has not been completely elucidated. However, it is clear that ciprofloxacin and other quinolones inhibit various activities of DNA gyrase, an enzyme essential for DNA synthesis.[1-6] DNA gyrase, also referred to as topoisomerase II, is capable of relaxing or introducing negative supercoils into DNA.[7-10] The enzyme is composed of two A subunits (MW=105,000) and two B subunits (MW=95,000).[9,10] The A subunit, encoded by *gyr*A (*nal*A), is associated with the introduction and rejoining of double-stranded nicks in DNA.[5,8-10] The B subunit, encoded by *gyr* B (*nal* C) is associated with ATP hydrolysis required for the supercoiling activity of DNA gyrase.[5,8-10] The A subunit of DNA gyrase is the direct target of the quinolones, while the B subunit is the target of novobiocin and the coumermycins.[5,8-10]

The quinolones do not appear to bind directly to the A subunit of DNA gyrase.[11] Rather, they appear to bind to DNA. In quinolone-treated cells a drug-gyrase-DNA complex is quickly formed, and an immediate reduction in DNA synthesis follows.[2,5] For gram-negative bacteria, inhibition of DNA gyrase activity is associated with in vitro antibacterial potency.[4,5,8] As shown in Table 1, ciprofloxacin is the most potent inhibitor of DNA gyrase from *Escherichia coli* and *Citrobacter freundii* and the most active drug against these organisms.[4,5,12,13] The association between antigyrase activity and antibacterial potency against gram-positive bacteria is not as great (Table 1).[14-16] When measured in tests with A subunits from *gyr*A mutants, the antigyrase effect of the quinolones was significantly diminished (Table 2).[6,8,13] However, MICs remained in the clinically achievable range for some agents. Thus, the close but not absolute association between antigyrase activity and antibacterial potency suggests that the quinolones may have additional as yet unrecognized targets in the cell. This possibility is greatest for some of the newer fluoroquinolones such as ciprofloxacin.

The precise mechanism responsible for the lethal effect of the quinolones is unknown. They are generally bactericidal for gram-negative bacteria regardless of the phase of growth.[17-20] This phase-independent effect is not seen with gram-positive bacteria, and it is more pronounced for ciprofloxacin and ofloxacin than other quinolones in tests with gram-negative organisms.[17-20] The quinolones also exhibit a post-antibiotic effect (defined as the amount of time required for bacterial growth to resume following removal of the antibiotic from the medium) for both gram-positive and gram-negative bacteria.[21-23] The bactericidal effects of the quinolones are diminished by inhibitors of protein or RNA synthesis as well as by excessive quinolone levels above the maximal bactericidal concentration.[1,18,24,25] However, the bactericidal effect of ciprofloxacin and ofloxacin is not completely abolished by these conditions.[1,18] The reversible bactericidal component may be produced by all quinolones while the irreversible component, to date seen only with ciprofloxacin and ofloxacin, may represent a second lethal effect.[1,25] The reversible component may be related to the ability of quinolones to induce synthesis of various components of the SOS-response, which is an important DNA repair mechanism in the bacterial cell.[2,10,26-31]

Inhibition of DNA synthesis by the quinolones leads to induction of the SOS-response possibly via a signal conveyed by single-stranded DNA tracts in the vicinity of the drug-gyrase-DNA complex.[2] This leads to cessation of cell division and an accumulation of several proteins associated with the SOS-response. One such protein, SfiA, inhibits cell division and could be responsible for the filamentation observed following quinolone administration.[2,10,31] Since continued induction of the SOS-response via any mechanism is lethal to the cell, and such induction would be prevented by inhibitors of protein or RNA synthesis, this may be the major factor responsible for the lethal effect of the quinolones. This possibility is further supported by reports that show: (a) SOS-induction is greatest at quinolone levels near the maximal bactericidal concentration;[30] (b) in vitro potency correlates well with SOS-induction potential;[31] (c) *gyr*A mutants show no induction of the SOS-response[2] and reportedly are resistant to the lethal effects of the newer quinolones;[32] and (d) mutations in one or more genes involved in the SOS-response produce altered susceptibility to the quinolones.[10,33] Thus, induction of the SOS-response may be very important in determining the lethal effect of the quinolones.

**Table 1.** Association between antigyrase activity* and antibacterial potency[†] for the quinolones

| Organism | Quinolone | Antigyrase Activity | Antibacterial Potency | Ref. |
|---|---|---|---|---|
| *Escherichia coli* KL-16 | | | | |
| | Ciprofloxacin | 0.78 | 0.013 | 14 |
| | Norfloxacin | 1.15 | 0.05 | |
| | Ofloxacin (±)[‡] | 0.98 | 0.05 | |
| | Ofloxacin (−) | 0.78 | 0.025 | |
| | Ofloxacin (+) | 7.24 | 1.56 | |
| *Escherichia coli* K12 | | | | |
| | Ciprofloxacin | 1.3 | 0.05 | 5 |
| | Norfloxacin | 3.3 | 0.1 | |
| | Pefloxacin | 4.5 | 0.2 | |
| | Ofloxacin | 6.3 | 0.15 | |
| | Nalidixic Acid | 64 | 4 | |
| *Escherichia coli* KL-16 | | | | |
| | Ciprofloxacin | 1.0 | ≤0.006 | 13 |
| | Norfloxacin | 2.4 | 0.05 | |
| | Ofloxacin | 3.1 | 0.05 | |
| | Enoxacin | 11.2 | 0.1 | |
| | Nalidixic Acid | >400 | 6.25 | |
| *Escherichia coli* KL-16 | | | | |
| | Ciprofloxacin | 0.25 | 0.02 | 6 |
| | Norfloxacin | 0.5 | 0.08 | |
| | Ofloxacin | 0.5 | 0.08 | |
| | Nalidixic Acid | 10-25 | 4 | |
| *Citrobacter freundii* IID976 | | | | |
| | Ciprofloxacin | 0.29 | 0.006 | 8 |
| | Norfloxacin | 0.50 | 0.05 | |
| | Ofloxacin | 0.52 | 0.05 | |
| | Fleroxacin | 0.55 | 0.05 | |
| | Nalidixic Acid | 14.2 | 3.13 | |
| *Micrococcus luteus* ATCC4698 | | | | |
| | CI-934 | 100 | 1 | 15 |
| | Ciprofloxacin | 200 | 1 | |
| | Ofloxacin | 800 | 2 | |
| | Fleroxacin | >800 | 8 | |
| | Norfloxacin | >800 | 8 | |
| | Pefloxacin | >800 | 16 | |
| | Enoxacin | >800 | 25 | |
| | Amifloxacin | >800 | 32 | |
| | Nalidixic Acid | >800 | 200 | |

***continued***

3

## Table 1. *Continued*

| Organism | Quinolone | Antigyrase Activity | Antibacterial Potency | Ref. |
|---|---|---|---|---|
| *Micrococcus luteus* ATCC4698 | Norfloxacin | 39 | 0.8 | 16 |
| | Ciprofloxacin | 78 | 0.8 | |
| | Ofloxacin | 156 | 2.0 | |
| | Amifloxacin | 312 | 128 | |
| | Nalidixic Acid | 625 | 256 | |

\* Expressed as 50% inhibitory concentration for DNA gyrase in μg/mL.
† Expressed as minimal inhibitory concentration in μg/mL.
‡ Indicates isomeric form.

## Table 2. Antigyrase activity of quinolones against *gyr*A mutant

| Organism | Quinolone | Antigyrase Activity in μg/mL | | MIC in mg/mL | | Ref. |
|---|---|---|---|---|---|---|
| | | Wildtype | gyrA | Wildtype | gyrA | |
| *Citrobacter freundii* IID976 | Ciprofloxacin | 0.29 | 5.2 | 0.006 | 0.10 | 8 |
| | Norfloxacin | 0.50 | 20.1 | 0.05 | 0.78 | |
| | Ofloxacin | 0.52 | 16.9 | 0.05 | 0.78 | |
| | Fleroxacin | 0.55 | 21.2 | 0.05 | 0.78 | |
| | Nalidixic Acid | 14.2 | >800 | 3.13 | >1,600 | |
| *Escherichia coli* NT525 | Ciprofloxacin | 0.1-0.25 | 5.0 | 0.005 | 0.08 | 6 |
| | Norfloxacin | 0.5 | >5.0 | 0.02 | 0.16 | |
| | Ofloxacin | 0.5 | >5.0 | 0.04 | 0.32 | |
| | Nalidixic Acid | 50 | >500 | 4 | 128 | |
| *Escherichia coli* KL-16/GN14181* | Ciprofloxacin | 1.0 | >800 | ≤0.006 | 25 | 13 |
| | Norfloxacin | 2.4 | >800 | 0.05 | 100 | |
| | Ofloxacin | 3.1 | >800 | 0.05 | 100 | |
| | Enoxacin | 11.2 | >800 | 0.1 | 100 | |
| | Nalidixic Acid | >400 | >800 | 6.25 | >400 | |

\* Wildtype and *gyr*A not isogenic.

The ability of ciprofloxacin and related compounds to cure plasmids from Enterobacteriaceae may represent an indirect effect of the drugs.[2,34-36] Plasmid curing appears to be more dependent upon the plasmid involved rather than on the quinolone or the concentration tested. It is likely that plasmid elimination results from the diminished expression of chromosomal genes necessary for plasmid maintenance.[2] Thus, the more reliant the plasmid is on chromosomal genes for its maintenance, the more likely it is to be lost under the DNA inhibitory effects of the quinolones.

## STRUCTURE/ACTIVITY RELATIONSHIPS

Quinolone inhibitors of the A subunit of DNA gyrase fall into two major chemical groups: the quinolines and the 1,8 naphthyridines (Table 3). The major difference between these two groups is the presence of a carbon at position 8 in the former and a nitrogen in the latter. Extensive studies have been performed on the structure/activity relationships of these compounds using for the most part antigyrase activity and/or antibacterial potency as indicators.[4,6,8,12,14,37,38] Antigyrase activity is generally considered to be a measure of target enzyme inhibition while antibacterial potency reflects cell penetration as well as target enzyme inhibition. Hence, certain compounds have good antigyrase activity but poor antibacterial activity.[4] These are considered to be poor permeants.

From the various structure/activity studies performed to date, a number of factors have been identified as important determinants of activity. The minimum structure required for activity is a 4-oxo-3 carboxylic acid array on a ring structure with nitrogen at position 1.[32] The potency of an agent can be improved and its antibacterial spectrum broadened by substituting fluorine on C-6 of this basic structure.[4,32,37] Increasing the number of fluorine atoms around the molecule is also associated with enhanced activity, especially against gram-positive bacteria.[4,32,37] At C-7, a piperazine ring is associated with enhanced potency, although many other substituents impart good activity to the molecule.[4,32,37] In a recent study utilizing computer automated structure evaluation, Klopman et al[37] proposed that cell permeation is controlled by the nature of the C-7 substituent, since for gram-negative bacteria, a piperazine or N-substituted piperazine increased activity.

The N-1 substituent has various effects. For those quinolones with a tricyclic configuration (N-1 to C-8) and a methyl group at C-3 (eg, ofloxacin, S-25930, S-25932, Table 3), two isomeric configurations are possible. Studies by a number of investigators have shown that the S(–) isomer has significantly greater antigyrase activity and antibacterial potency than the R(+) isomer.[6,12,14,32,38] Other alterations at N-1 have minimal effects on activity.

Using all of the elements shown to maximize the potency and antibacterial spectrum of the quinolones, Klopman et al[37] have recently predicted the structure of a hypothetical quinolone that should have maximal effects. This molecule incorporates

Table 3. Structure/activity relationships for the quinolines* and 1,8 naphthyridines[†]

| Compound | R1 | R6 | R7 | X | R8 | Antimicrobial Potency (MIC$_{50}$ in µg/ml)[‡] | | | |
|---|---|---|---|---|---|---|---|---|---|
| | | | | | | E. coli | P. aeruginosa | S. aureus | B. fragilis |
| Nalidixic Acid | C$_2$H$_5$ | H | CH$_3$ | N | | 2 - 4 | 64->128 | 16 - 128 | 64 - >128 |
| Enoxacin (AT-2266, CI-919) | C$_2$H$_5$ | F | (piperazinyl) | N | | 0.06 - 0.25 | 0.25 - 2.0 | 0.5 - 2 | 12.5 - 32 |
| T-3262 (A-61827, A-60969) | (difluorophenyl cyclopropyl) | F | (aminopyrrolidinyl) | N | H | 0.01 - 0.03 | 0.2 - 0.25 | 0.01 - 0.06 | 0.78 - 1 |
| Ciprofloxacin (Bay-o-9867) | (cyclopropyl) | F | (piperazinyl) | C | H | 0.008-0.06 | 0.06 - 0.25 | 0.12 - 0.5 | 4 - 8 |
| Norfloxacin (AM-715, MK-0366) | C$_2$H$_5$ | F | (piperazinyl) | C | H | 0.03 - 0.25 | 0.25 - 1.6 | 0.25 - 2 | 6.3 -100 |
| A-56620 | (fluorophenyl) | F | (piperazinyl) | C | H | 0.03 - 0.06 | 0.25 - 1.0 | 0.25 - 0.5 | 4 |
| Pefloxacin (1589RB) | C$_2$H$_5$ | F | (methylpiperazinyl) | C | H | 0.06 - 0.25 | 1.0 - 2.0 | 0.12 - 0.5 | 8 - 16 |
| Amifloxacin (WIN 49,375) | HNCH$_3$ | F | (methylpiperazinyl) | C | H | 0.02 - 0.5 | 1.0 - 4.0 | 0.78 - 2.0 | 16 |
| Lomefloxacin (NY-198, SC-47111) | C$_2$H$_5$ | F | (methylpiperazinyl) | C | F | 0.03 - 0.2 | 1.0 - 3.13 | 0.78 - 1.56 | 8 - 16 |
| Difloxacin (A-56619) | (fluorophenyl) | F | (methylpiperazinyl) | C | H | 0.06 - 0.25 | 2.0 - 4.0 | 0.12 - 0.25 | 2 - 4 |

| Compound | R$_1$ | R$_6$ | 7-substituent | X | R$_8$ | | | | |
|---|---|---|---|---|---|---|---|---|---|
| Fleroxacin (AM-833, Ro 23-6240) | CH$_2$CH$_2$F | F | [4-methylpiperazinyl, H$_3$C–N ring] | C | F | 0.05 - 0.12 | 0.5 - 4.0 | 0.25 -1.0 | 2 - 8 |
| Temafloxacin (A-62254) | [2,4-difluorophenyl] | F | [3-methylpiperazinyl, N–CH$_3$ ring] | C | H | 0.06 - 0.12 | 1.0 - 2.0 | 0.12 - 0.5 | 1 - 2 |
| E-3846 | [cyclopropyl] | F | | | H | 0.12 | 2.0 | 0.03 | |
| Irloxacin (E-3432) | CH$_2$CH$_5$ | F | [piperazinyl ring] | C | H | 0.5 | 4.0 | 0.06 | |
| E-3604 | CH$_2$CH$_2$F | F | [piperazinyl ring] | C | H | 0.25 | 4.0 | 0.03 | |
| Cl-934 | CH$_2$CH$_2$F | F | [3-(aminomethyl)pyrrolidinyl, H$_2$N ring] | C | F | 0.12 - 0.25 | 2.0 - 12.5 | 0.03 - 0.5 | 4 - 6.3 |
| Ofloxacin (DL-8280) | C$_3$H$_6$O (cyclic from N$_1$ to X) | F | [4-methylpiperazinyl, H$_3$C–N ring] | C | | 0.02 - 0.25 | 0.5 - 1.56 | 0.12 - 2.0 | 0.78 - 4 |
| S-25930 | C$_4$H$_8$ (cyclic from N$_1$ to X) | F | CH$_3$ | C | | 0.12 - 0.25 | 4.0 | 0.12 | 2 - 16 |
| S-25932 | C$_4$H$_8$ (cyclic from N$_1$ to X) | F | [imidazolyl ring] | C | | 0.12 - 0.25 | 4.0 - 8.0 | 0.25 | 1 - 16 |

\* x = C    † x = N    ‡ See text for references. Range of reported values shown.

a thiazolidine ring at C-7 with fluorines at C-6 and C-8 and an ethyl substituent at N-1. The validity of this prediction awaits synthesis and testing of the compound.

## RESISTANCE

Shortly after the introduction of nalidixic acid, the first of the clinically useful quinolones, the emergence of resistance during therapy of urinary tract infections was noted.[39] Thus, during the development of the new fluoroquinolones, the subject of resistance has been scrutinized intensely. Numerous studies on the occurrence of and mechanisms responsible for resistance to the fluoroquinolones have been conducted both in vitro and in vivo and in clinical trials.

Single-step mutations resulting in diminished susceptibility to the new fluoro-quinolones do not occur as frequently as with nalidixic acid.[1,17,40-52] Other than *Staphylococcus aureus* and *Pseudomonas aeruginosa,* such mutants rarely display resistance to the more potent of the new fluoroquinolones, such as ciprofloxacin, at concentrations above 1 µg/mL (Table 4).[42,46,53] Selection of mutants with higher levels of resistance usually requires multiple serial passages on quinolone-containing media (Table 5).[24,44,46-54] However, regardless of whether single- or multiple-step mutants are examined, the relative in vitro potency of the new fluoroquinolones generally stays the same as that observed with wild-type strains. This can best be illustrated by comparing the MICs of ciprofloxacin to those of other quinolones in tests against quinolone-resistant mutants (Table 6).[41,44,46,51] All mutants selected by one of the newer fluoroquinolones show some degree of cross-resistance with other quinolones. However, some have been selected that show cross-resistance to β-lactam antibiotics, aminoglycosides, chloramphenicol, tetracycline, and/or trimethoprim.[40-42,44,51,55-58] A few quinolone-resistant mutants that are hypersusceptible to β-lactam antibiotics and aminoglycosides have also been described.[6,57,58] Thus, it is apparent that multiple mechanisms are responsible for quinolone resistance.

The mechanisms responsible for altered susceptibility to the newer quinolones have been studied extensively.[1,6,44,55] All described to date have involved mutations in chromosomal genes, many of which have been mapped in *Escherichia coli* and *Ps. aeruginosa* (Table 7).[6,40,41,56,57,59-62] Two general categories of mechanisms have been described: those that involve DNA gyrase and those that do not. Mutations involving the A subunit of DNA gyrase usually produce high level resistance to nalidixic acid and a lower level of resistance to the fluoroquinolones (Table 2). However, a clinical isolate of *Escherichia coli* recovered from a patient with a urinary tract infection was found to be a *gyr*A mutant and highly resistant to the new fluoroquinolones (Table 2).[13] Thus, various mutations within *gyr*A may lead to different levels of resistance. Mutations in the B subunit of DNA gyrase produce variable effects.[59,60] Mutation in one location within *gyr*B (*nal*C) produces hypersusceptibility to the fluoroquinolones but reduced susceptibility to nalidixic acid. A second mutation in *gyr*B (*nal*D) appears

Table 4. Resistance to quinolones among single-step mutants

| Organism | Quinolone* | MIC in µg/mL | | Fold Increase | Ref. |
|---|---|---|---|---|---|
| | | Wildtype | Mutant | | |
| *Escherichia coli* | | | | | |
| | Nalidixic Acid | 4 | 128 | 32 | 42 |
| | Nalidixic Acid | 2 | 128 | 64 | 46 |
| | Ciprofloxacin | ≤0.03 | 0.25 | 8 | |
| | A-56620 | 0.03 | 0.5 | 16 | |
| | Nalidixic Acid | 1 | 32 | 32 | 53 |
| | Norfloxacin | 0.06 | 8 | 64 | |
| *Klebsiella pneumoniae* | | | | | |
| | Nalidixic Acid | 4 | 128 | 32 | 42 |
| | Norfloxacin | 0.06 | 4 | 64 | |
| | Ciprofloxacin | 0.03 | 0.25 | 8 | |
| | Nalidixic Acid | 1 | 64 | 64 | 53 |
| | Norfloxacin | 0.06 | 32 | 312 | |
| *Serratia marcescens* | | | | | |
| | Nalidixic Acid | 16 | 64 | 4 | 42 |
| | Norfloxacin | 0.5 | 4 | 8 | |
| | Ciprofloxacin | 0.25 | 1 | 4 | |
| *Pseudomonas aeruginosa* | | | | | |
| | Norfloxacin | 0.5 | 4 | 8 | 42 |
| | Ciprofloxacin | 0.12 | 2 | 16 | |
| | Norfloxacin | 0.06 | 8-16 | 128-256 | 46 |
| | Ciprofloxacin | 0.12 | 4 | 32 | |
| | Difloxacin | 1 | 16-64 | 16-64 | |
| | A-56620 | 0.5 | 8 | 16 | |

* Quinolone used to select mutant. MIC is for same quinolone.

to increase resistance to all quinolones. Each of these mutations within *gyr*B involves a single nucleotide change, which in turn produces a lysine to arginine or aspartic acid to glutamic acid transition.[59,60]

Mutations unrelated to DNA gyrase also produce resistance to the quinolones. Many of these appear to involve permeation of the quinolones into the gram-negative cell (Table 7).[6,40-42,56-58] The quinolones penetrate into the gram-negative cell by pas-

Table 5. Selection of quinolone-resistant mutants by serial passage in drug-containing media

| Organism | Quinolone* | MIC in µg/mL Wildtype | Mutant | No. of Transfers | Ref. |
|----------|-----------|---------|--------|------------------|------|
| *Escherichia coli* | | | | | |
| | Ciprofloxacin | 0.06 | 8 | 14 | 44 |
| | Norfloxacin | 0.06 | 16 | 14 | |
| | Ofloxacin | 0.12 | 8 | 14 | |
| | Enoxacin | 0.25 | 16 | 14 | |
| | Ciprofloxacin | ≤0.008 | 0.03 | 10 | 46 |
| | A-56620 | 0.015 | 0.12 | 10 | |
| | Norfloxacin | 0.03 | 0.06 | 10 | |
| | Difloxacin | 0.12 | 2 | 10 | |
| | Nalidixic Acid | 4 | 64 | | |
| | T-3262 | 0.03 | 0.25 | 14 | 50 |
| | Temafloxacin | 0.06 | 4 | 14 | 51 |
| | Lomefloxacin | 0.12 | 1 | 15 | 52 |
| *Pseudomonas aeruginosa* | | | | | |
| | Ciprofloxacin | 0.12 | 2 | 14 | 44 |
| | Norfloxacin | 0.12 | 16 | 14 | |
| | Ofloxacin | 0.25 | 16 | | |
| | Enoxacin | 0.5 | 32 | 14 | |
| | Ciprofloxacin | 0.12 | 4 | 10 | 46 |
| | A-56620 | 0.25 | 4 | 10 | |
| | Norfloxacin | 0.5 | 16 | 10 | |
| | Difloxacin | 2 | 64 | 10 | |
| | T-3262 | 0.03 | 4 | 14 | 50 |
| | Temafloxacin | 0.25 | 8 | 14 | 51 |
| | Lomefloxacin | 1 | 8 | 15 | 52 |

*continued*

## Table 5. *Continued*

| Organism | Quinolone* | MIC in µg/mL | | No. of Transfers | Ref. |
|---|---|---|---|---|---|
| | | Wildtype | Mutant | | |
| *Staphylococcus aureus* | | | | | |
| | Ciprofloxacin | 0.25 | 64 | 14 | 44 |
| | Norfloxacin | 0.5 | 64 | 14 | |
| | Ofloxacin | 0.25 | 64 | 14 | |
| | T-3262 | 0.12 | 0.5 | 14 | 50 |
| | Lomefloxacin | 0.5 | 2.0 | 15 | 52 |

\* Quinolone used to select mutant. MIC is for same quinolone.

## Table 6. Cross-resistance among the quinolones

| Organism | Mutant Selected with: | MIC in µg/mL for: | | Ref. |
|---|---|---|---|---|
| | | Ciprofloxacin | Other Quinolones Tested* | |
| *Escherichia coli* | | | | |
| | Ciprofloxacin | 1.0 | NFX-4.0; OFX-4.0; ENX-8.0; PFX-8.0 | 44 |
| | Difloxacin | 0.03 | NFX-0.12; DFX-2; A-56620-0.25; NA-32 | 46 |
| | A-55620 | 0.015 | NFX-0.03; DFX-1; A-56620-0.12; NA-8 | 46 |
| | Temafloxacin | 0.5 | OFX-4; TFX-4 | 51 |
| | Norfloxacin | 0.2 | NFX-0.4; OFX-0.4; FRX-0.4; NA-100 | 41 |
| *Pseudomonas aeruginosa* | | | | |
| | Ciprofloxacin | 1 | NFX-4; OFX-8; ENX-8; PFX-16 | 44 |
| | Difloxacin | 4 | NFX-8; DFX-64; A-56620-8 | 46 |
| | A-55620 | 2 | NFX-8; DFX-32; A-56620-4 | 46 |
| | Temafloxacin | 0.25 | OFX-4; TFX-8 | 51 |

\* DFX = Difloxacin, ENX = Enoxacin, FRX = Fleroxacin, NA = Nalidixic Acid, NFX = Norfloxacin
OFX = Ofloxacin, TFX = Temafloxacin

11

Table 7. Chromosomal locations of mutations causing quinolone resistance in
*Escherichia coli* and *Pseudomonas aeruginosa*

| Gene | Function | Map Location | Ref. |
|------|----------|--------------|------|
| *Escherichia coli* | | | |
| gyrA (*nal*A,*nfx*A,*cfx*A) | A subunit of DNA gyrase | 48' | 6,40 |
| *gyr*B (*nal*C,*nal*D) | B subunit of DNA gyrase | 83' | 6,59,60 |
| *nal*B | Permeability (?) | 58' | 6 |
| *mar*A (*nor*B,*cfx*B) | Permeability (?) | 34' | 6,40,41,61 |
| *nfx*B | Permeability (?) | 19' | 6,41 |
| *nor*C | Permeability (?) | 8' | 6,41 |
| *Pseudomonas aeruginosa* | | | |
| *gyr*A (*nal*A) | A subunit of gyrase | Between *hex*-9001+*leu*-10 | 62 |
| (*nfx*A) | | Between *hex*-9005+*leu*-9001 | 57 |
| (*cfx*A) | | 39' | 56 |
| *nal*B | Permeability (?) | Near *pyr*B | 57 |
| (*cfx*B) | | Near *pyr*B52 | 56 |
| *nfx*B | Permeability (?) | Between *pro*B+*ilv*BC | 57 |

sive diffusion through both the porins (outer membrane proteins, OMPs) and exposed lipid domains on the outer membrane of the organisms.[63,64] The relative importance of each pathway to a given quinolone is influenced by its hydrophobicity.[63] Thus, it is not surprising that alterations in OMPs or lipopolysaccharides of gram-negative cells influence susceptibility to the quinolones.[6,40-42,56-58,65] Mutations that diminish the expression of OMPs generally increase quinolone resistance four-fold, while mutations leading to lipopolysaccharide deficiency increase susceptibility to the quinolones, especially the more hydrophobic compounds. When mutations affecting permeation are involved, cross-resistance between the quinolones and chemically unrelated antibiotics is often encountered.[40-42,44,51,55-58,65]

The development of resistance to the newer quinolones has been examined in several pharmacodynamic and animal models of infection. In an in vitro model that mimics human pharmacokinetics, Blaser et al[66] showed that bacteria exposed to enoxacin were efficiently killed if peak concentrations were eight times the MIC. However, if such concentrations were not achieved, organisms 4- to 8-fold less susceptible to the drug developed, and subsequent doses had little or no bactericidal effect. Similar results were observed in an in vitro model that simulates cystitis.[67,68] Emergence of resistance during quinolone treatment of experimental pyelonephritis in mice has been studied by Fernandes et al.[46] No resistance was observed when mice were infected with *E. coli,* but mutants 2- to 64-fold less susceptible to the quinolones were recovered when mice were infected with *Ps. aeruginosa.* This difference may again be a reflection of the greater peak-to-MIC ratio for *E. coli* than for *Ps. aeruginosa* achieved in this model. The emergence of resistance during quinolone therapy has been examined in various other animal models. In rats with chronic *Pseudomonas* pneumonia given subtherapeutic doses of enoxacin daily for 10 weeks, Scribner et al[47] observed no emergence of resistance. However, Michéa-Hamzehpour et al[69] did observe resistance in intraperitoneal *Pseudomonas* infections in mice. This resistance was more likely if a high challenge inoculum was used or if talcum was added to the challenge inoculum. Resistance was less likely if the quinolone was used in combination with ceftazidime or amikacin. In a rabbit model of endocarditis, emergence of resistance to the quinolones was observed with both *Staphylococcus aureus* and *Ps. aeruginosa.*[70,71] In the *Pseudomonas* endocarditis model, emergence of resistance was associated with the inability to sterilize aortic vegetations.[70] The emergence of resistance during ciprofloxacin therapy of lethal systemic infections in mice induced by a variety of gram-negative and gram-positive organisms was observed infrequently in studies by Sanders et al.[72] Among 100 isolates recovered from treated mice, only five showed fourfold or greater increases in MIC to one of the study drugs. In no instance was this decreased susceptibility associated with diminished efficacy of the drug.

Overall, the emergence of resistance during quinolone therapy has been infrequent in the animal models studied to date. When it has occurred, it has usually been associated with conditions that lessen the likelihood of achieving a peak-to-MIC ratio of eight or more. This critical ratio probably reflects the fact that single-step mutations toward quinolone resistance usually involve 4- to 8-fold increases in MICs. Thus, it is not surprising that most of the emergence of resistance seen in the animal models has been with organisms with MICs near 1 µg/mL for the quinolones (eg, *Pseudomonas,* staphylococci). Single-step mutations in these organisms would result in MICs above achievable peak serum levels for most quinolones.

A number of clinical investigators have reported emergence of resistance during therapy with the newer quinolones. To date, only a few reports involve infections with organisms other than *Pseudomonas.*[73-81] These include infections due to staphylococci,[73-75] a pancreatic abscess due to *Campylobacter jejuni,*[76] one case of gonorrhoea,[77] and various infections due to Enterobacteriaceae.[73,78-81] Most instances of resistance reported to date involve *Pseudomonas* infections. In patients not suffering from cystic fibrosis (CF), emergence of resistance is usually associated with clinical failure or relapse and failure to eradicate *Pseudomonas* from the site of infection.[58,75,81-84] In patients with CF, most respond clinically despite the development of resistance by the infecting strain and its persistence in sputum.[81,85-88] The precise rate of emergence of resistance during therapy of acute exacerbations of bronchopulmonary *Pseudomonas* infections in cystic fibrosis varies widely from study to study. This is most likely due to differences in the methodology used to detect resistance[88] as well as the therapeutic regimen involved.[89] In general, resistance is more likely to develop during prolonged courses of therapy and retreatment with the quinolones. Although clinical evidence suggests that some of these resistant pseudomonads may persist and spread to other patients who have not received a quinolone,[85] a reduced virulence of such strains has recently been documented by Ravizzola et al[90] in tests with mice. The clinical consequences of secondary spread of these pseudomonads may therefore be limited.

## ANTIMICROBIAL SPECTRUM AND POTENCY

The antimicrobial spectrum and relative in vitro potency of the fluoroquinolones can best be assessed by comparisons of the concentrations required to inhibit 50% of the strains examined (ie, $MIC_{50}$). This factor closely reflects the relative intrinsic potencies of the drugs since: (a) it does not include results obtained with the few quinolone-resistant strains encountered in many studies; and (b) the entire range of MICs obtained with most species is very narrow for these drugs. For the new fluoroquinolones, which include pefloxacin, enoxacin, amifloxacin, norfloxacin, ciprofloxacin, and ofloxacin, $MIC_{50}s$ have been summarized in several large reviews.[17,55,91-95] Although not as extensively studied, similar data are available for those fluoroquinolones still in the early development stage, including difloxacin,[92,96-98] fleroxacin,[95,99-105] lomefloxacin,[52,99,106] temafloxacin,[51,107] irloxacin,[108] T-3262,[50,109,110] A-56620,[92,96-98] E-3846,[111] E-3604,[112] CI-934,[92,113-117] S-25930,[49,118,119] and S-25932.[49,118,119] By combining data from these in vitro studies, the antimicrobial spectrum and relative potency of the various fluoroquinolones can be derived.

The general antimicrobial spectrum of the fluoroquinolones is summarized in Table 3. These drugs are highly active against most aerobic and facultative gram-negative bacteria, as indicated by $MIC_{50}s$ of $\leq 0.5$ µg/mL for *Escherichia coli*. They are moderately active against *Ps. aeruginosa*. Among fluoroquinolones, ciprofloxacin is the single most active compound against gram-negative bacteria, with $MIC_{50}s$ usually <1 µg/mL. Most fluoroquinolones are only moderately active against gram-positive bacteria, as indicated by $MIC_{50}s$ of 0.5-1.0 µg/mL for *Staphylococcus aureus*. However, the activity against gram-positive bacteria of several newer quinolones (eg, T-3262, E-3846, E-3604, irloxacin) is greatly improved, with $MIC_{50}s$ for staphylococci of <0.1/mL.[50,108-112] Similarly, the anti-anaerobic activity of the fluoroquinolones is generally poor. However, $MIC_{50}s$ of T-3262 range from 0.78 to 1 µg/mL for *Bacteroides fragilis*.[50,109,110] Thus, this compound may possess clinically useful activity against obligate anaerobes. With this general description of the antimicrobial spectrum, a more specific examination of the organisms within the spectrum reveals a few additional differences among the fluoroquinolones.

Virtually every genus and species within the family Enterobacteriaceae is highly susceptible to most fluoroquinolones (Table 8). The enteropathogens among the Enterobacteriaceae, Vibrionaceae and *Campylobacter* spp. are also highly sensitive,[49-52,55,92,96,97,107,110,120-122] as are most of the fastidious gram-negative bacteria among the Pasteurellaceae, Neisseriaceae, and *Bordetella pertussis* (Table 8).[49-52,55,92,96,99,107,110,119,123-127] The few fastidious gram-negative bacilli that are not highly susceptible to the fluoroquinolones include *Brucella melitensis, Bordetella bronchiseptica, Gardnerella vaginalis,* and *Streptobacillus moniliformis* (Tables 9 and 10).[55,122,126,128-133] Among the aerobic gram-negative bacilli, most species of *Pseudomonas, Flavobacterium,* and *Acinetobacter* are moderately susceptible to the fluoroquinolones (Table 9).[50-52,92,94,96,99,103,106,118,119,134-137] Strains of *P. maltophilia, P. cepacia, P. pseudomallei,* and *Alcaligenes* spp. are generally resistant (MICs >2 µg/mL) to the fluoroquinolones (Table 10).[49-52,55,97,101,103,106,109,115,118,135,138,139] However, MICs against *P. maltophilia* for T-3262 are usually below 2 µg/mL.[50,109] Thus, this new quinolone may offer an advantage over other compounds against certain pseudomonads.

**Table 8.** Gram-negative bacteria highly susceptible to most fluoroquinolones

| **Enterobacteriaceae** | **Vibrionaceae** |
|---|---|
| *Escherichia* | *Vibrio* |
| *Shigella* | *Aeromonas* |
| *Salmonella* | *Plesiomonas* |
| *Citrobacter* | |
| *Serratia* | |
| *Enterobacter* | **Pasteurellaceae** |
| *Hafnia* | *Haemophilus influenzae* |
| *Klebsiella* | *H. ducreyi* |
| *Proteus* | *Pasteurella multocida* |
| *Providencia* | |
| *Morganella* | **Neisseriaceae** |
| *Yersinia* | *Neisseria* |
| | *Branhamella (Moraxella)* |
| **Other Genera** | |
| *Campylobacter* | |
| *Bordetella pertussis* | |

Table 9. Gram-negative bacteria moderately susceptible to fluoroquinolones

| | |
|---|---|
| *Pseudomonas aeruginosa* | *Flavobacterium* spp. |
| *P. fluorescens* | *Acinetobacter* spp. |
| *P. stutzeri* | *Brucella melitensis* |
| *P. picketti* | *Bordetella bronchiseptica* |
| *P. putida* | *Bordetella parapertussis* |
| *P. mendocina* | |
| *P. alcaligenes* | |
| *P. pseudoalcaligenes* | |
| *P. testosteroni* | |
| *P. diminuta* | |

Table 10. Gram-negative bacteria relatively resistant to fluoroquinolones

*P. cepacia*
*P. maltophilia*
*Alkaligenes* spp.
*Gardnerella vaginalis*
*P. pseudomallei*

The in vitro activity of most of the fluoroquinolones against gram-positive organisms is not as great as that against gram-negative organisms (Table 3).[49-51,55,94-97,99,101,106,107,110,113-115,119] However, MICs are 1 µg/mL or less for many streptococci and staphylococci, including methicillin-resistant staphylococci. Several new quinolones have greatly improved activity against gram-positive bacteria.[50,108-112] These include T-3262, irloxacin, E-3604, and E-3846. The MICs of these compounds are generally <0.25 µg/mL for streptococci, <1 µg/mL for enterococci, and <0.1 µg/mL for staphylococci. The greater activity of T-3262 against gram-positive bacteria is also reflected in tests with *Listeria* and corynebacteria.[49-51,97,102,113] Isolates of *Nocardia* and *Actinomyces* are generally resistant to the fluoroquinolones,[129,140-142] as are most species of mycobacteria.[55,72,143-149] However, for some strains of mycobacteria, MICs are within the clinically achievable range.

Obligate anaerobes (both gram-positive and gram-negative) are generally not susceptible to the fluoroquinolones at concentrations <1µg/mL (Table 3).[49-52,55,92,94,95,99,100,103,104,106,107,109,110,115,117,119,136] However, recent studies with T-3262 suggest that this quinolone may be active against a number of anaerobes.[50,109,110] MICs of 1 µg/mL or less were obtained in most tests with *Bacteroides* spp, *Clostridium perfringens*, *Peptococci*, and *Peptostreptococci*.

Most mycoplasmas,[128,150-152] chlamydia,[126,128,152-155] and *Legionella*[50-52,55,94,106,107,110,156,157] examined to date have been inhibited by fluoroquinolones at concentrations between 0.5-1 µg/mL (Table 11). Although the clinical relevance of this in vitro activity has yet to be established, the fluoroquinolones do appear to be effective against experimental *Legionella* pneumonia in guinea pigs.[158,159] Several studies have examined the in vitro activity of the fluoroquinolones against rickettsiae and *Coxiella burnetii*.[160,161] MICs have ranged from 0.5 to 4 µg/mL. Ciprofloxacin has been shown to be effective in the treatment of scrub typhus in a mouse model,[162] and has been used successfully in five patients with Mediterranean spotted fever.[163] Thus, the fluoroquinolones may have a role in the treatment of rickettsial diseases in humans.

## CONCLUSION

The new fluoroquinolones are a welcome extension of the antibiotic armamentarium. They are highly potent bactericidal agents, especially for gram-negative bacteria. Their unique mechanism of action limits cross-resistance with other antibiotic classes and, to date, has not been subject to plasmid-mediated resistance. Their antimicrobial spectrum suggests that they will become very useful agents for the treatment of a variety of infections.

**Table 11.** In vitro susceptibility of other organisms to fluoroquinolones

| Moderately Susceptible | Relatively Resistant |
|---|---|
| Staphylococcus | Listeria |
| Streptococcus* | Obligate anaerobes* |
| Mycoplasmas† | Nocardia |
| *Chlamydia trachomatis*† | Actinomyces |
| Legionella† | Mycobacteria* |
| Rickettsia† | Ureaplasmas |
| *Coxiella burnetii*† | |

\* Some exceptions noted in text.
† Clinical implications of in vitro activity not established.

17

# REFERENCES

1. Smith JT: The mode of action of 4-quinolones and possible mechanisms of resistance. J Antimicrob Chemother 1986;18(suppl D):21-29.

2. Courtright JB, Turowski DA, Sonstein SA: Alteration of bacterial DNA structure, gene expression, and plasmid encoded antibiotic resistance following exposure to enoxacin. J Antimicrob Chemother 1988;21(suppl B):1-18.

3. Crumplin GC, Kenwright M, Hirst T: Investigations into the mechanism of action of the antibacterial agent norfloxacin. J Antimicrob Chemother 1984;13(suppl B):9-23.

4. Domagala JM, Hanna LD, Heifetz CL, et al: New structure-activity relationships of the quinolone antibacterials using the target enzyme. The development and application of a DNA gyrase assay. J Med Chem 1986;29:394-404.

5. Tabary X, Moreau N, Dureuil C, et al: Effect of DNA gyrase inhibitors pefloxacin, five other quinolones, novobiocin, and clorobiocin on *Escherichia coli* topoisomerase I. Antimicrob Agents Chemother 1987;31:1925-1928.

6. Hooper DC, Wolfson JS: Mode of action of the quinolone antimicrobial agents. Rev Infect Dis 1988;10(suppl 1):S14-S21.

7. Gellert M, Mizuuchi K, O'Dea MH, et al: DNA gyrase: an enzyme that introduces superhelical turns into DNA. Proc Natl Acad Sci USA 1976;73:3872-3876.

8. Aoyama H, Sato K, Fujii T, et al: Purification of *Citrobacter freundii* DNA gyrase and inhibition by quinolones. Antimicrob Agents Chemother 1988;23:104-109.

9. Maxwell A, Gellert M: Mechanistic aspects of DNA topoisomerases. Adv Prot Chem 1986;38:69-107.

10. Drlica K: Biology of bacterial deoxyribonucleic acid topoisomerases. Microbiol Rev 1984;48:273-289.

11. Shen LL, Pernet AG: Mechanism of inhibition of DNA gyrase by analogues of nalidixic acid: The target of the drugs is DNA. Proc Natl Acad Sci USA 1985;82:307-311.

12. Wolfson JS, Hooper DC, Ng EY, et al: Antagonism of wild-type and resistant *Escherichia coli* and its DNA gyrase by the tricyclic 4-quinolone analogs ofloxacin and S-25930 stereoisomers. Antimicrob Agents Chemother 1987;31:1861-1863.

13. Sato K, Inoye Y, Fujii T, et al: Purification and properties of DNA gyrase from a fluoroquinolone-resistant strain of *Escherichia coli*. Antimicrob Agents Chemother 1986;30:777-780.

14. Imamura M, Shibamura S, Hayakawa I, et al: Inhibition of DNA gyrase by optically active ofloxacin. Antimicrob Agents Chemother 1987;31:325-327.

15. Fu KP, Grace ME, McCloud SJ, et al: Discrepancy between the antibacterial activities and the inhibitory effects on *Micrococcus luteus* DNA gyrase of 13 quinolones. Chemotherapy 1986;32:494-498.

16. Zweerink MM, Edison A: Inhibition of *Micrococcus luteus* DNA gyrase by norfloxacin and 10 other quinolone carboxylic acids. Antimicrob Agents Chemother 1986;29:598-601.

17. Wolfson JS, Hooper DC: The fluoroquinolones: structures, mechanisms of action and resistance, and spectra of activity *in vitro*. Antimicrob Agents Chemother 1985;28:581-586.

18. Zeiler H-J, Grohe K: The in vitro and in vivo activity of ciprofloxacin. Eur J Clin Microbiol 1984;3:339-343.

19. Zeiler H-J, Voigt W-H: Efficacy of ciprofloxacin in stationary-phase bacteria in vivo. Am J Med 1987;82(suppl 4A):87-90.

20. Chalkley LJ, Koornhof HJ: Antimicrobial activity of ciprofloxacin against *Pseudomonas aeruginosa, Escherichia coli,* and *Staphylococcus aureus* determined by the killing curve method: antibiotic comparisons and synergistic interactions. Antimicrob Agents Chemother 1985;28:331-342.

21. Neu HC, Chin N-X, Mandell W: The post-antimicrobial suppressive effect of quinolone agents. Drug Exptl Clin Res 1987;13:63-67.

22. Fuursted K: Post-antibiotic effect of ciprofloxacin on *Pseudomonas aeruginosa.* Eur J Clin Microbiol 1987;6:271-274.

23. Craig WA, Gudmundsson S: The post antibiotic effect, in Lorian V (ed), *Antibiotics in Laboratory Medicine,* ed. 2. Baltimore, Williams & Wilkins, pp 515-536, 1986.

24. Reeves DS, Bywater MJ, Holt HA, et al: *In vitro* studies with ciprofloxacin, a new 4-quinolone compound. J Antimicrob Chemother 1984;13:333-346.

25. Diver JM, Wise R: Morphological and biochemical changes in *Escherichia coli* after exposure to ciprofloxacin. J Antimicrob Chemother 1986;18(suppl D):31-41.

26. Little JW, Mount DW: The SOS regulatory system of *E. coli.* Cell 1982;29:11-22.

27. Krueger JH, Walker GC: *groEL* and *dnaK* genes of *Escherichia coli* are induced by UV irradiation and nalidixic acid in an *htpR*[+]-dependent fashion. Proc Natl Acad Sci USA 1984;81:1499-1503.

28. Engle EC, Manes SH, Drlica K: Differential effects of antibiotics inhibiting gyrase. J Bacteriol 1982;149:92-98.

29. Gudas LJ, Pardee AB: Model for regulation of *Escherichia coli* DNA repair functions. Proc Natl Acad Sci USA 1975;72:2330-2334.

30. Phillips I, Culebras E, Moreno F, et al: Introduction of the SOS response by new 4-quinolones. J Antimicrob Chemother 1987;20:631-638.

31. Piddock LJV, Wise R: Induction of the SOS response in *Escherichia coli* by 4-quinolone antimicrobial agents. FEMS Microbiol Lett 1987;41:289-294.

32. Crumplin GC: Aspects of chemistry in the development of the 4-quinolone antibacterial agents. Rev Infect Dis 1988;10(suppl 1):S2-S9.

33. Piddock LJV, Wise R: Induction of the recA protein in *E. coli* by newer 4-quinolones, abstract no. 949. Program and abstracts of the 26th Interscience Conference of Antimicrobial Agents and Chemotherapy, Washington, September 28-October 1, 1986.

34. Weisser J, Wiedemann B: Elimination of plasmids by new 4-quinolones. Antimicrob Agents Chemother 1985;28:700-702.

35. Michel-Briand Y, Uccelli V, Laporte J-M, et al: Elimination of plasmids from Enterobacteriaceae by 4-quinolone derivatives. J Antimicrob Chemother 1986;18:667-674.

36. Weisser J, Weidemann B: Elimination of plasmids by enoxacin and ofloxacin at near inhibitory concentrations. J Antimicrob Chemother 1986;18:575-583.

37. Klopman G, Macina OT, Levinson ME, et al: Computer automated structure evaluation of quinolone antibacterial agents. Antimicrob Agents Chemother 1987;31:1831-1840.

38. Gerster J, Rohlfing S, Pecore S, et al: Synthesis, absolute configuration, and antibacterial activity of 6, 7-dihydro-5,8-dimethyl-9-fluoro-1-oxo-1H, 5H-benzo[ij]quinolizine-2-carboxylic acid. J Med Chem 1987;30:839-843.

39. Ronald AR, Turck M, Petersdorf RG: A critical evaluation of nalidixic acid in urinary-tract infections. N Engl J Med 1966;275:1081-1089.

40. Hooper DC, Wolfson JS, Souza KS, et al: Genetic and biochemical characterization of norfloxacin resistance in *Escherichia coli*. Antimicrob Agents Chemother 1986;29: 639-644.

41. Hirai K, Aoyama H, Suzue S, et al: Isolation and characterization of norfloxacin-resistant mutants of *Escherichia coli* K-12. Antimicrob Agents Chemother 1986;30:248-253.

42. Sanders CC, Sanders WE Jr, Goering RV, et al: Selection of multiple antibiotic resistance by quinolones, beta-lactams, and aminoglycosides with special reference to cross-resistance between unrelated drug classes. Antimicrob Agents Chemother 1984; 26:797-801.

43. Cullmann W, Stieglitz M, Baars B, et al: Comparative evaluation of recently developed quinolone compounds - with a note on the frequency of resistant mutants. Chemotherapy 1985;31:19-28.

44. Neu HC: Bacterial resistance to fluoroquinolones. Rev Infect Dis 1988;10(suppl 1): S57-S63.

45. Aoyama H, Sato K, Kato T, et al: Norfloxacin resistance in a clinical isolate of *Escherichia coli*. Antimicrob Agents Chemother 1987;31:1640-1641.

46. Fernandes PB, Hanson CW, Stamm JM, et al: The frequency of *in vitro* resistance development to fluoroquinolones and the use of a murine pyelonephritis model to demonstrate selection of resistance *in vivo*. J Antimicrob Chemother 1987;19:449-465.

47. Scribner RK, Welch DF, Marks MI: Low frequency of bacterial resistance to enoxacin *in vitro* and in experimental pneumonia. J Antimicrob Chemother 1985;16:597-603.

48. Heifetz CL, Bien PA, Cohen MA, et al: Enoxacin: *in vitro* and animal evaluation as a parenteral and oral agent against hospital bacterial isolates. J Antimicrob Chemother 1988;21(suppl B):29-49.

49. Neu HC, Chin N-X: *In vitro* activity of two new quinolone antimicrobial agents, S-25930 and S-25932 compared with that of other agents. J Antimicrob Chemother 1987;19:175-185.

50. Espinosa AM, Chin N-X, Novelli A, et al: Comparative *in vitro* activity of a new fluorinated 4-quinolone, T-3262 (A-60969). Antimicrob Agents Chemother 1988;32: 663-670.

51. Chin N-X, Figueredo VM, Novelli A, et al: *In vitro* activity of temafloxacin, a new difluoro quinolone antimicrobial agent. Eur J Clin Microbiol Infect Dis 1988;7:58-63.

52. Chin N-X, Novelli A, Neu HC: *In vitro* activity of lomefloxacin (SC-47111;NY-198), a difluoroquinolone 3-carboxylic acid, compared with those of other quinolones. Antimicrob Agents Chemother 1988;32:656-662.

53. Duckworth GJ, Williams JD: Frequency of appearance of resistant variants to norfloxacin and nalidixic acid. J Antimicrob Chemother 1984;13(suppl B):33-38.

54. Limb DI, Dabbs DJW, Spencer KC: *In vitro* selection of bacteria resistant to the 4-quinolone agents. J Antimicrob Chemother 1987;19:65-71.

55. Sanders CC: Ciprofloxacin: *in vitro* activity, mechanism of action and resistance. Rev Infect Dis 1988;10:516-527.

56. Robillard NJ, Scarpa AL: Genetic and physiological characterization of ciprofloxacin resistance in *Pseudomonas aeruginosa* PAO. Antimicrob Agents Chemother 1988;32: 535-539.

57. Hirai K, Suzue S, Irikura T, et al: Mutations producing resistance to norfloxacin in *Pseudomonas aeruginosa*. Antimicrob Agents Chemother 1987;31:582-586.

58. Daikos GL, Lolans VT, Jackson GG: Alterations in outer membrane proteins of *Pseudomonas aeruginosa* associated with selective resistance to quinolones. Antimicrob Agents Chemother 1988;32:785-787.

59. Yamagishi J-I, Yoshida H, Yamayoshi M, et al: Nalidixic acid-resistant mutations of the *gyr*B gene of *Escherichia coli*. Mol Gen Genetics 1986;204:367-373.

60. Yamagishi J-I, Furutani Y, Inoue S, et al: New nalidixic acid resistance mutations related to deoxyribonucleic acid gyrase activity. J Bacteriol 1981;148:50-58.

61. George AM, Levy SB: Gene in the major cotransduction gap of the *Escherichia coli* K-12 linkage map required for the expression of chromosomal resistance to tetracycline and other antibiotics. J Bacteriol 1983;155:541-548.

62. Rella M, Haas D: Resistance of *Pseudomonas aeruginosa* PAO to nalidixic acid and low levels of β-lactam antibiotics: mapping of chromosomal genes. Antimicrob Agents Chemother 1982;22:242-249.

63. Chapman JS, Georgopapadakou NH: Routes of quinolone permeation in *Escherichia coli*. Antimicrob Agents Chemother 1988;32:438-442.

64. Bedard J, Wong S, Bryan LE: Accumulation of enoxacin by *Escherichia coli* and *Bacillus subtilis*. Antimicrob Agents Chemother 1987;32:1348-1354.

65. Hirai K, Aoyama H, Irikura T, et al: Differences in susceptibility to quinolones of outer membrane mutants of *Salmonella typhimurium* and *Escherichia coli*. Antimicrob Agents Chemother 1986;29:535-538.

66. Blaser J, Stone BB, Groner MC, et al: Comparative study with enoxacin and netilmicin in a pharmacodynamic model to determine importance of ratio and antibiotic peak concentration to MIC for bactericidal activity and emergence of resistance. Antimicrob Agents Chemother 1987;31:1054-1060.

67. Greenwood D, Osman M, Goodwin J, et al: Norfloxacin: activity against urinary tract pathogens and factors influencing the emergence of resistance. J Antimicrob Chemother 1984;13:315-323.

68. Muranaka K, Greenwood D: The response of *Streptococcus faecalis* to ciprofloxacin, norfloxacin and enoxacin. J Antimicrob Chemother 1988;21:545-554.

69. Michéa-Hamzehpour M, Auckenthaler R, Regamey P, et al: Resistance occurring after fluoroquinolone therapy of experimental *Pseudomonas aeruginosa* peritonitis. Antimicrob Agents Chemother 1987;31:1803-1808.

70. Bayer AS, Hirano L, Yih J: Development of β-lactam resistance and increased quinolone MICs during therapy of experimental *Pseudomonas aeruginosa* endocarditis. Antimicrob Agents Chemother 1988;32:231-235.

71. Kaatz GW, Barriere SL, Schaberg D, et al: The emergence of resistance to ciprofloxacin during treatment of experimental *Staphylococcus aureus* endocarditis. J Antimicrob Chemother 1987;20:753-758.

72. Sanders CC, Sanders WE Jr, Goering RV: Overview of preclinical studies with ciprofloxacin. Am J Med 1987;82(suppl 4A):2-11.

73. Desplaces N, Gutmann L, Carlet J, et al: The new quinolones and their combinations with other agents for therapy of severe infections. J Antimicrob Chemother 1986;17(suppl A):25-39.

74. Smith G-M, Cashmore C, Leyland MJ: Ciprofloxacin-resistant staphylococci. Lancet 1985;2:949.

75. Humphreys H, Mulvihill E: Ciprofloxacin-resistant *Staphylococcus aureus*. Lancet 1985;2:383.

76. Altwegg M, Burnens A, Zollinger-Iten J, et al: Problems in identification of *Campylobacter jejuni* associated with acquisition of resistance to nalidixic acid. J Clin Microbiol 1987;25:1807-1808.

77. Wagenvoort JHT, Van der Willigen AH, Van Vliet HJA, et al: Resistance of *Neisseria gonorrhoeae* to enoxacin. J Antimicrob Chemother 1986;18:429.

78. Follath F, Bindschedler M, Wenk M, et al: Use of ciprofloxacin in the treatment of *Pseudomonas aeruginosa* infections. Eur J Clin Microbiol 1986;5:236-240.

79. Cheng AF, Li MKW, Ling TKW, et al: Emergence of ofloxacin-resistant *Citrobacter freundii* and *Pseudomonas maltophilia* after ofloxacin therapy. J Antimicrob Chemother 1987;20:283-285.

80. Mehtar S, Drabu Y, Blakemore P: Ciprofloxacin in the treatment of infections caused by gentamicin-resistant gram-negative bacteria. Eur J Clin Microbiol 1986;5:248-251.

81. Chapman ST, Speller DCE, Reeves DS: Resistance to ciprofloxacin. Lancet 1985;2:39.

82. Eron LJ, Harvey L, Hixon DL, et al: Ciprofloxacin therapy of infections caused by *Pseudomonas aeruginosa* and other resistant bacteria. Antimicrob Agents Chemother 1985;27:308-310.

83. Crook SM, Selkon JB, McLardy Smith PD: Clinical resistance to long-term oral ciprofloxacin. Lancet 1985;1:1275.

84. Azadian BS, Bendig JWA, Samson DM: Emergence of ciprofloxacin-resistant *Pseudomonas* after combined therapy with ciprofloxacin and amikacin. J Antimicrob Chemother 1986;18:771.

85. Roberts CM, Batten J, Hodson ME: Ciprofloxacin-resistant *Pseudomonas*. Lancet 1985;1:1442.

86. Scully BE, Parry MF, Neu HC, et al: Oral ciprofloxacin therapy of infections due to *Pseudomonas aeruginosa*. Lancet 1986;1:819-822.

87. Miller MG, Ghoneim AT, Littlewood JM: Use of enoxacin in a patient with cystic fibrosis. Lancet 1985;1:646.

88. Stutman HR: Summary of a workshop on ciprofloxacin use in patients with cystic fibrosis. Pediatr Infect Dis J 1987;6:932-935.

89. Sanders WE Jr: Efficacy, safety and potential economic benefits of oral ciprofloxacin in the treatment of infections. Rev Infect Dis 1988;10:528-543.

90. Ravizzola G, Pirali F, Paolucci A, et al: Reduced virulence in ciprofloxacin-resistant variants of *Pseudomonas aeruginosa* strains. J Antimicrob Chemother 1987;20:825-829.

91. Bergan T: Quinolones, in Peterson PK, Verhoef J (eds), *Antimicrobial Agents Annual 1.* Amsterdam, Elsevier Science Publishers, 1986, pp 164-178.

92. King A, Phillips I: The comparative *in- vitro* activity of eight newer quinolones and nalidixic acid. J Antimicrob Chemother 1986;18(suppl D):1-20.

93. Grüneberg RN: Future development of quinolones and possible therapeutic applications, in Percival A (ed), *Quinolones - Their Future in Clinical Practice.* London Royal Society of Medicine Services, 1986, pp 65-71.

94. Janknegt R: Fluorinated quinolones. Pharma Weekbld 1986;8:1-21.

95. Mitsuhashi S: Comparative antibacterial activity of new quinolone-carboxylic acid derivatives. Rev Infect Dis 1988;10(suppl 1):S27-S31.

96. Stamm JM, Hanson CW, Chu DTW, et al: *In vitro* evaluation of A-56619 (difloxacin) and A-56620: New aryl-fluoroquinolones. Antimicrob Agents Chemother 1986;29:193-200.

97. Eliopoulos GM, Moellering AE, Reiszner E, et al: *In vitro* activities of the quinolone antimicrobial agents A-56619 and A-56620. Antimicrob Agents Chemother 1985;28:514-520.

98. Barry AL, Jones RN, Thornsberry C, et al: *In vitro* activity of the aryl-fluoroquinolone A-56619 and A-56620 and evaluation of disc susceptibility tests. Eur J Clin Microbiol 1986;5:18-22.

99. Wise R, Andrews JM, Ashby JP, et al: *In vitro* activity of lomefloxacin, a new quinolone antimicrobial agent, in comparison with those of other agents. Antimicrob Agents Chemother 1988;32:617-622.

100. Manek N, Andrews JM, Wise R: *In vitro* activity of Ro 23-6240, a new difluoro-quinolone derivative, compared with that of other antimicrobial agents. Antimicrob Agents Chemother 1986;30:330-332.

101. Fuchs PC, Jones RN, Barry AL, et al: Ro 23-6240 (AM-833), a new fluoroquinolone: *In vitro* antimicrobial activity and tentative disk diffusion criteria. Diagn Microbiol Infect Dis 1987;7:29-35.

102. Verschraegen G, Claeys G, Van den Abeele AM: Comparative *in vitro* activity of the new quinolone fleroxacin (RO 23-6240). Eur J Clin Microbiol Infect Dis 1988;7:63-66.

103. Clarke AM, Zemcov SJV: *In vitro* activity of the new 4-quinolone compound RO 23-6240. Eur J Clin Microbiol 1987;6:161-164.

104. Chin N-X, Brittain DC, Neu HC: *In vitro* activity of Ro 23-6240, a new fluorinated 4-quinolone. Antimicrob Agents Chemother 1986;29:675-680.

105. Hirai K, Aoyama H, Hosaka M, et al: *In vitro* and *in vivo* antibacterial activity of AM-833, a new quinolone derivative. Antimicrob Agents Chemother 1986;29:1059-1066.

106. Hirose T, Okezaki E, Kato H, et al: *In vitro* and *in vivo* activity of NY-198, a new defluorinated quinolone. Antimicrob Agents Chemother 1987;31:854-859.

107. Hardy DJ, Swanson RN, Hensey DM, et al: Comparative antibacterial activities of temafloxacin hydrochloride (A-62254) and two reference fluoroquinolones. Antimicrob Agents Chemother 1987;31:1768-1774.

108. Coll R, Esteve M, Moros M, et al: *In vitro* antibacterial activity of irloxacin (E-3432) on clinical isolates. Drugs Exptl Clin Res 1987;13:75-77.

109. Fujimaki K, Noumi T, Saikawa I, et al: *In vitro* and *in vivo* antibacterial activities of T-3262, a new fluoroquinolone. Antimicrob Agents Chemother 1988;32:827-833.

110. Fernandes PB, Chu DTW, Swanson RN, et al: A-61827(A-60969) a new fluoronaphthyridine with activity against both aerobic and anaerobic bacteria. Antimicrob Agents Chemother 1988;32:27-32.

111. Gargallo D, Moros M, Coll R, et al: Activity of E-3846, a new fluoroquinolone, *in vitro* and in experimental cystitis and pyelonephritis in rats. Antimicrob Agents Chemother 1988;32:636-641.

112. Xicota MA, Coll R, Esteve M, et al: *In vitro* antibacterial activity of E-3604, a new 6-fluoroquinolone, on clinical isolates. Drugs Exptl Clin Res 1987;13:133-136.

113. Eliopoulos GM, Reiszner E, Caputo GM, et al: *In vitro* activity of CI-934, a new quinolone antimicrobial, against gram-positive bacteria. Diagn Microbiol Infect Dis 1986;5:341-344.

114. Smith RP, Baltch AL, Hammer MC, et al: *In vitro* activity of CI-934 and other antimicrobial agents against gram-positive and gram-negative bacteria. Clin Ther 1986;9:106-118.

115. Fuchs PC, Barry AL, Jones RN, et al: C-934, a new difluoroquinolone: *In vitro* antibacterial activity and proposed disk diffusion test interpretive criteria. Diagn Microbiol Infect Dis 1987;6:185-192.

116. Verbist L: Comparative *in vitro* activity of the new quinolone CI-934. Eur J Clin Microbiol 1986;5:343-345.

117. Cohen MA, Griffin TJ, Bien PA, et al: *In vitro* activity of CI-934, a new quinolone carboxylic acid active against gram-positive and gram-negative bacteria. Antimicrob Agents Chemother 1985;28:766-772.

118. Rolston KVI, Ho DH, LeBlanc B, et al: *In vitro* evaluation of S-25930 and S-25932, two new quinolones, against aerobic gram-negative isolates from cancer patients. Antimicrob Agents Chemother 1987;31:102-103.

119. Piddock LJV, Andrews JM, Diver JM, et al: *In vitro* studies of S-25930 and S-25932, two new 4-quinolones. Eur J Clin Microbiol 1986;5:303-310.

120. Van der Auwera P, Scorneaux B: *In vitro* susceptibility of *Campylobacter jejuni* to 27 antimicrobial agents and various combinations of β-lactams with clavulanic acid or sulbactam. Antimicrob Agents Chemother 1985;28:37-40.

121. San Joaquin VH, Scribner RK, Pickett DA, et al: Antimicrobial susceptibility of *Aeromonas* species isolated from patients with diarrhea. Antimicrob Agents Chemother 1986;3:794-795.

122. Ling J, Kam KM, Lam AW, et al: Susceptibilities of Hong Kong isolates of multiply resistant *Shigella* spp. to 25 antimicrobial agents, including ampicillin plus sulbactam and new 4-quinolones. Antimicrob Agents Chemother 1988;32:20-23.

123. Doern GV, Tubert TA: *In vitro* activities of 39 antimicrobial agents for *Branhamella catarrhalis* and comparison of results with different quantitative susceptibility test methods. Antimicrob Agents Chemother 1988;32:259-261.

124. Appleman ME, Hadfield TL, Gaines JK, et al: Susceptibility of *Bordetella pertussis* to five quinolone antimicrobic drugs. Diagn Microbiol Infect Dis 1987;8:131-133.

125. Kurzynski TA, Boehm DM, Rott-Petri JA, et al: Antimicrobial susceptibilities of *Bordetella* species isolated in a multicenter pertussis surveillance project. Antimicrob Agents Chemother 1988;32:137-140.

126. Lebowitz LD, Saunders J, Fehler G, et al: *In vitro* activity of A-56619 (difloxacin), A-56620, and other new quinolone antimicrobial agents against genital pathogens. Antimicrob Agents Chemother 1986;30:948-950.

127. Sanson-LePors M-J, Casin IM, Thebault M-C, et al: *In vitro* activities of U-63366, a spectinomycin analog; roxithromycin (RU 28965), a new macrolide antibiotic; and five quinolone derivatives against *Haemophilus ducreyi*. Antimicrob Agents Chemother 1986;30:512-513.

128. Tjiam KH, Wagenvoort JHT, van Klingeren B, et al: *In vitro* activity of the two new 4-quinolones A56619 and A56620 against *Neisseria gonorrhoeae, Chlamydia trachomatis, Mycoplasma hominis, Ureaplasma urealyticum,* and *Gardnerella vaginalis.* Eur J Clin Microbiol 1986;5:498-501.

129. Felmingham D, O'Hare MD, Robbins MJ, et al: Comparative *in vitro* studies with 4-quinolone antimicrobials. Drugs Exp Clin Res 1985;11:317-329.

130. Gobernado M, Cantón E, Santos M: *In vitro* activity of ciprofloxacin against *Brucella melitensis.* Eur J Clin Microbiol 1984;3:371.

131. Bosch J, Linares J, Lopez de Goicoechea MJ, et al: *In vitro* activity of ciprofloxacin, ceftriaxone and five other antimicrobial agents against 95 strains of *Brucella melitensis.* J Antimicrob Chemother 1986;17:459-461.

132. Machka K: *In vitro* activity of ciprofloxacin and norfloxacin against *Gardnerella vaginalis.* Eur J Clin Microbiol 1984;3:374.

133. Edwards R, Finch RG: Characterization and antibiotic susceptibilities of *Streptobacillus moniliformis.* J Med Microbiol 1986;21:39-42.

134. Husson MO, Izard D, Bouillet L, et al: Comparative *in vitro* activity of ciprofloxacin against non-fermenters. J Antimicrob Chemother 1985;15:457-462.

135. Appelbaum PC, Spangler SK, Sollenberger L: Susceptibility of non-fermentative gram-negative bacteria to ciprofloxacin, norfloxacin, amifloxacin, pefloxacin and cefpirome. J Antimicrob Chemother 1986;18:675-679.

136. Jacobus NU, Tally FP, Barza M: Antimicrobial spectrum of WIN 49375. Antimicrob Agents Chemother 1984;26:104-107.

137. Stiver HG, Bartlett KH, Chow AW: Comparison of susceptibility of gentamicin-resistant and susceptible "*Acinetobacter anitratus*" to 15 alternative antibiotics. Antimicrob Agents Chemother 1986;30:624-625.

138. Chau PY, Ng WS, Leung YK, et al: *In vitro* susceptibility of strains of *Pseudomonas pseudomallei* isolated in Thailand and Hong Kong to some newer β-lactam antibiotics and quinolone derivatives. J Infect Dis 1986;153:167-170.

139. Puthucheary SD, Parasakthi N: Antimicrobial susceptibility of *Pseudomonas pseudomallei.* J Antimicrob Chemother 1987;20:921-922.

140. Gombert ME, Aulicino TM, duBouchet L, et al: Susceptibility of *Nocardia asteroides* to new quinolones and β-lactams. Antimicrob Agents Chemother 1987;31:2013-2014.

141. Southern PM, Kutscher AE, Ragsdale R, et al: Susceptibility *in vitro* of *Nocardia* species to antimicrobial agents. Diagn Microbiol Infect Dis 1987;8:119-122.

142. Auckenthaler R, Michéa-Hamzehpour M, Pechére JC: *In-vitro* activity of newer quinolones against aerobic bacteria. J Antimicrob Chemother 1986;17(suppl B):29-39.

143. Pattyn SR, Van Caekenberghe DL, Verhoeven JR: *In vitro* activity of five new quinolones against cultivable mycobacteria. Eur J Clin Microbiol 1987;6:572-573.

144. Berlin OGW, Young LS, Bruckner DA: *In vitro* activity of six fluorinated quinolones against *Mycobacterium tuberculosis*. J Antimicrob Chemother 1987;19:611-615.

145. Davies S, Sparham PD, Spencer RC: Comparative *in vitro* activity of five fluoro-quinolones against mycobacteria. J Antimicrob Chemother 1987;19:605-609.

146. Easmon C, Verity L: Effect of RO 23-6240 on sensitive and resistant intracellular mycobacteria. Eur J Clin Microbiol 1987;6:165-166.

147. Texier-Maugein J, Mormède M, Fourche J, et al: *In vitro* activity of four fluoroquino-lones against eighty-six isolates of mycobacteria. Eur J Clin Microbiol 1987;6:584-586.

148. Johnson SM, Roberts GD: *In vitro* activity of ciprofloxacin and ofloxacin against the *Mycobacterium avium-intracellulare* complex. Diagn Microbiol Infect Dis 1987;7:89-91.

149. Ernst F, Van Der Auwera P: *In vitro* activity of fleroxacin (RO 23-6240), a new fluoro-quinolone, and other agents, against *Mycobacterium* spp. J Antimicrob Chemother 1988;21:501-504.

150. Krausse R, Ullmann U: Comparative *in vitro* activity of fleroxacin (Ro 23-6240) against *Ureaplasma urealyticum* and *Mycoplasma hominis*. Eur J Clin Microbiol Infect Dis 1988;7:67-69.

151. Fallon RJ: *In vitro* sensitivity of legionellas, meningococci and mycoplasmas to ciprofloxacin and enoxacin. J Antimicrob Chemother 1985;15:787-789.

152. Ridgway GL, Mumtaz G, Gabriel FG, et al: The activity of ciprofloxacin and other 4-quinolones against *Chlamydia trachomatis* and *Mycoplasmas* in vitro. Eur J Clin Microbiol 1984;3:344-346.

153. Aznar J, Caballero MC, Lozano MC, et al: Activities of new quinolone derivatives against genital pathogens. Antimicrob Agents Chemother 1985;27:76-78.

154. Heessen FWA, Muytjens HL: In vitro activities of ciprofloxacin, norfloxacin, pipemidic acid, cinoxacin, and nalidixic acid against *Chlamydia trachomatis*. Antimicrob Agents Chemother 1984;25:123-124.

155. How SJ, Hobson D, Hart CA, et al: A comparison of the *in vitro* activity of antimicrobi-als against *Chlamydia trachomatis* examined by giemsa and a fluorescent antibody stain. J Antimicrob Chemother 1985;15:399-404.

156. Fallon RJ: *In vitro* sensitivity of legionellas and mycoplasmas to amifloxacin. J Anti-microb Chemother 1988;21:381-382.

157. Havlichek D, Saravolatz L, Pohlod D: Effect of quinolones and other antimicrobial agents on cell-associated *Legionella pneumophila*. Antimicrob Agents Chemother 1987;31:1529-1534.

158. Saito A, Koga H, Shigeno H, et al: The antimicrobial activity of ciprofloxacin against *Legionella* species and the treatment of experimental *Legionella* pneumonia in guinea pigs. J Antimicrob Chemother 1986;18:251-260.

159. Havlichek D, Pohold D, Saravolatz L: Comparison of ciprofloxacin and rifampicin in experimental *Legionella pneumophila* pneumonia. J Antimicrob Chemother 1987;20:875-881.

160. Raoult D, Roussellier P, Balicher V, et al: *In vitro* susceptibility of *Rickettsia conorii* to ciprofloxacin as determined by suppressing lethality in chicken embryos and by plaque assay. Antimicrob Agents Chemother 1986;29:424-425.

161. Yeaman MR, Mitscher LA, Baca OG: *In vitro* susceptibility of *Coxiella burnetii* to antibiotics, including several quinolones. Antimicrob Agents Chemother 1987;31:1079-1084.

162. McClain JB, Joshi B, Rice R: Chloramphenicol, gentamicin and ciprofloxacin against murine scrub typhus. Antimicrob Agents Chemother 1988;32:285-286.

163. Raoult D, Gallais H, De Micco P, et al: Ciprofloxacin therapy for Mediterranean spotted fever. Antimicrob Agents Chemother 1986;30:606-607.

# PHARMACOKINETICS AND TISSUE PENETRATION OF FLUOROQUINOLONES

# 2

*Jerome J. Schentag*
*David E. Nix*

## INTRODUCTION

Ciprofloxacin is the first fluoroquinolone to be marketed in the U.S. for the treatment of systemic infections. It combines a favorable pharmacokinetic profile (long half-life, extensive tissue distribution, low serum protein binding, and two-pathway elimination kinetics) with excellent in vitro activity against many of the commonly encountered hospital pathogens. Ciprofloxacin is readily assayed using HPLC,[1] and many studies of its pharmacokinetics have been performed in both volunteers and patients. Accordingly, it serves as a prototype for discussion of the pharmacokinetic properties of the entire group of fluoroquinolones. Several recent reviews of ciprofloxacin and other fluoroquinolones have been published.[2,3]

## ABSORPTION

The primary advantage of fluoroquinolones over parenteral antibiotics is oral administration. In many cases, oral dosing with fluoroquinolones can replace parenteral regimens or serve as oral continuation therapy after initial treatment with parenteral agents. Although bioavailability is good with these agents, it is not always complete. Norfloxacin has not been definitively studied, but oral bioavailability has been estimated to be only 30-50%.[4] Bioavailability ranges between 50-100% for the other fluoroquinolones.[2] The bioavailability of ciprofloxacin ranges from 54-85%. In one study the bioavailability of orally administered ciprofloxacin ranged from 75% with a 500 mg dose to 54% with a 750 mg dose.[5] Other investigators,[6,7] however, have been unable to confirm this dose dependency, as the area under the curve (AUC) was found to be proportional to dose. Enoxacin, lomefloxacin (NY-198), pefloxacin, ofloxacin, amifloxacin, and fleroxacin all appear to have bioavailabilities approaching 100%.[8-12]

Oral absorption of fluoroquinolones is rapid, with the peak serum concentration of most fluoroquinolones occurring within 1 to 3 hours after a dose.[2,8] Food delays slightly the time at which the peak serum concentration is reached but produces negligible effects on the AUC. Thus, fluoroquinolones may be taken with meals, which is particularly useful in situations where this practice may minimize gastrointestinal distress.

Although food does not affect the absorption of fluoroquinolones, these drugs are greatly affected by antacids containing $Al^{3+}$ and $Mg^{2+}$.[13] Marked (50-90%) reduction in the AUC has been observed frequently in normal volunteer interaction studies.[14,15] An example of the reduction in serum concentrations associated with antacids is shown in Figure 1. Data from one volunteer given Maalox® concurrently with ciprofloxacin are compared with data from the same volunteer given an identical dosage of ciprofloxacin alone. The interaction appears to be the result of a complex formed between the 3 carboxyl-4-oxo functional groups on the quinolone and the metal ion (Figure 2). The resulting complex is microbiologically inactive. The time of fluoroquinolone administration (in relation to the antacid) can be manipulated to avoid the interaction. Specifically, if the antacid is given 2-4 hours *following* fluoroquinolone administration, the interaction is minimized.[13] Antacids should therefore not be ad-

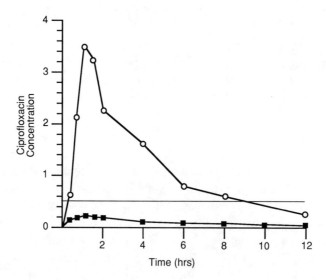

Figure 1.   Serum concentrations of ciprofloxacin alone ( ○ ) versus those following administration with antacid ( ■ ). The MIC value for susceptible *Pseudomonas* is shown on the figure as a reference point for therapeutic serum concentrations.

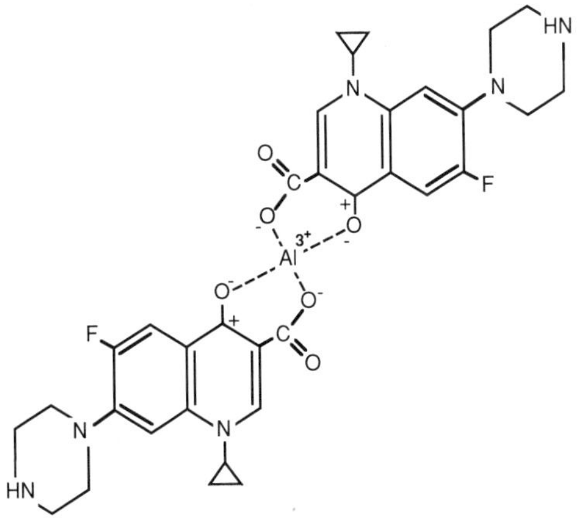

Figure 2. Structural interaction between aluminum ($Al^{3+}$) and two ciprofloxacin molecules.

ministered for at least four hours prior to a fluoroquinolone dose.[13] This strategy allows the antibiotic to be absorbed before the antacid is given, minimizing direct contact in the gastrointestinal tract. The interaction can be avoided entirely by using $H_2$-receptor antagonists rather than antacids for gastric acid control in ciprofloxacin- and ofloxacin-treated patients.[16] This strategy, however, should not be used with enoxacin, since administration of ranitidine significantly decreases plasma levels of this antibiotic.[14] The mechanism of this interaction is not clear, but since enoxacin is less soluble at pH levels above 3.0, perhaps decreased dissolution results from the higher gastric pH following ranitidine administration.

As shown in Figure 1, oral absorption of ciprofloxacin produces rapid peak serum concentrations that exceed the minimum inhibitory concentrations (MICs) of commonly treated bacteria. In the presence of antacids, mean peak serum concentrations in these volunteers did not reach the MIC, illustrating the danger of the drug-antacid interaction. This interaction has also been noted in patients and has been associated with clinical failure.[17]

## DISTRIBUTION

With doses of 400-500 mg and peak serum concentrations between 1.5 and 5 mg/L, the volume of distribution for fluoroquinolones ranges from 1.1 to 2.0 L/kg. With this distribution volume and serum half-life ranging between 3-6 hours, fluoroquinolones would be expected to reach steady-state at extravascular sites in the first 24 hours of therapy.[18] Accordingly, investigators seeking to determine steady-state tissue to serum ratios must wait until the third or fourth dose to collect tissue samples. Earlier sampling (before steady-state equilibrium) would lower the measured tissue to serum ratio. This is also the case if samples are taken within 15-30 minutes after rapid IV infusion of a dose. During this time interval the serum concentrations are high because of a poor equilibrium between intravascular and extravascular spaces.

The fluoroquinolones differ markedly from the β-lactams and aminoglycosides in their distribution profile. None of the newer fluoroquinolones is significantly bound to plasma proteins, and all are distributed widely throughout the body. They achieve tissue to serum ratios in excess of 2:1 at most tissue sites.[2,11] In contrast, β-lactams seldom have tissue to serum ratios in excess of 0.4:1.[18,19] Aminoglycosides achieve high concentrations in kidney, but here they are highly bound and produce toxicity.[20] Elsewhere, they demonstrate tissue to serum ratios less than 0.5:1.[21]

To reach a tissue to serum ratio in excess of 1:1, a drug must penetrate the cell membrane and be found within the cell at concentrations that are at least equal to serum. The only other means to achieve ratios in excess of 1:1 is for the drug to undergo extensive tissue binding.[18] Fluoroquinolones exceed the 1:1 ratio because they are found in cell cytoplasm in concentrations similar to blood, and they also bind to intracellular organelles in concentrations higher than in serum. This observation contrasts fluoroquinolones with β-lactams and aminoglycosides, which penetrate cell membranes poorly[19,22] and have tissue to serum ratios less than 1:1.

A listing of quinolone tissue to plasma ratios in extravascular tissue sites is shown in Table 1.[23] Although these are data from animals, they are representative of human studies.[24-26] The only sites which demonstrate low concentrations of fluoroquinolones are the brain and cerebrospinal fluid (CSF). It is assumed that fluoroquinolones penetrate into the central nervous system poorly, but the mechanism could also be an active removal process from CSF.[27] Further study is needed to clarify the mechanism.

For most body sites, the mechanism of quinolone distribution is passive diffusion across cell membranes, followed by intracellular ionic binding. Fluoroquinolones diffuse passively between blood, interstitial fluid, and various body compartments. Excretory sites such as liver and kidney therefore display the highest tissue to serum ratios. Tissues with greater numbers of binding sites would be expected to accumulate higher tissue to serum ratios. Sites such as the prostate, with its acidic pH, have increased distribution ratios due to ion trapping.[2,3] Body fluids such as synovial fluid, pleural fluid, and non-inflammatory wound exudates would be expected to have steady-state concentrations similar to those achieved in serum if blood flow is good to that site.[2,18] If blood flow is altered, then extravascular peaks may be lower and/or extravascular AUC reduced.[18,22]

Infected sites have higher quinolone tissue to serum ratios than normal tissues of the same type.[28] This is presumably a result of quinolone binding to the accumulated

**Table 1.** Tissue to plasma concentration ratios for pefloxacin (PFX), ciprofloxacin (CFX), and enoxacin (ENX) in animals after chronic dosing

| Tissue | PFX (dog) | CFX (Rhesus monkey) | ENX (dog) |
|---|---|---|---|
| Brain | 0.4 | undectable | 0.2 |
| Liver | 9.8 | 19.4 | 2.9 |
| Kidney | 4.8 | 4.7 | 5.0 |
| Heart | 4.0 | 2.1 | 2.7 |
| Lung | 2.8 | 2.3 | 1.5 |
| Spleen | 4.7 | 3.8 | 2.5 |
| Thymus | — | 3.2 | — |
| Muscle | 3.4 | 8.1 | 2.1 |

Adapted with permission from Nix and Schentag.[23]

white blood cells. With the increased movement of white blood cells to infected sites, the number of available binding sites increases. Two important consequences result from this tissue distribution profile:

- Fluoroquinolones diffuse into cells, offering the potential for activity against intracellular pathogens; and
- With high cellular uptake and associated large volumes of distribution, serum concentrations at a given dosage will be lower than those achieved with β-lactams or aminoglycosides.

For example, with their typical volumes of distribution, the peak serum concentrations after a 500 mg dose of ciprofloxacin, a cephalosporin, or an aminoglycoside (amikacin) are 3.0 μg/mL, 40 μg/mL, and 30 μg/mL, respectively. If all three antibiotics had a volume of distribution of 0.2 L/kg, their peaks would be identical. Thus, increased intracellular penetration is an advantage for fluoroquinolones if the pathogens are also located intracellularly. If the pathogens are in the blood or interstitial fluid, then the larger volume of distribution requires that higher dosages be used to produce infection site concentrations above the MIC. Persistence at some infection sites and longer serum half-life values are secondary benefits of wider extravascular distribution. The clinical value of the higher tissue to serum ratios in infected tissue has not been demonstrated, although theoretical advantages certainly exist.

## METABOLISM

In general, metabolic transformation of fluoroquinolones occurs at two sites: the 7-piperazine ring and the formation of glucuronides at position 3. Figure 3 illustrates ciprofloxacin and its known piperazine side chain metabolites. Metabolism is extensive (85%) with pefloxacin, moderate (25-40%) with ciprofloxacin and enoxacin, and minimal (<20%) with norfloxacin, amifloxacin, lomefloxacin (NY-198), and ofloxacin.[2] The metabolism of norfloxacin is similar to ciprofloxacin, after accounting for the lower bioavailability of norfloxacin. Following an oral dose, metabolites of both drugs appear rapidly in serum.

Intact ciprofloxacin and possibly its piperazine metabolites are excreted in bile. The portion of ciprofloxacin that is excreted in bile is also subject to reabsorption, particularly if it is not bound to intestinal contents. Small quantities of glucuronide metabolites are sometimes detected in urine and bile. Glucuronides are generally not enterohepatically recycled unless they are cleaved within the small intestine by glucuronidases. If this occurs, absorption and continued enterohepatic cycling of the cleaved product are expected. Metabolic and elimination pathways for fluoroquinolones are shown in Figure 4.

Fluoroquinolone metabolites are either inactive (glucuronides) or substantially less active (piperazine derivatives) than their parent compounds. Fluoroquinolones that are metabolized and also excreted via the kidney have half-life values in the range of 3-5 hours. This is the case with norfloxacin, ciprofloxacin, and enoxacin. Pefloxacin, which is metabolized but not excreted renally, has a long serum half-life (10 hrs), while ofloxacin and lomefloxacin, which are not metabolized, have half-lives in the range of 8-10 hours. Thus, fluoroquinolones that are excreted predominantly by either the renal or hepatic route have longer serum half-lives than those that are cleared by both pathways together (two-pathway drugs). A characteristic advantage of two-pathway drugs is their lack of significant accumulation in patients with either renal or hepatic disease. Either of these pathways, when intact, will protect against excessive serum accumulation in patients with failure of the organ system responsible for clearance.

The serum half-life of ciprofloxacin increases only minimally in patients with renal failure, because most of a dose is metabolized despite the absence of renal excretory pathways. The half-life of ciprofloxacin also does not substantially increase in patients with liver disease, since in this condition most of the ciprofloxacin dose passes into the urine as unchanged drug; ie, one pathway compensates for defects in the other.[1,23] Patients with renal failure who are given ofloxacin or lomefloxacin, and patients with liver failure who are given pefloxacin, which is not excreted renally, have dramatic increases in the serum half-life and require dosage adjustment to prevent excessive serum accumulation if the primary clearance organ fails.[29,30]

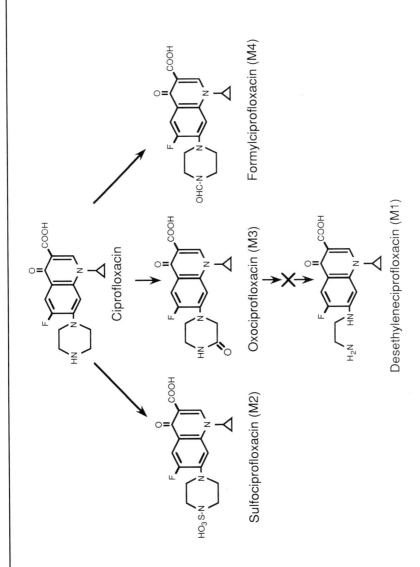

Figure 3.    Ciprofloxacin and its metabolites.

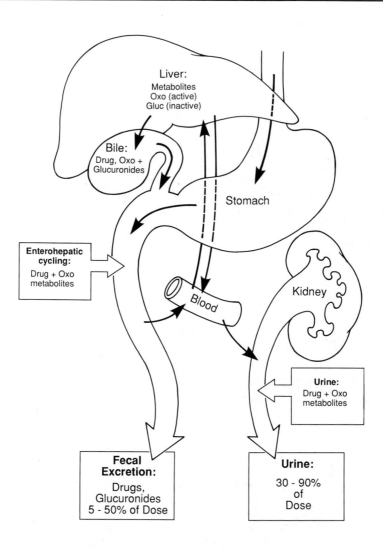

Figure 4.   Quinolone disposition in the body.

Much confusion exists regarding fluoroquinolone dosage adjustment in patients with renal and hepatic disease. Even fluoroquinolones metabolized via both pathways demonstrate some alteration in half-life. Therefore, it may be less confusing to reduce all quinolone dosages to some degree in patients with severe renal disease. Patients with hepatic disease require little dosage adjustment, except in the case of pefloxacin, which requires dosage adjustments in patients with hepatic disease but probably not in those with renal failure.[30]

## RENAL EXCRETION, DOSAGE ADJUSTMENT, AND DIALYSIS

Most fluoroquinolones are eliminated by the kidneys, as would be expected for these water soluble compounds. Mechanisms of renal elimination for some fluoro-quinolones (eg, enoxacin, ciprofloxacin) include both glomerular filtration and tubular secretion, as evidenced by their decreased elimination when administered concomitantly with probenecid.[31] The renal clearance of ciprofloxacin is approximately 230 mL/min in patients with normal renal function, with renal clearance declining to 18 mL/min in those with renal failure.[32]

Both ciprofloxacin and its metabolites are excreted in urine, and there is a relationship between creatinine clearance and total clearance.[33] The non-zero intercept on the graph of creatinine clearance versus total clearance represents metabolic (non-renal) clearance, as is typical of two-pathway drugs. The moderate slope of these graphs illustrates the rationale for mild dosage adjustments in patients with renal impairment.[33] Dialysis removes little of these highly tissue partitioned antibiotics, although there may be transient shortening of half-life during dialysis. Ciprofloxacin is poorly removed by hemodialysis, and although supplemental dosing is not required to compensate for dialysis removal, dosing should be started at the end of a dialysis session.[2]

## ELIMINATION

As shown in Figure 4, fluoroquinolones undergo complex elimination processes, in contrast to the single pathway (renal) excretion characteristics of aminoglycosides and most β-lactam antibiotics. Metabolites as well as unchanged drug are found in urine and bile. Some of the metabolites are enterohepatically recycled, and these metabolites (as well as unchanged drug) are found in high concentrations in feces.[23,34,35] Depending on the compound, as much as 50% of elimination is via the feces, while the other 50% is via the urine (Figure 4). The two-pathway drugs such as ciprofloxacin display this urine-fecal elimination, while single-pathway fluoro-quinolones such as ofloxacin are not eliminated in feces to as great a degree. All of the fluoroquinolones are found in high concentrations in the gastrointestinal tract. This is undoubtedly an advantage in the treatment of gastrointestinal infections. The fortu-itous lack of anaerobic activity allows the high gastrointestinal concentrations of these drugs to be reached without causing disruption of anaerobic gastrointestinal flora.[20,34]

The disadvantage of this complexity in disposition is the need to understand which of the main elimination pathways is most important for each of the fluoroquinolones, as a prelude to dosage adjustments in diseased patients. Ofloxacin, fleroxacin, and lomefloxacin are predominantly renally eliminated, and require dosage adjustment in renally impaired patients (but probably not in those with hepatic disease). Pefloxacin, however, is predominantly metabolized and requires dosage adjustment in those with hepatic but not renal disease. Since ciprofloxacin, norfloxacin, and enoxacin are two-pathway drugs, they may or may not require dosage adjustments. All fluoroquinolones will require major adjustments in dosage in patients with combined renal/hepatic failure, although guidelines to estimate the degree of dosage adjustment required have not been established.[23]

Fluoroquinolone metabolites are sufficiently inactive to contribute little to overall antimicrobial action. However, the toxicity of metabolites remains largely unstudied in humans and should be considered a potential factor if unanticipated adverse affects appear in patients with organ dysfunction given regular dosages. All two-pathway drugs have the potential for marked accumulation in serum and tissues of patients with hepatorenal failure.

## PHARMACOKINETICS IN SPECIAL POPULATIONS

As is the case with many other drugs, mild declines in total clearance, renal clearance, and non-renal clearance of fluoroquinolones have been observed in elderly patients.[36] Some authors attribute this to age, although most attribute it to the age-related decline in renal function and possibly hepatic function. Given the safety of the newer quinolones, it does not seem prudent to adjust dosages solely on the basis of age, since the risks of underdosing appear to be greater than the risks of toxicity. However, elderly patients who have concomitant renal or hepatic diseases require the same dosage adjustments as younger patients with similar degrees of organ dysfunction.

Patients with cystic fibrosis handle these agents in a manner similar to age-matched normals.[37,38] Fluoroquinolone dosages are often higher in cystic fibrosis patients, but in this case higher dosages can be justified on the basis of the high MICs of the infecting pathogens (eg, *Pseudomonas aeruginosa*). At present, little is known about the disposition of these drugs in the pediatric population.

## DRUG INTERACTIONS

In addition to the well documented interaction with antacids, some of the fluoroquinolones reduce the clearance of theophylline, caffeine, warfarin, and other metabolized drugs.[39,40] Enoxacin has the most potent interaction with theophylline,[40] followed by ciprofloxacin[41] and ofloxacin.[42] Some of the nonsteroidal anti-inflammatory agents (NSAIDs) can lower seizure thresholds in patients receiving some fluoroquinolones by a mechanism as yet uncharacterized.[43] At the moment, support for the NSAID interaction comes primarily from animal models, although a few serious central nervous system events have been noted in patients.[44]

# RELATIONSHIPS BETWEEN PHARMACOKINETICS AND MICROBIOLOGICAL ACTIVITY

As shown in Figure 1, a relationship between the cure of infection and achievement of quinolone serum concentrations above the MIC has been assumed. Such relationships are reasonably well supported for β-lactams in both animals[45-47] and humans.[48] β-lactams are most effective if the serum concentration is maintained above the MIC, since they lack post-antibiotic effects (PAEs) against gram-negative organisms.[45,46,48] Thus, the optimal dosing interval for these drugs is one that maintains the serum concentration above the MIC or minimum bactericidal concentration (MBC) for the greatest amount of time.[46,48]

Aminoglycosides may offer the potential for longer dosing intervals than expected on the basis of the amount of time over the MIC, since they demonstrate PAEs in vitro and in vivo.[49,50] This observation, along with their lower nephro- and ototoxic potential in intermittent regimens,[50,51] has led to their use at intervals equal to the time above the MIC plus the duration of PAE.[52] Intervals of 8 to 12 hours are typical for aminoglycosides.

Fluoroquinolones also show PAEs in vitro,[53] but apparently only on the first dose or exposure.[54] Therefore, it may be prudent to give ciprofloxacin via dosing regimens designed to maintain serum concentrations above the MIC for the entire dosing interval, as suggested by recent animal studies.[54] Nix et al tested this principle in patients with pneumonia caused by gram-negative bacteria and found a relationship between the amount of time that ciprofloxacin concentrations exceeded MIC and eradication of the infecting bacteria.[55] These results require confirmation in larger studies, but they strongly suggest that the PAE must be tested in pre-exposed and stationary-phase bacteria, as well as in the usual log growth populations. The problem is that quinolone-susceptible bacteria have potentially different MICs (3-5 fold or greater range) depending on the patient and level of organ impairment. Both sources of variance contribute to the variability in test results for a particular organism. Both quinolone blood levels and drug half-lives vary in individual patients, resulting in variation in the amount of time that serum and tissue levels exceed a particular MIC (3-10 fold range). Thus, methods for dosage regimen design that rely on the integration of serum concentrations with bacterial MICs require control of both pharmacokinetics and adjustment for individual bacterial MICs. This adaptive approach is termed "dual individualization."[19,55] The greatest value of this technique lies in its ability to determine optimal drug dosages and dosing intervals in small numbers of treated patients. Studies performed with ciprofloxacin show ideal dosage regimens to be those which maintain concentrations above the MIC for the entire dosing interval.[55] If this can be accomplished, most respiratory pathogens can be eradicated in three days or less.[56]

## CONCLUSION

In summary, ciprofloxacin and other fluoroquinolones possess a highly favorable set of pharmacokinetic properties, the chief advantages being their oral mode of administration and large volumes of distribution. Knowledge of the effects of disease state on pharmacokinetics allows selection of dosages, and the interaction between MICs and serum concentrations determines the dosing interval.

# REFERENCES

1. Nix DE, DeVito JM, Schentag JJ: Liquid chromatographic determination of ciprofloxacin in serum and urine. Clin Chem 1985;31:684-686.

2. Neuman M: Clinical pharmacokinetics of the newer antimicrobial 4-quinolones. Clin Pharmacokinetics 1988;14:96-121.

3. LeBel M: Ciprofloxacin: Chemistry, mechanism of action, resistance, antimicrobial spectrum, pharmacokinetics, clinical trials, and adverse reactions. Pharmacotherapy 1988;8(1):3-33.

4. Adhami S, Wise R, Wiston D, Crump B: The pharmacokinetics and tissue penetration of norfloxacin. J Antimicrob Chemother 1984;13:87-92.

5. Höffken G, Lode H, Prinzing C, Borner K, Koeppe P: Pharmacokinetics of ciprofloxacin after oral and parenteral administration. Antimicrob Agents Chemother 1985;27:375-379.

6. Tartaglione TA, Raffalovich AC, Poynor WJ, Espinel-Ingroff A, Kerkering TM: Pharmacokinetics and tolerance of ciprofloxacin after sequential increasing oral doses. Antimicrob Agents Chemother 1986;29:62-66.

7. Gonzalez MA, Uribe F, Moisen SD, Fuster AP, Selen A, Welling PG, Painter B: Multiple-dose pharmacokinetics and safety of ciprofloxacin in normal volunteers. Antimicrob Agents Chemother 1984;26:741-744.

8. Wise R, Lister D, McNulty CAM, Griggs D, Andrews JM: The comparative pharmacokinetics of five quinolones. J Antimicrob Chemother 1986;18(suppl D):71-81.

9. Frydman AM, LeRoux Y, LeFebvre ME, Djebbar F, Fourtillian JB, Galliott J: Pharmacokinetics of pefloxacin after repeated IV and oral doses of 400 mg in healthy volunteers. J Antimicrob Chemother 1986;17(suppl B):65-69.

10. Lode H, Höffken G, Olschewski P, Sievers B, Kirch A, Borner K, Koeppe P: Pharmacokinetics of ofloxacin after parenteral and oral administration. Antimicrob Agents Chemother 1987;31:1338-1342.

11. Johnson JA, Benziger DP: Metabolism and disposition of amifloxacin in laboratory animals. Antimicrob Agents Chemother 1985;27:774-781.

12. Weidekamm E, Stockel K, Dell D: Single-dose pharmacokinetics of the new quinolone fleroxacin (RO 23-6240) in humans. Rev Infect Dis 1988;10(suppl 1):594-595.

13. Schentag JJ, Watson WA, Nix DE, Sedman AJ, Frost RW, Letteri J: Time dependent interactions between antacids and quinolone antibiotics, abstract PPG-6. Clin Pharmacol Ther 1988;43:135.

14. Grasela TH, Schentag JJ, Sedman AJ, Wilton JH, Thomas DJ, Schultz RW, Lebsack ME, Kinkel AW: Inhibition of enoxacin absorption by antacids or ranitidine. Antimicrob Agents Chemother 1989;33:615-617.

15. Shiba K, Saito A, Miyahara T, Tachizawa H, Fugimoto T: The effect of aluminum hydroxide on the pharmacokinetics of new quinolones in humans. 15th International Congress of Chemotherapy, Istanbul, Turkey, July 19-24, 1987, Abstract 247, p 144.

16. Lode H: Drug interactions with quinolones. Rev Infect Dis 1988;10(suppl 1):S132-S136.

17. Preheim LC, Cuevas TA, Roccaforte JS, Mellencamp MA, Bittner MJ: Ciprofloxacin and antacids. Lancet 1986;2:48.

18. Schentag JJ, Gengo FM: Principles of antibiotic tissue penetration and guidelines for pharmacokinetic analysis. Med Clin N Am 1982;66:39-49.

19. Schentag JJ, Swanson DJ, Smith IL: Dual individualization - antibiotic dosage calculation from the integration of in vitro pharmacodynamics and in vivo pharmacokinetics. J Antimicrob Chemother 1985;15(suppl A):47-57.

20. Schentag JJ, Cumbo TJ, Jusko WJ, Plaut ME: Gentamicin tissue accumulation and nephrotoxic reactions. JAMA 1978;240:2067-2069.

21. Schentag JJ, Jusko WJ, Vance JW, Cumbo TJ, Abrutyn E, DeLattre M, Gerbracht LM: Gentamicin disposition and tissue accumulation on multiple dosing. J Pharmacokin Biopharm 1977;5:559-577.

22. Whelton A, Stout RL: An overview of antibiotic tissue penetration, in Cunha BA, Ristuccia AM (eds), *Antimicrobial Therapy*. New York, Raven Press, 1984, pp 81-94.

23. Nix DE, Schentag JJ: The quinolones: An overview and comparative appraisal of their pharmacokinetics and pharmacodynamics. J Clin Pharmacol 1988;28:169-173.

24. Ciprofloxacin Investigators Brochure (1986). Miles Pharmaceuticals, West Haven, Connecticut.

25. Enoxacin Investigators Brochure (1985). Warner-Lambert, Ann Arbor, Michigan.

26. Montay G, Goueffon Y, Roquet F: Absorption, distribution, metabolic fate, and elimination of pefloxacin mesylate in mice, rats, dogs, monkeys, and humans. Antimicrob Agents Chemother 1984;25:463-472.

27. Ziemniak JA, Shank RG, Schentag JJ: The partitioning of cimetidine into canine cerebrospinal fluid. Drug Metab Disp 1984;12:217-221.

28. Gerding DN, Hitt JA: Tissue penetration of the new quinolones in humans. Rev Infect Dis, in press.

29. Fillastre JP, Leroy A, Humbert G: Ofloxacin pharmacokinetics in renal failure. Antimicrob Agents Chemother 1987;31:156-160.

30. Danan G, Montay G, Cunci R, Erlinger S: Pefloxacin kinetics in cirrhosis. Clin Pharmacol Ther 1985;38:439-442.

31. Wingender W, Graefe K-H, Gau W, Förster D, Beermann D, Schacht P: Mechanism of renal excretion of ciprofloxacin in humans. Chemiotherapia 1985;4(suppl 2):403-404.

32. Boelaert J, Valcke Y, Schurgers M, Daneels R, Rosseneu M, Rousseel M, Bogaert MG: The pharmacokinetics of ciprofloxacin in patients with impaired renal function. J Antimicrob Chemother 1985;16:87-93.

33. Drusano GL, Weir M, Forrest A, Plaisance K, Emm T, Standiford HC: Pharmacokinetics of IV ciprofloxacin in patients with various degrees of renal function. Antimicrob Agents Chemother 1987;31:860-864.

34. Edlund C, Lidbeck A, Kager L, Nord CE: Effect of enoxacin on colonic microflora of healthy volunteers. Eur J Clin Microbiol 1987;6:298-300.

35. Brumfitt W, Franklin I, Grady D, Hamilton-Miller JMT, Iliffe A: Changes in the kinetics of ciprofloxacin and fecal flora during administration of a 7 day course to human volunteers. Antimicrob Agents Chemother 1984;26:757-761.

36. LeBel M, Barbeau G, Bergeron MG, Roy D, Vallée F: Pharmacokinetics of ciprofloxacin in elderly patients. Pharmacotherapy 1986;6:87-91.

37. LeBel M, Bergeron MG, Vallée F, Fiset C, Chasse G, Bigonesse P, Rivard G: Pharmacokinetics and pharmacodynamics of ciprofloxacin in cystic fibrosis. Antimicrob Agents Chemother 1986;30:260-266.

38. Goldfarb J, Wormser GP, Inshiosa MA, Guiden G, Diaz M, Mascia AV: Single dose pharmacokinetics of oral ciprofloxacin in patients with cystic fibrosis. J Clin Pharmacol 1986;26:222-226.

39. Wijnands W, van Herwaarden CLA, Vree TB: Enoxacin raises plasma theophylline concentrations. Lancet 1984;2:108-109.

40. Wijnands W, Vree TB, van Herwaarden CLA: Enoxacin decreases the clearance of theophylline in man. Br J Clin Pharmacol 1985;20:583-588.

41. Nix DE, De Vito JM, Whitbread MA, Schentag JJ: Effects of multiple dose oral ciprofloxacin on the pharmacokinetics of theophylline and indocyanine green. J Antimicrob Chemother 1987;19:263-269.

42. Gregoire SL, Grasela TH, Freer JP, Tack KJ, Schentag JJ: Inhibition of theophylline clearance by coadministered ofloxacin without alteration of theophylline effects. Antimicrob Agents Chemother 1987;31(3):375-378.

43. Morikawa K, Nagato O, Kubo S, Kato H, Yamamoto K: Unusual CNS toxic action of new quinolones, abstract 255. Program and abstracts of the 27th Interscience Conference on Antimicrobial Agents and Chemotherapy, New York, October 4-7, 1987.

44. Smith CR: Adverse effects of the fluoroquinolones. J Antimicrob Chemother 1987;19: 709-712.

45. Vogelman B, Gudmundsson S, Craig WA: Correlation of pharmacokinetic parameters of beta-lactam and aminoglycoside antibiotics with efficacy against gram negative bacilli in an animal model, abstract 24. Program and abstracts of the 24th Interscience Conference on Antimicrobial Agents and Chemotherapy, Washington, October 8-10, 1984.

46. Vogelman B, Gudmundsson S, Turnidge J, Leggett J, Craig WA: In vivo post antibiotic effect in a thigh infection in neutropenic mice. J Infect Dis 1988;157:287-298.

47. Gengo FM, Mannion TW, Nightingale CH, Schentag JJ: Integration of pharmacokinetics and pharmacodynamics of methicillin in the curative treatment of experimental endocarditis. J Antimicrob Chemother 1984;14:619-631.

48. Schentag JJ, Smith IL, Swanson DJ, DeAngelis C, Fracasso JE, Vari A, Vance JW: Role for dual individualization of cefmenoxime. Am J Med 1984;77(suppl 6A):43-50.

49. Gerber AU, Craig WA, Brugger H-P, Feller C, Vastola AP, Brandel J: Impact of dosing intervals on activity of gentamicin and ticarcillin against *Pseudomonas aeruginosa* in granulocytopenic mice. J Infect Dis 1983;147:910-917.

50. Bennett WM, Plamp CE, Gilbert DN, Parker RA, Porter GA: The influence of dosage regimen on experimental gentamicin nephrotoxicity: Dissociation of peak serum levels from renal failure. J Infect Dis 1979;140:576-580.

51. Reiner NE, Bloxham DD, Thompson WL: Nephrotoxicity of gentamicin and tobramycin given once daily or continuously in dogs. J Antimicrob Chemother 1978;4(suppl A):85-101.

52. McCormick JP, Schentag JJ: The potential impact of quantitative susceptibility tests on the design of aminoglycoside regimens. Drug Intell Clin Pharm 1987;21:187-191.

53. Gudmundsson S, Vogelman B, Wolz S, Craig WA: The in-vivo PAE of newer antimicrobials, abstract 546. Program and abstracts of the 25th Interscience Conference on Antimicrobial Agents and Chemotherapy, Minneapolis, September 29-October 2, 1985.

54. Michéa-Hamzehpour M, Auckenthaler R, Regamey P, Pechère JC: Resistance occurring during/after fluoroquinolone therapy of experimental *Pseudomonas aeruginosa* peritonitis. Antimicrob Agents Chemother 1987;31:1803-1808.

55. Nix DE, Sands MF, Peloquin CA, Vari AJ, Cumbo TJ, Vance JW, Fracasso JE, Schentag JJ: Dual individualization of intravenous ciprofloxacin in patients with nosocomial lower respiratory tract infections. Am J Med 1987;82(suppl 4A):352-356.

56. Peloquin CA, Cumbo TJ, Nix DE, Sands MF, Schentag JJ: Intravenous ciprofloxacin in patients with nosocomial lower respiratory tract infections: Impact of plasma concentrations, organism MIC, and clinical condition on bacterial eradication. Arch Intern Med 1989;149:2269-2273.

# FLUOROQUINOLONE THERAPY OF URINARY TRACT INFECTIONS  **3**

*Knud T. Nielsen*
*Jørn Aagaard*
*Paul O. Madsen*

## INTRODUCTION

The treatment of urinary tract infections (UTIs) has changed considerably over the past 10 to 15 years with the advent of new antimicrobials with favorable pharmacokinetics, broad antibacterial spectra, and competitive prices. The importance of such drugs is apparent when one considers that 10-20% of all women will develop urinary tract infection during their lifetime[1-3] and that 40% of all nosocomial infections are UTIs, most of which are caused by a transurethral catheter.[4]

This chapter will compare the newest group of antimicrobials, fluoroquinolones, to those antimicrobials currently used in the treatment of UTIs. Several studies of quinolone treatment of complicated and uncomplicated UTI and bacterial prostatitis have been published and will be reviewed. The use of quinolone prophylaxis in recurrent UTI, chronic bacterial prostatitis, and transurethral prostatic surgery will also be reviewed. Since only limited data are available on quinolone therapy in patients with asymptomatic bacteriuria, the treatment of these patients will not be discussed.

## Definitions

Before discussing therapeutic results in UTI, certain terms must be defined. *Urinary tract infection* is the presence of a specified number of bacteria in an uncontaminated urine sample from a patient with clinical symptoms. *Significant bacteriuria* has been defined as $10^5$ organisms in 1 mL of a clean-voided urine specimen from a noncatheterized patient.[5-7] Some authors consider this level to be too high, since approximately half of all symptomatic patients have colony counts well below this number.[8,9] A cutoff level of $10^2$ organisms/mL has been proposed.[10] Despite these

45

controversies, the definition of significant bacteriuria as $10^5$ colony-forming units/mL (cfu/mL) is used in most of the studies cited in this chapter unless otherwise stated. In patients with transurethral catheters long-term, Stark and Maki found that a level of $10^2$ cfu/mL will progress to higher levels and that treatment may be necessary if the patient is symptomatic.[4] Growth of more than one strain of organism in a urine specimen usually indicates contamination during sampling. However, mixed infections do occur, so the results from a culture should always be considered in light of the patient's symptoms.

The goal of treatment of urinary tract infections is to sterilize the urine.[3] Once the urine is sterilized, further treatment depends on the type and severity of the initial infection. After completion of therapy, the urinary tract may be colonized again. A recurrent infection can be categorized as either a relapse or a reinfection. Relapse is defined as isolation of the original organism in a symptomatic patient after initial eradication, while reinfection signifies colonization of the urinary tract with a new pathogen after previous successful treatment. Most recurrent UTIs are caused by reinfections from the fecal or vaginal reservoir.[3] Superinfection is present if the patient is infected with an additional organism during antimicrobial treatment.

When discussing and comparing various treatments, different endpoints and definitions of cure are often employed. The separation of therapeutic response into symptomatic and bacteriologic cure makes it easier to compare the results of different studies. However, bacteriologic treatment success has been defined as a reduction in colony count from $>10^5$ to $<10^5$ cfu/mL[11] or to $<10^4$ cfu/mL,[12] while still more restrictive criteria such as sterile urine are used by other investigators.[3]

In view of the problems in interpreting treatment results, the reader should keep in mind that comparison of minimal inhibitory concentrations (MICs) among antimicrobials does not necessarily reflect in vivo efficacy in terms of sterilizing the urine. Several factors such as pharmacokinetics, protein binding, ionization, excretion of the drug, and pH at the infected site will affect the clinical outcome. These variables are of special concern in the treatment of prostate infections.[13,14]

## Drug Concentration in Urine

In order to sterilize urine, a urine antimicrobial concentration of at least five times the MIC is generally necessary.[15] The urine concentration of ciprofloxacin reaches very high levels. Gonzalez et al[16] reported that two hours after a 250 mg oral dose of ciprofloxacin, the urine concentration ranged between 205 and 261 µg/mL; at 12 hours it was between 32 and 34 µg/mL. In elderly patients, urine concentrations ranged between 17.4 and 200 µg/mL 1-6 hours after a single 100 mg oral dose of ciprofloxacin.[17] Although somewhat lower than the concentrations reported in younger persons, these levels of ciprofloxacin are far above the MICs for relevant urinary pathogens (see chapter 1). Other clinically available fluoroquinolones, such as norfloxacin and cinoxacin, reach similarly high urine levels.

## Effect on Fecal Flora

Since most recurrent UTIs are reinfections,[3] a suitable drug for long-term prophylaxis would be one that alters the flora in feces and vagina and, most importantly, decreases the population of coliform bacteria. Ciprofloxacin was excreted in feces in high concentrations (185-2220 µg/g) following seven days of treatment with 500 mg twice daily.[18] The aerobic flora was changed considerably, with total absence of coliforms and decreased concentrations of streptococci and staphylococci. Anaerobes developed resistance to ciprofloxacin, but there was little change in their numbers. One week after cessation of treatment, the fecal flora had returned to normal. Similar effects on gram-negative bacteria and anaerobes were reported by Enzensberger et al.[19] Norfloxacin eradicated uropathogens in the feces in 14 of 15 patients, whereas trimethoprim-sulfamethoxazole (TMP-SMX) eradicated uropathogens in 8 of 14 patients; the two drugs had the same effect on the periurethral flora.[20] Enoxacin had the same effect as ciprofloxacin on fecal flora, even though it was excreted in lower concentrations.[21]

## UNCOMPLICATED URINARY TRACT INFECTIONS

Evaluation of fluoroquinolone therapy in uncomplicated UTI is difficult because a large proportion of patients have sterile urine after placebo therapy. In one study,[22] 71% of patients had sterile urine one month after placebo therapy and 80% were still uninfected at five-month follow-up. Thus, in order to demonstrate a significant treatment effect, a baseline cure rate of at least 70-80% should be obtained.

The typical patient, a woman with a symptomatic bladder infection, can be treated quite easily. A decade or more ago, therapy was often continued for several days; however, studies showed no difference between long- and short-term treatment.[23-25] Currently, single-dose therapy is accepted as the primary treatment,[26] and it can be used in first-time infected patients without obtaining a urine culture. The result of treatment will guide decisions on further therapy.[27] In an open, nonrandomized study,[28] two single oral doses of ciprofloxacin, 100 and 250 mg, were compared in 38 women. Cure rates of 84% and 89%, respectively, were obtained at the five-day follow-up; the corresponding four-week cure rates were 74% and 79%, respectively. These results are in the same range as those reported for single doses of amoxicillin (3 grams) and TMP-SMX (480 mg/2400 mg).[29,30] Interestingly, in a study of 39 women with uncomplicated bladder infections, 92% were cured at the seven-day follow-up using a single 500 mg dose of kanamycin administered intramuscularly.[31]

It is difficult to compare the cure rates in these studies due to the relatively small number of patients enrolled. In a report by Arcieri et al[32] describing their extensive clinical experience in open and controlled studies with ciprofloxacin administered orally, 465/514 (90%) patients with UTIs had sterile urine at short-term follow-up, and 83% of the patients evaluated at four weeks had sterile urine. The usual dose in these patients was 250 mg twice daily for a median duration of 10 days. These data confirm the efficacy of ciprofloxacin in the treatment of UTIs, but as pointed out by the authors, the patient population was heterogeneous with respect to both gender and severity of infection.

In a double-blind trial, 60 women with uncomplicated UTI were randomized to receive either ciprofloxacin 250 mg twice daily (n=30) or cinoxacin 500 mg twice daily (n=30), both given orally.[33] At the 4- to 6-week follow-up, 35 patients were evaluable for efficacy. Clinical cure was 80% in the ciprofloxacin group and 73% in the cinoxacin group. Three patients in the ciprofloxacin group had superinfection with enterococci, *K. oxytoca, E. coli*, or *Lactobacillus,* while three patients in the cinoxacin group had persistence of *E. coli.* A similar incidence of superinfection has been reported by other authors. Saaveda et al[34] reported their findings in 29 patients, most of whom had complicated UTI, who were treated with ciprofloxacin 500 mg twice daily for 1-2 weeks. Three of these patients developed superinfection with *Proteus, Pseudomonas* or *Citrobacter.* A very high rate of superinfection (8/32 patients, 25%) was also reported by Ryan et al,[35] who treated 32 patients with ciprofloxacin 500 mg orally. Superinfections were caused primarily by *Candida* and enterococci. These patients, however, many of whom were elderly, had significant primary disease such as diabetes mellitus and urological disorders. In addition, cultures of bladder urine generally revealed *Pseudomonas* or other organisms that were resistant to TMP-SMX before initial treatment.

The treatment of uncomplicated UTIs is fairly routine, and the quinolones do not seem to produce substantially better cure rates than other antibiotics, based on information from available studies. Furthermore, the difference in cost between a standard treatment such as sulfamethoxazole and a fluoroquinolone argues in favor of using the older agent. In patients who are allergic to the current drug of choice, TMP-SMX or ampicillin, the fluoroquinolones are a sensible alternative, administered orally as a single dose (eg, ciprofloxacin 250 mg or norfloxacin 400 mg).

## FLUOROQUINOLONE THERAPY OF COMPLICATED URINARY TRACT INFECTIONS

In this review, *complicated UTI* is defined as an infection in a patient with an indwelling catheter or anatomically abnormal urinary tract, or one that is caused by multi-resistant bacteria. Several studies of ciprofloxacin in complicated UTI have been published, but most of these are based on open and/or nonrandomized trials with small numbers of patients.[34-43] However, some conclusions can be drawn from these studies. Cure rates between 85% and 93% were reported in four studies[35,37,38,40] involving elderly patients and patients with infections caused by *Pseudomonas aeruginosa* or multi-resistant bacteria. Ciprofloxacin was administered orally in doses ranging from 250 mg to 500 mg twice daily for 5-17 days. Only a few recurrences were noted, and resistance to ciprofloxacin did not develop. The latter was the case in a study of 29 patients with multiple sclerosis, most of whom had indwelling catheters.[41] After seven days of treatment with ciprofloxacin 100 mg twice daily, 14 patients (48%) had bacteriological cure, while 5 had superinfections with *Pseudomonas, Streptococcus faecalis,* or *Klebsiella* spp. One patient was reinfected with a ciprofloxacin-resistant *Pseudomonas* strain. In a randomized, double-blind study comparing different dosage levels of ciprofloxacin, 84% were cured 5-9 days after treatment with 250 mg of ciprofloxacin twice daily for seven days.[11] This result was similar to the cure rates obtained using 500 mg and 750 mg twice daily.

Leigh et al[44,45] reported that norfloxacin produced cure rates in the same range as ciprofloxacin (85-95%); the cure rate with amoxicillin was lower but not significantly different (75%). In an open, multicenter study of 226 evaluable patients with UTIs,[12] norfloxacin 400 mg twice daily or TMP-SMX 160/180 mg twice daily was administered for at least seven days to 29 and 20 patients, respectively. Cure rates at the short-term follow-up were similar (28 of 29 on norfloxacin and 18 of 20 on TMP-SMX). In another randomized, double-blind multicenter study involving 1369 patients with lower and upper UTIs, no differences in efficacy between norfloxacin and TMP-SMX were found.[46] Oral enoxacin 200 mg administered twice daily for 6-14 days was evaluated in 28 patients with complicated UTIs.[47] Immediately after treatment, bacteriological cure was obtained in 96% of the patients, while the short-term cure rate was 72%. Similar results were obtained in a comparison of ciprofloxacin 500 mg daily with norfloxacin 800 mg daily.[48]

Ciprofloxacin and ofloxacin were compared in a small double-blind study in 35 patients with complicated UTI.[49] Bacteriological cure 10 days after treatment was 66% for ofloxacin and 50% for ciprofloxacin. However, no conclusions can be drawn as to differences in efficacy between the two drugs because of the small number of patients studied. The same is true of the report by Delia et al[50] in which 30 patients with uncomplicated UTIs (n=12) and serious recurrent UTIs (n=18) were treated with ofloxacin 300 mg three times daily for a mean of 14 days. Twenty-two patients (73%) had sterile urine at the 1 and 3-4 week follow-up periods. Of the remaining 8 patients, 6 were initially cured but relapsed, and one patient became reinfected (original pathogen *E. coli;* reinfecting isolate *S. faecalis).* Another patient was infected with *Ps. aeruginosa* and did not respond to ofloxacin therapy. The patient improved following treatment with ceftazidime.

Table 1.  Treatment of complicated urinary tract infections

BACTERIOLOGICAL CURE

| Drug/Dose/Duration | Number of Patients | Short-term* | Study design | Ref. |
|---|---|---|---|---|
| Ciprofloxacin | | | | |
| 500 mg x2, 7-28 d | 30 | 93% (28/30) | Open | 35 |
| Ciprofloxacin | | | | |
| 250 mg x2, 7 d | 43 | 84% (36/43) | Double-blind | 11 |
| 500 mg x2, 7 d | 37 | 87% (32/37) | randomized | |
| 750 mg x2, 7 d | 43 | 86% (37/43) | | |
| Norfloxacin | | | | |
| 400 mg x2, 10 d | 29 | 97% (28/29) | Open randomized | 12 |
| TMP/SMX | | | | |
| 160/800 mg x2, 10 d | 20 | 90% (18/20) | | |
| Enoxacin | | | | |
| 200 mg x2, 6-14 d | 25 | 72% (18/25)† | Open | 47 |
| Ciprofloxacin | | | | |
| 250 mg x2, 7 d | 17 | 47% (8/17) | Double-blind | 49 |
| Ofloxacin | | | randomized | |
| 100 mg x2, 7 d | 18 | 66% (12/18) | | |
| Ofloxacin | | | | |
| 300 mg x3, 9-26 d | 30 | 73% (22/30) | Open | 50 |

* Short term: follow-up evaluation 5-10 days after treatment.
† 5-14 day follow-up.

The overall impression from the published data, some of which are outlined in Table 1, is that complicated urinary tract infections such as upper tract infection, catheter-associated symptomatic bacteriuria, infections caused by multi-resistant organisms, and infections in anatomically abnormal urinary tracts can be safely and effectively treated with low doses of oral fluoroquinolones for 1-2 weeks. However, there is a need for properly designed double-blind studies with larger patient populations in order to compare different fluoroquinolones and to evaluate their long-term efficacy.

In summary, these data indicate that compared with current standard treatments, ciprofloxacin may be a cost-effective alternative to parenteral therapy in complicated UTI. The fact that the drug can be given on an outpatient basis further decreases the cost of therapy.

## BACTERIAL PROSTATITIS

The incidence of chronic and acute bacterial prostatitis is difficult to ascertain. Since antimicrobial therapy has a low long-term success rate (30-70%) in chronic bacterial prostatitis, it is fortunate that patients with this condition are not commonly encountered in clinical practice.[51] In the acutely inflamed prostate, antimicrobial therapy is usually effective, because these drugs typically diffuse freely from serum to the infected tissue. It is probable that any antimicrobial with the appropriate spectrum of activity that reaches sufficiently high serum concentrations can be used.[52] In the majority of cases, the pathogens isolated include Enterobacteriaceae, but *Pseudomonas* and enterococci can also be cultured.[52-54]

The study by Stamey et al[13] sheds light on several factors governing drug diffusion into the prostate. The ability of an antimicrobial agent to diffuse from serum into the prostatic acini is dependent on the drug's lipid solubility, its $pK_a$, and degree of protein binding. After the drug reaches the prostatic acini, the concentration attained is influenced by the pH of the prostatic secretion in relation to the serum pH and by whether the antimicrobial agent acts as an acid or a base. Using dog models, various antimicrobials have been infused and their concentrations in prostatic secretions and prostatic tissue measured.[13,55-57] A relationship between the concentration of the drug in the prostatic fluid and in plasma can be expressed using a rearrangement of the Henderson-Hasselbach equation.[58] This equation explains why drugs like ampicillin and the cephalosporins, with a low $pK_a$ and low lipid solubility, are not excreted in prostatic fluid and therefore may be inappropriate in the treatment of acute bacterial prostatitis. At higher pH values in prostatic fluid, as seen in chronic prostatitis, even these acidic drugs may reach therapeutically acceptable levels.[59]

Some criticism of the dog model has emerged, since the pH of prostatic secretion in dogs is acidic (6.5), whereas the pH of prostatic secretion is 8 in most patients with chronic bacterial prostatitis. Despite reservations concerning the dog model, comparisons between various quinolones have shown that the concentration of enoxacin in prostatic secretions is between 1.3-1.8 times the concurrent serum concentration, whereas ciprofloxacin and norfloxacin reach concentrations in prostatic secretions that are about one-half the serum concentration.[60] Studies in humans, however, have shown that all three quinolones attain concentrations in the prostatic tissue that are

1.9-2.5 times the serum concentration.[61] Ofloxacin was also found to concentrate in prostatic tissue, reaching levels 3.2 times the serum concentration.[62]

Clinical studies comparing different antibiotic treatments of chronic bacterial prostatitis are difficult to carry out due to the low incidence of the disease. This makes it difficult to enroll enough patients to provide adequate data for statistical analysis. The infecting organisms are the same as those which cause acute prostatitis. The predominant isolate is *E. coli*, but *Klebsiella, Proteus, Enterobacter*, and *Pseudomonas* are also occasionally cultured. The use of localization studies, as described by Meares and Stamey,[63] to verify the diagnosis and monitor the treatment result is essential in these trials.

Thirty-nine patients with chronic bacterial prostatitis were treated with oral ciprofloxacin 500 mg twice daily for a median period of 29 days.[64] The data, gathered from several separate studies, showed clinical success at the short-term evaluation in 77% (30/39) of patients, while bacteria were eradicated in all patients. The results of long-term follow-up at 6-12 months are lacking; the longest follow-up period reported was 10 weeks. Eight of 37 patients were considered treatment failures. Of these, 6 had reinfection or relapse, 1 had superinfection, and 1 required surgery because of persistent symptoms. The reinfections were caused by *Streptococcus* (n=3), *Pseudomonas* (n=1), *Citrobacter* (n=1), and *Klebsiella* (n=1) species. This report demonstrates that oral ciprofloxacin may have a high short-term cure rate in the treatment of chronic bacterial prostatitis, but its long-term efficacy is still unknown.

Weidner et al[65] treated 12 patients for two weeks with 500 mg ciprofloxacin twice daily. At the 12-month follow-up, clinical cure had been achieved in 5 patients, all of whom were infected with *E. coli,* while 2 patients had partial responses. Failures were encountered in patients infected with *Enterococcus* and *Pseudomonas* species. Based on the favorable pharmacokinetics and high concentration of the drug in the prostate, further evaluation of ciprofloxacin in chronic bacterial prostatitis is clearly warranted.

To date, no studies have compared the efficacy of various fluoroquinolones in the treatment of chronic bacterial prostatitis. Similarly, information on the comparative efficacy of standard drugs versus the quinolones is lacking. The available data on TMP-SMX indicate that 4-16 weeks of treatment will cure between 32% and 71% of patients, but long-term follow-up data are unavailable.[66-68] Carbenicillin indanyl sodium is currently the only antibiotic approved by the FDA for the treatment of bacterial prostatitis. Theoretically, the diffusion of carbenicillin into the prostate should be negligible, since the drug is an acid. However, the high pH (8) of prostatic fluid in patients with chronic infection facilitates diffusion of acidic drugs, and this may explain how carbenicillin indanyl sodium works. Oliveri et al[69] reported a 68% bacteriological cure rate after four weeks of carbenicillin indanyl sodium oral therapy, but they provided no information about long-term results. Other acidic drugs such as penicillins and cephalosporins would be expected to be equally effective.

Resistance to carbenicillin indanyl sodium among *Pseudomonas* species has emerged, underscoring the need for new antimicrobials with broad spectra and a low rate of microbial resistance. The fluoroquinolones, with their low MICs against most pathogens isolated in patients with chronic bacterial prostatitis, lack of plasmid-transferable resistance, and very low incidence of spontaneous mutational resistance,[33,38] seem promising in the treatment of chronic bacterial prostatitis. Furthermore, long-term low-dosage suppressive therapy is safe because of the low incidence (<7% in a large series) of clinically significant side effects.[32]

## PROPHYLACTIC USE OF FLUOROQUINOLONES IN UTIs

Prophylactic use of antimicrobial therapy is indicated to prevent recurrent UTIs in women, in patients with chronic bacterial prostatitis, and in those undergoing transurethral surgery. As mentioned above, the fluoroquinolones (eg, norfloxacin, ciprofloxacin, enoxacin) alter the fecal flora and consequently decrease the chance of reinfection of the urinary tract from the fecal reservoir, but no published study has compared the efficacy of the various fluoroquinolones for long-term prophylaxis in women with recurrent UTI or in men with chronic bacterial prostatitis.

The question of antimicrobial prophylaxis in transurethral resection of the prostate (TURP) has been extensively debated.[70] Most surgeons agree that preoperative bacteriuria, regardless of symptoms, should be treated, because bacteremia and septicemia are dramatically increased when invasive procedures are carried out on the urinary tract in the presence of infected urine.[71,72] In clinical practice, the result of a preoperative urine culture is not usually known until after surgery. Some reports indicate a high incidence (11%-70%) of significant bacteriuria ($10^5$ cfu/mL) in the first week after surgery in patients with preoperatively sterile urine.[73,74] This seems to be correlated with an increased risk for developing bacteremia and septicemia.[72] Therefore, the value of routine administration of various prophylactic antibiotics to all patients undergoing TURP, including those with preoperative sterile urine, has been evaluated in several studies.

Over the years the duration and time of initiation of antimicrobial prophylaxis in relation to surgery has been narrowed to a short (usually 24-48 hrs) perioperative period[75-81] or a single dose given just before surgery.[82-84] Two studies evaluated oral ciprofloxacin as a three-day perioperative course of 250 mg twice daily[80] and as short (1-2 days) or long (8-9 days) prophylaxis using a double dosage (500 mg twice daily).[81] In these trials, the incidence of significant postoperative bacteriuria decreased from 38% and 19.4% in the placebo groups to 6% and 2.5-3.4% in the prophylaxis groups, respectively.[80,81] In one of these studies, the duration of postoperative hospital stay was significantly shorter in the prophylaxis group.[80] No patient who received prophylaxis in either study developed postoperative bacteremia or septicemia, whereas five patients in the control groups did. In a prospective, randomized, double-blind trial, single doses of ciprofloxacin 300 mg or cefotaxime 1 gram IV were compared as prophylaxis preoperatively in 76 evaluable patients who underwent transurethral surgery.[82] One patient in the ciprofloxacin group and three patients in the cefotaxime group developed bacteriuria postoperatively. Placebo-controlled studies with quinolones,[80,81] cephalosporins,[83] and penicillins,[84] have all confirmed the value of antibiotic prophylaxis in reducing postoperative bacteriuria in TURP (Table 2).

The advantages of the fluoroquinolones are their convenience and decreased cost compared with parenteral antibiotics. In the study by Grabe et al,[81] a relatively long period of prophylaxis was used. However, the study by Christensen et al[82] suggests that a single perioperative dose of prophylactic treatment is as effective as an extended period of treatment. At present, it is not possible to provide a clear-cut recommendation as to which antimicrobial to use, but routine short-term, perioperative prophylaxis for all patients undergoing TURP is recommended.

**Table 2.** Incidence of postoperative bacteriuria after transurethral surgery in prospective randomized controlled trials on antibiotic prophylaxis

| Drug | Number of Patients | Administration | % Postoperative Bacteriuria | Statistics | Ref. |
|---|---|---|---|---|---|
| Ciprofloxacin | 50 | 3 days | 6% | p=0.002 | 80 |
| Placebo | 51 | | 38% | | |
| Ciprofloxacin | 29 | Until catheter removal (mean 1.5 days) | 3% | | 81 |
| Ciprofloxacin | 40 | 8-9 days | 3% | p=0.05 | |
| Placebo | 31 | Until catheter removal | 19% | | |
| Ciprofloxacin | 37 | 1 dose | 3% | NS† | 82 |
| Cefotaxime | 39 | 1 dose | 8%* | | |
| Ceftriaxone | 66 | 1 dose | 3% | p<0.05 | 83 |
| Placebo | 63 | | 13% | | |
| Mezlocillin | 49 | 1 dose | 18% | p<0.05 | 84 |
| Placebo | 51 | | 51% | | |

* 4-6 weeks postoperatively
† Not significant

# REFERENCES

1. Kass EH, Savage W, Santamarina BAG: The significance of bacteriuria in preventive medicine, in Kass EH (ed), *Progress in Pyelonephritis*. Philadelphia, FA Davis Co, 1965, p 3.

2. Freedman LR, Phair JP, Seki M, et al The epidemiology of urinary tract infections in Hiroshima. Yale J Biol Med 1965;37:262-282.

3. Stamey TA: Urinary tract infections in women, in Stamey TA (ed), *Pathogenesis and Treatment of Urinary Tract Infections*. Baltimore, Williams & Wilkins, 1980, pp 122-209.

4. Stark RP, Maki DG: Bacteriuria in the catheterized patient. N Engl J Med 1984;311:560-564.

5. Kass EH, Finland M: Asymptomatic infections of the urinary tract. Trans Assoc Am Physicians 1956;69:56-64.

6. Kass EH: Bacteriuria and the diagnosis of infections of the urinary tract, with observations on the use of methionine as a urinary antiseptic. Arch Intern Med 1957;100:709-714.

7. Kass EH: Role or asymptomatic bacteriuria in the pathogenesis of pyelonephritis, in Quinn EL, Kass EH (eds), *Biology of Pyelonephritis*. Boston, Little, Brown & Co, 1957, pp 399-412.

8. Monzon OT, Ory EM, Dobson HE, et al: A comparison of bacterial counts of the urine obtained by needle aspiration of the bladder, catheterization and midstream-voided methods. N Engl J Med 1958;259:764-767.

9. Goldberg LM, Vosti KL, Rantz LA: Microflora of the urinary tract examined by voided and aspirated urine culture, in Cass EH (ed), *Progress in Pyelonephritis*. Philadelphia, FA Davis, 1965, pp 545-549.

10. Stamm WE, Counts GW, Running KR, et al: Diagnosis of coliform infection in acutely dysuric women. N Engl J Med 1982;307:463-468.

11. Gasser TC, Graversen PH, Madsen PO: Treatment of complicated urinary tract infections with ciprofloxacin. Am J Med 1987;82(suppl 4A):278-279.

12. Sabbaj J, Hoagland VL, Shih WJ: Multiclinic comparative study of norfloxacin and trimethoprim-sulfamethoxazole for treatment of urinary tract infections. Antimicrob Agents Chemother 1985;27:297-301.

13. Stamey TA, Meares EM, Winningham DG: Chronic bacterial prostatitis and the diffusion of drugs into prostatic fluid. J Urol 1970;103:187-194.

14. Barza M, Cuchural G: The penetration of antibiotics into the prostate in chronic bacterial prostatitis. Eur J Clin Microbiol 1984;3:503-505.

15. Wolfson JS, Hooper DC: The fluoroquinolones: structures, mechanisms of action and resistance, and spectra of activity in vitro. Antimicrob Agents Chemother 1985;28:581-586.

16. Gonzalez MA, Uribe F, Moisen SD, et al: Multiple-dose pharmacokinetics and safety of ciprofloxacin in normal volunteers. Antimicrob Agents Chemother 1984;26:741-744.

17. Ball AP, Fox C, Ball ME, et al: Pharmacokinetics of oral ciprofloxacin, 100 mg single dose, in volunteers and elderly patients. J Antimicrob Chemother 1986;17:629-635.

18. Brumfitt W, Franklin I, Grady D, et al: Changes in the pharmacokinetics of ciprofloxacin and fecal flora during administration of a 7-day course to human volunteers. Antimicrob Agents Chemother 1984;26:757-761.

19. Enzenberger R, Shah PM, Knothe H: Impact of oral ciprofloxacin on the faecal flora of healthy volunteers. Infection 1985;13:273-275.

20. Haase DA, Harding GKM, Thomson MJ, et al: Comparative trial of norfloxacin and trimethoprim-sulfamethoxazole in the treatment of women with localized, acute, symptomatic urinary tract infections and antimicrobial effect on periurethral and fecal microflora. Antimicrob Agents Chemother 1984;26:481-484.

21. Edlund C, Lidbeck A, Kager L, et al: Comparative effects of enoxacin and norfloxacin on human colonic microflora. Antimicrob Agents Chemother 1987;31:1846-1848.

22. Mabeck CE: Treatment of uncomplicated urinary tract infection in non-pregnant women. Postgrad Med J 1972;48:69-75.

23. Gossius G, Vorland L: A randomised comparison of single-dose vs. three-day and ten-day therapy with trimethoprim-sulfamethoxazole for acute cystitis in women. Scand J Infect Dis 1984;16:373-379.

24. Tolkoff-Rubin NE, Weber D, Fang LST, et al: Single-dose therapy with trimethoprim-sulfamethoxazole for urinary tract infection in women. Rev Infect Dis 1982;4:444-448.

25. Counts GW, Stamm WE, McKevitt M, et al: Treatment of cystitis in women with a single dose of trimethoprim-sulfamethoxazole. Rev Infect Dis 1982;4:484-490.

26. Rubin RH: Infections of the urinary tract, in Rubenstein E, Federman DD, (eds), *Scientific American Medicine*. New York, Scientific American, Inc, 1985, pp 1-10.

27. Wilhelm MP, Edson RS: Antimicrobial agents in urinary tract infections. Mayo Clin Proc 1987;62:1025-1031.

28. Garlando F, Reitiker S, Tauber MG, et al: Single-dose ciprofloxacin at 100 versus 250 mg for treatment of uncomplicated urinary tract infections in women. Antimicrob Agents Chemother 1987;31:354-356.

29. Bailey RR, Abbott GD: Treatment of urinary tract infection with a single dose of amoxycillin. Nephron 1977;18:316-320.

30. Bailey RR, Abbott GD: Treatment of urinary tract infection with a single dose of trimethoprim-sulfamethoxazole. Can Med Assoc J 1978;118:551-553.

31. Ronald AR, Boutros P, Mourtada H: Bacteriuria localization and response to single-dose therapy in women. JAMA 1976;235:1854-1856.

32. Arcieri G, August R, Becker N, et al: Clinical experience with ciprofloxacin in the USA. Eur J Clin Microbiol 1986;5:220-225.

33. Goldstein EJC, Kahn RM, Alpert ML, et al: Ciprofloxacin versus cinoxacin in therapy of urinary tract infections:A randomized, double-blind trial. Am J Med 1987;82(suppl 4A):284-287.

34. Saavedra S, Ramírez-Ronda CH, Nevárez M: Ciprofloxacin in the treatment of urinary tract infections caused by *Pseudomonas aeruginosa* and multiresistant bacteria. Eur J Clin Microbiol 1986;5:255-257.

35. Ryan JL, Berenson CS, Greco TP, et al: Oral ciprofloxacin in resistant urinary tract infections. Am J Med 1987;82(suppl 4A):303-306.

36. Cox C: Brief report:Ciprofloxacin in the treatment of urinary tract infections caused by Pseudomonas species and organisms resistant to trimethoprim/sulfamethoxazole. Am J Med 1987; 82(suppl 4A):288-289.

37. Preheim LC, Cuevas TA, Roccaforte JS, et al: Oral ciprofloxacin in the treatment of elderly patients with complicated urinary tract infections due to trimethoprim/sulfamethoxazole-resistant bacteria. Am J Med 1987;82(suppl 4A):295-300.

38. Kamidono S, Arakawa S: Brief report:Ciprofloxacin treatment of complicated urinary tract infections. Am J Med 1987;82(suppl 4A):301-302.

39. Giamarellou H, Galanakis N, Dendrinos C, et al: Evaluation of ciprofloxacin in the treatment of *Pseudomonas aeruginosa* infections. Eur J Clin Microbiol 1986;5:232-235.

40. Mehtar S, Drabu Y, Blakemore P: Ciprofloxacin in the treatment of infections caused by gentamicin-resistant gram-negative bacteria. Eur J Clin Microbiol 1986;5:248-251.

41. Van Poppel H, Wegge M, Dammekens H, et al: Ciprofloxacin in the treatment of urinary tract infection in patients with multiple sclerosis. Eur J Clin Microbiol 1986;5:251-253.

42. Finch R, Whitby M, Craddock C, et al: Clinical evaluation of treatment with ciprofloxacin. Eur J Clin Microbiol 1986;5:257-259.

43. Boerema J, Boll B, Muytjens H, et al: Efficacy and safety of ciprofloxacin (Bay o 9867) in the treatment of patients with complicated urinary tract infections. J Antimicrob Chemother 1985;16:211-217.

44. Leigh DA, Emmanuel FXS: The treatment of *Pseudomonas aeruginosa* urinary tract infections with norfloxacin. J Antimicrob Chemother 1984;13(suppl B):85-88.

45. Leigh DA, Smith EC, Marriner J: Comparative study using norfloxacin and amoxicillin in the treatment of complicated urinary tract infections in geriatric patients. J Antimicrob Chemother 1984;13(suppl B):79-83.

46. The Urinary Tract Infection Study Group: Coordinated multicenter study of norfloxacin versus trimethoprim-sulfamethoxazole treatment of symptomatic urinary tract infections. J Infect Dis 1987;155:170-177.

47. Naber KG, Sorgel F, Gutzler F, et al: In vitro activity, pharmacokinetics, clinical safety and therapeutic efficacy of enoxacin in the treatment of patients with complicated urinary tract infections. Infection 1985;13:219-224.

48. Naber K, Bartosik-Wich B: Therapie komplizierter harnwegsinfektionen mit norfloxacin versus ciprofloxacin. Fortschr Antimikr Antineopl Chemother 1984;3:749-758.

49. Kromann-Andersen B, Sommer P, Pers C, et al: Clinical evaluation of ofloxacin versus ciprofloxacin in complicated urinary tract infections. Infection 1986;14(suppl 4):305-306.

50. Delia S, De Simone C, Vullo V, et al: Ofloxacin: Clinical evaluation in urinary and respiratory infections. Infection 1986;14(suppl 4):297-299.

51. Meares EM Jr: Prostatitis syndromes: New perspectives about old woes. J Urol 1980;123:141-147.

52. Ristuccia AM, Cunha BA: Current concepts in antimicrobial therapy of prostatitis. Urology 1982;20:338-345.

53. Goldfarb M: Clinical efficacy of antibiotics in treatment of prostatitis. Urology 1984; 24(suppl 6):12-13.

54. Shortliffe LMD: Prostatitis: Still a diagnostic and therapeutic dilemma. West J Med 1983; 139:542-544.

55. Fimodt-Møller PC, Dørflinger T, Madsen PO: Distribution of ciprofloxacin in the dog prostate and various tissues. Urol Res 1984;12:283-286.

56. Dørflinger T, Madsen PO: Enoxacin concentration in the prostatic tissue, prostatic secretion, interstitial fluid, and other tissues: An experimental study in dogs. J Int Biomed Info Data 1985;6:41-44.

57. Maigaard S, Frimodt-Møller N, Hoyme U, et al: Rosoxacin and cinoxacin distribution in prostate, vagina and female urethra. Invest Urol 1979;17:149-152.

58. Jacobs MH: Some aspects of cell permeability to weak electrolytes. Cold Spring Harbor Symp Quant Biol 1940;8:30.

59. Fair WR, Cordonnier JJ: The pH of prostatic fluid: A reappraisal and therapeutic implications. J Urol 1978;120:695-698.

60. Dørflinger T, Larsen EH, Glasser TC, et al: The concentration of various quinolone derivatives in the dog prostate, in Weidner W, (ed), *Therapy of Prostatitis: Experimental and Clinical Data.* Munchen, W Zuckschwerdt, 1986, pp 35-39.

61. Dørflinger T, Larsen EH, Glasser TC, et al: The concentration of various quinolone derivatives in the human prostate, in Weidner W (ed), *Therapy of Prostatitis: Experimental and Clinical Data.* Munchen, W Zuckschwerdt, 1986, pp 40-44.

62. Claes R, Dusart Y, Dupont JC, et al: Diffusion of oral ofloxacin (Hoe 280) into human prostatic tissue: Assessment by an improved high-performance liquid chromatographic method. Infection 1968;14(suppl 4):263-265.

63. Meares EM, Stamey TA: Bacteriologic localization patterns in bacterial prostatitis and urethritis. Invest Urol 1968;5:492-518.

64. Childs SJ: Treatment of chronic bacterial prostatitis with ciprofloxacin. Infect Surg 1987;6:649-651.

65. Weidner W, Schiefer HG, Dalhoff A: Treatment of chronic bacterial prostatitis with ciprofloxacin. Results of a one-year follow-up study. Am J Med 1987;82(suppl 4A):280-283.

66. Drach GW: Trimethoprim sulfamethoxazole therapy of chronic bacterial prostatitis. J Urol 1974;111:637-639.

67. McGuire EJ, Lytton B: Bacterial prostatitis: Treatment with trimethoprim-sulfamethoxazole. Urology 1976;7:499-500.

68. Pfau A, Sacks T: Chronic bacterial prostatitis: New therapeutic aspects. Br J Urol 1976;48:245-253.

69. Oliveri RA, Sachs RM, Caste PG: Clinical experience with geocillin in the treatment of bacterial prostatitis. Curr Ther Res 1979;25:415-421.

70. Grabe M: Antimicrobial agents in transurethral prostatic resection. J Urol 1987; 138:245-252.

71. Sullivan NM, Sutter VL, Mims NM, et al: Clinical aspects of bacteremia after manipulation of the genitourinary tract. J Infect Dis 1973;127:49-55.

72. Cafferkey MT, Falkiner FR, Gillespie WA, et al: Antibiotics for the prevention of septicaemia in urology. J Antimicrob Chemother 1982;9:471-477.

73. Fair WR: Perioperative use of carbenicillin in transurethral resection of the prostate. Urology 1986;27(suppl 2):15-18.

74. Grabe M, Forsgren A: Impact of short perioperative courses of cefotaxime on aerobic bacterial flora in patients undergoing transurethral prostatic resection. Eur J Clin Microbiol 1985;4:24-29.

75. Iversen P, Madsen PO: Short-term cephalosporin prophylaxis in transurethral surgery. Clin Ther 1982;5(suppl A):58-66.

76. Prokocimer P, Quazza M, Gibert C, et al: Short-term prophylactic antibiotics in patients undergoing prostatectomy; report of a double-blind randomized trial with 2 intravenous doses of cefotaxime. J Urol 1986;135:60-64.

77. Falkiner FR, Ma PTS, Murphy DM, et al: Antimicrobial agents for the prevention of urinary tract infection in transurethral surgery. J Urol 1983;129:766-768.

78. Grabe M, Forsgren A, Hellsten S: The effectiveness of a short perioperative course with pivampicillin/pivmecillinam in transurethral prostatic resection: Clinical results. Bacteriological results. Scand J Infect Dis 1986;18:567-573.

79. Goldwasser B, Bogokowski B, Nativ O, et al: Prophylactic antimicrobial treatment in transurethral prostatectomy. How long should it be instituted? Urology 1983;22:136-138.

80. Murdoch DA, Badenoch DF, Gatchalian ER: Oral ciprofloxacin as prophylaxis in transurethral resection of the prostate. Br J Urol 1987;60:153-156.

81. Grabe M, Forsgren A, Björk T, et al: Controlled trial of a short and prolonged course with ciprofloxacin in patients undergoing transurethral prostatic surgery. Eur J Clin Microbiol 1987;6:11-17

82. Christensen MM, Nielsen KT, Knes JM, et al: Brief report: Single-dose preoperative prophylaxis in transurethral surgery. Ciprofloxacin versus cefotaxime. Am J Med 1989;87(suppl 5A):258S-260S.

83. Finkelstein LH, Arsht DB, Manfrey SJ, et al: Ceftriaxone in the prevention of postoperative infection in patients undergoing transurethral resection of the prostate. Am J Surg 1984;148:19-21.

84. Charton M, Dosne B, Escovar P, et al: Traitement prophylactique minute des infections urinares aprs resection endoscopique de la prostate. Presse Med 1984;13:545.

# FLUOROQUINOLONES IN SKIN AND SKIN STRUCTURE INFECTIONS  **4**

*Lawrence J. Eron*

## INTRODUCTION

Infections of the skin and skin structure may be categorized as either primary cellulitis and pyoderma or as secondary invasion of wounds. Staphylococci and streptococci are the principal bacteria that cause cellulitis and pyoderma. With impetigo or erysipelas, Group A Streptococcus produces a rapidly evolving cellulitis that may develop in an exceedingly short period of time. However, its management is very straightforward. Rapid institution of oral penicillin, an oral cephalosporin, or erythromycin invariably reverses the process, with little morbidity and only rare adverse drug reactions.

Secondary wound invasion may not be as simple, both because of underlying diseases in the host and because of the involvement of more resistant bacteria. Perhaps the most challenging example is that of the diabetic patient with an infected plantar ulcer. The diabetic patient may have a defect in the external "armor" through which bacteria may easily pass. In the normal host bacteria are eliminated easily, but in the diabetic, either due to impaired circulation to the lower extremity or to a subtle defect in the polymorphonuclear leukocyte, an infectious process is more likely to develop.[1]

## INFECTION IN THE DIABETIC FOOT

Although many diabetic foot infections are caused by *Staphylococcus aureus*, these infections may be polymicrobial and involve other organisms such as Group B Streptococcus, anaerobes, facultative gram-negative bacilli, or even *Streptococcus faecalis*.[2] The exact role of each bacterial species in the pathogenic process has not yet been clearly delineated, but most therapeutic strategies utilize broad spectrum antibiotic coverage if there is no material to culture or if analysis of purulent wound drainage reveals polymicrobial flora.[1] In both cases the clinician may feel more comfortable if *S. aureus*, streptococcus (Group B), and/or anaerobic organisms are included in the spectrum of the antibiotic chosen (often clindamycin, cefoxitin, cefazolin, or nafcillin). Although these antibiotics possess good activity against methicillin-sensitive *S. aureus*, they are not active against gram-negative bacilli that are cephalothin-resistant (such as *Pseudomonas aeruginosa*, *Serratia marcescens*, and *Enterobacter* species), and are especially ineffective against methicillin-resistant *Staphylococcus aureus* (MRSA). While aminoglycosides are effective against many of these gram-negative pathogens, and vancomycin is active against MRSA, their toxicity and cost limit their usefulness. As MRSA infections become more widespread in the hospital and the community, the need for alternatives to vancomycin will become increasingly critical. This is particularly true in the treatment of the diabetic patient, who can ill afford the ototoxicity or nephrotoxicity that can occur with vancomycin, especially if diabetic retinopathy or Kimmelstiel-Wilson nephropathy complicate the clinical picture. The new fluorinated quinolones may be useful here if their in vivo efficacy matches their in vitro potency against MRSA.

## TRAUMATIC PSEUDOMONAS FOOT INFECTION

One of the most difficult clinical problems arises from a simple nail puncture of the plantar surface of the foot. Because *Ps. aeruginosa* colonizes the tissues, it may be driven deeply into the foot by the nail.[3] The clinician should attempt to clean the wound of all debris and foreign material. Because it is difficult to completely cleanse this type of contaminated wound, antibiotics should be administered. However, since otherwise healthy patients with this problem are usually managed on an outpatient basis, the use of parenteral agents such as aminoglycosides (tobramycin), third-generation cephalosporins (ceftazidime), acylureidopenicillins (azlocillin, mezlocillin, piperacillin), or carbapenems (imipenem) is not feasible. Fluoroquinolones may be utilized in this setting, however, due to their activity against *Ps. aeruginosa* and ability to be given orally.

Oral administration is also less costly than parenteral administration, since it does not involve extra equipment or labor to prepare admixtures for infusion (see chapter 15). These qualities also make quinolones useful in the hospital setting in more serious infections. However, by force of habit, clinicians usually rely on intravenous antibiotics in the hospital setting: (1) for reliable drug absorption; (2) to obtain high serum levels; and (3) because the only antibiotics active against cephalothin-resistant gram negative bacilli or MRSAs in the past were parenteral antibiotics.

## OVERALL CLINICAL EXPERIENCE WITH ORAL CIPROFLOXACIN

A large clinical experience has been compiled with ciprofloxacin in skin and skin structure infections. In 218 cases of skin and skin structure infections in the U.S.,[6] ciprofloxacin produced an overall cure rate of 71%, an improvement rate of 21%, and a failure rate of 8%. Bacterial pathogens were eradicated in 82% of cases, including 93 of 111 instances of *Ps. aeruginosa* (89%), 39 of 40 cases of *Enterobacter* spp. (98%), 8 of 10 cases of *Serratia* spp. (80%), and 6 of 9 *Acinetobacter* spp. (67%). If only monomicrobial *Ps. aeruginosa* infections are considered, an efficacy rate of 89% (51 of 57 cured or improved) and a cure rate of 68% (39 of 57 cured) were observed (Table 1). If all monomicrobial infections caused by cephalothin-resistant gram negative bacilli are combined, an efficacy rate of 92% (79 of 86 cases) and a cure rate of 74% (64 of 86 cases) were obtained.

In an open trial, Eron et al[4] reported their results in 26 patients with *Pseudomonas* infections who were treated with ciprofloxacin. Sixteen of 26 patients were cured, 5 improved, and 5 failed, for a response rate of 86%. The five who failed were diabetics with *Pseudomonas* infections of the lower extremities; in four of these, ciprofloxacin-resistant strains of *Ps. aeruginosa* emerged during therapy. Scully et al[5] reported a 73% response rate in 15 skin/skin structure infections caused by *Ps. aeruginosa*. Clinical failure again correlated with the emergence of resistance to ciprofloxacin as well as with underlying disease (usually diabetes). The emergence of resistant strains during the course of therapy may result from the conversion of a previously sensitive *Pseudomonas* strain to a resistant one or to superinfection with a new *Pseudomonas* strain that is resistant to ciprofloxacin.

Table 1.  Clinical efficacy of ciprofloxacin in the treatment of monomicrobial infections of skin and skin structures

| | Number of Patients (%) | | |
|---|---|---|---|
| | Cure | Improvement | Failure |
| *Pseudomonas aeruginosa* | 39 (68) | 12 (21) | 6 (11) |
| *Enterobacter* spp. | 8 (80) | 1 (10) | 1 (10) |
| *Serratia marcescens* | 3 (100) | 0 | 0 |
| *Citrobacter diversus* | 6 (100) | 0 | 0 |
| *Escherichia coli* | 14 (88) | 2 (12) | 0 |
| *Staphylococcus aureus* | 74 (84) | 12 (14) | 2 (2) |
| Group A streptococci | 11 (100) | 0 | 0 |
| Non-A, Group D streptococci | 6 (86) | 1 (14) | 0 |
| Anaerobes | 3 (100) | 0 | 0 |

From Am J Med 1987;82(suppl 4A):224-226.

Clinical efficacy rates for all infections (both mono- and polymicrobial) were tabulated according to bacterial strains (Table 2). Unexpectedly good efficacy rates were noted for anaerobic infections, which is surprising given the relatively low in vitro activity of ciprofloxacin against anaerobes. Cure was observed in 10 patients (56%), improvement in 3 (17%), and failure in 5 (28%). These five infections involved Peptococcus (n=1), Peptostreptococcus (n=2), and *Bacteroides species* (n=2). Fass[7] reported excellent cure rates for infections caused by *Ps. aeruginosa* (11 of 13) and anaerobic bacteria (4 of 5). Greenberg et al[8] reported an efficacy rate of 90% in 20 skin/skin structure infections. Wood and Logan[9] treated 21 patients and obtained a 95% efficacy rate in infections caused by S. aureus and Streptococcus Group A. Parish and Witkowski[10] treated 148 cases of various types of pyoderma caused mostly

Table 2. Clinical efficacy of ciprofloxacin in the treatment of all infections (including polymicrobial) of skin and skin structures

|  | Number of Patients (%) | | |
|---|---|---|---|
|  | Cure | Improvement | Failure |
| *Pseudomonas aeruginosa* | 69 (62) | 30 (27) | 12 (11) |
| *Enterobacter* spp. | 30 (75) | 8 (20) | 2 (5) |
| *Serratia marcescens* | 6 (67) | 1 (11) | 2 (22) |
| *Proteus* (indole-positive) | 13 (76) | 4 (24) | 0 |
| *Citrobacter diversus* | 12 (70) | 3 (18) | 2 (12) |
| *Klebsiella* spp. | 29 (71) | 10 (24) | 2 (5) |
| *Morganella morganii* | 10 (83) | 2 (17) | 0 |
| *Providencia stuartii* | 9 (90) | 1 (10) | 0 |
| *Acinetobacter anitratus* | 7 (70) | 2 (20) | 1 (10) |
| *E. coli* | 52 (78) | 12 (18) | 3 (4) |
| *S. aureus* | 141 (75) | 37 (20) | 10 (5) |
| Group A streptococci | 22 (76) | 5 (17) | 2 (7) |
| Non-A, D streptococci | 23 (68) | 10 (29) | 1 (3) |
| Enterococci | 12 (48) | 11 (44) | 2 (8) |
| Anaerobes | 10 (56) | 3 (17) | 5 (27) |

From Am J Med 1987;82(suppl 4A):224-226.

by staphylococci (61 cases) but in 16 instances by anaerobes, again with excellent efficacy rates (88.5% overall). Twelve of the 16 anaerobic infections responded satisfactorily. Valainis et al[11] noted an 85% satisfactory response rate in 33 courses of antibiotic, while Pien and Yamane[12] treated 19 patients, 13 of whom were infected with *Ps. aeruginosa*, again with excellent results.

These excellent efficacy rates for ciprofloxacin in the treatment of infections of skin and skin structure are especially notable, since they involved large numbers of cephalothin-resistant gram-negative bacilli. Indeed, the efficacy rates for ciprofloxacin in *Pseudomonas* infections are comparable to those for piperacillin[13,14] (72% and 56%), ceftazidime[15,16] (92% and 88%), imipenem[17] (95%), and tobramycin[18] (83%).

## COMPARISON OF ORAL CIPROFLOXACIN WITH INTRAVENOUS CEFOTAXIME

Comparisons between oral ciprofloxacin and intravenous cefotaxime indicate that ciprofloxacin is as effective as cefotaxime in the treatment of infections of skin and skin structure caused by *S. aureus*, *S. pyogenes*, and gram-negative bacilli, both cephalothin-sensitive and cephalothin-resistant. For example, Self et al[19] randomized 89 patients to receive oral ciprofloxacin and intravenous placebo, or oral placebo and intravenous cefotaxime and evaluated the two groups in a double-blind fashion. Cures were reported in 89% of those who received ciprofloxacin and in 93% of those who received cefotaxime. There were no differences between the two groups in terms of length of hospitalization, complication rate, or adverse reactions. In an identical study, Ramirez-Ronda et al[20] reported cure rates of 79% and 68%, respectively, in 60 patients. Perez-Ruvalcaba et al[21] reported cure rates of 77% and 76%, respectively, in 61 episodes, and Parish and Asper[22] observed cure rates of 88% and 69%, respectively, in their study of 56 patients. The combined experience,[23] in which 196 received oral ciprofloxacin and 204 received intravenous cefotaxime, revealed clinical cure rates of 78% with each drug, clinical failure rates of 2% with ciprofloxacin and 6% with cefotaxime, bacteriological eradication rates of 91% and 89%, respectively, and adverse drug reactions in 14% and 11% of cases, respectively. All 29 isolates of *Ps. aeruginosa* were eradicated by ciprofloxacin, compared with 12 of 21 with cefotaxime. Interestingly, the organisms with the poorest response to ciprofloxacin were streptococci (84% eradicated).

Orally administered ciprofloxacin achieves equivalent results to intravenously administered cefotaxime in the treatment of infections of skin and skin structure, although in the studies reported above, the pathogens were predominantly gram-positive cocci and cephalothin-sensitive gram-negative bacilli. Cephalothin-resistant gram-negative bacilli were the causative organisms in only a minority of the cases.

## OVERALL EFFICACY OF OTHER FLUOROQUINOLONES

Compared with ciprofloxacin, relatively few studies have been published describing the activity of the other quinolones. Enoxacin was compared to cephalexin in a double-blind trial[24] involving 36 patients with staphylococcal skin and skin structure infections. Cure rates were similar (43% vs. 50%, respectively). In an open study,[25] enoxacin produced a satisfactory response rate in 91% of patients with a wide variety of skin and skin structure infections. Ofloxacin was compared to cephalexin in two multicenter trials involving 263 and 400 patients, respectively.[26] Cure rates in the first study were 91% and 90%, respectively, and in the second study, 93% and 94%, respectively. Enoxacin and ofloxacin appear to be equivalent to cephalexin in the treatment of staphylococcal and streptococcal infections, but very little can be said about the efficacy of these two drugs for the treatment of infections caused by cephalothin-resistant gram-negative bacilli.

## FLUOROQUINOLONES IN STAPHYLOCOCCAL INFECTIONS

Trials with ciprofloxacin have indicated that this drug is effective in the treatment of infections caused by cephalothin-resistant gram-negative bacilli that heretofore were treatable only with parenteral antibiotics.[27] In vitro data[28] also suggest that ciprofloxacin may be useful in the treatment of MRSAs that up to now have required intravenous vancomycin. Mulligan et al[29] treated 14 episodes of MRSA colonization and 11 were eradicated. This success was tempered by the development of resistance to ciprofloxacin in seven treatment episodes. In a study using ofloxacin to treat skin and skin structure infections caused by methicillin-sensitive *S. aureus*, eradication of nasal colonization was also studied. Ofloxacin eradicated nasal carriage in 14 of 15 cases.[26] This impressive effect may be due to the ability of the fluorinated quinolones to concentrate in respiratory mucosal tissue.

Not all studies indicate a uniformly excellent response to ciprofloxacin for infections caused by *S. aureus* strains. In a report of 17 infections caused by methicillin-sensitive *S. aureus* severe enough to necessitate hospitalization, Righter reported five clinical failures and 12 bacteriological failures (71%).[30] These results conflict with those reported in the U.S. multicenter trials in which 124/148 (84%) staphylococcal infections were eradicated. The small size of the Righter study or the relative severity of the infections may account for the discrepancy. This study, however, serves to reinforce the need for close clinical monitoring of patients with severe staphylococcal infections who are treated with ciprofloxacin.

## CONCLUSION

Fluorinated quinolones such as ciprofloxacin, enoxacin, and ofloxacin are effective in the treatment of skin and skin structure infections caused by a variety of bacteria, including cephalothin-sensitive organisms such as *Staphylococcus aureus, Streptococcus pyogenes, E. coli,* and *Klebsiella pneumonia*e. In addition, ciprofloxacin is effective in the treatment of infections caused by cephalothin-resistant gram-negative bacilli, including *Ps. aeruginosa, Serratia marcescens,* and *Enterobacter* species. Orally administered ciprofloxacin is as effective as intravenously administered cefotaxime in the treatment of skin and skin structure infections, especially when these infections are caused by staphylococci and streptococci. Ciprofloxacin may be useful in helping to eradicate nasal colonization by methicillin-resistant *S. aureus.* In addition, fluoroquinolones may be a therapeutic alternative to vancomycin for infections caused by methicillin-resistant *S. aureus.* Finally, the oral administration of fluorinated quinolones may facilitate outpatient therapy and reduce the cost of drug administration when used in hospitalized patients.

# REFERENCES

1. Gibbons GW, Eliopoulos GM: Infection of the diabetic foot, in Kozak GP, Hoar CS, Rowbotham JL, Wheelock FC Jr, Gibbons GW, Campbell DWB (eds), *Management of Diabetic Foot Problems*. Philadelphia, WB Saunders, 1984, pp 97-102.

2. Axler DA: Microbiology of diabetic foot infections. J Foot Surg 1987;26(suppl):S3-S6.

3. Greene NE, Bruno J: Pseudomonas infections of the foot after puncture wounds. South Med J 1980;73:146-149.

4. Eron LJ, Harvey L, Hixon DL, et al: Ciprofloxacin therapy of infections caused by Pseudomonas aeruginosa and other resistant bacteria. Antimicrob Agents Chemother 1985;28:308-310.

5. Scully BE, Neu HC, Parry MF, et al: Oral ciprofloxacin therapy of infections due to Pseudomonas aeruginosa. Lancet 1985;1:819-822.

6. Arcieri G, August R, Becker N, et al: Clinical experience with ciprofloxacin in the USA. Eur J Clin Microbiol 1986;5:220-225.

7. Fass RJ: Treatment of skin and soft tissue infections with oral ciprofloxacin. J Antimicrob Chemother 1986;18(suppl D):153-157.

8. Greenberg RN, Kennedy DJ, Reilly PM, et al: Treatment of bone, joint, and soft tissue infections with oral ciprofloxacin. Antimicrob Agents Chemother 1987;31:151-155.

9. Wood MJ, Logan MN: Ciprofloxacin for soft tissue infections. J Antimicrob Chemother 1986;18(suppl D):159-164.

10. Parish LC, Witkowski JA: The quinolones and dermatologic practice. Int J Dermatol 1986;25: 351-356.

11. Valainis GT, Pankey GA, Katner HP, et al: Ciprofloxacin in the treatment of bacterial skin infections. Am J Med 1987;82(suppl 4A):230-232.

12. Pien FD, Yamane KK: Ciprofloxacin treatment of soft tissue and respiratory infections in a community outpatient practice. Am J Med 1987;82(suppl 4A):236-238.

13. Eron LJ, Goldenberg RI, Poretz DM, et al: Piperacillin therapy for Pseudomonas infections. South Med J 1983;76:859-862.

14. Simon GL, Snydman DR, Tally FP, et al: Clinical trial of piperacillin with acquisition of resistance by Pseudomonas and clinical relapse. Antimicrob Agents Chemother 1980; 18:167-170.

15. Clumeck N, Van Laethem Y, Gordts BL, et al: Use of ceftazidime in the therapy of serious infections, including those due to multiresistant organisms. Antimicrob Agents Chemother 1983;24:176-188.

16. Eron LJ, Park CH, Hixon DL, et al: Ceftazidime in patients with Pseudomonas infections. J Antimicrob Chemother 1983;12(suppl A): 161-169.

17. Calandra GB, Hesney M, Grad C: A multiclinic randomized study of the comparative efficacy, safety, and tolerance of imipenem (cilastatin) and moxalactam. Eur J Clin Microbiol 1984;3:478-487.

18. Bendusch CL, Weber R: Tobramycin sulfate: A summary of worldwide experience from clinical trials. J Infect Dis 1976;134(suppl):S219-S234.

19. Self PL, Zeluff BA, Sollo D, et al: Use of ciprofloxacin in the treatment of serious skin and skin structure infections. Am J Med 1987;82(suppl 4A):239-241.

20. Ramirez-Ronda CH, Saavedra S, Rivera-Vázquez CR: Comparative, double-blind study of oral ciprofloxacin and intravenous cefotaxime in skin and skin structure infections. Am J Med 1987;82(suppl 4A):220-223.

21. Perez-Ruvalcaba JA, Quintero-Perez NP, Morales-Reyes JJ, et al: Double-blind comparison of ciprofloxacin with cefotaxime in the treatment of skin and skin structure infections. Am J Med 1987;82(suppl 4A):242-246.

22. Parish LC, Asper R: Systemic treatment of cutaneous infections. Am J Med 1987; 82(suppl 4A):381-386.

23. Arcieri G, Griffith E, Gruenwaldt G, et al: Ciprofloxacin update on clinical experience. Am J Med 1987;82(suppl 4A):381-386.

24. King L, Vire CG: Comparison of enoxacin and cephalexin in the treatment of patients with skin and skin structure infections, in Ishigami J (ed), *Recent Advances in Chemotherapy*. Tokyo, University of Tokyo Press, 1985, pp 1751-1752.

25. Mensing H: Ergebnisse der bechandlung bakterieller entzundungen der haut mit enoxacin. Infection 1986;14(suppl 3):S217-S218.

26. Data on file, Ortho Pharmaceuticals, Raritan, New Jersey.

27. Eron L: Therapy of skin and skin structure infections with ciprofloxacin. Am J Med 1987;82(suppl 4A):224-226.

28. Smith SM, Eng RHK: Activity of ciprofloxacin against methicillin-resistant Staphylococcus aureus. Antimicrob Agents Chemother 1985;27:688-691.

29. Mulligan ME, Ruane PJ, Johnston L, et al: Ciprofloxacin for eradication of methicillin-resistant Staphylococcus aureus colonization. Am J Med 1987;82(suppl 4A):215-219.

30. Righter J: Ciprofloxacin treatment of *Staphylococcus aureus* infections. J Antimicrob Chemother 1987;20:595-597.

# FLUOROQUINOLONES IN BONE AND JOINT INFECTIONS   **5**

*Jon T. Mader*

## INTRODUCTION

The quinolones are DNA gyrase inhibitors, of which the prototype is nalidixic acid. Over the past several years, many new fluorinated derivatives of the quinolones have been synthesized. Recently, the use of the fluoroquinolones for the treatment of bone and joint infections has received much attention in the literature. Although fluoroquinolones appear to have several unique advantages, the one most often cited is their oral mode of administration, resulting in an estimated savings of $1,600 per patient on antibiotic costs alone over traditional treatment protocols.[1] This estimate does not include other cost-saving factors such as shortened hospital stays and reduced relapse/failure rates.

Another distinct advantage of the fluoroquinolones is their wide spectrum of activity. With few exceptions the fluoroquinolones are active against most aerobic gram-positive and gram-negative bacteria, including the most frequently isolated strains in the United States for the period 1971-1982. These include *Staphylococcus aureus, Staphylococcus epidermidis, Escherichia coli, Pseudomonas aeruginosa, Streptococcus faecalis, Klebsiella pneumoniae, Proteus mirabilis*, and *Haemophilus influenzae*.[2] In addition, the fluoroquinolones are active against *Mycobacterium tuberculosis, Mycobacterium fortuitum, Chlamydia trachomatis, Mycoplasma hominis*, and *Rickettsia conorii*.[2]

Ciprofloxacin is the fluoroquinolone most often utilized in the treatment of bone and joint infections. Compared to nalidixic acid, the fluoroquinolones are much less neurotoxic and not highly protein-bound, ranging from 14 to 30%.[3] In addition, ciprofloxacin is 100 times more potent, has a greater spectrum of activity, and promotes less resistance than nalidixic acid.[4] The bioavailability of ciprofloxacin in bone has been found to be 2.4 µg/mL at 12 hours post dosing with 500 mg.[2] Desplaces and Acar[5] reported that good penetration and storage in inorganic bone, as well as an oral half life of approximately four hours, made ciprofloxacin particularly useful for the treatment of bone and joint infections. However, the use of ciprofloxacin in bone infections must be confined to adult populations. The administration of any of the fluoroquinolones, particularly nalidixic acid, before closure of the epiphyses is contraindicated due to potential collagen changes.[4,6]

## ADULT OSTEOMYELITIS

Traditionally, osteomyelitis has been classified as acute or chronic. Generally, newly recognized bone infections are considered acute, whereas a relapse of a treated infection and/or a failure to respond to the usual measures of management represent a chronic process. The hallmarks of chronic osteomyelitis are a nidus of infected dead bone or scar tissue, an ischemic soft tissue envelope, and a refractory clinical course.[7] However, this simplistic approach ignores the defensive and restorative capabilities of the host, the site and extent of bony and soft tissue involvement, and the characteristics of the infective process. All of these factors influence medical and surgical management, as well as the anticipated outcome.

## *Staging of Osteomyelitis*

Recently, a classification system for chronic osteomyelitis has been offered by Cierny and colleagues[7,8] that takes into account contributing factors and provides some consistent terminology as a basis for comparison of treatment protocols and

**Table 1.** Classification system developed by Cierny and Mader

**Anatomic Types**
Stage 1 – Medullary osteomyelitis
Stage 2 – Superficial osteomyelitis
Stage 3 – Localized osteomyelitis
Stage 4 – Diffuse osteomyelitis

**Physiologic Class**
A Host – Normal host
B Host – Systemic compromise (Bs)
Local compromise (Bl)
C Host – Treatment worse than the disease

response (Table 1). Their staging system combines four anatomical disease types and three physiologic host categories to identify and define 12 discrete clinical stages of osteomyelitis. In stage 1 or medullary osteomyelitis the primary lesion is endosteal. Regardless of the etiology of the infection, its characteristics — ischemic scar, chronic granulations, and splinter sequestra within the medullary canal — are the same. In stage 2 or superficial osteomyelitis the problem is on the bone surface and represents a true contiguous focal lesion. The infection results from a compromised soft tissue envelop that initiates or perpetuates an exposure infection of the bone. Localized osteomyelitis (stage 3) involves full thickness cortical sequestration. It is a discrete lesion within a stable bony segment. Stage 4 or diffuse osteomyelitis represents a permeative, circumferential, or through and through disease of hard and soft tissue.

Physiologic classifications of the host include host A, a patient having normal physiologic response to infection and surgery, and host B, a compromised patient. This group is further divided into those with local deficiencies in healing and those with systemic compromise (Table 2). The final category, host C, represents a patient in whom the treatment or results of treatment are more compromising than the disease itself.

When anatomical and physiological categories are combined, a very comprehensive description is possible. For example, a Stage 4Bs osteomyelitis would represent a diffuse infective process in a systemically compromised host. This staging system has been used to determine optimal treatment protocols and to provide a replicable framework within which to evaluate the efficacy of a variety of antimicrobial, surgical, and adjunctive approaches used for the treatment of this recalcitrant disease.

Table 2. Systemic or local factors that affect immune surveillance, metabolism, and local vascularity

| Systemic (Bs) | Local (Bl) |
|---|---|
| Malnutrition | Chronic lymphedema |
| Renal or hepatic failure | Venous stasis |
| Diabetes mellitus | Major vessel compromise |
| Chronic hypoxia | Arteritis |
| Immune deficiency | Extensive scarring |
| Malignancy | Radiation fibrosis |
| Extremes of age | Small vessel disease |
| Immunosuppression | Complete loss of local sensation |
| Tobacco abuse | |

## *Treatment of Osteomyelitis*

Cierny et al[8] employ an evaluation and treatment protocol that includes all aspects of the following:

1.  Patient evaluation;
2.  Staging assessment;
3.  Identification of microorganisms; and
4.  Selection and administration of antibiotics.

Generally, unless the patient is critically ill, antibiotics are not started until the results of sensitivity studies are known. An optimal antibiotic provides a minimal inhibitory concentration (MIC) at least eight times less than the expected serum concentrations. Parenteral antibiotics, or more recently oral fluoroquinolones, are continued for four weeks after the last major debridement surgery.

5. Surgery is performed three to seven days after the initiation of appropriate antibiotics. Stabilization is provided prior to or after debridement where indicated. All avascular scar and bone are removed. A "second look" debridement procedure is performed five to seven days after the first debridement surgery, if necessary, to remove any remaining necrotic bone and to manage dead space. Ongoing host alteration is accomplished through patient education, nutritional supplementation, and hyperbaric oxygen therapy where indicated.[6-8]

Hospitalization is usually required, especially when aggressive debridement is necessary.[8] However, many patients may be released from the hospital shortly after the last debridement procedure to undergo additional parenteral antibiotic therapy on an outpatient basis using an indwelling Hickman, Broviac, or Groshong catheter. Unfortunately, for some patients and in some situations, this does not present a viable treatment option. In these cases, the development of an effective broad spectrum oral antibiotic agent has been helpful both in eradicating the disease and in reducing the length of hospital confinement.

## JOINT INFECTIONS IN ADULTS

### *Infectious Arthritis*

Infectious arthritis is a suppurative process in a joint space and is monarticular in 90% of cases.[9] However, it may also represent a metastatic spread of infection from a distant site. Hematogenous inoculation has occurred in cases of pneumonia, empyema, and osteomyelitis.[9-12] Any bacteremia may produce infection in a joint as well as in its neighboring tendon sheaths. Bacterial arthritis may also occur as contiguous extension into a joint space from an adjacent osteomyelitic process.[9] Bacterial arthritis as an extension of osteomyelitis is most often seen in children under one year of age, because the capillaries still perforate the epiphyseal growth plate. In the child aged one year or older, the growth plate is avascular and the infection is confined to the bone unless the metaphysis is intracapsular. Thus, cortical perforation of a metaphyseal infection at the proximal radius, humerus, or femur infects the elbow, shoulder, or hip joint.[9] In adults the infection may again involve the joint, since the growth plate has been resorbed.

A bacterial polyarthritis is sometimes seen as a manifestation of disseminated gonococcal infections.[12] This occurs most commonly in persons under the age of 30.[10]

## Etiology

Although any joint can be involved in bacterial arthritis, the highest incidence occurs in the knee (47%), followed by the shoulder (15%), sternoclavicular joint (9%), elbow (11%), wrist (7%), ankle (7%), interphalangeal and metacarpal joints (1%), and sacroiliac joint (2%).[11]

Several factors predispose to the development of a bacterial arthritis. Steroid therapy, either intra-articular or systemic,[9,11-15] and intra-articular invasion for drug therapy or for aspiration was implicated in 23% of cases reported by Kelly et al.[13] Wilkins et al[10] reported a 25% incidence of iatrogenic trauma in their open study. Degenerative joint disease also predisposes to bacterial arthritis, as does any condition, such as gout, which chronically traumatizes a joint.[10,11,12,16-18] Kelly et al[13] cited pre-existing arthritis in 24% of their series.

Underlying conditions or medications that alter host response or integrity, particularly those which interfere with the host's ability to eradicate or control infections, also predispose to bacterial arthritis. These factors include systemic steroid administration, cytotoxic therapy,[11,13] diabetes mellitus,[11-13,17] leukemia,[19] substance abuse,[10-13,15] cancer,[11,12] chronic granulomatous disease, cirrhosis,[11,12] and hypogammaglobulinemia.[11] In addition, older patients who have other chronic conditions which require frequent hospitalizations are especially prone.[10,12,13] Patients aged 60 or older who had concomitant chronic illnesses accounted for 50% of bacterial arthritis cases in one series.[10] Any trauma or surgery that threatens the integrity of a joint can also predispose to infection.[13,20]

The causative organisms of bacterial arthritis have been tabulated by a number of authors. Kelly et al[13] identified the following incidence: *S. aureus* (70%), *Haemophilus influenzae* (1%), *Streptococcus* spp. (17%), gram-negative bacilli (8%), and anaerobic organisms (1%). *S. aureus* is invariably the most common infecting agent in cases of bacterial arthritis, perhaps due to the increased prevalence of this organism in hospitalized patients.[11-13,21] In one series, 20% of the bacterial arthritis cases occurred in patients who had recently been discharged from the hospital.[10] Adult bacterial arthritis caused by *Streptococcus pyogenes* has also been reported.[13]

Gram-negative bacilli engender the most virulent type of bacterial arthritis,[9,11,12] with *Escherichia coli* and *Ps. aeruginosa* the most common organisms.[12] Bacterial arthritis caused by *Neisseria gonorrhoeae* is considered more benign.[11,21] Goldenberg and colleagues[11,12] reported an increase in the incidence of gram-negative bacillary arthritis: 22%-26% in their series compared to 7% of cases reviewed earlier (1947-1967). Since infections caused by gram-negative bacilli usually occur as a result of a debilitating disease or a chronic arthritis,[13] the increased incidence may be indicative of the increasing proportion of older persons in the United States.

## Clinical Course in Bacterial Arthritis

Classically, patients with nongonococcal arthritis present with fever, pain in and restricted movement of affected joint(s), and 90% present with joint effusions.[9] In older individuals with a history of chronic degenerative joint disease, a definitive diagnosis may be delayed because symptoms are erroneously attributed to the underlying condition rather than to an infectious process. Misleading presenting symptoms may also be seen in bacterial arthritis of the hip and sacroiliac joints where pain may be referred to the abdomen or knee.[22]

The presenting symptoms of bacterial arthritis in disseminated gonococcal infections may be insidious, with migratory polyarthralgias, fever, dermatitis and tenosynovitis being the most common. Only 30 to 40% of these patients present with the classic bacterial arthritis symptoms.[12]

Laboratory studies in patients with bacterial arthritis usually show an elevated erythrocyte sedimentation rate (ESR).[9] Usually an elevation in blood leukocyte counts does not occur in adults. A purulent or serosanguineous joint effusion is evident. Synovial fluid leukocyte counts are >100,000/cc in 30-50% of the cases.[9] Goldenberg and Reed[12] reported that more than 90% of the patients in their series demonstrated greater than 85% polymorphonuclear leukocytes in synovial exudate. Blood cultures are positive in 50% of non-gonococcal bacterial arthritis cases, but in only 20% of gonococcal infections.[12] Gram stains are not reliable or specific; Goldenberg and Reed found only 75% to be positive in patients with staphylococcal infections, 50% with gram-negative bacillary arthritis, and <25% with gonococcal arthritis.[12] Although roentgenographic changes may be inconclusive, distention of the joint capsule and some soft tissue swelling may be seen in disease of greater than two weeks duration.[12] Magnetic resonance imaging can provide evidence of bacterial arthritis earlier in the course of the disease than can radionuclide bone scans.[23] However, computerized tomography has no defined role in the diagnosis of bacterial arthritis.

## Treatment

Mielants et al[24] have offered a useful paradigm for the medical management of bacterial arthritis. Their regimen identifies three distinct phases of treatment. Phase I commences with diagnosis and subsequent identification of a causative organism.

During this phase of treatment, parenteral antibiotics are begun. Antibiotic infusions are continued for 14 to 21 days if the infection is staphylococcal or gram-negative;[25] daily needle aspiration of the joint is performed; continuous ice packing is employed; and relative immobilization through the use of a splint or traction is recommended. Absolute immobilization of the affected joint is contraindicated because muscle atrophy, articular adhesions, and joint stiffness may result. Phase II begins when the joint effusion has disappeared. During this phase, parenteral antibiotics are continued and intensive joint and muscle rehabilitation is begun. Phase III occurs when the ESR returns to pre-infection levels. Rehabilitation continues until no further improvement in function is noted.[21]

Wilkins et al[10] have indicated that eradication of the organism is more vital than removal of the exudate from the joint. Argen et al[17] agree that repeated aspirations are necessary to relieve joint pressure and to remove necrotic material and autolytic enzymes produced by cellular breakdown. Other investigators feel that aspiration provides an additional modality for monitoring the infection. Analysis of the exudate can assist in ensuring appropriate antibiotic choice and in assessing bactericidal activity as well as disease progression.[11,12,15] Goldenberg and Reed[12] recommend needle aspirations once or even twice daily during the first 5-7 days to evaluate the efficacy of antibiotic therapy. Leukocyte counts, cultures, and tube dilution determinations of the joint fluid are also recommended.[12]

Open surgical drainage of the joint is necessary in joints not easily accessible by needle aspiration or those in which adhesions or loculations are present.[9,11,12] The use of closed versus open drainage remains an issue of some controversy. Goldenberg and Cohen[11] reported an 80% recovery rate in a group of patients with bacterial arthritis who underwent medical management with closed drainage as compared with a 47% recovery rate in a group undergoing medical management with open surgical drainage. Generally, closed drainage is advised, at least initially.[9,11,12,25] Indications for the use of open surgical drainage include hip infections,[9,11,25] presence of loculations, coexistent osteomyelitis,[11] persistence of fluid neutrophil counts above 25,000/cc, or persistence of positive fluid cultures despite antibiotic therapy.[25] Intra-articular antibiotic administration is inadvisable because of the risks of developing clinical synovitis, increased joint trauma, and iatrogenic infection.[25]

## Prognosis

Wilkins et al[10] have reported a 50-60% treatment response with *S. aureus* bacterial arthritis compared to a 30-60% rate with *Pneumococcus*. Goldenberg and Cohen[11] reported complete recovery in 21% of gram-negative infections, 73% of *S. aureus*, 85% of *Strep. hemolyticus,* and 94% of *S. pneumoniae.*

Several factors have an impact on the recovery of patients with bacterial arthritis. Of greatest significance is the duration of the infection prior to the onset of therapy. A strong relationship exists between poor treatment response and delay of treatment.[9,12,21] Smith[9] observed a 67% recovery rate when treatment was delayed for less than seven days compared to a 27% rate when treatment was delayed for more than seven days. The findings of Wilkins et al,[10] however, do not strongly support this observation. They suggest that diagnostic delays often occurred in cases where the infectious process was insidious or the presenting symptoms masked by concomitant chronic illness. Poor recovery rates in this patient population may be more a function of the debilitation of severely compromised hosts than of a delay in treatment. Overall, underlying or predisposing conditions have been strongly implicated in poor treatment results. Most often cited are diabetes mellitus, rheumatoid arthritis, severe renal insufficiency, and the existence of prior joint disorders.[9,11,12,21]

Synovial fluid leukocyte values have been used as a predictor of treatment response. Goldenberg and Cohen[11] found that patients who had a marked fall in mean synovial counts by the end of the first week of therapy eventually had good treatment results. The site of the infectious process also plays a role in treatment response. In general, infections in large, easily accessible joints have the best prognosis.[9-12]

## FLUOROQUINOLONES IN BONE AND JOINT INFECTIONS

## *Comparative Studies*

Etesse et al[26] evaluated 43 patients with chronic osteomyelitis in a study comparing the diffusion of ciprofloxacin, ofloxacin, and pefloxacin in bone tissue. Patients were randomly assigned to one of three treatment groups: Group 1 (16 patients) received 500 to 750 mg of ciprofloxacin twice a day, Group 2 (12 patients) received 200 mg of ofloxacin twice a day, and Group 3 (15 patients) received 400 mg of pefloxacin twice a day. Seven days after the initiation of oral fluoroquinolone therapy and one to two hours after the last dose of the drug, bone specimens were obtained by biopsy from the iliac crest or were taken from the site of infection during surgery. Concurrent serum levels of each drug were also obtained. In all cases the level of the fluoroquinolone in bone was at least two times greater than the MIC for the infecting organism. Bone levels were highest for pefloxacin. The ratio of the level of drug in bone to the MIC ranged from 5.2 to 142.3 for ciprofloxacin, 1.4 to 202 for pefloxacin, and 3.0 to 78 for ofloxacin.[26]

In a similar study, Fong et al[27] evaluated 28 patients undergoing surgery for either hip or knee replacement (n=18) or debridement of osteomyelitis (n=10). Patients were randomly assigned to receive a single dose of ciprofloxacin 500 mg, 750 mg, or 1 gram 2-4 hours before surgery. Cortical bone and muscle samples were taken at the time of surgery. The results indicated that ciprofloxacin given at a dosage of 750 mg bid provided adequate concentrations in bone and soft tissue to treat most osteomyelitis and soft tissue infections.[27]

Mader et al[28] compared oral ciprofloxacin 750 mg bid with intravenous nafcillin, clindamycin, and gentamicin in 39 patients with osteomyelitis of greater than 20 months duration. In all cases treatment continued for four weeks following the last debridement surgery. They reported arrest rates of 79% at 17.2 months follow-up with oral ciprofloxacin and 83% at 15.3 months follow-up for the standard parenteral regimens. One of the three treatment failures with ciprofloxacin occurred in a patient with hardware in place, and one occurred in a stage B compromised host (alcohol and tobacco abuser). The final failure was due to persistence of a sensitive strain of *Streptococcus faecalis*.[28] In a randomized study, Greenberg et al[29] found ciprofloxacin 750 mg bid to be as effective as parenteral antibiotics in the treatment of chronic osteomyelitis. Parenteral agents employed in the study included amikacin, ampicillin, aztreonam, ceftazidime, azlocillin, cefotaxime, clindamycin, cefoperazone, cefoxitin, ceftriaxone, gentamicin, imipenem, piperacillin, tobramycin, and vancomycin. Fifteen of 30 patients were cured with ciprofloxacin at the conclusion of therapy, compared to a 65% cure rate in 16 patients who received other agents. Both groups were followed for 1 to 13 months. In addition to the cost effectiveness of an oral agent, these authors found that side effects with ciprofloxacin were significantly less severe than those seen with parenteral agents; in five of the latter cases a change in antimicrobial therapy was required due to adverse events. No patient had to be switched from ciprofloxacin to another agent due to intolerable side effects.[29]

Desplaces and Acar[5] compared treatment results using pefloxacin alone and in combination with rifampin, a β-lactam, or an aminoglycoside in osteomyelitis patients with and without foreign bodies present. Seven of 9 patients with metal hardware who received pefloxacin alone were considered cured after a follow-up of more than one year. Ten of 11 patients without metal hardware were considered cured at follow-up of more than two years. When pefloxacin was combined with rifampin, cure was achieved in all 3 patients with metal hardware and in all 11 patients without metal. No failures were seen in the pefloxacin plus rifampin groups. In the pefloxacin plus β-lactam/aminoglycoside group, 8 of 9 patients with metal hardware and 8 of 9 without foreign material were cured after a follow-up of 1-3 years.[5]

## Open Clinical Trials

At least one clinical trial of patients with chronic osteomyelitis caused by *Pseudomonas aeruginosa* infection has been reported.[30] Twelve patients received oral ciprofloxacin 500 mg bid or 750 mg bid for a period of 7 days to 4 months. The authors reported a 92% clinical response rate (cure plus improvement) after a follow-up of at least six months. The bacteriological eradication rate was 83%, and persistence was reported in 2 patients. In another small clinical trial, Solbiati et al[31] reported bacteriologic eradication of *S. aureus* in all four cases of chronic osteomyelitis using oral ciprofloxacin.

Slama[32] reviewed 23 cases of gram-negative or polymicrobial osteomyelitis, both acute and chronic types, treated with ciprofloxacin 750 mg bid. Cure was achieved in 17 of 23 cases, and recurrences occurred within six weeks of the end of therapy in two of these. This study did not differentiate between clinical results in acute versus chronic cases. Thus, it is difficult to draw conclusions regarding efficacy, since acute and chronic osteomyelitis are not equivalent conditions.

Scully and Neu[33] reported on 12 cases of osteomyelitis and septic arthritis treated with ciprofloxacin. Clinical improvement was noted in 10 of 12 patients, and bacteriologic eradication was achieved in 10 of 12. Both treatment failures were due to the emergence of resistant organisms.[33]

In a series of 22 osteomyelitis patients without metal appliances who were treated with ciprofloxacin, Greenberg et al[34] reported a cure rate of 64% (14 of 22) after follow-up of more than one year. Two treatment failures and four relapses due to methicillin resistant *S. aureus* were noted. These investigators also observed that ciprofloxacin did not eradicate osteomyelitis or skin and soft tissue infections in patients with underlying metal appliances, although the drug did reduce or eliminate the drainage.[34] A number of other open clinical trials indicated failure or relapse in patients who had metal appliances in place,[5,28,29,35] or who were systemically or locally compromised.[28,33,34,36,37] These findings emphasize the importance of rigorous and thorough medical and surgical management, as well as long-term follow-up for these patients.

## Joint Infections

Few studies have evaluated the use of fluoroquinolones specifically in joint infections. Typically, data from bone and joint infections are reported together under the broad heading "bone and joint infections." This approach prevents objective assessment of fluoroquinolone efficacy in these two quite different infectious processes. Although extension of an infection from joint to bone or from bone to joint is seen, isolating the precipitating focus and extent of the infection is crucial to treatment and to anticipation of outcome.

Bayer et al[38] reported equal efficacy of ciprofloxacin and ceftriaxone in reducing the mean counts of *E. coli* in infected synovia in experimentally induced arthritis in a rabbit model. Greenberg et al[34] reported on three cases of human joint infection treated with ciprofloxacin. One was cured at 19 month follow-up; another with an infected prosthetic hip relapsed two weeks after completion of therapy, and one patient with a prosthetic knee was a treatment failure due to the development of resistance by *S. aureus* and *Ps. aeruginosa*.

Peyramond et al[35] evaluated ofloxacin in their report of osteoarthritis patients treated for infections involving limbs, spine, major joints, soft tissue abscesses or fistulas, infected prostheses or bacteremia. Twenty patients received oral ofloxacin

200 to 400 mg bid, and 3 received ofloxacin in combination with rifampin, doxycycline, or amikacin. Seventeen of 20 had good clinical results, and 16 of 20 showed bacteriologic eradication at follow-up (range 1 to 19 months). Of the 3 treatment failures, 2 were attributable to resistant organisms and 1 to an infected hip prosthesis.[35]

## Resistance to Fluoroquinolones

Very low frequencies (between $10^{-7}$ and $10^{-9}$) of resistant mutants have been reported for *Enterobacter cloacae, Serratia marcescens, Ps. aeruginosa,* and *Streptococcus faecalis* using concentrations of ciprofloxacin that were four to eight times the MIC.[39] In a series of experimental *Ps. aeruginosa* osteomyelitis in a rabbit model, Norden and Shinners[40] found that the emergence of resistant strains accounted for 20% of the treatment failures in the animals. Moreover, a resistant strain of *Ps. aeruginosa* was isolated on agar containing twice the MIC of ciprofloxacin. These mutants were 2 to 64 times more resistant to ciprofloxacin and showed complete cross resistance to nalidixic acid, ofloxacin, enoxacin, and norfloxacin. This occurred by mutation of the gene for DNA gyrase.[41]

Clinical treatment failures due to resistant strains of *Ps. aeruginosa* have been reported in several series with ciprofloxacin.[30,33,34,36] However, ciprofloxacin has been shown to interact additively with tobramycin and azlocillin against *Pseudomonas aeruginosa.*[42] Chin et al[43] demonstrated that ciprofloxacin plus azlocillin was synergistic for about 30% of *Ps. aeruginosa* (including β-lactam resistant strains), with a 2-4-fold decrease in the $MIC_{90}$.

Another resistant organism commonly reported in clinical studies with ciprofloxacin, pefloxacin, and ofloxacin is *S. aureus.*[5,33-35] In an in vitro study, Smith and Robert[44] did not find any advantage using a combination of ciprofloxacin and vancomycin over ciprofloxacin alone in the treatment of resistant *S. aureus*. However, in another in vitro study, ciprofloxacin and ofloxacin inhibited growth of methicillin resistant *S. aureus* at lower concentrations than did amifloxacin, enoxacin, or norfloxacin.[45] Hackbarth et al[46] found that when ciprofloxacin was combined with rifampin against methicillin sensitive *S. aureus*, the effect on bactericidal activity was additive and the development of rifampin-resistant organisms was inhibited. Likewise, Weinstein et al[47] reported that ciprofloxacin combined with rifampin enhanced the serum bactericidal activity against oxacillin-sensitive and resistant *S. aureus* compared with ciprofloxacin alone. Henry et al[48] have shown that the combination of ciprofloxacin and rifampin was additive and possibly synergistic against methicillin-resistant *S. aureus* (MRSA) in rats. No rifampin-resistant MRSA developed in rats treated with the combination of ciprofloxacin and rifampin. Further studies are in progress to define the efficacy of ciprofloxacin and rifampin in the treatment of methicillin-sensitive and resistant *S. aureus*.

The persistence of *Streptococcus faecalis* was observed by Desplaces and Acars[5] and Mader et al[28] following treatment with ciprofloxacin and pefloxacin, respectively.[5,28] In addition, two clinical superinfections — one with *Ps. maltophilia* and one with *Ps. aeruginosa* — have been reported.[34,49] Caution and judgment must be exercised in the application and administration of the fluoroquinolones in order to guard against further proliferation of resistant mutants.

## Side Effects of Fluoroquinolone Therapy in Bone and Joint Infections

Because of reports that high doses of nalidixic acid and quinolones cause articular cartilage damage in young animals,[50,51] there has been some concern regarding the long-term use of these agents in humans. However, despite the lengthy course of treatment usually required for bone and joint infections, no cartilage toxicity has been seen in ciprofloxacin-treated patients. In fact, clinical studies using the fluoroquinolones for the treatment of patients with bone and joint infections indicate an infrequent incidence of relatively minor side effects with these agents.

In the studies reviewed in this chapter, gastrointestinal symptoms comprised the most frequently reported side effects. Nausea, epigastric pain, mild abdominal cramping, diarrhea, and constipation were reported.[5,28,29,35,36] None of these effects necessitated discontinuation of the therapy.

Neurological symptoms including dizziness, blurred vision, and photosensitivity occurred in a few patients.[29,36] Skin rashes were also noted in a few patients.[5,28,34,37] Minor elevations in liver enzymes were documented.[29,34,35,37] In all, only four cases of side effects required cessation of the quinolone therapy: one for dizziness,[36] one for esophagitis,[28] and two for rash.[5,33] Generally, the side effects responded well to conventional palliative measures such as use of antacids[28] or the application of anti-pruritic lotions.[28]

## SUMMARY

The oral fluoroquinolones have produced excellent clinical responses in a number of specific studies of bone and joint infections. However, any conclusions regarding the use of these agents over traditional therapy must be made with caution. This limitation arises from the failure of many studies to isolate the antibiotic effect from other factors which can impact significantly on patient response and prognosis.

One variable in the published reports of fluoroquinolone use in osteomyelitis is the use of aggressive surgical debridement as a routine part of the treatment plan. In addition, other factors vary widely among the published reports, including: (1) the duration of the infection and outcome of prior treatment efforts; (2) the underlying constitutional status of the patient with regard to potential for revascularization of compromised tissue and adequacy of the immune response; (3) the determination of cure, relapse, and/or failure rates based on varying follow-up intervals; and (4) variability in dosage and length of treatment regimens. Despite these variations, a review of the literature offers the clinician some direction for decision-making, as long as the inconsistencies are heeded. In general, the fluoroquinolones seem to be effective, safe, and practical agents for the treatment of bone and joint infections.

# REFERENCES

1. Nightingale GH, Gousse GC: Streamlining antibiotic therapy with oral quinolones: A commentary for P&T Committee Members. Hosp Form 1988;23(suppl B):32-37.

2. Fallon RJ, Brown WM: *In vitro* sensitivity of Legionella, Meningococcus, and Mycoplasmas to ciprofloxacin and enoxacin. Antimicrob Agents Chemother 1985;75:787-788.

3. Anderson RC, Goldstein EJ: The introduction of the quinolones: A new class of anti-infectives. Hosp Form 1987;22:36-47.

4. Bosso DA, Gentry LO, Neu HC, et al: A review of ciprofloxacin's effectiveness, clinical uses, and other P&T Committee concerns. Hosp Form 1988;23(suppl B):10-18.

5. Desplaces N, Acar JF: New quinolones in the treatment of joint and bone infections. Rev Infect Dis 1988;10(suppl 1):S179-S183.

6. Christ W, Lehner TI, Ulbrick KB: Specific toxicological aspects of the quinolones. Rev Infect Dis 1988;1(suppl I):S141-S146.

7. Cierny G, Mader JT: Infections of the bones, in Spittell JA (ed), *Clinical Medicine 2.* Philadelphia, Harper & Row, 1986, pp 1-11.

8. Cierny G, Mader JT, Pennick JJ: A clinical staging system for osteomyelitis. Contemp Ortho 1985;10:17-37.

9. Smith JW: Infectious arthritis, in Mandell GL, Bennett JE (eds), *Principles and Practices of Infectious Disease.* New York, John Wiley & Sons, 1985, pp 698-704.

10. Wilkins RF, Healey LA, Decker JL: Acute infectious arthritis in the aged and chronically ill. Arch Intern Med 1960;106:354-364.

11. Goldenberg DL, Cohen AS: Acute infectious arthritis. Am J Med 1976;60:369-377.

12. Goldenberg DL, Reed JI: Bacterial arthritis. N Engl J Med 1985;312:764-767.

13. Kelly PJ, Martin WJ, Coventry MB: Bacterial (suppurative) arthritis in the adult. J Bone Joint Surg 1970;52A:1595-1602.

14. Gowans DC, Granieri PA: Septic arthritis: Its relation to intra-articular injections of hydrocortisone acetate. N Engl J Med 1959;261:502-504.

15. Mills LC, Boylston B, Greene JA, et al: Septic arthritis as a complication of orally given steroid therapy. JAMA 1957;164:1310-1314.

16. Kellgren OH, Ball J, Fairbrother RW, et al: Suppurative arthritis complicating rheumatoid arthritis. Br Med J 1958;1:1193-1200.

17. Argen RJ, Wilson CH, Wood P: Suppurative arthritis. Arch Intern Med 1966;117:661-666.

18. Bunn D: Pyoarthritis: its treatment and the role of adrenal steroids in its pathogenesis. Trans Am Clin Climatol Assoc 1957;69:9-19.

19. Cunningham IJ, Hitchcock ER, Watson AB: Interphalangeal joint infection. Br Med J 1959;1:139-141.

20. Chartier Y, Martin WJ, Kelly PJ: Bacterial arthritis: Experience with the treatment of 77 patients. Ann Intern Med 1959;50:1462-1474.

21. Keiser H, Ruben FL, Wolinsky E, Kushner I: Clinical forms of gonococcal arthritis. N Engl J Med 1968;279:234-240.

22. Schmid FR: Infectious arthritis and osteomyelitis. Primary Care 1984;11:295-306.

23. Hendrix RW, Fisher MR: Imaging of septic arthritis. Clin Rheumatol Dis 1986;12:459-487.

24. Mielants H, Rhondt E, Gofthals L, et al: Long term functional results of the non-surgical treatment of common bacterial infection of joints. Scand J Rheumatol 1982;11:101-105.

25. LeFrock JL, Kannangara DW: Bacterial arthritis, in Kass EH, Platt R (eds), *Current Therapy in Infectious Diseases*. St. Louis, The CV Mosby Co, 1984, pp 262-264.

26. Etesse H, Garraffo R, Dellamonica P, et al: Diffusion of pefloxacin into bone and the treatment of osteomyelitis. Antimicrob Agents Chemother 1986;17(suppl B):93-102.

27. Fong TW, Ledetter WH, Vanderbroucke AC, et al: Ciprofloxacin concentrations in bone and muscle after oral dosing. Antimicrob Agents Chemother 1986;29:405-408.

28. Mader JT, Welch PH, Cantrell JS, et al: Randomized evaluation of ciprofloxacin versus best appropriate therapy for the treatment of adult osteomyelitis. Am Fed Clin Res South Sect, 1988.

29. Greenberg RN, Tice AD, Marsh DJ, et al: Randomized trial of ciprofloxacin compared with other antimicrobial therapy in the treatment of osteomyelitis. Am J Med 1982; 82(suppl 4A):266-269.

30. Giamarellou H, Galanakis N, Dendrinos C, et al: Evaluation of ciprofloxacin in the treatment of *Pseudomonas aeruginosa* infections. Eur J Clin Microbiol 1986;5:232-235.

31. Solbiati M, DeChecci G, Agueci A, et al: Clinical evaluation of ciprofloxacin in the treatment of severe infections. Rev Infect Dis 1988;10(suppl 1):S191.

32. Slama TG: Ciprofloxacin in the treatment of gram negative osteomyelitis. Rev Infect Dis 1988;10(suppl 1):S190.

33. Scully MB, Neu HC: Treatment of serious infections with intravenous ciprofloxacin. Am J Med 1982;82(suppl 4A):369-375.

34. Greenberg RN, Kennedy DJ, Reilly PM, et al: Treatment of bone, joint, and soft-tissue infections with oral ciprofloxacin. Antimicrob Agents Chemother 1987;131:151-155.

35. Peyramond D, Biron F, Lucht F, et al: Treatment of bacterial osteoarthritis with ofloxacin. Rev Infect Dis 1988;10(suppl 1):S187.

36. Tice AD, Marsh PK, Craven PC: Ciprofloxacin administered as therapy for osteomyelitis. Rev Infect Dis 1988;10(suppl 1):S187.

37. Giamarellou H, Galanakis N: Use of intravenous ciprofloxacin in difficult-to-treat infections. Am J Med 1987;82(suppl 4A):346-351.

38. Bayer AS, Norman DC, Blumquist IK: Comparative efficacy of ciprofloxacin and ceftriaxone in experimental arthritis by *Escherichia coli*. Rev Infect Dis 1988;10(suppl 1):S184.

39. Chin NX, Neu HC: Ciprofloxacin a quinolone carboxyl acid compound active against aerobic and anaerobic bacteria. Antimicrob Agents Chemother 1984;25:319-326.

40. Norden CW, Shinners E: Ciprofloxacin as therapy for experimental osteomyelitis caused by *Pseudomonas aeruginosa*. J Infect Dis 1985;151:291-294.

41. Robillard WJ, Alphonse LS: Genetic and physiological characteristics of ciprofloxacin resistance in *Pseudomonas aeruginosa*. Antimicrob Agents Chemother 1988;32:535-539.

42. Chalkley LJ, Koornhof HJ: Antimicrobial activity of ciprofloxacin against *Pseudomonas aeruginosa, Escherichia coli,* and *Staphylococcus aureus* determined by the killing curve method: Antibiotic comparisons and synergistic interactions. Antimicrob Agents Chemother 1985;28:331-342.

43. Chin N-X, Jules K, Neu HC: Synergy of ciprofloxacin and azlocillin in vitro and in a neutropenic mouse model of infection. Eur J Clin Microbiol 1986;5:23-28.

44. Smith SM, Robert HK: Activity of ciprofloxacin against methicillin resistant *Staphylococcus aureus.* Antimicrob Agents Chemother 1985;27:688-691.

45. Smith SM: *In vitro* comparison of A56619, A56620, amifloxacin, ciprofloxacin, enoxacin, norfloxacin, and ofloxacin against methicillin resistant *Staphylococcus aureus.* Antimicrob Agents Chemother 1986;29:325-326.

46. Hackbarth CJ, Chambers HF, Sande MA: Serum bactericidal activity of rifampin in combination with other antimicrobial agents against *Staphylococcus aureus.* Antimicrob Agents Chemother 1986;29:611-613.

47. Weinstein MP, Deeter RG, Swanson KA, et al: Serum bactericidal activity of ciprofloxacin alone and in combination with rifampin or clindamycin versus oxacillin-susceptible and -resistant *S. aureus* in healthy elderly volunteers, abstract A-15. Presented at the Annual Meeting of the American Society for Microbiology, New Orleans, May 14-18, 1989.

48. Henry NK, Rouse MS, Whitesell AL, et al: Treatment of methicillin-resistant Staphylococcus aureus experimental osteomyelitis with ciprofloxacin or vancomycin alone or in combination with rifampin. Am J Med 1987;82(suppl 4A):73-75.

49. Ramirez CA, Bran JL, Mejia CR, et al: Open prospective study of the clinical efficacy of ciprofloxacin. Antimicrob Agents Chemother 1985;28:128-132.

50. Christ W, Lehnert T, Ulbrich B: Specific toxicologic aspects of the quinolones. Rev Infect Dis 1988;10(suppl 1):S141-146.

51. Mayer DG: Overview of toxicological studies. Drugs 1987;34(suppl 1):150-153.

# CIPROFLOXACIN FOR RESPIRATORY TRACT INFECTIONS  6

*Faroque A. Khan*

## INTRODUCTION

The past decade has seen major advances in the development of antibiotics for parenteral use. However, it has not been possible to develop orally administered derivatives of the aminoglycosides and most extended-spectrum penicillins and cephalosporins. Oral therapy (with the exception of penicillins combined with a β-lactamase inhibitor) had therefore not progressed significantly until the development of potent fluoroquinolones in the 1980s, allowing for the first time effective oral therapy of serious infections caused by multiply resistant bacteria.

The earliest quinolone, nalidixic acid, was developed in the 1960s. Nalidixic acid was adequate for the treatment of urinary infections caused by some gram-negative organisms, but it did not penetrate tissue sufficiently after oral dosing to be of use in systemic infections. The rather rapid development of resistance and superinfection with resistant organisms such as *Pseudomonas aeruginosa* were additional problems.

The newer fluoroquinolones possess pharmacologic and antimicrobial properties that make them suitable for the treatment of systemic infections as well as urinary tract infections.[1] They have excellent tissue penetration after oral dosing, resulting in tissue concentrations that are well above the minimum inhibitory concentrations (MICs) for most gram-negative and gram-positive pathogens encountered in daily practice. Ciprofloxacin, for example, is active against common respiratory tract pathogens such as *Haemophilus influenzae, Streptococcus pneumoniae, Branhamella catarrhalis,* and *Ps. aeruginosa.* About 90% of *Pseudomonas* strains are inhibited by <1 µg/mL of ciprofloxacin. Some activity against *Legionella,*[2] chlamydia,[2] and mycobacteria[3] has also been demonstrated. Resistance to ciprofloxacin is slow to develop; spontaneous mutants occur at $10^{-7}$ to $10^{-11}$ colony-forming units.[4] Ciprofloxacin is also effective against β-lactamase producers and methicillin-resistant *Staphylococcus aureus.*[3]

Of those agents currently available or under investigation, ciprofloxacin is among the most attractive in terms of its potency, bactericidal activity, and pharmacokinetics. In vitro studies have shown that ciprofloxacin is active against gram-positive, gram-negative, and multi-drug resistant bacteria, as well as chlamydia, mycobacteria, and *Legionella* (Table 1).[5-7] Clinical trials in Europe and the United States have demonstrated that ciprofloxacin is effective against a variety of respiratory tract infections.

## COMMON PATHOGENS IN RESPIRATORY TRACT INFECTIONS

Bacterial species usually associated with acute infections of the bronchi in patients with chronic bronchitis or asthma include *Haemophilus influenzae, H. parainfluenzae, Streptococcus pneumoniae, Branhamella catarrhalis*, and *Neisseria* spp. *Klebsiella* and *Pseudomonas* spp. have also been isolated from these patients, but with less frequency than those listed above.[8] A survey of bacterial species recovered from the sputum of patients with acute bacterial infection over a two-year period (1984 to 1986) showed that *H. influenzae* occurred with the greatest frequency; *Haemophilus* spp. and *Streptococcus pneumoniae* accounted for 61% of all pathogens recovered.[8] Other pathogens included *S. aureus, Serratia marcescens*, and various streptococci.

Oral ciprofloxacin is quite effective in the treatment of various forms of respiratory tract infections. Gleadhill et al[9] compared the efficacy and safety of oral ciprofloxacin 500 mg bid with amoxicillin 250 mg tid in patients with respiratory infections (eg, pneumonia, acute bronchitis, exacerbation of chronic lung disease). Forty-eight patients were randomly assigned to a 10-day treatment course of each drug; 26

**Table 1.** Sensitivity of common respiratory tract infection pathogens to ciprofloxacin

| Sensitive (MIC <1 µg/mL) | Intermediate (MIC 1-2 µg/mL) | Resistant (MIC >2 mg/mL) |
|---|---|---|
| *Branhamella catarrhalis* | *Streptococcus pneumoniae* | Anaerobic cocci |
| *Hemophilus influenzae* | Other streptococci | *Bacteroides* spp. |
| *Klebsiella* spp. | | *Pseudomonas maltophilia* |
| *Neisseria* spp. | | *Pseudomonas cepacia* |
| *Pseudomonas aeruginosa* | | |
| *Staphylococcus aureus* | | |
| *Serratia marcescens* | | |

in the ciprofloxacin group and 22 in the amoxicillin group. All patients were evaluable for efficacy. Ciprofloxacin was found to be as effective as amoxicillin, with a successful outcome in 81% and 82% of cases, respectively. In the 28 patients in whom a specific bacterial cause was determined, the bacterial eradication rates were higher for ciprofloxacin than for amoxicillin (87% versus 64%). Amoxicillin was unsuccessful in eradicating infections caused by *B. catarrhalis*. Both regimens were safe and produced few adverse effects.[9]

Kobayashi[10] reported on a large, multi-center, open trial in 571 patients in Japan. Most patients received 600 mg of ciprofloxacin daily. Clinical efficacy was evaluated in 542 patients, and safety was evaluated in 568. Clinical efficacy was good-to-excellent in 81% of patients with pneumonia and 71% with chronic bronchial infections. Overall, the bacteriologic eradication rate was 68%; with *Haemophilus influenzae* the rate was 91%. No serious side effects were reported.

Davies et al[11] compared four different regimens of oral ciprofloxacin with pefloxacin in 80 hospitalized patients with acute purulent bronchitis. Pretreatment sputum isolates included *Haemophilus influenzae, Streptococcus pneumoniae, Branhamella catarrhalis*, and *Pseudomonas aeruginosa*. Twenty patients received oral ciprofloxacin 500 mg twice a day, 40 received 750 mg twice a day, and 20 received 1000 mg twice a day for 10 days. The 750 mg doses were supplied in two separate batches. At the end of treatment (day 11), 65 patients (81%) had achieved good responses. However, one week later, this figure had dropped to 53% (42 patients). There were no significant differences in response rates between the three ciprofloxacin regimens. Most failures were due to resistance or recurrence of *S. pneumoniae* infection, which occurred in 17 patients, or failure to eradicate *Pseudomonas*, which occurred in 5 of 9 patients. These authors concluded that the poor results in patients with *S. pneumoniae* was due to failure of ciprofloxacin to exceed the MIC of this pathogen, as reflected by mean sputum concentrations on the first day of treatment of only 1-2 µg/L. Nevertheless, the poor clinical results of this study are in contrast to those reported by a number of other investigators.[9,10,12,13]

Raoof et al[13] reported on the efficacy and safety of oral ciprofloxacin 750 mg administered twice daily to 129 patients with respiratory tract infections. Ciprofloxacin showed broad in vitro antimicrobial activity and was highly effective against both gram-negative and gram-positive organisms. The clinical cure rate was 96%. In 8 of the 129 patients, *Streptococcus pneumoniae* was the only isolate; the MICs for four of these isolates were high (0.5, 1.0, 1.0, 4.0 µg/L). Nevertheless, in these 8 patients, the high MICs did not interfere with the effectiveness of ciprofloxacin. In 7 of the 8 patients, clinical and bacteriological cures were achieved; the eighth patient had an underlying history of intravenous drug abuse that may have contributed to the failure of the ciprofloxacin regimen.

Wollschlager et al[12] reported on a prospective, randomized, double-blind, study in which ciprofloxacin 750 mg twice a day was compared with ampicillin 500 mg po given 4 times a day in the treatment of 87 patients with bacterial respiratory tract infection. Forty-five patients received ciprofloxacin and 42 received ampicillin. Results indicated that ciprofloxacin was as effective as ampicillin and produced a 98% clinical cure rate. Significantly more pretreatment bacterial isolates were susceptible to ciprofloxacin (p<0.05), and ciprofloxacin produced a significantly higher rate of sputum sterilization than ampicillin (p<0.05). Ciprofloxacin showed broad in vitro antibacterial activity, with low MICs for gram-negative organisms. Ciprofloxacin was well tolerated and produced few adverse effects. Patients who received ciprofloxacin had a significantly lower incidence of diarrhea than patients who received ampicillin (p<0.05). These investigators concluded that ciprofloxacin was an effective and well tolerated treatment for bacterial bronchitis.

Wollschlager et al[14] also reported on the effectiveness of oral ciprofloxacin in the treatment of 14 adult patients with bacterial pneumonia, 13 of whom had underlying lung disease. These patients received ciprofloxacin 750 mg twice daily for a mean duration of 11.5 days. At the end of treatment, 12 of the 14 (86%) were cured. All of the isolates, including *S. pneumoniae* in 5 patients and *Haemophilus influenzae* in 4, were sensitive to ciprofloxacin, and only 2 pathogens persisted in this group. Ernst et al[15] also reported on the effectiveness of ciprofloxacin 750 mg twice a day in 25 patients with pneumonia, of whom 19 had bacterial isolates from sputum or blood. All patients improved.

Based on an analysis of the reported studies, it is apparent that oral ciprofloxacin is effective in the treatment of bacterial respiratory tract infection, including both bronchitis and pneumonia.

## CYSTIC FIBROSIS

A number of studies have reported on the effectiveness of oral ciprofloxacin in the treatment of bacterial respiratory infections in cystic fibrosis (CF). Scully et al[16] reported on 39 bacterial infections in 18 patients with CF. Thirteen had severe exacerbations, 19 had moderate ones, and 7 had mild ones. The dose of ciprofloxacin ranged from 750 mg to 2250 mg/day, with a mean of 1800 mg/day, and the duration of treatment ranged from 10-42 days, with a mean of 16 days. The clinical response was excellent in 32/39 (82%) of patients. There was little correlation between failure to respond and pretreatment MICs. None of the patients had eradication of *Pseudomonas* from the sputum. In general, those who had not required treatment during the previous three months had susceptible organisms. When ciprofloxacin resistance did develop, no concomitant β-lactam or aminoglycoside resistance was encountered. The authors concluded that oral ciprofloxacin was comparable or superior to parenteral therapy with azlocillin, ticarcillin, piperacillin, ceftazidime, cefsulodin, or aztreonam. However, all patients had an increase in post-treatment MICs and clear emergence of resistance. As a result, these authors concluded that long-term continuous outpatient use of ciprofloxacin in patients with CF would result in the loss of efficacy of this agent. To prevent this from occurring, they recommended intermittent therapy with ciprofloxacin, alternating with other agents. Although fluoroquinolones are not recommended for use in the pediatric age group because of their adverse effect on cartilage, these authors suggested that CF treatment may be one pediatric situation in which ciprofloxacin should be used.[16]

Goldfarb et al[17] reported on the use of ciprofloxacin for acute pulmonary exacerbations of CF in 30 patients. These patients had 43 isolates of *Ps. aeruginosa* and 15 of *Ps. cepacia,* all of which were resistant to azlocillin and tobramycin. All patients improved on oral ciprofloxacin 750 mg tid for 21 days. The drug was well tolerated. The authors concluded that ciprofloxacin monotherapy is safe and effective in treating acute pulmonary exacerbations in young adults with CF. These patients carried resistant organisms and had failed on prior courses of conventional agents. Although all patients improved clinically, there was no protracted suppression of the infecting *Pseudomonas* strain. MIC values increased over the course of therapy, with all patients carrying ciprofloxacin-resistant strains at the end of therapy. Thus, although clinically effective, ciprofloxacin appears to have limited microbiologic success in treating acute pulmonary exacerbations in CF.

Bosso et al[18] reported on the effectiveness of ciprofloxacin versus tobramycin plus azlocillin in adult patients with pulmonary exacerbations of CF. Twenty patients (10 in each group) were randomly assigned either to ciprofloxacin 750 twice a day or tobramycin plus azlocillin, each given for 14 days. The authors found that ciprofloxacin was therapeutically equal to the intravenous antibiotics in the treatment of adult patients with CF who were experiencing pulmonary exacerbations associated with susceptible bacteria. They concluded that in patients with ciprofloxacin-sensitive organisms, ciprofloxacin offers several advantages over conventional therapy, including oral administration, an improved safety profile, a lack of need to monitor serum concentrations, low toxicity, and cost-effectiveness.

Rubio[19] reported on 26 courses of ciprofloxacin 750 mg twice a day in 11 patients with CF and compared the results to those in 11 patients who received tobramycin and azlocillin intravenously for two weeks. The results were comparable and there was no emergence of resistant strains in this study. No significant difference in MICs was found before and after treatment with ciprofloxacin.

Shalit et al[20] studied two dosage regimens of ciprofloxacin for the treatment of chronic respiratory infections in patients with CF. Twenty-nine adult patients were randomly assigned to either ciprofloxacin 750 or 1000 mg every 12 hours for two weeks. Fifteen of the 28 evaluable patients improved clinically and none deteriorated. Higher doses did not enhance clinical response. After 14 days, 14/23 patients (61%) had resistant *Ps. aeruginosa* and after 21 days, this number increased to 70% (16/23 patients). Outpatient treatment was associated with clinical improvement regardless of emergence of resistant *Ps. aeruginosa,* and adverse reactions were infrequent.

Oral ciprofloxacin is of special interest in the treatment of patients with CF because of its activity against *Ps. aeruginosa, S. aureus,* and *Haemophilus influenzae,* the three pathogens that commonly cause exacerbations in this disease. Although the emergence of resistance is disturbing, it does not necessarily predict clinical failure. Ciprofloxacin might be useful following maximum suppression of *Ps. aeruginosa* by parenteral agents. Most authors recommend that ciprofloxacin be used intermittently in the management of the recurrent pulmonary exacerbations in patients with CF.

## INTRAVENOUS CIPROFLOXACIN FOR SEVERE RESPIRATORY TRACT INFECTIONS

Khan and Basir[21] compared the safety and efficacy of sequential intravenous/oral ciprofloxacin to ceftazidime in a prospective clinical trial in patients with moderate-to-severe respiratory tract infections (RTIs). Sixty-six patients received IV ciprofloxacin (200-300 mg twice daily) followed by oral ciprofloxacin (500 mg twice daily) and 56 received intravenous ceftazidime (1-2 grams 2-3 times daily). Ciprofloxacin was as effective as ceftazidime and produced a 91% clinical cure rate. Significantly ($p<0.05$) more pretreatment bacterial isolates were susceptible to ciprofloxacin (98.3%; 167 of 170 isolates) than to ceftazidime (91.8%; 156 of 170 isolates). In addition, ciprofloxacin produced a significantly higher rate of sputum sterilization than ceftazidime. Ciprofloxacin showed broad in vitro antibacterial activity with particularly low MICs for gram-negative organisms. Ciprofloxacin was well tolerated and produced few adverse effects. Three of the 66 patients in the ciprofloxacin group and 6 of the 56 patients in the ceftazidime group developed superinfection. Ciprofloxacin is an effective and well-tolerated treatment for severe RTI; it has the advantages of broad in vitro antibacterial activity, bid dosing, and sequential availability in an oral or intravenous (not yet commercially available) formulation.

## CIPROFLOXACIN IN THE TREATMENT OF RESPIRATORY TRACT INFECTIONS CAUSED BY *S. PNEUMONIAE*

The role of ciprofloxacin in the treatment of infections caused by gram-positive bacteria, particularly *Streptococcus pneumoniae,* has not been fully established due to laboratory reports of high MICs.[13,21] However, clinical results in patients treated with ciprofloxacin have indicated that the high MICs do not impair the effectiveness of the drug. The reasons for this interesting discrepancy are perhaps related to the ability of ciprofloxacin to penetrate into tissue compartments. The fluoroquinolones are able to penetrate into the bronchial lining and achieve high concentrations in the lung, bronchial mucosa, and sputum.

Results obtained in nine studies reported from Europe[9,11,22,23] Japan,[10] and the USA[13,16,21,24] of ciprofloxacin in the treatment of RTI caused by *S. pneumoniae* are shown in Table 2. Although the number of patients in each study is small, the total number of patients is 102. In analyzing these studies, several observations can be made:

1. The clinical cure rate was 95% (72/76 patients were reported cured).
2. Davies et al[11] reported that only 9/26 patients improved; the remaining 17 patients failed therapy, and 21 of the 48 *S. pneumoniae* isolates persisted after completion of therapy. The reason for the discrepancy in results between this and the other studies of ciprofloxacin in treating *S. pneumoniae* RTIs is not clear at the present time.
3. The MICs for *S. pneumoniae* reported in these studies varied widely, which is consistent with earlier in vitro studies carried out with ciprofloxacin and *S. pneumoniae*.

It appears that high MICs do not necessarily portend therapeutic failure. The explanation for the demonstrated effectiveness of ciprofloxacin against *S. pneumoniae* can be found in its pharmacokinetics. Ciprofloxacin has a high volume of distribution, which suggests that its concentration in tissues can exceed serum levels for prolonged periods of time. Enoxacin, pefloxacin, and ofloxacin all have pharmacokinetics similar to ciprofloxacin.

Bergogne-Bérézin et al[25] assessed the penetration of ciprofloxacin into bronchial secretions in 21 patients who were given a single oral dose of 500 mg. Ten successive samples of sputum were collected over a 12-hour period. The serum levels peaked at $2.2 \pm 1.3$ µg/L at two hours post-dose and decreased slowly to $0.6 \pm 0.4$ µg/L at six hours. The corresponding mean bronchial levels were $0.44 \pm 0.34$ µg/L at two hours, which remained stable until six hours (range $0.56 \pm 0.98$ µg/L). This level was well above the ciprofloxacin MICs for most pathogens that cause respiratory tract infections. The bronchial/serum ratio was 0.19 µg/L at two hours and 0.95 µg/L at six hours. In another study, Bergogne-Berezin[26] reported on the penetration of ciprofloxacin into lung parenchymal tissue. Following a preoperative infusion of ciprofloxacin 100 mg, surgical samples of the lung were obtained. The lung tissue level exceeded the corresponding serum level by 300-900%. Ciprofloxacin also achieved a high concentration in the pleural fluid, with the peak level obtained 6-9 hours after drug administration. After 24 hours, the mean concentration of ciprofloxacin in pleural fluid was 0.9 µg/mL.

Shlenkhoff et al[27] reported on 14 patients who had been premedicated with 100 mg of intravenous ciprofloxacin prior to thoracic surgery. Four groups received injec-

Table 2. Ciprofloxacin in the treatment of *S. pneumoniae* respiratory tract infections

| Ref. | Number of Patients | Number of *S. pneumoniae* Isolates | MIC Range µg/mL | Mean | Clinical | Bacteriologic | Ciprofloxacin Dose |
|---|---|---|---|---|---|---|---|
| 9 | 7 | 12 | 0.85-3.40 | 1.56 | C 7/7 | E 7/12 | 500 mg PO x 2 |
| 10 | 25 | 42 | N.A. | N.A. | C 23/25<br>F 2/25 | E 29/42 | 200-1200 mg PO daily |
| 11 | 26* | 48 | 0.25-2<br>0.25-7 | 0.73 pre Rx<br>0.93 post Rx | I 9/26<br>F 17/26 | P 13/42<br>P 21/48 | 70% received 600 mg daily<br>500 mg x 2<br>750 mg x 2<br>1000 mg x 2 |
| 13 | 7 | 8 | 0.008-4.0 | N.A. | C 7/7 | E 6/8 | 750 mg PO x 2 |
| 15 | 6 | 6 | N.A. | N.A. | C 6/6 | N.A. | 750 mg PO x 2 |
| 21 | 9 | 9 | 0.5-2 | 1.1 | C 8/9<br>F 1/9 | E 8/9 | IV 200 mg x 2 for 3-5 days<br>followed by oral 500 mg x 2 |
| 22 | 3 | 3 | 0.15-0.5 | 0.255 | C 1/3<br>I 2/3 | E 2/3<br>P 1/3 | 750 mg PO x 2<br>250 mg PO x 2 |
| 23 | 78 | 12 | 0.5-1 | N.A. | C 73/78 | N.A. | 200 mg IV x 2 for 2-10 days<br>followed by 500 mg PO x 2 |
| 24 | 7 | 7 | 1-8 | N.A. | C 7/7 | E 7/7 | 500 mg PO x 2 |

\* Eleven patients had one isolate and 15 had more than one isolate.

Legend: C = cured, F = failure, I = improvement, E = eradication, P = persistence, N.A. = not available

tions 1, 2, 3, and 4 hours before tissue sampling. The results showed that the penetration of ciprofloxacin into lung tissue was marked, with the tissue level significantly exceeding the corresponding serum concentration. These authors found a lung/serum distribution ratio of 195-753% at 1 hour, 545-1044% at 2 hours, 675% at 3 hours, and 800-1000% at 4 hours.

Honeybourne et al[28] studied ciprofloxacin bronchial levels in 15 patients who received 500 mg of the drug twice daily for four days. Bronchial biopsy samples were assayed for drug levels. Timed biopsies and venipunctures were performed after the final dose. The serum levels ranged between 1-9 µg/mL while the bronchial levels ranged between 1.1 and 17.3 µg/g. The average penetration of the drug into bronchial mucosa was 161% but was quite variable. Although the sputum levels were low, the bronchial mucosa levels were very high.

Marlin et al[29] studied the enoxacin distribution ratio between plasma and bronchial mucosa after distribution equilibrium was established. They also compared the absolute bronchial mucosal concentration achieved with the in vitro bactericidal activity of enoxacin. Eighteen patients received enoxacin 400 mg twice daily for four days; on the fifth morning a 500 mg dose of enoxacin was given to all 18 patients. Bronchial mucosal biopsies and plasma samples were obtained at 3, 4, or 5 hours in six patients each, and the samples were assayed for enoxacin by high-pressure liquid chromatography. These investigators concluded that equilibrium between bronchial mucosa and plasma is achieved within three hours of dosing. The mean bronchial mucosal concentration for all patients was 47.8 µg/g, and the mean plasma concentration was 1.1 µg/mL. These data suggest the possibility of active transport into the bronchial mucosa, while avid drug binding to tissue macromolecules may account for the extensive accumulation of fluoroquinolones in the bronchial respiratory tract.

Reid et al[30] studied three groups of 10 patients who were undergoing diagnostic fiberoptic bronchoscopy. Patients were randomized to receive a single dose of ciprofloxacin, either 250 mg orally, 750 mg orally, or 200 mg intravenously. The oral dose was given three hours before bronchoscopy, while the 30-minute intravenous infusion was completed one hour before the procedure was performed. Serum samples and tissue biopsies of bronchial mucosa were obtained during bronchoscopy. Ciprofloxacin concentrations were assayed using high pressure liquid chromatography. Results are shown in Table 3. This unique feature of excellent penetration into the respiratory tract helps clarify the apparent paradox in the clinical results obtained with ciprofloxacin in the treatment of *S. pneumoniae* infection. The very high lung parenchymal and bronchial tissue levels achieved with ciprofloxacin apparently overcome the marginal MICs for *S. pneumoniae* and help explain the excellent clinical results reported by several authors.[9,10,13,16,21-24]

It appears that ciprofloxacin will play a major role in the treatment of various respiratory tract infections in the years to come. Oral ciprofloxacin will be particularly useful in the treatment of pulmonary exacerbations caused by gram-negative bacteria,

Table 3. Concentration of ciprofloxacin in serum and bronchial mucosa

| Dose | Route | Time After Administration (hours) | Mean Serum Level (μg/L) | Mean Bronchial Tissue Level (μg/kg) | Ratio of Tissue/Serum Concentration (range) |
|---|---|---|---|---|---|
| 250 mg | PO | 3.4 | 0.39 | 2.02 | 1.80-12.41 |
| 750 mg | PO | 3.4 | 2.01 | 4.86 | 1.58-6.00 |
| 200 mg | IV | 0.9 | 0.88 | 4.05 | 1.77-17.2 |

Adapted from Reid et al.[30]

as in patients with chronic obstructive pulmonary disease[10,13] and cystic fibrosis,[16-20] and in elderly patients, diabetics, and alcohol abusers, all of whom have an increased likelihood of developing gram-negative respiratory tract infections.[31] Ciprofloxacin is not recommended for the treatment of aspiration pneumonia and anaerobic infections. Once the intravenous formulation of ciprofloxacin becomes available, it will be an attractive antimicrobial therapy for serious respiratory tract infections. Preliminary results suggest that intravenous/oral ciprofloxacin is as effective as ceftazidime in the treatment of serious bacterial respiratory tract infections.[21] Although fluoroquinolones such as ciprofloxacin are effective against *S. pneumoniae,* penicillin is still the antibiotic of choice in cases in which *S. pneumoniae* is known to be the causative pathogen, particularly when the patient is young. In cases of mixed infections or when the pathogens are unknown, ciprofloxacin is a good choice, particularly if the patient is elderly.[32]

# REFERENCES

1. Walker RC, Wright AJ: The quinolones. Mayo Clinic Proc 1987;62:1007-1012.

2. Bauernfeind A: Antimicrobial activity of ciprofloxacin: an overview, in Neu HC, Weuta H (eds), *1st International Ciprofloxacin Workshop*. Amsterdam, Excerpta Medica, 1985, pp 7-11.

3. Sanders CC, Sanders WE, Jr., Goering RV: Overview of preclinical studies with ciprofloxacin. Am J Med 1987;82(suppl 4A):2-11.

4. Hooper DC, Wolfson JS, Ng EY et al: Mechanisms of action of and resistance to ciprofloxacin. Am J Med 1987;82 (suppl 4A):12-20.

5. Van Caekenberghe DL, Pattyn SR: In vitro activity of ciprofloxacin compared with those of other new fluorinated piperazinyl-substituted quinolone derivatives. Antimicrob Agents Chemother 1984;25:518-521.

6. Fenlon CH, Cynamon MH: Comparative in vitro activities of ciprofloxacin and other 4-quinolones against Mycobacterium tuberculosis and Mycobacterium intracellulare. Antimicrob Agents Chemother 1986;29:386-388.

7. Bure A, Desplaces N, Pangon B, et al: In vitro activity of ciprofloxacin, pefloxacin and ofloxacin against Legionella. Proceedings of the 14th International Congress of Chemotherapy, Kyoto, Japan, June 23-28, 1985, pp 37-74.

8. Chodosh S: Acute bacterial exacerbations in bronchitis and asthma. Am J Med 1987; 82(suppl 4A):154-163.

9. Gleadhill IC, Ferguson WP, Lowry RC: Efficacy and safety of ciprofloxacin in patients with respiratory tract infections in comparison with amoxycillin. J Antimicrob Chemother 1986;18(suppl D):133-138.

10. Kobayashi H: Clinical efficacy of ciprofloxacin in the treatment of patients with respiratory tract infections in Japan. Am J Med 1987;82(suppl 4A):169-173.

11. Davies BI, Maesen FPV, Baur C: Ciprofloxacin in the treatment of acute exacerbations of chronic bronchitis. Eur J Clin Microbiol 1986;5(2):226-231.

12. Wollschlager CM, Raoof S, Khan FA, et al: Controlled, comparative study of ciprofloxacin versus ampicillin in treatment of bacterial respiratory tract infections. Am J Med 1987;82(suppl 4A):164-168.

13. Raoof S, Wollschlager C, Khan F: Treatment of respiratory tract infections with ciprofloxacin. J Antimicrob Chemother 1986;18(suppl D):139-145.

14. Wollschlager CM, Raoof S, Khan FA: Oral ciprofloxacin in the treatment of 14 patients with bacterial pneumonia. NY State J Med 1987;87(6):330-333.

15. Ernst JA, Sy ER, Colon LH, et al: Ciprofloxacin in the treatment of pneumonia. Antimicrob Agents Chemother 1986;29(6):1088-1089.

16. Scully BE, Nakatomi M, Ores C, et al: Ciprofloxacin therapy in cystic fibrosis. Am J Med 1987;82(suppl 4A):196-201.

17. Goldfarb J, Stern RC, Reed MD, et al: Ciprofloxacin monotherapy for acute pulmonary exacerbations of cystic fibrosis. Am J Med 1987;82(suppl 4A):174-179.

18. Bosso JA, Black PG, Matsen JM: Ciprofloxacin versus tobramycin plus azlocillin in pulmonary exacerbations in adult patients with cystic fibrosis. Am J Med 1987;82(suppl 4A):180-184.

19. Rubio TT: Ciprofloxacin: Comparative data in cystic fibrosis. Am J Med 1987;82(suppl 4A):185-188.

20. Shalit I, Stutman HR, Marks MI, et al: Randomized study of two dosage regimens of ciprofloxacin for treating chronic bronchopulmonary infection in patients with cystic fibrosis. Am J Med 1987;82(suppl 4A):189-195.

21. Khan F, Basir R: Controlled comparative study of sequential intravenous-oral ciprofloxacin versus ceftazidime in the treatment of serious bacterial respiratory tract infections. Chest 1989;96:528-537.

22. Esposito S, Galante D, Bianchi W, et al: Efficacy and safety of oral ciprofloxacin in the treatment of respiratory tract infections associated with chronic hepatitis. Am J Med 1987;82(suppl 4A):211-214.

23. Chrysanthopoulos CJ, Skoutelis AT, Starakis JC, et al: Use of intravenous ciprofloxacin in respiratory tract infections and biliary sepsis. Am J Med 1987;82(suppl 4A):357-359.

24. Fass RJ: Efficacy and safety of oral ciprofloxacin in the treatment of serious respiratory infections. Am J Med 1987;82(suppl 4A):202-207.

25. Bergogne-Bérézin E, Berthelot G, Even P, et al: Penetration of ciprofloxacin into bronchial secretions. Eur J Clin Microbiol 1986;5(2):197-200.

26. Bergogne-Berezin E: Penetration of ciprofloxacin into tissue: a review, in Neu HC, Weuta H (eds), *Proceedings of the 1st International Ciprofloxacin Workshop*. Amsterdam, Excerpta Medica, 1986, pp 183-188.

27. Schlenkhoff D, Knopf J, Dalhoff A: Penetration of ciprofloxacin into human lung tissue, in Neu HC, Weuta H (eds), *Proceedings of the 1st International Ciprofloxacin Workshop*. Amsterdam, Excerpta Medica 1986, pp 157-159.

28. Honeybourne D, Wise R, Andrews JM: Ciprofloxacin penetration into lungs. Lancet 1987;1:8540.

29. Marlin GE, Brande PD, Whelan AJ, et al: Penetration of enoxacin into human bronchial mucosa. Am Rev Resp Dis 1986;134:1209-1212.

30. Reid TMS, Gould IM, Goldner D, et al: Respiratory tract penetration of ciprofloxacin, in Neu HC, Lode H, Percival A (eds), *Proceedings of the International Workshop*. Naples, Florida, 1989, p 37.

31. Wollschlager CM, Khan FA, Khan A: Utility of radiography and clinical features in the diagnosis of community-acquired pneumonia. Clinics Chest Med 1987;8:393-404.

32. Raju L, Khan F: Pneumonia in the elderly. Geriatrics 1988;43:51-62.

# FLUOROQUINOLONES IN SEXUALLY TRANSMITTED DISEASES     7

*Peter G. Pappas*

## INTRODUCTION

The appropriate therapy for sexually transmitted diseases (STDs) has been a topic of increasing interest and constant evolution over the last 15 years. As new pathogens have been described and as established pathogens (eg, *Neisseria gonorrhoeae* and *Haemophilus ducreyi*) have developed resistance to conventional therapeutic agents, the need for new and more effective antimicrobial agents has become apparent. For example, due to the increasing frequency of penicillinase-producing and chromosomally-mediated resistant strains of *N. gonorrhoeae*, ceftriaxone has become the treatment of choice for gonococcal infections.[1] Likewise, the development of trimethoprim-sulfamethoxazole (TMP/SMX) resistance among *H. ducreyi* isolates has led to the widespread use of ceftriaxone for primary therapy of chancroid in areas where these resistant strains are prevalent.[2] Infections due to *C. trachomatis* remain difficult to manage even though effective therapeutic agents such as tetracycline and erythromycin exist. Because of frequent adverse effects and the need for prolonged therapy with these agents, poor patient compliance, and therapeutic failures are common. As a result, alternative antichlamydial agents are needed.

The fluoroquinolones represent a new therapeutic alternative for many of the common sexually transmitted diseases. These agents have excellent in vitro activity against strains of *N. gonorrhoeae* (including plasmid-mediated and chromosomally-mediated resistant strains) and *H. ducreyi*.[3,4] The fluoroquinolones also have variable in vitro activity against *C. trachomatis* and *U. urealyticum*.[3]

## Neisseria gonorrhoeae

Gonococcal infections are among the most common sexually transmitted diseases in developed countries and the most commonly recognized sexually transmitted diseases in developing countries. The recognition of plasmid-mediated resistance to penicillin and tetracycline and chromosomally-mediated resistance to a number of antimicrobial agents has led to the widespread use of ceftriaxone to replace conventional therapy with penicillin, amoxicillin, or tetracycline.[5] In developing countries, spectinomycin is the most commonly available alternative therapy for resistant *N. gonorrhoeae,* even though it is expensive and its supply is frequently limited. Although both ceftriaxone and spectinomycin have been effective in the treatment of gonococcal infections where resistance to conventional agents has developed, resistance to spectinomycin has occurred with increasing frequency.[6] Ceftriaxone and spectinomycin are effective as single doses for the treatment of uncomplicated infections, but intramuscular injection is required and neither agent is active against other common genital pathogens such as *Chlamydia trachomatis, Ureaplasma urealyticum,* or *Mycoplasma hominis.* Also, both drugs are relatively expensive compared to many available oral regimens.

The fluoroquinolones are exceedingly effective agents against most strains of *N. gonorrhoeae,* including strains with plasmid- or chromosomally-mediated resistance to the penicillins, cephalosporins, tetracycline, erythromycin, and spectinomycin.[7] The minimum inhibitory concentrations (MICs) of selected fluoroquinolones for *N. gonorrhoeae* are listed in Table 1. These agents possess uniformly low MICs for *N. gonorrhoeae* and very favorable pharmacokinetic features that include excellent oral absorption and extended half-lives.[8] Together, these features make the fluoroquinolones potentially very valuable as primary therapy for uncomplicated gonococcal infections.

Gonococcal resistance to the fluoroquinolones has been encountered infrequently. Two recent reports describe resistance to enoxacin occurring in the clinical setting. In one report,[9] gonococcal resistance to enoxacin occurred in two patients while on therapy and was associated with clinical failure in both. In another report Joyce et al[10] found gonococcal resistance to enoxacin in the Philippines associated with its widespread use. These considerations may eventually limit the usefulness of fluoroquinolones in the treatment of infections due to *N. gonorrhoeae.*

Table 1. Minimum inhibitory concentrations (MIC) for *Neisseria gonorrhoeae*

|  | MIC$_{50}$ (µg/mL) | MIC$_{90}$ (µg/mL) |
| --- | --- | --- |
| Norfloxacin | .025 | 0.1 |
| Ciprofloxacin | .0015 | .003 |
| Ofloxacin | .0125 | .05 |
| Enoxacin | .0125 | 1.6 |
| Pefloxacin | .015 | .06 |

## Norfloxacin

The published clinical studies on the use of fluoroquinolones for infections due to *N. gonorrhoeae* have largely focused on uncomplicated urogenital infections. Crider et al[11] reported a comparative trial of oral norfloxacin 600 mg twice daily and intramuscular spectinomycin 2 grams in 92 U.S. naval personnel in the Philippines with uncomplicated gonococcal urethritis. Seventy-three percent of the isolates of *N. gonorrhoeae* were either penicillinase producers or were penicillinase negative but had an MIC to penicillin of 2.0 μg/mL or greater. All patients in both groups responded clinically and microbiologically. In this trial the MICs of norfloxacin were <0.5 μg/mL for all strains and there were no spectinomycin resistant isolates.[11]

In an uncontrolled, non-comparative trial,[12] Romanowski studied norfloxacin in 56 patients with uncomplicated gonococcal infections. All isolates were inhibited by 0.05 μg/mL norfloxacin, and no penicillinase-producing organisms were isolated. All 56 patients with urogenital infection and 6 patients with concomitant anorectal infections were cured. A single treatment failure was noted in one woman with pharyngeal infection. In another trial carried out in Rwanda, Bogaerts et al[13] compared a single oral dose of norfloxacin 800 mg with thiamphenicol 2.5 grams in 168 patients with uncomplicated gonococcal urethritis or cervicitis. Penicillinase-producing strains were isolated from 66 (39%) patients, and all strains were inhibited by 0.12 μg/mL norfloxacin. Ninety-seven percent (119/122) of the patients in the norfloxacin group were cured clinically and microbiologically, while only 35 of 46 patients (76%) in the thiamphenicol group responded to therapy. Recently, Cameron et al[14] compared a single oral dose of norfloxacin 800 mg with spectinomycin 2 grams administered intramuscularly in 92 East African males with gonococcal urethritis. All strains were susceptible to norfloxacin and spectinomycin, and 41% were penicillinase positive. All but one patient in each group was clinically and microbiologically cured.

Based on these studies, it is apparent that a single 800 mg dose or two 600 mg doses of norfloxacin is effective treatment for uncomplicated gonococcal infections in men and women. This effectiveness extends to penicillinase-producing strains and chromosomally-mediated resistant strains of *N. gonorrhoeae*. The usefulness of norfloxacin for the treatment of anorectal or pharyngeal gonococcal infections appears promising but requires further study.

## Ciprofloxacin

Ciprofloxacin is the best studied of the fluoroquinolones in acute gonococcal infections. Among the fluoroquinolones it has the greatest activity against *N. gonorrhoeae*, with MICs ranging between 0.0015 and 0.03 μg/mL.[3,15] Roddy et al[15] studied 100 men with uncomplicated gonorrhea caused by β-lactamase negative strains of *N.*

*gonorrhoeae.* Patients received a single oral dose of ciprofloxacin 250 mg or ampicillin 3.5 g plus probenecid 1.0 g administered orally. All 49 men treated with ciprofloxacin and 47 (92%) of 51 men treated with ampicillin and probenecid were cured at the urethral site. One of five patients with concomitant anorectal gonorrhea treated with ciprofloxacin remained culture positive. In a study of 164 male patients with gonococcal urethritis, a Dutch group reported a cure rate of 100% in patients receiving single oral doses of ciprofloxacin 250 mg or 500 mg.[16] In this group of patients, only 7 β-lactamase positive strains were isolated, and no spectinomycin-resistant strains were encountered. In a smaller study, Shahmanesh et al[17] compared single oral doses of ciprofloxacin 100 mg and 250 mg in 44 men with gonococcal urethritis. All patients were culture negative on the day following treatment. All patients remained culture negative at 14 days post-treatment, including the 19 patients who had received 100 mg of ciprofloxacin. In another study, Loo et al[18] reported that a single 250 mg dose of ciprofloxacin was effective in eradicating urethral, pharyngeal, and rectal isolates of *N. gonorrhoeae* in all 54 men who were treated. Finally, Szarmach et al[19] studied 100 males with acute gonococcal urethritis in a dose-decreasing study and reported that a single oral dose of ciprofloxacin 100 mg was effective in all 30 patients who received this dose. One treatment failure was noted in a patient with "chronic and subacute" gonococcal urethritis who received 250 mg of ciprofloxacin.

These data indicate that a single oral dose of ciprofloxacin 100 mg, 250 mg, or 500 mg is effective in eradicating urethral infections with *N. gonorrhoeae.* Limited data suggest that single-dose ciprofloxacin may be effective treatment for gonococcal infections of the rectum and pharynx, but more controlled trials are necessary.

## Ofloxacin

Ofloxacin is an investigational fluoroquinolone with excellent activity against *N. gonorrhoeae.* Minimum inhibitory concentrations are somewhat higher (0.0125-0.05 μg/mL) than those for ciprofloxacin,[3] but its extended half-life (7-8 hrs) may give ofloxacin a pharmacokinetic advantage, particularly with single-dose therapy. Black et al[20] compared a single oral 400 mg dose of ofloxacin with amoxicillin 3 grams plus probenecid 1 gram administered orally to 201 patients with urethral or cervical infection due to *N. gonorrhoeae.* Thirty patients had concomitant rectal infections, and 16 patients had concomitant pharyngeal infections. Overall, 99 of 100 patients (99%) receiving ofloxacin were cured, including all 13 (100%) with rectal gonorrhea. One failure occurred in a patient with pharyngeal infection. By comparison, 97 of 101 patients (97%) who received conventional therapy were cured. Only one patient with pharyngeal gonorrhea and none of 17 patients with rectal gonorrhea failed conventional therapy.

Boslego et al[21] compared ofloxacin 300 mg twice daily to doxycycline 100 mg twice daily, each given for 7 days, in 64 army recruits with urethritis. All 30 patients with gonorrhea who received ofloxacin were cured, compared with 29 (85%) of 34 patients who received doxycycline. Judson et al[22] reported a microbiologic cure rate of 100% in 43 patients receiving single oral 400 mg or 600 mg doses of ofloxacin for uncomplicated gonorrhea. They also reported a 97% cure rate in 73 patients given ofloxacin 300 mg twice daily for 7 days. Ariyarit et al[23] compared single 200 mg and 400 mg doses of ofloxacin in 220 Thai men with uncomplicated gonorrhea. All patients in both arms of the study were cured; 48% of the strains were penicillinase-producing, but the MIC of ofloxacin for *N. gonorrhoeae* remained quite low (0.008-0.063 µg/mL) in this study.[23] Chan et al[24] reported a 100% cure rate in 59 patients with uncomplicated gonorrhea who were given a single oral dose of either 400 mg or 600 mg of ofloxacin.

These studies indicate that ofloxacin is effective in the treatment of uncomplicated gonorrhea at a single oral dose of 200 mg, 400 mg, or 600 mg. As with norfloxacin and ciprofloxacin, single-dose ofloxacin appears to be effective in rectal and pharyngeal gonorrhea, but more studies are needed to determine optimal therapy.

## Enoxacin

Enoxacin is an investigational oral fluoroquinolone with activity against *N. gonorrhoeae*, although its activity is generally less than that of the other fluoroquinolones (Table 1). Shapiro et al[25] reported excellent in vitro activity for enoxacin against 23 strains of *N. gonorrhoeae*, including 15 resistant strains. The drug has good oral absorption and a half-life of 6-7 hours.

A number of clinical trials have documented the usefulness of enoxacin in uncomplicated gonorrhea. Notowicz et al[26] reported a cure rate of 100% in 22 patients given a single oral dose of 600 mg of enoxacin or two 400 mg doses of enoxacin four hours apart. Van der Willigen et al[9] reported a comparative trial of single 200 mg or 400 mg doses of enoxacin in 155 patients with uncomplicated gonorrhea. Cure rates of 90% (69/77) and 92% (72/78) were achieved with the 200 mg and 400 mg doses, respectively. Two patients developed resistance to enoxacin while on therapy (both were infected with penicillin-sensitive organisms). The same group reported a similar trial in 86 women comparing single 200 mg or 400 mg doses of enoxacin for uncomplicated urogenital gonorrhea. Cure rates of 100% (46/46) and 98.7% (39/40) were achieved with 400 mg and 200 mg of enoxacin, respectively.[27] Recently, Handsfield et al[28] compared a single oral 400 mg dose of enoxacin to 250 mg of ceftriaxone in 196 men and women with gonorrhoea. Eradication of *N. gonorrhoeae* from the urethra or cervix occurred in all patients. Five patients in this study had concomitant pharyngeal infection, 3 of whom received enoxacin and 2 of whom received ceftriaxone.

All three enoxacin recipients failed therapy, while both patients treated with ceftriaxone were cured.

Enoxacin in a single 200 mg or 400 mg dose is effective against *N. gonorrhoeae* but clearly has the least activity in vitro of the agents discussed here. Clinical trials have demonstrated a somewhat lower cure rate when compared to other fluoroquinolones for uncomplicated gonococcal urogenital infection, and the persistence of gonococcal pharyngeal infection in one trial is cause for some concern. Also, the development of resistance by gonococci to enoxacin while on therapy may limit the usefulness of this and other fluoroquinolones in the treatment of gonorrhea.

## Chlamydia trachomatis and Ureaplasma urealyticum

*Chlamydia trachomatis* is the main etiologic agent of male nongonococcal urethritis (NGU) and its counterpart in females, mucopurulent cervicitis.[29] *C. trachomatis* is probably the most common sexually transmitted disease in the United States and Western Europe, surpassing both gonorrhea and syphilis in frequency. *Ureaplasma urealyticum* is also a common etiologic agent of NGU, and it can be recovered from 20-30% of patients with NGU in the absence of other pathogens.[30] *C. trachomatis* and *U. urealyticum* may exist as sole pathogens, or they may coexist in the same patient. Depending on the population surveyed, *C. trachomatis* has also been isolated in as many as 40% of patients with gonococcal urethritis. Both organisms are recognized causes of endometritis and pelvic inflammatory disease (salpingitis); chlamydia is an etiologic agent in epididymitis, pharyngitis, proctitis, and probably prostatitis in sexually active persons.

The in vitro activities of the fluoroquinolones against *C. trachomatis* and *U. urealyticum* are shown in Tables 2 and 3. Although most of the fluoroquinolones have some activity against *C. trachomatis,* one would predict from these values that ofloxacin and ciprofloxacin are the most clinically active antichlamydial agents in this

Table 2.   Minimum inhibitory concentrations (MICs) for *C. trachomatis*

|  | $MIC_{50}$ (µg/mL) | $MIC_{90}$ (µg/mL) |
|---|---|---|
| Norfloxacin | 8.0 | 16.0 |
| Ciprofloxacin | 0.5 | 2.0 |
| Ofloxacin | 0.5 | 2.0 |
| Enoxacin | 8.0 | 16.0 |
| Fleroxacin | 1.5 | 2.5 |

Table 3. Minimum inhibitory concentrations (MICs) for *U. urealyticum*

|  | MIC$_{50}$ (µg/mL) | MIC$_{90}$ (µg/mL) |
|---|---|---|
| Norfloxacin | 16.0 | 32.0 |
| Ciprofloxacin | 16.0 | 32.0 |
| Ofloxacin | 4.0 | 8.0 |
| Enoxacin | 32.0 | 64.0 |
| Pefloxacin | 4.0 | 8.0 |

group. The high MICs of both enoxacin and norfloxacin for *C. trachomatis* make these agents potentially less effective for chlamydia infections. All of these agents are somewhat less active against *U. urealyticum* (Table 3), and good clinical data to support their usefulness in ureaplasma infections is generally lacking.

The fluoroquinolones have been studied less extensively in NGU and mucopuru-lent cervicitis than in gonococcal infections. Many of the clinical trials using fluoro-quinolones in gonococcal infections have reported concomitant isolation of *C. trachomatis* and *U. urealyticum* in these patients, and it is apparent from these studies that single-dose therapy which is effective in gonococcal infections is ineffective in the treatment of chlamydia or ureaplasma infections. For example, Roddy et al[15] found persistent *C. trachomatis* following a single oral dose of ciprofloxacin 250 mg in 10 of 11 patients co-infected with *N. gonorrhoeae* and *C. trachomatis*. Likewise, Tegelberg-Stassen et al[16] noted post-gonococcal urethritis (PGU) in 31 (36%) of 85 and 21 (27%) of 79 of patients receiving a single oral dose of either 250 mg or 500 mg of ciprofloxacin, respectively. Chlamydia and ureaplasma cultures were not done as part of this study. Shahmanesh et al[17] also noted no effect on *C. trachomatis* and PGU in 44 men given a single oral dose of either 100 mg or 250 mg of ciprofloxacin for gonococcal urethritis.[17] Van der Willigen et al[9] reported no effect of enoxacin on post-treatment *C. trachomatis* cultures in 155 patients treated with either a single 200 mg or 400 mg dose. In this study, 34% of patients developed PGU and 17% were culture positive for *C. trachomatis*. Loo et al[18] reported PGU in 21 (45%) of 47 men who had received a single oral dose of ciprofloxacin 250 mg, and *C. trachomatis* was isolated from 16 (76%) of 21 individuals following treatment. Finally, Ariyarit et al[23] reported PGU in 43 (24%) of 181 patients who were treated with ofloxacin 400 mg, but chlamydia cultures were not reported as part of the study. It is clear from these studies that single-dose ciprofloxacin (250 or 500 mg), ofloxacin (200 or 400 mg), or enoxacin (200 mg or 400 mg) are ineffective in the treatment of *C. trachomatis* urethritis in males.

Ofloxacin is one of the most active fluoroquinolones in vitro against *C. trachomatis* (MIC 0.5-2.0 µg/ml), although it is significantly less active against *U. urealyticum* (MIC 4.0-8.0 µg/ml).[3] Several published trials support the usefulness of ofloxacin in NGU. Boslego et al[21] compared oral ofloxacin 300 mg twice daily to oral doxycycline 100 mg twice daily (both given for seven days) in 45 patients with NGU. Clinical cure was achieved with ofloxacin in 25 (95%) of 26 patients compared to 15 (79%) of 19 patients in the doxycycline group. Chlamydia cultures were initially positive in 18 ofloxacin recipients, and 3 remained culture positive at follow-up. In a similar study, Judson et al[22] compared seven day regimens of ofloxacin 300 mg bid or doxycycline 100 mg bid in patients with NGU. The microbiologic cure rate in ofloxacin recipients was 82% (31/38) for chlamydia isolates and 67% (6/9) for ureaplasma isolates. Fransen et al[31] reported a comparative trial in 40 patients with *C. trachomatis* urethritis or cervicitis using doxycycline 200 mg daily for 10 days versus ofloxacin 200 mg twice daily for 9 days. Clinical and microbiologic cure was achieved in 11 (100%) of 11 male and 8 (80%) of 10 female ofloxacin recipients. All nineteen doxycycline recipients were clinically and microbiologically cured. Lastly, Morel et al[32] reported 5 adult males with chlamydia urethritis clinically and microbiologically cured following treatment with ofloxacin 200 mg twice daily for 14 days.

Unpublished studies of the use of ofloxacin in NGU suggest similar success rates. Stein and Saravolatz[33] compared ofloxacin 300 mg twice daily versus doxycycline 100 mg twice daily in 44 patients with NGU. Both drugs were given for seven days. All patients were microbiologically cured including 29 patients with *C. trachomatis* and 10 patients with *U. urealyticum.* One clinical failure occurred in the doxycycline group. Tack et al[34] reported data from a collection of five studies using ofloxacin 300 mg twice daily for 7 days in the treatment of NGU. In 64 (88%) of 73 *C. trachomatis* infections the organism was eradicated after therapy. Not surprisingly, only 24 (69%) of 35 *U. urealyticum* isolates were eradicated. Finally, Vilata et al[35] compared two different ofloxacin regimens (200 mg tid for 7 days or 200 mg bid 5 days) with minocycline 100 mg twice daily for 7 days in patients with NGU. All patients were culture positive for *C. trachomatis, U. urealyticum,* or both organisms at study entry. Efficacy as measured by eradication of the infecting organisms was similar for all groups; 90% (36/40) with minocycline, 87.5% (35/40) with high-dose ofloxacin, and 92.5% (37/40) with the lower dose of ofloxacin.

Ciprofloxacin and ofloxacin are similarly active in vitro against *C. trachomatis* (MIC 0.5-2.0 µg/ml), but ciprofloxacin is considerably less active than ofloxacin versus *U. urealyticum* (MIC 16-32 µg/ml).[3] Fong et al[36] compared oral ciprofloxacin 750 mg twice daily for 7 days to oral doxycycline 100 mg twice daily for 7 days in 145 patients with NGU. Response rates were similar for both groups with 37 (52.1%) of 71 patients cured with ciprofloxacin and 45 (60.8%) of 74 patients cured with doxycycline. In patients with only chlamydia isolated, significantly more were cured with doxycycline (75%) than with ciprofloxacin (45%). In addition, *C. trachomatis* was re-cultured from 15 (68%) of 22 men treated with ciprofloxacin but only from 3 (15%) of 20 men treated with doxycycline. In contrast, patients infected with only *U. urealyticum* responded better to ciprofloxacin (69% cured) than to doxycycline (45% cured). In a similar study, Arya et al[37] found ciprofloxacin to be ineffective in eradicating *C. trachomatis* from urethral cultures in 11 (79%) of 14 men following treatment. Somewhat better results were seen against *U. urealyticum,* but these authors concluded that ciprofloxacin was of little value in the treatment of *C. trachomatis* urethritis in men.

Norfloxacin, with an MIC of 8.0-16.0 µg/ml for *C. trachomatis* and 8.0- 64.0 µg/ml for *U. urealyticum,* has been largely unsuccessful in the treatment of NGU. Bowie et al treated a group of men with NGU with norfloxacin 400 mg twice daily for 10 days.[38] Shortly following therapy, 21 (84%) of 25 men who were initially positive for *C. trachomatis* had the organism re-isolated. Ultimately all but one patient had a microbiologic relapse within the first six weeks following therapy. Patients with only *U. urealyticum* isolated did much better, however, and 17 (63%) of 27 remained culture negative following therapy. These results indicate no role for norfloxacin in the treatment of urogenital infections due to *C. trachomatis.*

Fleroxacin is an investigational agent with moderate activity against *C. trachomatis* (MIC 1.5-2.5 µg/ml).[39] Unique features of this drug include nearly complete oral absorption and a long half-life (10-11 hrs.). Gundersen and Zahm[40] reported 11 patients with positive urogenital cultures for *C. trachomatis* given 400 mg of fleroxacin orally once daily for 7 days. Nine (82%) of 11 patients were cured at early follow-up (one week); however, only 6 (60%) of 10 remained culture-negative at final follow-up (2-3 weeks). An Austrian group studied 22 patients with *C. trachomatis* urethritis or cervicitis given fleroxacin 400 mg once daily for 7 days. Only 1 patient remained culture positive at one week follow-up, and 2 were culture positive at four-week follow-up.[41] Bowie and Willetts[42] studied varying doses of fleroxacin (400, 600, and 800 mg) given once daily for 7 days in patients with genital chlamydia or ureaplasma infections. In this study, fleroxacin failed to reliably eradicate *C. trachomatis* from men and was inconsistent against *U. urealyticum.*

In conclusion, although all of the fluoroquinolones possess activity against *C. trachomatis* and *U. urealyticum,* only ofloxacin and to some extent ciprofloxacin have shown reasonably reliable activity in the treatment of these infections. There appears to be no role for norfloxacin in chlamydia infections, and inconsistent results with the investigational agent fleroxacin for the treatment of NGU are worrisome.

## Pelvic Inflammatory Disease

Pelvic inflammatory disease (PID), including acute and chronic endometritis, salpingitis, and tubo-ovarian abscess, is a major cause of morbidity and an occasional cause of mortality among young sexually active females, accounting for approximately one million cases annually in the U.S.[43] The major bacteriologic causes of pelvic inflammatory disease include *N. gonorrhoeae, C. trachomatis,* genital mycoplasmas, aerobic streptococci (especially Group B streptococcus) and anaerobic bacteria (especially *Bacteroides* spp.). In addition to the acute morbidity of pelvic inflammatory disease, PID is a major factor in female infertility and the development of ectopic pregnancies.

Conventional therapy for PID has generally included the use of an agent with activity against *N. gonorrhoeae,* aerobic streptococci, and anaerobic bacteria combined with an antichlamydial agent. An example of this combination is cefoxitin or ceftizoxime plus doxycycline. Another "gold standard" therapy for PID has been an aminoglycoside (gentamicin or tobramycin) plus clindamycin. Clindamycin has antichlamydial activity in addition to being an excellent drug against aerobic streptococci, staphylococci, and anaerobic bacteria. Parenteral agents are frequently given for 3-4 days followed by an oral regimen to complete a 10-14 day course of therapy.

The fluoroquinolones have not been used extensively in pelvic inflammatory disease, and no published studies comparing their efficacy to conventional therapy are available. However, several abstracts examining the efficacy of these agents in PID have recently appeared. Crombleholme et al[44] reported a comparative trial of the efficacy of ciprofloxacin administered alone versus a combination of gentamicin and clindamycin in 54 patients with PID. Pretreatment cervical and endometrial cultures were obtained on all patients. *N. gonorrhoeae* was isolated from 61% of patients, *C. trachomatis* from 7.4%, *M. hominis* from 61%, *U. urealyticum* from 67%, and anaerobes from 70%. Clinical cure was noted in 24 (92%) of 26 patients in the ciprofloxacin group and 28 (100%) of 28 patients in the gentamicin-clindamycin group. One ciprofloxacin failure had persistent *C. trachomatis* after 14 days of therapy, and the other developed a pelvic abscess requiring other therapy. A study of outpatient therapy of PID in 72 women compared oral ofloxacin 400 mg twice daily for 10 days to cefoxitin 2 grams intramuscularly plus 1 gram probenecid orally followed by oral doxycycline 100 mg twice daily for 10 days.[45] Cervical and endometrial cultures for *N. gonorrhoeae* and *C. trachomatis* were obtained in all patients at entry. Thirty-five (94.6%) of 37 women in the ofloxacin group were clinically cured, compared with 34 (97.1%) of 35 patients treated with the cefoxitin/doxycycline regimen. No bacteriologic failures were noted; however, all "clinical failures" occurred in women with *N. gonorrhoeae* salpingitis.[45] In another study, Thadepalli et al[46] compared the efficacy of intravenous ciprofloxacin for 3 days followed by oral ciprofloxacin 500 mg twice daily for 10 days, to intravenous gentamicin and clindamycin for three days followed by oral clindamycin 300 mg four times daily for 14 days in women with pelvic infections. Forty-six women with salpingitis (n=30), endometritis (n=5), septic abortion (n=3), paraovarian abscess (n=2), chronic PID (n=5) or infected tubal pregnancy (n=1) were included in this study. *N. gonorrhoeae* and *C. trachomatis* were the most common bacterial isolates in these women. Clinical cures occurred in 20/22 women in the ciprofloxacin group and in 22/24 in the gentamicin/clindamycin group. Clinical recurrences were seen in one patient from each group, and surgery was required in one patient from each group.[46]

These unpublished studies suggest that monotherapy with ciprofloxacin or ofloxacin may have a role in the treatment of PID due to susceptible organisms. The relative inactivity of the fluoroquinolones against most anaerobic bacteria and the frequent occurrence of these organisms in PID, however, are major points of concern.

## *Haemophilus ducreyi (Chancroid)*

Chancroid is a common sexually transmitted ulcerative disease seen mostly in the tropics, but an increase in the number of cases of chancroid in the U.S. and Europe has led to a greater awareness of this disease.[47] Conventional therapy for chancroid has included erythromycin, TMP/SMX (single- or multiple-dose), and more recently, ceftriaxone. However, with the development of resistance to some of the conventional therapies (eg, TMP/SMX), the introduction of new therapies is essential.

The fluoroquinolones all have excellent in vitro activity against various strains of *H. ducreyi* (Table 4), which has led to their use in clinical trials for treatment of chancroid.[4,48] Naamara et al[49] compared a single oral 500 mg dose of ciprofloxacin, ciprofloxacin 500 mg twice daily for 3 days, and TMP/SMX (160 mg/800 mg) twice daily for 3 days in 122 patients with chancroid. All 40 patients given ciprofloxacin for 3 days were clinically and bacteriologically cured, while 2 (5%) of 41 patients in the single-dose ciprofloxacin and 3 (7%) of 41 patients in the TMP/SMX groups failed therapy. Bodhidatta et al[50] administered a single oral 500 mg dose of ciprofloxacin or two 500 mg doses of ciprofloxacin four hours apart to 180 patients with chancroid. Of the *H. ducreyi* culture positive patients, 43 (100%) of 43 in the single-dose cipro-

**Table 4.** Minimum inhibitory concentrations (MICs) for *Haemophilus ducreyi*

| | MIC$_{50}$ (µg/mL) | MIC$_{90}$ (µg/mL) |
|---|---|---|
| Norfloxacin | 0.12 | 0.12 |
| Ciprofloxacin | 0.03 | 0.03 |
| Ofloxacin | 0.03 | 0.03 |
| Enoxacin | 0.12 | 0.12 |
| Pefloxacin | 0.12 | 0.12 |

floxacin group and 43 (98%) of 44 in the two-dose ciprofloxacin group were cured. Of the culture-negative patients, 42 of 45 (93%) in the 500 mg ciprofloxacin group and 46 of 48 (96%) in the 1000 mg group were cured. In both studies, inguinal buboes often progressed to suppuration despite antimicrobial therapy.

Mensing studied enoxacin in the treatment of chancroid in 7 patients.[51] Patients were given oral enoxacin 400 mg twice daily for 7 to 12 days (until healing of lesions). All patients were cured on this regimen. MacDonald et al[52] reported the use of single oral dose fleroxacin (200 or 400 mg) in 49 East African men with chancroid, 11 of whom were co-infected with HIV-1. Overall, 23 (88.5%) of 26 patients treated with 200 mg of fleroxacin and 18 (78.3%) of 23 patients treated with 400 mg of fleroxacin were cured. Furthermore, microbiologic cure occurred in 8 (73%) of 11 patients who were seropositive for HIV-1 as compared to 35 (95%) of 37 patients seronegative for HIV-1. In a similar study, Miller et al[53] reported the efficacy of single dose fleroxacin (200 mg or 400 mg) in the treatment of chancroid in 33 South African mine workers. Only one patient in the low-dose (200 mg) group had a microbiologic failure, but 3 (16%) of 19 in this group were clinical failures compared to only 1 (7%) of 14 in the 400 mg fleroxacin group.

Based on these data, it appears that oral ciprofloxacin in one or two 500 mg doses is effective therapy for chancroid. Additionally, oral enoxacin in single 400 mg dose or in multiple doses is reasonably effective therapy for chancroid. Finally, fleroxacin appears to be effective as a single dose (200 or 400 mg) against *H. ducreyi*, although it may be less effective in HIV-1 seropositive patients.

## Treponema pallidum (Syphilis)

The fluoroquinolones have not been studied extensively in the treatment of syphilis. To date, no clinical trials to determine the efficacy of the fluoroquinolones for the treatment of syphilis are available. Veller-Fornasa et al[54] reported rather disappointing results in an experimental trial of ofloxacin given to rabbits infected intratesticularly with *T. pallidum*. Three days after infection, 10 rabbits were given 100 mg ofloxacin orally for 3 consecutive days; 9 rabbits were given procaine penicillin, and 7 rabbits were left untreated. All of the untreated and ofloxacin-treated rabbits developed syphilitic orchitis seven days after inoculation. Three additional rabbits infected with treponemes obtained from ofloxacin-treated rabbits developed syphilitic orchitis and positive serologic tests for syphilis. All penicillin treated rabbits remained serologically negative for syphilis and did not develop syphilitic orchitis.[54] Based on these limited data, the fluoroquinolones cannot be recommended for the treatment of syphilis in any stage.

## Bacterial Vaginosis

Bacterial vaginosis (formally non-specific vaginitis) is felt to be a synergistic vaginal mucosal infection caused by overgrowth of *Gardnerella vaginalis,* anaerobic bacteria including *Bacteroides* and *Mobiluncus* spp., *Corynebacterium* spp., and facultative aerobic bacteria. Few published studies exist detailing the efficacy of fluoroquinolones in the treatment of bacterial vaginosis. Carmona et al[55] described the use of ciprofloxacin in 22 women with bacterial vaginosis. Patients were given oral ciprofloxacin 500 mg twice daily for 7 days. Sixteen of 22 (73%) patients had clinical and bacteriologic cures, while 4 of 22 (18%) patients had clinical cures without bacteriologic eradication. Two patients (9%) failed therapy clinically. Interestingly, "clue cells," the pathognomonic marker for bacterial vaginosis, were not eradicated in 11 of 17 women with clinical cures, making this an unreliable marker for response to therapy. In an unpublished study of three different quinolones (ofloxacin, ciprofloxacin, norfloxacin) in bacterial vaginosis, Alegente et al[56] reported limited efficacy for ciprofloxacin (500 mg bid for 7 days) and ofloxacin (300 mg bid for 7 days) in the treatment of bacterial vaginosis. In this study, 7 of 10 (70%) patients in the ciprofloxacin group and 7 of 10 (70%) patients in the ofloxacin group responded to therapy, compared with only 4 of 10 (40%) patients in the norfloxacin group. Conclusions as to the utility of the fluoroquinolones in this disorder cannot be drawn based on these limited data.

## CONCLUSION

The fluoroquinolones represent a new class of antimicrobial agents that have activity against a number of sexually transmitted pathogens. These drugs are particularly active against penicillin-susceptible and penicillin-resistant strains of *N. gonorrhoeae.* Clinical trials suggest that single-dose ciprofloxacin, norfloxacin, ofloxacin, and enoxacin are effective in curing virtually 100% of cases of uncomplicated urogenital gonorrhea. The fluoroquinolones also have exceptional activity against *H. ducreyi* and appear to be at least as effective as existing standard therapy.

Single-dose ciprofloxacin and ofloxacin appear to be effective in eradicating most cases of chancroid, although multiple doses are necessary to achieve a cure in 100% of cases. The best regimen for chancroid remains to be determined and awaits the results of well-controlled clinical trials. Unfortunately, with the possible exception of ofloxacin, none of the fluoroquinolones is sufficiently active against *C. trachomatis* to be considered first-line therapy. Clinical trials suggest ofloxacin may be as effective as doxycycline for uncomplicated chlamydia urethritis and cervicitis, but more clinical trials are necessary to determine the exact role of this agent in chlamydia infections.

Increasing clinical experience suggests a possible role for ciprofloxacin and ofloxacin in the outpatient treatment of PID caused by *N. gonorrhoeae* and *C. trachomatis*, but published clinical trials are lacking to support their broad use in PID. The use of fluoroquinolones in incubating syphilis must be discouraged at present. Ultimately the role of the fluoroquinolones in sexually transmitted diseases will be determined by the results of well-controlled clinical trials and whether significant levels of resistance to these agents develop in sexually transmitted pathogens.

# REFERENCES

1. 1989 Sexually Transmitted Diseases Treatment Guidelines. Morbid Mortal Wkly Rep 1989;38(suppl 8):21-27.

2. Ronald AR, Plummer FA: Chancroid and *Haemophilus ducreyi.* Ann Intern Med 1985; 102:705-707.

3. Aznar J, Caballero MC, Lozano MC, et al: Activities of new quinolone derivatives against genital pathogens. Antimicrob Agents Chemother 1985;27:76-78.

4. Wall RA, Mabey DCW, Bello CSS, et al: The comparative *in-vitro* activity of twelve 4-quinolone antimicrobials against *Haemophilus ducreyi.* J Antimicrob Chemother 1985;16:165-168.

5. Hook EW III, Holmes KK: Gonococcal infections. Ann Intern Med 1985;102;229-243.

6. Johnson SR, Morse SA: Antibiotic resistance in *Neisseria gonorrhoeae:* genetics and mechanisms of resistance. Sex Trans Dis 1988;15:217-224.

7. Wolfson JS, Hooper DC: The fluoroquinolones: structures, mechanisms of action and resistance, and spectra of activity in vitro. Antimicrob Agents Chemother 1985;28:581-586.

8. Hooper DC, Wolfson JS: The fluoroquinolones: pharmacology, clinical uses, and toxicities in humans. Antimicrob Agents Chemother 1985;28:716-721.

9. Van der Willigen AH, van der Hoek JCS, Wagenvoort JHT, et al: Comparative double-blind study of 200- and 400-mg enoxacin given orally in the treatment of acute uncomplicated urethral gonorrhea in males. Antimicrob Agents Chemother 1987;31:535-538.

10. Joyce MP, Aying BB, Vaughan GH: In vitro sensitivity of *Neisseria gonorrhoeae* to quinolone antibiotics in the Philippines (abstract E19). Sixth Pathogenic Neisseria Conference, Pine Mountain, Georgia, 16-21 October, 1988.

11. Crider SR, Colby SD, Miller LK, et al: Treatment of penicillin-resistant *Neisseria gonorrhoeae* with oral norfloxacin. New Engl J Med 31984;11:137-139.

12. Romanowski B: Norfloxacin in the therapy of gonococcal infections. Scand J Infect Dis 1986;48(suppl):40-45.

13. Bogaerts J, Tello WM, Verbist L, et al: Norfloxacin versus thiamphenicol for treatment of uncomplicated gonorrhea in Rwanda. Antimicrob Agents Chemother 1987;31:434-437.

14. Cameron D, Plummer F, D'Costa L, et al: Therapy with single dose norfloxacin or spectinomycin for gonococcal urethritis in men, abstract 1160. Twenty-eighth Interscience Conference on Antimicrobial Agents and Chemotherapy, Los Angeles, October, 1988.

15. Roddy RE, Handsfield HH, Hook EW III: Comparative trial of single-dose ciprofloxacin and ampicillin plus probenecid for treatment of gonococcal urethritis in men. Antimicrob Agents Chemother 1986;30:267-269.

16. Tegelberg-Stassen MJAM, van der Hoek JCS, Mooi L, et al: Treatment of uncomplicated gonococcal urethritis in men with two dosages of ciprofloxacin. Eur J Clin Microbiol 1986;5:244-246.

17. Shahmanesh M, Shukla SR, Phillips I, et al: Ciprofloxacin for treating urethral gonorrhoea in men. Genitourin Med 1986;62:86-87.

18. Loo PS, Ridgway GL, Oriel JD: Single dose ciprofloxacin for treating gonococcal infections in men. Genitourin Med 1985;61:302-305.

19. Szarmach H, Weuta H, Podziewski J, et al: Ciprofloxacin in acute male gonorrhea. Arzneim-Forsch/Drug Res 1986;36(II):1840-1842.

20. Black JR, Handsfield HH, Hook EW III: Single dose ofloxacin vs. amoxicillin plus probenecid for treatment of uncomplicated gonococcal infection. Rev Infect Dis 1989; 11(suppl 5):1313-1314.

21. Boslego JW, Hicks CB, Greenup R, et al: A prospective randomized trial of ofloxacin vs. doxycycline in the treatment of uncomplicated male urethritis. Sex Trans Dis 1988; 15(4):186-191.

22. Judson FN, Beals BS, Tack KJ: Clinical experience with ofloxacin in sexually transmitted disease. Infection 1986;14(suppl 4):S309-S310.

23. Ariyarit C, Panikabutra K, Chitwarakorn A, et al: Efficacy of ofloxacin in uncomplicated gonorrhoea. Infection 1986;14(suppl 4):S311-S313.

24. Chan ASC, Tank KC, Fung KK, et al: Single dose ofloxacin in treatment of uncompli- cated gonorrhoea. Infection 1986;14(suppl 4):S314-S315.

25. Shapiro MA, Heifetz CL, Sesnie JC: Comparative in-vitro activity of enoxacin against penicillinase- and non-penicillinase-producing *Neisseria gonorrhoeae*. Sex Trans Dis 1987;14:111-112.

26. Notowicz A, Stolz E, van Klingeren B: A double blind study comparing two dosages of enoxacin for the treatment of uncomplicated urogenital gonorrhoea. J Antimicrob Chemother 1984;14(suppl C):91-94.

27. Tegelberg-Stassen MJAM, van der Willigen AH, van der Hoek JCS, et al: Treatment of uncomplicated urogenital gonorrhoea in women with a single oral dose of enoxacin. Eur J Clin Microbiol 1986;5:395-398.

28. Handsfield HH, Black JR, Hook EW III: Comparative trial of single-dose enoxacin vs. ceftriaxone for treatment of uncomplicated gonorrhea. Rev Infect Dis 1989;11(suppl 5): 1315-1316.

29. Brunham RC, Paavonen J, Stevens CE, et al: Mucopurulent cervicitis - the ignored counterpart in women of urethritis in men. New Engl J Med 1984;311:1-6.

30. Bowie WR: Urethritis in Males, in KK Holmes, PA Mardh, PF Sparling, Wiesner PJ (eds), *Sexually Transmitted Diseases*. New York, McGraw-Hill, 1984, pp 638-650.

31. Fransen L, Avonts D, Piot P: Treatment of genital chlamydia infection with ofloxacin. Infection 1986;14 (suppl 4):S318-S320.

32. Morel P, Casin I, Bianchi A, et al: Traitement pare ofloxacin (RU 43280) des urethrites, masculines bacteriennes non compliquees. Pathologie Biologie 1986; 34(5):502-504.

33. Stein GE, Saravolatz LD: Randomized clinical study of ofloxacin and doxycycline in the treatment of NGU and cervicitis. Rev Infect Dis 1989;11(suppl 5):1272.

34. Tack KJ, Callery SV, Smith JA, et al: Ofloxacin in the treatment of sexually transmitted diseases. Rev Infect Dis 1989;11(suppl 5):1282-1283.

35. Vilata JJ, Garcia-de-Lomas J, Sanchez J, et al: A double- blind randomized study compar- ing two ofloxacin regimens vs. minocycline in the treatment of NGU. Rev Infect Dis 1989;11(suppl 5):1285-1286.

36. Fong IW, Linton W, Simbul M, et al: Treatment of nongonococcal urethritis with cipro- floxacin. Am J Med 1987;82(suppl 4A):311-316.

37. Arya OP, Hobson D, Hart CA, et al: Evaluation of ciprofloxacin 500 mg twice daily for one week in treating uncomplicated gonococcal, chlamydia, and non-specific urethritis in men. Genitourin Med 1986;62:170-174.

38. Bowie WR, Willetts V, Sibau L: Failure of norfloxacin to eradicate *Chlamydia trachomatis* in nongonococcal urethritis. Antimicrob Agents Chemother 1986;30:594-597.

39. Oriel JD: Use of quinolones in chlamydia infection. Rev Infect Dis 1989;11(suppl 5): 1273-1276.

40. Gundersen T, Zahm F: Fleroxacin in the treatment of urogenital infections caused by *Chlamydia trachomatis*. Rev Infect Dis 1989;11(suppl 5):1278-1279.

41. Soltz-Szots J, Schneider S, Mailer H: Efficacy of and tolerance to fleroxacin in the treatment of chlamydial urethritis and cervicitis. Rev Infect Dis 1989;11(suppl 5):1280-1281.

42. Bowie WR, Willetts V: Double-blind evaluation of fleroxacin for treatment of *C. trachomatis* infection. Rev Infect Dis 1989;11(suppl 5):1284.

43. Sweet RL: Pelvic inflammatory disease: etiology, diagnosis and treatment. Sex Trans Dis 1981;8:308-315.

44. Crombleholme WR, Schachter J, Sweet RL: Ciprofloxacin vs. clindamycin plus gentamicin in the treatment of acute pelvic inflammatory disease. Rev Infect Dis 1989;11(suppl 5):S1312-S1315.

45. Wendel GD, Cox SM, Theriot SK, et al: Ofloxacin in the treatment of acute salpingitis. Rev Infect Dis 1989;11(suppl 5):S1314-S1315.

46. Thadepalli H, Mathai D, Savage E, et al: Ciprofloxacin therapy for pelvic inflammatory disease (PID) in hospitalized patients, abstract 1169. Program and abstracts of the 28th Interscience Conference on Antimicrobial Agents and Chemotherapy, Los Angeles, October 23-26, 1988.

47. Schmid GP, Sanders LL, Blount JH, et al: Chancroid in the United States: Reestablishment of an old disease. JAMA 1987;258:3265-3268.

48. Sturm AW: Comparison of antimicrobial susceptibility patterns of fifty-seven strains of *Haemophilus ducreyi* isolated in Amsterdam from 1978 to 1985. J Antimicrob Chemother 1987;19:187-191.

49. Naamara W, Plummer FA, Greenblatt RM, et al: Treatment of chancroid with ciprofloxacin: A prospective, randomized clinical trial. Am J Med 1987;82(suppl 4A):317-320.

50. Bodhidatta L, Taylor DN, Chitwarakorn A, et al: Evaluation of 500- and 1,000-mg doses of ciprofloxacin for the treatment of chancroid. Antimicrob Agents Chemother 1988; 32:723-725.

51. Mensing H: Treatment of chancroid with enoxacin. Acta Dermatol Venereol (Stockholm) 1985;65:455-457.

52. MacDonald KS, Cameron DW, D'Costa LJ, et al: Evaluation of fleroxacin as single-dose oral therapy for chancroid. Rev Infect Dis 1989;11(suppl 5):1319-1320.

53. Miller SD, Exposto F, Dangor Y, et al: A dose-finding study of fleroxacin in the treatment of chancroid. Rev Infect Dis 1989;11(suppl 5):S1310-1311.

54. Veller-Fornasa C, Tarantello M, Cipriani R, et al: Effect of ofloxacin on *Treponema pallidum* in incubating experimental syphilis. Genitourin Med 1987;63:214-218.

55. Carmona O, Hernandez-Gonzalez S, Kobelt R: Ciprofloxacin in the treatment of nonspecific vaginitis. Am J Med 1987;82(suppl 4A):321-323.

56. Alegente G, Marchi B, Mugnaini F, et al: Treatment of *Gardnerella vaginalis* syndrome with new quinolones: preliminary results. Rev Infect Dis 1989;11(suppl 5):1308.

# FLUOROQUINOLONES IN THE TREATMENT OF INFECTIOUS DIARRHEA  8

*Larry J. Goodman*
*John Segreti*
*Gordon M. Trenholme*

## INTRODUCTION

Acute diarrheal illnesses are among the most common infectious syndromes worldwide. Nevertheless, some basic questions concerning infectious diarrhea remain unanswered. Although a number of organisms have been associated with diarrheal illness, the majority of patients with acute diarrhea have no pathogen identified. The challenge of identifying an organism from among the myriad of non-pathogens in the most heavily contaminated specimen (stool) sent to the microbiology laboratory remains a formidable one. Even when a pathogen is identified, the benefit of specific antimicrobial therapy is uncertain in most situations. Furthermore, whether the therapeutic outcome depends on levels of antimicrobial agent in the serum, stool, gut wall, or some combination of these, is unknown.

The new fluoroquinolones have excellent in vitro activity against most enteric bacterial pathogens. Stool concentrations of these agents are high, and serum concentrations are many times greater than the minimum inhibitory concentrations (MICs) for susceptible organisms. Plasmid-mediated resistance to the fluoroquinolones has yet to be reported, a factor of particular significance for enteric infections, which occur in the ultimate in vivo mixing house — the colon. Finally, early human studies have demonstrated that the fluoroquinolones effectively eradicate many enteric bacterial pathogens from the stool, and in several studies, shorten the duration of clinical illness.

# IN VITRO ACTIVITY OF NEW FLUOROQUINOLONES AGAINST ENTERIC BACTERIAL PATHOGENS

The in vitro activity of ciprofloxacin, norfloxacin, temafloxacin, difloxacin, and nalidixic acid has been compared with agents commonly used to treat bacterial enteritis, including erythromycin, trimethoprim-sulfamethoxazole (TMP-SMX), chloramphenicol, ampicillin, and doxycycline, against isolates of *Campylobacter jejuni, Campylobacter coli, Salmonella* spp., *Shigella* spp., *Yersinia enterocolitica*, and *Vibrio* spp.[1-3] These results are shown in Table 1. The fluoroquinolones were more active than any of the other agents tested. *Aeromonas hydrophila* and *Plesiomonas shigelloides* are also usually susceptible ($MIC_{90}$ <0.25 µg/mL). Other investigators have also found that the fluoroquinolones, including norfloxacin, ciprofloxacin, enoxacin, pefloxacin, ofloxacin, and fleroxacin, have significant activity against common enteric pathogens.[4-7]

Most of the currently available fluoroquinolones have relatively little activity against anaerobes. It is therefore not surprising that these agents have little in vitro activity against *Clostridium difficile*. Against 15 *C. difficile* isolates, the $MIC_{90}$ for ciprofloxacin was 16 µg/mL (range=8-32 µg/mL).[1] Possibly because the fluoroquinolones cause minimal disruption of the anaerobic flora in the gut, or due to the high concentration of fluoroquinolones excreted in the stool, the development of *C. difficile* colitis as a complication of fluoroquinolone therapy is rare.[8]

# ANIMAL STUDIES

The excellent in vitro activity of the fluoroquinolones against enteric bacterial pathogens led to the evaluation of these agents in vivo. Several animal studies preceded human clinical trials, and despite the limitations of animal studies, provided some insights into the potential uses of the fluoroquinolones.

In the only primate study, 23 marmosets were treated.[9] All animals were chronically excreting *Campylobacter jejuni* or *Campylobacter coli*. Eleven animals received ciprofloxacin and 12 animals received erythromycin. Antimicrobial agents were administered by gastric tube in a 5 mg dose twice a day for 5 days, a dosage chosen to approximate the dosages used in humans.

Within 48 hours of initiating treatment, stool cultures from all animals in both groups became negative for *Campylobacter* species. However, six animals in the erythromycin group relapsed shortly after therapy was completed. During the eight-week follow-up period, *Campylobacter* was not isolated from any animal that received ciprofloxacin. This difference was statistically significant (p<0.01, Fisher's exact test). The mean ciprofloxacin stool level in these animals was 49.2 µg/g, while the mean erythromycin stool level was 14.4 µg/g.

**Table 1.** Comparative activity of four fluoroquinolones and five other antimicrobial agents against enteric bacterial pathogens

| Antimicrobial Agent | MIC$_{90}$ ($\mu$g/mL) | | | | | |
|---|---|---|---|---|---|---|
| | Campylobacter jejuni (n=46) | Campylobacter coli (n=26) | Salmonella spp. (n=28) | Shigella spp. (n=20) | Yersinia enterocolitica (n=17) | Vibrio spp. (n=10)* |
| Ciprofloxacin | 0.25 | 0.25 | 0.03 | 0.015 | 0.015 | <0.008 |
| Norfloxacin | 1.0 | 1.0 | 0.06 | 0.03 | 0.125 | 0.03 |
| Temafloxacin | 0.125 | 0.125 | 0.125 | 0.03 | 0.06 | 0.25 |
| Difloxacin | 0.25 | 0.25 | 0.25 | 0.125 | 0.125 | 0.125 |
| Nalidixic Acid | 8.0 | 4.0 | 4.0 | 4.0 | 2.0 | 0.25 |
| TMP/SMX[†] | 2.0 | >8.0 | 0.5 | 0.5 | 0.25 | 0.03 |
| Ampicillin | 8.0 | 8.0 | 2.0 | 128.0 | 128.0 | 8.0 |
| Doxycycline | 8.0 | 16.0 | 16.0 | 16.0 | 2.0 | 0.25 |
| Erythromycin | 1.0 | >32.0 | >32.0 | 64.0 | >32.0 | 4.0 |

* Because only 10 organisms were tested, the MIC$_{50}$ for each agent is given.
† Trimethoprim-sulfamethoxazole. Only the trimethoprim concentration was recorded. The ratio of trimethoprim to sulfamethoxazole was 1:19.
Adapted from Goodman et al,[1] Fliegelman et al,[2] and Segreti et al.[3]

*Salmonella,* an intracellular pathogen, presents a difficult treatment problem, particularly in immunocompromised patients. Antibiotic therapy aimed at eradicating *Salmonella* species from the stool of humans has had limited success, both for patients with acute diarrhea and for asymptomatic chronic *Salmonella* carriers. The previously demonstrated in vitro activity of the fluoroquinolones against *Salmonella* species[1-3] and the ability of the fluoroquinolones to penetrate phagocytic cells suggested that these agents might be effective.[10]

CBA and A/J mice are relatively resistant to subcutaneous challenge with *Salmonella typhimurium* ($LD_{50}$ >$10^6$ cfu). Ciprofloxacin (10 mg/kg) for 5 days beginning the sixth day after infection dramatically reduced mortality compared to placebo for mice challenged with 5 x $10^6$ and $10^7$ cfu.[11] In this same study, ciprofloxacin was also more effective than chloramphenicol in reducing mortality and the percentage of large bowel carriage in these animals. These investigators also studied infection in Balb/C mice, which, unlike the above strains, have no natural resistance to *Salmonella*. Balb/C mice were challenged with $10^3$ cfu of *Salmonella typhimurium* administered subcutaneously. Ciprofloxacin therapy significantly reduced liver and spleen counts of *Salmonella* in these mice compared to placebo; however, mortality figures for treated and untreated mice were similar.

In normal and immunocompromised mice, oral ciprofloxacin was compared to ampicillin or chloramphenicol in the treatment of murine typhoid caused by *Salmonella typhimurium*.[12] High-dose oral ciprofloxacin (100 mg/kg bid) administered from days 3-28 after a lethal dose of *Salmonella* cured 80% of immunocompromised mice. Similar dosage regimens of ampicillin and chloramphenicol were significantly less effective (p<0.001), as was a lower dose (20 mg/kg bid) and a shorter course (12 days) of ciprofloxacin.

These animal data suggest that the fluoroquinolones might be more effective in eradicating *Campylobacter* and *Salmonella* from the stool than agents currently used for these infections. Also, prolonged quinolone therapy (3-4 weeks) for the most compromised host with salmonellosis might be more effective than a similar course of ampicillin or chloramphenicol. However, since animal studies are limited in their ability to predict the response seen in human infections, clinical studies were conducted to define the role of the fluoroquinolones in human enteric disease.

## CLINICAL STUDIES

### *Prophylaxis of Travelers' Diarrhea*

Three studies evaluating the efficacy of fluoroquinolones for prevention of diarrhea in travelers have been published. Norfloxacin 200 mg bid was compared to placebo for the prevention of diarrhea in travelers to Western Europe, Asia, Africa, or Latin America.[13] Fifty-six patients received norfloxacin, and 59 received placebo. Six patients in the norfloxacin group developed diarrhea compared to 20 in the placebo group (p<0.01). When travelers to Western Europe were excluded (leaving those who traveled to Asia, Africa, or Latin America) the difference was even more striking (4/32 versus 16/30). The mean duration of symptoms in the placebo group was 3.6 days, while all patients in the norfloxacin group who developed symptoms had them for one day or less. Adverse effects were mild and rare.

Norfloxacin 400 mg once daily for 14 days was compared to placebo for the prevention of travelers' diarrhea in adults traveling to Guadalajara, Mexico.[14] Four of the 56 patients (7%) in the norfloxacin group developed diarrhea compared with 36 of 59 (61%) in the placebo group (p<0.01). In this study the fecal flora was also monitored weekly for the development of norfloxacin resistance. None was seen.

In a study of travelers visiting Tunisia, ciprofloxacin 500 mg once daily was compared to placebo for the prophylaxis of travelers' diarrhea.[15] One of 25 subjects (4%) who received ciprofloxacin developed diarrhea compared to 18 of 28 patients (64%) in the placebo group. No difference in photosensitivity (sunburn/rash) was noted between the two groups.

For comparison purposes, Dupont et al[16] have previously reported that 1 of 57 travelers (2%) who received TMP/SMX 160/800 mg daily for prophylaxis of travelers' diarrhea in Mexico developed diarrhea, compared to 8 of 58 patients (14%) who received TMP/SMX 200 mg daily and 10 of 30 (33%) who received placebo.

These data demonstrate that both ciprofloxacin and norfloxacin are effective agents for the prophylaxis of travelers' diarrhea in adults. The routine use of antibiotics for the prophylaxis of travelers' diarrhea for all travelers to high-risk areas remains controversial. Concerns include the development of antimicrobial resistance, drug side effects, and cost. These, coupled with the relatively benign course of travelers' diarrhea for most healthy persons, and the availability of alternative prophylactic measures (diet restrictions, bismuth subsalicylate) have led many experts to conclude that antibiotic prophylaxis should be restricted to special circumstances only.[17] Studies evaluating the cost-effectiveness of antibiotic prophylaxis utilizing decision analysis, as outlined by Reeves et al,[18] are needed to further resolve this question.

## Treatment of Travelers' Diarrhea

In a study of the treatment of acute diarrhea acquired by travelers to Mexico, ciprofloxacin 500 mg bid was compared with TMP/SMX 160/800 mg bid and with placebo.[19] Both ciprofloxacin and TMP-SMX were significantly more effective than placebo (p<0.0001) for the treatment of diarrhea in this group. *Shigella* and enterotoxigenic *Escherichia coli* were the most common pathogens identified. A favorable clinical response was seen in patients with enterotoxigenic *Escherichia coli,* invasive pathogens, or unknown pathogens (patients with negative cultures), regardless of which antimicrobial agent they received. In this study, early antimicrobial therapy shortened the duration of diarrhea from an average of 81 hours (placebo) to 29 hours (ciprofloxacin) and 20 hours (TMP/SMX) measured from the time therapy was initiated.

In a double-blind, placebo-controlled study of acute diarrhea in travelers to West Africa, patients were randomized to receive oral fleroxacin 400 mg daily for 2 days, a single dose of fleroxacin 400 mg, or placebo.[20] Of 195 tourists enrolled, 156 were evaluable. The main reason for patient withdrawal from the study was concomitant medication use. Fleroxacin in either dosage regimen was more effective than placebo in resolving diarrhea and associated symptoms (p<0.01).

## Treatment of Acute Diarrheal Disease in Non-Travelers

A number of studies have evaluated fluoroquinolone therapy in patients with acute diarrhea. Specifically, does therapy shorten the duration of diarrhea, decrease associated symptoms, and/or hasten the eradication of the pathogen from the stool in such patients? In most of the studies reported below, treatment was initiated at the time of presentation, prior to the availability of culture results.

In a double-blind study of 85 patients hospitalized with acute enterocolitis, ciprofloxacin 500 mg bid for 5 days was compared to placebo.[21] Of 38 patients in the ciprofloxacin group, 16 had *Salmonella,* 19 had *Campylobacter,* and 3 had *Shigella.* In the placebo group, 21 patients had *Salmonella,* 11 had *Campylobacter,* and 6 had *Shigella.* Overall, patients in the ciprofloxacin group had a significantly shorter duration of fever (1.3 vs. 3.1 days, p<0.05) and a significantly shorter duration of diarrhea (1.5 vs. 2.9 days, p<0.001). Patients with *Salmonella* and *Campylobacter* who received ciprofloxacin also had a shorter duration of diarrhea than those who received placebo (1.9 vs. 3.4 days, and 1.1 vs. 2.2 days, respectively; p<0.01). Ciprofloxacin was also more effective than placebo in eradicating pathogens from the stool. All pathogens in the ciprofloxacin group were eradicated within 48 hours, whereas only four pathogens in the placebo group were eradicated at the end of the five-day treatment period. There were four relapses (all *Salmonella)* in the ciprofloxacin group. Pre- and post-treatment MICs for these isolates were identical.

In a randomized, double-blind study of adults with acute diarrhea, Goodman et al[22] compared a five-day course of ciprofloxacin 500 mg bid with TMP/SMX 160/180 mg bid or placebo. Patients were for the most part previously healthy outpatients. Patients were started on therapy the day of presentation. Fifty-six of 59 patients (95%) in the ciprofloxacin group and 49 of 56 patients (87%) in the TMP/SMX group were cured or improved during the five-day treatment period, compared with 45 of 58 patients (77%) in the placebo group. The difference in clinical response for ciprofloxacin compared with placebo was significant (p<0.05). Ciprofloxacin was also more effective than TMP/SMX and placebo in eradicating bacterial enteric pathogens from the stool (p<0.001) and shortening the duration of diarrhea. Two patients with *Campylobacter* infections developed resistance to ciprofloxacin while on therapy.

Dupont et al[23] reported the results of studies conducted in seven countries by Merck Sharp and Dohme in 392 persons with acute diarrhea who were treated with either norfloxacin 400 mg twice daily, norfloxacin 400 mg three times daily, or TMP/SMX 160 mg/800 mg twice daily. Clinical cure rates were similar in both norfloxacin groups (89% vs. 91%), compared with a 78% cure rate in patients who received TMP/SMX. In nearly all patients the bacterial pathogen isolated from pre-treatment stool specimens was eradicated (105 of 106 with either dose of norfloxacin and 49 of 52 with TMP/SMX).

Two studies have evaluated single-dose fluoroquinolone therapy for shigellosis. In the first of these, norfloxacin 800 mg was compared to 5 days of TMP/SMX in patients presenting with dysentery.[24] Of 55 patients with shigellosis, 29 received norfloxacin and 26 received TMP/SMX. No significant differences between groups were seen with respect to mean duration of illness (2.5 days with norfloxacin vs. 2.0 days with TMP/SMX) or the number of unformed stools passed after beginning therapy (9.7 with norfloxacin vs. 7.6 with TMP/SMX).

In a second study, ofloxacin was used to treat patients with shigellosis.[25] The first seven patients received ofloxacin 200 mg every 8 hours for 1 day. All had negative stool cultures by the second post-treatment day. The next 14 patients received ofloxacin 400 mg as a single dose. In the patients who received single-dose therapy, 13/14 had negative stool cultures by treatment day 2.

The results of two non-comparative open studies also suggest that fluoroquinolone therapy may play a role in the treatment of diarrheal disease. In one of these studies, 57 patients with acute diarrhea were treated with norfloxacin 400 mg bid for 3 days.[26] All patients had more than four stools in the previous 24 hours and required hospitalization. Pathogens most frequently isolated included *Plesiomonas shigelloides* (n=13 isolates), *Shigella* species (n=13), *Vibrio parahaemolyticus* (n=9), *Vibrio cholera* (n=7), and *Salmonella* species (n=5). Twenty-eight patients had negative stool cultures after one day of therapy; all patients had negative stool cultures after two days of treatment. One patient with *Salmonella* had a subsequent positive stool culture after therapy was completed.

In a second non-comparative study, 11 patients with acute enterocolitis without bacteremia (6 patients with *Shigella* species, 5 with *Salmonella* species) and 10 patients with *Salmonella* bacteremia were treated with ofloxacin 200 mg bid.[27] The duration of therapy ranged between 6 and 30 days. All bacterial strains were susceptible to ofloxacin. All patients were cured without sequelae. The pathogen was eradicated in each case by the third day.

These studies demonstrate that fluoroquinolones are effective in eradicating susceptible pathogens from the stool and may shorten the clinical illness in adults with acute diarrhea by about one day if treatment is initiated on presentation. For the controlled studies outlined above, enrollment criteria selected for a moderately-to-se-verely ill patient population. There is little information on the clinical effect of treating patients with mild-to-moderate diarrheal illness with fluoroquinolones. Additionally, concerns about cost, the effect of antibiotic treatment on community microbial resis-tance patterns, drug side effects, as well as the relatively limited clinical benefits of therapy, underscore the need for further studies to establish the role of therapy in this setting. Further evaluation of shorter courses of treatment is also needed.

## Treatment of Typhoid Fever

In an open study, oral ciprofloxacin 500 mg bid was administered to 38 patients with bacteremia (positive blood or bone marrow culture) caused by *Salmonella typhi*.[28] The mean duration of therapy was 13.7 days. Favorable clinical and bacterio-logical responses were seen in 37 of 38 patients. In a prospective, randomized trial, pefloxacin 400 mg was compared with co-trimoxazole 160 mg/800 mg for the treat-ment of typhoid fever.[29] The antibiotics were administered orally twice daily for 14 days. All 42 patients studied were cured. No relapses or persistent excretion of *Salmo-nella* occurred. Patients in the pefloxacin group had fewer febrile days and a more rapid resolution of symptoms.

## Chronic Salmonella Carriers and Recurrent Salmonella Infections in Human Immunodeficiency Virus (HIV)-Positive Patients

The chronic *Salmonella* carrier (>1 year) and the HIV-positive patient with recur-rent *Salmonella* infections (usually bacteremic) represent particularly difficult treat-ment problems. A small number of patients with chronic *Salmonella* infections have been treated with fluoroquinolones. In one study,[30] 5 of 6 patients who were chroni-cally excreting a nontyphoidal *Salmonella* were cured after receiving 500 mg of oral ciprofloxacin bid for 4 weeks. Gotuzzo et al[31] carried out a study with 24 chronic typhoid carriers who were randomized to receive either norfloxacin 400 mg bid for 28 days (n=12) or placebo (n=12). Eleven of the norfloxacin-treated patients had nega-tive stool and bile cultures after therapy. All 12 placebo-treated patients remained culture positive. Eleven of these patients were then treated with norfloxacin; seven of these became culture negative. After one year, 18 of the 23 (78%) treated patients remained culture-negative. In an open study, 12 chronic *Salmonella* carriers were treated with ciprofloxacin 750 mg bid for 28 days.[32] At one year, 10 of these patients remained culture negative.

Although the number of patients in these studies is too small to permit definitive conclusions, ciprofloxacin and norfloxacin appear to be promising agents for the eradication of *Salmonella* from the chronic carrier. Further studies with particular attention to the presence of obstruction or stones in the biliary tract, as well as a follow-up period of up to two years, are needed.

Jacobson et al[33] treated four patients with acquired immunodeficiency syndrome (AIDS) and recurrent *Salmonella* bacteremia with ciprofloxacin 750 mg bid for 1-8 months. None of these patients was bacteremic while receiving ciprofloxacin. However, bacteremia did recur in one patient after therapy was stopped.

## OTHER POTENTIAL USES OF FLUOROQUINOLONES IN GASTROINTESTINAL TRACT INFECTIONS

The fluoroquinolones may also play a role in the treatment of other infectious processes that can involve the gastrointestinal tract, although clinical data are currently not available. The first of these, *Clostridium difficile* associated diarrhea, is among the most common nosocomial infections. Although the in vitro activity of the fluoroquinolones against *C. difficile* is not impressive, the development of *C. difficile* disease during fluoroquinolone therapy is rare, possibly due to the high concentrations of drug excreted in the stool (exceeding the MIC for *C. difficile*). Based on this and minimal anecdotal experience, some have suggested that fluoroquinolones might be effective therapy for *C. difficile* diarrhea.[34-36] Clinical studies are necessary to answer this question.

*Mycobacterium avium* complex is a relatively common infectious complication of AIDS. When the gastrointestinal tract is involved, patients usually have fever, weight loss, and diarrhea. Antimicrobial therapy of this infection has produced disappointing results. Recently, a multiple drug regimen including ciprofloxacin has shown some promise in clinical studies with small numbers of patients.[37]

The third organism for which the fluoroquinolones may have a therapeutic role is *Helicobacter pylori* (previously *Campylobacter pylori*). This organism has been associated with type B gastritis and peptic ulcer disease.[38,39] *H. pylori* is susceptible to a number of antimicrobial agents including ampicillin, metronidazole, and bismuth salts. Treatment with these agents hastens histologic healing and clearing of the organism. Although relapse is common, it is less common if *H. pylori* is eradicated.[40] The in vitro activity of the fluoroquinolones against *H. pylori*, and the ability of the quinolones to penetrate intracellularly, suggest that these agents may be useful in the treatment of this organism.[41]

## CONCLUSION

The fluoroquinolones are a promising group of agents for the treatment of bacterial enteric infections. In addition to excellent in vitro activity against most bacterial enteric pathogens, they are effective in eradicating susceptible pathogens from the stool and for the prophylaxis of travelers' diarrhea. These agents also appear useful in eradicating *Salmonella* from the stool, even in chronic carriers. This may significantly change the current approach to this difficult treatment problem. Equally exciting are the reports that fluoroquinolones shorten the clinical illness in adult non-travelers with acute diarrhea and suppress *Salmonella* bacteremia in HIV-positive patients with previously recurrent disease. The high levels achieved in stool, excellent in vitro activity, and relative safety make the fluoroquinolones ideal agents for further evaluation in the treatment of infectious diarrhea and other gastrointestinal infections.

# REFERENCES

1. Goodman LJ, Fliegelman RM, Trenholme GT, et al: Comparative in vitro activity of ciprofloxacin against Campylobacter spp. and other bacterial enteric pathogens. Antimicrob Agents Chemother 1984;25:504-506.

2. Fliegelman RM, Petrak RM, Goodman LJ, et al: Comparative in vitro activities of twelve antimicrobial agents Campylobacter species. Antimicrob Agents Chemother 1985;27: 429-430.

3. Segreti J, Nelson JA, Goodman LJ, et al: In vitro activities of lomefloxacin and temafloxacin against pathogens causing diarrhea. Antimicrob Agents Chemother 1989; 33:1385-1387.

4. Verbist L: Comparative in vitro activity of RO 23-6240, a new trifluorinated quinolone. J Antimicrob Chemother 1987;20:363-372.

5. Goldstein E: Norfloxacin, a fluoroquinolone antibacterial agent. classification, mechanism of action, and in vitro activity. Am J Med 1987;82(suppl 6B):3-17.

6. Neu HC, Chin N-X: In vitro activity of two new quinolone antimicrobial agents, S-25903 and S-25932 compared with that of other agents. J Antimicrob Chemother 1987;19:175-185.

7. Ling J, Kam KM, Lam AW, et al: Susceptibilities of Hong Kong isolates of multiply resistant Shigella spp. to 25 antimicrobial agents, including ampicillin plus sulbactam and new 4-quinolones. Antimicrob Agents Chemother 1988;32:20-23.

8. Arcieri G, Griffith E, Gruenwaldt G, et al: Ciprofloxacin: An update on clinical experience. Am J Med 1987;82(suppl 4A):381-386.

9. Goodman LJ, Kaplan RL, Petrak RM, et al: Effects of erythromycin and ciprofloxacin on chronic fecal excretion of Campylobacter species in marmosets. Antimicrob Agents Chemother 1986;29:185-187.

10. Easmon CSF, Crane JP: Uptake of ciprofloxacin by macrophages. J Clin Pathol 1985; 38:442-444.

11. Easmon CS, Blowers A: Ciprofloxacin treatment of systemic salmonella infection in sensitive and resistant mice. J Antimicrob Chemother 1985;16:615-619.

12. Brunner H, Zeiler H-J: Oral ciprofloxacin treatment for Salmonella typhimurium infection of normal and immunocompromised mice. Antimicrob Agents Chemother 1988;32:57-62.

13. Wistrom J, Norrby SR, Burman LG, et al: Norfloxacin versus placebo for prophylaxis against travelers' diarrhea. J Antimicrob Chemother 1987;20:563-574.

14. Johnson PC, Ericsson CD, Morgan DR, et al: Lack of emergence of resistant fecal flora during successful prophylaxis of travelers' diarrhea with norfloxacin. Antimicrob Agents Chemother 1986;30:671-674.

15. Rademaker CMA, Hoepelman IM, Wolfhagen MJHM, et al: Results of a double-blind placebo-controlled study using ciprofloxacin for prevention of travelers' diarrhea. Eur J Clin Microbiol Infect Dis 1989;8:690-694.

16. Dupont HL, Ericsson CD, Johnson PC, et al: Antimicrobial agents in the prevention of travelers' diarrhea. Rev Infect Dis 1986;8(suppl 2):S167-S171.

17. NIH Consensus Development Conference on Travelers' Diarrhea. JAMA 1985;253: 2700-2704.

18. Reeves RR, Johnson PC, Ericsson CD, et al: A cost-effectiveness comparison of the use of antimicrobial agents for the treatment or prophylaxis of travelers' diarrhea. Arch Intern Med 1988;148:2421-2427.

19. Ericsson CD, Johnson PC, Dupont HL, et al: Ciprofloxacin or trimethoprim-sulfamethoxazole as initial therapy for travelers' diarrhea. Ann Intern Med 1987;106:216-220.

20. Steffen R, Jori R, DuPont HL, et al: Fleroxacin, a long-acting fluoroquinolone as effective therapy for travelers' diarrhea. Ann Intern Med 1987;106:216-220.

21. Pichler HET, Diridl G, Stickler K, et al: Clinical efficacy of ciprofloxacin compared with placebo in bacterial diarrhea. Am J Med 1987;82(suppl 4A):329-332.

22. Goodman LJ, Trenholme GM, Segreti J, et al: Empiric antimicrobial therapy of domestically acquired acute diarrhea in urban adults. Arch Intern Med 1990:150:541-546.

23. Dupont HL, Corrado ML, Sabbaj J: Use of norfloxacin in the treatment of acute diarrheal disease. Am J Med 1987;82(suppl 6B):79-83.

24. Gotuzzo E, Oberhelman RA, Maguina C, et al: Comparison of a single dose treatment with norfloxacin and standard five day treatment with trimethoprim-sulfamethoxazole for acute shigellosis in adults. Antimicrob Agents Chemother 1989;33:1101-1104.

25. Akalur HE, Firat M, Unol S, et al: Clinical efficacy of single dose or one day treatment with ofloxacin in shigellosis. Rev Infect Dis 1989;(suppl 5):S1152-S1153.

26. Lolekha S, Patanacharoen S: Clinical and microbiologic efficacy of norfloxacin for the treatment of acute diarrhea. Rev Infect Dis 1988;10:S210-S211.

27. Tigoud S, Lucht F, Peyramond D, et al: Use of ofloxacin for the treatment of enteric infections. Rev Infect Dis 1988;10:S207.

28. Ramirez CA, Bran JL, Mejia CR, et al: Open, prospective study of the clinical efficacy of ciprofloxacin. Antimicrob Agents Chemother 1985;28:128-132.

29. Hajji M, el-Mdaghri N, Benbachir M, et al: Prospective randomized comparative trial of pefloxacin versus cotrimoxazole in the treatment of typhoid fever in adults. Eur J Clin Microbiol Infect Dis 1988;7:361-363.

30. Diridl G, Pichler H, Wolf D: Treatment of chronic salmonella carriers with ciprofloxacin. Eur J Clin Microbiol 1986;5:260-261.

31. Gotuzzo E, Guerra JG, Benavente L, et al: Use of norfloxacin to treat chronic typhoid carriers. J Infect Dis 1988;157:1221-1225.

32. Ferreccio C, Morris JG, Jr., Valdivicso C, et al: Efficacy of ciprofloxacin in the treatment of chronic typhoid carriers. J Infect Dis 1988;157:1235-1239.

33. Jacobson MA, Hahn SM, Gergerding JL, et al: Ciprofloxacin for *Salmonella* bacteremia in the acquired immunodeficiency syndrome (AIDS). Ann Intern Med 1989;110:1027-1029.

34. Loge RV: Oral fluoroquinolone therapy for *Clostridium difficile* enterocolitis. JAMA 1989;261:2063-2064.

35. Maggiolo F, Bianchi W, Ohnmeiss H: A new approach to the treatment of pseudomembranous colitis? J Infect Dis 1989;160:170-171.

36. Lettau LA: Oral fluoroquinolones therapy in *Clostridium difficile* enterocolitis (letter). JAMA 1988;260:2216-2217.

37. Young LS: *Mycobacterium avium* complex infection. J Infect Dis 1988;157:863-867.

38. Anderson LP, Holk S, Povlsen CD, et al: *Campylobacter pyloridis* in peptic ulcer disease. I. Gastric and duodenal infection caused by *C. pyloridis*: histological and microbiological findings. Scand J Gastroenterol 1987;22:219-224.

39. Goodwin CS, Marshall PJ, Blinlow ED, et al: Prevention of nitroimidazole resistance in *Campylobacter pylori* by co-administration of colloided bismuth subcitrate: clinical and *in vitro* studies. J Clin Pathol 1988;41:207-210.

40. Marshall BJ, Goodwin CS, Warren JR, et al: Prospective double-blind trial of duodenal ulcer relapse after eradication of *C. pylori*. Lancet 1988;2:1439-1442.

41. McNulty CA, Dent JC: Susceptibility of clinical isolates of *Campylobacter pylori* to twenty-one antimicrobial agents. Eur J Clin Microbiol Infect Dis 1988;7:566-569.

# THE USE OF FLUOROQUINOLONES IN NEUTROPENIC PATIENTS $\quad$ 9

*Donna Przepiorka*

## INTRODUCTION

Infection is a major cause of mortality in patients with neutropenia. A review of the literature of the 1970s revealed that infection was the cause of death in nearly 75% of patients with acute leukemia.[1] Predisposing factors that occurred as a result of intensive chemotherapy included profound and prolonged neutropenia as well as injury to the mucosal barriers in the pharynx and gastrointestinal tract. Careful comparison of organisms causing infection with those isolated from surveillance cultures in the same patient demonstrated that the majority of infections in neutropenic patients were caused by endogenous flora.[2] The organisms isolated most commonly were aerobic gram-negatives, and mortality was highest (70%) in patients infected with *Pseudomonas* spp.[1]

With the initiation of empiric broad spectrum antibiotic coverage as standard care in febrile neutropenic patients, early mortality from infection has decreased substantially in the 1980s. Aerobic gram-positive organisms, while not a major cause of mortality, now comprise the most common isolates.[3,4] Polymicrobic infections and infections due to multiply-resistant gram-negative bacteria remain an all too common cause of death. The challenge for the 1990s is to identify antibiotics with little toxicity that have a broad spectrum of activity, are effective against multiply-resistant organisms, can be used to prevent as well as treat infections without selecting for resistant organisms, and can be administered without great expense.

## RATIONALE FOR THE USE OF FLUOROQUINOLONES IN NEUTROPENIC PATIENTS

Since endogenous flora appear to account for the majority of infections in neutropenic patients, one might expect that infections would be prevented if one could eliminate all flora and prevent recolonization from exogenous sources. Such total

131

decontamination has been accomplished using oral nonabsorbable antibiotics and mouthwash, bactericidal skin cleansers and creams, germ-free food, and strict isolation in laminar air-flow rooms. However, the cost and labor involved preclude application of this approach to all patients. Using an animal model, Van der Waaij et al[5] have demonstrated the importance of anaerobic flora of the gut in prevention of colonization with new aerobic gram-negative bacteria. Thus, antibiotics that eliminate aerobic flora without affecting anaerobic flora should decrease the risk of infection from endogenous flora without allowing acquisition of new aerobic organisms. In theory, such selective decontamination could provide a more practical means of infection prevention in neutropenic patients.

The initial studies of infection prevention utilizing nalidixic acid, the first quinolone, showed that it was effective in the elimination of aerobic gut flora and reduction of infections.[6-8] Furthermore, the duration of neutropenia for patients receiving nalidixic acid was shorter than for those receiving trimethoprim/sulfamethoxazole (TMP/SMX).[7] Unfortunately, nalidixic acid lacked activity against *Pseudomonas* and was associated with greater acquisition of resistant organisms.[7,8]

The fluoroquinolones are much improved analogues of nalidixic acid. The addition of a fluorine atom at position 6 and a piperazine group at position 7 of the quinolone ring has broadened the spectrum of activity of these agents and increased their efficacy against *Pseudomonas*. The fluoroquinolones have clinically useful activity against nearly all aerobic gram-positive and gram-negative bacteria, but most anaerobes are not susceptible.[9] The mutation rate in vitro for resistance to fluoroquinolones is much less than for nalidixic acid,[10] so development of fluoroquinolone-resistant organisms is less likely to be a problem than with nalidixic acid. In addition, the fluoroquinolones do not possess activity against fungi per se, but enhancement of the antifungal activity of other drugs by a fluoroquinolone has been reported.[11] Thus, the fluoroquinolones provide the appropriate spectrum of activity for selective decontamination of neutropenic patients.

The mechanism of action of the fluoroquinolones is inhibition of the bacterial enzyme DNA gyrase (topoisomerase II).[10] This mechanism is not shared by any other class of antibiotics used frequently in a clinical setting. Thus, cross-resistance between a fluoroquinolone and other antibiotics due to a mutation in the target site is unlikely. The mechanism of resistance to fluoroquinolones is chromosomally-mediated, which limits the spread of resistance. Resistance to most other antibiotics is plasmid-mediated, and frequently one plasmid contains the genes for resistance to several different antibiotic classes. Plasmid-mediated antibiotic resistance leads to rapid spread of the multiply-resistant phenotype. Because of differences in the nature of resistance to fluoroquinolones in comparison to other antibiotics, many multiply-resistant organisms are still susceptible to the fluoroquinolones. This confers a special advantage on the fluoroquinolones for neutropenic patients.

Serious adverse effects due to fluoroquinolone therapy are rare.[12-14] Specifically, renal failure, inhibition of platelet function, inhibition of clotting factor synthesis, hepatic dysfunction, and *C. difficile* diarrhea occur less frequently than reported for most aminoglycosides and β-lactams. Overall, the spectrum of activity and patient tolerability of the fluoroquinolones suggest that these drugs could have wide application in the neutropenic population.

## EFFECT OF ORAL FLUOROQUINOLONES ON ENDOGENOUS FLORA

The effect of oral ciprofloxacin on endogenous gut flora has been studied extensively (Table 1).[15-19] Changes in gut flora in volunteers receiving oral ciprofloxacin reflect to a large extent the in vitro sensitivity data. Gram-negative bacilli are most sensitive. Colony counts decreased 4-7 logs/gram feces within 3-5 days of starting therapy and returned to baseline within 7-14 days after therapy was discontinued. Ciprofloxacin-resistant gram-negatives were not noted in normal volunteers given short courses of ciprofloxacin, but Rozenberg-Arska et al[16] found resistant organisms in leukemia patients receiving a prolonged course of therapy for infection prophylaxis.

The effect of oral ciprofloxacin on aerobic gram-positive bacteria was variable. Colony counts of enterococci decreased moderately in 2 of 4 studies, and staphylococci decreased moderately in 2 of 3 studies. Diphtheroids were followed in only one study, and these were essentially unaffected. Ciprofloxacin did not have much effect on gut anaerobes. In fact, Brumfitt et al[15] reported an increase in the incidence of ciprofloxacin-resistant anaerobes in volunteers after 7 days of treatment. However, there was no outgrowth of *C. difficile,* and no reports of diarrhea or enterocolitis.

The effects of oral ofloxacin and norfloxacin on gut flora are similar to those of ciprofloxacin.[18,20,21] Gram-negative bacilli decrease rapidly and return quickly after cessation of therapy, while anaerobes remain stable. In one comparative study of ciprofloxacin and ofloxacin, van Saene et al[20] reported that anaerobes and enterococci were reduced to a greater extent and yeast outgrowth was significantly higher in those receiving ciprofloxacin. However, Shah et al[18] found no differences in the effects of ofloxacin and ciprofloxacin on gut flora.

Few studies of the effects of oral fluoroquinolones on pharyngeal flora have been reported, and the results are contradictory. Lipsky et al[22] compared ofloxacin, cephalexin, clindamycin, and erythromycin in the eradication of *S. aureus* nasal colonization. Ofloxacin was effective in 93% of the patients, and 6/6 patients were still free of *S. aureus* when tested 3 weeks after completing therapy. Only clindamycin showed similar efficacy. Bergan et al[17] found little change in the salivary flora in

Table 1. Effect of oral ciprofloxacin on gut flora

| Organism | Decrease in Organisms (log/gram feces) | | | | |
| --- | --- | --- | --- | --- | --- |
| | 15* | 16 | 17 | 18 | 19 |
| Corynebacteria | — | — | I | — | — |
| Staphylococci | >2 | — | I | >3 | — |
| Enterococci | >2 | I | >2 | — | I |
| Enterobacteria | >5 | >4 | >5 | >7 | >4 |
| Total anaerobes | I | — | — | I | — |
| Bacteroides | — | I | >3 | — | — |
| Clostridia | I | I | I | — | — |
| Anaerobic cocci | — | I | I | — | — |
| Anaerobic bacilli† | — | I | I | — | — |
| Yeast | I | I | — | I | I |
| Dose (mg) bid | 500 | 500 | 500 | 200-500 | 100 |
| Duration (days) | 7 | 42 | 5 | 7-10 | 6 |

* Reference
† Gram-positive bacilli
I = Insignificant change

volunteers treated with oral ciprofloxacin for 5 days. Only *Neisseria* spp. were decreased significantly. In contrast, Appelbaum et al[23] reported a dramatic reduction in both aerobic and anaerobic flora after just two doses of ciprofloxacin 750 mg. Colony counts of *Neisseria, Hemophilus,* enterobacteria, and anaerobic cocci were reduced 8-10 logs. Staphylococci, streptococci, and *Bacteroides* were least sensitive. This profile is similar to the reductions in gut flora after oral ciprofloxacin discussed above.

The relative resistance of anaerobes as defined by in vitro sensitivity testing is based on the fact that the $MIC_{90}$ of anaerobes (4-16 µg/mL) frequently exceeds the serum levels that can be maintained in vivo. Fluoroquinolone fecal levels of 200-2000 µg/g can be achieved with oral dosing,[15] so anaerobes should be inhibited. While the clinical studies demonstrate that oral fluoroquinolones can be used effectively for selective decontamination of the gastrointestinal tract, the basis for maintenance of the anaerobic flora in the presence of high fecal levels of drug is unclear. In vitro studies carried out by Goldstein et al[24] may partially explain the inconsistency. These investigators reported that there is a rather substantial inoculum effect on the activity of norfloxacin against anaerobes but not against *E. coli.* When the inoculum density was raised to a level more like that in fecal samples, the minimum bactericidal concentration (MBC) for *E. coli* was still within the range of drug levels achieved in vivo, but the MBCs for many of the anaerobes far exceeded even the high fecal levels of norfloxacin. Thus, one might be able to push the dose of a fluoroquinolone to achieve levels that exceed the MBC of aerobic gram-negatives while maintaining selectivity in gut decontamination.

## EFFICACY OF ORAL FLUOROQUINOLONE PROPHYLAXIS IN NEUTROPENIC PATIENTS

Ciprofloxacin, norfloxacin, and ofloxacin have been tested in studies of infection prophylaxis in patients with neutropenia (Table 2).[16,21,25-28] Most of these patients were leukemics who were receiving conventional chemotherapy, so the neutropenia was severe and prolonged. The oral fluoroquinolone was administered from the start of chemotherapy to resolution of neutropenia or institution of systemic antibiotics. No study showed a decrease in fatal infections in the fluoroquinolone group, but modern empiric systemic antibiotic therapy was probably responsible for the remarkably low incidence of fatal infections overall (average 7.2%). Karp et al[21] reported a significant delay in the onset of first fever in patients receiving norfloxacin in comparison to those receiving placebo, but no difference was found when norfloxacin was compared to other oral prophylactic regimens.[27,28] A decrease in the incidence of microbiologically-documented gram-negative infections was noted in nearly all studies. In the reports listed in Table 2, only 3% of patients receiving fluoroquinolone prophylaxis developed gram-negative infections, in comparison to 19% of those receiving placebo or conventional regimens. Thus, in parallel with the reduction in gram-negative flora in the gut, gram-negative infections are substantially reduced in neutropenic patients receiving oral fluoroquinolone prophylaxis.

Three major sources of failure were noted in these studies. Gram-positive cocci were by far the most common causative organisms isolated from patients who developed infection while on oral fluoroquinolone therapy. Gram-positive infections occurred in 27% of the patients on fluoroquinolone prophylaxis (vs. 19% of those receiving placebo or a conventional regimen). In many of these cases the infecting organism was also found in the oropharynx or the infection was catheter-related. Since the concentration of fluoroquinolones in the saliva rarely approaches that in the feces, selective decontamination of the pharynx is unlikely to be efficient in neutropenic patients, nor will skin flora be successfully eliminated at the dosages of fluoroquinolone used for oral prophylaxis, especially if aseptic catheter technique is not stringently followed. The utility of fluoroquinolone decontamination thus seems to be

Table 2. Efficacy of oral fluoroquinolone prophylaxis in neutropenic patients

| Ref. | Drug(s) | No. of Patients | No. with Infections | Documented Infections | Gram-Negative | Gram-Positive | Anaerobic | Invasive Fungal |
|---|---|---|---|---|---|---|---|---|
| 16 | Ciprofloxacin | 15 | 9 | 5 | 0 | 4 | 1 | 0 |
| 25 | Ciprofloxacin vs. | 28 | 18 | 5 | 0 | 4 | 1 | 0 |
|  | T/S + Colistin | 28 | 21 | 14 | 7 | 7 | 0 | 0 |
| 26 | Norfloxacin vs. | 36 | — | 17 | 0 | 13 | 0 | 4 |
|  | Vancomycin + Polymyxin | 30 | — | 18 | 6 | 6 | 0 | 6 |
| 21 | Norfloxacin vs. | 35 | 35 | — | 4 | 16 | 1 | 10 |
|  | Placebo | 33 | 33 | — | 13 | 13 | 0 | 8 |
| 27 | Norfloxacin vs. | 31 | — | 9 | 0 | 9 | 0 | 0 |
|  | T/S | 32 | — | 8 | 4 | 2 | 0 | 3 |
| 28 | Norfloxacin ± Vancomycin | 48 | 27 | 7 | 1 | 6 | 0 | 0 |
|  | Vancomycin + Polymyxin + Neomycin | 48 | 31 | 7 | 2 | 5 | 0 | 0 |

T/S = Trimethoprim/sulfamethoxazole

limited to the gastrointestinal tract. Attention must be paid to good oral hygiene and aseptic catheter care independent of the regimen used for selective decontamination, since the flora in these areas are generally not affected sufficiently.

The second major cause of failure was invasive fungal infection. In theory, selective decontamination should have maintained colonization resistance and minimized overgrowth of yeast. However, as pointed out by Counts et al,[29] once systemic antibiotics have been started as empiric therapy for fever, selectivity of decontamination is lost. Thus, fungal colonization of the gut, as seen in these studies, was not totally unexpected, since many patients required empiric systemic antibiotics. In addition, it is unlikely that selective decontamination of the gut would have any effect on the progression of *Aspergillus* colonization to invasive infection in the airways. In the fluoroquinolone prophylaxis studies, the incidence of invasive fungal infections was highest when no prophylactic oral fungal agent was used. In the three studies that included oral amphotericin in the prophylaxis regimen,[16,25,28] no invasive fungal infections occurred. Thus, it may be wise to utilize an oral antifungal agent prophylactically as an adjunct in selective decontamination of patients with prolonged neutropenia.

Finally, despite the lack of emergence of resistant organisms in normal volunteers receiving short courses of oral fluoroquinolones, fluoroquinolone-resistant organisms have been isolated from neutropenic patients receiving prolonged courses of fluoroquinolones as infection prophylaxis. The resistant organisms isolated from surveillance cultures of neutropenic patients were *S. epidermidis, Pseudomonas*, and *Acinetobacter.* Twenty-three fluoroquinolone-resistant organisms were isolated from 145 neutropenic patients receiving oral fluoroquinolone prophylaxis.[16,21,25-27] Despite the number of resistant organisms, only one patient had a documented infection involving a resistant organism. This is less than expected from previous studies of infections caused by colonizing organisms in neutropenic patients not receiving fluoroquinolone prophylaxis.[2] This may be explained in part by the fact that the mechanism of resistance and the mode of resistance transfer for the fluoroquinolones are different from those of the β-lactams and aminoglycosides usually employed for empiric therapy. As a result, conventional empiric therapy may be successful in patients who had received oral fluoroquinolones as infection prophylaxis, even if these patients harbor fluoroquinolone-resistant organisms. This is in contrast to the selection of multiply-resistant organisms in patients receiving TMP/SMX as infection prophylaxis.[30] Thus, a major advantage may exist for the use of a noncross-resistant antibiotic for infection prophylaxis in neutropenic patients.

## EFFICACY OF INTRAVENOUS CIPROFLOXACIN IN THE TREATMENT OF INFECTIONS IN NEUTROPENIC PATIENTS

In vitro studies indicate that ciprofloxacin inhibits growth of a broad spectrum of organisms, including *Pseudomonas* and *Staphylococcus*. However, when treating neutropenic patients, bactericidal rather than bacteriostatic activity is required. Investigations in several neutropenic animal models have shown that in the absence of granulocytes, ciprofloxacin alone or in combination with a β-lactam has significant bactericidal activity in vivo against species of *Pseudomonas*[31,32] and *Staphylococcus*,[33] suggesting that it may be an appropriate antibiotic for treatment of infections in neutropenic patients.

The first neutropenic patients treated with ciprofloxacin had life-threatening infections due to multiply resistant *Salmonella* or *Pseudomonas*.[34-37] Ciprofloxacin 200 mg (directly or following a 400 mg loading dose) was administered intravenously twice daily alone or in addition to multiple other antibiotics. All patients improved. One patient with *Pseudomonas* sepsis and cellulitis relapsed when ciprofloxacin was discontinued after 15 days of therapy while he was still neutropenic.[36] This experience underscores the requirement for adequate antibiotic coverage until resolution of neutropenia in patients with tissue infections.

Wood and Newland[35] used intravenous ciprofloxacin 200 mg twice daily to treat patients with neutropenic fever unresponsive to first-line empiric antibiotics. Of 10 evaluable patients, complete resolution occurred in 6 and improvement in 1. Two patients with *Pseudomonas aeruginosa* bacteremia and one with *E. coli* bacteremia failed to respond. In vitro antibiotic sensitivities of the organisms were not reported. Considering that these patients had already failed first-line therapy, the response rate of 70% was sufficient to justify further prospective studies.

Intravenous ciprofloxacin alone and in combination with other agents has been tested as first-line empiric therapy for neutropenic fever (Table 3).[38-45] Smith et al[38] reported 64% improvement in febrile neutropenic patients treated with intravenous ciprofloxacin alone, but only 50% of the patients with documented bacteremias improved. In comparative studies, intravenous ciprofloxacin plus benzylpenicillin,[41,43] netilmicin,[42] or azlocillin[44] was as effective as a combination of an aminoglycoside and a β-lactam in the treatment of neutropenic fever. The best results have been reported by Smith et al[45] using intravenous ciprofloxacin and vancomycin. Overall, 77% of the febrile neutropenic patients improved, including 75% of the bacteremic patients. Moreover, adverse reactions were rare and mild. This is superior to the results of studies using two β-lactams or a combination of an aminoglycoside and a β-lactam.[46,47]

*Pseudomonas* accounted for the majority of failures of intravenous ciprofloxacin in the treatment of neutropenic patients. In vitro testing revealed that some of these organisms were still sensitive to ciprofloxacin, so the reason for failure was not clear

**Table 3.** Efficacy of intravenous ciprofloxacin in the treatment of infections in neutropenic patients

| Ref. | No. of Patients | Regimen | Infection | Response |
|---|---|---|---|---|
| 34 | 1 | Cipro | *Salmonella* abscess | Resolution and eradication |
| 35 | 10 | Cipro | Sepsis | 4/7 improved |
| | | | Other | 3/3 improved |
| 36 | 2 | Cipro | *Pseudomonas* sepsis | 2/2 improved |
| 37 | 3 | Cipro | *Pseudomonas* | 3/3 improved |
| 38 | 10 | Cipro | Fever | Overall 64% improved (50% of bacteremic pts.) |
| 39 | 30 | Cipro | Mixed | Overall 73% improved (100% of bacteremic pts.) |
| 40 | 21 | Cipro | Fever | Overall 48% improved |
| | 25 | Ceftaz | | Overall 52% improved |
| 41 | 18 | Cipro + BPCN | Fever | Overall 33% resolved (39% of documented infections) |
| | 20 | Net + BPCN | | Overall 30% resolved (27% of documented infections) |
| 42 | 59 | Cipro + Net | Fever | Overall 68% responded (52% of bacteremic pts.) |
| | 59 | Pip + Net | | Overall 66% responded (40% of bacteremic pts.) |
| 43 | 50 | Cipro + BPCN | Fever | Overall 66% improved |
| | 46 | Net + Pip | | Overall 65% improved |
| 44 | 25 | Cipro + Azlo | Fever | Overall 56% improved (67% of bacteremic pts.) |
| | 54 | Ceftaz + Amik | | Overall 67% improved (78% of bacteremic pts.) |
| 45 | 35 | Cipro + Vanco | Fever | Overall 77% improved (75% of bacteremic pts.) |

Amik = amikacin, Azlo = azlocillin, BPCN = benzylpenicillin, Ceftaz = ceftazidime, Cipro = ciprofloxacin, Net = netilmicin , Pip = piperacillin, Vanco = vancomycin

initially. Dudley et al[48] have investigated the bactericidal activity of ciprofloxacin in an in vitro model system. When using a regimen of ciprofloxacin 200 mg every 12 hours, they found that drug levels were maintained sufficiently high enough to be bactericidal for *E. coli* but not for *Ps. aeruginosa*. Thus, dosing of ciprofloxacin more frequently than every 12 hours may be required in neutropenic patients if *Pseudomonas* is to be covered adequately.

## ADVERSE EFFECTS OF FLUOROQUINOLONES IN NEUTROPENIC PATIENTS

Reviews of the side effects of fluoroquinolones in clinical trials have revealed relatively few serious adverse reactions.[13,14] The excellent safety profile extends to the neutropenic population as well. Corrado et al[49] reported that drug-related adverse effects occurred in only 2 of 139 neutropenic patients receiving norfloxacin for infection prophylaxis. This incidence was comparable to the placebo group and less than in patients who received TMP/SMX or vanco/colistin. In double-blind trials comparing norfloxacin with placebo for infection prophylaxis, the most common side effects were rash, nausea and diarrhea, but the incidence of these in the norfloxacin group was no greater than in the placebo group.[49] The experience with the other fluoroquinolones is much smaller but equally benign.

The excellent tolerability profile of these agents has a favorable impact on patient acceptance of therapy. In the prophylaxis studies, compliance with oral fluoroquinolone therapy generally exceeded 90%, and in several studies the oral fluoroquinolone was tolerated better than TMP/SMX or vanco/colistin.[25,26]

Despite the safety of oral fluoroquinolones as demonstrated in the initial clinical trials, the number of neutropenic patients evaluated during prolonged therapy is relatively small. Several special problems may arise in the neutropenic population, including myelosuppression, nephrotoxicity, and drug interactions. Future studies should address these concerns by monitoring neutropenic patients who receive prophylactic fluoroquinolone therapy.

The risk of myelosuppression during fluoroquinolone therapy occurs because the eukaryotic topoisomerase is also sensitive to these drugs (albeit to a much lesser degree than the prokaryotic topoisomerase),[50,51] so eukaryotic cell growth, including bone marrow, can be inhibited. Negishi et al[52] reported that murine granulocyte/macrophage and erythroid colony-forming units grown in vitro were inhibited by ofloxacin, norfloxacin, and nalidixic acid at concentrations $\geq 100$ mg/L. Human marrow colony-forming units were suppressed with pefloxacin at $\geq 100$ mg/L and ciprofloxacin at $\geq 25$ mg/L.[53] Somekh et al[54] also tested ciprofloxacin for myelosuppression in vivo. Incubation of syngeneic marrow for one hour with ciprofloxacin at 0.5-50 mg/L had no effect on engraftment in lethally-irradiated mice. However, when the animals were injected with ciprofloxacin 100 mg/kg/day for 8 days after transplantation, splenic uptake of $^{125}$IUDR was reduced to 30% of control, and the frequency of splenic colony-forming units was only 14% of control. Blood levels one hour after administration of ciprofloxacin were about 10 mg/L. This is about twice what is achieved in humans following a single 1000 mg dose of ciprofloxacin orally.

A review of the adverse effects of fluoroquinolones in non-neutropenic patients has revealed only a single case of neutropenia in a patient treated with ciprofloxacin,[13] and mild leukopenia (white blood cell count 3000-4000 per μL) occurred in less than 0.5% of patients treated with other fluoroquinolones.[51] Delays in resolution of aplasia after conventional chemotherapy or marrow transplantation have not been reported in patients who received ciprofloxacin 500 mg or norfloxacin 400 mg orally twice daily as prophylaxis. Close monitoring of hematopoiesis is warranted when there is impairment of fluoroquinolone clearance or when one of these agents is used concurrently with another drug that by itself is only minimally myelosuppressive.

Nephrotoxicity is a rare adverse effect of fluoroquinolone therapy in non-neutropenic patients. A decrease in renal function as assessed by BUN, serum creatinine, or creatinine clearance occurred in less than 0.2% of nearly 1700 patients in the initial clinical trials of ciprofloxacin.[13] The potential for nephrotoxicity resulting from fluoroquinolone therapy was first appreciated in preclinical toxicity studies. Animals that received high doses of ciprofloxacin for prolonged periods were noted to have elevations of BUN and creatinine.[55] Examination of the urine revealed acicular crystals and proteinuria. In some animals, histologic examination revealed an inflammatory foreign-body reaction in the distal renal tubules believed to be due to the crystals precipitated there.[55] The relative lack of nephrotoxicity in humans is thought to be due to the fact that human urine is acidic, and fluoroquinolone solubility is increased in acidic solutions. Urine from the species used in preclinical studies was alkaline, and this predisposed to crystallization of the drug in the renal tubules, especially when high doses were used. Neutropenic patients who receive nephrotoxic antibiotics, especially amphotericin, frequently develop a distal renal tubular acidosis with alkaline urine. In addition, many patients are given intravenous bicarbonate to prevent uric acid nephropathy while receiving chemotherapy. As a result of alkalinization of the urine, these patients may be at increased risk for impairment of renal function during fluoroquinolone therapy.

Patients receiving multiple medications often experience drug interactions. Medications taken concurrently may decrease the efficacy of fluoroquinolones. The best example is the reduction in the bioavailability of ciprofloxacin when it is administered orally with a magnesium-containing antacid.[56] In addition, the fluoroquinolones may also alter the efficacy or enhance the toxicity of other drugs. Ciprofloxacin is metabolized by the hepatic P-450 system, and its use may inhibit clearance of other drugs utilizing the same metabolic pathway.[57] Several reports of patients receiving fluoroquinolones describe increased serum levels of xanthine derivatives like theophylline[56] and caffeine,[58] probably due to inhibition of xanthine metabolism. Such an effect on drug clearance can lead to potentially serious adverse effects in patients receiving drugs at the maximum tolerated dosage, especially if the therapeutic index is narrow. One such drug is cyclosporin A (CSA). Elston and Taylor[59] have reported CSA-associated nephrotoxicity when patients receiving CSA are given ciprofloxacin concurrently. However, Hooper et al[60] found no change in CSA trough concentrations in two patients treated with ciprofloxacin. In a study of renal transplant recipients, Lang et al[61] reported a rise in serum creatinine in 4 of 10 patients on CSA when ciprofloxacin was administered, but no change was found in the single-dose pharmacokinetics of CSA. Given such contradictory reports, further investigation in marrow transplant recipients is clearly warranted.

There has been little study of the interactions between fluoroquinolones and other drugs administered to neutropenic patients. As fluoroquinolones are used more frequently in neutropenic patients, drug interactions may become more apparent.

## CONCLUSION

In vitro studies predicted that the fluoroquinolones would be useful in infection prevention in neutropenic patients because of their broad spectrum of activity against clinically important organisms and lack of activity against organisms responsible for colonization resistance, and because of their low mutation rate for development of drug resistance. Clinical studies of infection prevention using oral fluoroquinolones revealed a tremendous decrease in the enteric gram-negative content, accompanied by a decrease in gram-negative infections. Selective decontamination of the oropharynx was less successful, so infections due to organisms seeded from the oropharynx remained a problem, as did catheter-related infections. In addition, fungal infections were more frequent when patients did not receive antifungal prophylaxis along with the fluoroquinolone. Overall, the safety and utility of oral fluoroquinolones in prevention of gram-negative infections in neutropenic patients was well-documented, but aseptic catheter technique, oral hygiene and antifungal agents must remain part of the infection prophylaxis regimen to make a significant impact.

In vitro studies also predicted that the fluoroquinolones would be useful for treatment of infection in clinical settings in which broad spectrum agents or agents with activity against multiply-resistant organisms are required. Fluoroquinolones have been used successfully for the treatment of infections due to multiply-resistant organisms in neutropenic patients. However, the most effective dosing regimen, especially for infections involving *Pseudomonas,* has not been determined. In studies of empiric therapy in patients with neutropenic fever, the combination of ciprofloxacin and vancomycin provided sufficiently broad coverage to be comparable to double β-lactam therapy or combination aminoglycoside and β-lactam therapy. Controlled clinical trials will be required to confirm the apparent equivalence of these regimens.

These studies indicate that the fluoroquinolones definitely have a place in the treatment of neutropenic patients. Further experience with these drugs in this population will determine the optimum method of use, and as more patients are treated, the questions regarding potential adverse effects will be answered.

# REFERENCES

1. Ketchel SJ, Rodriguez V: Acute infections in cancer patients. Semin Oncol 1978;5:167-179.

2. Newman KA, Schimpff SC, Young VM, et al: Lessons learned from surveillance cultures in patients with acute nonlymphocytic leukemia. Am J Med 1981;70:423-431.

3. Wade JC, Schimpff SC, Newman KA, et al: *Staphylococcus epidermidis:* An increasing cause of infections in patients with granulocytopenia. Ann Intern Med 1982;97:503-510.

4. Meyers JD, Atkinson K: Infection in bone marrow transplantation. Clin Haematol 1983;12:791-811.

5. Van der Waaij D, Berghuis JM, Lekkerkerk JEC: Colonization resistance of the digestive tract in conventional and antibiotic-treated mice. J Hyg 1971;69:405-411.

6. Sleijfer DT, Mulder NH, de Vries-Hospers HG, et al: Infection prevention in granulocytopenic patients by selective decontamination of the digestive tract. Eur J Cancer 1980;16:859-869.

7. Wade JC, de Jongh CA, Newman KA, et al: Selective antimicrobial modulation as prophylaxis against infection during granulocytopenia: Trimethoprim-sulfamethoxazole vs. nalidixic acid. J Infect Dis 1983;147:624-634.

8. Bow EJ, Rayner E, Scott BA, et al: Selective gut decontamination with nalidixic acid or trimethoprim-sulfamethoxazole for infection prophylaxis in neutropenic cancer patients: Relationship of efficacy to antimicrobial spectrum and timing of administration. Antimicrob Agents Chemother 1987;31:551-557.

9. Fass RJ: In vitro activity of ciprofloxacin (Bay o 9867). Antimicrob Agents Chemother 1983;24:568-574.

10. Hooper DC, Wolfson JS, Ng EY, et al: Mechanisms of action of and resistance to ciprofloxacin. Am J Med 1987;82(suppl 4A):12-20.

11. Walsh TJ, Newman KR, Moody M, et al: Trichosporonosis in patients with neoplastic disease. Medicine 1986;65:268-279.

12. Bergan T: Pharmacokinetic differentiation and consequences for normal microflora. Scand J Infect Dis 1986;49:91-99.

13. Ball P: Ciprofloxacin: An overview of adverse experiences. J Antimicrob Chemother 1986;18:187-193.

14. Corrado ML, Struble WE, Peter C, et al: Norfloxacin: Review of safety studies. Am J Med 1987;82(suppl 6B):22-26.

15. Brumfitt W, Franklin I, Grady D, et al: Changes in the pharmacokinetics of ciprofloxacin and fecal flora during administration of a 7-day course to human volunteers. Antimicrob Agents Chemother 1984;26:757-761.

16. Rozenberg-Arska M, Dekker AW, Verhoef J: Ciprofloxacin for selective decontamination of the alimentary tract in patients with acute leukemia during remission induction treatment: The effect on fecal flora. J Infect Dis 1985;152:104-107.

17. Bergan T, Delin C, Johansen S, et al: Pharmacokinetics of ciprofloxacin and effect of repeated dosage on salivary and fecal microflora. Antimicrob Agents Chemother 1986;29:298-302.

18. Shah PM, Enzensberger R, Glogau O, et al: Influence of oral ciprofloxacin or ofloxacin on the fecal flora of healthy volunteers. Am J Med 1987;82(suppl 4A):333-335.

19. van Saene JJM, van Saene HKF, Geitz JN, et al: Effects of ciprofloxacin on the intestinal flora. Rev Infect Dis 1988;10:198-212.

20. van Saene HKF, Lemmens SEB, van Saene JJM: Gut decontamination by oral ofloxacin and ciprofloxacin in healthy volunteers. J Antimicrob Chemother 1988;22(suppl C):127-134.

21. Karp JE, Merz WG, Hendricksen C, et al: Oral norfloxacin for prevention of gram-negative bacterial infections in patients with acute leukemia and granulocytopenia. Ann Intern Med 1987;106:1-7.

22. Lipsky BA, Pecoraro RE, Hanley ME: Eradication of *Staphylococcus aureus* nasal colonization by ofloxacin & other antibiotics, abstract 1040. Program and abstracts of the 27th annual Interscience Conference on Antimicrobial Agents and Chemotherapy, New York, October 4-7, 1987.

23. Appelbaum PC, Spangler SK, Strauss M: Reduction of oral flora with ciprofloxacin in healthy volunteers. J Antimicrob Chemother 1988;21:243-249.

24. Goldstein EJC, Citron DM, Corrado ML: Effect of inoculum size on in vitro activity of norfloxacin against anaerobic bacteria. Am J Med 1987;82(suppl 6B):84-86.

25. Dekker AW, Rozenberg-Arska M, Verhoef J: Infection prophylaxis in acute leukemia: A comparison of ciprofloxacin with trimethoprim-sulfamethoxazole and colistin. Ann Intern Med 1987;106:7-12.

26. Winston DJ, Ho WG, Nakao SL, et al: Norfloxacin versus vancomycin/polymyxin for prevention of infections in granulocytopenic patients. Am J Med 1986;80:884-890.

27. Bow EJ, Rayner E, Louie TJ: Comparison of norfloxacin with cotrimoxazole for infection prophylaxis in acute leukemia. Am J Med 1988;84:847-854.

28. Schmeiser T, Kurrle E, Arnold R, et al: Norfloxacin for prevention of bacterial infections during severe granulocytopenia after bone marrow transplantation. Scand J Infect Dis 1988;20:625-631.

29. Counts GW, Pallansch P, Jansen S, et al: Selective and total decontamination of marrow transplant patients using ciprofloxacin: Additional impact of systemic antibiotics on intestinal flora. abstract 959. Program and abstracts of the 27th Interscience Conference on Antimicrobial Agents and Chemotherapy, New York, October 4-7, 1987.

30. Hamilton DJ, Ulness BK, Baugher LK, et al: Comparison of a novel trimethoprim-sulfamethoxazole-containing medium with kanamycin agar for isolation of antibiotic-resistant organisms from stool and rectal cultures of marrow transplant patients. J Clin Microbiol 1987;25:1886-1890.

31. Gordin FM, Hackbarth CJ, Scott KG, et al: Activities of pefloxacin and ciprofloxacin in experimentally induced *Pseudomonas* pneumonia in neutropenic guinea pigs. Antimicrob Agents Chemother 1985;27:452-454.

32. Fu KP, Hetzel N, Gregory FJ, et al: Therapeutic efficacy of cefpiramide-ciprofloxacin combination in experimental pseudomonas infections in neutropenic mice. J Antimicrob Chemother 1987;20:541-546.

33. Peterson LR, Fasching CE, Moody JA, et al: Vancomycin, cephalothin, oxacillin, ciprofloxacin, azlocillin, and ciprofloxacin plus azlocillin therapy of *S. aureus* and *S. epidermidis* in a neutropenic site model, abstract 168. Program and abstracts of the 27th Interscience Conference on Antimicrobial Agents and Chemotherapy, New York, October 4-7, 1987.

34. Patton WN, Wmith GM, Leyland MJ, et al: Multiply resistant *Salmonella typhimurium* septicaemia in an immunocompromised patient successfully treated with ciprofloxacin. J Antimicrob Chemother 1985;16:667-669.

35. Wood ME, Newland AC: Intravenous ciprofloxacin in the treatment of infection in immunocompromised patients. J Antimicrob Chemother 1986;18(suppl D):175-178.

36. Bendig JWA, Kyle PW, Giangrande PLF, et al: Two neutropenic patients with multiple resistant *Pseudomonas aeruginosa* septicaemia treated with ciprofloxacin. J Royal Soc Med 1987;80:316-317.

37. Barnes RA, Rogers TR: Response rates to a staged antibiotic regimen in febrile neutropenic patients. J Antimicrob Chemother 1988;22:759-763.

38. Smith GM, Leyland MJ, Farrell ID, et al: Preliminary evaluation of ciprofloxacin, a new 4-quinolone antibiotic, in the treatment of febrile neutropenic patients. J Antimicrob Chemother 1986;18(suppl D):165-174.

39. Rolston KVI, Haron E, Cunningham C, et al: Intravenous ciprofloxacin for infections in cancer patients. Am J Med 1989;87(suppl 5A):261S-265S.

40. Bayston KF, Want S, Cohen J: A prospective, randomized comparison of ceftazidime and ciprofloxacin as initial empiric therapy in neutropenic patients with fever. Am J Med 1989;87(suppl 5A):269S-273S.

41. Wood ME, Newland AC: Ciprofloxacin + benzyl penicillin in the treatment of fever in neutropenia, abstract 1252. Program and abstracts of the 27th Interscience Conference on Antimicrobial Agents and Chemotherapy, New York, October 4-7, 1987.

42. Chan CC, Oppenheim BA, Anderson H, et al: Randomised prospective trial comparing the efficacy of netilmicin & ciprofloxacin versus netilmicin & piperacillin as empirical antibiotic therapy in febrile neutropenic patients, abstract 1250. Program and abstracts of the 27th Interscience Conference on Antimicrobial Agents and Chemotherapy, New York, October 4-7, 1987.

43. Kelsey SM, Wood ME, Shaw E, et al: Intravenous ciprofloxacin as empirical treatment of febrile neutropenic patients. Am J Med 1989;87(suppl 5A):274S-277S.

44. Flaherty JP, Waitley D, Edlin B, et al: Multicenter, randomized trial of ciprofloxacin plus azlocillin versus ceftazidime plus amikacin for empiric treatment of febrile neutropenic patients. Am J Med 1989;87(suppl 5A):278S-282S.

45. Smith GM, Leyland MJ, Farrell ID, et al: A clinical, microbiological and pharmacokinetic study of ciprofloxacin plus vancomycin as initial therapy of febrile episodes in neutropenic patients. J Antimicrob Chemother 1988;21:647-655.

46. Dejace P, Klastersky J: Comparative review of combination therapy: Two beta-lactams versus beta-lactam plus aminoglycoside. Am J Med 1986;80(suppl 6B):29-38.

47. Anaissie EJ, Fainstein V, Bodey G, et al: Randomized trial of beta-lactam regimens in febrile neutropenic cancer patients. Am J Med 1988;84:581-589.

48. Dudley MN, Mandler HD, Gilbert D, et al: Pharmacokinetics and pharmacodynamics of intravenous ciprofloxacin. Am J Med 1987;82(suppl 4A):363-368.

49. Corrado ML, Struble WE, Hesney M: The tolerability profile of prophylactic norfloxacin in neutropenic patients. Eur J Cancer Clin Oncol 1988;24(suppl 1):S29-S33.

50. Hussy P, Maass G, Tümmler B, et al: Effect of 4-quinolones and novobiocin on calf thymus DNA polymerase $\alpha$ primase complex, topoisomerases I and II, and growth of mammalian lymphoblasts. Antimicrob Agents Chemother 1986;29:1073-1078.

51. Halkin H: Adverse effects of the fluoroquinolones. Rev Infect Dis 1988;10:S258-S267.

52. Negishi M, Young C, Suzuki H: Effect of ofloxacin on the hematopoietic stem cells and comparison with other antimicrobial agents. Proceedings of the 14th International Congress of Chemotherapy, Kyoto, pp 861-862, 1985.

53. Somekh E, Douer D, Shaked N, et al: The effect of ciprofloxacin and pefloxacin on human bone marrow stem cells and leukemic cells, abstract 953. Program and abstracts of the 27th Interscience Conference on Antimicrobial Agents and Chemotherapy, New York, October 4-7, 1987.

54. Somekh E, Lev B, Schwartz E, et al: The effect of ciprofloxacin and pefloxacin on bone marrow engraftment in the spleen of mice. J Antimicrob Chemother 1989;23:247-251.

55. *Ciprofloxacin Product Information Monograph - Compendium of Preclinical and Clinical Data.* New York, Marcel Dekker, Inc, 1988.

56. Lode H: Drug interactions with quinolones. Rev Infect Dis 1988;10:S132-S136.

57. Ludwig E, Szekely E, Csiba A, et al: The effect of ciprofloxacin on antipyrine metabolism. J Antimicrob Chemother 1988;22:61-67.

58. Staib AH, Stille W, Dietlein G, et al: Interaction between quinolones and caffeine. Drugs 1987;34(suppl 1):170-174.

59. Elston RA, Taylor J: Possible interaction of ciprofloxacin with cyclosporin A. J Antimicrob Chemother 1988;21:679-680.

60. Hooper TL, Gould FK, Swinburn CR, et al: Ciprofloxacin: A preferred treatment for legionella infections in patients receiving cyclosporin A. J Antimicrob Chemother 1988; 22:952-953.

61. Lang J, Finaz de Villaine J, Garraffo R, et al: Cyclosporine (cyclosporin A) pharmacokinetics in renal transplant patients receiving ciprofloxacin. Am J Med 1989;87(suppl 5A):82S-85S.

# BRONCHOPULMONARY INFECTIONS IN CYSTIC FIBROSIS: PATHOPHYSIOLOGY AND TREATMENT   10

*Michael D. Reed*
*Jeffrey L. Blumer*

## INTRODUCTION

Cystic fibrosis (CF) is the most common lethal genetic disorder affecting caucasians and the most common hereditary disease in the United States. The significant advances achieved over the past few years in the localization and identification of the CF gene[1-3] are overshadowed only by the elusiveness of the specific underlying metabolic defect. This complex disorder affects the exocrine glands and thus either directly or indirectly affects all body organs. As a clinical syndrome, CF is characterized by an elevated sweat chloride, chronic obstructive pulmonary disease, and exocrine pancreatic insufficiency. Although the diagnosis of CF is generally made during early infancy, CF is no longer a disease confined to infants and young children. The median survival of these patients now exceeds 25 years,[4] which accounts for the gradual increase in admission of CF patients to adult hospital wards.

According to early nineteenth century German folklore, "the child will soon die whose brow tastes salty when kissed."[5] This description is considered by many to be one of the earliest references to the clinical syndrome of CF. The association of the pulmonary and digestive symptoms of CF was first described in 1936 by Fanconi and colleagues (as cited in Wood et al[5]) as cystic pancreatic fibrosis and bronchiectasis. Cystic fibrosis as a distinct entity was first reported in 1938 by Anderson,[6] who described the disorder as cystic fibrosis of the pancreas. Great strides have been made in our understanding of the pathophysiology, genetics, and therapy of this complex disorder since these landmark descriptions.

## EPIDEMIOLOGY AND INCIDENCE

Population genetics data strongly support the belief that CF is inherited as an autosomal recessive trait;[3,7] approximately 1 in every 2000 live caucasian and 1 in every 8000 live black births in the United States have CF. The occurrence of CF in the American Indian is rare. These frequencies suggest that approximately 5% of U.S. caucasians are heterozygous carriers. The highest incidence of CF appears to be in Central Europe and the British Isles;[3] in contrast, an incidence rate of 1 in 90,000 births has been reported for Orientals.[8] Considering that the homozygous individual rarely reproduces, there should be a strong inherent selection against the disease allele; ie, a genetic lethal. However, this is obviously not the case. Explanations for the continued high incidence of the disease gene include the possibility of some selective advantage for the carrier state; multiple loci; and/or the unlikely possibility of continued mutations.[3,9]

## PATHOGENESIS AND PATHOPHYSIOLOGY

The past few years have witnessed important advances in knowledge of the primary metabolic abnormality in CF. This marked increase in our knowledge stems from the advances recently made in the understanding of electrolyte transfer by the epithelial cell. Abnormalities in epithelial cell electrolyte permeability are currently considered to be the cellular defect in CF. Studies in several CF organ systems have shown decreased sodium and chloride permeability, with an abnormality in the chloride channel representing the primary ionic defect.[2,10] Abnormalities in cellular chloride and sodium homeostasis have been described in the epithelium of the three primary organs involved in CF (sweat gland, pancreas, and the airways). The sweat gland normally conserves sodium and chloride via sodium reabsorption. In CF patients the sweat gland reabsorbs sodium at a nearly normal rate but the "channel" is impermeable to the counter ion, chloride. As a result, chloride and to a lesser extent sodium are concentrated in the sweat of CF patients.[2] Similarly, reabsorption of sodium and chloride across airway epithelium is a normal process whereby transepithelial electrolyte transport regulates the composition and quantity of respiratory secretions. In CF patients there appears to be a relative inability to secrete chloride into the airway lumen. This "chloride block" leads to a decreased passive flow of water and results in thick desiccated respiratory secretions. Dehydrated, tenacious respiratory secretions, which are classically associated with CF, compromise mucociliary transport, obstruct airways, and serve as a viable environment for bacterial colonization and infection.[2,4,5,11-15]

Chronic progressive obstructive pulmonary disease is responsible for 95% of the morbidity and mortality in CF. It appears that the early pulmonary changes of dilatation and hypertrophy of the bronchial glands are due to inflammation not associated with

150

infection.[4,5,11] The abundance of thick tenacious secretions and consequent mucus plugging of both small and large airways leads to chronic air trapping, bronchiectasis and atelectasis, all of which promote bacterial growth. One of the hallmarks of CF is chronic and recurrent infectious bronchitis and bronchopneumonia; extrapulmonary infections are unusual in these patients. This chronic colonization and infection appear to contribute further to the ongoing tissue damage and pulmonary compromise.[4,5,11-15]

## PULMONARY MICROBIOLOGY

The respiratory flora of CF patients usually include *Staphylococcus aureus* and *Haemophilus influenzae* initially, followed by the addition of *Pseudomonas aeruginosa*.[4,5,12-15] Other bacterial pathogens found in respiratory secretions of patients with CF include *Streptococcus pneumoniae, Escherichia coli, Klebsiella* spp., *Proteus* spp., *Serratia* spp., *Citrobacter* spp., group A streptococci, and a host of non-fermenting gram-negative bacilli, including *Ps. maltophilia, Ps. fluorescens, P. alcaligenes* and *Achromobacter xylosoxidans*.[14-17] These latter microorganisms are isolated sporadically, whereas *Ps. aeruginosa* and *S. aureus* comprise the primary pathogens which chronically reside in the lungs of CF patients. Recent data have shown that respiratory viruses may also be responsible for precipitating some of the pulmonary exacerbations associated with the disease.[18,19] Of more importance, however, is the suggestion that viral upper respiratory tract infections may influence markedly the natural history of CF pulmonary exacerbations by interfering with the host-bacteria interaction.[19] The role and prevalence rate of anaerobic bacteria, atypical mycobacteria, and fungi on the progression of the pulmonary diseases remains to be more fully described.[15,16,18,19]

The relative frequency with which respiratory pathogens are isolated from CF patients appears to have changed over the past four decades.[16,18-20] *S. aureus* was believed by many to be the primary pathogen invading and subsequently chronically residing in the lungs of CF patients, followed by *Ps. aeruginosa*. Mearns et al[20] described a decrease in the isolation of *S. aureus* at initial hospitalization in their group of CF patients; 86% during 1950-1957 versus only 30% in 1969-1971. The reason for this apparent change in *S. aureus* isolation is unclear, although some investigators have speculated that it resulted from increased use of antistaphylococcal antibiotics and possibly from improved infection control measures in newborn nurseries.[14] In contrast to these data, a number of centers have demonstrated that *Ps. aeruginosa* as well as other pathogens may initially colonize the lung of these patients.[14-16,21] Other investigators, however, have been unable to corroborate this so-called shift in respiratory tract flora.[15] Thus, the significance of this apparent change in bacterial flora remains unclear.

*Ps. aeruginosa* is the species of bacteria most frequently isolated from the sputum of CF patients.[15,22] The reason for its prevalence is unknown but may reflect the extraordinary metabolic and genetic versatility of this pathogen.[14] One of the most characteristic features of *Ps. aeruginosa* isolated from CF patients is the ability of the microorganism to produce mucoid alginate.[15] Though extremely common in CF patients, mucoid strains of *Ps. aeruginosa* are only rarely isolated from non-CF patients.[5,12-17,22,23] The production of this exopolysaccharide mucoid slime[23-27] and the formation of microcolonies in the lungs of these patients[15,28,29] appears to be a result of the CF lung environment and the remarkable ability of the pathogen to adapt.[30] Most mucoid strains of *Ps. aeruginosa* isolated from CF patients will revert in vitro to the non-mucoid variant.[15,31] Mucoid variants of other pathogens including *E. coli*, *Klebsiella*, and *Enterobacter* spp., have been isolated from the sputum of these patients.[32,33] Although the source and mode of transmission of *Ps. aeruginosa* among CF patients remain a topic of considerable debate,[14,15] these data suggest that environmental factors are primary determinants.

Recently, *Ps. cepacia* has emerged as a frequent and important respiratory tract pathogen in CF patients.[14,15,34-36] Initial reports from the Toronto CF Center[34] described three distinct clinical patterns; the most ominous was a rapidly deteriorating clinical course associated with fever, leukocytosis, and an increased mortality in patients in whom *Ps. cepacia* was isolated. Chronic "asymptomatic" colonization with *Ps. cepacia,* with or without co-isolation of *Ps. aeruginosa,* and a progressive deterioration over months with recurrent fever, progressive weight loss, and repeat hospitalizations have also been described.[34] Similar experiences have been reported by other North American CF centers.[14,35] Due to the highly variable clinical course associated with *Ps. cepacia* colonization and the high likelihood of nosocomial spread of the pathogen,[14,15] specific infection control measures including patient isolation and improved equipment decontamination techniques were immediately undertaken by CF treatment centers.[14,15,34-37] As a result of more careful measures to combat the nosocomial spread of *Ps. cepacia* among CF patients, its incidence has declined rapidly.[37] Nevertheless, our understanding of the pathogenicity and virulence of *Ps. cepacia* colonization/infection in CF is limited.[36] With the exception of ciprofloxacin and possibly ceftazidime, *Ps. cepacia* is resistant to most antibiotics in vitro, further hampering attempts to evaluate patient response to therapeutic intervention.

The etiologic basis for the chronic harboring of pathogens in the respiratory secretions and lung parenchyma of CF patients remains unknown. Although abnormalities in local pulmonary host defenses have been demonstrated, extrapulmonary immune status in these patients is intact and competent.[14,38] It appears that defects in pulmonary host defenses in these patients are in fact a result of chronic infection and not an etiologic factor in the evolution of the chronic infection.[14,38-40] Phagocytic activity of both normal and CF alveolar macrophages can be inhibited in vitro by serum from CF patients whose lungs are chronically colonized by *P. aeruginosa*.[14,39,40] Because this inhibition is specific for *Ps. aeruginosa,* inhibitory activity appears to be antibody-mediated. Available data suggest that nonopsonic antibodies compete with opsonic $IgG_3$ coating the bacteria, thus inhibiting phagocytosis.[14] This defective opsonophagocytosis effectively neutralizes the pulmonary macrophage in an otherwise immunocompetent host.[39]

## DRUG THERAPY OF CYSTIC FIBROSIS

The primary goals of therapy are to maintain adequate nutrition and to prevent progression of the pulmonary involvement. At present, the emphasis of pharmaco-therapy is directed at reducing the pulmonary complications of the syndrome that are responsible for 95% of the associated morbidity and mortality.[4,5] However, despite the massive amount of reported experience, the exact role of infection as an etiologic factor in the initiation and progression of CF pulmonary disease remains ill-defined.[4,12,19] Nevertheless, most authorities agree that bacterial, and possibly, viral infections are central to the progression of the associated lung disease.[4,5,11-15,19,41]

Nearly 85% of CF patients suffer from exocrine pancreatic insufficiency,[5] which is responsible for the observed maldigestion, malabsorption, failure to gain weight, and growth retardation. Modifications in diet combined with advances in pancreatic enzyme replacement preparations have led to substantial improvements in the nutri-tional care of these patients.[42,43] It is not unusual for these patients to require specific food substitutes and multivitamin supplementation (especially the fat-soluble vita-mins A, D, E, and K).

Multiple therapeutic modalities including chest physiotherapy, pharmacologic aerosols, bronchodilators, and repeated courses of high dose, potent, broad-spectrum antibiotics are currently recommended for the treatment of pulmonary exacerba-tions.[4,5,12-15] At present, no uniform recommendations exist regarding the use of these or other therapeutic interventions in the care of CF patients. In fact, multiple therapeu-tic modalities are often used in differing combinations at different times and at differ-ent intervals depending upon the individual CF treatment center. Such an approach has hampered efforts to develop and define specific therapeutic guidelines for the treatment of these patients. The lack of a specific definition of what constitutes an acute "pulmonary exacerbation" of the disease,[4] combined with the known differences in drug disposition profiles in CF patients as compared to unaffected controls,[44-46] com-pounds these difficulties and more importantly, serves as a perpetual source fueling the "controversies."

An acute pulmonary exacerbation of CF is a difficult clinical entity to define. In a recent international workshop on CF held at the Rotterdam Medical School,[47] the participants were unable to formulate a consensus opinion regarding a definition of a "CF infectious exacerbation." This difficulty is in part due to the fact that *an acute pulmonary exacerbation represents a constellation of clinical signs and symptoms that is difficult to quantify.* One clinical definition of an acute pulmonary exacerbation of the disease, based on clinical criteria, is satisfied when a CF patient is experiencing four or more of the following symptoms: (1) increased productive cough; (2) change in volume, appearance and/or color of sputum; (3) increased respiratory rate or dyspnea; (4) progressive physical findings on chest auscultation; (5) new infiltrate on chest x-ray; (6) deterioration in pulmonary function as revealed by pulmonary function testing; (7) decreased appetite or weight loss; or (8) fever. Similar clinical definitions are used by others.[5,12-14,41,48]

Chronic bacterial colonization of the lower respiratory tract, and in particular, colonization with mucoid variants of *Pseudomonas* spp. and other bacteria, are hallmarks of an acute pulmonary exacerbation and are pathognomonic.[4,5,12-15] This phenomenon is uncommon in the sense that bacteria chronically reside in a normally sterile anatomic site regardless of the repeated use of appropriate and aggressive antibiotic therapy. Despite these unusual characteristics, the principles behind antibiotic selection for the treatment of CF-associated endobronchial infection are essentially no different from those used to design therapy for any infectious disease or more specifically, bronchopneumonia. Pharmacologic considerations include the antibacterial activity of the antibiotic against the pathogen, achievable concentrations of the drug at the infectious site, stability of the drug within the infectious milieu, and the efficacy and safety profile of the drug.

Despite its variable usefulness in the evaluation of lower respiratory tract bacteriology and infections in general, sputum collection and culture are routinely performed on CF patients and are frequently used to direct antibiotic therapy.[5,12,14] In CF patients, standard techniques used to culture respiratory secretions have been shown to accurately reflect the bacteriology of the respiratory tract. Thomassen et al[49] compared bacteriologic cultures of sputum to specimens obtained at thoracotomy in 17 CF patients and found that all organisms isolated from the surgical specimens were also isolated from sputum culture. Sputum or deep throat cultures are plated on 5% sheep's blood, chocolate and mannitol salt agars, and incubated at 35°C in 5% $CO_2$ for 24 hours. To enhance growth of *Ps. cepacia* and slow-growing *Pseudomonas* spp., cultures are incubated further at room temperature or 35°C for an additional 24 hours.[14] Standard agar dilution or micro- or macrodilution broth techniques are used widely to quantitate antibiotic minimum inhibitory concentrations against sputum isolates.[14]

Many microbiology laboratories servicing CF centers classify *Ps. aeruginosa* isolates into distinct morphologic categories (eg, mucoid, rough, smooth, classic, gelatinous or dwarf).[22,50] A sputum culture from one CF patient may yield a number of different *Ps. aeruginosa* morphotypes. Some investigators have recommended that each morphotype be tested individually to ascertain its in vitro antibiotic susceptibility.[14,22,50] The clinical significance of such extensive isolation and in vitro culture and sensitivity testing for directing antibiotic selection and patient clinical response remains unknown. Considering the frequent repetitive exposure of CF patients to high-dose broad spectrum antibiotics, it is not unusual for many of these patients, particularly as they get older, to harbor microorganisms that are highly resistant to most available antibiotics. Representative in vitro antibiotic susceptibility data for aminoglycosides against gentamicin-resistant *Ps. aeruginosa* CF sputum isolates are shown in Table 1.[51] In vitro antibiotic susceptibility data for broad-spectrum β-lactam and quinolone antibiotics against *Ps. aeruginosa* and *Ps. cepacia* isolates are shown in Tables 2 and 3, respectively.[52] Considering the highly desirable antibacterial spectrum of the newer fluoroquinolone antibiotics[53-55] and their favorable pharmacokinetic characteristics, it is likely that their use will increase in CF patients over the next few years (see below). Table 4 shows representative, comparative in vitro antibacterial activity of a number of the available and investigational fluoroquinolone antibiotics against a large number of bacterial species that can be isolated from the sputum of CF patients.

## PHARMACOKINETIC-PHARMACODYNAMIC PRINCIPLES OF THERAPY

The inherent antibacterial activity of an antibiotic and its concentration at the infected focus are important determinants of effective therapy. Both of these factors reflect complex interactions that comprise the pharmacodynamic and pharmacokinetic characteristics of each antibiotic. The pharmacokinetic and pharmacodynamic

Table 1. Comparative in vitro activity of aminoglycoside antibiotics against 30 *Ps. aeruginosa* sputum isolates from CF patients

| Antibiotic | Minimum Inhibitory Concentration (μg/mL) | | % Resistant |
|---|---|---|---|
| | Median | Range | |
| Gentamicin* | 64 | 16->256 | 100 |
| Amikacin[†] | 64 | 2-512 | 87 |
| Kanamycin[†] | 512 | 64->512 | 100 |
| Netilmicin* | 256 | 4->512 | 97 |
| Tobramycin* | 16 | 2->128 | 77 |
| Streptomycin[†] | 512 | 32->512 | 100 |

* Resistance defined as MIC ≥8 μg/mL.
† Resistance defined as MIC ≥32 μg/mL.
Adapted from McNeil et al.[51]

155

**Table 2.** Susceptibility of 32 *Ps. aeruginosa* sputum isolates from CF patients

| Antibiotic | MIC$_{50}$ | MIC$_{90}$ | MIC Range |
|---|---|---|---|
| Ciprofloxacin | 0.5 | 0.5 | ≤0.06-1 |
| Norfloxacin | 2 | 2 | ≤0.06-8 |
| Azlocillin | 64 | >64 | 1->64 |
| Mezlocillin | >64 | >64 | 8->64 |
| Aztreonam | 8 | 32 | 0.5->64 |
| Ceftazidime | 4 | 32 | 0.25->64 |
| Cefsulodin | 8 | >64 | 0.06->64 |
| Imipenem | 4 | 16 | 0.5-32 |

MIC = minimum inhibitory concentration (mg/L)
Inoculum 10$^6$ colony forming units/mL
Adapted from Klinger and Aronoff.[52]

**Table 3.** Susceptibility of 34 *Ps. cepacia* sputum isolates from CF patients

| Antibiotic | MIC$_{50}$ | MIC$_{90}$ | MIC Range |
|---|---|---|---|
| Ciprofloxacin | 4 | 16 | ≤0.06-1 |
| Norfloxacin | 16 | 32 | 0.125-32 |
| Azlocillin | 64 | >64 | 4->64 |
| Mezlocillin | 64 | >64 | 1->64 |
| Aztreonam | 32 | >64 | 1->64 |
| Ceftazidime | 4 | 16 | 0.5->64 |
| Cefsulodin | >64 | >64 | 2->64 |
| Imipenem | 16 | 32 | 0.25->64 |

MIC = minimum inhibitory concentration (mg/L)
Inoculum 10$^6$ colony forming units/mL
Adapted from Klinger and Aronoff.[52]

properties of a number of drugs have been shown to be different in CF patients as compared with unaffected individuals. In 1975 Jusko et al[56] were the first to describe differences in the disposition profile of a drug in CF patients. These investigators described a significantly decreased area under the serum concentration time curve (AUC), with resultant increased plasma clearance (Cl) and renal clearance (Cl$_R$) of dicloxacillin in 10 CF patients as compared with 8 unaffected controls. The same

**Table 4.** In vitro activity of selected fluoroquinolones against pathogens that may be isolated from the sputum of patients with CF

| Pathogen | Minimum Inhibitory Concentration (MIC90) µg/mL | | | | |
|---|---|---|---|---|---|
| | Ciprofloxacin | Enoxacin | Norfloxacin | Ofloxacin | Pefloxacin |
| *Staphylococcus aureus** | 1.0 | 3.1 | 6.3 | 0.4 | 0.5 |
| *Streptococcus pneumoniae* | 2.0 | 16.0 | 4.0 | 2.0 | 4.0 |
| *Haemophilus influenzae** | 0.016 | 0.12 | 0.06 | 0.06 | 0.06 |
| *Escherichia coli* | 0.03 | 0.4 | 0.12 | 0.2 | 0.25 |
| *Klebsiella pneumoniae* | 0.12 | 2.0 | 1.6 | 0.2 | 2.0 |
| *Enterobacter* spp. | 0.06 | 0.8 | 0.4 | 0.8 | 1.0 |
| *Pseudomonas aeruginosa* | 0.5 | 2.0 | 2.0 | 2.0 | 2.0 |
| *Pseudomonas cepacia* | 8.0 | 2.0 | 16.0 | 16.0 | 8.0 |
| *Bacteroides fragilis* | 8.0 | 3.2 | 128.0 | 4.0 | 8.0 |
| *Serratia marcescens* | 0.5 | 2.0 | 1.0 | 1.0 | 1.0 |

* Includes β-lactam-resistant strains.
Adapted from Wolfson and Hooper.[53]

group subsequently published similar findings with methicillin.[57] Since these early reports, a number of carefully controlled pharmacologic studies have clearly demonstrated differences in the pharmacokinetic profiles of a large number of drugs in CF patients as compared with unaffected controls.[44-46] These agents represent a diverse group of compounds that rely on both the kidney and the liver as their primary route(s) of body clearance and include penicillins,[56-61] cephalosporins,[62-69] aminoglycosides,[70-75] trimethoprim and sulfamethoxazole,[76] cimetidine,[77] theophylline,[78,79] furosemide,[80] N-benzoyl-tyrosyl-para-aminobenzoic acid,[81] and albuterol.[82] The observed pharmacokinetic differences for many of these agents are summarized in Table 5.[83] In contrast, the pharmacokinetics of ciprofloxacin appear similar in CF patients and unaffected controls (Table 6).[84-88]

In general, changes in drug pharmacokinetics in CF patients include an increased apparent volume of distribution, enhanced body clearance, and resultant decreased serum drug concentrations (Table 5). These data appear somewhat paradoxical in view of CF-associated pathophysiology (ie, cor pulmonale, focal biliary cirrhosis), which would be expected to impair rather than enhance drug elimination. The mechanism(s) underlying these disease-specific differences in pharmacokinetics are unknown. Attempts to identify alterations in the functional capacity of the kidney in CF patients have revealed conflicting results. Berg et al[89] and Michalsen et al[90] described an increased glomerular filtration rate and tubular secretion in CF subjects, whereas Arvidsson et al,[66] Spino et al,[91] and others[44] have observed no differences in renal function (ie, glomerular filtration rate, effective renal plasma flow, or tubular secretion) in CF subjects. Fewer studies have attempted to evaluate hepatic capacity. The reasons for these discrepancies are unknown but may be due, in part, to differences in the age of study subjects and severity of disease at the time of enrollment.[46] More recent data have suggested the possibility of a link between the observed enhanced biotransformation of drugs and the genetic defect in CF.[79,92]

Most clinicians treating CF patients select antibiotic regimens based upon identification and in vitro susceptibility testing of isolates cultured from sputum samples. Numerous investigators have demonstrated that antibiotic concentrations in respiratory secretions in excess of the minimum inhibitory concentration (MIC) of the pathogen are necessary for successful treatment of pulmonary infections.[93-97] The concept of a blood-bronchus barrier, analogous but dissimilar to the blood-brain-barrier, has been used to assess the characteristics of drug penetration into pulmonary secretions.[93] The ability of a drug to penetrate into respiratory secretions depends upon multiple physicochemical factors including molecular size, lipid solubility, and the degree of ionization at serum and biologic fluid pH. Studies performed in animals and CF patients suggest that larger molecular size may favor the accumulation of drugs into bronchial secretions.[98-100] This finding is in contrast to data on drug penetration into other physiologic compartments such as the cerebrospinal fluid,[101] and may be a result of trapping lower molecular weight compounds in mucin pores.[93,96,98,100,102] The

Table 5. Pharmacokinetic differences of selected drugs in CF patients compared to unaffected control subjects

| Pharmacokinetic Parameter Estimates | Drug | Values Compared to Unaffected Controls |
|---|---|---|
| Bioavailability | Chloramphenicol | Decreased |
| | Ciprofloxacin | No Difference |
| Volume of Distribution | Aminoglycosides* | Increased |
| | Cloxacillin | Increased |
| | Azlocillin | Increased |
| | Piperacillin | Increased |
| | Ceftazidime | Increased |
| | Theophylline | Increased |
| | Cimetidine | Increased |
| Protein Binding | Cloxacillin | No Difference |
| | Dioloxacilin | No Difference |
| | Ceftazidime | No Difference |
| | Gentamicin | No Difference |
| | Theophylline | Decreased |
| Body Clearance | Aminoglycosides | Increased |
| | Cloxacillin | Increased |
| | Azlocillin | Increased |
| | Piperacillin | Increased |
| | Ceftazidime | Increased |
| | Theophylline | Increased |
| | Trimethoprim | Increased |
| | Sulfamethoxazole | Increased |
| | Cimetidine | Increased |
| | Ciprofloxacin | No Difference |

\* Gentamicin, tobramycin, amikacin
Adapted from Blumer et al.[83]

rate at which a drug accumulates in respiratory secretions also appears to be an important factor in determining clinical efficacy.[97] In addition, the unionized and more lipid soluble form of a drug favors tissue penetration.[101] The pH of infected bronchi is often more acidic than normal tissue and blood,[103,104] and may also influence the local accumulation of drug. Less well studied is the influence of drug protein binding on the rate and amount of drug penetration into respiratory secretions. Since the degree of protein binding influences the ability of a drug to cross membranes, a

**Table 6.** Controlled pharmacokinetic evaluation of ciprofloxacin in CF patients

| Pharmacokinetic Parameter | Specific Controlled Study | | | |
|---|---|---|---|---|
| | Bender et al[84] | | LeBel et al[85] | |
| | CF | Control | CF | Control |
| No. of subjects studied | 7 | 11 | 11 | 12 |
| Ka (hr$^l$) | — | — | 1.1 (0.5)* | 1.8 (1.3) |
| T$_{1/2}$ (hr) | 5.1 (2) | 4.4 (0.8) | 2.6 (1)* | 3.9 (1) |
| Cl/F (l/hr) | — | — | 49.7 (17)$^\dagger$ | 54.5 (15) |
| Cl$_R$ (l/hr) | 17 (10)$^\dagger$ | 14 (0.7)$^\dagger$ | 28.4 (10)$^\dagger$ | 23.8 (8) |
| Vdss (l/kg) | — | — | 2.1 (0.8)* | 3.8 (0.9) |
| C$_{max}$ (mg/l) | 5.6 (2.4) | 3.9 (0.9) | 2.8 (0.6) | 2.3 (0.8) |
| T$_{max}$ (hr) | 1.9 (1) | 1.1 (0.4) | 1.6 (0.6) | 1.3 (0.5) |
| Dose (mg) | 1000 | 1000 | 500 | 500 |
| Fe (% dose) | 41 (9) | 35 (9) | | |
| Assay used | microbiologic | | HPLC | HPLC |
| Shwachman score$^\ddagger$ | — | — | 72 (14) | — |
| Hospitalized | yes | — | No | — |
| Patient age (yrs) | — | — | 21 (2) | 22 (2) |

***continued***

similar relationship would be expected within the lung.[93-97,105] These concepts relative to overall drug penetration into respiratory secretions have lead to the clinical practice of more frequent dosing with certain antibiotics (eg, aminoglycosides and β-lactams) to achieve high peak serum concentrations on the assumption that higher (and possibly more effective) biologic fluid concentrations of the drug will be achieved.[97,102,106-108] Substantial clinical experience supports this practice for treating pulmonary infections with certain antibiotics, although more data are needed to describe the relationships between these variables and clinical response.[97,102,106-108]

Prior to the availability of newer β-lactam and fluoroquinolone antibiotics possessing consistent, potent activity against multiple gram-negative pathogens including *Ps. aeruginosa,* the administration of antibiotics via aerosol or direct endotracheal instillation was promoted by some investigators.[109-111] This method of drug administration is an attempt to provide increased "topical" concentrations of antibiotics which do not appear to penetrate respiratory secretions effectively, while reducing the likelihood of systemic toxicity. In addition, greater local concentrations of antibiotics, particularly the polymyxins and aminoglycosides, are believed to partially overcome

## Table 6. *Continued*

| Pharmacokinetic Parameter | Davis et al[86] | | Reed et al[87] | |
|---|---|---|---|---|
| | CF | Control | CF | Control |
| No. of subjects studied | 12 | 12 | 6 | 6 |
| Ka (hr[l]) | 0.9 (0.4) | 1.9 (1) | 1.3 (0.9) | 1.8 (1.8) |
| $T_{1/2}$ (hr) | 4.7 (0.8) | 5.2 (0.8) | 4.5 (1) | 4.8 (0.8) |
| Cl/F (l/hr) | 44 (16) | 52 (28) | 27.3 (2.5)[‡] | 30.5 (4.5)[‡] |
| $Cl_R$ (l/hr) | 14 (6) | 17 (5) | 5.7 (1.9)[‡] | 5.1 (2.4)[‡] |
| Vdss (l/kg) | 2.9 (0.8) | 2.4 (0.4) | 2.8 (0.5) | 3.2 (0.6) |
| $C_{max}$ (mg/l) | 3.2 (1) | 3.3 (1.3) | 4.7 (1.7) | 3.8 (0.7) |
| $T_{max}$ (hr) | 2.2 (0.9) | 1.5 (0.9) | 2.3 (0.6) | 1.3 (0.4) |
| Dose (mg) | 750 | 750 | — | — |
| Fe (% dose) | — | — | 42 (7.9) | 39 (5.1) |
| Assay used | HPLC | HPLC | HPLC | HPLC |
| Shwachman score[‡] | 55 | — | 74 (11) | — |
| Hospitalized | No | — | No | — |
| Patient age (yrs) | 18-34 | 23-32 | 18-25 | 20-28 |

\* Statistically significant (p<0.01) compared with control.
† mL/min/kg
‡ From Shwachman and Kulczycki.[88]
 Ka = absorption rate constant, $T_{1/2}$ = elimination half-life, Cl/F = body clearance/bioavailability, $Cl_R$ = renal clearance, Vdss = volume of distribution at steady state, $C_{max}$ = maximum serum ciprofloxacin concentration, $T_{max}$ = time to maximum serum ciprofloxacin concentration, Fe (% dose) = percent of drug dose excreted in the urine over the sample collection period

the substantial decrease in antibiotic bioactivity observed when these agents interact with purulent material present in infectious foci.[15,30,98-100,112-117] Despite these potential theoretical advantages, the role of antibiotic aerosols or direct endotracheal instillation in clinical practice remains ill-defined.[118-120]

The adverse influence of cystic fibrosis sputum on the bioactivity of certain antibiotics further complicates an already challenging therapeutic problem.[100,113,114,116] Sputum from CF patients produces disease-induced alterations in drug pharmacokinetics and pharmacodynamics. Mendelman et al[100] and Levy et al[116] have meticulously evaluated and described the antagonism of aminoglycoside antibacterial bioactivity by CF sputum. These data serve as a foundation, but can only partially explain the inability to sterilize CF sputum despite prolonged (2-4+ weeks) high-dose antibiotic therapy. Preliminary data[121] with ciprofloxacin and ceftazidime (which support previous data with carbenicillin)[114] suggest that these agents are less sensitive to the antagonistic effects of CF sputum than polymyxins[114] and aminoglycoside[100,116] antibiotics. This apparent adverse effect of CF sputum on aminoglycoside antibiotics may also be a result of the mucoid slime coating of certain bacteria. The negatively charged exopolysaccharide may retard the diffusion of positively charged aminoglycosides, preventing them from reaching their target receptors.[98,99,102,115,117] Diffusion of neutral or negatively charged β-lactam and fluoroquinolone antibiotics does not appear to be affected.[115,121] Moreover, the ability of mucoid *Ps. aeruginosa* to aggregate into microcolonies in the respiratory tract of CF patients and become embedded within the exopolysaccharide layer(s) of certain bacteria would be expected to further antagonize the activity of antibiotics.[28-30]

## ANTIMICROBIAL THERAPY OF ACUTE PULMONARY EXACERBATIONS OF CYSTIC FIBROSIS

Antimicrobial therapy for acute pulmonary exacerbations of CF remains a hotly debated issue among clinicians who care for these patients.[4,5,12-14,122] The logic of initiating antimicrobial therapy specifically directed against bacteria that reside chronically in a normally sterile anatomic site (the lung) appears obvious. Many believe that the improved patient survival witnessed over the past two decades is in large part due to advances in antimicrobial therapy, methods of administering these agents (ie, increased understanding of pharmacokinetics), and more aggressive therapeutic regimens (ie, larger drug doses and prolonged [2 week] treatment courses).[4,5] Numerous clinical trials, both controlled and uncontrolled, have evaluated the role of various antibiotics and combination regimens in CF, particularly those with antibacterial activity against *Pseudomonas* spp.[4,5,123-126] The prevalence of this perspective over the past two decades has served as the foundation supporting the large number of varying and often times uncontrolled evaluations of the plethora of available antibiotics.[123-139] Despite this wealth of published experience, no data exist to indicate an absolute therapeutic superiority of one antibiotic regimen over another. At present, other differences among therapies including cost, safety, and ease of drug administration are often used to favor one drug regimen over another. Difficulties in interpreting the clinical trial literature on antibiotic therapy in CF result from: (1) heterogeneity in the patient population and disease severity; (2) lack of a uniform definition of pulmonary exacerbation; (3) small numbers of patients in many studies; and (4) relative insensitivity of the outcome indicators employed.[4,41,47] Interpretation is further complicated by the fact that bacteria are rarely, if ever, eradicated from the lower respiratory tract of these patients, and that no correlation has been identified among: (1) clinical and bacteriologic outcomes; (2) changes in sputum colony counts; (3) initial pathogen susceptibility patterns; or (4) the emergence of pathogen resistance during therapy, regardless of the therapeutic regimen employed.

Very few well-designed, controlled studies have evaluated the role of intensive antipseudomonal therapy in the treatment of CF patents experiencing an acute pulmonary exacerbation of their disease. Since 1980, four studies have been reported; two were placebo-controlled[140,141] and in two the non-antipseudomonal antibiotic treatment arm consisted of cloxacillin[142] or oxacillin.[143] Overall, antipseudomonal antibiotic therapy (ie, tobramycin or ceftazidime monotherapy versus placebo; carbenicillin versus cloxacillin; and carbenicillin/oxacillin/sisomicin versus oxacillin) was found to be beneficial in two studies,[140,143] whereas no difference was found in the other two studies.[141,142] The discrepancy in the conclusions from these studies has led to confusion among clinicians and patients, and has served to heighten controversy regarding the desirability and/or effectiveness of antibiotic therapy.[133] In a critical evaluation of the design and mechanics of these studies, Levy[41] has offered some possible explanations for the disparate findings, including: (1) differences in illness severity among study subjects; (2) use of an antistaphylococcal antibiotic as a "placebo"; (3) suboptimal antibiotic dosage in at least one study; and (4) differences in outcome indicators. In addition, these study results should be interpreted relative to the boundaries of their study design; ie, immediate results following a single therapeutic intervention. However, CF is a chronic progressive disorder, and these studies offer no information relative to the long-term effects of such an antibiotic treatment plan, or the possible effects of chronically treating pulmonary exacerbations without antibiotics.[4] Most authorities continue to believe that antipseudomonal antibiotics are an important component of any therapeutic regimen for CF patients.

The ideal antibiotic regimen for the in-hospital treatment of an acute pulmonary exacerbation of CF has not yet been identified. However, most CF treatment centers use one of the following regimens as primary therapy: (1) an aminoglycoside (eg, tobramycin or amikacin) combined with a β-lactam (eg, mezlocillin, piperacillin, or ticarcillin-clavulanate); (2) a cephalosporin (eg, ceftazidime or cefsulodin); or (3) ceftazidime monotherapy.[133] Other centers often employ three drugs; an aminoglycoside, a β-lactam, and an antistaphylococcal antibiotic (eg, nafcillin or oxacillin) or clindamycin. The decision to use specific antibiotics and in particular combinations is most often directed by the results of sputum culture and sensitivity[5,12,14] and/or the patient's clinical response to a previous antibiotic regimen. Antibiotic therapy is usually continued for 2 to 3 weeks depending on the clinical response. Due to the disease-influenced (altered) pharmacokinetics described for most antibiotics in CF (Table 5), current dosage recommendations suggest that larger doses be administered more frequently to CF patients than to unaffected individuals. Although such a therapeutic approach appears justified, very little data exist to support this practice. In a recent randomized, double-blind evaluation of three different daily doses of ceftazidime monotherapy in hospitalized CF patients,[129] one group was unable to identify any greater benefit from high-dose versus conventional dose ceftazidime (ie, 150 mg/kg/day). Similar findings were reported by Strandvik.[107]

More recently, the antibiotic treatment of CF patients has focused on the new fluoroquinolone class of antibiotics. The first clinically important 4-quinolone antibiotic, nalidixic acid, was introduced in 1963. However, unfavorable pharmacokinetic characteristics combined with patient intolerance and frequent pathogen resistance precluded the use of nalidixic acid for infections outside the urinary tract.[144] Nevertheless, renewed interest in this class of compounds helped bolster the development and release of several new fluoroquinolone antibiotics. These newer agents possess favorable pharmacokinetic characteristics with a broadened spectrum of antibacterial activity combined with a dramatic reduction in the development of pathogen resistance as compared with previous analogues.[144] Ciprofloxacin represents the first commercially available orally administered fluoroquinolone that possesses consistent potent in vitro activity against *Ps. aeruginosa* (Table 3). These pharmacologic characteristics suggest that ciprofloxacin as well as some of the newer congeners would be useful both in ambulatory and hospital care of patients experiencing an acute pulmonary exacerbation of CF.[134-139,145,146] A number of clinical evaluations have been performed with this drug in CF patients.[145] As with other antibiotic evaluations in CF patients, study populations differed widely relative to patient characteristics, disease duration and severity, and criteria used to determine therapeutic response. Nevertheless, pooling of available published experience has revealed a clear positive response in patients receiving oral ciprofloxacin. Most importantly, the magnitude of favorable therapeutic response in these studies was similar to that observed in patients receiving combination antibiotic therapy (ie, aminoglycoside and azlocillin).[145] Furthermore, available biologic fluid distribution data have demonstrated consistent and impressive sputum penetration of ciprofloxacin following 750 and 1000 mg oral doses.[85,87,135]

The pharmacologic and clinical data presented above have fostered tremendous interest in ciprofloxacin and in future fluoroquinolone analogues for the treatment of CF patients. This interest, however, is tempered by concern regarding possible fluoroquinolone-induced joint damage which has restricted the use of these agents to patients whose skeletal growth is complete (ie, patients >18 years of age).[144,145] Preliminary toxicity studies using rodent and juvenile canine models have shown destructive lesions of growing cartilage following the administration of these agents.[144-148] Reports of arthropathy in teenage CF patients have appeared in the literature, further suggesting caution in the use of this class of compounds in younger CF patients.[146,149] A recently held workshop on ciprofloxacin use in CF stressed the need for critical controlled evaluations of this compound in younger patients.[146] From this workshop, guidelines for the use of these agents in CF patients were generated and include the following:

1. Ciprofloxacin monotherapy may be a very useful alternative to parenteral antibiotic therapy for CF patients ≥18 years of age.

2. Information regarding the efficacy and safety of ciprofloxacin in patients <18 years of age is limited, and thus its use in these patients should be considered investigational.

3. Data currently available suggest that the duration of ciprofloxacin therapy be limited to 2-4 weeks. Repeated courses may be appropriate in patients with advanced disease.

4. No data are available to address the appropriateness or usefulness of ciprofloxacin as a prophylactic agent, either intermittently or on a continuous basis, in patients with stable disease or mild pulmonary exacerbations.

## EVALUATION OF ANTIBIOTIC THERAPY

Collectively, CF patients represent a very heterogenous group. The extent of exocrine pancreatic insufficiency and lung involvement varies widely from patient to patient. This heterogeneity is partially responsible for the large variation observed in the clinical course of patients, their clinical response to therapeutic intervention, and in the data reported from studies of CF patients. Although investigators have made concerted efforts to group patients based upon similar laboratory data and/or by similar clinical scores (eg, NIH score, Shwachman-Kulczycki score, etc.), heterogeneity among reported study populations remains high.[88,150-155] The evaluation of antibiotic efficacy in hospitalized CF patients is difficult and further confounded by the fact that multiple therapeutic modalities are employed, with no consistent method for assessment of efficacy. Investigators have used a number of subjective and objective parameters to sequentially monitor a patient's treatment course in an attempt to quantitate changes in clinical status.[41,48,62,121] Some of these parameters are outlined in Table 7.[156] Despite the clinical availability/utility of these parameters and their apparent pathophysiologic relationship(s), none has been shown to discriminate objectively between various therapeutic interventions. In summary, an understanding of the limitations of currently employed pharmacodynamic criteria is necessary in order to make a critical interpretation of the available data.

Table 7. Parameters commonly employed to evaluate the efficacy of therapeutic intervention in CF patients

CLINICAL PARAMETERS*
    Nutritional history/body weight
    Resting/sleeping respiratory rate
    Body temperature
    Chest auscultation
    Pulmonary function testing
    Chest roentgenogram

SPUTUM PARAMETERS[†]
***Composition***
    Proteins (albumin/transferrin)
    DNA
    Electrolytes (potassium/chloride)

***Microbiology/Volume***
    Descriptive morphotype
    Colony count
    MIC/MBC

BIOCHEMICAL PARAMETERS
    White blood cell count (differential)
    Erythrocyte sedimentation rate
    Arterial blood gas

CLINICAL SCORES[‡]
    Shwachman and Kulczycki [88]
    Taussig et al [150]
    Brasfield et al [151]
    Others

* Evaluation usually determined as change in parameter relative to change in therapeutic intervention.
† Parameter change frequently highly variable.
‡ Composites of certain above parameters.
DNA = deoxyribonucleic acid
MIC = minimum inhibitory concentration
MBC = minimum bactericidal concentration
Adapted from Kearns and Reed.[156]

# REFERENCES

1. Wainwright BJ, Scambler PJ, Schmidtke J, Watson EA, Law HY: Localization of cystic fibrosis locus to human chromosome, 7cen-q22. Nature 1985;318:384-385.

2. Welsh MJ, Fick RB: Cystic fibrosis. J. Clin Invest 1987;80:1523-1526.

3. Kane K: Cystic fibrosis: recent advances in genetics and molecular biology. Ann Clin Lab Sci 1988;18:289-296.

4. Wood RE, Leigh MW: What is a "pulmonary exacerbation" in cystic fibrosis? (editorial). J Pediatr 1987;111:841-842.

5. Wood RE, Boat TF, Doershuk CF: State of the art: cystic fibrosis. Am Rev Resp Dis 1976;113:833-878.

6. Anderson DH: Cystic fibrosis of the pancreas and its relation to celiac disease: a clinical and pathologic study. Am J Dis Child 1938;56:344-399.

7. Colten HR: Genetics of cystic fibrosis (editorial). J Pediatr 1986;109:154-155.

8. Wright SE, Morton NE: Genetic studies on cystic fibrosis in Hawaii. Am J Hum Genet 1968;20:157-169.

9. Klinger KW: Genetics of cystic fibrosis. Semin Resp Med 1985;6:243-251.

10. Welsh MJ: Electrolyte transport by airway epithelia. Physiol Rev 1987;67:1143-1184.

11. Kuzemko JA: Evolution of lung disease in cystic fibrosis. Lancet 1983;1:448-449.

12. Marks MI: The pathogenesis and treatment of pulmonary infections in patients with cystic fibrosis. J Pediatr 1981;98:173-179.

13. Davis PB: Pathophysiology of pulmonary disease in cystic fibrosis. Semin Resp Med 1985;6:261-270.

14. Thomassen MJ, Demko CA, Doershuk CF: Cystic fibrosis: a review of pulmonary infections and interventions. Pediatr Pulmonol 1987;3:334-351.

15. Hoiby N: Haemophilus influenzae, Staphylococcus aureus, Pseudomonas cepacia, Pseudomonas aeruginosa in patients with cystic fibrosis. Chest 1988;94(suppl);97S-102S.

16. Hoiby N: Microbiology of lung infections in cystic fibrosis patients. Acta Paediatr Scand 1982;301(suppl C): 33-54.

17. Klinger JD, Thomassen MJ: Occurrence and antimicrobial susceptibility of gram-negative nonfermentative bacilli in cystic fibrosis patients. Diagn Microbiol Infect Dis 3 1985;149-158.

18. Peterson NT, Hoiby N, Mordhorst CH, Lind K, Flensborg EW, Bruun B: Respiratory infections in cystic fibrosis patients caused by virus, chlamydia and mycoplasma: possible synergism with Pseudomonas aeruginosa. Acta Paediatr Scand 1981;70:623-628.

19. Wang EEL, Prober CG, Manson B, Corey M, Levinson H: Association of respiratory viral infections with pulmonary deterioration in patients with cystic fibrosis. N Engl J Med 1984;311:1653-1658.

20. Mearns MB, Hunt GH, Rushworth R: Bacterial flora of respiratory tract in patients with cystic fibrosis, 1950-1971. Arch Dis Child 1972;47:902-927.

21. May JR, Herrick NC, Thompson D: Bacterial infection in cystic fibrosis. Arch Dis Child 1972;47:908-912.

167

22. Thomassen MJ, Demko CA, Boxerbaum B, Stern RC, Kuchenbrod PJ: Multiple isolates of Pseudomonas aeruginosa with differing antimicrobial susceptibility patterns from patients with cystic fibrosis. J Infect Dis 1979;140:873-880.

23. Doggett RG: Incidence of mucoid Pseudomonas aeruginosa from clinical sources. Appl Microbiol 1969;18:936-937.

24. Doggett RG, Harrison GM, Stillwell RN, Walles ES: An atypical Pseudomonas aeruginosa associated with cystic fibrosis of the pancreas. J Pediatr 1966;68:215-221.

25. Miller RV, Rubero VJR: Mucoid conversion by phages of Pseudomonas aeruginosa strains from patients with cystic fibrosis sera. J Clin Microbiol 1984;19:717-719.

26. Speert DP, Lauton D, Mutharia LM: Antibody to Pseudomonas aeruginosa mucoid exopolysaccharide and to sodium alginate in cystic fibrosis sera. Pediatr Res 1984; 18:431-433.

27. Ramphal R, Pier GB: Role of Pseudomonas aeruginosa mucoid exopolysaccharide in adherence to tracheal cells. Infect Immunol 1985;47:1-4.

28. Lam J, Chan R, Lam K, Costerton JW: Production of mucoid microcolonies by Pseudomonas aeruginosa within infected lungs in cystic fibrosis. Infect Immunol 1980;28:546-556.

29. Costerton JW, Lam J, Lam K, Chan R: The role of the microcolony mode of growth in the pathogenesis of Pseudomonas aeruginosa infections. Rev Infect Dis 1983;5(suppl 5):S867-S873.

30. Govan JRW, Harris GS: Pseudomonas aeruginosa and cystic fibrosis: unusual bacterial adaptation and pathogenesis. Microbiol Sci 1986;3:302-308.

31. Govan JRW, Fyfe JAM, McMillan C: The instability of mucoid Pseudomonas: fluctuation test and improved stability of the mucoid form in shaken culture. J Gen Microbiol 1979;110:229-232.

32. Macone AB, Pier GB, Pennington JE, Matthews WJ Jr, Goldman DA: Mucoid Escherichia coli cystic fibrosis. New Engl J Med 1981;304:1445-1449.

33. Kelly NM, Falkiner FR, Keane CT, Fitzgerald MX, Tempany E: Mucoid gram-negative bacilli in cystic fibrosis (letter). Lancet 1983;1:705.

34. Isles A, Maclusky I, Corey M, Gold R, Prober C, Fleming P, Levison H: Pseudomonas cepacia infection in cystic fibrosis: an emerging problem. J Pediatr 1984;104:206-210.

35. Thomassen MJ, Demko CA, Klinger JD, Stern RC: Pseudomonas cepacia colonization among patients with cystic fibrosis. Am Rev Resp Dis 1985;131:791-796.

36. Goldman DA, Klinger JD: Pseudomonas cepacia: biology, mechanisms of virulence, epidemiology. J Pediatr 1986;108(suppl):806-812.

37. Thomassen MJ, Demko CA, Doershuk CF, Stern RC, Klinger JD: Pseudomonas cepacia: decrease in colonization in cystic fibrosis patients. Am Rev Resp Dis 1986; 134:669-671.

38. Schiotz PO: Systemic and mucosal immunity and non-specific defense mechanisms in cystic fibrosis. Acta Paediatr Scand 1982;301(suppl):55-62.

39. Doring G, Albus A, Hoiby N: Immunologic aspects of cystic fibrosis. Chest 1988; 94(suppl):S109S-S114S.

40. Thomassen MJ, Demko CA, Wood RE, Tandler B, Dearborn D, Boxerbaum B, Kuchenbrod PJ: Ultrastructure and function of alveolar macrophages from cystic fibrosis patients. Pediatr Res 1980;14:715-721.

41. Levy J: Antibiotic therapy in cystic fibrosis: Evaluation of efficacy. Chest 1988; 94(suppl):S150-S154.

42. Cho YW, Aviado PM: Pancreatic enzyme preparations, with special reference to enterically coated microspheres of pancrelipase. J Clin Pharmacol 1981;21:224-237.

43. Niessen KH, Konig J, Molitor M, Neef B: Studies on the quality of pancreatic preparations: Enzyme content, prospective bioavailability, bile acid pattern and contamination with purines. Eur J Pediatr 1983;141:23-29.

44. Prandota J: Drug disposition in cystic fibrosis: Progress in understanding pathophysiology and pharmacokinetics. Pediatr Infect Dis J 1986;6:1111-1126.

45. de Groot R, Smith AL: Antibiotic pharmacokinetics in cystic fibrosis: Differences and clinical significance. Clin Pharmacokinet 1987;13:228-253.

46. Prandota J: Clinical pharmacology of antibiotics and other drugs in cystic fibrosis. Drugs 1988;35:542-578.

47. Kenbijn KF: Conference summary. Chest 1988;94(suppl):S167-S169.

48. Smith AL, Redding G, Doershuk C, Goldman D, Gore E, Hilman B, Marks, M, Moss R, Ramsey B, Rubio T, Schwartz RH, Thomassen MJ, Williams-Warren J, Weber A, Wilmott RW, Wilson HD, Yogev R: Sputum changes associated with therapy for endobronchial exacerbation in cystic fibrosis. J Pediatr 1988;112:547-554.

49. Thomassen MJ, Klinger JD, Badger SJ, van Heeckeren DW, Stern RC: Cultures of thoracotomy specimens confirm usefulness of sputum cultures in cystic fibrosis. J Pediatr 1984;104:352-356.

50. Irvin RT, Govan JWR, Fyfe JAM, Costerton JW: Heterogeneity of antibiotic resistance in mucoid isolates of Pseudomonas aeruginosa obtained from cystic fibrosis patients. Role of outer membrane proteins. Antimicrob Agents Chemother 1981;19:1056-1063.

51. McNeil WF, John JF Jr, Twitty JA: Aminoglycoside resistance in Pseudomonas aeruginosa isolated from cystic fibrosis patients. Am J Clin Pathol 1984;81:742-747.

52. Klinger JD, Aronoff SC: In vitro activity of ciprofloxacin and other antibacterial agents against Pseudomonas aeruginosa and Pseudomonas cepacia from cystic fibrosis patients. J Antimicrob Chemother 1985;15:679-684.

53. Wolfson JS, Hooper DC: The fluroquinolones: structures, mechanisms of action and resistance, and spectra of activity in vitro. Antimicrob Agents Chemother 1985;28:581-586.

54. Hooper DC, Wolfson JS: The fluroquinolones: pharmacology, clinical uses and toxicities in humans. Antimicrob Agents Chemother 1985;28:716-721.

55. Stutman HR: Summary of a workshop on ciprofloxacin use in patients with cystic fibrosis. Pediatr Infect Dis J 1987;6:932-935.

56. Jusko WJ, Mosovich LL, Gerbracht LM, Mattar ME, Yaffe SJ: Enhanced renal excretion of dicloxacillin in patients with cystic fibrosis. Pediatrics 1975;56:1038-1044.

57. Yaffe SJ, Gerbracht LM, Mosovich LL, Mattar ME, Danish M, Jusko WJ: Pharmacokinetics of methicillin in patients with cystic fibrosis. J Infect Dis 1977;135:828-831.

58. Spino M, Chai RP, Isles AF, Theissen JJ, Tesore A, Gold R, MacLeod SM: Cloxacillin absorption and disposition in cystic fibrosis. J Pediatr 1984;105:829-835.

59. Bosso JA, Saxon BA, Herbst JJ, Matsen JM: Azlocillin pharmacokinetics in patients with cystic fibrosis. Antimicrob Agents Chemother 1984;25:630-632.

60. Jacobs RF, Trang JM, Kearns GL, Warren RH, Brown AL, Underwood FL, Kluza RB: Ticarcillin/clavulanic acid pharmacokinetics in children and young adults with cystic fibrosis. J Pediatr 1985;106:1001-1007.

61. Reed MD, Stern RC, Myers CM, Klinger JD, Yamashita TS, Blumer JL: Therapeutic evaluation of piperacillin for acute pulmonary exacerbations in cystic fibrosis. Pediatr Pulmonol 1987;3:101-109.

62. Kercsmar CM, Stern RC, Reed MD, Myers CM, Murdell D, Blumer JL: Ceftazidime in cystic fibrosis: pharmacokinetic and therapeutic response. J Antimicrob Chemother 1983;12(suppl A):289-295.

63. Strandvik B, Malmborg AS, Alfredson H, Ericsson A: Clinical results and pharmacokinetics of ceftazidime treatment in patients with cystic fibrosis. J Antimicrob Chemother 1983;12(suppl A):283-287.

64. Leeder JS, Spino M, Isles AF, Tesoro AM, Gold R, MacLeod SM: Ceftazidime disposition in acute and stable cystic fibrosis. Clin Pharmacol Ther 1984;36:355-362.

65. Nahata MC, Lubin AH, Visconti JA: Cephalexin pharmacokinetics in patients with cystic fibrosis. Dev Pharmacol Ther 1984;7:221-228.

66. Arvidsson A, Alván G, Strandvik B: Difference in renal handling of cefsulodin between patients with cystic fibrosis and normal subjects. Acta Paediatr Scand 1983;72:293-294.

67. Reed MD, Stern RC, Yamashita TS, Ackers I, Myers CM, Blumer JL: Single dose pharmacokinetics of cefsulodin in patients with cystic fibrosis. Antimicrob Agents Chemother 1984;25:579-581.

68. Hedman A, Adan-Abdi Y, Alván G, Strandvik B, Arvidsson A: Influence of the glomerular filtration rate on renal clearance of ceftazidime in cystic fibrosis. Clin Pharmacokinet 1988;15:57-65.

69. Lietman PS: Pharmacokinetics of antimicrobial drugs in cystic fibrosis: β-lactam antibiotics. Chest 1988;94(suppl):S115-S119.

70. Kearns GL, Hilman BC, Wilson JT: Dosing implications of altered gentamicin disposition in patients with cystic fibrosis. J Pediatr 1982;100:312-318.

71. Levy J, Smith AL, Koup JR, Williams-Warren J, Ramsey B: Disposition of tobramycin in patients with cystic fibrosis: a prospective controlled study. J Pediatr 1984;105:117-124.

72. Vogelstein B, Kowarski AA, Lietman PS: The pharmacokinetics of amikacin in children. J Pediatr 1977;91:333-339.

73. Michalsen H, Bergen T: Pharmacokinetics of netilmicin in children with and without cystic fibrosis. Antimicrob Agents Chemother 1981;19:1029-1031.

74. Hendeles L, Iafrate RP, Stillwell PC, Mangos JA: Individualizing gentamicin dosage in patients with cystic fibrosis: limitations to pharmacokinetic approach. J Pediatr 1987;110:303-310.

75. Horrevorts AM, Driessen OMJ, Michel MF, Kerrebijn KF: Pharmacokinetics of antimicrobial drugs in cystic fibrosis: aminoglycoside antibiotics. Chest 1988;94 (suppl): S120-S125.

76. Reed MD, Stern RC, Bertino JS Jr, Myers CM, Yamashita TS, Blumer JL: Dosing implications of rapid elimination of trimethoprim-sulfamethoxazole in patients with cystic fibrosis. J Pediatr 1984;104:303-307.

77. Ziemniak JA, Assael BM, Padoan R, Schentag JJ: The bioavailability and pharmacokinetics of cimetidine and its metabolites in juvenile cystic fibrosis: age related differences as compared to adults. Eur J Clin Pharmacol 1984;26:183-189.

78. Isles AF, Spino M, Tabachnik E, Levison H, Theissen J, MacLeod S: Theophylline disposition in cystic fibrosis. Am Rev Resp Dis 1983;127:417-421.

79. Knoppert DC, Spino M, Beck R, Thiessen JJ, MacLeod SM: Cystic fibrosis: enhanced theophylline metabolism may be linked to the disease. Clin Pharmacol Ther 1988;44:254-264.

80. Alván G, Beerman B, Hjelte L, Lind M, Lindholm A, Strandvik B: Increased nonrenal clearance and increased diuretic efficacy of furosemide in cystic fibrosis. Clin Pharmacol Ther 1988;44:436-441.

81. Koren G, Weizman Z, Forstner G, MacLeod SM, Durie PR: Altered PABA pharmacokinetics in cystic fibrosis: implications for bentiromide test. Digest Dis Sci 1985;30:928-932.

82. Vaisman N, Koren G, Goldstein D, Canny G, Tan YK, Soldin S, Pencharz P: Pharmacokinetics of inhaled salbutamol in patients with cystic fibrosis versus healthy young adults. J Pediatr 1987;111:914-917.

83. Blumer JL, Stern RC, Yamashita TS, Myers CM, Reed MD: Cephalosporin therapeutics in cystic fibrosis. J Pediatr 1986;108(suppl):854-860.

84. Bender SW, Dalhoff A, Shah PM, Strehl H, Posselt HG: Ciprofloxacin pharmacokinetics in patients with cystic fibrosis. Infection 1986;14:17-21.

85. LeBel M, Bergeron MG, Vallée F, Fiset C, Chasse G, Bigonesse P, Rivard G: Pharmacokinetics and pharmacodynamics of ciprofloxacin in cystic fibrosis patients. Antimicrob Agents Chemother 1986;30:260-266.

86. Davis RL, Koup JR, Williams-Warren J, Weber A, Heggen L, Stempel D, Smith AL: Pharmacokinetics of ciprofloxacin in cystic fibrosis. Antimicrob Agents Chemother 1987;31:915-919.

87. Reed MD, Stern RC, Myers CM, Yamashita TS, Blumer JL: Lack of unique ciprofloxacin pharmacokinetics in patients with cystic fibrosis. J Clin Pharmacol 1988; 28:691-699.

88. Shwachman H, Kulczycki LL: Long-term study of 105 patients with cystic fibrosis. Am J Dis Child 1958;96:6-15.

89. Berg U, Kusoffsky E, Strandvik B: Renal function in cystic fibrosis with special reference to the renal sodium handling. Acta Paediatr Scand 1982;71:833-838.

90. Michalsen H, Monn E, Bergen T, Churgand J, Johannessen JV: Renal biopsies in cystic fibrosis. Pathol Res Pract 1984;178:261-267.

91. Spino M, Chai RP, Isles AF, Balfe JW, Brown RG, Thiessen JJ, MacLeod SM: Assessment of glomerular filtration rate and effective renal plasma flow in cystic fibrosis. J Pediatr 1985;107:64-70.

92. Kearns GL, Mallory GB Jr, Crom WR: Use of model substrates to evaluate hepatic drug clearance in cystic fibrosis. Clin Res 1988;36:55A.

93. Pennington JE: Penetration of antibiotics into respiratory secretions. Rev Infect Dis 1981;3:67-73.

94. Schentag JJ, Gengo FM: Principles of antibiotic tissue penetration and guidelines for pharmacokinetic analysis. Med Clin North Am 1982;66:39-49.

95. Vogelman B, Craig WA: Kinetics of antimicrobial activity. J Pediatr 1996; 108(suppl): 835-840.

96. Smith BR, LeFrock JL: Bronchial tree penetration of antibiotics. Chest 1983;83:904-908.

97. Drusano GL: Role of pharmacokinetics in the outcome of infections. Antimicrob Agents Chemother 1988;32:289-297.

98. Saggers BA, Lawson D: Some observations on the penetration of antibiotics through mucous in vitro. J Clin Pathol 1966;19:313-317.

99. Saggers BA, Lawson D: In vitro penetration of antibiotics into sputum in cystic fibrosis. Arch Dis Child 1968;43:404-409.

100. Mendelman PM, Smith AL, Levy J, Weber A, Ramsey B, Davis RL: Aminoglycoside penetration, inactivation and efficacy in cystic fibrosis sputum. Am Rev Resp Dis 1985; 132:761-765.

101. Reed MD: Current concepts in clinical therapeutics: bacterial meningitis in infants and children. Clin Pharm 1986;5:798-809.

102. Nichols WW, Dorrington SM, Slack MPE, Walmsley HL: Inhibition of tobramycin diffusion by binding to alginate. Antimicrob Agents Chemother 1988, 32:518-523.

103. Matthews LW, Spector S, Lemm J, Potter JL: Studies on pulmonary secretions I. The overall chemical composition of pulmonary secretions from patients with cystic fibrosis;bronchiectasis and laryngectomy. Am Rev Resp Dis 1963;88:199-204.

104. Bodem CR, Lampton LM, Miller DP, Tarka EF, Everett ED: Endobronchial pH. Relevance to aminoglycoside activity in gram negative bacillary pneumonia. Am Rev Resp Dis 1983, 127:39-41.

105. Wise R: The clinical relevance of protein binding and tissue concentrations in antimicrobial therapy. Clin Pharmacokinet 1986, 11:470-482.

106. LeBel M, Spino M: Pulse dosing versus continuous infusion of antibiotics: pharmacokinetic-pharmacodynamic considerations. Clin Pharmacokinet 1988;14:71-95.

107. Strandvik B: Antibiotic therapy of pulmonary infections in cystic fibrosis: dosage schedules and duration of treatment. Chest 1988;94(suppl):S146-S149.

108. Klastersky J, Thys JP, Mombelli G: Comparative studies of intermittent and continuous administration of aminoglycosides in the treatment of bronchopulmonary infections due to gram-negative bacteria. Rev Infect Dis 1981;3:74-83.

109. Gough PA, Jordans NS: A review of the therapeutic efficacy of aerosolized and endotracheally instilled antibiotics. Pharmacotherapy 1982;2:367-377.

110. Klastersky J, Thys JP: Local antibiotic therapy for bronchopneumonia, in Pennington JE (ed), *Respiratory Infections: Diagnosis and Management*, Raven Press, New York 1983, pp 481-489.

111. Stout SA, Derendorf H: Local treatment of respiratory infections with antibiotics. Drug Intell Clin Pharm 1987;21:322-329.

112. Potter JL, Matthews LW, Spector S, Lemm J: Complex formation between basic antibiotics and deoxyribonucleic acid in human pulmonary secretions. Pediatrics 1965;36: 714-720.

113. Bryant RE, Hammond D: Interaction of purulent material with antibiotics used to treat Pseudomonas infections. Antimicrob Agents Chemother 1974;6:702-707.

114. Davis DS, Bruns WT: Effects of sputum from patients with cystic fibrosis on the activity in vitro of 5 antimicrobial drugs on Pseudomonas aeruginosa. Am Rev Resp Dis 1978; 117:176-178.

115. Slack MPE, Nichols WW: The penetration of antibiotics through sodium alginate and through the exopolysaccharide of a mucoid strain of Pseudomonas aeruginosa. Lancet 1981;2:502-503.

116. Levy J, Smith AL, Kenny MA, Ramsey B, Schoenknecht FD: Bioactivity of gentamicin in purulent sputum from patients with cystic fibrosis or bronchiectasis: comparison with activity in serum. J Infect Dis 1983;148:1069-1076.

117. Costerton JW, Cheng KJ, Geesey GG, Ladd TI, Nickel JC, Dasgupta M, Marrie TJ: Bacterial biofilms in nature and disease. Ann Rev Microbiol 1987;41:435-464.

118. Hodson ME: Antibiotic treatment: aerosol therapy. Chest 1988;94(suppl):S156-S160.

119. Jensen T, Pedersen SS, Garne S, Heilmann C, Hoiby N, Koch C: Colistin inhalation therapy in cystic fibrosis patients with chronic Pseudomonas aeruginosa lung infection. J Antimicrob Chemother 1987;19:831-838.

120. Schaad UB, Wedgwood-Krucko J, Suter S, Kraemer R: Efficacy of inhaled amikacin as adjunct to intravenous combination therapy (ceftazidime and amikacin) in cystic fibrosis. J Pediatr 1987;111:599-605.

121. Reed MD, Goldfarb J, Crenshaw D: Lack of correlation between clinical response and sputum quantitative cultures in patients with cystic fibrosis, abstract 798. Program and abstracts of the 27th Interscience Conference on Antimicrobial Agents and Chemotherapy. New York, October, 1987.

122. Marks MI: Pulmonary infections in patients with cystic fibrosis: where to now? J Pediatr 1986;108:483-485.

123. Boxerbaum B: The art and science of the use of antibiotics in cystic fibrosis. Pediatr Infect Dis 1982;1:381-383.

124. Pines A, Raafat H, Plucinski K: Gentamicin and colistin in chronic purulent bronchial infection. Br Med J 1967;2:543-545.

125. Boxerbaum B, Doershuk CF, Pittman S, Matthews LW: Use of carbenicillin in patients with cystic fibrosis. J Infect Dis 1970;122(suppl):S59-S61.

126. Marks MI, Prentice R, Swarson R, Cotton EK, Eickhoff TC: Carbenicillin and gentamicin: pharmacologic studies in patients with cystic fibrosis and pseudomonas pulmonary infections. J Pediatr 1971;79:822-828.

127. Hoogkamp-Korstanje JAA, vander Laag J: Piperacillin and tobramycin in the treatment of Pseudomonas lung infections in cystic fibrosis. J Antimicrob Chemother 1983;12:175-183.

128. McLaughlin FJ, Matthews WJ Jr, Streider DJ, Sullivan B, Taneja A, Murphy P, Goldman DA: Clinical and bacteriological responses to three antibiotic regimens for acute exacerbations of cystic fibrosis: ticarcillin-tobramycin, azlocillin-tobramycin and azlocillin-placebo. J Infect Dis 1983;147:559-567.

129. Gold R, Overmeyer A, Knie B, Fleming PC, Levison H: Controlled trial of ceftazidime vs. ticarcillin and tobramycin in the treatment of acute respiratory exacerbations in patients with cystic fibrosis. Pediatr Infect Dis 1985;4:172-177.

130. Jackson MA, Kusmiesz H, Shelton S, Prestidge C, Kramer RI, Nelson JD: Comparison of piperacillin vs. ticarcillin plus tobramycin in the treatment of acute pulmonary exacerbations of cystic fibrosis. Pediatr Infect Dis J 1986;5:440-443.

131. Reed MD, Stern RC O'Brien CA, Crenshaw DA, Blumer JL: Randomized double-blind evaluation of ceftazidime dose ranging in hospitalized patients with cystic fibrosis. Antimicrob Agents Chemother 1987;31:698-702.

132. Bosso JA, Block PG: Controlled trial of aztreonam vs. tobramycin and azlocillin for acute pulmonary exacerbations of cystic fibrosis. Pediatr Infect Dis J 1988;7:171-176.

133. Michel BC: Antibacterial therapy in cystic fibrosis: a review of the literature published between 1980 and February 1987. Chest 1988;94(suppl):S129-S140.

134. Smith MJ, Hodson ME, Batten JC: Ciprofloxacin in cystic fibrosis (letter). Lancet 1986;1:1103.

135. Goldfarb J, Stern RC, Reed MD, Yamashita TS, Myers CM, Blumer JL: Ciprofloxacin monotherapy for acute pulmonary exacerbations of cystic fibrosis. Am J Med 1987; 82(suppl 4A): 174-179.

136. Bosso JA, Black PG, Matsen JM: Ciprofloxacin versus tobramycin plus azlocillin in pulmonary exacerbations in adult patients with cystic fibrosis. Am J Med 1987;82(suppl 4A): 180-184.

137. Hodson ME, Roberts CM, Butland RJA, Smith MJ, Batten JC: Oral ciprofloxacin compared with conventional intravenous treatment for Pseudomonas aeruginosa infection in adults with cystic fibrosis. Lancet 1987;1:235-237.

138. Shalit I, Stutman HR, Marks MI, Chartrand SA, Hilman BC: Randomized study of two dosage regimens of ciprofloxacin for treating chronic bronchopulmonary infection in patients with cystic fibrosis. Am J Med 1987;82(suppl 4A):189-195.

139. Rubio TT, Shapiro C: Ciprofloxacin in the treatment of pseudomonas infection in cystic fibrosis patients. J Antimicrob Chemother 1986;18(suppl D):147-152.

140. Wientzen R, Prestidge CB, Kramer RI, McCracken GH, Nelson JD: Acute pulmonary exacerbations in cystic fibrosis: a double-blind trial of tobramycin and placebo therapy. Am J Dis Child 1980;134:1134-1138.

141. Gold R, Carpenter S, Heurter H, Corey M, Levison H: Randomized trial of ceftazidime versus placebo in the management of acute respiratory exacerbations in patients with cystic fibrosis. J Pediatr 1987;111:907-913.

142. Beaudry PH, Marks MI, McDougall D, Desmond K, Rangel R: Is anti-Pseudomonas therapy warranted in acute respiratory exacerbations in children with cystic fibrosis? J Pediatr 1980;97:144-147.

143. Hyatt AC, Chipps BE, Kumor KM, Mellits ED, Lietman PS, Rosenstein BJ: A double-blind controlled trial of anti-Pseudomonas chemotherapy of acute respiratory exacerbations in patients with cystic fibrosis. J Pediatr 1981;99:307-311.

144. Reed MD, Blumer JL: Urologic pharmacology in the office setting. Urol Clin North Am 1988;15:737-751.

145. LeBel M: Ciprofloxacin: chemistry, mechanism of action, resistance, antimicrobial spectrum, pharmacokinetics, clinical trials and adverse reactions. Pharmacotherapy 1988;8:3-33.

146. Stuttman HR: Summary of a workshop on ciprofloxacin use in patients with cystic fibrosis. Pediatr Infect Dis J 1987;6:932-935.

147. Ingham B, Brentnall DW, Dale EA, McFadzean JA: Arthropathy induced by antibacterial fused N-alkyl-4-pyridone-3-carboxylic acids. Toxicol Letts 1977;1:21-26.

148. Gough A, Barsorim NJ, Mitchell L, McGuire EJ, DeLa Iglesia FA: Juvenile canine drug-induced arthropathy: clinicopathological studies on articular lesions caused by oxolinic and pipemidic acids. Toxicol Appl Pharmacol 1979;51:177-187.

149. Alfaham M, Holt ME, Goodchild MC: Arthropathy in a patient with cystic fibrosis taking ciprofloxacin. Br Med J 1987;295:699.

150. Taussig LM, Kattwinkel J, Friedewald WT, DiSant'Agnese PA: A new prognostic score and clinical evaluation for cystic fibrosis. J Pediatr 1973;88:380-390.

151. Brasfield D, Hicks G, Soon SJ, Tiller RE: The chest roentgenogram in cystic fibrosis: a new scoring system. Pediatrics 1979;63:24-29.

152. Blumer JL, Stern RC, Klinger JD, Yamashita TS, Myers CM, Blum A, Reed MD: Ceftazidime therapy in patients with cystic fibrosis and multiply-drug-resistant Pseudomonas. Am J Med 1985;79(suppl 2A):37-46.

153. Govan JRW, Doherty C, Glass S: Rational parameters for antibiotic therapy in cystic fibrosis. Infection 1987;15:300-308.

154. Glass S, Hayward C, Govan JRW: Serum C-reactive protein in assessment of pulmonary exacerbations and antimicrobial therapy in cystic fibrosis. J Pediatr 1988;113:76-79.

155. Bosso JA, Walker KB: Lack of correlation between objective indicators and clinical response scores during antimicrobial therapy for acute pulmonary exacerbations of cystic fibrosis. Clin Pharm 1988;7:897-901.

156. Kearns GL, Reed MD: Clinical pharmacokinetics in infants and children: a reappraisal. Clin Pharmacokin 1989;17(suppl 1):29-67.

# USE OF FLUOROQUINOLONES IN THE TREATMENT OF SURGICALLY RELATED INFECTIONS

# 11

*Larry H. Danziger*
*Keith A. Rodvold*
*Thomas A. Stellato*

## INTRODUCTION

The use of antimicrobial agents for the treatment of surgical infections and for prophylaxis in surgery has proven to be effective and is accepted medical practice. With the introduction of new, broad-spectrum antimicrobial agents, the selection of the most appropriate agent in these clinical settings is constantly being reevaluated.

Antimicrobial agents account for a major portion of the pharmacy budget, with upwards of 30-50% of the antimicrobial budget aimed at prophylaxis.[1] With the introduction of prospective payment systems, the need to limit costs takes on even greater importance. Strategies aimed at achieving this goal include administering the least toxic antimicrobial agent for the shortest possible effective course, selecting antimicrobial agents with longer half-lives so that fewer doses are required, using single rather than multiple-drug regimens, and using oral dosage forms over parenteral administration whenever possible.

## WOUND INFECTIONS

Wound infections following surgical procedures are still an important source of morbidity in hospitalized patients. It has been estimated that the overall wound infection rate in the U.S. is approximately 7.5%.[2] In 1967 it was estimated that both direct and indirect costs associated with wound infections were approximately $9.8 billion.[3,4] Cruse recently suggested that wound infections in the 1980s delay a patient's discharge and may add between $5,000-$10,000 per hospitalization.[5]

Table 1. Wound infection classification*

| Categories | Percentage of all Infections |
|---|---|
| Clean | 1.5-5.1% |
| Clean-Contaminated | 8-10% |
| Contaminated | 15% |
| Dirty and/or Infected | 25-40% |

* Incidence of wound infection when antibiotics not used. Adapted from references 2,4.

Surgical procedures have been categorized according to the type of operation and the risk for subsequent wound infection (Table 1). *Clean wounds* are those in which no inflammation is encountered, no break in surgical technique occurs, and the respiratory, alimentary, and genitourinary tracts are not entered. *Clean-contaminated wounds* are those in which the alimentary tract or respiratory tract is entered without major spillage. *Contaminated wounds* are those in which a major break in aseptic technique or gross spillage from the alimentary tract has occurred, or those that are fresh or traumatic in nature. *Dirty* and/or *infected wounds* refer to situations in which frank pus or a perforated viscus was found.

Many factors are associated with patient resistance to wound infection. These include age, weight, nutritional status, remote infections, other concomitant disease(s), and surgical technique. The clinical manifestations of wound infections are often dependent on the site and the microorganism(s) involved. The microorganisms most often associated with wound infections are those which comprise the normal skin flora.[6] However, over the past decade, gram-negative bacteria have taken on an increasingly important role (Table 2).

Under normal circumstances the skin and subcutaneous tissues are resistant to infection. Even when high concentrations of bacteria have been injected into soft tissue a subsequent infection rarely occurs. Various conditions are necessary for wound infection to occur and include: (1) the presence of large concentrations of bacteria ($10^5$ microorganisms); (2) occlusion of the blood supply to the tissue in question; (3) availability of proper nutrients; and (4) the presence of a foreign body or debris in the wound.[7,8]

## Tissue Penetration

Several studies of the pharmacokinetics and antibacterial activity of the fluoroquinolones have indicated that these agents are active against the likely pathogens

Table 2.  Bacteriology of surgical wound infections

| Pathogen | Incidence of Infection |
| --- | --- |
| *Staphylococcus aureus* | 19.0% |
| Enterococci | 11.4% |
| *Escherichia coli* | 11.4% |
| *Staphylococcus epidermidis* | 8.4% |
| *Pseudomonas aeruginosa* | 8.1% |
| *Enterobacter* spp. | 6.9% |
| *Proteus* spp. | 5.0% |
| *Klebsiella* spp. | 4.8% |
| *Bacteroides* spp. | 4.4% |

Adapted from reference 6.

associated with wound infections and that adequate concentrations are achieved in the target tissue.[9,10] Fluoroquinolones reach concentrations at the operative sites that exceed the minimum inhibitory concentrations (MICs) for many of the organisms that cause infections. The extended elimination half-life of fluoroquinolones should permit the use of a single dose in settings that require no more than one day of antimicrobial coverage.

## EFFECT ON FECAL FLORA

The use of antimicrobial agents may have either desirable or undesirable effects on the flora of the gastrointestinal (GI) tract. Various antimicrobial agents have a dramatic impact on the flora of the GI tract. Alterations in this flora may cause disastrous effects in certain patient populations. Sparing of the anaerobic flora is thought to be of value in preventing serious bacterial overgrowth syndromes, as sometimes occurs in immunocompromised hosts.[10] Anaerobes rarely cause infections and are important in protecting the patient by competitively preventing colonization by potentially pathogenic aerobic organisms.

Since fluoroquinolones achieve high concentrations in stool after oral administration, their impact on the fecal flora in both volunteers and patients has been examined.[11-13] The fluoroquinolones dramatically reduce the bacterial counts of Enterobacteriaceae, generally within 3-5 days after oral therapy has been initiated.[10,14] The effect of the fluoroquinolones on staphylococci and streptococci is not as dra-

179

matic as is seen with the gram-negative aerobes. Most fluoroquinolones have very little if any activity against anaerobes. This apparent lack of activity against anaerobic bacteria occurs in spite of the tremendous concentrations that these compounds reach in the gastrointestinal tract after oral dosing. Some researchers have speculated that these drugs are bound to fecal material, which decreases the amount of free active drug available,[15] or that the anaerobic bacteria rapidly develop resistance to the fluoroquinolones.[13]

After withdrawal of antimicrobial therapy, fecal bacterial counts return to normal with in 3-4 weeks. To date no studies have reported problems with bacterial over-growth or superinfections with resistant microorganisms during or after fluoroquino-lone therapy. No overgrowth of *Pseudomonas* and only one case of overgrowth by *Candida albicans* have been reported.[11] Thus, the available data indicate that no deleterious effect on colonic bacteria will be encountered when the fluoroquinolones are used.

## TREATMENT OF SURGICAL INFECTIONS

### Biliary Tract

Some studies have reported that bacterial infection of the bile (bactibilia) occurs in up to 90% of patients with cholelithiasis.[16] The most common microorganisms isolated are *Escherichia coli*, *Klebsiella* spp. and *Enterococcus* spp.[17] The fluoro-quinolones have excellent activity against most of the pathogens found in biliary tract infections and achieve high bile and gallbladder tissue concentrations.[18] These char-acteristics make them ideally suited for use either in the treatment or prevention of biliary tract infections.

Despite this theoretical advantage of the fluoroquinolones, only limited data are available regarding their use in the treatment of biliary tract infections.[18-21] Much of what data is available must be extracted from large open trials evaluating the use of fluoroquinolones in the treatment of various infections. Chrysanthopoulos et al[19] treated 30 patients with biliary tract infections with ciprofloxacin. Patients received ciprofloxacin 200 mg intravenously every 12 hours for 3-8 days followed by 750 mg orally twice daily for an additional 3-5 days. The treatment outcome was completely successful in 25/30 (83%) patients. Unfortunately, biliary tract cultures were not obtained during the course of this study. Three of the five failures had empyema of the gall bladder, and the remaining two patients had an associated pancreatic carcinoma.

Yura et al[18] reported results in 23 patients treated with lomefloxacin (14 with acute cholecystitis and 9 with acute cholangitis). The drug was given orally at 300-600 mg/day for 3 to 11 days. Patients treated for acute cholecystitis had a 93% response rate, and those treated for acute cholangitis had a 67% response rate.

In the largest group of patients reported to date, Chacon et al[20] compared pefloxacin to the combination of ampicillin plus gentamicin in patients with either cholecystitis and/or cholangitis. Of 98 evaluable patients, 51 received pefloxacin 400 mg every 8 hours either intravenously or orally. Ampicillin was administered orally (1 gram intravenously every 6 hours for 3-4 days and then 0.5 grams every 6 hours thereafter) with intramuscular gentamicin (80 mg every 8 hours). The diagnoses were confirmed surgically in 68/98 of these patients. Therapy lasted an average of 8 days in the pefloxacin group and 8.5 days in the ampicillin plus gentamicin group. All patients in the pefloxacin group were cured and 44/47 in the comparative group were treated successfully.

Ciprofloxacin has also been used successfully for the treatment of patients with recurrent cholangitis after hepatic portoenterostomy. Houwen et al[21] administered ciprofloxacin 25-50 mg twice daily to three infants suffering from cholangitis secondary to portoenterostomy for biliary atresia. None of the infants had a recurrence of cholangitis.

## Intra-abdominal Infections

Despite improvements over the last 15 years in preoperative, intraoperative, and postoperative care, infections still account for major morbidity and mortality associated with surgery of the gastrointestinal tract. Infections of the abdominal cavity (peritonitis or abscess) often occur after trauma to or surgery of the GI tract. Mortality rates associated with intra-abdominal abscesses have ranged from 3-50% depending on the location and nature of the infectious process.[22,23]

The approach to treatment for intra-abdominal infections includes adequate drainage (surgical or radiologic), elimination of any ongoing source of infection, and appropriate antimicrobial therapy. Clindamycin/aminoglycoside combinations have been considered the traditional approach to therapy, generally resulting in cure/improvement rates of 80% or better.[24]

Since these intra-abdominal infections are generally caused by bacteria residing in the GI tract, the antimicrobial agent(s) selected should have activity against these same microorganisms and be able to penetrate the site of infection (intra-abdominal cavity). The fluoroquinolones have excellent activity against the gram-negative aerobes[10] and *may* have some activity against the anaerobic bacteria of the GI tract.[25] The fluoroquinolones have been shown to penetrate into the peritoneal cavity, the active site of infection.[26,27]

Evaluation of multiple fluoroquinolones in the treatment of experimental intra-abdominal infections has shown that these agents reach the site of infection and have efficacy equal to the comparative antimicrobial regimens.[28-30] Unfortunately, only limited data exists concerning the use of fluoroquinolones in humans for the treatment

181

of intra-abdominal infections, with much of the data being anecdotal. The data reviewed below has been extracted from larger open trials evaluating the use of the fluoroquinolones in the treatment of various types of severe infections.

Nine trials involving 48 patients treated with either pefloxacin or ciprofloxacin for some type of intra-abdominal infection are shown in Table 3.[31-39] Of these 48 patients, 38 (79%) had either improvement or cure of their infectious process. Because of the concern that the fluoroquinolones are not very active against anaerobes, in some trials either clindamycin or metronidazole was added to the treatment regimen. Interestingly, no mention of an anaerobic agent was made in over half the trials, yet positive outcomes were still achieved with fluoroquinolone therapy alone. These patients received 2-4 days of intravenous fluoroquinolone therapy which was then followed up with oral therapy for various periods of time.

The view that any regimen used in the treatment of intra-abdominal infections must have activity against bowel anaerobes implies that the fluoroquinolones will not have a role as monotherapy in this setting. More data comparing the fluoroquinolones (in combination with an anaerobic agent) with the standard combination therapies are necessary before any recommendations for their use can be made.

## ANTIMICROBIAL PROPHYLAXIS

Factors that affect the choice of an antimicrobial for prophylaxis include spectrum of activity, ability to penetrate into the surgical site, elimination half-life, adverse reactions, and cost of the prophylaxis regimen.

Fluoroquinolones have several characteristics that make them effective, convenient, and inexpensive agents for use as perioperative prophylaxis.[40] The following analysis is a review of the available data regarding the *potential* use of fluoroquinolones as prophylactic agents in abdominal, cardiac, and urologic surgery.

## Colorectal

There is convincing evidence that a variety of oral and parenteral antimicrobial regimens are effective in reducing the infection rate following colorectal surgery. For fluoroquinolones, most studies thus far have focused on the relationship between drug administration and tissue concentrations. The first of these studies was reported by Silverman et al,[41] who reported ciprofloxacin concentrations of >5 mg/kg in the jejunal wall after a dose of 200 mg. Brismar et al[25] administered oral ciprofloxacin 750 mg every 12 hours for two doses 24 hours prior to surgery and 400 mg of intravenous ciprofloxacin at the time of anesthesia induction and 12 hours later to 21 patients undergoing colorectal surgery. Ciprofloxacin concentrations in the intestinal mucosa ranged from 2.7 to 37.8 mg/kg of tissue sample and fecal concentrations were 858 mg/kg. These concentrations were associated with marked suppression of both

**Table 3.** Fluoroquinolones in the treatment of intra-abdominal infections

| Ref. | Drug/Dose | Number of Evaluable Patients | Infection Type | Cure/ Improvement |
|------|-----------|------------------------------|----------------|-------------------|
| 31 | Pefloxacin* | 2 | Intra-abdominal abscess | 2/2 |
| 32 | Pefloxacin[†‡] | 2 | Hepatic abscess | 2/2 |
|    |           | 1 | Pancreatic abscess | 0/1 |
|    |           | 1 | Ovarian abscess | 1/1 |
|    |           | 1 | Diffuse peritonitis | 1/1 |
| 33 | Ciprofloxacin[§‡] | 1 | Liver abscess | 1/1 |
| 34 | Ciprofloxacin[‖ ‡] | 2 | Intra-abdominal abscess | 2/2 |
| 35 | Ciprofloxacin[†] | 9 | Intra-abdominal (unknown) | 9/9 |
| 36 | Ciprofloxacin[¶] | 2 | Intra-abdominal | 2/2 |
|    |           | 1 | Subphrenic abscess | 1/1 |
| 37 | Ciprofloxacin[#] | 9 | Appendicitis | 8/9 |
|    |           | 3 | Cholangitis | |
|    |           | 2 | Nongonococcal PID | |
| 38 | Ciprofloxacin[†] | 3 | Intra-abdominal | 5/6 |
|    |           | 1 | Subphrenic abscess | |
|    |           | 1 | Hepatic abscess | |
|    |           | 1 | Retroperitoneal abscess | |
| 39 | Ciprofloxacin[**,‡] | 6 | Intra-abdominal (unknown) | 5/6 |

* 400 mg IV three times daily for 5 days, then 400 mg IV twice daily for 5 more days
† Regimen was not adequately specified.
‡ Metronidazole or clindamycin was added if anaerobes were suspected.
§ 200 mg IV q12 hrs 3-5days, then 500 mg PO BID for a total of 7-14 days
‖ 200 mg IV q12 hrs
¶ 500 mg or 750 mg PO q12hrs
# 750 mg PO q12 hrs for 7-13 days
** 200 mg IV q12 hrs for at least 2 days, then 750 mg PO BID by at least day 4

aerobic and anaerobic bacteria in the lower intestinal tract during the surgical procedure and immediate postoperative period.

Two brief reports have evaluated the prophylactic efficacy of fluoroquinolones in elective colorectal surgery. Offer et al[42] compared the safety and efficacy of metronidazole 500 mg every 8 hours for one day with either two doses of intravenous ciprofloxacin 200 mg or cefazolin 2 grams administered every 8 hours for three days. Prophylaxis was successful in 31 of 34 patients who received ciprofloxacin compared with 31 of 36 patients who received cefazolin. The only adverse effect reported was a swelling in the forearm of a patient who received ciprofloxacin.

Cooreman et al[43] compared a combination of intravenous metronidazole 500 mg every 8 hours for one day with either pefloxacin (800 mg at time of intervention followed by 400 mg at 8 and 16 hours afterwards) or cefuroxime 750 mg every 8 hours for one day. Prophylaxis was successful in 42 of 45 patients who received pefloxacin and 39 of 45 patients who received cefuroxime. The prophylactic failures in the pefloxacin group were limited to *Candida* species and *Streptococcus faecalis*. Prophylactic failures in the cefuroxime group included a wide variety of pathogens including *Streptococcus faecalis*, *Klebsiella pneumoniae*, *Haemophilus influenzae*, *Escherichia coli*, *Staphylococcus epidermidis*, and *Pseudomonas aeruginosa*.

The results of these studies suggest that the fluoroquinolones are suitable agents for antimicrobial prophylaxis of infections associated with colorectal surgery. Clindamycin or metronidazole may be safely added to provide anaerobic coverage.

## Biliary Tract

Prophylactic antimicrobial agents are recommended in patients who undergo surgery for chronic calculous cholecystitis and who have clinical risk factors or a positive intraoperative Gram-stain showing the presence of bacteria in bile. The risk factors for the presence of bacteria in the biliary tract include: (1) previous biliary tract operation; (2) age over 70 years; (3) surgery performed on an emergency basis; (4) jaundice; (5) fever or chills within one week of surgery; (6) diabetes mellitus; and (7) surgery performed within one month of an acute attack of cholecystitis. Clinical studies with fluoroquinolones thus far have evaluated efficacy and tissue penetration. Kujath randomly assigned 200 patients to receive either single-dose ciprofloxacin 200 mg intravenously or ceftriaxone 2 grams intravenously prior to biliary tract surgery.[44] Two postoperative wound infections occurred in the ciprofloxacin group and one in the ceftriaxone group. In the 20 patients who received ciprofloxacin, gallbladder tissue probes were used to determine the tissue levels. The tissue level of ciprofloxacin in the gallbladder wall at 65-70 minutes was $4.5 \pm 2.35$ µg/gm of tissue. The concentration of drug in gallbladder bile was $2.43 \pm 1.86$ µg/mL, which was lower than that in liver bile (56.8 ± 21.6 µg/mL). These bile concentrations exceeded the MIC of the isolated pathogens by several-fold. Similar gallbladder wall tissue concentrations have been reported by Silverman et al[41] and Kogler et al.[45]

Cooreman has reported the results of 112 patients randomly assigned to receive either intravenous pefloxacin 400 mg or intravenous cefazolin 2 grams prior to elective biliary tract surgery.[46] Of 98 evaluable patients, prophylaxis was successful in 49 of 50 pefloxacin patients and 46 of 48 cefazolin patients. One patient from each group developed a wound abscess that required drainage. The other cefazolin patient had an intra-abdominal infection caused by *Klebsiella pneumoniae* and *Pseudomonas aeruginosa*. Adverse effects included six instances (three in each treatment group) of local irritation at injection site, one episode of anaphylactic shock with pefloxacin, and one episode of rash in a cefazolin patient.

The fluoroquinolones seem to have potential for the prophylaxis of infections associated with biliary tract surgery. Concentrations in the gallbladder and bile well exceed the MICs for susceptible bacteria known to cause biliary tract infections.

## CARDIAC SURGERY

Prophylactic antimicrobial agents can decrease the incidence of infection after open heart surgery, including valvular procedures and coronary artery bypass grafts. Antimicrobial prophylaxis for cardiopulmonary bypass surgery should be directed against staphylococci and gram-negative bacilli, which account for the majority of bacterial infections. The pharmacokinetics and antimicrobial spectrum of fluoroquinolones make these agents suitable for use in the prophylaxis of infections associated with open-heart surgery. The objectives of the completed studies to date have been to determine the concentrations in blood and tissues and to evaluate the influence of hemodilution and initiation of cardioplegia.

The penetration of ciprofloxacin into heart muscle, skeletal muscle, heart valves, sternal bone marrow, and mediastinal fat has been studied by several investigators.[47-49] After a single 200 mg dose of intravenous ciprofloxacin, respective tissue concentrations were 3.82 ± 1.34 µg/g in heart muscle, 1.79 ± 0.60 µg/g skeletal muscle, and 1.04 ± 0.53 µg/g in mediastinal fat.[47] There was also good penetration into heart valves and sternal bone marrow when ciprofloxacin was given prophylactically as either a single 400 mg intravenous dose prior to surgery or by combining a single intravenous dose with doses of 750 mg orally every 12 hours for 48 hours preceding surgery.[49] These characteristics explain why sternal wound infections can be successfully treated with the combination of intravenous/oral ciprofloxacin and surgical debridement.[50]

The disposition of intravenous ciprofloxacin 300 mg and pefloxacin 600 mg has been studied during cardiopulmonary bypass.[50,51] The serum concentrations of both fluoroquinolones exceed the MICs of sensitive strains throughout the entire operative procedure. Hemodilution and cardioplegia had minimal effect on the serum concentrations. Concentrations of pefloxacin in atrial tissue, myocardium, and heart valves were $11.6 \pm 4.7$ µg/g, $25.0 \pm 7.9$ µg/g, and $5.1 \pm 1.5$ µg/g, respectively.[51] Pefloxacin levels in heart valves have also been shown to persist for up to 24 hours after a single intravenous dose of 800 mg.[52]

Whether fluoroquinolones are effective agents for prophylaxis in cardiac surgery has not been answered. Auger et al[53] randomized 111 patients to receive either pefloxacin 400 mg intravenously prior to surgery and every 12 hours thereafter, or cefazolin 1 gram intravenously prior to surgery and every 6 hours thereafter for a total of two days. The preliminary results of this study reported colonization at culture sites in 14 of the patients receiving pefloxacin and 11 of the patients receiving cefazolin. In addition, one patient who received cefazolin developed mediastinitis caused by a cefazolin-resistant strain of *Staphylococcus epidermidis*. Further trials examining the role of fluoroquinolones in cardiac surgery prophylaxis are currently being conducted in several centers across the U.S.

## UROLOGICAL

Any antimicrobial agent selected for prophylaxis in patients undergoing urologic surgery should attain high urinary concentrations, have a low toxic potential, and be active selectively against the common organisms encountered in the urinary tract. Two of the most common microorganisms are *Escherichia coli* and *Streptococcus faecalis*.

The use of prophylactic antimicrobial agents to prevent genitourinary tract infections after transurethral surgery (TURP) remains controversial. Some experts believe antimicrobial prophylaxis may be of benefit in averting postoperative bacteriuria in patients with sterile urine who undergo TURP while other authors recommend short-term preoperative prophylaxis for all patients undergoing TURP.

Several randomized studies have assessed the efficacy of oral ciprofloxacin versus placebo in TURP prophylaxis (Table 4). Both single-dose and short courses of oral ciprofloxacin significantly decreased the incidence of postoperative bacteriuria when compared with the placebo groups.[54-56] Similar results have also been reported for oral enoxacin therapy.[57]

Three studies have compared the prophylactic role of ciprofloxacin with cefotaxime administered as a single intravenous dose (Table 4).[58-60] The incidence of significant postoperative bacteriuria ranged from 0% to 8% in the ciprofloxacin groups and 2% to 16% in the cefotaxime groups. These studies demonstrate that a single intravenous dose of ciprofloxacin was as effective as a single dose of cefotaxime in reducing the incidence of infection following TURP procedures.

There is a general agreement that antimicrobial agents should be administered prior to TURP in patients with positive urine cultures. Norfloxacin 400 mg twice daily was compared with trimethoprim-sulfamethoxazole (TMP/SMX) 160 mg/800 mg twice daily in patients with known bacteriuria who were undergoing TURP.[61] Bacteriologic evidence of genitourinary tract infection was found in 31.5% of patients who received TMP/SMX and in 23.8% of those who received norfloxacin. These results suggest that norfloxacin is at least as effective as TMP/SMX in reducing postoperative bacteriuria.

At present, there are no guidelines on which to base the prophylactic use of fluoroquinolones. As new fluoroquinolones are developed, their efficacy and safety in prophylactic regimens will require critical evaluation in well-controlled, prospective clinical trials. The optimal dose and frequency of administration need to be determined, since shorter periods of prophylaxis would reduce costs and presumably be associated with a lower risk for the development of resistant bacteria and adverse reactions.

## SUMMARY

The studies reviewed offer an assessment of the therapeutic potential of the fluoroquinolones as antimicrobial agents for the treatment and prophylaxis of infections commonly associated with gastrointestinal, cardiac, and urological surgery. The broad spectrum of activity and excellent tissue penetration of the fluoroquinolones suggest they would be effective agents at the site of surgical infections. In addition, the favorable pharmacokinetic profile, minimal toxicity, and the availability of both oral and parenteral routes of administration make fluoroquinolones attractive alternatives to agents commonly used in surgical patients.

**Table 4.** Incidence of postoperative bacteriuria after transurethral surgery in prospective randomized controlled trials

| Drugs Tested | Number of Patients* | Administration | % Postoperative Bacteriuria | Reference |
|---|---|---|---|---|
| Ciprofloxacin | 50 | 250 mg orally q12hrs x 3 days | 6% | 54 |
| Placebo | 51 | | 38% | |
| Ciprofloxacin | 29 | 500 mg orally q12hrs x 3-4 days | 3% | 55 |
| Ciprofloxacin | 40 | 500 mg orally q12hrs x 8-9 days | 3% | |
| Placebo | 31 | | 19% | |
| Ciprofloxacin | 47 | single 500 mg oral dose | 2% | 56 |
| Placebo | 42 | | 43% | |
| Enoxacin | 39 | 200 mg oral q12hrs x 2 days | 9% | 57 |
| Placebo | 39 | | 43% | |
| Ciprofloxacin | 45 | single 300 mg IV dose | 0% | 58 |
| Cefotaxime | 47 | single 1 gm IV dose | 2% | |
| Ciprofloxacin | 50 | single 300 mg IV dose | 8% | 59 |
| Cefotaxime | 45 | single 1 gm IV dose | 16% | |
| Ciprofloxacin | 37 | single 300 mg IV dose | 3% | 60 |
| Cefotaxime | 39 | single 1 gm IV dose | 8% | |

* All patients had sterile urine preoperatively.

# REFERENCES

1. Danziger L, Hassan E: Antimicrobial prophylaxis of gastrointestinal surgical procedures and treatment of intraabdominal infections. Drug Intell Clin Pharm 1987;21:406-416.

2. National Research Council Division of Medical Sciences, Ad Hoc Committee of the Committee of Trauma: Postoperative wound infections: the influence of ultraviolet irradiation of the operating room and other factors. Ann Surg 1964;160(suppl 2):1-192.

3. Cruse PJE: Incidence of wound infection on the surgical services. Surg Clin N Am 1975;55:1269-1275.

4. Cruse PJE, Foord R: The epidemiology of wound infection: a 10-year prospective study of 62 wounds. Surg Clin N Am 1980;60:27-40.

5. Cruse PJE: Wound Infections: Epidemiology and Clinical Characteristics, in Howard RJ, Simmons RL (eds), *Surgical Infectious Diseases*, ed 2. Norwalk, Appleton & Lange, 1988, pp 319-329.

6. Morbidity Mortality Weekly Report 1983;33:955.

7. Roettinger W, Edgerton MT, Kurtz LD, et al: Role of inoculation size as a determinant of infection in soft tissue wounds. Am J Surg 1973;126:354-358.

8. Rodeheaver GT, Pettry D, Turnbull V, et al: Identification of the wound infections-potentiating factors in soil. Am J Surg 1974;128:8-13.

9. Gerding DN, Hitt JA: Tissue penetration of the new quinolones in humans. Rev Infect Dis 1989;11(suppl 5):S1046-S1057.

10. Paton JH, Reeves DS: Fluoroquinolone antibiotics: microbiology pharmacokinetics and clinical use. Drugs 1988;36:193-228.

11. Scully BE, Jules K, Chin N-X, et al: Effect of ciprofloxacin on fecal flora of patients with cystic fibrosis and other patients treated with oral ciprofloxacin. Am J Med 1987;82(suppl 4A):336-338.

12. Shah PM, Enzensberger, Glogau O, et al: Influence of oral ciprofloxacin or ofloxacin on the fecal flora of healthy volunteers. Am J Med 1987;82(suppl 4A):333-335.

13. Brumfitt W, Franklin I, Grady J, et al: Changes in the pharmacokinetics of ciprofloxacin and fecal flora during administration of a 7 day course to human volunteers. Antimicrob Agents Chemother 1984;26:757-761.

14. Campoli-Richards D, Monk JP, Price A, et al: Ciprofloxacin a review of its antibacterial activity, pharmacokinetic properties and therapeutic use. Drugs 1988;35:373-447.

15. Edlund C, Lindqvist L, Nord C: Norfloxacin binds to human fecal material. Antimicrob Agents Chemother 1988;32:1869-1874.

16. Tabata M, Nakayama F: Bacteria and gallstones: etiological significance. Dig Dis Sci 1981;26:218-224.

17. Chetlin SH, Elliot DW: Biliary bacteremia. Arch Surg 1971;102:303-307.

18. Yura J, Shinagawa N, Mizuno A, et al: Biliary excretion of lomefloxacin in human and its clinical efficacy for biliary tract infection. 28th Interscience Conference on Antimicrobial Agents and Chemotherapy, October 24-25, Los Angeles, CA 1988.

19. Chrysanthopoulos CJ, Byileveld CM, Vreis-Hospers HG, et al: Use of ciprofloxacin in biliary sepsis (letter). Infection 1987;16:249.

20. Chacon JP, Criscuolo PD, Kobata CM et al: Pefloxacin vs. ampicillin plus gentamicin for the treatment of biliary tract infections. Rev Infect Dis 1989;11(suppl 5):1299.

21. Houwen RH, Bijileveld CM, De Vreis-Hospers, et al: Ciprofloxacin for cholangitis after hepatic portoenterostomy (letter). Lancet 1987;1:1367.

22. Wittmann DH: Intraabdominal infections. World J Surg 1990;14:145-147.

23. Altemeir WA, Gilbertson WR, Fullen WD, et al: Intra-abdominal abscesses. Am J Surg 1973;125:70-79.

24. Gorbach SL: Anaerobic infections: treatment of intraabdominal sepsis. Ann Int Med 1975;83:377-379.

25. Brismar B, Edlund C, Malmborg A, et al: Ciprofloxacin concentrations and impact of the colon microflora in patients undergoing colorectal surgery. Antimicrob Agents Chemother 1990;34:481-483.

26. Weberley J, Ashby J, Donovan I, et al: Intraperitoneal penetration of pefloxacin. Rev Infect Dis 1989;11(suppl 5):1294.

27. Dan M, Serour F, Goera A, et al: Penetration of norfloxacin into abdominal wall muscle tissue. Infection 1989;17:249.

28. Lahnborg G, Nord CE: Effect of ciprofloxacin compared to gentamicin in the treatment of experimental intraabdominal infections in rats. Scand J Infect Dis 1989;60(suppl): 35-38.

29. Tudor RG, Youngs DJ, Yoshioka K, et al: A comparison of the penetration of two quinolones into intra-abdominal abscess. Arch Surg 1988;123:1487-1490.

30. Esposito S: Activity of ciprofloxacin in the treatment of experimental intra-abdominal abscesses in mice. Clin Ther 1989;11:32-37.

31. Ramirez FH, Hidalgo H: Comparison of pefloxacin vs. cefotaxime for the treatment of patients with severe bacterial infection. Rev Infect Dis 1989;11(suppl 5):1169.

32. Giamarellou H, Galankis N, Davoulous G, et al: Pefloxacin for the treatment of gram negative infections. Rev Infect Dis 1989;11(suppl 5):1165.

33. Meyers B, Mendelson MH, Tortosa-Sarni M, et al: Parenteral and oral ciprofloxacin for the treatment of patients with serious infections. Rev Infect Dis 1989;11(suppl 5):1162.

34. Levine D, McNeil P, Lerner S, et al: Randomized, double-blind study of intravenous ciprofloxacin versus ceftazidime for the treatment of serious infections. Rev Infect Dis 1989;11(suppl 5):1173.

35. Modai J: Treatment of patients with serious infections with ciprofloxacin. Rev Infect Dis 1989;11(suppl 5):1177.

36. Scully BE, Neu HC: Oral ciprofloxacin therapy of infection caused by multiply resistant bacteria other than *Pseudomonas aeruginosa*. J Antimicrob Chemother 1986;18(suppl D):179-185.

37. Leal del Rosal P, Riosvelasco A, Leal del Rosal L, et al: Clinical evaluation of ciprofloxacin in surgical field. Proceedings of a Ciprofloxacin Workshop: 14th International Congress of Chemotherapy, Kyoto, Japan, 1985, pp 57-60.

38. Giamarellou H, Galanakis N, Dendrinos C, et al: Evaluation of ciprofloxacin in the treatment of *Pseudomonas aeruginosa* infections. Eur J Clin Microbiol 1986;5:232-235.

39. Gelfand MS, Simmons BP, Craft R, et al: Brief report: clinical study of intravenous and oral ciprofloxacin in complicated bacterial infections. Am J Med 1989;87(suppl 5A):235S-237S.

40. Nord CE: Surgical prophylaxis and treatment of surgical infections with fluoroquinolones. Rev Infect Dis 1989;11(suppl 5):S1287-S1291.

41. Silverman SH, Johnson M, Burdon DW, et al: Pharmacokinetics of single dose intravenous ciprofloxacin in patients undergoing gastrointestinal surgery. J Antimicrob Chemother 1986;18:107-112.

42. Offer C, Weuta H, Bodner E: Efficacy of perioperative prophylaxis with ciprofloxacin or cefazolin in colorectal surgery. Infection 1988;16(suppl 1):S46-S47.

43. Cooreman F, Ghyselen J, Penninckx F, et al: Pefloxacin vs. cefuroxime for prophylaxis of infections after elective colorectal surgery. Rev Infect Dis 1989;11(suppl 5):S1301.

44. Kujath P: Brief report: Antibiotic prophylaxis in biliary tract surgery: Ciprofloxacin versus ceftriaxone. Am J Med 1989;87(suppl 5A):255S-257S.

45. Kogler J, Hancke E, Marklein G, et al: Ciprofloxacin for single shot prophylaxis during cholecystectomy. Infection 1989;17:174-175.

46. Cooreman F: Pefloxacin vs. cefazolin as single-dose prophylaxis in elective biliary tract surgery. Rev Infect Dis 1989;11(suppl 5):S1300.

47. Schmidt W, Eigel P, Zurcher J, et al: Ciprofloxacin as prophylaxis in open-heart surgery: distribution into serum, myocardium, skeletal muscle, and mediastinal fat. Rev Infect Dis 1989;11(suppl 5):S1016.

48. Mertes PM, Voiriot P, Dopff C, et al: Penetration of ciprofloxacin into heart valves, myocardium, mediastinal fat, and sternal bone marrow in humans. Antimicrob Agents Chemother 1990;34:398-401.

49. Pryka RD, Rodvold KA, Ting W, et al: Effect of cardiopulmonary bypass on ciprofloxacin disposition (abstract). Clin Pharmacol Ther 1990;47:154.

50. Soroko T, Morrison S, Khosdal A, et al: Brief report: Ciprofloxacin treatment of sternal wound infections following open heart surgery. Am J Med 1989;87(suppl 5A):240S-242S.

51. Girard C, Brun Y, Etienne J, et al: Pefloxacin in cardiac surgery: influence of cardiopulmonary bypass and cardioplegia on serum and tissue concentrations. Rev Infect Dis 1989;11(suppl 5):S1010.

52. Brion N, Lessana A, Mosset F, et al: Penetration of pefloxacin in human heart valves. J Antimicrob Chemother 1986;17(suppl B):89-92.

53. Auger P, Leclerc Y, Pelletier LC, et al: Efficacy and safety of pefloxacin vs. cefazolin as prophylaxis in elective cardiovascular surgery. Rev Infect Dis 1989;11(suppl 5):S1302-S1303.

54. Murdoch DA, Badenoch DF, Gatchalian ER: Oral ciprofloxacin as prophylaxis in transurethral resection of the prostate. Br J Urol 1987;60:153-156.

55. Grabe M, Forsgren A, Björk T, et al: Controlled trial of a short and a prolonged course with ciprofloxacin in patients undergoing transurethral prostatic surgery. Eur J Clin Microbiol 1987;6:11-17.

56. Shearman CP, Silverman SH, Johnson M, et al: Single dose, oral antibiotic cover for transurethral prostatectomy. Br J Urol 1988;62:434-438.

57. Desai KM, Abrams PH, White LO: A double-blind comparative trial of short-term orally administered enoxacin in the prevention of urinary infection after elective transurethral prostatectomy: a clinical and pharmacokinetic study. J Urol 1988;139:1232-1234.

58. Gombert ME, DuBouchet L, Aulicino TM, et al: Brief report: Intravenous ciprofloxacin versus cefotaxime prophylaxis during transurethral surgery. Am J Med 1989;87(suppl 5A):250S-251S.

59. Cox CE: Comparison of intravenous ciprofloxacin and intravenous cefotaxime for antimicrobial prophylaxis in transurethral surgery. Am J Med 1989;87(suppl 5A):252S-254S.

60. Christensen MM, Nielsen KT, Knes J, et al: Brief report: Single-dose preoperative prophylaxis in transurethral surgery: Ciprofloxacin versus cefotaxime. Am J Med 1989; 87(suppl 5A):258S-260S.

61. Adolfsson J, Kohler C, Falck L: Norfloxacin versus trimethoprim-sulfamethoxazole: a study in patients with known bacteriuria undergoing transurethral resection of the prostate. Scand J Urol Nephrol 1989;23:255-259.

# FLUOROQUINOLONES FOR THE TREATMENT OF FOOT INFECTIONS IN PATIENTS WITH DIABETES MELLITUS

# 12

*Dale N. Gerding*
*Lance R. Peterson*

## INTRODUCTION

Foot infections are one of the most costly complications of diabetes mellitus. They account for more days of hospitalization than any other complication of diabetes and are responsible for the majority of nontraumatic amputations among patients in the United States.[1,2] Peripheral neuropathy, with its attendant loss of sensation in the foot, and lack of adequate arterial circulation to the lower extremity, are common pathological changes in diabetes and are believed to be primarily responsible for the development of these infections. At our institution,* peripheral neuropathy has been associated with the vast majority of patients with foot ulceration. Lack of sensation in the foot leads not only to the development of foot ulceration, but also results in failure to recognize the ulceration and delay in seeking medical care for the problem.

## TYPES OF INFECTION

Foot infections generally can be divided into those that involve the soft tissues and skin and those that involve the bone. Although this distinction may be somewhat artificial, it is important in terms of selection and duration of antimicrobial therapy as well as the ultimate prognosis for cure. Infection of soft tissue or skin is usually manifested by cellulitis that originates from the site of abrasion or ulceration, often over bony prominences on the feet, particularly the digits and the metatarsal heads. Caution is required when evaluating any soft tissue infection, as small ulcerations

* VA Medical Center, Minneapolis, Minnesota.

may overlie large soft tissue defects that do not become apparent until the ulcer is probed.

Bone infection or osteomyelitis is involved in at least 13% of all patients with diabetic foot ulcerations.[3] Published reports have emphasized the poor prognosis of patients with osteomyelitis and diabetes.[3-5] However, a retrospective review of 51 patients with osteomyelitis and diabetes has revealed that the prognosis is much better than previously thought.[6] Most of these patients had bone infection involving the distal metatarsal or proximal phalanges or both. Twenty-seven patients (53%) had good outcomes of their osteomyelitis, with limb preservation at follow-up (an average of 19 months after treatment). Seven of the patients had a local incision and drainage procedure at the time of their acute infection. The remainder received no surgical therapy. Fifteen of these patients (29%) required a below knee amputation and 9 underwent local amputations of the digits of the feet. Factors associated with a good outcome (ie, resolution of infection) included the presence of edema or swelling at the infection site and a duration of antibiotic therapy of at least four weeks for intravenously administered drugs and 10 weeks if combination intravenous plus oral therapy was utilized.

The data also indicate that bacteremia, the presence of gangrene, and the absence of swelling are associated with a poor clinical response and often surgical amputation. In three published reports, 27/27 patients with gangrene, 10/13 without local swelling, and 10/15 with bacteremia required amputation during initial hospitalization.[6-8] These data also indicate that in diabetic patients, a long duration of appropriate spectrum antibiotic therapy is associated with an increase in the rate of cure of osteomyelitis.

## INFECTING ORGANISMS

Foot infections in diabetic patients are typically polymicrobial in origin; that is, multiple bacterial species are isolated from the site of the infection. Depending upon the technique used to obtain cultures, usually between 3 and 6 different bacterial species will be isolated from a diabetic foot infection.[7,9-12] The best method to obtain culture specimens from foot infections remains controversial, and the relative merits of the various methods have been discussed in detail by Sapico et al.[10] The usual methods are a simple swab of the infected ulcer site, a curettage of the base of the ulcer, or a needle aspiration of the deep tissues lying beneath the ulcer; the latter is achieved by passing the needle through uninfected or uninvolved skin that has been prepped with an antiseptic prior to aspiration. Use of the simple ulcer swab usually yields a higher number of bacterial species than the other methods, while the needle aspiration is usually associated with the lowest number of bacterial species. The major problem with the use of the needle aspiration technique is that it cannot be determined with certainty whether the needle has passed into the area of infected tissue, and consequently, falsely negative cultures may result. Although surface cultures have been deemed "unreliable," a careful analysis of these specimens by Wheat et al[9] suggests that if the bacterial population from an unreliable swab specimen is treated with appropriate antimicrobial agents, the agents will cover the bacterial species recovered from a so-called reliable specimen in 93% of cases.

The specific bacteria causing these infections are listed in Table 1. The three major groups are: (1) gram-positive aerobic or facultatively anaerobic bacteria, primarily *Staphylococcus aureus* and a variety of streptococci and enterococci; (2) gram-negative aerobic or facultative bacilli typified by species of *Proteus, Klebsiella, Enterobacter* and *E. coli;* and (3) anaerobic bacteria, specifically gram-positive anaerobes such as *Peptococcus* and *Peptostreptococcus* spp. Although the pathogenicity of *Bacteroides fragilis* in foot infections has been emphasized, it is not isolated as frequently as are gram-positive anaerobes. However, it is not clear whether the failure to isolate *B. fragilis* reflects insufficient care in performing anaerobic cultures or a failure of the organism to be present in large enough numbers of infections.[7-10,12] The bacteriology of osteomyelitis of the diabetic foot appears to be very similar to that of infections limited to the soft tissues.[6]

## SUITABILITY OF FLUOROQUINOLONES FOR THE TREATMENT OF FOOT INFECTIONS

Fluoroquinolones are antimicrobial agents that possess a very broad spectrum of antibacterial activity against gram-negative aerobic and facultative bacilli.[13-16] Organisms of the Enterobacteriaceae family are particularly susceptible, as are enteric pathogens such as *Salmonella, Shigella, Yersinia, Campylobacter,* and *Vibrio.*[13-16] In addition, meningococci, gonococci, and *Haemophilus influenza* are highly susceptible.[15,16] These agents are also quite active against staphylococci, including methicillin-resistant strains.[13-16] Activity against streptococci including the enterococci is only modest, however, with minimum inhibitory concentrations (MICs) ranging from approximately 2 μg/mL to >16 μg/mL. Strictly anaerobic bacteria, with the exception of some anaerobic gram-positive cocci, are generally quite resistant to all of the fluoroquinolones.[13-16] Modest activity against Clostridial species may be present.[13] In general, the fluoroquinolones as a group cannot be considered reliably active against anaerobic bacteria.[15]

Given the polymicrobial nature of foot infections in diabetic patients, it is clear that the fluoroquinolones are not active in vitro against the entire spectrum of infecting agents. As mentioned earlier, fluoroquinolones have little useful activity against anaerobic bacteria and to some extent the streptococci.[8,13-15] However, limited clinical data suggest that ciprofloxacin may be quite effective in the treatment of diabetic foot infections and that the use of an additional agent directed specifically against anaerobic

Table 1. Bacteriology of foot infections in patients with diabetes mellitus*

| ORGANISMS | NUMBER OF ISOLATES |
|---|---|
| **Aerobic and Facultative Isolates** | 313 |
| Gram-positive | |
|    *Streptococcus* spp. | 48 |
|    *Staphylococcus aureus* | 42 |
|    *Enterococcus* spp. | 42 |
|    Coagulase-negative staphylococci | 36 |
|    Gram-positive bacilli | 21 |
|    Total | 189 |
| Gram-negative | |
|    *Proteus* spp. | 37 |
|    *Escherichia coli* | 17 |
|    *Enterobacter* spp. | 15 |
|    *Klebsiella* spp. | 15 |
|    *Pseudomonas aeruginosa* | 13 |
|    Other gram-negative bacilli | 31 |
|    Gram-negative cocci | 2 |
|    Total | 130 |
| **Anaerobic Isolates** | 180 |
| Gram-positive | |
|    *Peptococcus* spp. | 54 |
|    *Peptostreptococcus* spp. | 25 |
|    *Clostridium* spp. | 21 |
|    Other gram-positive bacilli | 15 |
|    Total | 115 |
| Gram-negative | |
|    *Bacteroides fragilis* group | 36 |
|    *Bacteroides melaninogenicus* group | 16 |
|    Other *Bacteroides* spp. | 9 |
|    *Veillonella* spp. | 1 |
|    Other gram-negative bacilli | 3 |
|    Total | 65 |

* Data compiled from 127 patients in references 7,9,10,12. Cultures were obtained by ulcer curette, aspiration and biopsy, or deep tissue biopsy.

bacteria may not be necessary. However, if anaerobic infection is likely, the use of metronidazole or clindamycin in combination with a fluoroquinolone is appropriate.

The advantages of the fluoroquinolone antibiotics, which include their ease of administration and excellent tissue penetration,[17] make them attractive agents for the treatment of diabetic foot infections. In addition, the long serum half-life of most of these agents allows them to be administered orally on a twice-daily basis, and thus should aid in patient compliance.

In addition to their broad antibacterial spectrum, oral bioavailability, and favorable pharmacokinetics, the fluoroquinolones also possess excellent tissue penetration properties. Although specific data regarding penetration into sites of infection in the diabetic foot are not available, such data are available for skin and bone. Fluoroquinolone concentrations in skin, as performed by the skin blister model in humans, are shown in Table 2, along with comparative data for selected non-fluoroquinolone antibiotics.[17,18] Comparable data for bone penetration are shown in Table 3.

Penetration of fluoroquinolones into skin, as measured by the blister fluid model, is exceptionally good,[17] particularly when the comparison is made by using the area under the curve (AUC) method. Data using this method suggest that the fluoroquinolones are actually concentrated within the blister sites. Because most of these studies are performed with an inflammatory blister, it is possible that the large influx of polymorphonuclear leukocytes (PMNs) may actually enhance the penetration of the fluoroquinolones into these sites since some of these drugs are concentrated intracellularly in PMNs.[17]

The degree to which fluoroquinolones and selected additional antimicrobials penetrate into PMNs is shown in Table 4.[17,18] Fluoroquinolones appear to be concentrated within PMNs from two-fold to 14-fold. The ability of the PMN to concentrate fluoroquinolones into abscess sites has been shown in an experimental model.[19] Both ciprofloxacin and fleroxacin were shown to be concentrated in the pus of abdominal abscesses in an experimental rat model.[19] Although the specific mechanism has not been elucidated, the fact that the fluoroquinolones are highly concentrated within PMNs and that many PMNs are found within abscesses suggests that this is the explanation for the very high drug concentrations at these sites. If true, delivery of high concentrations of quinolones to the abscesses of the foot in diabetic patients may be possible, assuming that the vascular supply to the foot is sufficient for the PMNs to reach the infection.

Data on bone penetration of the fluoroquinolones, as measured by the ratio of the concentration of drug at the site compared with concentration in serum ranges from 27% to well over 300% depending on the time at which the measurement is made relative to drug administration (Table 3). These data also compare very favorably with the concentrations achieved with other antimicrobial agents.[18]

Table 2. Concentrations of selected fluoroquinolones and other antimicrobial agents in blister fluid

| Fluoroquinolone | Method of Admin. | Dose (G) (multiple or single) | Serum concentration mean (range) | Time serum obtained (h) | Site concentration mean (range) | Time site specimen obtained (h) | Ratio of site/serum (%) | Ratio of AUC site/serum (%) | Notes* |
|---|---|---|---|---|---|---|---|---|---|
| Ciprofloxacin | PO | 0.5 (S) | 2.3±0.7 | 1.3 | 1.4±0.4 | 2.6 | 43 | 117 | CB |
| Ciprofloxacin | IV | 0.1 (S) | 2.0 | PEAK | 0.6±0.2 | 1.3 | 65 | 121 | CB,E |
| Ciprofloxacin | PO | 0.5 (S) | 2.8±0.4 | 1.4 | 0.8±0.2 | 2.5 | 28 | 56 | SB |
| Ciprofloxacin | PO | 0.5 (M) | 3.5±1.3 | 1.0 | 1.9±0.7 | 2.5 | 57 | 85 | SB |
| Enoxacin | PO | 0.6 (S) | 3.7±0.5 | 1.9 | 2.9±0.5 | 3.7 | 78 | 114 | CB |
| Enoxacin | IV | 0.4 (S) | 5.5±1.8 | PEAK | 2.2±0.5 | 0.5 | 40 | 133 | CB |
| Fleroxacin | PO | 0.4 (S) | 6.1±2.2 | 0.7 | 3.8±0.6 | 4.0 | 62 | 90 | CB |
| Ofloxacin | PO | 0.6 (S) | 10.7±6.4 | 1.2 | 5.2±6.9 | 5.3 | 49 | 125 | CB |
| Norfloxacin | PO | 0.4 (S) | 1.5±0.1 | 1.5 | 1.0±0.3 | 2.3 | 67 | 105 | CB |
| Pefloxacin | IV | 0.4 (S) | 5.1 | PEAK | 3.3±0.7 | 1.8 | 66 | 133 | CB,E |
| Pefloxacin | PO | 0.4 (S) | 6.6±1.3 | 0.8 | 3.9±0.7 | 2.4 | 59 | 99 | CB |
| Other Selected Antimicrobial Agents | | | | | | | | | |
| Cefotaxime | IM | 1.0 (S) | 17.5 | 2.0 | 7.0 | 2.0 | 40 | NA | CB |
| Ceftazidime | IV | 1.0 (S) | 24.3±2.2 | 2.0 | 18.3±2.4 | 2.0 | 75 | NA | CB |
| Cephalexin | PO | 1.0 (S) | 23.3 | 1.5-2.0 | 13.7 | 1.5-2.0 | 59 | NA | CB |
| Amoxicillin | IV | 1.0 (S) | 15.0 | 2.0 | 6.0 | 2.0 | 40 | NA | CB |
| Ampicillin | PO | 0.6 (S) | 3.1±0.5 | 2.0 | 1.5±0.3 | 2.0 | 48 | NA | CB |
| Erythromycin | PO | 0.5 (S) | 2.5 | 3.0 | 0.2 | 3.0 | 8 | NA | SB |
| Rifampin | PO | 0.5 (S) | 13.2(10.0-16.0) | 3.0 | 2.7(2.7-2.8) | 6.9 | 20 | NA | SB |
| Sulfamethoxazole | PO | 1.6 (S) | 103±10 | 2.0 | 11±3 | 2.0 | 11 | NA | SB |
| Trimethoprim | PO | 0.3 (S) | 2.8±0.4 | 2.0 | 1.5±0.4 | 2.0 | 54 | NA | SB |

S = single; M = multiple; CB = cantharides blister; SB = suction blister; E = extrapolated from graphs; NA = data not available
Adapted from Gerding and Hitt[17] and Gerding et al.[18]

# Table 3. Concentrations of selected fluoroquinolones and other antimicrobial agents in bone

| Fluoroquinolone | Method of Admin. | Dose (G) (multiple or single) | Serum concentration mean (range) | Time serum obtained (h) | Site concentration mean (range) | Time site specimen obtained (h) | Ratio of site/serum (%) | Notes* |
|---|---|---|---|---|---|---|---|---|
| Ciprofloxacin | PO | 0.5 (S) | 1.4 (0.4-2.0) | 1.5-4.5 | 0.4 (0.2-0.9) | 1.5-4.5 | 28 | R,Q,C,U |
| Ciprofloxacin | PO | 0.75 (S) | 2.6 (0.9-3.8) | 1.5-4.5 | 0.7 (0.2-1.4) | 1.5-4.5 | 27 | R,Q,C,U |
| Ciprofloxacin | PO | 1.0 (S) | 2.9 (0.9-4.4) | 1.5-4.5 | 1.6 (1.0-2.4) | 1.5-4.5 | 55 | R,Q,C,U |
| Ciprofloxacin | IV | 0.20 (S) | 1.5 (±0.2) | 1.2 | 6.9 (±0.8) | 1.2 | 460 | H,E,R, |
| Enoxacin | PO | 0.4 (S) | 2.O (±0.4) | 1.5-5.5 | 0.7 (±0.3) | 1.5-5.5 | 35 | R,Q,C,U |
| Enoxacin | IV | 0.4 (S) | 1.8 (±0.4) | 1.5-5.5 | 0.9 (±0.5) | 1.5-5.5 | 50 | R,Q,C,U |
| Enoxacin | IV | 0.4 (M) | 3.1 (±0.9) | 1.5-5.5 | 1.1 (±0.5) | 1.5-5.5 | 35 | R,Q,C,I |
| Enoxacin | PO | 0.4 (M) | 2.8 (±1.6) | 1.5-5.5 | 1.3 (±1.6) | 1.5-5.5 | 46 | R,Q,C,I |
| Pefloxacin | IV/PO | 0.4 (M) | 9.2 (3.5-17.3) | 2.0 | 4.1 (0.3-10.2) | 2.0 | 44 | I,R,Q,B |
| Ofloxacin | PO | 0.4 (S) | 2.0 | 4.5 | 1.22 | 4.5 | 61 | Q,U,R |

## Other Selected Antimicrobial Agents

| Fluoroquinolone | Method of Admin. | Dose (G) (multiple or single) | Serum concentration mean (range) | Time serum obtained (h) | Site concentration mean (range) | Time site specimen obtained (h) | Ratio of site/serum (%) | Notes* |
|---|---|---|---|---|---|---|---|---|
| Cefamandole | IV | 2.0 (S) | 74±6 | 0.9 | 9.4±1.1 | 0.9 | 13 | U |
| Cefazolin | IV | 1.0 (S) | 80 | 0.7 | 30 | 0.7 | 38 | U,C |
| Cefotaxime | IV | 2.0 (S) | 61 | 0.5-1.0 | 5.4 | 0.5-1.0 | 9 | U,C |
| Cefoxitin | IV | 2.0 (S) | 39 | 1.2 | 6.3 | 1.2 | 16 | U |
| Ceftazidime | IV | 2.0 (S) | 37 | 2.0 | 20 (10-25) | 2.0 | 55 | U,C |
| Ceftizoxime | IV | 1.0 (M) | 34±6.9 | 1.0 | 6.3±4.6 | 1.0 | 19 | U |
| Cefuroxime | IV | 3.0 (S) | 60 | 1.5 | 12 | 1.5 | 20 | U |
| Azlocillin | IV | 5.0 (S) | 14.3 | 1.0 | 24(±1.4) | 0.8-1.5 | 17 | U |
| Dicloxacillin | PO | 0.5 (S) | 13±2.5 | 1.5 | 2.0±0.5 | 1.5 | 15 | U |
| Oxacillin | IV | 1.0 (S) | 19 (5-33) | 1.0 | 2.1(0.3-14.5) | 1.0 | 11 | U |
| Clindamycin | PO | 0.3 (S) | 2.8±1.2 | 1.5 | 0.6±0.4 | 1.5 | 21 | U |
| Erythromycin | PO | 0.5 (S) | 1.3 (0.1-2.1) | 1.0 | 0.2±0.1 | 1.5 | 18 | U |
| Rifampin | PO | 0.6 (M) | 8.9±2.3 | 3.0 | 1.7±1.0 | 3.0 | 20 | U,C |

* S= single dose; M = multiple dose; R = tissue rinsed; Q = quinolone extraction (from bone); C = correction for blood contamination;
U = uninfected; I = infected; H = bone homogenized; E = extrapolated from graphs; N = no details given for bone extraction or preparation
Adapted from Gerding and Hitt [17] and Gerding et al. [18]

Table 4. Concentrations of selected fluoroquinolones and other antimicrobial agents in polymorphonuclear leukocytes

| Fluoroquinolone | Extracellular Concentration (μg/mL) | Cellular Concentration (μg/mL) | Cellular to Extracellular Concentration (%) | Notes* |
|---|---|---|---|---|
| Ciprofloxacin | 20 | 120-140 | 600-700 | SO |
| Ciprofloxacin | 2 | 7.8 | 390 | CW |
|  | 5 | 9.8 | 200 | CW |
| Ciprofloxacin | 50 | 175 | 349 | SO |
| Enoxacin | 10 | 40 | 400 | CW |
|  | 20 | 72 | 360 | CW |
| Norfloxacin | 50 | 112 | 224 | SO |
| Norfloxacin | 5-10 | 35-140 | 700-1400 | SO |
| Ofloxacin | 50 | 408 | 815 | SO |
| Pefloxacin | 50 | 145 | 290 | SO |
| **Other Selected Antimicrobial Agents** |  |  |  |  |
| Gentamicin | 18 | 15 | 84 | SO |
| Cefamandole | 10 | <1 | <10 | SO |
| Cefazolin | 10 | <1 | <10 | SO |
| Ampicillin | 100 | 7.7 | 7.7 | CL |
| Penicillin G | 10 | 4-6 | 40-60 | SO |
| Chloramphenicol | 10 | 22.3 | 223 | SO |
| Clindamycin | 10 | 111 | 1110 | SO |
| Erythromycin | 18 | 254 | 1332 | SO |
| Rifampin | 20 | 47 | 233 | SO |

* SO = silicone oil; CW = centrifugation and washing; CL = cell lysis
  Adapted from Gerding and Hitt [17] and Gerding et al.[18]

## CLINICAL EXPERIENCE WITH FLUOROQUINOLONES IN DIABETIC FOOT INFECTIONS

Available data on the efficacy of the fluoroquinolones for the treatment of skin and soft tissue infections report response rates ranging from 69-97%.[20] Data regarding the treatment of osteomyelitis are more limited but suggest excellent results with ciprofloxacin and pefloxacin.[20]

Specific data on the use of fluoroquinolones in the treatment of foot infections in diabetic patients are presently limited to two studies of ciprofloxacin.[8,21] Peterson et al[8] treated 48 patients with peripheral vascular disease, 46 of whom had diabetes mellitus. These patients were randomized to receive oral ciprofloxacin 750 mg bid or 1000 mg bid for the treatment of osteomyelitis or soft tissue infection. The duration of therapy was three months for patients with osteomyelitis and three weeks for those with soft tissue infection. The diagnosis of osteomyelitis was made on the basis of radiographs of the foot or bone scans. Patients entered into this protocol were treated with local care of the infection site, including debridement of the wound and removal of surface eschars, calluses, and necrotic material. Maintenance of the infection site was achieved through the alternating use of wet and dry gauze dressings. Local antimicrobial or topical therapy was not used, and patients were instructed to avoid weight-bearing on the affected limb.

Criteria for entry into the study included a history of diabetes mellitus or peripheral vascular disease and a foot lesion of sufficient severity to require hospitalization. Signs of local infection included local heat, edema, drainage, erythema, and pain. Fever greater than 37.8° C was also considered evidence of active infection. Patients were monitored for chemistry and hematology laboratory abnormalities during the study as well as for evidence of healing of the infected site. The pharmacokinetics of ciprofloxacin were assayed in both serum and urine, and in selected patients the concentration of ciprofloxacin in stool was assayed.

Cultures of foot lesions were obtained by needle aspiration and/or swab culture of the ulcer and were processed for both aerobic and anaerobic bacteria by standard methods. Susceptibility to ciprofloxacin was determined in cation supplemented Mueller-Hinton or Wilkins-Chalgren media.

All patients were followed for one year after entry into the study to assess the long-term outcome and need for re-treatment as well as amputation. The need for either additional antimicrobial treatment of the same lesion or limb amputation was considered a failure of therapy. Responses to therapy were measured both acutely (through the period of treatment) and long-term (up to one year). Data from cultures of the infection sites are shown in Table 5 and reveal a comparable spectrum of organisms to those reported by other investigators, with the exception that the mean number of organisms isolated was slightly less than in previous studies (1.8 organisms per infected site). The organisms isolated from aspirates were primarily *S. aureus* and

Table 5. Bacteriology of foot infections treated with ciprofloxacin

| Organism | Aspirate Culture* | Swab Culture |
|---|:---:|:---:|
| **Aerobes** | | |
| S. aureus | 12 | 13 |
| S. epidermidis | 9 | 18 |
| Group D streptococci | 4 | 12 |
| Other gram-positive cocci | 5 | 11 |
| Enterobacteriaceae | 5 | 10 |
| Other gram-negative bacilli | 4 | 9 |
| Corynebacteria | 1 | 19 |
| **Anaerobes** | | |
| Anaerobic gram-positive cocci | 11 | ND[†] |
| Anaerobic gram-positive bacilli | 2 | ND |
| Anaerobic gram-negative bacilli | 1 | ND |
| Number of organisms/patient | 1.8 | 1.9 |

\* Thirty of 46 aspirates yielded positive cultures.
† Anaerobic culture not done on swab cultures.
Adapted from Peterson et al.[8]

anaerobic gram-positive cocci while *S. epidermidis*, Corynebacterium, *S. aureus,* and enterococci were isolated from swab cultures. Seventy-seven percent (36 of 47) of infections were polymicrobial. Of the monomicrobial infections, 6 were due to *S. aureus* alone, and 5 were due to *S. epidermidis* as a single species. Two patients were bacteremic, one with *S. aureus* and one with *S. epidermidis*. Overall, 95% of bacteria were susceptible to ciprofloxacin at a concentration of 1.0 µg per mL or less.

Serum concentrations of ciprofloxacin peaked at 2.5 µg/mL two hours after a dose of 750 mg and 3.1 µg/mL two hours after the 1000 mg dosage. The half-life was 5.3 to 6 hours, reflecting the older age of the patients receiving treatment. The concentration of ciprofloxacin in the stool of patients ranged from approximately 1 to 1100 µg per gram of stool. Higher stool concentrations were generally recorded later in the therapeutic course.

Three patients were unevaluable. One patient underwent amputation of his foot within 24 hours of enrollment and two discontinued therapy after 20 and 34 days, respectively, because of nausea and vomiting in the first case and severe anxiety in the second. As a result, there were 23 evaluable patients in the 750 mg bid group and 22 evaluable patients in the 1000 mg bid group. Overall, 31 of the evaluable patients had osteomyelitis and 16 had soft tissue infection. Acute response to therapy was excellent, with 43 of 47 patients (91%) able to leave the hospital; however, 4 of these 43 patients subsequently did not complete their planned course of therapy either because of amputation or relapse of infection, thus necessitating a change in treatment.

The long-term outcome of the patients at one-year follow-up is shown in Table 6. There were no significant differences in outcomes between patients who received the 1500 mg/day dose as compared to those who received the 2000 mg/day dose. The results indicate that 19/29 patients (65%) with osteomyelitis and 8/16 (50%) with soft tissue infection or cellulitis had a favorable response. When the two types of infection were combined, 27 of 45 patients (60%) had a favorable long-term outcome. Nine of 45 patients (20%) required an amputation at some point during the one-year follow-up period. Average length of hospitalization for these patients was only 6.3 days.

The outcome of patients treated with ciprofloxacin has been compared retrospectively to that of a similar group of patients treated at the Minneapolis and Wadsworth Veterans Administration Medical Centers in the period just prior to this study.[7] Patients in that study were treated with either cefoxitin or ceftizoxime using a randomized, double-blind protocol and followed for one year before the code was broken. Patients with osteomyelitis were treated for approximately 30 days while those with soft tissue infection and cellulitis were treated for 10 days. At one year the successful outcome for the cefoxitin and ceftizoxime groups was 28% and 36%, respectively, as

Table 6. Clinical outcome of patients with foot infections treated with ciprofloxacin

| | Outcome No. Patients/No. Treated (%)* |
|---|---|
| One Year Successful Outcome: | |
| Osteomyelitis | 19/29 (65) |
| Soft tissue/cellulitis | 8/16 (50) |
| All infections | 27/45 (60) |
| Number of amputations | 9/45 (20) |

* Data pooled for dosages of 1500 mg/day and 2000 mg/day. Duration of treatment was three months for osteomyelitis and three weeks for soft tissue/cellulitis.
Adapted from Peterson et al.[8]

compared with 60% for patients treated with ciprofloxacin in the present study. Similarly, the percentage of patients in the cefoxitin and ceftizoxime groups who required amputations was 44% and 36%, respectively. This compares with 20% (9/45) of patients in the present study who required amputations. The duration of hospitalization for patients treated with cefoxitin and ceftizoxime was 18.6 and 20 days, respectively.

In the study by Peterson et al,[8] the long-term outcome correlated with the presence of ulcer healing at the time of cessation of antibiotic therapy. For patients whose ulcer was healed when antibiotic therapy was stopped, 14 of 15 (93%) ultimately went on to achieve a successful one-year outcome. In contrast, only 13 of 30 (43%) patients whose ulcers had failed to heal at the time therapy was discontinued achieved a successful outcome at one year (p<0.01). The superior outcome of patients treated to closure of their ulcers was evident in both those with soft tissue infection (p<0.03) as well as those with osteomyelitis (p<0.04) Thus, the superior outcome of patients treated with ciprofloxacin as compared with those treated with cefoxitin and ceftizoxime may, in part, be related to the longer duration of therapy possible in these patients. Clearly, prolonged duration of therapy is achieved more readily with an oral agent such as ciprofloxacin than with an intravenously administered drug.

Results of a similar ciprofloxacin study have been reported by Beam et al in abstract form.[18] In this study, 42 patients were treated initially with intravenous ciprofloxacin at a dosage of 200 mg every 12 hours for 5-14 days. This was followed by oral administration of ciprofloxacin at a dosage of either 500 or 750 mg every 12 hours for 2-4 weeks. The primary bacterial organisms isolated were staphylococci (n=33), streptococci (n=32), Enterobacteriaceae (n=30), Pseudomonads (n=10), and anaerobes (n=9). Clinical outcome was good in 39 of 42 patients, but clinical follow-up was limited to only three months. Patients were able to be discharged from the hospital as soon as they were switched to oral therapy.

Although both of these ciprofloxacin studies demonstrate excellent clinical outcomes in foot infections among diabetics, the number of anaerobic bacterial isolates was small. In the study by Peterson et al[8] only 14 anaerobic bacteria were isolated, most of which were anaerobic gram-positive cocci. In the study by Beam et al[21] only 9 strictly anaerobic bacteria were isolated. For anaerobic gram-positive cocci, the $MIC_{50}$ of ciprofloxacin was 1.0 µg/mL and the $MIC_{90}$ was 8.0 µg/mL, which suggests that the drug possesses modest activity against these organisms.[8] The MIC of Group D streptococci isolated in the study by Peterson et al[8] ranged from 1.0 to 4.0 µg/mL, a level comparable to the peak blood levels achieved in serum for the study drug. Definitive data regarding the efficacy of ciprofloxacin in patients with high concentrations of anaerobic bacteria isolated from foot ulcers remains unanswered; however, it is possible that activity against every organism isolated in a mixed infection may not be necessary. In particular, the drainage and opening of the often closed infections of the foot may be sufficient to inhibit further growth of anaerobic bacteria. This, coupled with the elimination of susceptible aerobic and facultative bacteria, may be all that is necessary to achieve a successful clinical outcome.

## SUMMARY

Foot infections in diabetic patients involving skin, soft tissue or bone are caused by a mixture of bacterial organisms including aerobic gram-positive, gram-negative, and anaerobic types. Several characteristics of the fluoroquinolone antibiotics make them attractive therapeutic agents for the treatment of these infections, including their broad spectrum of activity, oral bioavailability, and favorable pharmacokinetics. The latter includes a long serum half-life, high concentrations in skin and bone, and concentration within polymorphonuclear leukocytes. The relative lack of activity of the fluoroquinolones against anaerobic bacteria and their marginal activity against streptococci is a cause for concern. Clinical experience in diabetic foot infections to date is limited to two studies using ciprofloxacin. In the best documented study, patients receiving ciprofloxacin had better results than those who received cefoxitin or ceftizoxime in previous trials.

Based on the results of this present study, ciprofloxacin should be used at a dosage of at least 750 mg bid and the duration of therapy should be at least three weeks for soft tissue infections and three months for osteomyelitis. In addition, patients may benefit from an even longer course of therapy if their ulcers have not healed at the time that treatment would normally be discontinued. However, this impression requires confirmation. It appears that fluoroquinolones have excellent potential to achieve favorable treatment outcomes in diabetic patients, even though these drugs have been evaluated without the addition of specific antimicrobial agents with anaerobic activity. The addition of drugs such as metronidazole or clindamycin may further improve the therapeutic outcome in patients with serious lower extremity infections.

# REFERENCES

1. Gibbons GW, Eliopoulous GM: Infection of the diabetic foot, in Kozak GP, Campbell D, Hoar CS, et al (eds), *Management of Diabetic Foot Problems*. New York, WB Saunders, 1984, pp 97-102.

2. Leichter SB, Allweis P, Harley J, et al: Clinical characteristics of diabetic patients with serious pedal infections. Metabolism 1988;37(suppl 1):22-24.

3. Kozak GP, Rowbotham JL: Diabetic foot disease: A major problem, in Kozak GP, Campbell D, Hoar CS, et al (eds), *Management of Diabetic Foot Problems*. New York, WB Saunders, 1984, pp 1-8.

4. Hirschmann JV: Osteomyelitis, in Petersdorf RG, Braunwald E, Isselbacher KJ, et al (eds), *Harrison's Principles of Internal Medicine*. New York, McGraw-Hill, 1987, pp 1910-1912.

5. Little JR, Kobayashi GS, Sonnenwirth AC: Infection of the diabetic foot, in Levin ME, O'Neal LW (eds), *The Diabetic Foot*. St. Louis, The CV Mosby Co, 1983, pp 133-147.

6. Bamberger DM, Daus GP, Gerding DN: Osteomyelitis in the feet of diabetic patients. Am J Med 1987;83:653-660.

7. Hughes CE, Johnson CC, Bamberger DM, et al: Treatment of long-term follow-up of foot infections in patients with diabetes or ischemia: A randomized, prospective, double-blind comparison of cefoxitin vs. ceftizoxime. Clin Ther 1987;10(suppl A):36-49.

8. Peterson LR, Lissack LM, Canter K, et al: Therapy of lower extremity infections with ciprofloxacin in patients with diabetes mellitus, peripheral vascular disease, or both. Am J Med 1989;86:801-808.

9. Wheat LJ, Allen SD, Henry M, et al: Diabetic foot infections. Arch Intern Med 1986; 146:1935-1940.

10. Sapico FL, Witte JL, Canawati HN, et al: The infected foot of the diabetic patient: Quantitative microbiology and analysis of clinical features. Rev Infect Dis 1984;6(suppl 1):S171-S176.

11. Fierer J, Daniel D, Davis C: The fetid foot: Lower extremity infections in patients with diabetes mellitus. Rev Infect Dis 1979;1:210-217.

12. Louie TJ, Bartlett JG, Tally FP, et al: Aerobic and anaerobic bacteria in diabetic foot ulcers. Ann Intern Med 1976;85:461-463.

13. Bergan T: Quinolones, in Peterson PK, Verhoef J (eds), *The Antimicrobial Agents Annual 1*. Amsterdam, Elsevier, 1986, pp 164-178.

14. Bergan T: Quinolones, in Peterson PK, Verhoef J (eds), *The Antimicrobial Agents Annual 2*. Amsterdam, Elsevier, 1987, pp 169-183.

15. Saunders CC: Ciprofloxacin: *In vitro* activity, mechanism of action, and resistance. Rev Infect Dis 1988;10:516-527.

16. Vassey CM, Baltch AL, Smith RP: Comparative antimicrobial activity of enoxacin, ciprofloxacin, amifloxacin, norfloxacin and ofloxacin against 177 bacterial isolates. J Antimicrob Chemother 1986;17:623-628.

17. Gerding DN, Hitt JA: Tissue penetration of the new quinolones in humans. Rev Infect Dis 1989;11(suppl 5):S1046-S1057.

18. Gerding DN, Peterson LR, Hughes CE, et al: Extravascular antimicrobial distribution in man, in Lorian V (ed), *Antibiotics in Laboratory Medicine*. Baltimore, Williams & Wilkins, 1986, pp 938-994.

19. Tudor RG, Youngs DJ, Yoshioka K, et al: A comparison of the penetration of two quinolones into intra-abdominal abscess. Arch Surg 1988;123:1487-1490.

20. Bergan T: Quinolones, in Peterson PK, Verhoef J (eds), *The Antimicrobial Agents Annual 3*. Amsterdam, Elsevier, 1988, pp 177-202.

21. Beam TR, Guitierrez I, Powell S, et al: Prospective study of the efficacy and safety of ciprofloxacin IV/PO in the treatment of diabetic foot infections, abstract. Second International Symposium on New Quinolones, Geneva, Switzerland, August 25-27, 1988, p 176.

# THE USE OF FLUOROQUINOLONES IN MISCELLANEOUS INFECTIONS **13**

*Bruce E. Kreter*
*Bennett Lorber*

## INTRODUCTION

The use of fluoroquinolones to treat urinary tract, skin and soft tissue, bone and joint, gastrointestinal, and lower respiratory tract infections is well established. Their efficacy in specialized groups, such as neutropenic or cystic fibrosis patients, is currently under investigation. In this chapter, data are presented regarding the use of fluoroquinolones to treat central nervous system infections, endocarditis, ocular infections, typhoid fever, malignant otitis externa, Lyme disease, nocardiosis, malaria, and mycobacterial infections, including leprosy. The use of these drugs to eradicate the carrier state of salmonellae, meningococci, and staphylococci is also discussed.

## CENTRAL NERVOUS SYSTEM INFECTIONS

Successful treatment of bacterial meningitis requires the use of bactericidal antibiotics that penetrate the blood-brain barrier in sufficient concentrations to eradicate the pathogenic organisms causing the disease. Most cases of bacterial meningitis in patients over two months of age are caused by *Haemophilus influenzae, Neisseria meningitidis,* and *Streptococcus pneumoniae.* Gram-negative meningitis caused by Enterobacteriaceae or *Pseudomonas aeruginosa* may occur in the post-neurosurgical setting. The drugs of choice for the common bacterial meningitides have traditionally been ampicillin plus chloramphenicol in pediatric patients, and penicillin in adults; more recently the third-generation cephalosporins have been used in both pediatric and adult patients.

The fluoroquinolones have excellent in vitro activity against many of the gram-negative bacteria that cause meningitis, particularly *N. meningitidis, H. influenzae,* the Enterobacteriaceae and *Pseudomonas.* Minimum inhibitory concentrations (MICs) as low as 0.008 µg/mL have been reported for ciprofloxacin against *N. meningitidis.*[1]

However, the fluoroquinolones do not have reliable bactericidal activity against the streptococci, which frequently cause both pediatric and adult meningitis. Because of their in vitro activity, the fluoroquinolones have been evaluated in both animal and human studies with regard to pharmacokinetic disposition in the central nervous system (CNS) and efficacy in treating meningitis. The use of fluoroquinolones in the treatment of central nervous system infections has recently been reviewed by Norrby.[2]

Montay et al[3] evaluated the pharmacokinetics of pefloxacin and its metabolites in various laboratory mammals. Brain tissue levels of pefloxacin were 10-20% of concurrent serum concentrations in rats and 25-30% of concurrent serum concentrations in dogs. Tran Van Tho et al[4] studied the central nervous system distribution of enoxacin in dogs with healthy meninges and in dogs with experimental meningitis. In both models, cerebrospinal fluid (CSF) levels were in excess of reported MICs for both *H. influenzae* and *N. meningitidis*. Levels in meningitic dogs were approximately twice those in healthy dogs, demonstrating that fluoroquinolone penetration of the meninges may be dependent on the degree of inflammation present.

Sobieski and Scheld evaluated the activities of ciprofloxacin and ofloxacin in experimental *H. influenzae* meningitis in rabbits.[5] The concentrations of both drugs in cerebrospinal fluid were in excess of the MICs for *H. influenzae*. Shibl et al[6] and Hackbarth et al[7] studied the effects of pefloxacin and ciprofloxacin on experimental gram-negative meningitis in rabbits. The CNS penetration of pefloxacin was 26-33% in normal rabbits and 51% in infected animals. Time-kill curves demonstrated that the drug was as effective as cefotaxime in clearing experimentally-induced *E. coli* meningitis. Ciprofloxacin penetrated uninfected rabbits to a lesser extent (4%) than animals experimentally infected with *Ps. aeruginosa* (18%). As the dose of ciprofloxacin was increased, the rate of bacterial killing also increased proportionally. Ciprofloxacin was comparable to ceftazidime and tobramycin in this model.

The pharmacokinetic distribution of ciprofloxacin, ofloxacin, and pefloxacin into the human CNS has been studied by many researchers, both in patients with meningitis and in healthy volunteers. Bassaris et al[8] measured the CSF concentrations of ciprofloxacin by lumbar puncture following two 200 mg intravenous doses. At one hour the CSF concentrations ranged from 0.01 to 0.12 µg/mL. Ciprofloxacin IV (200 mg every 12 hours for 3 doses) was administered to 23 patients with meningitis being treated with antibiotics other than fluoroquinolones.[9] The concentration of ciprofloxacin in CSF ranged from 0.35 to 0.56 µg/mL. Valainis et al[10] studied the penetration of 500 mg of oral ciprofloxacin into the CNS of one patient by sampling intraventricular CSF obtained from an Ommaya reservoir. The peak CSF level achieved was 7.5% of the peak serum concentration. Kitzes-Cohen et al[11] evaluated the CSF penetration of a single 500 mg oral dose of ciprofloxacin in 48 patients undergoing diagnostic lumbar puncture who presented without inflammation of the meninges. Mean peak CSF concentration was achieved 4 hours after drug administration and reached a level of 0.14 µg/mL. Area under the concentration curve determinations in both serum and CSF demonstrated approximately 10% penetration of the central nervous system by ciprofloxacin.

In nine patients treated with intravenous amoxicillin (100 mg/kg/d) and ofloxacin (200 mg orally twice daily), the CSF concentration of ofloxacin was reported to reach levels between 50 and 60% of concurrent serum levels.[12] Diagnostic CSF taps in 17 patients with neurological disease revealed 47 to 87% penetration by ofloxacin.[13] Wolff et al[14] reported 52-58% penetration of oral or intravenous pefloxacin into CSF in 15 patients with bacterial meningitis or ventriculitis. Similar results were reported by Dow et al[15] after a single 400 mg intravenous dose of pefloxacin was given to nine patients with hydrocephalus. Korinek et al[16] evaluated brain tissue levels of pefloxacin after different doses were administered to 30 patients undergoing neurosurgical procedures. Levels in tumor tissue were higher than in surrounding normal brain tissue and in some cases exceeded concurrent serum levels.

Information regarding the therapeutic applications of fluoroquinolones to the treatment of meningitis is available from a handful of case reports. Buckley[17] reported the successful ciprofloxacin treatment of a patient with chronic relapsing meningitis due to *Ps. aeruginosa* who had failed conventional therapy. Millar et al[18] successfully treated a 56-year-old man with a post-neurosurgical, multi-resistant, *Ps. aeruginosa* meningitis with ciprofloxacin (200 mg IV every 12 hours) and tobramycin (120 mg IV every 8 hours) after failure of cefotaxime and gentamicin. Isaacs et al[19] successfully treated a premature infant with recurrent, multi-resistant, *Ps. aeruginosa* ventriculitis with intravenous ciprofloxacin for 28 days. A 78-year-old woman with a post-laminectomy wound infection and meningitis caused by *Morganella morganii* was successfully treated with intravenous pefloxacin.[20] Bertrand et al[21] reported the successful treatment of a patient with purulent meningitis as part of an open trial using ofloxacin for various infections.

It appears that the fluoroquinolones achieve adequate levels in the CSF; penetration is superior in patients with inflamed meninges. Ofloxacin and pefloxacin attain higher concentrations in the CSF than ciprofloxacin, possibly because of their relatively low degree of ionization at serum pH and their greater lipid solubility. The fluoroquinolones should not be used empirically in infections of the central nervous system because of their unreliable activity against streptococci and lack of activity against anaerobic bacteria (common causes of brain abscess). However, these agents may prove useful for the treatment of resistant gram-negative bacterial meningitides.

## REFERENCES

1.  Felmingham D, Wall RA: The comparative activity of twelve 4-quinolone antimicrobials and sulphadiazine against *Neisseria meningitidis*. Drugs Exp Clin Res 1985; 11(7):427-429.

2.  Norrby SR: 4-Quinolones in the treatment of infections of the central nervous system. Rev Infect Dis 1988;10:(suppl 1):S253-S255.

3.  Montay G, Goueffon Y, Roquet F: Absorption, distribution, metabolic fate, and elimination of pefloxacin mesylate in mice, rats, dogs, monkeys, and humans. Antimicrob Agents Chemother 1984;25:463-472.

4.  Tran Van Tho, Armengaud A, Davet B: Diffusion of enoxacin into the cerebrospinal fluid in dogs with healthy meninges and with experimental meningitis. J Antimicrob Chemother 1984;14(suppl C):57-62.

5.  Sobieski MW, Scheld WM: Comparative activity of ciprofloxacin and ofloxacin in experimental *H. influenzae* meningitis, abstract No. 216. Program and abstracts of the 24th Interscience Conference on Antimicrobial Agents and Chemotherapy, Washington, October 8-10, 1984.

6.  Shibl AM, Hackbarth CJ, Sande MA: Evaluation of pefloxacin in experimental *Escherichia coli* meningitis. Antimicrob Agents Chemother 1986;29(3):409-411.

7.  Hackbarth CJ, Chambers HF, Stella F, et al: Ciprofloxacin in experimental *Pseudomonas aeruginosa* meningitis in rabbits. J Antimicrob Chemother 1986;18(suppl D):65-69.

8.  Bassaris H, Papadakis N, Gogos C, et al: Penetration of ciprofloxacin into CSF through non-inflamed meninges, [abstract]. Program and abstracts of the International Congress for Infectious Disease, Cairo, Egypt, 1985.

9.  Wolff M, Boutron L, Singlas E, et al: Penetration of ciprofloxacin into cerebrospinal fluid of patients with bacterial meningitis. Antimicrob Agents Chemother 1987;31(6):899-902.

10. Valainis G, Thomas D, Pankey G: Penetration of ciprofloxacin into cerebrospinal fluid. Eur J Clin Microbiol 1986;5:206-207.

11. Kitzes-Cohen R, Miler A, Gilboa A, et al: Penetration of ciprofloxacin into the cerebrospinal fluid. Rev Infect Dis 1987;10(suppl 1):S256-S257.

12. Stahl JP, Croize J, Lefebvre MA, et al: Diffusion of ofloxacin into the cerebrospinal fluid in patients with bacterial meningitis. Infection 1986;14(suppl 4):S254-S255.

13. Stubner G, Weinrich W, Brands U: Study of the cerebrospinal fluid penetrability of ofloxacin. Infection 1986;14(suppl 4):S250-S253.

14. Wolff M, Regnier B, Daldoss C, et al: Penetration of pefloxacin into CSF of patients with meningitis. Antimicrob Agents Chemother 1984;26:289-291.

15. Dow J, Chazal J, Frydman AM, Janny P, et al: Transfer kinetics of pefloxacin into CSF after one hour IV infusion of 400 mg in man. J Antimicrob Chemother 1986;17(suppl B): 81-87.

16. Korinek AM, Montay G, Bianchi A, et al: Penetration of pefloxacin into human brain tissue. Rev Infect Dis 1988;10(suppl 1):S257.

17. Buckley R: Safety and efficacy of chronic oral ciprofloxacin suppressive therapy in a patient with chronic relapsing pseudomonas meningitis, abstract No. 256. Abstracts of the International Symposium on New Quinolones, Geneva, July 17-19, 1986.

18. Millar MR, Bransby-Zachary MA, Tompkins DS, et al: Ciprofloxacin for *Pseudomonas aeruginosa* meningitis [letter]. Lancet 1986;1:1325.

19. Isaacs D, Slack MPE, Wilkinson AR, et al: Successful treatment of pseudomonas ventriculitis with ciprofloxacin. J Antimicrob Chemother 1986;17:535-538.

20. Isaacs RD, Ellis Pegler RB: Successful treatment of *Morganella morganii* meningitis with pefloxacin mesylate. J Antimicrob Chemother 1987;20(5):769-770.

21. Bertrand A, Janbon F, Despaux E, et al: Ofloxacin (RU 43280). Clinical study. Pathol Biol (Paris) 1987;35(5):629-633.

# ENDOCARDITIS

The new fluoroquinolone antibiotics have poor activity against the streptococcal strains commonly responsible for bacterial endocarditis.[1-3] However, the activity of fluoroquinolones against staphylococci (both methicillin-sensitive and methicillin-resistant) makes these drugs worthy of study as potential therapeutic agents for endocarditis due to these increasingly prevalent pathogens. In addition, the activity of quinolones against *Pseudomonas aeruginosa* warrants their consideration for the treatment of endocarditis due to this organism.

To date, little information has been published regarding the efficacy of fluoroquinolones in human endocarditis. Daikos et al[4] treated two patients with incurable *Ps. aeruginosa* endocarditis with oral ciprofloxacin for 3 1/2 months and 22 months, respectively. Bacteremia cleared and symptoms improved; the drug was well tolerated and blood isolates after treatment showed limited progression of resistance to ciprofloxacin. Additional clinical studies will likely be forthcoming since pharmacokinetic and animal model data are encouraging.

Numerous studies have shown the efficacy of quinolones in animal models of staphylococcal endocarditis. These include pefloxacin for both methicillin-susceptible and methicillin-resistant *S. aureus*,[5] enoxacin for methicillin-resistant *S. aureus*,[6] and difloxacin for methicillin-sensitive *S. aureus*.[7] In one study,[8] the combination of fosfomycin and pefloxacin was more effective than either agent alone in sterilizing cardiac vegetations due to methicillin-resistant *S. aureus*.

Ciprofloxacin is the most widely studied of the fluoroquinolones in endocarditis. Several animal studies have shown it to be effective for staphylococcal endocarditis due to methicillin-susceptible as well as resistant strains.[9-12] In one study of methicillin-susceptible *S. aureus* endocarditis,[13] progressive resistance of the test strain was observed in 12.5% of animals treated with ciprofloxacin. In a study of the in vitro interaction between ciprofloxacin and vancomycin against 9 *S. epidermidis* isolates from patients with endocarditis,[14] killing curves demonstrated early antagonism between the two agents.

*Ps. aeruginosa* endocarditis has been notoriously difficult to treat medically, and surgical intervention is often necessary. In two animal studies,[15,16] ciprofloxacin compared favorably to combination therapy with an antipseudomonal penicillin plus an aminoglycoside. In another animal study,[17] ciprofloxacin was significantly more effective than this combination. In none of these studies did emergence of resistance become a problem; however, in a study of pefloxacin the MICs of organisms from 30% of vegetations obtained on day 10 of therapy were 4- to 8-fold higher than those of the parent strain used to induce infection.[18]

In summary, preliminary data from in vitro and animal model studies are encouraging and suggest that fluoroquinolones may prove useful in endocarditis, particularly that due to methicillin-resistant *S. aureus*. The potential for emergence of resistance during the necessarily long course of therapy must be evaluated, but further clinical trials are warranted.

## REFERENCES

1. Etienne J, Coulet M, Brun Y, et al: Susceptibilities of streptococcal strains associated with infective endocarditis to nine antibiotics. Chemotherapy 1988;34:113-116.

2. Fernandez-Guerrero M, Rouse MS, Henry NK, et al: In vitro and in vivo activity of ciprofloxacin against enterococci isolated from patients with infective endocarditis. Antimicrob Agents Chemother 1987;31:430-433.

3. Ingerman M, Pitsakis PG, Rosenberg A, et al: β-lactamase production in experimental endocarditis due to aminoglycoside resistant *Streptococcus faecalis*. J Infect Dis 1987;155:1226-1232.

4. Daikos GL, Katpalia SB, Lalans VT, et al: Long-term oral ciprofloxacin: Experience in the treatment of incurable infective endocarditis. Am J Med 1988;84:786-790.

5. Sullam PM, Tauber MG, Hackbarth CJ, et al: Pefloxacin therapy for experimental endocarditis caused by methicillin-susceptible or methicillin-resistant strains of *Staphylococcus aureus*. Antimicrob Agents Chemother 1985;27:685-687.

6. Gilbert M, Boscia JA, Kobasa WD, et al: Enoxacin compared with vancomycin for the treatment of experimental methicillin-resistant *Staphylococcus aureus* endocarditis. Antimicrob Agents Chemother 1986;29:461-463.

7. Boscia JA, Kobasa WD, Kaye D: Comparison of difloxacin, enoxacin, and cefazolin for the treatment of experimental *Staphylococcus aureus* endocarditis. Antimicrob Agents Chemother 1988;32:262-264.

8. Thauvin C, Lemeland JF, Humbert G, et al: Efficacy of pefloxacin-fosfomycin in experimental endocarditis caused by methicillin-resistant *Staphylococcus aureus*. Antimicrob Agents Chemother 1988;32:919-921.

9. Perrone CM, Malinverni R, Glauser MP: Treatment of *Staphylococcus aureus* endocarditis in rats with coumermycin A1 and ciprofloxacin, alone or in combination. Antimicrob Agents Chemother 1987;31:539-543.

10. Carpenter TC, Hackbarth CJ, Chambers HF, et al: Efficacy of ciprofloxacin for experimental endocarditis caused by methicillin-susceptible or -resistant strains of *Staphylococcus aureus*. Antimicrob Agents Chemother 1986;30:382-384.

11. Kaatz GW, Barriere SL, Schaberg DR, et al: Ciprofloxacin versus vancomycin in the therapy of experimental methicillin-resistant *Staphylococcus aureus* endocarditis. Antimicrob Agents Chemother 1987;31:527-530.

12. Fernandez-Guerrero M, Rouse MS, Henry N, et al: Ciprofloxacin therapy of experimental endocarditis caused by methicillin-susceptible or methicillin-resistant *Staphylococcus aureus*. Antimicrob Agents Chemother 1988;32:747-751.

13. Katz GW, Barriere SL, Schaberg DR, et al: The emergence of resistance to ciprofloxacin during treatment of experimental *Staphylococcus aureus* endocarditis. J Antimicrob Chemother 1987;20:753-758.

14. Paton JH, Williams EW: Interaction between ciprofloxacin and vancomycin against staphylococci. J Antimicrob Chemother 1987;20:251-254.

15. Struck RW, Gratz JC, Maserati R, et al: Comparison of ciprofloxacin with azlocillin plus tobramycin in the therapy of experimental *Pseudomonas aeruginosa* endocarditis. Antimicrob Agents Chemother 1985;28:428-432.

16. Bayer AS, Kim KS: In vivo efficacy of azlocillin and amikacin versus ciprofloxacin with and without amikacin in experimental right-sided endocarditis due to *Pseudomonas aeruginosa*. Chemotherapy 1986;32:364-373.

17. Bayer AS, Blomquist IK, Kim KS: Ciprofloxacin in experimental aortic valve endocarditis due to *Pseudomonas aeruginosa*. J Antimicrob Chemother 1986;17:641-649.

18. Bayer AS, Hirano L, Yih J: Development of beta-lactam resistance and increased quinolone MICs during therapy of experimental *Pseudomonas aeruginosa* endocarditis. Antimicrob Agents Chemother 1988;32:231-235.

## INFECTIONS OF THE EYE

The treatment of ophthalmic infections is frequently difficult; despite clinical signs suggesting the presence of infection, pathogenic organisms are difficult to isolate. In addition, the degree of ocular penetration of many antibiotics is either unknown or has been inadequately studied. The antibacterial spectrum and tissue distribution characteristics of the fluoroquinolones make them potentially useful drugs for ocular infections, including endophthalmitis due to staphylococci, Enterobacteriaceae, *Pseudomonas* and other gram-negative bacteria.

Cataract extraction procedures provide a convenient model for the study of the ophthalmic pharmacokinetics of antibacterial agents. Aqueous humor, vitreous humor and the opacified lens can be obtained from otherwise healthy patients undergoing surgery. The patient population tends to be older, however, which may influence the renal elimination and thus the ocular penetration of some fluoroquinolones.

Numerous authors have investigated the pharmacokinetic distribution of ciprofloxacin, pefloxacin, and ofloxacin in human subjects undergoing cataract removal procedures (Table 1).[1-10] In these studies, the antibiotics were administered at different times, by different routes, and at different dosages prior to surgery; however, some overall conclusions are possible. Of the three study drugs, pefloxacin reached the highest levels in aqueous humor (0.75 to 2.66 µg/mL), followed by ofloxacin and ciprofloxacin. Vitreous humor levels were measured in two studies;[1,5] ciprofloxacin reached a level of 0.4 µg/mL six hours after a 400 mg intravenous dose and pefloxacin reached levels of up to 36% of corresponding serum levels after a single 800 mg intravenous dose. The lenticular penetrations of pefloxacin and ofloxacin have been studied by Salvanet et al[8] and Fisch et al.[10] Uptake into the lens appears to lag behind corresponding plasma levels, reaching a peak many hours after plasma concentrations become undetectable. Relatively low levels of ofloxacin were found in the lenses of 20 patients studied by Fisch et al, whereas pefloxacin slowly accumulated in the lenses of 20 patients studied by Salvanet et al, reaching a concentration of 0.43 µg/mL 24 hours after administration.

Despite the available pharmacokinetic data in humans, the therapeutic efficacy of fluoroquinolones in eye infections has been studied only in animal models. Sugar et al[11] compared topical placebo, enoxacin (3 mg/mL and 10 mg/mL) and gentamicin sulfate (3 mg/mL) in a rabbit model of *Pseudomonas* keratitis. Two drops of solution were administered every hour for 24 hours, after which time the corneas were analyzed for bacterial counts. Enoxacin treated animals demonstrated an approximate 5000-fold reduction in bacterial counts when compared to controls. No significant differences were seen between the two strengths of enoxacin solution and gentamicin. Topical ciprofloxacin (3 mg/mL) was compared to saline-treated control rabbits in another study of experimental *Pseudomonas* keratitis by O'Brien et al.[12] Eradication of all bacterial colony forming units occurred in ciprofloxacin-treated animals, compared

**Table 1.** Human pharmacokinetic studies of fluoroquinolone concentrations in the eye

| Reference | Total number of patients | Drug/Dose/Route | Time of level | Peak level in aqueous humor µg/mL | Vitreous humor µg/mL | Lens µg/g |
|---|---|---|---|---|---|---|
| 1 | 35 | Ciprofloxacin 400 mg IV x 1 | 1 hour | 0.27 | N/R | N/R |
| | | Ciprofloxacin 750 mg PO x 1 | 4 hours | 0.35 | N/R | N/R |
| | | Ciprofloxacin 750 mg PO x 2 | 12 hours | 0.33 | N/R | N/R |
| | | Ciprofloxacin 750 mg PO x 8 | 12 hours | 0.75 | N/R | N/R |
| 2 | 25 | Ciprofloxacin 200 mg IV x 2 | 1 hour | 0.21 | N/R | N/R |
| 3 | 16 | Ciprofloxacin 200 mg IV x 1 | 1 hour | 0.165 | N/R | N/R |
| 4 | 25 | Ciprofloxacin 1 g PO x 1 | 2 hours | 0.56 | N/R | N/R |
| 5 | 64 | Pefloxacin 400 mg IV x 1 | 1 hour | 0.60 | 0.5 | N/R |
| | | Pefloxacin 400 mg IV x 1 | 2 hours | 0.80 | 0.3 | N/R |
| | | Pefloxacin 800 mg IV x 1 | 1 hour | 2.70 | 0.4 | N/R |
| | | Pefloxacin 800 mg IV x 1 | 12 hours | 2.20 | 1.3 | N/R |
| 6 | 53 | Pefloxacin 400 mg IV x 1 | 6 hours | 1.40 | N/R | 0.20 |
| | | Pefloxacin 400 mg PO x 3 | 12 hours | 7.00 | N/R | 5.20 |
| | | Ofloxacin 400 mg PO x 1 | 2 hours | 1.00 | N/R | 0.04 |
| 7 | 35 | Pefloxacin 400 mg PO x 1 | "average level" | 0.95 | N/R | N/R |
| 8 | 20 | Pefloxacin 400 mg IV x 1 | 2 hours | 0.75 | N/R | 0.90 |
| | | Pefloxacin 400 mg IV x 1 | 6 hours | 1.45 | N/R | 0.20 |
| 9 | 30 | Ofloxacin 200 mg PO x 1 | 6 hours | 0.60 | N/R | N/R |
| 10 | 20 | Ofloxacin 400 mg PO x 1 | 2 hours | 1.00 | N/R | 0.04 |
| | | Ofloxacin 400 mg PO x 1 | 6 hours | 1.10 | N/R | 0.04 |

N/R = not reported

with 1-10 million organisms per mL recovered from controls. Aqueous humor concentrations of ciprofloxacin were higher in animals with debrided corneal epithelia than in those with intact epithelia. Davey et al[13] administered single intravitreous injections of ciprofloxacin, gentamicin and imipenem to rabbits with experimental *Pseudomonas* endophthalmitis. Therapy was begun either "early" (within 24 hours of inoculation) or "late" (48 hours after inoculation). Dose-response testing yielded better results for all three antibiotics in early treatment when 10 to 100 times the minimum bactericidal concentrations were achieved in the vitreous humor. None of the drugs had any appreciable activity when treatment was delayed by 48 hours after inoculation. This study underscores the necessity of prompt treatment of endophthalmitis. Delays in treatment impair antibiotic efficacy and may cause loss of vision in the affected eye.

Preliminary pharmacokinetic evidence demonstrates adequate fluoroquinolone penetration of the aqueous and vitreous humors as well as of the lens in human patients undergoing cataract removal procedures. Topical instillation of 3 mg/mL of either enoxacin or ciprofloxacin was effective in rabbit models of *Pseudomonas* keratitis, and the early intravitreous injection of ciprofloxacin resulted in markedly reduced bacterial counts in rabbits. The fluoroquinolones deserve attention for both the topical and systemic treatment of ocular infections. Recommendations for therapy must await the publication of human clinical trials.

## REFERENCES

1. Mounier M, Adenis JP, Denis F: Intraocular penetration of ciprofloxacin after infusion and oral administration. Pathol Biol (Paris) 1988;36(5 Pt 2):724-727.

2. Skoutelis AT, Gartaganis SP, Chrysanthopoulos CJ, et al: Aqueous humor penetration of ciprofloxacin in the human eye. Arch Ophthalmol 1988;106(3):404-405.

3. Behrens-Baumann W, Martell J: Ciprofloxacin concentrations in human aqueous humor following intravenous administration. Chemotherapy 1987;33(5):328-330.

4. Fern AI, Sweeney G, Doig M, et al: Penetration of ciprofloxacin into aqueous humor. Trans Ophthalmol Soc UK 1986;105(Pt 6):650-652.

5. Denis F, Mounier M, Adenis JP: Intraocular penetration of pefloxacin in man and rabbit. The aqueous humor and vitreous body. Pathol Biol (Paris) 1987;35(5 Pt 2):772-776.

6. Lafaix C, Salvanet A, Fisch A, et al: Diffusion of fluoroquinolones in the aqueous humor and crystalline lens. Pathol Biol (Paris) 1987;35(5 Pt 2):768-771.

7. Bron A, Talon D, Delbosc B, et al: Intracameral penetration of pefloxacin in man. J Fr Ophthalmol 1986;9(4):317-321.

8. Salvanet A, Fisch A, Lafaix C, et al: Pefloxacin concentrations in human aqueous humor and lens. J Antimicrob Chemother 1986;18(2):199-201.

9. Bron A, Talon D, Delbosc B, et al: Intracameral penetration of ofloxacin in man. J Fr Ophthalmol 1987;10(6-7):443-446.

10. Fisch A, Lafaix C, Salvanet A, et al: Ofloxacin in human aqueous humor and lens [letter]. J Antimicrob Chemother 1987;20(3):453-454.

11. Sugar A, Cohen MA, Bien PA, et al: Treatment of experimental *Pseudomonas* corneal ulcers with enoxacin, a quinolone antibiotic. Arch Ophthalmol 1986;104(8):1230-1232.

12. O'Brien TP, Sawusch MR, Dick JD, et al: Topical ciprofloxacin treatment of *Pseudomonas* keratitis in rabbits. Arch Ophthalmol 1988;106(10):1444-1446.

13. Davey PG, Barza M, Stuart M: Dose response of experimental *Pseudomonas* endophthalmitis to ciprofloxacin, gentamicin, and imipenem: Evidence for resistance to "late" treatment of infections. J Infect Dis 1987;155(3):518-523.

## TYPHOID AND OTHER ENTERIC FEVERS

Typhoid fever remains a major problem worldwide: the number of cases in the United States is increasing, and *Salmonella* spp. have become progressively resistant to antimicrobial agents in recent years.[1] The results of preliminary trials suggest that the fluoroquinolones may be particularly useful agents in the treatment of bacteremic *Salmonella* infections including typhoid fever. They may also be useful in eradicating the chronic typhoid carrier state.

As pointed out by Keusch,[2] success in treating invasive enteric infections correlates with in vitro susceptibility as well as with high concentrations of antibiotic in both the blood and the lumen of the gastrointestinal tract. Fluoroquinolones meet all three of these criteria. Ciprofloxacin, norfloxacin, and ofloxacin have each demonstrated marked in vitro activity against *Salmonella* spp. including *S. typhi*.[2,3] Minimum inhibitory concentrations for 90% of isolates are 0.02-0.097 mg/L.[2] In a study employing human volunteers,[4] serum bactericidal activity against 8 strains of *S. typhi* was measured following oral doses of ciprofloxacin (500 mg) and ofloxacin (200 mg). Both agents produced excellent bactericidal levels in serum (ciprofloxacin greater than ofloxacin), and kinetic studies showed both drugs to be superior to the classical anti-typhoid agents, chloramphenicol, amoxicillin, and trimethoprim-sulfamethoxazole.

Clinical studies evaluating the efficacy of the new quinolones in the treatment of enteric fevers, including typhoid fever, are beginning to appear in the literature. Tigaud et al[5] treated 10 patients with enteric fever with ofloxacin (200 mg bid orally); all patients recovered without sequelae or carriage of the *Salmonella* pathogens. In another study, 38 patients with culture-proven typhoid fever were treated with oral ciprofloxacin (500 mg bid) for 14 days.[6] Of the 36 patients completing the study, all had favorable clinical and bacteriologic outcomes. In a study comparing pefloxacin to trimethoprim-sulfamethoxazole in the treatment of typhoid fever, Hajji et al[7] reported comparable cure rates, but pefloxacin was better tolerated and produced clinical responses more rapidly. Thus, although clinical experience is still quite limited, the fluoroquinolones are clearly promising agents for the treatment of enteric fevers.

Treatment of chronic carriers of *S. typhi* is an important measure for controlling typhoid fever. Ampicillin or amoxicillin (6 grams daily for 4-6 weeks), with or without probenecid, is considered the treatment of choice for such patients. The efficacy of this regimen is hampered by low patient compliance, high rates of adverse drug effects, and high relapse rates (40-60%). Preliminary results suggest that the new quinolones may be particularly useful for eradicating the *S. typhi* carrier state. In a study using oral ciprofloxacin 750 mg orally for 28 days, Ferreccio et al treated 12 chronic carriers of *S. typhi*.[8] Ten patients had negative cultures at the one-year follow-up, including two patients who were known to have gallstones. One patient was culture positive (bile) three weeks after treatment, and one developed typhoid fever with a different *S. typhi* strain six months after treatment. The cure rate was 92% (11 of 12 patients). However, the authors expressed concern about adverse reactions; one patient had an allergic reaction and 3 had an unexplained fall in hemoglobin.

Norfloxacin (400 mg bid orally) was compared with placebo in a double-blind study of chronic typhoid carriers.[9] Eleven of 12 norfloxacin-treated individuals had negative stool and bile cultures post-treatment, whereas all placebo-treated patients were still positive. In a subsequent open trial, *S. typhi* was eradicated in 7 of 11 carriers, for an overall eradication rate of 78%.

These preliminary studies are encouraging and suggest that the quinolones may prove useful in the treatment of chronic carriers of *S. typhi*.

## REFERENCES

1. Bryan JP, Rocha HM, Scheld WM: Problems in salmonellosis: Rationale for clinical trials with newer β-lactam agents and quinolones. Rev Infect Dis 1986;8:189-207.

2. Keusch GT: Antimicrobial therapy for enteric infections and typhoid fever: State of the art. Rev Infect Dis 1988;10(suppl 1):S199-S205.

3. Hannan A: In vitro activity of ofloxacin against 210 clinical isolates of typhoid salmonellae. Infection 1986;14(suppl 4):S243-S244.

4. Trautmann M, Krause B, Birnbaum D, et al: Serum bactericidal activity of newer quinolones against Salmonella typhi compared with standard therapeutic regimens. Eur J Clin Microbiol 1986;5:297-302.

5. Tigaud S, Lucht F, Peyramond D, et al: Use of ofloxacin for the treatment of enteric infections. Rev Infect Dis 1988;10(suppl 1):S207.

6. Ramirez CA, Bran JL, Meija CR, et al: Open prospective study of the clinical efficacy of ciprofloxacin. Antimicrob Agents Chemother 1985;28:128-132.

7. Hajji M, el-Mdaghri N, Benbachir M, et al: Prospective randomized comparative trial of pefloxacin versus cotrimoxazole in the treatment of typhoid fever in adults. Eur J Clin Microbiol 1988;7:361-363.

8. Ferreccio C, Morris JG Jr, Valdivieso C, et al: Efficacy of ciprofloxacin in the treatment of chronic typhoid carriers. J Infect Dis 1988;157:1235-1239.

9. Gotuzzo E, Guerra JG, Benavente L, et al: Use of norfloxacin to treat chronic typhoid carriers. J Infect Dis 1988;157:1221-1225.

## INVASIVE EXTERNAL OTITIS

Invasive external otitis (malignant otitis externa) is an uncommon but potentially devastating infection that begins in the external ear canal and may progress rapidly to involve the skull, cranial nerves, meninges, and brain. This infection is seen primarily in elderly diabetics with no previous history of ear disease and is due to *Pseudomonas aeruginosa* in almost all instances. Treatment typically involves surgical debridement and prolonged courses (4-6 weeks) of intravenous antibiotics. The activity of the fluoroquinolones against *Pseudomonas aeruginosa* makes these agents potentially useful in this infection; indeed, they may obviate the need for prolonged intravenous antibiotic therapy and facilitate early hospital discharge and out-patient management.

A few investigators have reported the successful use of ciprofloxacin in the treatment of this infection.[1-5] Although the total number of cases is small, results are encouraging. Morrison and Bailey[3] treated two patients with relapsing invasive external otitis with oral ciprofloxacin (750 mg bid) following 6 weeks of traditional parenteral therapy (azlocillin and gentamicin). After six months both patients were cured.

Yu et al[4] treated 8 patients with oral ciprofloxacin (750 mg bid) in combination with rifampin (600 mg bid) for 6 to 8 weeks. All patients were elderly diabetics with *Ps. aeruginosa* infection and documented osteomyelitis. Seven of the 8 patients had failed prior parenteral antipseudomonal therapy. All patients responded to the oral regimen; however, one relapsed 4 months later. These authors concluded that the combination of oral ciprofloxacin with rifampin may be a major advance in the treatment of this difficult infection. Finally, Lang et al[5] treated 13 patients with oral ciprofloxacin (750 mg bid) alone for 6 weeks. Results were similar to those reported above; 12 of 13 were cured, and 1 recovered only after repeated surgery and being crossed over to traditional intravenous therapy. No emergence of resistance occurred during therapy.

## REFERENCES

1. Joachims HZ, Danino J, Raz R: Malignant external otitis: Treatment with fluoro-quinolones. Am J Otolaryngol 1988;9:102-105.

2. Sabater F, Mensa J, Domenech J, et al: Necrotizing external otitis treated with cipro-floxacin. A case report. J Laryngol Otol 1988;102:606-607.

3. Morrison GA, Bailey CM: Relapsing malignant otitis externa successfully treated with ciprofloxacin. J Laryngol Otol 1988;102:872-876.

4. Yu VL, Stoehr G, Rubin J, et al: Efficacy of oral ciprofloxacin plus rifampin for therapy of malignant otitis externa, abstract 188. Program and abstracts of the 27th Interscience Conference on Antimicrobial Agents and Chemotherapy. New York, October 4-7, 1987.

5. Lang R, Goshen S, Kitzes-Cohen R, et al: Ciprofloxacin in malignant otitis externa (MEO), abstract 337. Program and abstracts of the 28th Interscience Conference on Anti-microbial Agents and Chemotherapy. Los Angeles, October 23-26, 1988.

# LYME DISEASE

Lyme disease is a zoonotic spirochetal infection of humans caused by *Borrelia burgdorferi*. This spirochete is transmitted to humans from its common hosts - white-footed mice, raccoons, and deer, by ticks of the genus *Ixodes*. The symptoms of Lyme disease include local erythema at the site of the tick bite, a flu-like illness, and occasionally cardiac, neurological, and arthritic complications. Current drugs of choice for the treatment of Lyme disease include oral penicillins, oral tetracyclines, and parenteral third-generation cephalosporins.[1] Mursic et al[2] tested the susceptibility of *Borrelia burgdorferi* to 12 antibiotics including ofloxacin and ciprofloxacin. The third-generation cephalosporins and tetracycline showed the greatest activity against the pathogen, both in vitro using a broth dilution technique and in vivo with a gerbil model of borrelial infection. The in vitro $MIC_{90}$s of ciprofloxacin and ofloxacin were 2 µg/mL and 4 µg/mL, respectively. The two fluoroquinolones were not tested in the animal model since they exhibited only modest in vitro activity.

Meisel and Blenk[3] reported on the effectiveness of low dose (250 mg) oral ciprofloxacin given twice daily for various bacterial skin infections. They noted that all cases of pyoderma healed quickly, but relapses occurred in patients receiving six weeks of quinolone therapy for Lyme disease.

Since the data are limited to a single in vitro study and an open case series, the fluoroquinolones cannot be recommended for the treatment of Lyme disease. Tetracycline and penicillin remain the mainstays for oral treatment of early disease (erythema chronicum migrans), while third-generation cephalosporins are recommended for the later stages.[4]

# REFERENCES

1. Dattwyler RJ, Halperin JJ, Pass H, et al: Ceftriaxone as effective therapy in refractory Lyme Disease. J Infect Dis 1987;155:1322-1325.

2. Mursic VP, Wilske B, Schierz G, et al: In vitro and in vivo susceptibility of *Borrelia burgdorferi*. Eur J Clin Microbiol 1987;6(4):424-426.

3. Meisel C, Blenk H: The effectiveness of ciprofloxacin in bacterial skin infections. Zur wirksamkeit von ciprofloxacin bei bakteriellen hautinfektionen. Z-Hautkr 1988;63(12): 1016-1022.

4. Anonymous. Treatment of Lyme disease. Med Lett Drugs Ther 1988;30:65-66.

# NOCARDIOSIS

Nocardiae are aerobic, gram-positive, partially acid-fast, branching rods that rarely cause human disease. Pathogenic nocardial species include *Nocardia asteroides, Nocardia brasiliensis,* and *Nocardia caviae.* Infection is most frequently observed in immunocompromised hosts such as AIDS patients. Infection with *N. asteroides* commonly occurs as pneumonia, with or without brain abscess. Skin and soft tissue infections and osteomyelitis are the usual manifestations of *N. brasiliensis* infection.[1,2] The drug of choice for treating nocardial infections is trimethoprim/sulfamethoxazole, although amikacin, imipenem, and minocycline have also been used.[3]

In vitro susceptibility testing of *Nocardia* species to fluoroquinolones has yielded varying results. Berkey et al[4] evaluated the in vitro susceptibilities of 31 strains of *Nocardia* against a variety of antimicrobial agents. The most effective quinolone was PD-117558, an experimental carboxyquinolone currently under development. Ten of 23 strains of *N. asteroides* were susceptible to ciprofloxacin. Imipenem was the most active agent tested, inhibiting 90% of *N. asteroides* isolated at an MIC of 2 μg/mL.

Wallace and Steele[5] published guidelines for in vitro susceptibility testing of Nocardiae, including interpretive data for ciprofloxacin. They found that 13 of 55 isolates (24%) were susceptible using the disk diffusion method. Gombert et al[6] performed in vitro susceptibility testing of various fluoroquinolone and β-lactam antibiotics against 31 strains of *N. asteroides.* Ciprofloxacin inhibited the growth of 50% of strains with clinically achievable levels. Amikacin, imipenem, and minocycline were the most active agents tested, inhibiting 100% of the isolates.

Southern et al[7] tested the in vitro susceptibilities of 54 strains of *Nocardia* against various antimicrobial agents. Eighty-nine percent of strains were susceptible to ciprofloxacin at an MIC of 2 μg/mL. Auckenthaler et al[8] evaluated the in vitro susceptibilities of a variety of aerobic bacteria, including *Nocardia asteroides,* to ciprofloxacin, enoxacin, norfloxacin, ofloxacin, and pefloxacin. *Nocardia* were usually intermediately susceptible or resistant to these fluoroquinolones.

*Nocardia asteroides* has shown varying degrees of susceptibility to fluoroquinolones in vitro testing. Caution should be exercised before employing these agents to treat nocardiosis, either as primary or adjunctive therapy, since clinical efficacy in humans has not yet been demonstrated.

# REFERENCES

1. Smego RA Jr, Gallis HA: The clinical spectrum of *Nocardia brasiliensis* infection in the United States. Rev Infect Dis 1984;6(2):164-180.

2. Chazen G: Nocardia. Infect Control 1987;8(6):260-263.

3. Sanford JP: *Guide to Antimicrobial Therapy 1988*. Bethesda, Antimicrobial Therapy Inc, 1989, p 68.

4.  Berkey P, Moore D, Rolston KVI: In vitro susceptibilities of Nocardia species to newer antimicrobial agents. Antimicrob Agents Chemother 1988;32(7):1078-1079.

5.  Wallace RJ Jr, Steele LC: Susceptibility testing of Nocardia species for the clinical laboratory. Diagn Microbiol Infect Dis 1988;9(3):155-166.

6.  Gombert ME, Aulicino TM, duBouchet L, et al: Susceptibility of *Nocardia asteroides* to new quinolones and β-lactams. Antimicrob Agents Chemother 1987;31(12):2013-2014.

7.  Southern PM Jr, Kutscher AE, Ragsdale R, et al: Susceptibility in vitro of Nocardia species to antimicrobial agents. Diagn Microbiol Infect Dis 1987;8(2):119-122.

8.  Auckenthaler R, Michéa-Hamzehpour M, Pechère JC: In-vitro activity of newer quinolones against aerobic bacteria. J Antimicrob Chemother 1986;17(suppl B):29-39.

## TUBERCULOSIS AND ATYPICAL
## MYCOBACTERIAL INFECTIONS

Tuberculosis remains a major problem worldwide. For the first time in decades an increase in the number of new cases has been reported in the United States, probably related to the AIDS epidemic. Atypical mycobacterial infections, particularly those due to the *Mycobacterium avium* complex, have emerged as an important cause of morbidity in AIDS patients. The in vitro activity of the fluoroquinolones against mycobacteria and the fact that they are active intracellularly make these agents potentially useful in the treatment of tuberculosis and other mycobacterial diseases.[1]

Berlin et al[2] tested 35 clinical isolates of *M. tuberculosis* (24 susceptible and 11 resistant to conventional primary anti-tuberculosis drugs) for susceptibility to fluoroquinolones. The average MICs of isoniazid-susceptible organisms for ciprofloxacin, ofloxacin, enoxacin and norfloxacin were 1.0, 1.0, 2.0, 2.0 µg/mL respectively; resistant strains were usually inhibited within one dilution of these values. Using an agar dilution technique, Byrne et al[3] reported that difloxacin inhibited 50% of *M. tuberculosis* isolates at a concentration of 4 µg/mL; isoniazid-susceptible and -resistant strains were equally susceptible to difloxacin. Heifets and Lindholm-Levy[4] reported that ciprofloxacin and ofloxacin were bactericidal for 41 strains of *M. tuberculosis*, with MICs lower than achievable serum concentrations; ciprofloxacin MICs were lower than those for ofloxacin. Crowle et al[5] reported that ofloxacin was bactericidal for *M. tuberculosis* in cultured human macrophages at a concentration of 2 µg/mL. In a recent review, Tsukamura reported that ofloxacin 300 mg daily was clinically effective against drug resistant tuberculosis; however, in several patients organisms became resistant to ofloxacin.[6]

The *Mycobacterium avium* complex is not as susceptible to the fluoroquinolones. Variable in vitro results have been reported, and activity is method-dependent.[7] Heifets and Lindholm-Levy reported that the MIC of ciprofloxacin was lower than achievable serum levels for only 28% of 46 *M. avium* strains isolated from AIDS patients.[4] In another study[8] the $MIC_{90s}$ for ciprofloxacin and ofloxacin against 20 clinical isolates were 2 and 8 µg/mL, respectively. Some synergy has been demonstrated against *M. avium* complex strains when ciprofloxacin has been combined with traditional antimycobacterial agents.[9]

Other atypical mycobacteria including *M. fortuitum, M. smegmatis, M. kansasii, M. xenopi, M. scrofulaceum*, and *M. marinum* have been reported to be susceptible in vitro to fluoroquinolones.[10,11] The clinical efficacy of ofloxacin in a patient with *M. fortuitum* pulmonary infection has been described.[12] *M. chelonae* is generally not susceptible to quinolones.[10]

In summary, fluoroquinolones display variable activity against mycobacteria. Virtually all agents (ciprofloxacin, ofloxacin, enoxacin, norfloxacin, difloxacin) inhibit *M. tuberculosis* at achievable serum levels, with ciprofloxacin and ofloxacin

having the greatest activity.[13] Fluoroquinolones have the advantage of oral administration and may prove to be valuable agents for the treatment of mycobacterial infections.

## REFERENCES

1. Easmon CSF, Crane JP, Blowers A: Effect of ciprofloxacin on intracellular organisms: in-vitro and in-vivo studies. J Antimicrob Chemother 1986;18(suppl D):43-48.

2. Berlin OG, Young LS, Bruckner DA: In vitro activity of six fluorinated quinolones against *Mycobacterium tuberculosis*. J Antimicrob Chemother 1987;19:611-615.

3. Byrne SK, Crawford CE, Geddes GL, et al: In vitro susceptibilities of *Mycobacterium tuberculosis* to 10 antimicrobial agents. Antimicrob Agents Chemother 1988;32:1441-1442.

4. Heifets LB, Lindholm-Levy PJ: Bacteriostatic and bactericidal activity of ciprofloxacin and ofloxacin against *Mycobacterium tuberculosis* and *Mycobacterium avium* complex. Tubercle 1987;68:267-276.

5. Crowle AJ, Elkins N, May MH: Effectiveness of ofloxacin against *Mycobacterium tuberculosis* and *Mycobacterium avium,* and rifampin against *M. tuberculosis* in cultured human macrophages. Am Rev Resp Dis 1988;137:1141-1146.

6. Tsukamura M: Chemotherapy of lung tuberculosis by a new antibacterial substance ofloxacin (DL 8280), in Casal M, (ed), *Mycobacteria of Clinical Interest.* Amsterdam, Excerpta Medica, 1986, pp 234-240.

7. Inderlied CB, Young LS, Yamada JK: Determination of in vitro susceptibility of *Mycobacterium avium* complex isolates to antimycobacterial agents by various methods. Antimicrob Agents Chemother 1987;31:1697-1702.

8. Fenlon CH, Cynamon MH: Comparative in vitro activities of ciprofloxacin and other 4-quinolones against *Mycobacterium tuberculosis* and *Mycobacterium intracellulare*. Antimicrob Agents Chemother 1986;29:386-388.

9. Yajko DM, Kirihara J, Sanders C, et al: Antimicrobial synergism against *Mycobacterium avium* complex strains isolated from patients with acquired immune deficiency. Antimicrob Agents Chemother 1988;32:1392-1395.

10. Swenson JM, Wallace RJ Jr, Silcox VA, et al: Antimicrobial susceptibility of five subgroups of *Mycobacterium fortuitum* and *Mycobacterium chelonae*. Antimicrob Agents Chemother 1985;28:807-811.

11. Salfinger M, Hohl P, Kafader FM: Comparative in vitro activity of fleroxacin and other 6-fluoroquinolones against mycobacteria. J Antimicrob Chemother 1988;22(suppl D):55-63.

12. Ichiyama S, Tsukamura M: Ofloxacin and the treatment of pulmonary disease due to *Mycobacterium fortuitum*. Chest 1987;99:1110-1112.

13. Young LS, Berlin OGW, Inderlied CB: Activity of ciprofloxacin and other fluorinated quinolones against mycobacteria. Am J Med 1987;82(suppl 4A):23-26.

# LEPROSY

The observation that fluoroquinolones exhibit activity against atypical and tuberculous mycobacteria has led to interest in their use in the treatment of leprosy (Hansen's disease), a chronic infection caused by the slow growth of *Mycobacterium leprae* in cool body tissues. Current treatment consists of at least two years of dapsone plus either rifampin or clofazimine.[1]

In vitro susceptibility testing of *Mycobacterium leprae* is not possible due to the lack of a suitable culture medium. The mouse footpad model has become a reproducible standard for examining the effects of antimycobacterial drugs on bacterial growth. Guelpa-Lauras and colleagues have studied the effect of fluoroquinolones on the mouse footpad model of leprotic infection.[2,3] In their initial trial,[2] oral ciprofloxacin and pefloxacin were compared at two dosage levels with respect to the growth of a standard inoculum of *Mycobacterium leprae*. Ciprofloxacin given continuously at doses of either 50 mg/kg/day or 150 mg/kg/day did not inhibit the growth of *Mycobacterium leprae*. Pefloxacin, when administered at the lower dose, suppressed the rate of growth of the bacteria but did not prevent growth. The larger dose of pefloxacin inhibited the growth of *Mycobacterium leprae,* and the growth delay that followed discontinuation of pefloxacin suggested that 99% of the inoculated *Mycobacterium leprae* had been killed.

In a subsequent trial using the same mouse footpad model,[3] ofloxacin in similar low and high doses was compared with high-dose pefloxacin (150 mg/kg/day) and with prothionamide. All drugs were given in combination with dapsone. Growth delay was extended in all treated animals as compared with untreated controls. No regrowth of *Mycobacterium leprae* was observed in the animals treated for three months with high-dose ofloxacin. Pattyn also tested ofloxacin and pefloxacin in mice using the footpad model of infection.[4] Ofloxacin was superior to pefloxacin in comparable doses when bacterial growth was evaluated after one year of treatment. Adjusting for pharmacokinetic differences between mouse and man, a daily dose of approximately 400 mg of ofloxacin should be effective antimicrobial therapy for leprosy.

Ofloxacin and pefloxacin, two quinolones with good oral absorption and high lipophilicity, have proven the most effective fluoroquinolones against *Mycobacterium leprae*, particularly when combined with dapsone. However, dapsone given for extended periods of time with either rifampin or clofazimine, remains the mainstay of therapy for leprosy. Ofloxacin and pefloxacin may prove to be useful adjunctive drugs for this disease.

# REFERENCES

1.  Modlin RL, Rea TH; Leprosy: new insight into an ancient disease. J Am Acad Dermatol 1987;17(1):1-13.

2. Guelpa-Lauras CC, Perani EG, Giroir AM, et al: Activities of pefloxacin and ciprofloxacin against *Mycobacterium leprae* in the mouse. Int J Lepr Mycobact Dis 1987;55(1):70-77.

3. Grosset JH, Guelpa-Lauras CC, Perani EG, et al: Activity of ofloxacin against *Mycobacterium leprae* in the mouse. Int J Lepr Mycobact Dis 1988;56(2):259-264.

4. Pattyn SR: Activity of ofloxacin and pefloxacin against *Mycobacterium leprae* in mice, letter. Antimicrob Agents Chemother 31(4):671-672, 1987.

# MALARIA

Malaria remains a major health problem worldwide. The lack of an effective vaccine and the increasing prevalence of drug resistant strains make the search for new antimicrobial agents imperative. Recent reports suggest that the newer quinolones are active in vitro against both chloroquine-susceptible and -resistant strains of *Plasmodium falciparum*.[1] The mechanism of this activity is not fully understood and may be different from inhibition of DNA gyrase.

Following the chance discovery of the simultaneous eradication of *Plasmodium falciparum* and *Pseudomonas aeruginosa* by norfloxacin, Sarma[2] studied this agent in the treatment of uncomplicated falciparum malaria. Nine adult patients were given oral norfloxacin 400 mg every 12 hours for 3 days. All patients were cured without recrudescences over a 35-day follow-up. As pointed out in the editorial accompanying this report,[3] further study of fluoroquinolones in malaria is warranted, and particular attention must be given to their efficacy against multidrug-resistant strains of *P. falciparum*.

# REFERENCES

1. Divo AA, Sartorelli AC, Patton CL, et al: Activity of fluoroquinolone antibiotics against *Plasmodium falciparum* in vitro. Antimicrob Agents Chemother 1988;32:1182-1186.

2. Sarma PS. Norfloxacin: a new drug in the treatment of falciparum malaria. Ann Intern Med 1989;111:336-337.

3. Wyler DJ: Fluoroquinolones for malaria: the newest kid on the block? (editorial). Ann Intern Med 1989;111:269-270.

## ERADICATION OF NASOPHARYNGEAL CARRIAGE

The drugs currently employed for the chemoprophylaxis of invasive meningo-coccal disease are rifampin and minocycline, neither of which is ideal. Ciprofloxacin has been shown to be an effective agent for eradication of the nasopharyngeal carrier state caused by *Neisseria meningitidis*. In a double-blind study of army recruits in Finland,[1] meningococcal carriage was eliminated in 96% of those who received ciprofloxacin 250 mg bid for 2 days versus 13% of those given placebo. In another study, young adult persistent carriers of *N. meningitidis* were given either cipro-floxacin 500 mg every 12 hours for 5 days or an apparently identical placebo.[2] All ciprofloxacin-treated individuals had rapid elimination of meningococci and re-mained free of this organism at follow-up 13 days post-treatment. In contrast, the positivity rate in placebo-treated patients ranged from 66% to 95% at each of the sampling times. A recent smaller study involving 12 subjects indicated that a single dose of ciprofloxacin 750 mg was 92% effective.[3] The results of these studies are as good or better than those reported with minocycline and rifampin. Fluoroquinolones may prove to be useful agents for *N. meningitidis* chemoprophylaxis.

Eradication of *S. aureus* from the anterior nares to prevent recurrent furunculosis or nosocomial infection has proved to be a difficult problem. Although rifampin has been the most effective agent, emergence of resistance is a potential problem. Recent data indicate that ciprofloxacin and ofloxacin offer promise for eradicating nasal carriage due to both methicillin-susceptible and -resistant staphylococci.[4,5]

## REFERENCES

1. Renkonen O-V, Sivonen A, Visakorpe R: Effect of ciprofloxacin on carrier state of *Neisseria meningitis* in army recruits in Finland. Antimicrob Agents Chemother 1987;31:962-963.

2. Pugsley MP, Dworzack DL, Horowitz EA, et al: Efficacy of ciprofloxacin in the treatment of nasopharyngeal carriers of *Neisseria meningitidis*. J Infect Dis 1987;156:211-213.

3. Pugsley MP, Dworzack DL, Roccaforte JS, et al: An open study of the efficacy of a single dose of ciprofloxacin in eliminating the chronic nasopharyngeal carriage of *Neisseria meningitidis*. J Infect Dis 1988;157:852-853.

4. Smith SM, Eng RHK, Tecson-Tumang F: Ciprofloxacin therapy for methicillin-resistant *Staphylococcus aureus* infections or colonizations. Antimicrob Agents Chemother 1989;33:181-184.

5. Chow JW, Yu VL: *Staphylococcus aureus* nasal carriage in hemodialysis patients. Its role in infection and approaches to prophylaxis. Arch Intern Med 1989;149:1258-1262.

# ADVERSE REACTIONS TO FLUOROQUINOLONES 14

*W. Eugene Sanders, Jr.*

## OVERVIEW OF REACTIONS

The new fluoroquinolones appear to be relatively safe and effective antimicrobial agents. However, none of these drugs has been administered to a sufficient number of patients to permit the precise determination of rates of any given reaction or detection of relatively rare untoward effects.[1,2] For example, it has been estimated that aplastic anemia due to chloramphenicol, with a prevalence of 1:50,000, would require 150,000 patient exposures for observation.[2] Therefore, it is unlikely that an event occurring with similar frequency would be detected for the fluoroquinolones in general or for any single agent within the group. On the other hand, a sufficient number of patients have been treated with a few of the new agents (eg, enoxacin, pefloxacin, norfloxacin, ciprofloxacin, ofloxacin) to allow at least a profile of the more common reactions and a preliminary estimate of the rates of these events. The results presented in this paper are those obtained primarily with oral therapy.

To date, overall rates of adverse reactions appear to be low and comparable to or less than those observed with other classes of antimicrobial agents.[1-15] Rates in large clinical trials or in reviews of pooled data range from 2 to 25%, with a mean of approximately 4-8%. Disparities in rates among the publications cited appear to result from the use of different criteria for assessment of relationship to therapy and from variations in methods of data analysis. For example, some authors have determined rates on the basis of number of patients treated, while others have used the number of courses of therapy as the denominator in the calculation. Another factor that affects the incidence of adverse reactions is whether events considered only "possibly" or "remotely" related to the fluoroquinolones are included. Obviously, authors who include these less certain events will report higher rates. In addition to confounding methodologic variations, geographical differences may exist as well. Using similar definitions, rates of reactions to ciprofloxacin were determined separately for patients in Japan, Europe, and the United States. Schacht et al[8] noted rates of 3.0% in Japan and 6.7% in Europe and the United States. Using similar criteria, Arcieri et al[15] and Sanders[7] found that the incidence of adverse reactions was significantly less frequent abroad. Overall rates were four-fold less, while gastrointestinal, central nervous system, and cutaneous reactions were 3- to 8-fold less. At present, no explanation for these discrepancies has been put forward.

In general, adverse reactions to the fluoroquinolones have been innocuous or of mild to moderate severity. Reports of permanent disability or death have been extremely rare and of questionable relationship to fluoroquinolone therapy.[1-15] Severe reactions necessitating discontinuation of treatment have been infrequent (1.0-6.5%, with a mean of approximately 1.5%).[1-3,7,8] Results with individual drugs are comparable and are shown in Table 1.

Ciprofloxacin is representative of the quinolones in terms of the overall rate of adverse reactions. The characterization of reactions and their outcomes are summarized in Table 2. According to data submitted to the U.S. Food and Drug Administration,[7] 93% of all reactions are mild to moderate in severity. Serious reactions occurred in only 1.1% of total courses of ciprofloxacin. Signs and symptoms resolved or improved promptly in nearly all patients. Only one death was observed; it was considered "possibly" related the drug. The patient was an 80-year-old man who presented with infected decubitus ulcers. He was debilitated and malnourished; cardiac and renal failure precluded surgical debridement of the ulcers. Ciprofloxacin 1000 mg was administered daily for 12 days, as were eight other drugs. His death was attributed to pneumonia, sepsis, and renovascular failure.

## RISK FACTORS

Several groups of investigators have attempted to identify factors that might be associated with an increased risk of adverse reactions. Shah and Frech[12] suggested

Table 1. Adverse reactions to fluoroquinolones that necessitated discontinuation of therapy

| Fluoroquinolone | Rate (%) | Reference |
|---|---|---|
| Enoxacin | 2.6-6.5 | 2,3 |
| Pefloxacin | 1.3-2.2 | 2,3 |
| Norfloxacin | 1.0-1.2 | 2,3 |
| Ciprofloxacin | 1.2-2.9 | 2,7,8 |
| Ofloxacin | 1.4-1.7 | 2,3 |
| Pooled | 1.0-3.0 | 1,2 |

Table 2. Characteristics and outcome of 332 adverse reactions in 2236 courses of oral ciprofloxacin cited in the NDA to the U.S. Food and Drug Administration

| | | Courses with Reaction | |
| --- | --- | --- | --- |
| Parameter | Number | Percent of reactions | Percent of total courses |
| **Relationship to treatment** | | | |
| Highly probable | 24 | 7 | 1.1 |
| Probable | 127 | 38 | 5.7 |
| Possible | 181 | 55 | 8.1 |
| **Intensity** | | | |
| Mild | 158 | 48 | 7.1 |
| Moderate | 150 | 45 | 6.7 |
| Severe | 24 | 7 | 1.1 |
| **Countermeasure** | | | |
| None | 200 | 60 | |
| Rx discontinued permanently | 60 | 18 | |
| Rx discontinued, restarted | 4 | 1 | |
| Dosage reduced | 9 | 3 | |
| Treatment required | 31 | 9 | |
| Other | 28 | 8 | |
| **Outcome** | | | |
| Resolved | 252 | 76 | |
| Improved | 36 | 11 | |
| Unchanged | 5 | 2 | |
| Worse | 0 | 0 | |
| Death | 1 | 0 | |
| Insufficient data | 38 | 11 | |

Adapted from Sanders.[7]

that advancing age and increased duration of therapy predispose to toxicity. Schacht et al[10] and Sanders[7] have reported that gastrointestinal side effects of ciprofloxacin tend to occur more frequently with increasing dosage. However, others have been unable to identify any relationship between risk and dosage administered or age of patients. Holmes and associates[9] and Monk and Campoli-Richards[6] were unable to discern an association between dosage and risk in their reviews of experience with norfloxacin and ofloxacin, respectively. Similarly, Halkin[2] found no increased risk of reactions to ofloxacin and pefloxacin with advancing age. Increased risk of reactions has been noted in some patients given other drugs concurrently (see below).

## Gastrointestinal Tract

In supervised clinical trials, gastrointestinal side effects have been encountered most commonly.[2-4,6,9-11,14] Reported rates range from 1.0% to 20% of patients or courses of therapy. Most studies and reviews of pooled data report rates of approximately 3-7%. Results with quinolones individually and collectively are shown in Table 3.

Nearly all gastrointestinal effects have been innocuous or of mild-to-moderate severity. Nausea and diarrhea have been the most common complaints. Vomiting, epigastric burning, abdominal cramps, anorexia, and flatulence have been noted in decreasing order of frequency.[7,10] On occasion, gastrointestinal symptoms have been sufficiently severe to require discontinuation of the fluoroquinolone. Serious symptoms have resolved promptly with discontinuation of therapy. Occasional patients have responded to lowering the dosage.[7]

Pseudomembranous enterocolitis has rarely been reported in patients treated with the new fluoroquinolones.[7,10] A clear relationship to quinolone administration has been difficult to establish because of the nature of the underlying disease or administration of other antimicrobial agents concurrently or proximately. In the U.S., one patient among 2,203 treated with ciprofloxacin has reportedly developed pseudomembranous enterocolitis.[7] The patient responded promptly to metronidazole, and no sequelae were noted. A second patient treated with ciprofloxacin outside the U.S. developed the syndrome; however, moxalactam had also been administered.[10] The rarity of this syndrome is consistent with the relative lack of activity of most fluoroquinolones against the anaerobic components of the fecal flora.[6]

**Table 3.** Rates of gastrointestinal side effects of fluoroquinolones

| Fluoroquinolone | Rate (%) | Reference |
|---|---|---|
| Enoxacin | 3.4-3.8 | 2,3,14 |
| Pefloxacin | 4.2-5.6 | 2,3 |
| Norfloxacin | 2.1-4.5 | 2,3,9,14 |
| Ciprofloxacin | 2.1-8.1 | 2-4,10,14 |
| Ofloxacin | 2.6-3.0 | 2,3,6,11,14 |
| Pooled | 1.0-20.0 | 1,2 |

The overall incidence and relative frequency of gastrointestinal side effects have declined significantly (for at least one fluoroquinolone) with the transition from supervised clinical trials to post-marketing passive surveillance.[11] After the marketing of ofloxacin in Europe, reports of enteric side effects were exceeded by those of central nervous system and hypersensitivity reactions. This apparently lower incidence of side effects may relate to the fact that both patients and physicians have grown to accept and tolerate mild gastrointestinal symptoms during the course of antimicrobial therapy in general and therefore report these events less frequently with new agents.

## Central Nervous System

Adverse reactions involving the central nervous system are the second most commonly encountered. Rates of these reactions have ranged from 0.4 to 4.4%, with a mean for each drug of approximately 1.0%.[2-4,6,7,9,11,14] Rates for individual drugs are shown in Table 4.

The most commonly encountered symptoms are attributable to central nervous system stimulation. These include tremulousness, anxiety, nervousness, insomnia, euphoria, nightmares, hallucinations, mania, and frank psychoses.[1-15] Hallucinations are usually visual.[11] Paradoxically, some patients have reported somnolence as a side effect of these drugs.[5]

The stimulatory effects of the fluoroquinolones are thought to result from inhibition of binding of $\gamma$-aminobutyric acid (GABA), an inhibitory neurotransmitter, to receptors in the central nervous system.[1,14,16] The new fluoroquinolones appear to inhibit the binding of GABA in a dose-dependent manner.[14,16] The interaction appears to be a straightforward pharmacological antagonism.[16] Central nervous system stimulatory effects may also be augmented or potentiated as a result of interactions between fluoroquinolones and theophylline or caffeine (see below).

Since convulsions (tonic-clonic seizures) were reported with high doses of nalidixic acid,[17] investigators have been alert to this possibility with the new fluoro-

**Table 4.** Rates of central nervous system side effects of fluoroquinolones

| Fluoroquinolone | Rate (%) | Reference |
|---|---|---|
| Enoxacin | 1.1-1.2 | 2,3,14 |
| Pefloxacin | 0.9-1.1 | 2,3,14 |
| Norfloxacin | 0.8-1.7 | 2,3,9,14 |
| Ciprofloxacin | 0.4-4.4 | 2-4,7,10,14 |
| Ofloxacin | 0.9-1.0 | 2,3,6,11,14 |

quinolones. The recognition of inhibition of GABA binding gave additional cause for concern.[14,16] Despite close monitoring of patients, the precise role, if any, of the fluoroquinolones in the induction of seizures remains unclear. Convulsions have been reported during administration of nearly all of the new agents.[5,7,11,14,18] However, most patients who have experienced this adverse event have been predisposed by other factors, such as antecedent epilepsy, head trauma, cerebrovascular disease, severe renal disease, alcoholism, or drug abuse. For example, four patients with seizures during ciprofloxacin therapy were described in the New Drug Application to the U.S. Food and Drug Administration;[7] two had a history of alcoholism and two had epilepsy. In one of these patients, the seizure activity was also associated with high serum levels of theophylline. Similarly, of 9 patients with convulsions associated with ofloxacin, 2 had tetany, 2 had epilepsy, 1 gave a history of heminephrectomy and cerebral trauma, and for the remaining 4, no information was available.[11]

It is possible that one or more non-steroidal anti-inflammatory agents may interact with fluoroquinolones to result in convulsions.[5] The combination of fenbufen plus enoxacin has been observed "in rare instances to cause convulsions in humans."[5] In addition, fluoroquinolone administration has resulted in tonic convulsions in mice and rats pretreated with fenbufen.[5] Therefore, caution is advised when administering fluoroquinolones to patients receiving non-steroidal anti-inflammatory agents or to those with conditions predisposing to seizures. Further study of these possible associations is clearly necessary.

## Skin

Cutaneous reactions have occurred in from 0.4 to 2.4% of patients treated with fluoroquinolones.[2-4,7,9,14] Rates for individual drugs are shown in Table 5. There are no significant differences among the agents. Almost every known cutaneous manifestation of drug allergy or toxicity has been attributed to the fluoroquinolones. However,

Table 5. Rates of cutaneous reactions to fluoroquinolones

| Fluoroquinolone | Rate (%) | Reference |
|---|---|---|
| Enoxacin | 0.7 | 2,3,14 |
| Pefloxacin | 2.2-2.4 | 2,3 |
| Norfloxacin | 0.4-0.7 | 2,3,9,14 |
| Ciprofloxacin | 0.4-1.9 | 2-4,7,10,14 |
| Ofloxacin | 0.4-0.6 | 2,3,14 |
| Pooled Data | 0.5-2.2 | 2 |

the great majority of skin reactions have been innocuous. Maculopapular and other rashes, pruritus, palmoplantar erythema, local edema, and urticaria have been reported most often.[1,7,10,14]

## Musculoskeletal System

Reactions involving the musculoskeletal system have been uncommon. Occasional patients complain of arthralgia or myalgia without objective evidence of joint or muscle inflammation. Rates for individual fluoroquinolones range from 0.04 to nearly 1%.[3,4,6,8,10,11] These are shown in Table 6. None of these reactions has been severe. Tenosynovitis has been reported in several patients treated with norfloxacin.[13,19-21] Tendinitis occurred in two immunocompromised patients given the drug for prolonged periods.[19] At least two patients with joint swelling and tendinitis experienced recurrence of symptoms when rechallenged with norfloxacin. This provided convincing evidence of the role of the drug in this adverse event. Whether tenosynovitis is a reaction unique to norfloxacin or to fluoroquinolones in general is as yet unknown.

## Cartilage

All quinolones accumulate in cartilage, from which they disappear slowly.[1-3,5,22] In young animals and embryonic mice, blister formation progresses to ulceration and inhibition of growth.[1,5,23] Weight-bearing joints are most severely damaged. This problem is seen infrequently in adult animals. As a result of the cartilage damage observed in young animals, the fluoroquinolones have seldom been administered to children. However, the animal data *may* not be broadly applicable to humans. Nalidixic acid (the prototypic quinolone) causes the same damage to cartilage in laboratory animals but has been used in children for decades without reports of toxicity to cartilage or joints. Schaad and Wedgwood-Krucko[24] performed a retrospective

Table 6. Rates of musculoskeletal reactions to the fluoroquinolones

| Fluoroquinolone | Rate (%) | Reference |
|---|---|---|
| Enoxacin | 0.04 | 3 |
| Pefloxacin | 0.9 | 3 |
| Norfloxacin | 0.1 | 3 |
| Ciprofloxacin | 0.08-0.2 | 3,4,8,10 |
| Ofloxacin | <1.0 | 6,11 |

matched controlled study of 11 children who had received nalidixic acid for 9-600 days and 11 carefully matched children who had never received a quinolone. No evidence of arthropathy or inhibition of growth was found in the nalidixic acid-treated children in comparison to controls. The authors concluded that "quinolone-associated arthropathy does not occur in children, even after long-term therapy."

## Genitourinary Tract

Adverse effects involving the genitourinary tract have been encountered only rarely. Rates of these reactions range from 0 to 0.1% with pefloxacin,[2,3] 0.3-0.4% with ciprofloxacin,[2,10] and 0.3-1.0% with ofloxacin.[2-4] The vast majority of reactions have been mild.

Most of the quinolones may crystallize in urine at very high concentrations and at high urinary pH.[3] To date, this has not posed a significant clinical problem with any of the new quinolones.[1-15] Microscopic crystalluria that required repeated examinations of urine to be made was detected in only 2 of 2,203 patients treated with ciprofloxacin during supervised clinical trials.[7] Crystalluria was transient and not associated with symptoms or changes in renal function.

A very few patients have developed hematuria with or without deterioration in renal function during administration of fluoroquinolones.[3,25,26] No evidence of crystalluria has been noted in these individuals. The syndrome has been attributed to transient interstitial nephritis. Most authors have concluded that the fluoroquinolones are not primarily nephrotoxic agents and that the potential for crystalluria is not a significant concern.[1,3,5,7] Nonetheless, it may be prudent to maintain good hydration in patients given these drugs.

Several fluoroquinolones have been implicated in testicular damage in laboratory animals.[3,5,22] Decreased spermatogenesis, azoospermia, necrosis or atrophy have been noted alone or in combination in rats, dogs, and monkeys.[22] Norfloxacin, pefloxacin, enoxacin and pipemidic acid have been involved. Ofloxacin and ciprofloxacin appear to have little or no effect.[3,5,22] In humans, testicular damage does not appear to be a problem.[1-15]

## Ocular Reactions

Pefloxacin and rosoxacin induce cataracts in several species of laboratory animals.[5,11,27] For this reason, patients treated with the new quinolones have been monitored closely for evidence of oculotoxicity. Over 800 patients treated with ciprofloxacin were subjected to extensive ophthalmological testing and examinations, and no significant abnormalities were identified.[10] Only 7 ocular complaints have been registered during post-marketing surveillance of ofloxacin in Europe.[11] None was serious. Two patients complained of transient diplopia, and one reported a reversible change in color perception that resulted in a "purple veil" before the eyes.

## Photosensitivity Reactions

Photosensitivity reactions have been reported during administration of several old and new quinolones.[2,4,5,28-30] Nalidixic acid was noted to induce phototoxic bullous eruptions in 1969.[28] Meyer[30] noted photosensitivity reactions in 3 of 21 (14.3%) patients with cystic fibrosis given ofloxacin. By analyzing data supplied by the manufacturer, Halkin[2] determined that phototoxic reactions have occurred in nearly 1% of patients treated with pefloxacin. In one-quarter of these patients, therapy was discontinued as a result of the toxicity. Photosensitivity has been reported less frequently with other fluoroquinolones. Only three instances (0.03%) were identified among 8,861 patients treated with ciprofloxacin.[10]

## Allergy and Hypersensitivity

Each of the recognized manifestations of allergy and hypersensitivity has been observed in patients given the new fluoroquinolones.[1-15] Rates of clinically apparent reactions have generally been less than 1% in pooled data and with individual drugs. Eosinophilia may occur as an isolated event or in association with clinical manifestations of allergy. Reported cases of eosinophilia have varied from 0.2 to 2.0%.[2] Precise rates of sensitization cannot be determined at present because of the relatively small numbers of patients who have received more than one course of a given fluoroquinolone.

## ABNORMALITIES IN LABORATORY TESTS

Abnormalities in a variety of laboratory tests have been detected during supervised clinical trials with the new quinolones.[1-15] Rates have generally varied from a fraction of 1% to as high as 8%. There have been few differences among rates reported for individual drugs. However, Halkin[2] has reported higher rates of eosinophilia and abnormal tests of renal function in patients treated with ofloxacin. Abnormalities in hepatic enzymes and hematologic and renal function have been encountered most often. Many of these abnormalities were noted retrospectively. Changes in laboratory tests usually have been slight in degree, transient, and not associated with signs or symptoms of toxicity. Nearly all have returned to normal or to baseline after completion of therapy. Few have necessitated discontinuation of therapy. For example, 103 (1.6%) laboratory abnormalities were detected among the first 1,690 patients enrolled in trials of ciprofloxacin in Europe and the U.S.[8] Of these, 102 were of no consequence clinically. In one patient, a dramatic increase in alkaline phosphatase was noted. However, the level returned to normal within 7 days after therapy was discontinued.

## ADVERSE DRUG INTERACTIONS

### *Theophylline and Caffeine*

Recognition that administration of enoxacin raises plasma levels of theophylline has prompted extensive investigations of the potential for a similar interaction with other quinolones.[31-37] Collectively, these data suggest that the effect on theophylline pharmacokinetics is profound with enoxacin, moderate with pefloxacin and ciprofloxacin, and minimal or absent with ofloxacin, norfloxacin and nalidixic acid. Wijnands et al[37] have shown that enoxacin, pefloxacin, and ciprofloxacin: (a) elevate plasma concentrations of theophylline in human volunteers by 111%, 20%, and 23%, respectively, and (b) decrease clearance of theophylline by 64%, 29%, and 30%, respectively. No changes in plasma levels or clearance were noted with ofloxacin or nalidixic acid. Bowles et al[34] have shown that norfloxacin may slightly increase serum levels of theophylline without altering its mean clearance or half-life. Gregoire et al[35] demonstrated a subtle effect (approximately 10%) of ofloxacin on renal clearance, area-under-concentration-time curve, and average steady-state plasma concentration of theophylline. The mechanism of the pharmacokinetic changes appears to be inhibition of the hepatic mixed function oxidase system, with a resultant decrease in metabolism of theophylline and congeners.[37] Indirect evidence suggests that the 4-oxo-metabolite, and not the parent fluoroquinolone, is responsible for the effect.

Manifestations of theophylline toxicity, which may be heralded by nausea and vomiting, have been identified most often in patients treated with enoxacin.[14,31,32] The frequency appears to be less with ciprofloxacin and pefloxacin.[3,6,31-33,37,38] For this reason Wijnands et al[37] recommend that the theophylline dosage be halved and serum levels monitored daily in patients given enoxacin. With ciprofloxacin and pefloxacin, they recommend administration of theophylline in the usual dosage with periodic measurement of its concentration in serum. These recommendations appear rational in light of the pharmacokinetic data generated to date. However, the studies of Khan and Raoof[33] suggest that alterations in the metabolism of theophylline may not be the only pathogenetic mechanism for the observed toxicity. They noted increases in serum levels of theophylline in 20 of 33 (61%) patients given ciprofloxacin. The mean increase in serum concentration was 10 µg/mL. They determined that the greatest risk for increased serum levels was in elderly patients with chronic obstructive bronchopulmonary disease. Interestingly, five patients whose theophylline levels were *at or above* the putative "toxic level" (20 µg/mL) failed to develop any adverse signs or symptoms. Paradoxically, a few patients whose levels were in the therapeutic and presumably non-toxic range also developed symptoms resembling theophylline toxicity. These symptoms developed concurrently with rises in theophylline levels even though the new levels remained within the normal range. These observations suggest that factors other than the inhibition of metabolism of theophylline may be operative. It is possible that the new fluoroquinolones also interact at the end organ responsible for toxicity. Perhaps the inhibition of GABA binding to receptors alters the sensitivity of the nervous system to theophylline and its congeners. In view of these possibilities and until further data are available, caution is advised when administering any of the fluoroquinolones to patients receiving theophylline.

Some fluoroquinolones may also alter the metabolism of caffeine.[38,39] Enoxacin reportedly increases the mean elimination half-life of caffeine, while decreasing its plasma clearance and volume of distribution.[38,39] Ciprofloxacin also alters the pharmacokinetics of caffeine, but to a lesser extent. Ofloxacin appears to have little or no effect on the metabolic disposition of caffeine.

## Antacids

A variety of antacids has been shown to inhibit absorption of one or more of the fluoroquinolones from the gastrointestinal tract. Most of the data have been generated in studies with ciprofloxacin[40-42] and ofloxacin.[6,43] In patients with cystic fibrosis, pancreatic enzyme replacement therapy had no effect on the absorption and distribution of ciprofloxacin.[40] Binding of the fluoroquinolones to magnesium and aluminum ions may markedly diminish absorption of the drugs. Calcium has little or no effect. If antacids must be used in patients given fluoroquinolones, calcium salts would be preferable. Fortunately, ranitidine and congeners have no effect on absorption of ciprofloxacin or ofloxacin.

## Other Drugs

Interactions may occur with a variety of other drugs. However, data are scanty, and mechanism(s) of these putative interactions have not been ascertained. The renal excretion of ciprofloxacin is inhibited by probenecid and possibly by other weak acids.[44] No deleterious effects of this interaction have been noted to date. The new fluoroquinolones, especially enoxacin, pefloxacin, and ciprofloxacin, may alter levels of warfarin and related drugs that are metabolized by the same pathway as theophylline.[32] Monitoring of prothrombin times in patients on warfarin plus fluoroquinolones is advisable.[32] A single report has suggested possible potentiation of the nephrotoxicity of cyclosporin A by ciprofloxacin in a patient with a recently transplanted kidney.[45] This possibility should be examined with all the new fluoroquinolones. The interaction between non-steroidal anti-inflammatory agents and fluoroquinolones has been reviewed above.

## FUTURE DEVELOPMENTS

The fluoroquinolones as a group are relatively safe drugs. The pattern of reactions appears to be similar for each of the individual agents, but differences in rates or in severity among them may occur.

A number of important questions remain to be answered. (1) What are the relationships, if any, of the known adverse effects to dose and duration of therapy? (2) What are the risk factors for toxicity? (3) Are there any late effects such as carcinogenesis or mutagenesis? (4) What are the relative rates of reactions for the individual fluoroquinolones? (5) Are there idiosyncratic reactions that may be detected only after exposure of very large numbers of patients? (6) What are the molecular mechanisms of the known toxicities? (7) Are these drugs safe in children? Clearly, a great deal of work remains to be done. Much of it should be challenging and exciting for careful investigators.

# REFERENCES

1. Smith CR: The adverse effects of fluoroquinolones. J Antimicrob Chemother 1987;19: 709-712.

2. Halkin H: Adverse effects of the fluoroquinolones. Rev Infect Dis 1988;10(suppl 1):S258-S261.

3. Bergan T: Quinolones, in Peterson VK, Verhoef J (eds), *Antimicrobial Agents Annual 3.* Amsterdam, Elsevier Science Publishers BV, 1988, pp 177-202.

4. Arcieri G, Griffith E, Gruenwaldt G, et al: Ciprofloxacin: An update on clinical experience. Am J Med 1987;82(suppl 4A):381-386.

5. Christ W, Lehnert T, Ulbrich B: Specific toxicologic aspects of the quinolones. Rev Infect Dis 1988;10(suppl 1):S141-S146.

6. Monk JP, Campoli-Richards DM: Ofloxacin: A review of its antibacterial activity, pharmacokinetic properties and therapeutic use. Drugs 1987;33:346-391.

7. Sanders WE Jr: Efficacy, safety, and potential economic benefits of oral ciprofloxacin in the treatment of infections. Rev Infect Dis 1988;10:528-543.

8. Schacht P, Deck K, Arcieri G, et al: Overview of international clinical studies of ciprofloxacin, with special reference to safety, in Neu HC, Weuta H (eds), *1st International Ciprofloxacin Workshop Proceedings.* Amsterdam, Excerpta Medica, 1985, pp 435-445.

9. Holmes B, Brogden RN, Richards DM: Norfloxacin: A review of its antibacterial activity, pharmacokinetic properties and therapeutic use. Drugs 1985;30:482-513.

10. Schacht P, Arcieri G, Branolte J, et al: Worldwide clinical data on efficacy and safety of ciprofloxacin. Infection 1988;16(suppl):S29-S43.

11. Jungst G, Mohr R: Side effects of ofloxacin in clinical trials and in postmarketing surveillance. Drugs 1987;34(suppl 1):144-149.

12. Shah PM, Frech K: Overview of clinical experience with the quinolones, in Percival A (ed), *Quinolones Their Future in Clinical Practice.* London, Royal Society of Medicine Services, 1986, pp 29-43.

13. Hooper DC, Wolfson JS: The fluoroquinolones: Pharmacology, clinical uses, and toxicities in humans. Antimicrob Agents Chemother 1985;28:716-721.

14. Janknegt R: Fluorinated quinolones. A review of their mode of action, antimicrobial activity, pharmacokinetics and clinical efficacy. Pharm Weekly (Sci) 1986;8:1-21.

15. Arcieri G, August R, Becker N, et al: Clinical experience with ciprofloxacin in the USA. Eur J Clin Microbiol 1986;5:220-225.

16. Tsuji A, Sato H, Kume Y, et al: Inhibitory effects of quinolone antibacterial agents on γ-aminobutyric acid binding to receptor sites in rat brain membranes. Antimicrob Agents Chemother 1988;32:190-194.

17. Fraser AG, Harrower ADB: Convulsions and hyperglycaemia associated with nalidixic acid. Br Med J 1977;ii:1518.

18. Simpson JK, Brodie MJ: Convulsions related to enoxacin. Lancet 1985;2:161.

19. Bailey RR, Kirk JA, Peddie RA: Norfloxacin-induced rheumatic disease. N Zeal Med J 1983;96:590.

20. Deany NB, Vogel R, Vandenburg MJ, et al: Norfloxacin in acute urinary tract infections. Practitioner 1984;228:111-117.

21. Kirby CP: Treatment of simple urinary tract infections in general practice with a 3-day course of norfloxacin. J Antimicrob Chemother 1984;13(suppl B):107-112.

22. Mayer DG: Overview of toxicological studies. Drugs 1987;34(suppl 1):150-153.

23. Maghan B, Brentnall DW, Dale EA, et al: Arthropathy induced by antibacterial fused N-alkyl-4-pyridone-3-carboxylic acids. Toxicol Lett 1977;1:21-26.

24. Schaad UB, Wedgwood-Krucko J: Nalidixic acid in children: Retrospective matched controlled study for cartilage toxicity. Infection 1987;15:165-168.

25. Garlando F, Tanber MG, Joos B, et al: Ciprofloxacin-induced hematuria. Infection 1985; 13:177-178.

26. Boelaert J, deJaegere PP, Daneels R, et al: Case report of renal failure during norfloxacin therapy. Clin Nephrol 1986;25:272.

27. Schlüter G: Toxicology of ciprofloxacin, in Neu HC, Weuta H (eds), *1st International Ciprofloxacin Workshop Proceedings*. Amsterdam, Excerpta Medica, 1986, pp 61-67.

28. Birkett DA, Garretts M, Stevenson CJ: Phototoxic bullous eruptions due to nalidixic acid. Br J Dermatol 1969;81:342-344.

29. Epstein JH, Wintroub BU: Photosensitivity due to drugs. Drugs 1985;30:42-57.

30. Meyer H: Ofloxacin in cystic fibrosis. Drugs 1987;34(suppl 1):177-179.

31. Wijnands WJ, Van Herwaarden CLA, Vree TB: Enoxacin raises plasma theophylline concentrations. Lancet 1984;2:108-109.

32. Maessen FP, Teengs JP, Baur C, et al: Quinolones and raised plasma concentrations of theophylline. Lancet 1984;2:530.

33. Kahn F, Raoof S: Ciprofloxacin in the treatment of respiratory tract infections, in Neu HC, Weuta H (eds), *1st International Ciprofloxacin Workshop Proceedings*. Amsterdam, Excerpta Medica, 1985, pp 252-256.

34. Bowles SK, Popsvski Z, Rybak MJ, et al: Effect of norfloxacin on theophylline pharma-cokinetics at steady state. Antimicrob Agents Chemother 1988;32:510-512.

35. Gregoire SL, Grasela TH Jr, Freer JP, et al: Inhibition of theophylline clearance by coadministered ofloxacin without alteration of theophylline effects. Antimicrob Agents Chemother 1987;31:375-378.

36. Schwartz J, Jauregui L, Lettieri J, et al: Impact of ciprofloxacin on theophylline clearance and steady-state concentrations in serum. Antimicrob Agents Chemother 1988;32:75-77.

37. Wijnands WJA, Vree TB, Van Herwaarden CLA: The influence of quinolone derivatives on theophylline clearance. Br J Clin Pharmacol 1986;22:677-683.

38. Stille W, Harder S, Mieke S, et al: Decrease of caffeine elimination in man during co-administration of 4-quinolones. J Antimicrob Chemother 1987;20:729-734.

39. Staib AH, Stille W, Dietlein G, et al: Interaction between quinolones and caffeine. Drugs 1987;34(suppl 1):170-174.

40. Blumer JL: Efficacy and safety of ciprofloxacin in cystic fibrosis, in Neu HC, Weuta H (eds), *1st International Ciprofloxacin Workshop Proceedings*. Amsterdam, Excerpta Medica, 1985, pp 279-281.

41. Höffken G, Borner K, Glatzel PD, et al: Reduced enteral absorption of ciprofloxacin in the presence of antacids. Eur J Clin Microbiol 1985;4:345.

42. Preheim LC, Cuevas TA, Roccaforte JS, et al: Ciprofloxacin and antacids. Lancet 1986;2:48.

43. Maesen FPV, Davies BI, Geraedts WH, et al: Ofloxacin and antacids. J Antimicrob Chemother 1987;19:848-849.

44. Wingender I, Beermann D, Forster D, et al: Interactions of ciprofloxacin with food and drugs, in Neu HC, Weuta H (eds), *1st International Ciprofloxacin Workshop Proceedings*. Amsterdam, Excerpta Medica, 1985, pp 136-140.

45. Elston RA, Taylor J: Possible interaction of ciprofloxacin with cyclosporin A. J Antimicrob Chemother 1988;21:679-680.

# PHARMACOECONOMIC IMPLICATIONS OF ORAL FLUOROQUINOLONE THERAPY

# 15

*Joseph A. Paladino*

## INTRODUCTION

With the advent of the diagnosis-related group (DRG) classification system, prospective reimbursement programs have gained the attention of the medical community.[1] The economic survival of hospitals under the conditions of prospective reimbursement depends, to a large degree, on their policies, programs, and efficient allocation of personnel. Prospective reimbursement compels institutions to contain costs by decreasing both length-of-stay and the cost of hospital functions.[2]

Because of the increased emphasis on cost-containment, special attention has been directed towards pharmacy expenditures. Antibiotics comprise, by a substantial margin, the largest component of U.S. hospital drug purchases. Expenditures for systemic anti-infectives exceeded $1.4 billion in 1985; this was more than four times the amount spent on the second ranking category, cardiovascular drugs.[3]

One-third of hospitalized patients receive antibiotic medication.[4] For many infections a variety of antibiotics can be considered for use by the clinician, with the expectation of equal efficacy. These antibiotics are distinguished not only by cost but also by their adverse reaction profile and potential to promote the development of bacterial resistance.[5,6] Because of this opportunity for medication selection, risk-versus-benefit analysis (performed before ordering any treatment) becomes a preliminary process leading up to the consideration of cost-effectiveness. Pharmacy and Therapeutics (P&T) committees serve an increasingly important role in influencing drug use by : (1) developing and maintaining formularies that provide access to safe and effective medications without needless duplication or overlap; (2) establishing drug-use review (DUR) programs;[7-11] (3) enacting restrictive policies;[12] and (4) requiring the use of antibiotic order sheets.[13]

Early drug-use review standards of the Joint Commission for the Accreditation of Health Care Organizations (JCAHO) mandated that institutions evaluate antibiotic usage.[14] As reviewed by Todd et al,[7] the JCAHO has regularly expanded these standards, which now include the evaluation of drug use in general. For the past 10 years antibiotic prescribing has been audited through programs designed to evaluate such use as appropriate or inappropriate. Inappropriate use could apply to a case in which the ordered antibiotic would likely be effective, but another antibiotic should be prescribed because it is less expensive, has a lower potential to promote bacterial resistance, or a more favorable adverse effect profile.[6] Prospective and concurrent DUR programs are superior to retrospective efforts in that prospective programs have an immediate effect, are more efficient in saving money, and benefit patients directly.[8] These programs have consistently demonstrated the potential to save significant amounts of money while improving the usefulness of antibiotics.[9-11]

## INTRAVENOUS VERSUS ORAL ADMINISTRATION

The parenteral dosage formulation of a medication typically costs more than the same dose in an oral preparation.[15] Additionally, administering an intravenous dose requires more preparation, time, and materials than oral dosage forms. In a comprehensive paper on cost-effective antibiotic prescribing, Gleckman and Gantz[5] include switching from intravenous to oral antibiotics as one method of achieving cost savings without diminishing the quality of patient care. Written before the release of fluoroquinolones, their paper contains several specific examples of infections in which oral antibiotics have been used successfully, such as: (1) osteomyelitis and septic arthritis in children; and (2) acute, symptomatic, community-acquired bacterial pyelonephritis in women who do not appear to be "toxic." Their discussion notes that considerable cost savings can be achieved with oral therapy because the costs of intravenous sets and solutions and the personnel time necessary for dose preparation and infusion are eliminated. In addition, oral therapy avoids the risks inherent with intravenous medications, and when administered at home, supervised oral treatment is particularly cost-effective while patient comfort is enhanced.[5]

The cost-effectiveness of oral medication has been described in a number of published reports; these results are applicable to oral antimicrobial agents. Kimelblatt et al[16] noted that intravenous cimetidine, which costs 4-8 times more than the oral preparation, was inappropriately ordered 52% of the time, based on criteria developed with the cooperation of their gastroenterology department. This inappropriate use resulted in a projected annual excess expenditure of $14,727 on drug costs alone (in 1982 dollars). Interestingly, many of these patients were initially treated appropriately via the intravenous route, but should have been switched to oral therapy after oral restrictions were removed.[16] Wald et al[17] reviewed the records of 100 hospitalized medical and surgical patients who received cimetidine and found that more than $10,000 per year (in 1983) in drug costs could be saved if patients on intravenous cimetidine were switched to the oral route when feeding resumed.

Recent interest in the cost-containment aspect of oral medications is also reflected in papers presented on theophylline and other drugs.[18,19] Smith and Hill[18] monitored 10 target drugs that were being administered intravenously for at least 48 hours, and concomitantly with other medications by the oral or nasogastric routes. Contacting the prescribers resulted in 89% compliance with recommended regimen changes and subsequent annualized savings of more than $33,000. Based on a drug utilization review audit at a large private teaching hospital, Beckner and Hancock[19] projected an annualized savings potential of $10,800 in material costs if patients on intravenous theophylline were switched to the oral form of the drug.

## Drug Cost

The pressure of cost-containment provides the incentive for evaluating alternative treatment modalities. The following compares the cost of selected antibiotics for the treatment of a hypothetical urinary tract infection. Recognizing that alternative antibiotics might be chosen depending on in vitro susceptibility results, patient allergy history, and other clinical factors, consider the following agents and costs when purchased by a typical hospital: intravenous cefazolin 1 gm $2.50; intravenous gentamicin 80 mg $0.20; oral norfloxacin 400 mg $1.65; and oral ciprofloxacin 500 mg $1.57. Assuming efficacy to be similar among the four agents in this example, gentamicin would appear to be the most cost-effective therapy on the basis of drug cost alone. However, this simplistic comparison does not consider the ancillary costs associated with the use of intravenous medications.

## Incidental Costs

The estimated or calculated costs of ancillary materials needed to administer an intravenous dose are sometimes considered and should be added to the cost of the drug.[10,20] Typical incidental materials, listed in Table 1, contribute to the cost of administering intravenous medications. These ancillary charges may actually exceed the cost of the drug.[21] For example, the cost of a 1 gram vial of ampicillin is $0.71, while the cost of ancillary materials to administer that dose on a q6h regimen are $2.44. Some have compared patient charges rather than hospital costs, which produce larger differences between treatments. A survey of 39 hospital pharmacies revealed that the mean charges for antimicrobial agents whose costs range between $2.15-$3.08 per gram were $18.02-$20.42.[22] Other costs include nurse and pharmacist time, and the time spent taking inventory, ordering, and providing intravenous pumps and controllers. The hospital drug costs of seven days of treatment with selected antibiotics, including ancillary charges for materials listed in Table 1, are shown in Table 2.

**Table 1.** Incidental materials associated with intravenous medication use

**Per Dose**
Bag, bottle, or other container
Needle
Syringe
Alcohol swab
Diluent for reconstitution
Intravenous fluid for infusion
Label

**Divided Among Multiple Doses**
Intravenous tubing (primary, secondary sets)
Provision and maintenance of venous access

**Table 2.** Hospital drug and ancillary material costs of 7 days of antibiotic therapy

| Antibiotic | Regimen | Cost* |
|---|---|---|
| **Intravenous Antibiotics** | | |
| Cefazolin | 1 g q8h | $108 |
| Nafcillin | 2 g q4h | $210 |
| Vancomycin | 1 g q12h | $410 |
| Ceftazidime | 2 g q8h | $520 |
| Ceftriaxone | 1 g q24h | $192 |
| Tobramycin + Ticarcillin | 100 mg q12h 3 g q4h | $515 |
| Ampicillin + Gentamicin + Clindamycin | 1 g q6h 80 mg q8h 900 mg q8h | $480 |
| **Oral Antibiotics** | | |
| Ciprofloxacin | 750 mg po bid | $ 42 |
| Ciprofloxacin + Metronidazole | 750 mg po bid 500 mg po tid | $ 45 |

\* Costs shown reflect those for a typical hospital in 1988 and are less than list or average wholesale prices.

Drug costs, ancillary materials, and personnel costs will differ depending on the type of intravenous system used to deliver the medication. There are several types of small volume parenteral delivery systems through which intravenous medications can be supplied and administered, including metered chambers, minibags and minibottles, manufacturer's piggyback containers, and syringe administration sets.[23] For example, cefazolin is available premixed in a minibag, which removes the necessity of using many of the incidental materials listed in Table 1. However, this is offset by an increased cost of the minibag as compared to a vial.[15] In general, additional material costs associated with intravenous antibiotics are approximately $2-7 per dose. There is a certain amount of interinstitutional variability to this figure, which is affected by the size of the hospital and its equipment, policies, procedures, and purchasing system. For example, changing intravenous tubing sets every 48-72 hours lowers the per dose cost for each set compared with using a new set every day.

Most comparisons assign a constant ancillary cost to each dose. This practice does not adequately apportion the actual costs, except for the infrequent situation when an entirely new intravenous setup is used for each dose. For example, at one institution the ancillary materials charges for administering nafcillin every four hours and ceftriaxone once a day are $2.21 and $4.49 per dose, respectively. Each dose will require the use of certain supplies such as a needle and diluent, while the cost of the intravenous tubing set is divided among all doses administered within the 48 hour period that each intravenous tubing set is used.

Returning to the UTI example, the incidental materials charges are included with the per dose comparison and are shown in column 3 of Table 3. There are no additional costs associated with administering an oral medication as compared with a

Table 3. Cost comparison of selected antibiotics in the treatment of a model urinary tract infection

| Antibiotic | Drug | Drug plus ancillary materials* | Drug, ancillary materials and laboratory expenses† |
|---|---|---|---|
| Cefazolin 1 gm IV q8h | $2.50 | $5.15 | $108 |
| Gentamicin 80 mg IV q8h | $0.20 | $2.02 | $160 |
| Norfloxacin 400 mg po bid | $1.65 | $1.65 | $23 |
| Ciprofloxacin 500 mg po bid | $1.57 | $1.57 | $22 |

\* Costs shown reflect typical hospital acquisition costs per dose or item.
† Costs for seven days of therapy.

parenteral drug. By including the additional material costs a hospital will incur with the use of intravenous medication, it becomes cost-effective to use the oral rather than the intravenous antibiotics in this example, as shown in Table 3.

## Personnel Time Savings

Some investigators include personnel time in cost comparisons. Time-and-motion studies have quantified the time required to prepare and administer an intravenous dose. In a study of six hospitals, the mean time to prepare and administer an IV dose ranged from 1.9-9.5 minutes.[20] The contribution of reduced personnel time to actual cost savings is questionable, however, since a reduction in intravenous doses would probably not result in a reduction of personnel but perhaps might allow for some reallocation of personnel time. Acknowledging this, Tanner does not consider fringe-benefit costs in his calculation of the cost-benefit obtained with switching to a less-frequently administered cephalosporin.[20]

Concurrent with the advent of DRGs, the hospital pharmacy became a cost-conscious center rather than a profit-generating department, and the trend towards expanded dosing intervals became apparent. The introduction of newer medications with longer half-lives has allowed for longer dosing intervals, which saves time and expense.[20,24] However, by changing to extended half-life cephalosporins, no nursing expenses were recoverable, there was little chance of consistently reducing pharmacy compounding expenses, and pharmacy costs were potentially increased by the use of these more expensive antibiotics.[25] Yet, in another study in which similar methodology was employed, switching seven patients from intravenous to oral antibiotics was calculated to allow the re-allocation of one eight-hour nursing shift per 24 hours.[26]

## Therapeutic Drug Monitoring

Valid arguments exist for appropriate monitoring of renal function and serum concentrations of aminoglycosides.[27] Measuring one set of peak and trough concentrations of gentamicin, and measuring blood urea nitrogen and serum creatinine on three occasions, incurs an additional cost to the hospital of more than $100. Ordering a laboratory test ultimately contributes to the workload of many people and involves various materials and equipment. A nurse or ward secretary must complete a requisition; a nurse or phlebotomist must obtain the sample, which must be transported to and processed by the laboratory, which will then perform the quantitative analysis with appropriate controls, print the results, and transport those results to the nursing station for inclusion in the patient's chart. Many of these steps are subject to quality control or quality assurance procedures and record keeping. The additional costs of personnel time, inventory, and other activities required for therapeutic drug monitoring will not be considered here.

Adding the monitoring costs associated with gentamicin into the UTI example transforms gentamicin, with the lowest drug cost of $0.20 per dose, into the most expensive antibiotic to use. The costs for seven days of therapy, including ancillary material and laboratory costs, are shown in the last column of Table 3.

## Adverse Drug Effects

The possibility of adverse drug effects should not be ignored in any cost evaluation. Complications associated with intravenous drug delivery include sepsis, thrombosis, phlebitis, embolism, and drug precipitation. There may be other types of incompatibilities, infiltration, extravasation, and fluid overload associated with certain systems.[28] In addition, bleeding associated with β-lactam antibiotics could require costly treatment.[29]

The cost of treating either nephrotoxicity or bleeding is quite variable. Treatment options, duration of therapy, and cost of treatment depend on the degree of toxicity and underlying medical condition of the patient. The relative cost would depend on the true incidence of those adverse effects requiring treatment with the modalities considered in the cost analysis. For example, Holloway et al[30] used decision analysis to estimate incremental costs attributable to nephrotoxicity associated with gentamicin or tobramycin therapy. Their cost estimates ranged from $129 per case of mild nephrotoxicity to more than $300,000 to treat patients who require permanent hemodialysis, an extremely rare event. Whether adverse drug effects associated with oral fluoroquinolone therapy will be economically important is not yet clear.

## ORAL CIPROFLOXACIN STUDY

In order to evaluate the cost benefit associated with the use of oral ciprofloxacin, preliminary data from a current study at the author's institution was subjected to a cost analysis. The study is a clinical trial comparing oral ciprofloxacin with standard intravenous antibiotics in hospitalized patients with serious infections.

## Methodology

Hospitalized adult patients with serious, documented bacterial infections requiring intravenous antibiotic therapy were eligible for inclusion in the study. Patients were excluded if they were pregnant or were breastfeeding, or had serum creatinine >3.0 mg/dl, anaerobic bacteremia, cystic fibrosis, pelvic infections, or <1000/mm$^3$ polymorphonuclear leukocytes. Other exclusion criteria included chronic urinary catheterization and an inability to ingest and absorb oral medications.

All patients received intravenous antibiotics for three days. After 72 hours patients were randomized to remain on intravenous antibiotics or switch to oral ciprofloxacin

750 mg twice daily. To provide antibacterial coverage against anaerobes, oral metronidazole could be added to the regimen of patients receiving ciprofloxacin.

Data was collected on 46 evaluable patients. Infection sites (Table 4), cultured bacteria (Table 5), and initial intravenous antibiotics (Table 6) were similar in the two arms of the study. In the intravenous arm, 19 of 26 infections responded to therapy, while 24 of 25 infections in patients who were switched to oral ciprofloxacin responded satisfactorily. Response assessments were based on bacteriological results, temperature, white blood cell count and differential, other diagnostic and monitoring tests, and local signs and symptoms of infection. These are raw data only; complete results with statistical analysis will be published in a separate report. Nevertheless, these preliminary findings are consistent with those reported in other studies and demonstrate equal efficacy of oral ciprofloxacin and parenteral antibiotics in both respiratory and skin and soft tissue infections.[31-36]

## Cost Analysis

Table 7 lists the average cost per patient, including acquisition costs of the antibiotics, ancillary material costs associated with intravenous doses, and laboratory tests ordered specifically for therapeutic drug monitoring (serum drug concentration, BUN, and serum creatinine). Not included are allowances for pharmacy and nursing time, reduced length-of-stay, and ancillary costs not listed in Table 1.

The analysis in Table 7 compares costs in one group of patients with another. However, the typical prospective drug-use review program would evaluate benefit to a specific patient. For example, if a DUR program recommended that a patient receive cefazolin rather than cefotaxime, one might calculate a savings associated with the

Table 4. Study of oral ciprofloxacin vs. intravenous antibiotics: Infection site and number of cases

| | Number of Infections* | |
| --- | --- | --- |
| Infection Site | Parenteral | Parenteral, then oral ciprofloxacin |
| Respiratory tract | 6 | 3 |
| Skin and skin structure | 13 | 16 |
| Bone and joint | 2 | 3 |
| Bacteremia | 2 | 1 |
| Urinary tract | 3 | 1 |
| Malignant otitis externa | 0 | 1 |

\* Five of 46 evaluable patients each had two infection sites.

Table 5. Study of oral ciprofloxacin vs. intravenous antibiotics: Number of cultured bacteria

| | Number of Isolates* | |
| --- | --- | --- |
| Isolate | Parenteral | Parenteral, then oral ciprofloxacin |
| *Pseudomonas aeruginosa* | 6 | 9 |
| *Staphylococcus aureus* | 10 | 10 |
| *Staphylococcus epidermidis* | 2 | 1 |
| *Escherichia coli* | 2 | 4 |
| *Klebsiella pneumoniae* | 1 | 2 |
| *Enterobacter* spp. | 2 | 2 |
| *Serratia marcescens* | 0 | 1 |
| *Branhamella catarrhalis* | 1 | 0 |
| *Bacteroides fragilis* | 1 | 0 |
| Other | 2 | 3 |

\* Some sites were infected with more than one isolate.

Table 6. Study of oral ciprofloxacin vs. intravenous antibiotics: Antimicrobial agents used during the first three days of therapy*

| | Number of Treatments | |
| --- | --- | --- |
| Antibiotic | Parenteral | Parenteral, then oral ciprofloxacin |
| Aminoglycoside | 12 | 9 |
| Antipseudomonal penicillin | 6 | 4 |
| 1st generation cephalosporin | 9 | 2 |
| 3rd generation cephalosporin | 3 | 7 |
| Nafcillin | 2 | 8 |
| Vancomycin | 5 | 3 |
| Clindamycin | 2 | 3 |
| Imipenem | 0 | 1 |
| Other | 5 | 1 |

\* Most patients received an intravenous regimen containing more than one antibiotic.

DUR process by determining the difference in drug costs between the two agents, multiplied by the number of days on the new regimen. If the patient had remained on cefotaxime, the drug cost for treatment of that infection might have been $270. However, because the patient was switched to the less expensive cefazolin, the actual cost was only $110. Therefore, the savings in this particular example was $160.

By applying this type of DUR analysis to the data for the patients switched to oral ciprofloxacin in the current study, a more accurate estimate of cost savings emerged. Because individualization of antibiotic therapy (which may occur on treatment day 2 or 3 when culture and sensitivity results become available), may result in a more cost-effective treatment regimen, the daily cost of the appropriate intravenous antibiotic regimen was calculated and multiplied by the number of days of treatment received. A conservative estimate of the cost of drug monitoring laboratory tests was added. The average total antibiotic and associated materials costs for the patients who were switched to oral ciprofloxacin was $293. If these patients had remained on intravenous antibiotics (with appropriate modification of the regimen for culture and sensitivity results) for the same length of time they were on ciprofloxacin, the antibiotic costs would have been $1123. Thus, the projected average savings with ciprofloxacin was $830 per patient.

This savings was greater than predicted from Table 7 when comparing treatment arms, and perhaps reflects another event that may occur due to the ease of administration of oral medications. As suggested by Barriere,[37] it is likely that patients with serious or chronic infections may receive a longer course of treatment with oral ciprofloxacin than they would have received with intravenous antibiotics. Some of this savings may be offset by patients being switched to alternative, less expensive oral antibiotics. However, this option is not available to patients with systemic infections not amenable to oral antibiotic treatment other than with a fluoroquinolone.

When comparing the prices of oral antibiotics, it is probably more appropriate to consider the outpatient cost. Thus, the average wholesale price (AWP) will be used as a basis of comparison. The AWP is what a retail pharmacy would be expected to pay to obtain the medication, so charges to the patients will be higher (by several dollars)

Table 7. Study of oral ciprofloxacin vs. intravenous antibiotics: Average antibiotic and associated costs

|  | Parenteral | Parenteral, then oral ciprofloxacin |
| --- | --- | --- |
| Day 1-3/per day | $55 | $65 |
| Day 4+/per day | $47 | $6 |

after prices are marked up for professional fee, overhead, etc. An AWP cost comparison of seven days of therapy with selected oral antibiotics can be found in Table 8.

## Early Discharge

A more significant cost savings potential of oral fluoroquinolone therapy is due to early discharge from the hospital. For patients whose continued hospitalization is solely for the purpose of receiving intravenous antibiotics, a switch to oral fluoroquinolones and subsequent discharge will substantially reduce hospital costs. For

**Table 8.** Average wholesale price comparison of selected oral antibiotics

| Antibiotic | Dose | Cost per Week |
|---|---|---|
| Amoxicillin | 250 mg tid | $ 3 |
| | 500 mg tid | $ 6 |
| Amoxicillin/Clavulanic Acid | 250 mg tid | $19 |
| | 500 mg tid | $28 |
| Carbenicillin indanyl | 382 mg qid | $24 |
| | 764 mg qid | $48 |
| Cefaclor | 250 mg tid | $25 |
| | 500 mg tid | $48 |
| Cephalexin | 250 mg qid | $16 |
| | 500 mg qid | $29 |
| Cefuroxime axetil | 250 mg bid | $21 |
| | 500 mg bid | $41 |
| Ciprofloxacin | 250 mg bid | $24 |
| | 500 mg bid | $25 |
| | 750 mg bid | $49 |
| Dicloxacillin | 250 mg qid | $11 |
| | 500 mg qid | $20 |
| Norfloxacin | 400 mg bid | $28 |
| Trimethoprim-sulfamethoxazole | DS* bid | $ 8 |

\* Double-strength
Adapted from Lee.[15]

some patients, outpatient parenteral antibiotics programs already allow some savings to be realized.[38] However, parenteral antibiotic therapy is associated with certain incidental costs, regardless of whether it is administered on an outpatient or inpatient basis. Furthermore, intravenous antibiotics are more costly than oral ciprofloxacin; the hospital cost of ceftriaxone 1 gram is $23, while the AWP is $28.15 The hospital cost of ciprofloxacin 750 mg is $3, while the AWP is $3.49. Ancillary material costs will also be higher on an outpatient basis, since hospitals obtain lower pricing through competitive bidding related to volume purchasing. Thus, while home intravenous antibiotic programs can reduce hospitalization expenditures, costs are shifted to the outpatient setting.

The majority of patients who have benefitted from outpatient parenteral antibiotic programs have been those with infections requiring relatively long-term antibiotic therapy. However, most antibiotic usage is for shorter courses, often less than 10 days. The home antibiotic administration system is not usually activated for these patients, because the preparations for discharge on home intravenous antibiotics usually require several hospital days to accomplish. Use of oral fluoroquinolones can allow a greater number of patients to complete antibiotic therapy at home, with resultant benefits and savings associated with decreased hospital stay.

## CONCLUSION

Certainly the use of oral rather than intravenous medications is more comfortable for the patient and carries a decreased risk of adverse events. The use of oral fluoroquinolones may contribute to early discharge from the hospital while allowing the patient to remain on potent antibiotic therapy.

This chapter focuses on the economic benefit associated with switching from intravenous antibiotics to oral ciprofloxacin. Considering drug costs alone does not adequately reflect the actual costs of intravenous administration, as ancillary material and personnel costs can exceed the cost of the drug itself. The costs of treating many infections can be significantly reduced by using oral ciprofloxacin. Although the ultimate impact of treating infections with oral fluoroquinolones has yet to be realized, the economic implications are not likely to escape the watchful eye of governmental and other third-party payers responsible for health care reimbursement. Previously, most newly released antibiotics were more costly than those they replaced. While improved parenteral antibiotics may reduce hospital stay, they increase the hospital pharmacy budget.[25] In contrast, oral fluoroquinolones can contain hospitalization costs by decreasing the length-of-stay and reducing the pharmacy budget as well.

# REFERENCES

1. Eisenberg BS: Diagnosis-related groups, severity of illness and equitable reimbursement under medicare. Editorial. JAMA 1984;251:645-646.

2. Tanner DJ: Health care cost-containment in a changing health care world. Drug Intell Clin Pharm 1985;19:291-292.

3. Baum C, Kennedy DL: Hospital drug expenditures in 1985. Letter. Am J Hosp Pharm 1987;44:492-495.

4. Castle M, Wilfert CM, Cate TR, et al: Antibiotic use at Duke University Medical Center. JAMA 1977;237:2819-2822.

5. Gleckman R, Gantz NM: Cost-effective antibiotic prescribing. Pharmacotherapy 1983; 3:239-248.

6. Report from the Antimicrobial Agents Committee. J Infect Dis 1987;156:700-705.

7. Todd MW, Keith TD, Foster MT: Development and implementation of a comprehensive, criteria-based drug-use review program. Am J Hosp Pharm 1987;44:529-535.

8. Stolar MH: The case for prospective and concurrent drug utilization review. Qual Rev Bull 1982;8:6-10.

9. Abramowitz PW, Nold EG, Hatfield SM: Use of clinical pharmacists to reduce cefamandole, cefoxitin, and ticarcillin costs. Am J Hosp Pharm 1982;39:1176-1180.

10. Suzuki NT, Pelham LD: Cost benefit of pharmacist concurrent monitoring of cefazolin prescribing. Am J Hosp Pharm 1983;40:1187-1191.

11. Powers DA: Antimicrobial surveillance in a VAMC teaching hospital- resulting cost avoidance. Drug Intell Clin Pharm 1986;20:803-805.

12. Hayman JN, Sbravati EC: Controlling cephalosporin and aminoglycoside costs through pharmacy and therapeutics committee restrictions. Am J Hosp Pharm 1985;42:1343-1347.

13. Kowalsky SF, Echols RM, Peck F: Preprinted order sheet to enhance antibiotic prescribing and surveillance. Am J Hosp Pharm 1982;39:1528-1529.

14. Joint Commission on Accreditation of Hospitals, 1979 Edition. Accreditation Manual for Hospitals. Chicago: Joint Commission on Accreditation of Hospitals, p 95.

15. Lee FH (ed), *Blue Book. American Druggist, Annual Directory of Pharmaceuticals 1987-1988*. New York, The Hearst Corporation, 1987.

16. Kimelblatt BJ, Lerro RC, Franchak N, et al: Use review of cimetidine injection. Am J Hosp Pharm 1982;39:311.

17. Wald A, Britton L, Wing EJ: Inappropriate use of cimetidine in hospitalized patients. South Med J 1983;76:701-705.

18. Smith C, Hill TR: Cost impact of conversion of IV to PO therapy - a target program. Presented at the ASHP 22nd Annual Midyear Clinical Meeting, Atlanta, GA, 1987.

19. Beckner RR, Hancock D: Drug utilization review: Conversion of theophylline therapy from the intravenous to the oral route - a descriptive report. Presented at the ASHP 22nd Annual Midyear Clinical Meeting, Atlanta, GA, 1987.

20. Tanner DJ: Cost containment of reconstituted parenteral antibiotics: Personnel and supply costs associated with preparation, dispensing and administration. Rev Infect Dis 1984;6:S924-S937.

21. Aldis WL, Cowan D: Cost-effectiveness of antibiotic use, letter. JAMA 1984;252:3252.

22. Dudley M, Barriere S, Mills J: Cost comparisons among antimicrobial agents, letter. N Engl J Med 1982;307:689.

23. Rapp RP: Hospital intravenous drug administration in the era of prospective payment. Drug Intell Clin Pharm 1985;19:146-148.

24. Tartaglione TA, Polk RE: Review of the new second-generation cephalosporins: cefonicid, ceforanide, and cefuroxime. Drug Intell Clin Pharm 1985;19:188-198.

25. Scalley RD, Stuart CC: Is there cost reduction potential for extended half-life cephalosporins? Drug Intell Clin Pharm 1986;20:975-980.

26. Lincoln LL, Dudley MN: Effect of substitution of parenteral antibiotic therapy with oral agents on nurse staffing requirements determined by the GRASP system. Presented at the ASHP 22nd Annual Midyear Clinical Meeting, Atlanta, GA, 1987.

27. Lampasona V, Crass RE: Patient selection for serum gentamicin monitoring. Ther Drug Monit 1983;5:255-262.

28. Akers MJ: Current problems and innovations in intravenous drug delivery. Considerations in using the i.v. route for drug delivery. Am J Hosp Pharm 1987;44:2528-2530.

29. Sattler FR, Weitekamp MR, Ballard JO: Potential for bleeding with the new beta-lactam antibiotics. Ann Intern Med 1986;105(6):924-931.

30. Holloway JJ, Smith CR, Moore RD, et al: Comparative cost effectiveness of gentamicin and tobramycin. Ann Intern Med 1984;101:764-769.

31. Bosso JA, Black PG, Matsen JM: Ciprofloxacin versus tobramycin plus azlocillin in pulmonary exacerbations in adult patients with cystic fibrosis. Am J Med 1987;82(suppl 4A):180-184.

32. Rubio TT: Ciprofloxacin: comparative data in cystic fibrosis. Am J Med 1987;82(suppl 4A):185-188.

33. Self PL, Zeluff BA, Sollo D, et al: Use of ciprofloxacin in the treatment of serious skin and skin structure infections. Am J Med 1987;82(suppl 4A):239-241.

34. Parish LC, Asper R: Systemic treatment of cutaneous infections: A comparative study of ciprofloxacin and cefotaxime. Am J Med 1987;82(suppl 4A):227-229.

35. Pérez-Ruvalcaba JA, Quintero-Pérez NP, Morales-Reyes JJ, et al: Double-blind comparison of ciprofloxacin with cefotaxime in the treatment of skin and skin structure infections. Am J Med 1987;82(suppl 4A):242-246.

36. Ramirez-Ronda CH, Saavedra S, Rivera-Vázquez CR: Comparative, double-blind study of oral ciprofloxacin and intravenous cefotaxime in skin and skin structure infections. Am J Med 1987;82(suppl 4A):220-223.

37. Barriere SL: Economic impact of oral quinolones. Hosp Form 1987;22(suppl A):21-24.

38. Poretz DM, Eron LJ, Goldenberg RI, et al: Intravenous antibiotic therapy in an outpatient setting. JAMA 1982;248:336-339.

# NEW DEVELOPMENTS IN FLUOROQUINOLONE THERAPY 16

*Kenneth V. I. Rolston*

## INTRODUCTION

In recent years a large number of fluoroquinolones have been synthesized. Two of them, norfloxacin and ciprofloxacin, have been approved by the Food and Drug Administration for clinical use in the United States. The release of others such as ofloxacin, enoxacin, pefloxacin, and fleroxacin can be expected to occur within the next year or two. Other compounds as yet designated by numbers only (PD117,596, PD127-391, S-25930, etc.) are in the early stages of development. The newer fluoroquinolones are structurally related to nalidixic acid, which has been available for over 25 years.

Although some differences exist in individual antimicrobial activity, the newer fluoroquinolones are all much more active in vitro than nalidixic acid and have a broader spectrum of activity.[1] The fluoroquinolones are most active against aerobic gram-negative organisms; they are less active against streptococci, staphylococci, and anaerobes. Like nalidixic acid, these agents are well absorbed after oral administration; norfloxacin has the lowest and ofloxacin the greatest oral bioavailability. Other useful pharmacokinetic properties include low protein binding, wide distribution, and excellent penetration into many body tissues and fluids and into cells, resulting in activity against intracellular pathogens. In addition, these agents all have relatively long elimination half-lives in serum, which permits twice-daily administration in most instances.

Single-step resistance to the new fluoroquinolones occurs but is relatively infrequent.[2] While cross-resistance among the fluoroquinolones is common, cross-resistance with other classes of antimicrobial agents is rare. Combination with other antimicrobial agents is additive with regard to antimicrobial effects and generally does not result in significant synergy or antagonism.

The new fluoroquinolones represent a significant advance over older agents such as nalidixic acid and are useful in a number of clinical settings. Intense clinical research over the past decade has led to the establishment of various indications for their use. Future investigations are likely to identify additional areas of therapeutic application. Newer developments in fluoroquinolone therapy will be reviewed along with current indications for the use of these agents.

## CLINICAL USE OF FLUOROQUINOLONES

## *Urinary Tract Infections*

The usefulness of nalidixic acid and related compounds was limited by a narrow spectrum of activity that excluded all gram-positive and anaerobic organisms and aerobic gram-negative bacilli such as *Pseudomonas aeruginosa* and *Serratia marcescens*. Another major drawback was the rapid development of high-level resistance. In contrast, the newer fluoroquinolones are active against the majority of urinary pathogens, including those resistant to other antibiotics, and the risk of development of spontaneous resistance is low. These agents possess other properties that make them attractive for the treatment of urinary tract infections (UTIs). Adequate urinary levels are maintained even in the presence of renal insufficiency, and gastrointestinal concentrations are sufficient to eliminate potential uropathogens, thus decreasing the possibility of reinfection or superinfection with resistant organisms. Although the newer fluoroquinolones such as norfloxacin, ciprofloxacin, and ofloxacin are effective in the treatment of uncomplicated urinary tract infections, they should not supplant standard agents such as amoxicillin or trimethoprim-sulfamethoxazole (TMP/SMX), which are more appropriate in this setting. The fluoroquinolones, however, are extremely effective in the treatment of complicated UTIs, nosocomial UTIs (particularly those caused by multidrug resistant organisms), and in upper urinary tract disease (eg, pyelonephritis).[3] Since these infections often require lengthy antibiotic therapy, the availability of orally administered fluoroquinolones is an added attraction. Nevertheless, resistance is likely to develop with prolonged use as prophylaxis or chronic therapy in patients with obstructing renal lesions or kidney stones.

The fluoroquinolones have the ability to penetrate into prostatic tissue and fluid and are potentially useful agents for the treatment of bacterial prostatitis. Currently available data indicate that chronic bacterial prostatitis, particularly that caused by *Escherichia coli,* may respond to fluoroquinolone therapy.[4,5] In addition, relapses are more likely with infections caused by *Enterococcus* spp. and *Ps. aeruginosa*. Although initial results have been somewhat disappointing, fluoroquinolone therapy of prostatitis is probably as effective as therapy with any other currently available agent. More clinical information about the role of the fluoroquinolones in prostatic infection is needed before their efficacy can be fully assessed.

## Skin and Soft Tissue Infections

Skin and soft tissue infections such as pyoderma, impetigo, furunculosis, and simple cellulitis are often caused by staphylococci and streptococci. Of the currently available fluoroquinolones, ciprofloxacin is the most active against these organisms, with tissue levels generally above those required for inhibition. Although ciprofloxacin is effective in such infections, including those caused by methicillin-resistant *Staphylococcus aureus* (MRSA), reports of failures and the emergence of resistant organisms have appeared.[6,7] As a result, β-lactam agents, clindamycin, or TMP/SMX should be used instead of fluoroquinolones in these settings. Recent evidence indicates that the combination of ciprofloxacin and rifampin is more effective than ciprofloxacin alone for staphylococcal infections and is less likely to result in the emergence of resistant organisms.[8] However, the indiscriminate use of rifampin-containing regimens (other than in mycobacterial infections) should be avoided.

Other skin and soft tissue infections in which the newer fluoroquinolones are useful include mixed aerobic gram-negative infections such as decubitus ulcers and diabetic foot infections. Since anaerobic organisms are frequently isolated from such sources, it may be prudent to combine ciprofloxacin or other fluoroquinolones with metronidazole or clindamycin in order to provide activity against anaerobes. Because of its activity against *Ps. aeruginosa,* ciprofloxacin is extremely useful in the treatment of malignant otitis externa, an entity seen most often in diabetic patients. In this situation, the ability to administer the fluoroquinolones orally may reduce the duration of hospitalization or eliminate the need for intravenous antibiotic therapy.

## Bone and Joint Infections

The ease of administration of the fluoroquinolones and their penetration into bone make them very useful agents for the treatment of osteomyelitis. Clinical data with ciprofloxacin and ofloxacin indicate that for gram-negative osteomyelitis, these agents are at least as effective and potentially superior to currently available parenteral antibiotics.[9] Fleroxacin, an agent currently undergoing evaluation, has an elimination half-life of over 10 hours and produces high plasma concentrations with relatively low dosing.[10] This may make it possible to treat infections due to susceptible organisms with a once-daily dosage regimen.

The fluoroquinolones are also useful (particularly when combined with rifampin) for the treatment of osteomyelitis and sternotomy infections caused by staphylococci, including methicillin-resistant organisms. Newer agents being developed (PD117, 558, PD-117,596, PD-127,391) are extremely active against gram-positive cocci and inhibit the majority of staphylococcal and streptococcal species at concentrations of

0.06-0.12 μg/mL or less.[11-13] If these agents reach clinical trials, they should prove very effective against gram-positive organisms.

## Respiratory Tract Infections

Upper respiratory infections such as sinusitis and otitis may be effectively treated with ciprofloxacin and ofloxacin. However, the agents of choice in this setting are the β-lactams, TMP/SMX, and macrolides.

Mounting evidence indicates that the fluoroquinolones may be useful in the treatment of lower respiratory infections such as acute bronchitis and pneumonia.[14] Infections most likely to respond are those caused by gram-negative coccobacillary organisms, *H. influenzae* and *B. catarrhalis*. Fluoroquinolone treatment of infections caused predominantly by *S. pneumoniae* may be unsatisfactory in the presence of bacteremia. Persistence of *S. pneumoniae* in the sputum of patients treated with the fluoroquinolones has also been reported. In hospital acquired pneumonias, where aerobic gram-negative bacilli such as the Enterobacteriaceae and *Ps. aeruginosa* are common pathogens, the fluoroquinolones can be used as initial therapeutic agents. In patients with aspiration pneumonia caused by anaerobic and microaerophilic organisms such as *Fusobacterium* spp., *Bacteroides* spp., and microaerophilic streptococci, the fluoroquinolones are suboptimal agents and should not be used.

Newer fluoroquinolones under development, including PD-117,596 and PD-127,391, have good in vitro activity against gram-positive organisms including *S. pneumoniae* and anaerobes. These agents are likely to expand the role of the fluoroquinolones in the treatment of respiratory tract infections to include community-acquired infections and aspiration pneumonia.

Ciprofloxacin has been used successfully to treat infections in patients with cystic fibrosis (CF).[15] However, because of the potential for damage to cartilage that exists with all quinolones, they should not be used in children or adolescents younger than 14 years of age. In addition, prolonged use of ciprofloxacin in patients with CF results in the emergence of resistant organisms, particularly *Ps. aeruginosa*. Non-aeruginosa *Pseudomonas* spp. such as *Ps. cepacia* and *Ps. maltophilia* are less susceptible than *Ps. aeruginosa* and may occasionally cause superinfections. In patients with CF, ciprofloxacin should be alternated with other therapeutic regimens to prevent the selection of resistant organisms.

## Gastrointestinal Infections

Norfloxacin, ciprofloxacin, and other fluoroquinolones are active against the majority of organisms causing gastrointestinal infections. Diarrhea caused by *Campylobacter,* toxigenic *E. coli, Aeromonas* spp., *Shigella* spp., *Salmonella* spp. (including *S. typhi*), and *Vibrio* spp. (including *V. cholera*) is cured with rapid elimination of the organisms from the intestinal tract.[16] Some evidence suggests that norfloxacin and ciprofloxacin are superior to ampicillin, TMP/SMX, and chloramphenicol for the treatment of Salmonellosis in AIDS patients.[17,18] Fewer relapses and recurrent infections occur with the use of fluoroquinolones, due to the exquisite susceptibility of *Salmonella* spp. as well as the high biliary levels achievable with these agents; this allows eradication of the carrier state. Antibiotic therapy of *Salmonella* gastroenteritis is currently not recommended. However, in patients with AIDS, gastroenteritis usually precedes bacteremia or disseminated infection with *Salmonella* spp., and these patients do benefit from therapy with the new fluoroquinolones.[16] Similarly, the fluoroquinolones are effective in typhoid fever and in eliminating carriage of *S. typhi*.[19] Prolonged therapy may occasionally result in overgrowth of *Clostridium difficile* and colitis, since these organisms are not inhibited by the fluoroquinolones.

## Sexually Transmitted Diseases

All of the newer fluoroquinolones are highly effective as single-dose therapy of gonorrhea, including infections caused by penicillinase-producing *Neisseria gonorrhoeae*.[20-22] Although additional data are needed, these agents seem to be effective not only for gonococcal urethritis and cervicitis but also for pharyngeal and rectal infection. The fluoroquinolones are also very active against *Haemophilus ducreyi*, and limited clinical data indicate efficacy in the treatment of chancroid.[23] Doxycycline is more effective than the fluoroquinolones for the treatment of infections due to chlamydia. The efficacy of the fluoroquinolones against mycoplasma and ureaplasma genital infections has not been adequately established. The fluoroquinolones are not effective against *Treponema pallidum*, and are not recommended for the treatment of syphilis in any stage.

## Prophylaxis

Ciprofloxacin is effective in eliminating nasal and oropharyngeal carriage of *Neisseria meningitidis*.[24] It is relatively well tolerated, is generally effective against rifampin-resistant organisms, and does not induce much resistance among these organisms.[25]

Ciprofloxacin has also been used to eliminate colonization with methicillin-resistant *S. aureus* at various clinical sites. As indicated previously, ciprofloxacin in combination with rifampin is superior to ciprofloxacin alone against MRSA. Newer fluoroquinolones which are much more potent against gram-positive pathogens might be adequate as single agents for prophylaxis against MRSA. Clinical studies will be needed to determine the clinical value of these agents.

Both norfloxacin and ciprofloxacin have been used for prophylaxis in neutropenic patients undergoing chemotherapy or following bone marrow transplantation.[26,27]

Many investigators are concerned over the possibility of selection of resistant organisms or of superinfections with less susceptible gram-positive organisms. Excessive use of these agents for prophylaxis in cancer patients may lead to their elimination as useful therapeutic agents.

## Other Potential Indications

Many reports have indicated that *Helicobacter pylori* is susceptible in vitro to the fluoroquinolones.[28] Gastritis caused by this organism may respond to therapy with fluoroquinolones, but more data are needed before firm recommendations can be made. Failures with ofloxacin and norfloxacin have been reported.[29]

The diffusion of ciprofloxacin into cerebrospinal fluid is adequate to inhibit gram-negative organisms, and there are isolated reports of successful treatment of *Ps. aeruginosa* meningitis with this agent.[30,31] Routine use in meningitis with currently available agents is not possible due to lack of activity against *S. pneumoniae*. The lack of activity against streptococci also prevents routine use of fluoroquinolones in patients with endocarditis. However, they may be used in selected cases of gram-negative endocarditis and occasionally for *S. aureus* endocarditis when combined with rifampin. At present, clinical data in these settings are limited.

In vitro as well as animal and human data indicate that the fluoroquinolones may be effective in the treatment of *Legionella* pneumonia.[32-34] Ciprofloxacin may be preferable for the treatment of *Legionella* pneumonia in patients receiving cyclosporine since it does not seem to alter levels of this agent, whereas both erythromycin and rifampin cause dramatic alterations in cyclosporine levels.[35] Ciprofloxacin, however, must be used with caution since treatment failures have been reported.[36]

The fluoroquinolones have activity against mycobacteria including *Mycobacterium avium intracellulare* (MAI).[37] However, experimental animal studies and early clinical studies using ciprofloxacin in combination with amikacin and other agents for MAI infections in patients with AIDS have not been encouraging.[38] Some of the newer fluoroquinolones have in vitro activity against *Nocardia* spp. and may be of potential benefit in the treatment of nocardiosis, but clinical studies are lacking.[39]

The fluoroquinolones may also be of value in the treatment of ophthalmologic infections. Topical fluoroquinolones may be beneficial in bacterial conjunctivitis. Some evidence suggests that the fluoroquinolones penetrate into aqueous humor.[40,41] Studies need to be conducted to determine their penetration into vitreous humor and their efficacy in bacterial endophthalmitis.

The newer fluoroquinolones may also have a role in the treatment of Yersiniosis. Limited data on the successful use of ciprofloxacin in this setting have been published.[42] As with many other infections, more clinical data with the use of fluoroquinolones are needed before firm conclusions can be drawn.

Recent reports suggest that the newer quinolones including norfloxacin, ciprofloxacin, enoxacin, ofloxacin, amifloxacin, and pefloxacin are active in vitro against both chloroquine-susceptible and chloroquine-resistant strains of *Plasmodium falciparum*.[43] The mechanism of this activity is not fully understood and may be entirely different from inhibition of parasite DNA gyrase, since bacterial DNA gyrase inhibitors such as novobiocin and nalidixic acid do not diminish the activity of DNA gyrase isolated from *Plasmodium falciparum*.

The accidental observation of a cure of malaria in a patient who received norfloxacin for a concomitant bacterial infection suggested that the quinolones might be active in this disease.[44] In a subsequent trial by the same investigator, nine patients with uncomplicated falciparum malaria were treated with oral norfloxacin 400 mg every 12 hours for 3 days. All patients were apparently cured. These preliminary results are promising but further trials with larger numbers of patients are needed to clarify the role of the quinolones for the prophylaxis and therapy of human malaria, particularly multi-drug resistant falciparum malaria.

## Intravenous Fluoroquinolone Therapy

Although the availability of the newer fluoroquinolones for oral administration represents a major advantage in terms of ease of administration and cost, particularly in patients requiring prolonged antibiotic therapy, in certain clinical settings parenteral therapy is preferable. These include infections in critically ill patients, those unable to tolerate oral therapy, and patients with abnormalities that impede absorption from the gastrointestinal tract. Parenteral fluoroquinolone therapy has been evaluated in some of these situations.

Ciprofloxacin in combination with vancomycin was administered as initial therapy to febrile neutropenic patients and resulted in an overall response rate of 86%.[45] In most patients who responded, it was possible to change to oral ciprofloxacin after one week of parenteral therapy. In another recently conducted trial, ciprofloxacin plus netilmicin was found to be as effective as piperacillin plus netilmicin, but the ciprofloxacin regimen was far superior (86% response rate versus 43%) in the treatment of gram-negative bacteremia in febrile neutropenic patients.[46] This study also demonstrated that it was possible to switch from parenteral to oral therapy with ciprofloxacin.

In two separate open-ended trials, one with oral ciprofloxacin and the other with intravenous ciprofloxacin, overall response rates greater than 85% were achieved in neutropenic and non-neutropenic febrile cancer patients treated at the University of Texas M.D. Anderson Cancer Center.[47] These data indicate that parenteral fluoroquinolone therapy is promising for initial use in seriously ill patients, and that the ability to change to oral therapy helps simplify and reduce the overall costs associated with such treatment. Parenteral therapy with ciprofloxacin has also been used successfully for other serious infections including bacteremia, pneumonia, and cholangitis.[48-50] To date, no reports have described additional toxicity with parenteral use.

## SUMMARY

The fluoroquinolones are remarkable new agents that are safe and effective for a wide variety of infections. Oral fluoroquinolones provide an alternative to many currently used agents such as the aminoglycosides and β-lactams and enable the physician to administer outpatient therapy, thus reducing overall costs. The availability of parenteral forms of the newer fluoroquinolones will extend the usefulness of these agents to include seriously ill patients and those unable to tolerate oral therapy. More potent fluoroquinolones are being developed, with activity against gram-positive organisms and anaerobes. Longer-acting fluoroquinolones such as fleroxacin may also make once-daily therapy possible. The medical community needs to use these agents appropriately in order to preserve their overall usefulness. Misuse of these agents will quickly lead to the emergence of resistance and diminished efficacy.

# REFERENCES

1. Wolfson JS, Hooper DC: The fluoroquinolones: Structures, mechanisms of action and resistance, and spectra of activity in vitro. Antimicrob Agents Chemother 1985;28:581-586.

2. Hooper DC, Wolfson JS, Ng EY, et al: Mechanisms of action of and resistance to ciprofloxacin. Am J Med 1987;82(suppl 4A):12-20.

3. Gasser TC, Graversen PH, Madsen PO: Treatment of complicated urinary tract infections with ciprofloxacin. Am J Med 1987;82(suppl 4A):278-279.

4. Weidner W, Schiefer HG, Dalhoff A: Treatment of chronic bacterial prostatitis with ciprofloxacin: Results of a one-year follow-up study. Am J Med 1987;82(suppl 4A):280-283.

5. Childs SJ: Treatment of chronic bacterial prostatitis with ciprofloxacin. Infect Surg 1987;6:649-651

6. Piercy EA, Barbaro D, Luby JP, et al: Ciprofloxacin for methicillin-resistant *Staphylococcus aureus* infection. Antimicrob Agents Chemother 1989;33:128-130.

7. Ramirez-Ronda CH, Saavedra S, Rivera-Vázquez CR: Comparative, double-blind study of oral ciprofloxacin and intravenous cefotaxime in skin and skin structure infections. Am J Med 1987;82(suppl 4A):220-223.

8. Smith SM, Eng RHK, Tecson-Tumang F: Ciprofloxacin therapy for methicillin-resistant *Staphylococcus aureus* infections or colonization. Antimicrob Agents Chemother 1989;33:181-184.

9. Greenberg RN, Tice AD, Marsh PK, et al: Randomized trial of ciprofloxacin compared with other antimicrobial therapy in the treatment of osteomyelitis. Am J Med 1987;82(suppl 4A):266-269.

10. Wise R, Kirkpatrick B, Ashby J, et al: Pharmacokinetics and tissue penetration of RO23-6240, a new trifluoroquinolone. Antimicrob Agents Chemother 1987;31:161-163.

11. King A, Boothman C, Phillips I: The in-vitro activity of PD127,391, a new quinolone. J Antimicrob Chemother 1988;22:135-141.

12. Rolston KVI, Bodey GP: Activity of CI-934 against gram-positive bacteria. J Antimicrob Chemother 1986;18:768-769.

13. Rolston KVI, LeBlanc B, Gooch G, et al: In-vitro activity of PD117558, a new quinolone against bacterial isolates from cancer patients. J Antimicrob Chemother 1989;23:363-371.

14. Monk JP, Campoli-Richards DM: Ofloxacin: A review of its antibacterial activity, pharmacokinetic properties, and clinical use. Drugs 1987;33:346-391.

15. Scully BE, Nakatomi M, Ores C, et al: Ciprofloxacin therapy in cystic fibrosis. Am J Med 1987;82(suppl 4A):196-201.

16. DuPont HL, Corrado ML, Sabbaj J: The use of norfloxacin in the treatment of acute diarrheal disease. Am J Med 1987;82(suppl 6B):70-74.

17. Rolston KVI, Rodriguez S, Mansell PWA: Antimicrobial therapy of *Salmonella* infections in patients with the acquired immunodeficiency syndrome. Ann Intern Med 1988;108:309.

18. Heseltine PNR, Causey DM, Appleman MD, et al: Norfloxacin in the eradication of enteric infections in AIDS patients. Eur J Cancer Clin Oncol 1988;24(suppl 1):S25-S28.

19. Diridl G, Pichler H, Wolf D: Four weeks' treatment of adult chronic *Salmonella* carriers with ciprofloxacin and its influence on the faecal flora, in Neu HC, Weuta H (eds), *Proceedings First International Ciprofloxacin Workshop*. Amsterdam, Excerpta Medica, 1986, pp 370-372.

20. Notowicz A, Stolz E, van Klingeren B: A double blind study comparing two dosages of enoxacin for the treatment of uncomplicated urogenital gonorrhoea. J Antimicrob Chemother 1984;14(suppl C):91-94.

21. Oriel JD: Ciprofloxacin in the treatment of gonorrhoea and non-gonococcal urethritis. J Antimicrob Chemother 1986;18(suppl D):129-132.

22. Aznar J, Prados R, Herrera A, et al: Single doses of ofloxacin in uncomplicated gonorrhoea. Drugs 1987;34(suppl 1):107-110.

23. Bodhidatta L, Taylor DN, Chitwarakorn A, et al: Evaluation of 500- and 1000-mg doses of ciprofloxacin for the treatment of chancroid. Antimicrob Agents Chemother 1988; 32:723-725.

24. Pugsley MP, Dworzack DL, Horowitz EA, et al: Efficacy of ciprofloxacin in the treatment of nasopharyngeal carriers of *Neisseria meningitidis*. J Infect Dis 1987;156:221-213.

25. Berkey P, Rolston K, Zukiwski A, et al: Rifampin-resistant meningococcal infection in a patient given rifampin prophylaxis. Am J Infect Control 1988;16:250-252.

26. Karp JE, Merz WG, Hendricksen C, et al: Oral norfloxacin for prevention of gram-negative bacterial infections in patients with acute leukemia and granulocytopenia: A randomized, double-blind, placebo-controlled trial. Ann Intern Med 1987;106:1-7.

27. Dekker AW, Rozenberg-Arska M, Verhoef J: Infection prophylaxis in acute leukemia: A comparison of ciprofloxacin with trimethoprim-sulfamethoxazole and colistin. Ann Intern Med 1987;106:7-12.

28. Shungu DL, Nalin DR, Gilman RH, et al: Comparative susceptibilities of *Campylobacter pylori* to norfloxacin and other agents. Antimicrob Agents Chemother 1987;31:949-950.

29. Mertens JCC, Dekker W, Ligtvoet EEJ, et al: Treatment failure of norfloxacin against *Campylobacter pylori* and chronic gastritis in patients with nonulcerative dyspepsia. Antimicrob Agents Chemother 1989;33:256-257.

30. Hackbarth CJ, Chambers HF, Stella F, et al: Ciprofloxacin in experimental *Pseudomonas aeruginosa* meningitis in rabbits. J Antimicrob Chemother 1986;18(suppl D):65-69.

31. McClain JB, Rhoads J, Krol G: Cerebrospinal fluid concentrations of ciprofloxacin in subjects with uninflamed meninges. J Antimicrob Chemother 1988;21:808-809.

32. Moffie BG, Mouton RP: Sensitivity and resistance of *Legionella pneumophila* to some antibiotics and combinations of antibiotics. J Antimicrob Chemother 1988;22:457-462.

33. Nowicki M, Paucod JC, Bornstein N, et al: Comparative efficacy of five antibiotics on experimental airborne legionellosis in guinea pigs. J Antimicrob Chemother 1988; 22:513-519.

34. Winter JH, McCartney C, Bingham J, et al: Ciprofloxacin in the treatment of severe Legionnaires' disease. Rev Infect Dis 1988;10(suppl 1):218-219.

35. Hooper TL, Gould FK, Swinburn CR, et al: Ciprofloxacin: A preferred treatment for legionella infections in patients receiving cyclosporin A. J Antimicrob Chemother 1988;22:952-953.

36. Kurz RW, Graninger W, Egger TP, et al: Failure of treatment of legionella pneumonia with ciprofloxacin. J Antimicrob Chemother 1988;22:389-391.

37. Fenlon CH, Cynamon MM: Comparative in-vitro activities of ciprofloxacin and other 4-quinolones against *Mycobacterium tuberculosis* and *Mycobacterium intracellulare*. Antimicrob Agents Chemother 1986;29:386-388.

38. Inderlied CB, Kolonoski PT, Wu M, et al: Amikacin, ciprofloxacin, and imipenem treatment for disseminated *Mycobacterium avium* complex infection in beige mice. Antimicrob Agents Chemother 1989;33:176-180.

39. Berkey P, Moore D, Rolston K: In vitro susceptibilities of nocardia species to newer antimicrobial agents. Antimicrob Agents Chemother 1988;32:1078-1079.

40. Behrens-Baumann W, Martell J: Ciprofloxacin concentrations in human aqueous humor following intravenous administration. Chemotherapy 1987;33:328-330.

41. Fisch A, Lafaix C, Salvanet A, et al: Ofloxacin in human aqueous humor and lens. J Antimicrob Chemother 1987;20:453-454.

42. Hoogkamp-Korstanje JAA: Possible role of quinolones in Yersiniosis. Drugs 1987;34: 134-138.

43. Divo AA, Sartorelli AC, Patton CL, et al: Activity of fluoroquinolone antibiotics against *Plasmodium falciparum* in vitro. Antimicrob Agents Chemother 1988;32:1182-1186.

44. Sarma PS: Norfloxacin: A new drug in the treatment of falciparum malaria. Ann Intern Med 1989;111:336-337.

45. Smith GM, Leyland MJ, Farrell ID, et al: A clinical, microbiological and pharmacokinetic study of ciprofloxacin plus vancomycin as initial therapy of febrile episodes in neutropenic patients. J Antimicrob Chemother 1988;21:647-655.

46. Chan CC, Oppenheim BA, Anderson H, et al: Randomized trial comparing ciprofloxacin plus netilmicin versus piperacillin plus netilmicin for empiric treatment of fever in neutropenic patients. Antimicrob Agents Chemother 1989;33:87-91.

47. Rolston K, Haron E, Cunningham C, et al: Ciprofloxacin for infections in cancer patients. Rev Infect Dis 1989;11(suppl 5):1241-1242.

48. Giamarellou H, Galanakis N: Use of intravenous ciprofloxacin in difficult-to-treat infections. Am J Med 1987;82(suppl 4A):346-351.

49. Chrysanthopoulos CJ, Skoutelis AT, Starakis JC, et al: Use of intravenous ciprofloxacin in respiratory tract infections and biliary sepsis. Am J Med 1987;82(suppl 4A):357-359.

50. Scully BE, Neu HC: Treatment of serious infections with intravenous ciprofloxacin. Am J Med 1987;82(suppl 4A):369-375.

# INDEX

275

# NOTES

# NOTES

# NOTES

# NOTES

NOTES

NOTES

# NOTES